D1488340

The Trial of Curiosity

THE TRIAL
OF CURIOSITY

Henry James, William James,
and the Challenge
of Modernity

Ross Posnock

New York   Oxford

OXFORD UNIVERSITY PRESS

1991

Oxford University Press

Oxford   New York   Toronto
Delhi   Bombay   Calcutta   Madras   Karachi
Petaling Jaya   Singapore   Hong Kong   Tokyo
Nairobi   Dar es Salaam   Cape Town
Melbourne   Auckland

and associated companies in
Berlin   Ibadan

Copyright © 1991 by Oxford University Press, Inc.

Published by Oxford University Press, Inc.,
200 Madison Avenue, New York, New York 10016

Oxford is a registered trademark of Oxford University Press

All rights reserved. No part of this publication may be reproduced,
stored in a retrieval system, or transmitted, in any form or by any means,
electronic, mechanical, photocopying, recording, or otherwise,
without the prior permission of Oxford University Press.

Library of Congress Cataloging-in-Publication Data
Posnock, Ross.
The trial of curiosity : Henry James, William James,
and the challenge of modernity / Ross Posnock.
p.   cm.   Includes bibliographical references and index.
ISBN 0-19-506606-5
ISBN 0-19-507124-7 (pbk)
1. James, Henry, 1843–1916—Criticism and interpretation.
2. James, William, 1842–1910—Influence.
3. Modernism (Literature)—United States.   I. Title.
PS2124.P63 1991 813'.4—dc20
90-25621

The quotation from a letter by Henry James to Howard Sturgis
appearing on page 214 is reproduced by permission of the Houghton
Library, Harvard University.

2 4 6 8 9 7 5 3 1

Printed in the United States of America
on acid-free paper

TO

Karen Joy Shabetai

JAN 12 1994

Preface

This study began with the modest intention of taking Henry James seriously as an intellectual.[1] Despite the much-heralded shift in critical models in the last decade from various poststructuralisms to new historicisms, I believed that James remained, to a significant degree, underestimated as a cultural analyst. His major cultural critique, *The American Scene* (1907), an account of his 1904 repatriation, places James in the company of American social thinkers like Veblen, Dewey, Mead, and Bourne, and among such European theorists of urban modernity as Simmel and Weber, as well as their successors in and around the Frankfurt School. My corollary aim was to realign the Jamesian canon by treating his late novel *The Ambassadors* as well as his important late nonfiction—*The American Scene*, the prefaces, and the autobiographies—as an interconnected unit that, when read through and against these social thinkers, would reveal James's aesthetic, cultural, and psychological responses to modernity and their challenging, even radical, political implications.[2] A strikingly different Henry James would thus be revealed, someone who is more like Walt Whitman than Henry Adams in opening himself to incessant stimuli and relaxing the anxious Victorian ethos of strenuous masculinity. This James had hitherto been obscured by the prevailing tendency to treat *The American Scene* as an oddity in the Jamesian canon, the eccentric travelogue of a reactionary aesthete. All too often this work was minimized rather than read as a culminating act of analysis that extends the concerns of James's fiction. This segregation had muffled the subtle power of James's historical imagination, ensuring that his identity would remain more or less that of a genteel aesthete whose destiny, to quote John Carlos Rowe, "always seems to end in the intricacies of his late style and its retreat from life into the palace of art" (*Theoretical* 28).

Though my use of the past tense would suggest otherwise, the argument

I have sketched remains the basis of the present book: a study of Henry James in the context of modern cultural and social thought. Yet this description is, like my initial conception, misleadingly incomplete. Hence I use the past tense to signal distance from my original intention to take James seriously as an intellectual, a project complicated by my contextualist focus. For anyone seeking to place Henry James within an intellectual context, it is not long before William James's priority, which Henry found "proper and pre-appointed," asserts itself. Simply tracing the genealogy of the word "intellectual" to its first widely publicized American use leads to the figure whom Henry James acknowledges as his "inexhaustible authority," perennial mediator, and predecessor. William James in 1907 gave wide circulation to the term.

This fact, and the revisions it necessitated of my early intentions, can stand as a paradigm of how the present study evolved: I found "discrimination among the parts of my subject again and again difficult—so inseparably . . . did they seem to hang together." These are Henry James's words, taken from the first page of *A Small Boy and Others*, where he describes his "attempt to place together some particulars of the early life of William James and present him in his setting" (*Autobiography* 3). Henry's original effort at sketching a brief memoir of his elder brother turned into autobiography because his inveterate discrimination led him to compose a "picture of differences" not isolated and fixed but rather "fused and united and interlocked," so "prevailingly and almost exclusively" was life "conditioned" for him by William's "nearness" (4).

Precarious first intentions, the necessity of revision, the pleasure and difficulty of negotiating the shifting and permeable boundaries of self and other, the dialectic of identity and difference—all are matters of central concern throughout the late fiction and nonfiction. But nowhere are they more clearly dramatized than at the opening of *A Small Boy and Others*. There the novelist confronts the "promptest" of "very first perceptions"—that William occupies a "place in the world to which" Henry "couldn't at all aspire." And it is William who sets the terms that Henry will challenge as he works out what he called the very "different ends" of his intellectual life. In short, the author of a contextual study inevitably is placed in a position not unlike Henry's at the opening of his memoirs. What begins as one thing—an exclusive focus on Henry James as an intellectual—quickly becomes another—a study of the relation of Henry and William James and their response to modernity.

In a spirit of Jamesian revision, I should at this point qualify my emphasis on contextualism since it is not a wholly adequate description of my approach. My use of the word is apt to the extent that my intention is to practice a historicized intellectual history that treats ideas as emerging from and developing within "a complex series of overlapping fields" rather than as "free-floating essences evolving in proud disregard for mere social reality," to cite Richard Fox (xi). But this contextual approach to ideas only partly defines my method. Thanks to recent critiques of contextualism in intellectual history, I can describe my procedure more precisely as also being "comparative" in the sense used recently by historian David Harlan, who argues in favor of an alternative to radical contextualism's pursuit of textual origins and disdain for any kind of presentism. My effort is both contextualist—to situate the Jameses by returning them to their cultural contexts—and comparative— to resituate them in new and unexpected contexts constructed in light of contemporary interests. Among these interests is the current preoccupation with the changing figure of the intellectual in a culture that, until recently, equated the intellectual and the aesthetic with a transcendent realm of value. Modes of intellectual practice are currently being reexamined in our adamantly antiformalist and anti-idealist moment, where both Marxism and modernism have lost much of their oppositional authority.

I situate William and Henry James by juxtaposing them with contemporaneous historical figures whom they both knew: E. L. Godkin (chaps. 6 and 8), Charles Eliot Norton (chap. 8), Theodore Roosevelt (chaps. 1 and 10), and George Santayana (chap. 8). I also resituate the brothers in a comparative "exercise in theoretical confrontations," as John Patrick Diggins describes his comparative study of Thorstein Veblen. Among other pairs, my study juxtaposes Henry James and Walter Benjamin (chap. 6), William James and Theodor Adorno (chap. 5), and both Jameses with John Dewey and Adorno (chaps. 3–6). This comparative thrust dictates that my method be one of perspective by incongruity (to enlist a prime Jamesian value and to borrow Kenneth Burke's phrase) and acknowledges the value of "letting the present interrogate the past" (Harlan 608). Thus, my study seeks to make a virtue of "presentism, the scourge of professional historiography" (593). Whether we like it or not, the realization that our contemporary intellectual moment shapes how we construct any context seems a valuable recognition of presentism's ineradicability.

My placement of Henry and William James in a web of textual affiliations— literary, philosophical, political, sociological—has affinities with New Historicism's effort to rethink context and to reconceive literary history as an analysis of an ensemble of texts inhabiting a discursive field that breaks down the rigid distinction between primary and secondary works. To a less flamboyant degree, I share the New Historicist "strategy of the surprising juxtaposition,"[3] but I am not committed to dissolving the primacy of the individual subject or text into a larger network or structure of relations and commitments generated by what Walter Michaels calls a cultural logic. Unlike this Foucault-inspired strategy of assimilation, the present study situates (and resituates) the James family. One way I diverge from a New Historicist method of leveling is by investing not only William and Henry but also certain texts (*The American Scene* and the autobiography) with exceptional importance. Indeed, I argue that these works possess a culturally exemplary status.

In assessing and contextualizing Henry James's late nonfiction by treating him as a formidable cultural analyst, I have been inspired by the implicit precedent found in the work of two of the most distinguished critics of

James's fiction, Laurence B. Holland and Richard Poirier. According to the latter, Holland was the first to prove that "*in* his fiction, no less than in his essays, reviews and travel writing . . . James was always the critic at work, the greatest critic America has yet to produce." Poirier goes on to say that the "allegations . . . still being made" that James was "somehow insufficiently historical or that he was out of touch with American realities" indicate that "literary criticism never sufficiently takes advantage of its best findings in order to move forward to questions still unanswered" ("Forward" viii). The present study seeks to move forward by integrating literary and biographical criticism with social and cultural theory, thereby setting in motion multi-disciplinary interactions to promote new ways of thinking about the James brothers in the context of their time and ours.

Seattle
January 1991   R.P.

Acknowledgments

Part of chapter 10 first appeared in *Journal of American Studies* (21 [April 1987]) and parts of chapters 2 and 8 originally appeared in *Raritan* (8 [Winter 1989] and 10 [Winter 1991]). I am grateful to both journals for permission to reprint. My work benefited from a 1988 summer stipend from the National Endowment for the Humanities. A number of individuals have been generous with their time and interest and it is a pleasure to thank them here. I am grateful to David Bergman, Gordon Hutner, and Mary Esteve for their painstaking attention to various chapters. Robert Casillo offered crucial eleventh-hour advice; once again his erudition has put me in his debt. George Cotkin helped me rethink my response to William James. In his careful perusal of an early draft of the manuscript, Jonathan Freedman offered a host of valuable suggestions. At Oxford University Press, I have had the good fortune to work with William Sisler, Elizabeth Maguire, and Henry Krawitz. Both before and since his 1985 N.E.H. Summer Institute, Walter Michaels has incited me to historicize more rigorously. For support and encouragement of various kinds through the years, I wish to thank Martha Banta, William Cain, and Michael T. Gilmore. In Seattle I talked out many of my ideas with four colleagues whose curiosity remains inspiring: Daniel Silver, Douglas Collins, Charles Altieri, and John O'Neill. It is a special pleasure to acknowledge the many kindnesses of Richard Poirier. Now I know more vividly what Henry James meant when he called John La Farge "that rare thing, a *figure*."

My deepest and luckiest debt is recorded in the dedication.

Contents

The Trial of Curiosity

1

Introduction:
Master and Worm;
Anarchist and Idiot

Since this book, I hope, will interest not only literary critics but intellectual historians in various fields, it may seem perverse to begin with two concluding moments in Henry James's late fiction. But they provide a convenient point of entry to my set of concerns in the present study. Near the close of *The Ambassadors*, Maria Gostrey and Lambert Strether recall an earlier "curiosity felt by both of them as to where he would 'come out' " if his delicate mission to return Chad to America came "to smash." In the wake of Strether's botched mission, his Parisian pleasures, and his uncertain American future, they realize that "he was out, in truth, as far as it was possible to be" (342). Near the end of *The Golden Bowl*, James's last completed novel, Maggie Verver is close to reclaiming her straying husband and renewing their marriage on a new basis of sexual intensity. She compares her husband, an Italian prince "fixed in his place," with her own evolving status. Whereas Amerigo's place "was like something made for him beforehand," Maggie's "own had come to show simply as that improvised 'post'... of the kind spoken of as advanced" and serving "a settler or trader in a new country. ... The only geography marking it would be doubtless that of the fundamental passions" (516–17). What these passages disclose are characters' movements beyond the conventional codes that impose intelligibility upon individual behavior. James's late work is concerned not simply to celebrate these figures of illegibility, as might a Whitman or an Emerson, but to socialize them. James does so by redirecting their energy back toward a social order whose demands for legibility might then be challenged and modified. Thus relaxed, democratic psyches and social structures might be shaped by less coercive mappings.

The Golden Bowl marks the end of the so-called major phase of James's fiction. And there, in 1904, the canonical James ends. But James did not.

What he went on to create, as recent critics increasingly realize, was a second major phase (1907–14) of autobiography, cultural criticism, and aesthetics: *A Small Boy and Others*, *Notes of a Son and Brother*, *The American Scene*, and the New York Edition prefaces. The motto for this cluster of texts might be James's declaration in the preface to *The American Scene*: "I would stand on my gathered impressions. . . . I would in fact go to the stake for them." This sounds the most characteristic note—intimate, vulnerable, defiant—of his self-representation throughout the late nonfiction. As if inspired by the degree of exposure risked by his two greatest fictional creations, James comes out as far as possible and represents his self not as fixed beforehand by what he calls the "oppressive *a priori*" but as improvisational, "led . . . on and on" by the force of fundamental passions. With this mobile stance he greets American modernity, disembarking at Hoboken, New Jersey, on August 30, 1904, for a strenuous ten-month tour.

Arguably, my rhetoric seems rather inflated; after all, one might point out, I am describing the final works of an aging, genteel, celibate bachelor whose last books seem more absorbed in the consolations of memory than in anything else. But these oft-repeated facts of canonical wisdom are redolent of what James calls "fatal futility," for they inform only by simplifying, by smoothing out the incongruities that mark the texture of James's genius. These incongruities are present in the quotations at the start of this chapter and partly inspired my own language in the preceding paragraph. James heightens incongruity when he likens Maggie, his fabulously wealthy princess, to "some Indian squaw with a papoose on her back and barbarous beadwork to sell" (517). What does James intend by having the primitive jostle against the genteel, a tension echoed in his willingness to go to the stake and in likening himself (in his memoirs) to a subtle savage? Simply to pose this question suggests the reason for James's inflation of diction and metaphor: it is the means of making the question visible. His mock-heroic hyperbole functions less as satire than as the vehicle for expressing the return of inner and outer nature—that which is repressed by the violent strain of holding the bourgeois self together.

If bourgeois respectability in the late nineteenth-century capitalist world, says Sartre, embodies "antinature" (*Critique* 771–72), or the suppression of desire, in both of his major phases James in effect stages nature's revolt. Yet antinature—the condition of culture—"bears without cracking the strongest pressure" James throws on it (*Art* 304). Culture holds fast—Maggie's marriage is revived; Strether will go back to Woollett—but not before its dictatorship over nature has been toppled. The result is that nature and culture in his fiction, like the alien and the assimilated in *The American Scene*, exist in a relation of reciprocal incitation, each "eat[ing] round the edges" of the other's position, "baffling insidiously" the other's "ideal," as James describes the interplay of drama and picture in his aesthetics (*Art* 298). This volatile tension characterizes a dynamic, democratic social order that since the nineteenth century has been, in the words of one contemporary political theorist, "the theatre of an uncontrollable adventure" (Lefort 305). In turn, this "ungraspable society" engenders the bourgeois values and institutions designed to contain it. According to Lefort, the clash between indeterminacy and the cult of order produces a "certain vertigo" that, since Marx and Baudelaire, has been identified as modernity's hallmark. James defines the "very *donnée*" of twentieth-century America as the "great adventure of a society" where "fluctuations and variations, the shifting quantity of success and failure" render experience bewilderingly inconclusive (*Scene* 12).

Having punctured, if not overturned, the complacencies and confinements of the genteel, the Jamesian self finds the space to improvise new forms of identity and pleasure, including those found in exhilarating, isolating experiences of passion and exposure. My language may again seem slightly inflated, appropriate for more exuberant critics of Victorian repression—a Whitman, Wilde, or William James—than for decorous Henry James. It seems just as easy not to take Henry James seriously as a radical critic of the genteel as it is to dismiss Strether's coming out "as far as it was possible to be" as the trivial, if poignant, gropings of a late middle-aged widower. Both creator and character seem to epitomize what I am claiming they critique. Yet this skepticism may ultimately reflect less about Henry James and more about a reigning presupposition we have regarding the cultural critic—that the role entails heroic opposition and a shattering of conventions. To varying degrees the trio mentioned earlier willingly embrace this role.

This understanding of cultural critique forecloses a subtler, if less glamorous, alternative, one founded on the mundane fact that our experience of the social order is one of contradiction—that we are at once within and without it. Rather than being debilitating, the contradiction is productive for Henry James's relation to the genteel, since it permits him to tap the energy of its repressions as a source of critical power and excitement. On this dialectical basis, we can now take seriously James's and Strether's coming out "as far as it was possible to be" as the effort to make the bourgeois surface bear without cracking the pressure of the self stripping away its defenses to reach a point of maximum exposure to shock. In his coming out Strether discovers what James does in *Notes of a Son and Brother*—that for the "subject or victim" of "the play of strong imaginative passion" this passion "constitutes in itself an endless crisis," for it is "fed by every contact and every apprehension" (*Autobiography* 454). The word "imaginative" should not be understood as relegating passion to the merely vicarious. This is so predictable a reduction that it virtually defines what we mean by Jamesian. Yet James carefully avoids equating his passion with such diminishment. Instead, he finds this "passion strong enough to *be*... the very interest of life" (454). How James reaches this understanding of passion and what it means for his life and work are matters explored in the following pages.

In light of James's suggestion of a self aroused to a kind of perpetual crisis of sexual excitement, my invoking of Wilde and Whitman is not inappropriate after all. Like them, James converts the bourgeois self of control into a more supple mode that eludes social categories and is open to the play of the fundamental passions. But, unlike Wilde, James does not advertise his coming out with a yellow silk handkerchief and knee breeches. He does not follow Whitman in flaunting the aggressive seduction of himself and his reader. Nor does Henry partake of his elder brother's invitation to dive into the flux and dispense with words and concepts. James once referred to Wilde as an "unclean beast." Not until late in life did he acknowledge a significant rapprochement with Whitman's sensibility. Henry's response to William is, of course, more complex, and a major concern of this work will be to clarify their relationship. By exploring the dynamics of their fraternal bond, we will be in a better position to comprehend the evolution of their differing styles of self-representation and cultural criticism.

I

The different reactions of the two eldest James brothers to each other and to modernity comprise my main subject. If I grant primacy to Henry James, I do so with the full awareness that he makes the very notion of primacy problematic. So acute is his sense of our "exposed and entangled state" as "social creatures" (*Art* 65) that his version of Claude Lévi-Strauss's syllogism, "Whoever says Man says Language, and whoever says Language says Society" might read "Whoever says Man says Entanglement, and whoever says Entanglement says Social Creature." Entangled are public and private, psychology and sociology, aesthetic theory and cultural critique. Because James's late nonfiction is based on these entanglements, my reading of the memoirs, prefaces, and cultural criticism emphasizes how they interlock while preserving their differences. In their relationship William and Henry were also simultaneously interlocked and decisively different; reading them against each other illuminates their understandings of identity, imitation, curiosity, and pragmatism. For instance, William James's individualism posits that each "I" and each "you" keeps its own thoughts to itself: we speak not of this or that thought but "*my thought*, every thought being owned" (*Principles* 221). Henry James's memoirs dramatize an alternative to an atomized self. Ownership and separation are conspicuously absent in Henry's account of being "conditioned" by William's "nearness."

Far from being sterile or gloomy, William's sense of the closed, discontinuous nature of human subjectivity, what he calls that "unsharable feeling which each one of us has," is inseparable from his passionate advocacy of individual freedom (*Varieties* 499). His understanding of our ineradicable blindness to others led to a philosophy of pluralism that sought to escape intolerances and cruelties. And in his personal conduct James expressed the rarest generosity and tolerance toward all manner of alien being, especially those held in suspicion by the reigning orthodoxies. At the same time, William James was a self-declared Mugwump who upheld the patrician Victorian ethic of class responsibility. As a spokesman for what he called the college-bred intellectual class, James envisioned it as the American version of "the aristocracy in older countries. . . . Our motto, too, is *noblesse oblige*." James preferred to justify the elitism of the intellectual class by proclaiming that it stood for "ideal interests solely" (qtd. Matthiessen, *Family* 635). However, like any class, it possessed specific interests, including the sanctification of culture as a privileged realm of the well bred. In actuality (if not by William's design) the concept of "ideal interests" was aimed at insulating the elite from ever more ambitious and worrisome immigrant, feminist, black, and working-class demands.[1]

In light of this idealizing of the intellectual, it is ironic that seven years before James used the word in his 1907 address on "The Social Value of the College Bred," it had been employed in a working-class context—on New York City's Lower East Side. As Thomas Bender notes, it referred "to those immigrants who, under settlement house auspices or in cafe society, had formed study groups to incorporate into their lives American literature and culture" (228). In 1902 Hutchins Hapgood, an old-stock, Harvard-educated journalist and former student of William James, published *The Spirit of the Ghetto*, in which he observed "the intellectuals"—anarchists, socialists, editors, poets, playwrights. "At once neither orthodox Jews nor Americans . . . and in matters of taste and literary ideals . . . European rather than American," these intellectuals "gather every evening in cafes of the quarter and become habitually intoxicated with the excitement of ideas" (39–40).

In 1904 Henry James, another expatriate—neither wholly European nor wholly American—and lacking a college degree (he had left Harvard after a year), visited the Lower East Side and registered the presence of this new social type. Fascinated by the packed, roaring vitality of the New York ghetto, unlike "the dark, foul, stifling Ghettos of other remembered cities," James is equally intrigued by Bowery "beer-houses and cafes," where he feels "the immensity of the alien presence." These establishments make visible to the observer "the various possibilities of the waiting spring of intelligence . . . the germ of a 'public' " (*Scene* 133, 138). James is particularly taken by a German cafe where "exquisite," "contemplative stillness" reigns (203–4). Here intellectuals would prosper in the "friendly stillness" of this "modest asylum" and "tiny temple. . . . A new metaphysic might have been thought out or the scheme of a new war intellectualized" (204). The exquisite tone of this "pure and simple" cafe, serene and dignified "while the East Side roared," impresses James as embodying one of the "real triumphs of art . . . discriminations made and preserved in the face of no small difficulty" (203). These are the "discriminations in favor of taste produced not by the gilded and guarded 'private room,' but by making publicity itself delicate, making your barrier against vulgarity consist but in a few tables and chairs, a few coffee cups and boxes of dominoes." Large amounts of money "can always create tone," says James, but on the Bowery it is produced by the "practical subtlety of the spirit unashamed of its preference for the minor key" (203–4).

Here Henry nearly stands on its head the class snobbery and aesthetic idealism of genteel Anglo-Saxonism as he locates "exquisite tone" in supple, improvisational discrimination that manages to transform a clamorous public space into a "tiny temple" of tranquility built on a "few tables and chairs."

The "gilded and guarded 'private room' "—the gentile sanctuary of intellect—must now share American cultural capital with the hastily constructed
temples of immigrant culture. Erected in the very teeth of publicity, "like
a well-inserted wedge" amid the "loud surrounding triumphs," this alien
enclave is an ingenious triumph of art. The wit and audacity needed for
fashioning "discriminations . . . in the face of no small difficulty" are just
what is missing from inert, genteel culture—"gilded and guarded"—in its
privatized elitism. In contrast, the "new metaphysic" and "new war" theo-
rized by ghetto intellectuals suggest the fertility, and hint at the violence,
of this urban culture's iconoclastic energy. One reason Henry James is alert
and sympathetic to the new intellectuals of the new century, conceiving of
them as a social type not restricted to a college elite, is that they, like him,
are between cultures. Thus they escape the dictates of an American gentry
that conceives of the intellectual as serving "ideal interests" exempt from
matters of power and public life.

Nevertheless, Henry still maintains that culture requires a "barrier against
vulgarity." Yet he revises this patrician bias by defining that barrier not as
the insuperable, exclusive preserve of class privilege but as a few tables and
chairs. James savors art's heterogeneous power to effect a cunning reversal
or conversion that, in this case, triumphs "by making publicity itself delicate." Analogously, he writes in a notebook entry of the "sacred and salutary
refuge" granted by "the refreshment of art," locating such refuge in "resolute
. . . production," which has "purchased" and "acquired material" as "grist
to his mill" (*Notebooks* 61). The sacred and the profane, art and commerce—
all found, for instance, in the "contemplative stillness" of a Lower East Side
cafe—together comprise the "luminous paradise of art" (61) that is embedded within the marketplace of "modernity with its pockets full of money"
(*Scene* 155).

In the eyes of many cultural critics, instrumentality is the bane of modern
life and the enemy of high culture. But for James it is not opposed to but
inherent in aesthetic practice both as subject and technique. That "everything counts, nothing is superfluous" stands as the utilitarian imperative for
James, his characters, and his reader in their mapping of social and psychic
texts (*Art* 3). But this instrumental demand to make everything legible becomes less coercive than creative because James reveals the limits of the
instrumental. He discovers that dwelling within the act of artistic creation,
and in life, is "inevitable deviation": the "exquisite treachery even of the
straightest execution" or the "most mature plan" (*Art* 325). The artist's "real
triumph" is not in fleeing from the disciplinary or the instrumental but rather
in pursuing them to the exquisite point of "inevitable deviation" wherein
dialectical reversal occurs and the illegible—unassimilable particularity—
crystallizes. This dynamic process of conversion embodies the immanent
logic of aesthetic practice and orients Henry James's political critique of
American modernity.[2]

In James's response to the Lower East Side it is tempting to find some
condescending aestheticism, particularly his conversion of the beer hall into

a "tiny temple." Indeed, an element of slumming is built into his visit to the Lower East Side. But the charge of aestheticism, though reasonable, is misguided. As James declares at the start of his autobiography, image and scene are "the only terms in which life has treated me to experience" (4). The act of perception for James is not innocently transparent; rather, experience is framed, making both the framer and the framed, subject and object, inherently theatrical. But if perception is aesthetic, *aestheticism* (at least of the American genteel variety) is not the necessary consequence. In all likelihood a Brahmin aesthete would not enter the immigrant cafe, being sufficiently repulsed by "everything vulgar . . . that reigned" around it; or if he did enter he would distance it in a haze of blurry idealism. James invokes both possibilities but cancels them through his discriminating grasp of particularity, which renders his aestheticizing historically alert and precise. James's nongenteel aestheticism, in short, partakes to some degree of the European tradition of a Wilde, a William Morris, or an Arthur Symons in terms of their interest in working-class experience. But perhaps the most pertinent precedent for James's relish of the ghetto cafe was William Wetmore Story, the subject of a two-volume biography that James published the year before he visited America. This markedly un-Bostonian Brahmin expatriate (his father was an eminent judge and a founder of Harvard Law School) refused to "endure the restraint and bondage of Boston" (qtd. James, *Story* 1: 102). Instead he lived in Rome for over forty years, delighting in its dirt and bohemian cafes. In his guidebook to Rome he devoted an admiring chapter to the city's Jewish ghetto.[3]

James implies his preference for immersion rather than idealism in his final preface, where he dispenses with protective presuppositions by "shaking off all shackles of theory" (*Art* 336). Facilitating James's capacity for engagement is the often ignored or minimized fact that he did not consider himself a New Englander but a New Yorker, and thus never felt any special obeisance to Boston's cultural idealism. Indeed, as Charles Feidelson has suggested, James had no deeply felt class loyalties, a crucial insight with important implications (339).

One implication bears on the kind of late nineteenth-century intellectual William and Henry each became. As a public intellectual with a large following, William inherited a role that until the mid eighteenth century had been filled by a preacher (King 142). From his pulpit at Harvard he provided moral guidance founded on the practical value of self-trust, religious belief, and opposition to large institutions. Henry presents a more elusive profile. Unlike William, he was rarely active politically (his response to World War I being an exception) and was not a social critic in the sense of publishing letters and making speeches on behalf of the anti-imperialists, or preaching the virtues of the strenuous life or the need for a "moral equivalent of war." Indeed, Henry can be considered an American public intellectual only on a few occasions: his "American Letters," which appeared in a British magazine in the spring and summer of 1898, and, of course, *The American Scene*. His first letter, "The Question of the Opportunities," adumbrates the stance he will enact in his book on America. He addresses the "unique situation" of a "huge, homogenous, and fast-growing" reading public. Rather than lamenting "literature for the billion," James is intrigued by the unprecedented opportunities, not the least being "the critic's happy release from the cramped posture of foregone conclusions and narrow rules" (*Literary* 1: 651–53). As its governing premise, Henry's cultural criticism takes the "democratic era unreservedly for granted." We cannot and need not "meditate plans of escape" from the "inexorability" of the modern world. Escape is beside the point, not only because modernity shapes our psyches but also because its conditions are neither uniformly oppressive nor impervious to reform. To think otherwise is to surrender to "foregone conclusions." Unlike William, Henry does not regard bigness as inherently dehumanizing. Rather, he holds that modernity's very "vastness" might encourage expression of "sufficient vitality" to erupt "at points of proportionate frequency" (*Literary* 1: 690, 653).

Henry's tentative, open stance suggests one of his signal merits as a cultural critic: a willingness to recognize and submit to a new scale of values and new "importances" rather than to continue measuring by older standards. "Truly the Yiddish world was a vast world, with its own deeps and complexities," notes James. His respect for its integrity is part of his recognition that the scale of "importances" seems "strikingly shifted and reconstituted, in the United States, for the visitor attuned, from far back, to 'European' importances" (*Scene* 138). This rearrangement is perhaps most drastic in the New Jerusalem of the Lower East Side, where a "new style of poverty" is "everywhere insistent" (135–36). As William Boelhower has been virtually alone in observing, James employs a "revolutionary" method in confronting the alien: he abandons both "preestablished rules for ordering" impressions and an "aprioristic legitimizing frame" for a "fluid process of ethnic semiosis. . . . This means that the context is all; that no theoretical ordering can ever fly free of the tenuous ground of its own making" (22–24). What Boelhower calls revolutionary I call pragmatic. James's inordinate receptivity replaces theory with practice, the a priori with contingency, clarity with shock, information with immersion, and delineates the contours of a pragmatism that places the fact of urban modernity at its center. Unlike previous commentators, I find it important to discriminate among the various pragmatisms in order to define Henry's version.[4] While nourished by William's pragmatism, Henry is ultimately closer to John Dewey's, especially its historicist emphasis on man as culturally embedded.

By emphasizing Henry James as active, empirical, and pragmatic rather than fastidious, "gilded and guarded," the present study challenges the received conviction that James was "intensely concerned with the preservation of the world that nurtured him." Joel Porte has recently argued that on "returning to his native New York in 1904, James found himself horrified at an ethnic invasion that seemed palpably to threaten the essentially uniform Anglo-Saxon Christian culture that was the staple of his fiction" (141–42). This statement encapsulates canonical truth and echoes F. O. Matthiessen's famous judgment, made over forty years earlier, that in *The American Scene* James was drifting "dangerously close to a doctrine of racism."[5]

With a few notable exceptions, literary critics and intellectual historians continue to regard Henry James as an aloof, genteel elitist repulsed by immigrant New York and modernity in general.[6] The reasons for such misreadings are various, but they comprise a consistent pattern, with its own cultural and political significance, that I explore in chapter 3. Yet it is noteworthy that this popular misprision is linked to the oft-unspoken assumption that equates modernism and the literary intellectual with opposition to the alienation of twentieth-century urban life. In a perverse sense, by accusing James of anti-Semitism and racism one is calling him a high modernist. Such accusations are easy, since literary modernism is expected to coincide—and often does—with lament (be it from the left or right) over the state of the modern world. And such lamentation pervades the late nineteenth-century bourgeois/aristocratic milieu of Henry and William James. The subject deserves some mention here because its implications will be paramount in later chapters.

In a widely admired book Jackson Lears identified antimodernism as a major cultural tendency, particularly among patrician intellectuals from 1880 to 1920, many of whom were among Henry James's oldest friends. "Transatlantic in scope and sources, antimodernism drew on venerable traditions as well as contemporary cultural currents." Chief among its concerns was a quest for authentic, immediate experience that presumably had withered amid the vulgarities of the capitalist marketplace. Nurtured by "republican moralism" and romanticism, antimodernism was antiurban, extolling "childlike rusticity" and energetic physical activity over the abstract intellectualism of rationalism and positivism. Reacting against what Lears calls the "evasive banality of modern culture," replete with its "flatulent pieties" of progressive optimism, antimodernism often asserts "a vitalist cult of energy and process; and a parallel recovery of the primal, irrational forces in the human psyche." Lears notes that many antimodernists "yearned increasingly for oceanic dependence," a "desire to abandon autonomous selfhood and sink into a passive state of boundless union with all being" (57–58, 218).

Among the manifestations of American antimodernism were the Victorian cult of the strenuous life, the revival of Ruskin and Morris's Arts and Crafts Movement, and the rebirth of premodern religious awe, reflected in Victorian medievalism. Brooks and Henry Adams, Frank Norris, G. Stanley Hall, Charles Eliot Norton, James Russell Lowell, George Santayana, Mark Twain, Edith Wharton, and Randolph Bourne are among the many distinguished figures that Lears counts among the antimodernists. The variety of this group suggests that the antimodernist label flattens nearly as many distinctions as it crystallizes. For instance, Wharton, Bourne, and Santayana are arguably more distinctively modernist than antimodernist, an argument I make for these last two figures in later chapters. Despite the looseness of Lears's taxonomy, he does enlarge our understanding of this movement, which, until after 1910, was virtually synonymous with American Anglo-

Saxon high culture, the tradition that Santayana dubbed genteel. Antimodernism not only comprises much of the intellectual content of this tradition; its antidemocratic elitism supplied a framework of social values for some illustrious representatives of twentieth-century American poetic modernism, particularly the nexus of Pound, Eliot, Tate, and Ransom. Their aesthetics and politics are rooted in antiurban, religious, agrarian values. Regardless of its attacks on Victorian gentility, modernism represents, in large measure, a "radically detribalized gentility" (Habegger 291).

William James is also on Lears's list. His radical empiricism, vitalism, anti-intellectualism, and mysticism make him an exemplary antimodernist, yet he is also a most eloquent critic of antimodernism's nativist intolerance, pompous complacencies, and desiccated traditions. Henry James is significantly absent from Lears's anatomy of antimodernism. If this omission implies that Lears does not regard him as antimodernist, I concur. It is more accurate than historian James Gilbert's more typical estimate, which, instead of distinguishing between William and Henry, merges them in "romantic opposition" to modernity (210).

II

In the present study I argue that *The American Scene* constitutes a calculated act of affiliation with the new century and its endless possibilities. Addressing the United States near the end of his book, James distinguishes his perspective from that of the "painted savages you have dispossessed." While they rightfully begrudge "every disfigurement and every violence" that America has inflicted upon the land, James declares: "I accept your ravage" (463). Because he situates his response to modernity as necessarily belated rather than aboriginal, he is not drawn to a prelapsarian Eden of solitude and wholeness. Instead, James is preeminently concerned with representation, the shifting ground where art and social behavior interact. Skeptical and ironic toward all that purports to be natural, he believes in the primacy of imitation and theatricality. Moreover, he conceives of the self's relation to commodities as inevitably entwined not only with corporate manipulation but also with human expressiveness and creativity. Such a sensibility finds the Lower East Side a "rare experience," "so modernized . . . so little sordid, so highly 'evolved' " (*Scene* 133, 135). Like Hapgood, a thirty-three-year-old self-described "gentile" reporting "sympathetically" on the ghetto Jews (5), James, at sixty-one, bears direct witness to the transition from a Victorian culture of hierarchy and homogeneity to a more unsettling urban modernity.

I do not mean to suggest that James also shares Hapgood's missionary zeal for publicizing the glories of ghetto life. Unlike Hapgood, a self-conscious modernist intellectual, James never made a programmatic effort to include the immigrant in a new enfranchisement of American culture that Randolph Bourne called "trans-national." While we will see that in significant ways James is close to this project, his engagement with urban modernism is not without profound, freely confessed ambivalence and even acute unease.

The "East side cafes" may be "tiny temples," but they are also, to his ears, "torture-rooms of the living idiom" (*Scene* 139). Yet even in his "piteous gasp" he refuses to condemn "the accent of the very ultimate future" as bereft of unsuspected beauty.

In sum, Henry James may be mired in the nativist prejudices of his class, yet he is unique in submitting them to the "tonic shock" of total immersion. When he literally confronts and interacts with the object of his disgust in 1904, he revises his congealed responses and dependency on reified assumptions. In exploring New York City his powers of discrimination are put to their severest test, and they grow more inclusive than exclusive. His wayward, avid curiosity, which brings him to "the very heart of the New York whirlpool," embodies a dynamic of mobile involvements that puts him in contact with a variety of people, classes, institutions, and locales in his year of traveling from New Hampshire to California and from Florida to Chicago (134). To this array of experiences James reacts variously, alternately expressing contempt, condescension, exhilaration, fear, respect, pleasure, and nostalgia. But rather than surrendering to nostalgia, that prime antimodernist emotion, James savors it as a subject. He muses "on the oddity of our nature," which makes us tender toward "ghostly presences" such as those that haunt his walk down Charles Street in Boston (243–44).[7]

James makes nostalgia and its retreat from modernity the subject of a brief but telling interlude. During a visit to Washington Irving's home at Sunnyside in upstate New York, he self-consciously bathes in nostalgia. Sunnyside is now a tourist's shrine where the " 'little' American literary past" resides—but hardly in unmolested innocence. For "modernity, with its pockets full of money," has turned Irving's home into a museum, and Irving has been "doomed to celebrity." James invokes the "vague golden . . . haze" of the past that makes "sharp reflection of our own increase of arrangement and loss of leisure." Under the spell of "envy [that] exhausts . . . the futilities of discrimination," he is reduced to lamenting "*our* ugly era" of the "quickened pace, the heightened fever, the narrowed margin." If modernity means "rushing about and being rushed at," the premodern world of Sunnyside, like Irving himself, was "mild" and "pleasant," qualities whose blandness recalls the American literary past that James gently mocks as "little" (155–57).

James concludes his mixed homage by carefully noting that Sunnyside is the "last faint echo of a felicity forever gone. That is the true voice of such places, and not the imputed challenge to the chronicler or the critic" (157). Here James recovers his discrimination, which envy had exhausted earlier. Rather than a beckoning ideal challenging us to rediscover it "off somewhere in the hills," Sunnyside is extinct save as a preserved and "amplified" artifact of modernity. "With its terrible power of working its will . . . of gilding its toy," modernity has made a toy shrine of the "original modest house," whose " 'dear' old portrait prints [are] very dear today when properly signed and properly sallow." Modernity, James implies, is impossible to ignore, for its powerful "will" creates and not merely reflects reality: it makes our experience of Sunnyside at best a "qualified Sleepy Hollow" and turns into commodities the paraphernalia of our precious little past. And to imagine it possible to escape somehow or ignore modernity renders us as antique and irrelevant as "Rip Van Winkle" or a citizen of Sleepy Hollow "in some dreamland of old autumns." James invokes Rip Van Winkle as being "really at the bottom of it all," the "it" referring to the languorous "shimmer of association" in Sunnyside's inviting temptation to oblivion (154–55).

James's ironic performance at Sunnyside mimics many of the main tropes of antimodernist cultural response as he playfully mocks the genteel chronicler and critic, with their conventional gestures of lament and offended sensibility. As a "religiously preserved" monument to an idealized culture and nature, Sunnyside is a perfect stage upon which James can enact his nostalgic set piece. Amid the rural charm of the Hudson River valley, James hears echoes of the premodern "unimproved age, the age of processes still comparatively slow." Like Hawthorne before him, James dutifully laments the intrusion of "the railroad . . . thrust in at the foot of the slope" as an ugly reminder, indeed, the master symbol of industrial life. In this bucolic shrine "no deeper, softer dell," no more serene "primitive cell" could be imagined, wrapped in the "vague . . . haze" of "legend, of aboriginal mystery." Sunnyside becomes a somnolent paradise, tempting one to oceanic surrender and harmonious reunion with nature and our earliest origins (154–56).

But this haven, suffused with a premodern aura so seductive for the spiritually starved antimodernist, is a simulacrum. Eager to commemorate what it has dispossessed, "modernity" has preserved and enlarged this "gilded shell" of a tourist haunt. What James satirizes is the fashionable moral inflation of rusticity into a cult of purity that defines itself in opposition to the vulgarity of urban tumult. James's satire is not directed at country life per se. Indeed, in 1898 he had left London and a life of urban flânerie for the "so rural and tranquil" suburbs of Rye, fulfilling his "long unassuaged desire for a calm retreat" which would grant him the solitude to increase his rate of artistic production (*Letters* 4: 62). He was careful, however, to maintain a room in London to which he often returned. When Henry visited America in 1904, he enjoyed what he called the "real New England Arcadia" at William's country house in the White Mountains of Chocorua, New Hampshire.

III

Unlike Henry, William found deep pleasure and spiritual renewal in nature. Writing in 1895 from his favorite place, Keene Valley, New York, William tells his wife: "I begin to feel as if I were living on a normal moral plane again. It is curious how Society poisons me in seeming to take me away from the real springs of my life" (qtd. Bjork 202). William's Emersonian accents here can also be heard in his most characteristic political and cultural attitudes, which repeatedly protest the "bigness and greatness" of modern society, champion the embattled individual, and extol the redemptive powers of nature (*Letters* 2: 90; qtd. Matthiessen, *Family* 402). As it had for Emerson,

America remained nature's nation for James: "Bless the innocence," he wrote of his country in the wake of France's moral disgrace in the Dreyfus Affair, "we must thank God for America" (*Letters* 2: 100, 102).

William James's heroic individualism partly reflects his own philosophical eschewing of abstraction for the concrete. He enshrines tolerance of otherness—respect for particularity and multiplicity—as the guiding moral standard for the always precarious American democratic tradition. Thus he condemns the McKinley-Roosevelt administration's predatory expansion of empire as morally indefensible. To end this imperial policy of domination, James urged a return to "the older American beliefs" so that the country might once again "possess its ancient soul." In recovering the smallness of a preimperial America open to the alien, we could cast off our destructive "belief . . . in a national destiny which must be 'big' at any cost" (*Essays* [1987] 158, 157).

James articulated his social thought in a rhetoric of incomparable moral eloquence and passion, becoming a beloved cultural hero by the last decade of his life and remaining one in our own time.[8] His commitment to individual voluntarism, expressed in his pragmatism and political activity, acted as an inspiring therapeutic model for a college-educated audience in need of spiritual solace to confront the bewilderments of modernity. That James has remained vital testifies both to his compelling personal example and our own need for solace, particularly that afforded by his belief in "the morning freshness of the founding American myth," which conceives of the "individual as truly prior to society." These words by one contemporary celebrant of William James announce the philosopher's "return" as an event that will liberate "the imagination of the American literary humanist from its fascination with the French intellectual scene." James "recognizes but does not capitulate to the suffocating and tyrannous world that Foucault described" (Lentricchia 120, 104, 123). Even though the the current skeptical, historicist temper easily points up the deficiencies of James's Adamic myth, his existential anarchism remains seductive.[9] This suggests that the appeal of his romantic stance is emotional, rooted more in the stirring optimism of his individualism than in his engagement with history and its constraints.

Perhaps this is only to say that William James's politics belong to the nineteenth century. In a recent major study James Kloppenberg noted of the generation that matured intellectually in the 1870s and 1880s that their "ideas reflected a substantially different social reality from the world that dawned in the 1890s" (146). To Kloppenberg James's political thinking is valuable not for his personal, largely moral response to events but for philosophical reasons, particularly his pragmatic method of revisionary, historicist inquiry skeptical of all abstractions and untested pieties. This method (rather than his own practice of it) was James's legacy: his pragmatism "helped to nurture the seeds of a new political sensibility" (174). To those individuals like John Dewey, whose politics are of the twentieth century, this antidogmatic method helped make "available a new way of understanding a new world" (194). James "committed himself to no particular substantive program but instead to a style of inquiry" that would promote "critical historicism" in later thinkers whose worldviews were considerably less romantic (149, 110).[10]

This is a useful approach to James not least because it focuses attention on what I take to be most impressive about his own style of inquiry—its deliberate resistance to precise political identity. He defined himself politically "both within and against a Mugwump ideology," notes George Cotkin, who finds that James's "anarchistic edge" would "always prevent him from embracing any easily definable political attitude" (126, 17). This skeptical openness embodies the new understanding that James imparted, an openness that helps account for another aspect of his remarkable legacy—the variety of social critics he directly influenced. These included not only his philosophical colleagues (Dewey, Mead, and Cooley) but also his students (Walter Lippmann, Horace Kallen, and W.E.B. Du Bois) and admirers (Harold Laski and Randolph Bourne).[11]

William's open, unaffiliated style of inquiry, which conceives the aim of politics to be the circulation of differences rather than their imperial subjugation, bears striking similarities to the premises of Henry's pragmatist cultural criticism. Each brother practices his own mode of what I call a politics of nonidentity, a phrase that cannot avoid the paradox of trying to label a strategy dedicated to disrupting the compulsion to fix identity. Any definition is identification, and identity logic is our normal mode of thought. By positing a transparent coincidence between concepts and their objects, this logic tacitly excludes ambiguity, as the flux of reality is converted into the fixity of concepts. Confronted by a social and political order seeking to dissolve difference into a monolithic American identity, William and Henry were united in their suspicion of the assimilating, homogenizing thrust of totalizing systems. William sought to preserve the "unclassified residuum" (*Will* 223), Henry the "obstinate residuum" (*Scene* 124). The former's mode of preservation looks to the primitive power of nature and the innocence of the beleaguered individual (including those oppressed by imperial powers, ranging from the United States to medical licensing boards) as sources of value and intensity in an increasingly stultifying world. The latter honors the residuum, but he does so within the crucible of modernity—the city. In urban immersion, in flâneries that risk "a certain recklessness in the largest surrender to impressions," Henry recovers intensity and affirms the claim of the alien (*Scene* 3, 85).

Henry practices a politics of nonidentity in the course of his American journey, which, he tells us, is made under the "ensign" of the "*i*/legible word." He fancies that it "hangs in the vast American sky," signifying the unknowability of the nation's future (*Scene* 121–22). This ensign is apt, for James admires the illegible, the "unconverted residuum" embodied in the aliens he sees in New York, and regrets that they seem about to be absorbed into a homogenous social order. But rather than merely lamenting the American genius for social control—what he calls "hotel-spirit"—James fashions an immanent strategy that probes the workings of this spirit and finds that its mania for order creates its own disorder. Thus the extinction of the alien is not complete and "they may rise again . . . affirming their vitality and value" (129).

William sought to save the residuum from various forces, among them the devouring grasp of American imperialist aggression and German idealist philosophies. In early and late essays William criticized Hegel's "logic of identity" for its sacrifice of contingency and particularity to the abstract laws of an absolutist system. And in his 1899 campaign against imperialism William denounced Roosevelt as an "arch abstractionist" and accused him of practicing, in effect, a Hegelian politics of identity that "swamps everything together in one flood of abstract bellicose emotion" (*Essays* [1987] 164).[12] A year earlier Henry had leveled a similar attack at another dimension of Roosevelt's view of national identity. The latter's demand for one hundred percent Americanism, said Henry, threatened to "tighten the screws of the nationalist consciousness as they had never been tightened before" (*Literary* 1: 663). Henry regarded Roosevelt's disciplinary imperative of identity as expressing "the puerility of his simplifications" (665). William thought Roosevelt was "still mentally in the Sturm und Drang period of early adolescence" (*Essays* [1987] 163).

William and Henry's politics of nonidentity represent their shared effort at interrogating the dominant forms of authority and mastery in late nineteenth-century culture. The Jameses' most audacious mode of inquiry takes the form of a commitment to vulnerability and abjectness, as if liberating the infantile rage fueling imperialist jingoism and converting it into playful mockery of the rigidity of bourgeois character structure. Henry, the impeccable Master, relished bewilderment and more than once called himself a "worm," "most abject," a "suppliant flat-on-my-belly" (*Letters* 4: 689).[13] William describes his radical empiricism as lying "flat on its belly in the middle of experience, in the very thick of its sand and gravel" (*Pluralistic* 125). "Its world is always vulnerable," says William of the pluralistic vision, "its partisans must always feel to some degree insecure" (*Pragmatism* 290).[14] It is ironic, of course, to associate two grand figures with the deflation of grandeur. But their deflation was a strategic resistance to the suffocating, absolutist ideologies of mandarin culture. The willful loss of dignity is part of a dialectic that Adorno has identified: "Art partakes of weakness no less than of strength. In fact, the unconditional surrender of dignity may even become a vehicle of strength in modern art" (*Aesthetic* 58). This logic informs Henry's personal experiments with a more heterogeneous and marginal mode of being (which I term mimetic) that he developed in reaction to what he represented as William's invincible priority.

Encouraging Henry's flexibility was the support of a family where "the presence of paradox was so bright" that all five children "breathed inconsistency and ate and drank contradictions" (*Autobiography* 124). Thus a Jamesian spirit animates my revisionist stance, which finds incongruity and contradiction crucial to the identities of both men. In his memoirs Henry not only flaunts his abjectness and celebrates William's prowess but also carefully

conceals his elder brother's flounderings and his own near effortless achievement of professional and social success. William, a self-proclaimed, carefree
anarchist and a heroic exemplar of the strenuous life, also possessed another
identity as a lifelong neurasthenic who never lost a sense of anguished kinship
with the "green-skinned" epileptic "idiot" he confronted during his depression of the 1860s. In complicating the monochromatic, canonized images of
William and Henry as anarchist and master with the less familiar dimensions
of their identities as idiot and worm, I hope to reveal the meanings and
manifestations of their complex psychic economies.

IV

In the James family nothing was more vigorously interrogated than the self.
Echoing his Calvinist heritage, James senior called the self "the curse of
mankind." Recovering from his 1844 "vastation," which led to his religious
conversion to Swedenborgianism, the elder James thought "how sweet it
would be" to find himself no longer a man but a humble sheep (qtd. Matthiessen, *Family* 162). "To exalt humble and abase proud things was ever
the darling sport of his conversation," noted William of his father, and what
he most energetically sought to abase was the sovereign self of liberal individualism (168). Radically opposed to his friend Emerson's divinizing of
the unfettered self, Henry senior spent his life seeking to redeem man from
the disease of self-sufficiency by recalling him to the "society into which he
is born," for "Society is the movement of redemption, or the finished spiritual
work of God" (142–43). The elder James's embrace of the abject ("I . . . will
cherish the name of him alone whose insufficiency to himself is so abject
that he is incapable of realizing himself except in others") most directly
inspired William and Henry's own irreverence toward conventional modes
of authority and identity and their experiments in sailing what their father
called "that virgin, unexplored sea of Being" (153, 165). Each undertook
different explorations of that sea, but they were propelled by the belief that
no single form of selfhood was either preordained or sacrosanct; various forms
beckoned to be explored and fashioned from diverse experiences of abasement, conversion, and revision.[15]

These explorations were exhilarating but also perilous since the Jamesian
dialectic of abasement and renewal could inflict mental trauma. For William
and his father the dialectic was decisively shaped by the sudden fear that
temporarily overwhelmed each of them in their thirties. Father and son
overcame their shared sense of the self dissolving in terror by tenaciously
adhering to their habitual means of survival. The elder Henry retreated from
the world at large—where he was "left stranded high and dry," in William's
phrase—into the bosom of his family, which constituted virtually the only
audience for his gospel of anti-individualism (qtd. Matthiessen 140). William
"found salvation," as James Hoopes has noted, not, like his father, in "the
construction of a theology of selflessness" but "in self-confidence . . . in human freedom and ability" grounded in the will to believe (Hoopes 208).

Brother Henry, nurtured by the dialectic but spared its moment of terrible panic, was also spared what the panic bred in his father and brother—the compulsion of self-preservation. The consequence was that, unlike his father and William, Henry was comparatively free to sail the uncharted sea of Being. Spurning the serene obliviousness of his father's absorption in theological system-building and relaxing the vigilant will that was the motor of William's renewal, Henry submitted his own selfhood, and the very concept of self-hood, to an extended ordeal of vulnerability. This ordeal is the subject of his late autobiographical writings and of *The Ambassadors*, works central to this study.

The energy and freedom to remake the self were not extended to all members of the James family. The lives of the three youngest were, on the whole, frozen in the isolation of emotional failure. Alice, the only daughter, found life a "never-ending fight," a "hideous battle" that demanded "an acrid strain to stiffen the sinews" against the "multifold traps set for your undoing" (*Diary* 76, 149–50). After the family fashion, Alice sought survival by identifying with the abject: "I remind myself all the time of a coral insect," she remarked of her ceaseless cultivation of "inner consciousness" (109). It remained Alice's lot to articulate the dark side of the dangerous family dialectic of impotence and strength. The fragile interplay of failure and power that defined the family's creative economy produced in Alice James the will to construct only a memento mori—the diary of her inva-lidism—which she left as her memorial. Her willfully attenuated creativity (she began her diary three years before her death) testifies as much to her desire to publish her life as to her passionate refusal of any act of creative will save preparing for her own death. "I am working away as hard as I can to get dead as soon as possible," she wrote two years before finally accom-plishing the task that occupied most of her forty-four years (qtd. Yeazell 185). Schooled in the family's love of paradox, she could not resist converting her life's negativity into a certain intellectual vitality as she enacted her own prostrate version of the family dialectic. "Even *my* torpid career has not been without its triumphs to my own consciousness and therefore not to be pitied," she said in rebuking William. To his description of her as "impotent" she staunchly replied: "I consider myself one of the most potent creatures of my time" (106, 116). As Ruth Yeazell argues, Alice's cultivation of death is a "perverse kind of achievement," for the "very abjectness of her surrender leaves her curiously free" (2, 26).

Alice's confession, near the end of her life, that "I had to peg away pretty hard between 12 and 24, 'killing myself,' " can be read as a grotesquely literal version of her father's imperative of self-erasure. In the same diary entry her remark that she had absorbed "into the bone that the better part is to clothe oneself in neutral tints" anticipates her brother Henry's discovery of the creative possibilities in the "saving virtue of vagueness" (*Diary* 95). Unlike Henry's, Alice's willed effacement is not a means to an end but a permanent vocation in itself. She describes her adoption of "neutral tints" as her life's defining epiphany: "The knowledge crystallized within me of what Life meant for me . . . before which all mystery vanished" (95). Just as the coral, with which she identifies, grows by means of passive, repetitive accretion, so Alice's crystalline, neutered self endures a permanent but thriving stasis. Convinced that to "possess one's soul in silence" is her fate, Alice concludes her diary entry with fierce pride in her coral self:

> How profoundly grateful I am for the temperament which saves from the wretched fate of those poor creatures who never find their bearings, but are tossed . . . hither, thither and yon at the mercy of every event which o'ertakes them. Who feel no shame at being vanquished, or at crying out at the common lot of pain and sorrow, who never dimly suspect that the only thing which survives is the resistance we bring to life. (96)

Though heroic on one level (she is declaring her resistance to suicide), her defiance here is also unsettling in its celebration of emotional insulation as her elected form of existence.

Yet Alice only seems to carry to an extreme William's own understanding of the self as existing in "absolute insulation" (*Principles* 221). Her hermeticism was continually undermined by the strangely exultant receptivity of her diary, which functioned as a "receptacle" for what she called her "overflow" (*Diary* 105). Thus Alice's sensibility seems both to mock and affirm the experimental, risky openness that her father had made the family ideal; indeed, her tenacious commitment to death-in-life parodies Jamesian energy. Yet the power and truth of her grim parody resides in her lavish embrace of what that energy often sought to repress: passivity, renunciation, and insulation. These things were the perennial torments and temptations her father and two eldest brothers struggled with all their lives. In this context, William's pragmatism and Henry's "religion of doing" can be read as flights from the nightmare of inertia embodied in Alice, the most perverse flowering of the Jamesian genius.

V

Henry describes William's mind as "incapable of the shut door in any direction" (*Autobiography* 430). But it is a description equally apt regarding himself, for it helps explain what he means by his "incurable perversity" and "ambiguous economy." The engine of his openness, what drives his ordeal of vulnerability, is curiosity. In 1907 one observer of his American travels noted that Henry James had transgressed genteel boundaries; he attributed this to an intense "curiosity [James] displays toward things which it is our Anglo-Saxon instinct to avoid" (qtd. Gard 447).[16] On the most visible level, the word weaves through *The American Scene* from beginning to end. From the outset James finds the American spectacle a "challenge to intelligent curiosity" and "curiosity is fairly fascinated by the immensity" of the challenge (*Scene* 55). Later he discovers an affinity between curiosity and what I have been calling nonidentity or otherness. The "object" of "curiosity" is to look "over the alien shoulder . . . seeing, judging, building, fear-ing, reporting with the alien sense" (334–35). Since curiosity entwines self with other, one result is a "good deal of speculative tension" that James will consistently cultivate (335).

On a less visible level, Henry's embodiment of curiosity is comprised of overlapping psychological, cultural, critical, and sexual modalities. To illuminate how these dimensions reciprocally interact (and to avoid psychologism and other forms of reductionism) requires the flexible, nuanced concepts of dialectical thought. It also demands the perspectives of a variety of thinkers in several disciplines. These multiple vantage points partly comprise the web of textual affiliations in which I place the Jameses. Two strands of this web take on a special value in themselves, for they articulate a kinship unnoticed by intellectual histories. This occurs in the juxtaposition of Dewey and Adorno (chap. 5). Their affinity (which the latter acknowledged) constitutes a bridge between two traditions seldom brought together—German Critical Theory and American pragmatism—and provides a historical basis for my larger effort to read the James brothers against and within both schools of social thought. Emerging from this cross-fertilization of European and American traditions are the major concepts I use to elaborate William and Henry's various reconfigurations of identity and authority. Two have already been sketched: the deployment of an immanent logic of cultural critique and the practice of nonidentity thinking. Adorno is associated with both this method and thinking, and he (in conjunction with Benjamin) also furnishes a third concept—the mimetic—that is pivotal to my reading of Henry James. What Adorno calls aesthetic or mimetic behavior is a nonidentical mode of being and reason that dialectically sublates (canceling and preserving rather than simply opposing) the instrumental. Releasing all that rigid identity represses—spontaneity, expressiveness, and imitative, wordless impulse— mimetic reason and behavior survive in the modern world as remnants of the turbulent indeterminacies of the pre-Oedipal phase.[17] While Western rationality has stigmatized mimetic behavior as irrational and regressive, Henry James's curiosity nurtures a capacity for it, reinvesting it with productive potential. Tracing the various modalities of Jamesian curiosity will provide some sense of how the subsequent chapters unfold.

Henry James's curiosity is a form of psychic energy that shapes a selfhood at once instrumental and contemplative, permeable and hoarding. This doubleness, enacted in the diffuse, wayward movements of Henry's "gaping" urban perambulations, elicits unease in his elder brother. This reaction signals the defensiveness that sustains William's precarious psychic health. His equilibrium depends on a tense commitment to action, not prolonged contemplation. To assuage his unease William tends to regard Henry as basically powerless and passive (chap. 2). William's active blindness to Henry's "rare curiosity" anticipates the disciplinary procedures of literary canonization that repress Henry James as the peripatetic cultural critic animated by restless curiosity. Instead, it enshrines a reified image of James the master formalist. From Van Wyck Brooks in the twenties to contemporary deconstructionists, this domesticated Henry James is a caricature promoted by liberal and leftist critics alike. This consistent misprision (which William's reaction to Henry can be said to initiate) indicates that his psychic economy arouses a cultural anxiety. To understand this response requires philosophical models that reject liberalism's dualistic epistemology and aesthetic idealism (chap. 3). Thus Dewey's project—which revises William James's liberal ontology of self while reconceiving philosophy as cultural inquiry—is enlisted to help recover what canonization has repressed: Henry James the cultural analyst of modernity. Also relevant is the more radical, Marxist-derived social and aesthetic thought of Adorno and Benjamin. They provide perspectives useful for understanding not only Henry James's complex selfhood but also his style of cultural critique, in particular how it evolves and diverges from William's (chap. 4).

Their attitude toward curiosity is the crux of their differences. William's unease regarding Henry's ambiguous mode of being extends outward and shapes his problematic relation to modernity. Dewey and Adorno provide a context in which to discuss William James's radical empiricism as an escape from modernity's stifling of man's affective life. William's effort to give up the logic of identity for the immediacy and flux of "pure experience" has significant affinities with Dewey and Adorno. But, unlike William James, these thinkers (and Henry James) resist the irrational without embracing the instrumental by finding a mode of reason and behavior that Adorno dubs mimetic and that Henry embodies in his radical curiosity. The mimetic can be correlated with Henry James's fascination with the self's aesthetic behavior, the capacity for representation (or theatricality) that he finds the governing condition of social experience (chap. 5).

If the first half of this study constructs a more hospitable intellectual and philosophical tradition in which to locate Henry James, the second half interprets his major cultural works within this new context. The stylistic triumph of *The American Scene* is James's discovery of a form of cultural analysis that mimes the dissonant rhythms of his radical curiosity, which in turn feeds on shocks, contingencies, and the transitory attractions of urban minutiae. James's "traumatophilia" not only recalls Baudelaire's flaneur but also anticipates Walter Benjamin's celebration of this mode of being in his essays on Baudelaire as the emblematic figure of modernity. The form of critique Henry devises to enact his urban subjectivity strikingly prefigures Benjamin's own peripatetic analyses, which make immersion their guiding imperative (chap. 6).

In the last twelve years of his art and life, Henry James's representation of a restless curiosity comprises his effort to instill both in American gender and culture a certain vertiginous blurring that would make the self and social arrangements more flexible and thus more tolerant of a range of behaviors beyond conventional norms. In his prefaces he dubbed this sponsorship of otherness a "public and . . . civic use of the imagination" (*Art* 223) and it is in this light that his acts of cultural and psychic inquiry should be judged (chap. 7). His inquiry contests the hegemony of the genteel bourgeoisie— particularly its construction of American masculinity. Chapters 7, 8, and 9 comprise a virtual unit that discusses James's self and sexual representations in memoirs, a novel, and in the context of the cultural and sexual politics of the genteel bourgeois aristocracy. James's acquaintance with this milieu was facilitated by his close friendship with Howard Sturgis, an androgynous novelist and a cousin of George Santayana. All three men suffered under the "yoke" of the genteel (as Santayana termed it), and in response they each fashioned alternative forms of identity and sexuality that avoided the polarized psyche of the oedipally organized male (chap. 8). Rooted in libidinal sublimation rather than the repudiation of the feminine, Jamesian curiosity functions androgynously by partaking of the labile texture of pre-Oedipal identification with both sexes. His double identification constructs sexuality as pleasure in shock and friction itself, in sensation without a stable referent. This is what Strether discovers in Europe (chap. 9). What James discovers in America is that a fluidity of identification instills a capacity for a mutuality that is the basis of vital citizenship (chap. 10).

James's civic project—honoring difference without fetishizing it—must reckon with modernity's tensions. On the one hand, both his own mobile self shaped by the contingencies of urban life and his representations of an indeterminate sexuality correlate with a democratic dispersal of hierarchy. Thus, in 1914 he welcomes "the repudiation of the *distinctive*" as the "consummation" of the emancipated woman's "freedom to annex the male identity" (*Literary* 2: 780). Yet, on the other hand, this same social order threatens the freedom of this modern heterogeneous self. Even as it produces more open democratic subjects, modernity's instrumental mandate seeks to dissolve differences into a "single type" that is easier to control (*Scene* 427). James's project intuits that modernity's dialectic of freedom and control is always threatening to collapse into the latter term. Thus his urgent hope is that America will stop gloating about its "general conquest of nature and space" and attend to all that it has left "undone"—the creation of a more pluralistic democracy (463). The plague upon the American scene is an absence of the agonism crucial to a healthy politics and responsible citizenship, two checks upon the workings of the "hotel-spirit."

These concerns for fostering active citizenship and the messy heterogeneity of pluralism orient James's analysis, in *The American Scene*, of social control in the age of Teddy Roosevelt. Henry's ambivalence regarding modernity respects the finesse and reach of the "hotel-spirit" but criticizes its tranquilizing of subjectivity and depoliticizing of the social order. His anatomy of progressivism's technologies of control acknowledges their power not simply to influence but to constitute subjectivity. Yet James finds that, despite the best efforts of social technocracy, the project of modernity remains incomplete and incalculable. A "margin" of plasticity remains in American life, potentially able to fashion looser, more flexible social and psychic structures designed to release active curiosity. Henry James's stance, embodying a politics of nonidentity, is clarified by juxtaposing it with an array of Progressive social and cultural critics (chap. 10).

The preceding summary suggests that the Jamesian construction of curiosity is akin to what Raymond Williams calls a "structure of feeling actively lived and felt." A structure of feeling is "practical consciousness of a present kind, in a living and inter-relating continuity." Still in process and "in solution," curiosity is a "specific structure of particular linkages, particular emphases and suppressions" (*Marxism* 132–34). In other words, Jamesian curiosity is a pragmatic historical practice suspicious of any discourse equating the social with fixed or finished forms. An analogous commitment to revision will provide the present work with at least a measure of the requisite complexity to unsettle received opinion and to reanimate the contradictions and paradoxes within which Henry and William lived.

I
THE TRIAL
OF CURIOSITY

2

Henry and William James
and the Trial of Curiosity

"If we wish to act," says William James, "we should pause and wonder as little as possible." Otherwise we risk the vertiginous mental state of near paralysis that James dubs "ontological wonder-sickness," whereby "thought oscillating to and fro . . . finds no end, in wandering mazes lost" (*Will* 64, 66). It is probable that William was first exposed to the virus of "purely theoretic contemplation" when, as an adolescent, he strolled the streets of Paris and London with his brother, who somehow seemed immune to the sickness. Henry remarked that "we had done nothing, he and I, but walk about together . . . dawdle at shop-windows and buy watercolors and brushes" (*Autobiography* 170). But whereas Henry had no "quarrel" with "endlessly" walking and daubing, William, "looking back at it from after days . . . denounced it . . . as a poor and lamentable and arid time . . . missing such larger chances and connections." What William denounced as "poverty of life" Henry found a "medium so dense," "most expressive to myself of the charm and color of history and . . . of society" (171–72).

Passages such as this have helped form the now nearly indelible image of the contrasting temperaments of William and Henry. According to virtually all accounts, their relationship consisted of a series of neat dualisms: active, manly, inquisitive William versus contemplative, sissified, withdrawn Henry. In the words of Gerald Myers, William's most recent biographer, William "saw in Henry a passivity, a willingness to let life come to him, whereas William viewed himself as meeting life head-on. Henry was the serene observer, William the restless doer" (29). Like other critics and biographers before him, Myers leaves these polarities unchallenged.[1] This critical habit can be explained, if not justified, as a kind of deference to the brothers themselves, the ultimate source of these characterizations. William repeatedly feared that Henry would end up paralyzed and helpless. Throughout

27

his memoirs Henry depicted himself as grateful to live on the "crumbs" of William's "feast and the echoes of his life" (*Autobiography* 246). In short, these representations and the dualisms they generated are not false, but they are best viewed as partial and highly strategic, satisfying some emotional needs and investments of the brothers that are part of their larger, more intricate psychic economies. For instance, in *Pragmatism* William articulates one of his fondest self-representations when he sets his "radical pragmatist . . . a happy-go-lucky anarchistic sort of creature" against the "doctrinaire and authoritative complexion" of the rationalist mind. Rejecting the rationalist's "*must* be,*"* the pragmatist welcomes an "unfinished, growing" universe, a "tramp and vagrant world" that "leans on nothing" (124–25).

Some problems in William James's representation are exposed in a "psychological analysis" of the philosopher published in 1909, a year before his death, by one Edwin Tausch. The latter's most provocative claim is that a disturbing "bitterness of feeling" and "intolerance" against those who prize metaphysical speculation pervades James's "passionate anti-intellectual empiricism." Evidently James's self-advertised "happy-go-lucky" anarchism contained some of the despised dogmatism that he ascribed to doctrinaire rationalists. In his published response to Tausch, James appears to contest these claims: "My flux philosophy may well have to do with my extremely impatient temperament. I am a motor, need change, and get very quickly bored." What James says, in effect, is: you mistake impatience for intolerance. With this correction James hopes to close the gap Tausch has opened. But it is hard not to find bitterness in James's statement—quoted three times by Tausch—that "there is something diseased and contemptible, yea vile, in theoretic grubbing and brooding." Regardless of this animus, notes Tausch, James must necessarily "still believe in theoretic grubbing and brooding; he is still a philosopher" (15, 23–25).[2] What Tausch exposes is James's uneasy relation to philosophy itself. The discrepancy between William James's lavishly proclaimed anarchic insouciance and his "bitter" contempt for metaphysics will be explored in the present chapter. I intend not only to illuminate James's psychological complexity but also to dispute the dualistic structure of previous accounts of the relationship between William and Henry.

Seeking to understand William is the best way to appreciate Henry's kind of subjectivity. Although reading Henry through William is nothing new, I hope to avoid what this procedure typically yields (in the work of Edel and others): a picture of fierce rivalry on both sides that left Henry deformed by feelings of inferiority and repressed rage toward William. Myers, declaring himself "generally skeptical of Freudian interpretations of the brothers' relationship," tacitly rejects Edel's influential reading: "It was not fraternal rivalry or hidden animus that led William to separate himself from Henry, but rather a genuine difference in philosophical attitudes. We need not assume that such a difference tarnished their fraternal affection" (29). Myers here suggests a useful change of emphasis, one that can take the measure of Henry's statement to William in 1905: "To what different ends we have had to work out... our respective intellectual lives" (*Letters* 4: 383). To define these "different ends," any analysis must avoid the usual interpretive reflexes—particularly the reliance on an overly familiar Freudian scenario and the conventional oppositions of active versus passive. In the present chapter I hope to resist these reductive moves and to show that the psychological components of the Henry/William relationship are inseparable from its cultural aspects. The cultural moment that concerns us here is the late nineteenth- and early twentieth-century anxiety about and fascination with forms of being that resist normalization, the obedience to social techniques of domination that produce the subject. This process, which Foucault called the submission of subjectivity, was adumbrated by Nietzsche and several of his contemporaries, including the Jameses, who confronted these issues on their own terms.

I

Tausch's suggestion of conflict in William James's psyche remained tentative and unpursued, an unsolved "puzzle," says Tausch, "as long as we are not allowed a detailed account" of James's "mental development" (25). The detailed account, published in 1920 (in the form of James's letters and selected diary entries), revealed that James's "bitterness" was a reaction to his abulia, a near suicidal paralysis of will that plagued him in the late 1860s. James's letters and notes of this period describe what would come to be known as one of the representative cases of late nineteenth-century spiritual crisis.[3] James's neurasthenia—the word he preferred—recalls the early crises of Wordsworth, Mill, and Carlyle, whose various efforts in overcoming the disease of thought and self-consciousness helped inspire James's own struggle. Indeed, Carlyle's command to "get to work like Men!" would remain one of James's touchstones. In dramatic detail James's letters recount his struggle to surmount his obstructed will, which had produced a vexed, at times tormented, relation to philosophy. It is crucial to see how James resolved his crisis. A diary note of 1870 reads: "[I] care little for speculation, much for the form of my action... I will abstain from the mere speculation and contemplative *Grublei* in which my nature takes most delight" (*Letters* 1: 159). Thus the bitterness that Tausch sensed is born of love that has learned self-denial. If James's disdain for speculation is rooted in the imperative of self-preservation, it is also tinged with self-contempt.

Preservation, denial, and contempt merge to form a knot of repression— what James will call a "native hardness"—upon which he constructs a self (*Varieties* 110). "He had *made* himself... into a compulsively active man," emphasizes Richard Poirier, and this act of making is enacted throughout his life and is a major subject of his work (*Renewal* 197). His rigorous commitment to self-creation confirms what thinkers like Nietzsche, Freud, Adorno, and Foucault stress: the coercive character of identity and the entanglement of subjectivity and subjection. Sovereign man, "this master of a *free* will," wrote Nietzsche in 1887, is created by the "labor performed by man upon himself. . . . Ah, reason, seriousness, mastery over the affects . . . all these prerogatives and showpieces of man: how dearly they have been bought! how much blood and cruelty lie at the bottom of all 'good things'!" (59, 62). James's life and work are a monument to the self as a perpetual work of "labor," a structure of repression. But this is not to deny that the repression is dialectical, issuing in a philosophy of pragmatism that celebrates repression's opposite: the fact of vulnerability in a world of contingency, uncertainty, risk, change, "novelty and possibility forever leaking in" (qtd. Perry 2: 700).

At least two rhetorics coexist uneasily in William James: one stresses the self as an engine of rationalistic control, shaping its experience by ceaselessly selecting and eliminating, whereas the other delights in the futility of "all neat schematisms with permanent . . . distinctions, classifications with absolute pretensions, systems with pigeon holes" (qtd. Perry 2: 700).[4] On the one hand, James's belief in radical autonomy posits the individual keeping his own thoughts to himself; on the other, he preferred to believe in overlap and continuity among individual streams of consciousness and insisted on the reality of relations. One rhetoric doesn't cancel out the other; they are conjunctive and indicative of a more complicated, anxious temperament than James's public persona of happy anarchist suggests. The "bitterness" Tausch detected is one manifestation of this anxiety. Another is James's defensive habit of mind, a tendency toward rigid polarities that encourages "the love of unity at any cost," an impulse from which James proudly believed he was exempt (*Will* 136). A characteristic Jamesian dualism is his declaration, following Carlyle, that "conduct, not sensibility, is the ultimate fact" (*Will* 134). This distinction, evident throughout his work, sustains yet also limits him, causing, as we shall see, a certain blindness in James even as he pleads for openness and empathy.

As more than one commentator has observed, James spent most of his life making sure he would never repeat the debilitating, infantilizing experiences of 1867–73. His letters during that time convey his drastic enfeeblement. In 1869 he writes: "I am very much run down in nervous force and have resolved to read as little as I possibly can . . . and absolutely not study, i.e., read nothing which I can get interested in and *thinking* about" (qtd. Perry 1: 306). A year earlier he was (predictably) fascinated by and identified with a production of *Hamlet* he had seen, "this awful *Hamlet*, which groans and aches so with the mystery of things, with the ineffable . . . as if the tongue were mocking itself. So too, action seems idle" (272). With these statements in mind, James's bitterness toward speculation can be seen as marking the strain of exertion demanded in his effort to transform himself from a Hamlet into a radical pragmatist/anarchist. And it is as a triumph of will that James's life is often read. Certainly his momentous diary entry of April 30, 1870, encourages such a reading: "My first act of free will," he announced after reading Charles Renouvier, the philosopher of will, "shall be to believe in free will." Until recently this statement has been quoted by virtually every student of James's life as expressing his pivotal and inaugural enactment of the gospel of belief. As James's first and most influential biographer, Ralph Barton Perry, declared: "To believe *by* an act of will *in* the efficacy of the will—that is a gospel which fits the temper of action, and which may be used to bring the invalid warrior back to fighting trim" (324).

Recently Howard Feinstein has dissented from this view, stressing that the "cure"—belief in free will—was part of the disease: "Instead of freedom *of* the will, William needed to be free *from* the will" (310). Concurring with this judgment, Richard Poirier adds that James's April 30 diary entry merely perpetuates his problems "in terms by which he deludes even himself. What sounds like an affirmation of free will is really a denial of it, a determination to thwart it. . . . Ambitious to be a philosopher . . . he must forbid himself philosophy" (*Renewal* 65). As Feinstein shows, it is only James's "willful throttling of self" that permitted individuation from the two Henrys and stable maturity for William (326). Feinstein and Poirier's positing of "freedom *from* the will" is provocative but sketchy; this kind of freedom remains an ideal elaborated upon neither in these critics' discourse nor in James's own life. Yet James found it a persistently compelling, if elusive, ideal for both conscious and unconscious reasons. Because freedom from will goes to the heart of his dialectic of repression, which produces fascination with, and even advocacy of, unrepressed modes of being, it remains a subject worthy of exploration.

James's psychological fascination is not difficult to understand. Those who possess freedom from will have, as Adorno says, escaped the effort of keeping the I together. They indulge in the *Grüblei* James had once delighted in and renounced in the interest of achieving stable selfhood. But unrepressed individuals, perhaps because they remind him of the cost (Nietzsche's "blood and cruelty") of constructing his own self, also disturb him. Hence his admiration almost always involves his exiling them to the margins of social experience, where they are safely confined to the eccentric status of mystic, saint, or primitive. When he seems most tempted by states where a "magically irresponsible spell" reigns, where "nothing happens, nothing is gained, and there is nothing to describe," James is careful to restrict them to "the holidays of life," not its weekday activity (*Talks* 263). Regardless of his ambivalence toward the marginal, his respect for them grew in later life into a defense of the rights of the alien in general. Mental patients, believers in psychic research, and the people of the Philippines were among those for whom James demanded tolerance and acceptance.

James's courageous advocacy of the marginal and the transgressive, and his profound generosity toward those whose "oddities and eccentricities" he cherished was his attempt, says Poirier, to "release himself and the rest of us from any settled, coherent idea of the human" (65). But this judgment ignores the paradox that James's release from settled ideas of the human is conditioned by entrapment in an unquestioned belief—that the self is radically autonomous and defined by "absolute insulation." This belief partly comprises what Santayana called William's guiding assumption "that certain thoughts and hopes—those familiar to a liberal Protestantism—were every man's true friends in life. This assumption would have been hard to defend if he . . . had ever questioned it" (*Character* 85). A particularly vivid instance of the dialectic of repression informs James's essay "On a Certain Blindness in Human Beings" and unwittingly complicates its premise that we are all afflicted by blindness about the feelings of those different from ourselves.

Although Frank Lentricchia has recently found this essay to be rich in critical self-scrutiny, its self-reflexivity is compromised by James's dualisms. "Self-scrutiny" is indeed James's subject: he hopes that by confronting squarely the fact of human selfishness, tolerance will grow and a "live and let live attitude" will flourish. The need for such an attitude was imperative, James felt, given the immediate context of political intolerance—American imperialist aggression in the Philippines. But James's larger claim is that tolerance, in any context, is difficult, for it violates man's innate self-absorption. As "practical beings . . . with limited functions and duties to perform," we are so absorbed in our "vital secrets" that we are easily indifferent to the "significance of alien lives" (qtd. Matthiessen, *Family* 398). Although James's statements imply that he is describing man's ontological condition, his view is founded on a particular premise that he leaves unspoken—the insulation and instrumentality of possessive individualism. James assumes this individualism to be the transhistorical nature of man: "So blind and dead does the clamor of our practical interests make us to all other things, that it seems almost as if it were necessary to become worthless as a practical being . . . to have any perception of life's meaning on a large objective scale" (400). This polarity—blind practicality versus perceptive uselessness—defines the essay as a whole. James celebrates "your mystic, your dreamer, or your insolvent tramp or loafer" as agents of perception. Whitman embodies this dreamy loafer for James, who quotes from a letter in which the poet stares at the endless panorama of people as they stroll down Broadway. Attending to the "mere spectacle of the world's presence" is "the most fundamental way" of shedding our habitual blindness, for it permits one to "descend to a more profound and primitive level," which can be reached variously—by being "imprisoned or shipwrecked or forced into the army," or simply "living in the open air and on the ground" (402).

In his plea for the recognition and tolerance of otherness, James ignores the possibility that people other than Whitmanic primitives "are alive where we often are dead." His strict dichotomy sees either "savages and children of nature" or the self-absorbed bourgeoisie, repressed in its frenzy of activity (402). Ironically, James knew someone as fascinated as Whitman by the same Broadway spectacle, who often seemed so lost in dawdling and reverie over its endless panorama that he was mistaken for a dunce. But this same person had little of Whitman's ostentatious primitivism, which celebrated in "Song of Myself" the "scent of these armpits' aroma finer than prayer." Henry James's absence from his brother's essay suggests that the "certain blindness" is, on an unconscious level, a blindness to a brother who represents a difficult "third" category of selfhood unassimilable to William's binary structure. As a connoisseur of *Grüblei* par excellence, Henry's mode of being in many ways embodies the very behavior—"holiday" pleasure in merely dawdling and gaping—that William finds discomforting. And even more unnerving is that in his love of doing nothing Henry managed to avoid irresponsibility. Indeed, Henry's "silent pluck" (as William called it) accompanied his addiction to "dawdling" and helped him to create at such a rate that William was forced to confess in 1869: "I give up like a baby in comparison." But twenty years later, William's "maturity" evidently demanded a new psychic equilibrium: it was now Henry whom William believed to be helpless and powerless.

Henry's hovering presence about rather than in "On a Certain Blindness" makes him the unspeakable "alien" who reveals the blindness in William's effort to exercise self-scrutiny. But William grants Henry an oblique recognition near the end of the essay. He reports the words of a tribal "chieftain" to his white guest: "Ah! my brother, thou wilt never know the happiness of both thinking of nothing and doing nothing." "Ah! my brother"—this gratuitous phrase seems to express William's unconscious identification of Henry with the "chieftain," one of the "savages . . . of nature, to whom we deem ourselves so much superior." Yet, warns William, they "certainly are alive where we often are dead," blind as we are "to the fundamental static goods of life" (403). In his memoirs Henry would compare his "play of strong imaginative passion" to the way "the subtle savage puts" his ear to the ground to catch "some vibratory hum" (*Autobiography* 482). Such an existence has already found the remedy William prescribes—descent to a more "profound and primitive level" where doing nothing is imbued with creative fertility. Evidently this subtle primitivism is too close to life's "static goods" for William to embrace it comfortably. Such a state of freedom from will is inherently paradoxical to the philosopher of will.

Since will is the source of action, to be free from it would comprise freedom not to act, to speculate without making thoughts "instruments of action" (*Pragmatism* 97). Except for special cases, such freedom is little more than an invitation to morbidity, even to mental degeneration, as James stressed in his 1896 Lowell lectures: "an infinite *Grübelsucht*" creates a deadening skepticism and unreality. Although James offered this diagnosis with the (unacknowledged) conviction of personal experience, it represented the orthodox medical opinion of the day, which linked insanity to speculation, a view James adheres to in *The Principles of Psychology*. There he defines the "infinite *Grübelsucht*" as the "questioning mania," "the inability to rest in any conception and the need of having it confirmed and explained," which hinders all action (914). Nonpathological freedom is found not only in "chieftains" but also in mystics and saints, who attain equilibrium "not by doing, but by simply relaxing and throwing the burden down." This abandonment of self-responsibility involves a "melting" wherein "a native hardness must break down and liquefy" (*Varieties* 289, 110). The capacity for abandonment differentiates "religious as distinguished from moral practice." Of his own experience of religious practice, James remarks: "My own constitution shuts me out from their enjoyment almost entirely, and I can speak of them only at second hand" (379).

What decisively shaped James's constitution was an experience of a self liquefying not in ecstasy but in "panic fear." This notorious, much-discussed episode occurred sometime in 1870–72, when James felt a "horrible fear" of his own existence in the midst of "philosophic pessimism and general depression." His fear found its objective correlative in the image of an epileptic idiot he had once seen in an asylum, a "black-haired youth with greenish skin" who used to sit all day in a fetal position. "He sat there . . . moving nothing but his black eyes." This figure terrifies James because he recognizes him as an image of his own fear: *That shape am I*, I felt potentially." This shock at recognizing his own "merely momentary discrepancy from" the inert epileptic produces a visceral response in James: "It was as if something hitherto solid within my breast gave way entirely and I became a mass of quivering fear" (160). Here "freedom from will" reaches its most acutely morbid stage in an experience that seems a nightmare version of the "melting" selfhood of saintliness that James describes in *The Varieties of Religious Experience*. The epileptic's inertia, his absence of will, engenders in James a tormented mimicry of sympathetic identification as his "solid," stable selfhood gives way "entirely" and he is left a mass of "quivering fear."

To close this exposed, gaping self requires the exertion of will; James's determined belief in free will is the catalyst for his recovery, as he remakes the "shape" of panic fear into a shape built up on "habits of order." In his April 1870 diary entry he vows to "accumulate grain on grain of willful choice like a very miser." By inculcating habit and hoarding, or the habit of hoarding, salvation from panic fear is possible but not assured. Indeed, what gives dynamism and "the element of precipitousness" to James's vision of experience is the perpetual struggle between the selecting bias of the will and the mind's "theatre of simultaneous possibilities." Life's "dramatic interest" is rooted in its irreducible "zone of insecurity," a "dynamic belt of quivering uncertainty" that threatens to disrupt the self's efficiency unless one exercises careful vigilance (*Will* 193). The agencies of vigilance are various— habit, attention, belief, consent—but they all share a function: to impose order upon an "indistinguishable swarming continuum, devoid of distinction or emphasis" as a "sculptor works on his block of stone" (*Principles* 274–76). The result of this work is experience, which James defines as "what I agree to attend to" (380). By "picking out what to attend to, and ignoring everything else," the mind reveals its partiality, which is a condition of its efficiency (*Will* 165). Without the discipline and repetition of selection, which keeps sharp "the faculty of effort," we will not become the "mere walking bundle of habits" in which James takes such comfort. In his famous hymn to habit he calls it society's "most precious conservative agent. It alone is what keeps us all within the bounds of ordinance. . . . It is well for the world that in most of us, by the age of thirty, the character has set like plaster, and will never soften again" (*Principles* 126).

But "softening" does occur; even James admits to the "temporary melting moods" that the saint makes a way of life. But "with most of us," says James, "the customary hardness quickly returns" (*Varieties* 267). This "hard-

ness"—the merciful antidote to the liquid self of the saint or of "panic fear"—
is on guard against the enemy called distraction: "We all know this . . . state,
even in its extreme degree." A few times a day most of us become absorbed
in staring off into space, where "the eyes are fixed on vacancy . . . the attention is dispersed," and we surrender to the "empty passing of time"
(*Principles* 382). To be able to banish this "scattered condition of mind" is
to possess a precious faculty: the ability to "voluntarily bring back a wandering attention . . . is the very root of judgment, character, and will" (401).
A healthy will enables the self to insulate itself against distraction. And
"absolute insulation" is, for James, the law governing the relations among
minds: each personal consciousness "keeps its own thoughts to itself . . . as
if the elementary psychic fact were not *thought* . . . but *my thought*, every
thought being *owned*. . . . The breaches between such thoughts are the most
absolute breaches in nature" (221). But, in characteristic Jamesian fashion,
a law is declared only to be qualified. In the next chapter of *The Principles
of Psychology* James states that it would be rash "to be too sure" about insulation, given the "phenomena of thought transference, mesmeric influence,
and spirit control" that some authorities (including James) endorse. James
thus revises his law: "The definitively closed nature of our personal consciousness is probably an average statistical resultant of many conditions,
but not an elementary force or fact" (331).

What is so revealing about this amendment to the "law of absolute insulation" is what prompts it: only extreme phenomena (such as mesmerism)
give James pause. He does not seem to consider either the possibility that
his basic premise of monadic subjectivity may be too simple and constricted
a model or that the self is a social construct dependent on and conditioned
by others. In short, James excludes the open and intersubjective self posited
by his contemporary, George Herbert Mead. "Selves can only exist," says
Mead, "in definite relationships to other selves. No hard-and-fast line can
be drawn between our own selves and the selves of others" (*Mind* 164).
Perhaps James was disinclined to posit a social model of identity because
the dialectic of self and other inherent in social representation necessarily
compromises the will's freedom. In contrast, the insulated self assumes a
rigidly controlled will, the will of the rugged individualist to whom James
always gave priority: "Surely the individual . . . is the more fundamental
phenomenon" and the social institution "secondary" (*Memories* 102). James,
of course, does not deny that man and society interact; *The Principles of
Psychology* contains a famous and notably brief discussion of man's "social
self." But he conceives it narrowly as "the recognition which man gets from
his mates." For James the social self is not constitutive but merely one
among several selves. To claim, as did Mead, that "a person is a personality
because he belongs to a community" and internalizes its institutions (*Mind*
162) would likely strike James as a threat to what he celebrated—the sanctity
of the individual in all his idiosyncrasy.

James's capacious sympathy and receptivity toward others, particularly
toward people whose wills were somehow impaired, were largely neglected

in the popular image of him. By the time of his death, the prophet of pragmatism was regarded as so persuasive an advocate of "conduct, not sensibility," that James had (unwittingly) become the philosophical patron of the burgeoning efficiency movement. Indeed, Josiah Royce spent most of his memorial essay arguing that although James "shared in a rich measure" the values of the movement, his pragmatism was not "a sort of philosophic generalization of the efficiency doctrine" (31–32). Ironically, it was a distinguished advocate of efficiency, a proponent of the "instinct for workmanship" and a scourge of leisure, who offered one of the most telling critiques of pragmatism's preoccupation with practical action.

II

In 1906 Thorstein Veblen proposed that pragmatism's blind spot was its inability to account for what he called "idle curiosity." He found inadequate the pragmatic belief that intelligence is wholly functional and that motor responses to stimuli are discharged through some action or behavior—"a reasoned line of conduct looking to an outcome that shall be expedient for the agent" (*Science* 6). This account neglects another stimulus response that "does not spend itself in a line of motor conduct and does not fall into a system of uses." Pragmatically speaking, this response is "idle, unintended and irrelevant." Closely related to the aptitude for play, "idle curiosity" is the instinct, first exerting itself in myth and legend, that has urged mankind "toward a more and more comprehensive system of knowledge." In striking contrast is pragmatism's static and "didactic exhortations to thrift, prudence, equanimity, and shrewd management" (9). This appears to be an indictment of James's discussion of curiosity in *The Principles of Psychology*. In his chapter on instinct James stresses the transience of the instinct of curiosity: "Our purely intellectual zeal" ebbs as we grow into adulthood. "In each of us a saturation-point is soon reached . . . we settle into an equilibrium and live on what we learned when our interest was fresh and instinctive." James emphasizes that men "*cannot* get anything new. Disinterested curiosity is past, the mental grooves and channels set." The "natural conclusion" that James draws is that "instincts are implanted for the sake of giving rise to habits, and that, this purpose once accomplished," the instincts fade away (1021–22). James's divergence from Veblen is also made clear several pages later when he qualifies his remarks on curiosity by noting that "scientific curiosity" has nothing to do with instinctive curiosity and is only an "*incidental*" feature of our mental life (1046). For James, then, idle curiosity would resemble "freedom from will" as another potentially dangerous condition of distraction.[5]

Veblen, however, would concur with James on one point: curiosity (beyond the instinctive level) is the province of the scientist, whose "inquiry is as 'idle' as that of the Pueblo myth-maker" (*Science* 17). Veblen's emphasis on the idleness of science was likely influenced by his former professor, Charles S. Peirce, who defined true science as "the study of useless things. . . . It is destroyed as soon as it is made an adjunct to conduct." Peirce described his attitude as "Aristotelian," evidently an allusion to the ancient's valuation of theory over practice and the opening of his *Metaphysics*: "All men by nature desire to know. An indication of this is the delight we take in our senses; for even apart from their usefulness they are loved for themselves" (1: 55, 57, 618). Peirce's view of the scientist has been called sentimental and ahistorical in its insistence on the absolute purity of curiosity. Perhaps seeking to avoid Peirce's idealism and to account for contemporary reality while retaining the category of the useless, Veblen finds a mediating term, technology, which he defines as "the employment of scientific knowledge for useful ends." Despite the scientist's "idle" inquiry, "the canons of validity under whose guidance he works are those imposed by the modern technology.... His canons of validity are made for him by the cultural situation; they are habits of thought imposed on him by the scheme of life current in the community in which he lives" (16–17). While contemporary thinkers like Jacques Ellul would likely reject Veblen's effort to reconcile idle curiosity and technology, Veblen here shows an admirably keen awareness of the historically conditioned nature of curiosity.[6]

Curiosity's turbulent history has played a central role in defining "the legitimacy of the modern age," as Hans Blumenberg has argued in his book of the same title. Part of Blumenberg's massive study traces what he calls "the trial of theoretical curiosity" from the ancients' love of *curiositas* to twentieth-century technology. Blumenberg describes his subject, which is confined to Western European thought, as the process whereby curiosity, "a mark of youthfulness even in animals," becomes the "substratum around which historical articulation and focus set in. As a result of the discrimination against it, what was natural and went without saying is explicitly 'entered into' and accentuated" (234). Curiosity, then, is a concept and stance toward the world that is perennially contested. Although the " 'theoretical attitude' may be a constant of European history since the awakening of the Ionians' interest in nature," it became one of the epochal characteristics of the modern age only "after contradiction, restriction, competition, and the exclusiveness of other essential human interests had been set up in opposition to it" (380). Partially comprising this "opposition" was the medieval or, more specifically, Augustinian prohibition against curiosity as the vice of "ocular desire," an arrogant dispersal of attention from man's highest goal of otherworldly salvation, a verdict partly in response to the classical esteem of curiosity as "reposeful and bliss-conferring contemplation" (312, 385).

This Christian discrimination, in turn, generated curiosity's rehabilitation at the beginning of the modern age: the Enlightenment asserted man's right to an "unrestricted cognitive drive." But Enlightenment man's assertion, stresses Blumenberg, presupposes an altered concept of theory, a move from the contemplative classical ideal to an experimental one. Francis Bacon is usually credited with shaping this change, which reconceives theoretical knowledge as "ruthless curiosity" (Nietzsche's phrase), as power that must bear, says Bacon, "fruits and works" in practical usefulness. John Dewey

called Bacon the "real founder of modern thought," the "prophet of a pragmatic conception of knowledge" in his emphasis on "induction, experiment,
discovery and progress." Dewey suggests that William James might have
had Bacon in mind when he called pragmatism "a new name for an old way
of thinking" (*Reconstruction* 28, 34, 38). So thoroughly does Bacon pragmatize
the Aristotelian ideal of passive contemplation that, as Blumenberg observes,
"the pleasure of curiosity appears once more in its medieval signification . . .
[as] a standstill in the pursuit of knowledge, a forgetfulness of its original
purpose," which is to improve conditions (*Legitimacy* 388). In effect, Bacon
remade the "canons of validity," in Veblen's terms, to reflect the self-
understanding of an expanding capitalist and industrial society. Increasing
economic competition and technological innovation encourages inventive-
ness and utility, rendering pure theoretical curiosity "an attitude of ines-
capable resignation because it has no motive for its progress but rather dwells
persistently on each of its phenomena and loses itself in admiration of it"
(388). Such knowledge, says Bacon, resembles the sexual activity of a cour-
tesan, "which is for pleasure and not for fruit." Blumenberg sums up the
status of *curiositas* in the wake of Baconianism: "*Curiositas* has become a
worldly 'sin', the indolence of theory in theory itself, a failure in the exten-
siveness of the cognitive pretension as a result of its intensiveness" (388).
For Bacon the purity of theory comes to mean applied science and cooperative
research.

Veblen's strategy to redeem *curiositas* from sin and to reclaim the category
of idleness that pragmatism had ignored indicates that even in the late
nineteenth century the status of curiosity remained polemical, especially in
utilitarian cultures like those of England and America. In both countries
curiosity remained an attitude and a mode of being saturated in both medieval
and Christian interdictions and the Baconian revaluation of *curiositas*. For
instance, the ambiguities of curiosity figure prominently in Matthew Arnold's
argument, in 1865, that criticism is the "free play of the mind upon all
subjects" as "a pleasure in itself." Arnold illustrates his claim that for the
Englishman "practice is everything, a free play of mind nothing" by stating
that "it is noticeable that the word *curiosity*, which in other languages is used
in a good sense" to mean the autotelic attitude toward free play, has in
English "no sense of the kind, no sense but a rather bad and disparaging
one." Arnold laments this fact because "criticism, real criticism, is essentially
the exercise of" curiosity (246–47). Four years later, in *Culture and Anarchy*,
the subject has moved from defining the grounds of criticism to that of
culture. Arnold's advocacy of curiosity grows ambivalent. He begins by defending curiosity against the English bias for utility but ends by justifying
its disparagement as "frivolous and unedifying activity." He implicitly frames
his discussion as a conflict between the socialized impulses of "action" and
"doing good" versus the selfish "personal satisfaction" derived from gratifying curiosity's love of "pure knowledge" (472–74). This dualism of action
versus inwardness has deep roots in Arnold, appearing in his famous *Preface
to Poems* (1853), where he laments his age's passivity—"with us the expres-

sion predominates over the action"—and regrets indulgence in "the dialogue of the mind with itself" (185, 190).[7] Arnold's dichotomy strikingly recalls William James's celebration of will and impatience with speculation. James also shares Arnold's nervousness about curiosity as dangerous temptation. An exploration of the status of curiosity and its cognates—speculation, theoretic knowledge, wonder—in William James's life and work opens a rich vein of significance that reveals his powerful dialectic of repression.

III

The year 1872 found William strong enough to begin teaching at Harvard. But his battle with abulia, and the sense of inertia and hollowness it produced, remained too fresh to permit James to teach his deepest love, philosophy. He restricted himself to anatomy and physiology because he said their "concrete facts . . . form a fixed basis." Philosophy would put this stability in question because a philosopher "pledges himself publicly never to have done with doubt on these subjects." James found intolerable "the constant sense of instability generated by this attitude" (qtd. Perry 1: 343). But by 1879 he was able to teach philosophy because he had found a way to conceive of philosophy as a source of stability, like the natural sciences.

In the opening pages of his unintentionally autobiographical essay "The Sentiment of Rationality," James narrates the intricate, even painful, process of how he eased into philosophy. Written in 1877 and published in the year he began teaching philosophy, the essay's opening sentence asks why philosophers "philosophize at all?" Rationality is what they desire, but James's real interest is in defining its "subjective marks." What does rationality feel like? According to James, the movement from a "state of puzzle and perplexity to rational comprehension is full of lively relief and pleasure." This "feeling of the sufficiency of the present moment . . . this absence of all need to explain it, account for it, or justify it—is what I call the Sentiment of Rationality" (*Will* 57–58). This condition of "fluency" may be found in various ways, and he first examines the "theoretic way." James begins his essay by granting that theoretic philosophy—idealism—can attain its goal of satisfying the craving for simplicity, can succeed in classifying and abstracting from "concrete heterogeneity." The "relief of identification," which is the end of theoretic rationality, would appear to assimilate all into a unified system, and "no otherness being left to annoy us, we should sit down at peace . . . [with] no further considerations to spin" (63). But is this the peace of rationality? James says no. Contemplation does not end when mysteries and difficulties are resolved: "Our mind is so wedded to the process of seeing an *other* beside every item of its experience, that when the notion of an absolute datum is presented to it, it goes through its usual procedure and remains pointing at the void beyond, as if in that lay further matter for contemplation" (63).

Embodying the nagging possibility of "non-entity," this void exhales "the blighting breath of the ultimate Why?" (64). Why this world, this datum?

The void is the recognition of arbitrariness that leaves thought to stand "oscillating to and fro, wondering . . . and finds no end, in wandering mazes lost" (63). The allusion here is apt: like Milton's devils, forced to wander, James's situation is infernal. He dubs the craving for more explanation "ontological wonder-sickness." This memorable phrase tacitly connects philosophic anguish with James's personal crisis, the abulia that left him similarly "oscillating" with "the evil of feeling restless," as he wrote in a letter of 1867.

Clearly, theoretic reasoning, as James conceives it, fails to provide the "fluency" of rationality. The question remains as to how one exorcises the "ultimate Why?" One answer is familiar from our earlier discussion: to find "the peace of rationality" James moves to the margins, to the "ecstasy" of mysticism, as he admires Whitman's loafing on the grass. But this solution lacks "universality"; it is a "plaster but no cure" (65). James resolves the question in the same way he resolved his "panic fear"—with a leap of faith demanded by the fact that "ontological wonder-sickness" cannot be exorcised. "The bottom of being is left logically opaque to us, as something which we simply come upon and find." If we wish to act, if we wish to take control, we simply must "pause and wonder as little as possible" (64).[8]

With this directive we move from theoretical to practical rationality, where James can rejoice, free at last from "wonder-sickness." Practical action "will give back to the mind the free motion which has been blocked in the purely contemplative path" and "make the world seem rational again." James's philosophic project has now cleared away impediments and found its bearings; he can profess philosophy, confident of finding it a source of stability. "The Sentiment of Rationality" vividly confirms Gerald Myers's claim that "philosophizing was therapeutic for James" (413). But some of the paradoxes of James's therapy should be noted.

In abandoning wonder, that "issueless channel of purely theoretic contemplation," James refuses the classical explanation of why men philosophize. For Aristotle "it is owing to their wonder that men both now begin and at first began to philosophize. . . . A man who is puzzled and wonders thinks himself ignorant." Thus men pursue "science in order to know, and not for any utilitarian end" (*Metaphysics* bk. I, chap. 2). While not rejecting practical knowledge, the Greeks deemed it inferior. In contrast, James shares the Baconian impatience with *curiositas* as mere gaping at things. Seeking the purposeless knowledge of pure curiosity is precisely what must be avoided, says James, "if thought is not to stand forever pointing at the universe in wonder" (*Will* 65). Just as Howard Feinstein shows that a "willful throttling of self" is required for William to form a stable identity, a willful throttling of curiosity sets his philosophy in motion. Indeed, James's is a philosophy *of* motion so determined "to restore the fluent sense of life again" (as the measure, he says, of its "human success") that its ultimate logic is to abolish philosophy (*Radical* 45).[9]

James's pragmatism, like his psychology, radically seeks to curtail philosophy's tendency to wayward theoretical curiosity and wonder. Pragmatism's investment in control is easy to lose sight of amid James's extravagant rhetoric of endless process, vulnerability, risk, and change. But without this investment pragmatism would cease to be the way to philosophize without lapsing back into "wonder-sickness." James notes early on in *Pragmatism* that "the pragmatic method is primarily a method of settling metaphysical disputes that otherwise might be interminable" (32, 28). By tracing "practical consequences" and differences, disputes are terminated. "Man always wants his curiosity gratified for a particular purpose"; the human mind is "efficient" only "by narrowing its point of view. Otherwise what little strength it has is dispersed, and it loses its way altogether" (*Will* 165). Dispersal counts as "diseased curiosity," the vice of "subjectivism" and its literary counterpart, "romanticism." The "fatalism" that pervades both movements threatens to leave us lost in a "labyrinth" or on a "downward slope." "At what point on [it] are we to stop?" (136, 132–33).[10]

James's nervousness derives not only from his fear of regressing again to "panic fear" but also reacts to the particular climate of his upbringing. He grew up in a household where "useless curiosity" was pursued with a fervor that knew no bounds—neither geographic, intellectual, nor vocational. The James family patriarch was financially free to engage in unrestrained social and theological speculation. Had Blumenberg discussed the James family in his account of curiosity's historical articulation, he would have found a remarkable clash of classical, medieval, and modern attitudes, all interacting in an atmosphere of creative and destructive turbulence. The "waste" of "useless curiosity" was the keynote. The dispersion of *curiositas* was indeed so delirious that, judging from William's description in a letter of 1865, home sounded like a veritable madhouse, with "people swarming about . . . killing themselves with thinking about things that have no connection with their merely external circumstances, studying themselves into fevers, going mad about religion, philosophy, love . . . breathing perpetual heated gas and excitement, turning night into day" (qtd. Perry 1: 225).

Immersion in this overheated environment over a period of several years helped produce James's suicidal depression, a nineteenth-century version of acedia, the eighth deadly sin of Catholic doctrine, which Blumenberg has related to *curiositas*.[11] As a kind of torpor that paralyzes action, acedia can often be mistaken for laziness. But the indifference and apathy it creates betokens a spiritual desolation, a state Aquinas believed epitomized "the despondency and indolence of the man who has deviated from his vocation. . . . Acedia is a form of sadness that surrenders itself to its own heaviness and thereby turns away from the goal of its existence, indeed from all purposeful behavior and exertion whatever. *Curiositas* is only one of the forms that this purposelessness takes"(Blumenberg 334). In "straying toward illicit things" and "losing oneself in dispersion," man lapses from his "essential centering" and falls into purposeless curiosity (334).

Because of the Calvinist, utilitarian tenor of American culture, the elder Henry James's lavish flaunting of purposelessness created social embarrassment for his sons, as Henry says at several points in his memoirs. Their father's "freedom from pressure" in turn generated pressure—the conflicting demands of paternal and social norms. This conflict instilled in William a guilty relation to curiosity even as he was engulfed in it. His early twenties witnessed his "straying" and "dispersion"; his reading was desultory, and his interests constantly shifted from psychology to literature, or to philosophy. By the late 1860s this "dead drifting of my life," as William described this period, resulted in the brooding of acedia, inadvertently encouraged by his father's stress "just to *be* something, something unconnected with specific doing, something free and uncommitted" (*Autobiography* 268).

IV

The elder James's ostensibly emancipating directive damaged not only his eldest son but also his only daughter. By age nineteen Alice's self-described "violent turns of hysteria" had settled in for life and made any specific doing impossible (*Diary* 149). "There is a terrible sense," observes Ruth Yeazell, "in which the invalid daughter—unconnected and uncommitted with a vengeance—most closely fulfilled" her father's "splendidly liberating ambition" (20). Although her gender made it easier "just to *be* something" and to avoid the pressure of vocation, Alice was never to experience the pleasurable abandonment of merely being. Indeed, she described her temperament as "forbidding the abandonment of an inch or the relaxation of a muscle," for she had "imposed upon" herself the "duties of doctor, nurse, and strait-jacket" (*Diary* 149). As if in reaction to the self-dispersions of William's acedia, Alice willed herself to be a "hard core" of selfhood, void of curiosity and thus steadfast in her "resistance" to life (192, 96). Something of this logic is evident in her diary, where in a late entry she notes her "curious, given my inheritance and surroundings, complete absence of intellectual curiosity—philosophies and systems, theologies and sciences having ever been as dry husks" (216). Her tone here is archly ironic as she confesses her curious lack of curiosity, a lack belied by her diary's responsiveness and precision of observation. Yet Alice's statement should also be taken seriously as a clue to the workings of what she calls her "organization." In terms that strikingly recall the traditional anxiety regarding dispersed curiosity, she describes her incurious, "restricted nature" as not "generous" but at least "highly practical and time saving, in so far that it never runs you off the track. . . . So many seem to pass their lives starting afresh on every side track" (216). This wasteful pursuit of false starts and side tracks plagued William, whereas Alice was to feel "profoundly grateful" for a temperament "which saves one from the wretched fate of those who never find their bearings" (96). She was determined not to be "thrust forth weaponless to fight in the hideous battle" of life (76).

Within the James family Alice's adamant resistance to the vulnerabilities and relaxations of vagrant curiosity became a means of closing the self her father urged be kept open. But in a larger cultural context her defiance seemed indistinguishable from the "significant ego restriction" that characterized the "relation between hysterical character formation and female role socialization" in late nineteenth-century America (Smith-Rosenberg 212–13). This restriction included prohibition against "overt anger and violence as unfeminine and vulgar," as was "curiosity, intrusiveness, exploratory behavior" (212). In her occasional chafings against the repressions circumscribing the feminine, Alice revealed the self-abnegation demanded of her "miserable sex": "How sick one gets of being 'good', how much I should respect myself if I could burst out and make everyone wretched for 24 hours; embody selfishness" (212, 64). But to be selfish would transgress her own strictures against directly "rebellious" behavior, which she found more "comic" than "heroic in the eye of the cold-blooded observer" (119). Surrender became her mode of passive rebellion: "Surrender, smiling, if possible, is the only attainable surface which gives no hold to the scurvy tricks of Fortune" (119). The smooth surface of surrender protected her fortresslike self, whose "hard core" of identity received its objective correlative in the "unholy granite" lump of cancer in her breast (225). Alice's famously perverse sense of fulfilled aspirations upon being diagnosed as terminally ill testifies to her identification with cancer less as an enemy than an ally, an instrument of fortification that functioned, she said, to lift her "out of the formless vague" and to set her "within the very heart of the sustaining concrete" (207). The motor of her psychic economy, noted William, was an "imperious will," and for both will protected them from the anxiety of openness. Yet the forms of their defense were, of course, different: Alice willed surrender, while William willed action. "He is just like a blob of mercury," noted Alice, "you can't put a mental finger upon him" (57).

In contrast to both Alice and William, Henry seemed to conjoin both surrender and activity. He had been publishing since 1864, his incessant "taking in" through the senses yielding a giving out in "production" (*Autobiography* 493). This process, in effect, combines the stance of openness with Henry senior's other directive—"to convert and convert . . . everything that should happen to us, every contact, every impression and every experience" (123). Henry has described his cunning fusion of "gaping" and converting as "marked in [its] way by a rare curiosity and energy" (172). Rather than sharing William's sense of curiosity as dead drifting, Henry is full of the *energy* of curiosity and finds "no quarrel" with "conditions" that William denounced as "arid and lamentable." William's reaction—that having "endlessly walked and endlessly daubed" was a waste of time, a "poverty of life"—makes no sense to Henry, whose "steps," if "often hampered or mystified," were "absolutely never wasted" (174, 492). Indeed, so unbounded is his curiosity that even "waste" affects him as "blooming with interest" (125). What makes Henry's curiosity "rare" is that it is simultaneously autotelic, purposeless, and profitable—in short, a blending of classical and Baconian attitudes that refuses the oppositions that define both stances (172). Curiosity, as Henry embodies it, is neither theoretic nor instrumental but rather, in his words, a "deeply dissimulative process." For it appears at once as "a sort of fatalism of patience, spiritless in a manner, no doubt, yet with an inwardly active, productive and ingenious side" (158, 170). Curiosity's double movement begins with the "taking in" of impressions, "perhaps" the "greatest pleasure" Henry "was ever to know." But the relaxation involved in "taking in," usually during moments of ease—as when the young Henry lies on a hotel bed in London—is simultaneously an act of "seizing": "We seize our property by an avid instinct wherever we find it, and I must have kept seizing mine at the absurdest little rate" (158).

Henry's dispersed attention practices the "precious fine art" of "taking in" until it reaches an "active pitch," wherein it passes into its opposite— a receptivity so sensitive that a mere open window gives off the "hum of a thousand possibilities" (158). In other words, Henry dissolves the self-enclosure of autonomy and welcomes what would have been a nightmare for William. Henry is the chieftain whose "doing nothing" consists of "vision and nothing but vision." Sight offers "a plate for impressions to play on" in remarkable abundance because vision for Henry is a taking in of "the sense and image of it all," which doesn't culminate with him merely cherishing the urban spectacle (442). Rather, these impressions emit "some vibratory hum" that makes the pictorial "ever . . . the dramatic, the social, the effectively human aspect" (482). Like the Whitman of William's essay, Henry's self is a "window" open to what the novelist calls "the material pressure of things," which bombards him with the "force . . . of vibrations" (569).

Thus, the urgent plea that concludes "On a Certain Blindness"—a demand to "tolerate, respect, and indulge" others—is irrelevant to Henry. This demand is as empty of content as the very problem—blindness—that engenders the essay. From Henry's perspective William is scratching where it does not itch: already infiltrated by otherness, Henry never needed to be liberated from blindness. As a small boy among others, Henry's life was "conditioned"—he announces on the second page of his autobiography— "prevailingly and almost exclusively, during years and years," by William's nearness. And when William died, Henry felt as if "cut into, deep down, as an absolute mutilation" (qtd. Lewis 292). If blindness is the cost of "absolute insulation," vulnerability, in Henry's phrase, is the cost of an "exposed and entangled" self. Between this self and others there is "no hard-and-fast line," in Mead's words, that can be drawn. As Henry noted after William's death, "My life, thank God, is impregnated with him" (*Letters* 4: 562).

Although within the family, as Henry recalls, "I couldn't have been judged . . . reckless or adventurous," he is imbued with "wonder at the liberty of range and opportunity of adventure" he finds merely in being "somewhere— almost anywhere would do" (125, 16). Under cover of vagueness and seeming bewilderment, Henry conducts a "remarkably active life" that includes the fun of living by his "imagination in William's so adaptive skin," and delight in the fruits of his capacity for vicarious imagination—the "freshness of first creations" (412, 176, 493). He is referring to his earliest production of short stories for sale. These tales are created out of "an admirable commerce" between art and life, an "interpenetration . . . of borrowing and lending, taking and giving" (493). This incessant process (as incessant as capitalist trade), where vagueness and dawdling issue in production, defines Henry's psychic economy, one whose dialectical energy disturbs William's dualism of speculation opposed to action. Henry insists on their interpenetration: to "feel anything with force, whether for pleasure or for pain," is to feel it "as an immense little act or event of life" (569). One implication Henry James draws from equating feeling and action is his acute sense that "the varieties of his [William's] application had been as little wasted for him as those of my vagueness had really been for me" (498). Rather than being a passive escape from action, vagueness has varieties of application. Indeed, vagueness, at a certain pitch, is application, just as "passion"—as Henry says with reference to George Sand—which can always dependably "vibrate," "becomes to that extent action" (*Literary* 2: 767).

Instead of grasping that Henry was "actively inert in his own behalf" (to borrow his father's phrase), William and the majority of critics and biographers ignore this dialectic and focus solely on one moment—inertia. Thus the verdict of passivity and inferiority is handed down. But this judgment ignores what is crucial—the experimental "energy" of Henry's "rare curiosity"—a mode of being that challenges the monadic self his brother assumed was universal.[12] And this challenge refuses to abstract "idle curiosity" from history, from the "habits of thought . . . imposed" on man by his "cultural situation." Henry's critique is profoundly immanent, for he both depends on the very reflex inculcated by capitalism—the hoarding of private property—and submits this reflex to dialectical pressure. Thereby "absolute insulation" is overcome through stimulations of otherness.

The Henry James delineated in these last few pages—a self-described "subtle savage" rooted in a "more profound and primitive level" than "bourgeois circumspection"—is a Whitmanlike figure immersed in an "orgy of the senses" (242, 135). This James is not frequently recognized because repression is conspicuously absent. The repression that is said to define Henry's stance toward the world structures William's psyche. On one level, it is strange to suggest that the lifelong bachelor celibate is less repressed than the man of legendary gusto, a virile husband and father. Yet Henry's relation to repression is precisely what is in question. What he called his "rare curiosity" defines a self founded not on repression but sublimation. This distinction is not often made by Freud, but in an important discussion of sublimation he does distinguish between them.

V

Significantly, Freud's remarks, contained in his study of Leonardo da Vinci, concern the fate of curiosity after a "wave of energetic sexual repression" has terminated the period of infantile sexual researches. The goal of these researches had been mastery, "the infantile dream of a permanently pleasurable union with its surroundings," to which most minds remain unconsciously committed despite the renunciation that inevitably concludes investigation (White 106). Freud defines three possible outcomes resulting from the abandonment of infantile research. The first is characterized by "neurotic inhibition," where the "free activity of intelligence may be limited for the whole of the subject's lifetime" and curiosity remains permanently stunted (Freud 29). In the second outcome curiosity remains unconsciously attached to the dream of mastery as "perfect bliss" and expresses itself in "the form of compulsive brooding" (30).[13] This brooding sexualizes thinking itself, pervading it "with the pleasure and anxiety that belong to sexual processes proper." Thus the intelligence, impatient to reduce sexual tension, seeks an end to curiosity and finds a replacement for sexual satisfaction in settling and explaining things (30). Freud describes the third type of outcome as the "rarest and most perfect" type of sublimation: "The libido evades the fate of repression by being sublimated from the very beginning into curiosity." Although "here, too, the research becomes to some extent compulsive and a substitute for sexual activity," neurosis is absent because "there is no attachment to the original complexes of infantile sexual research" (30). In other words, the desire for mastery and "perfect bliss" (the content of the "original complexes") does not return from the unconscious to limit curiosity. Thus "the instinct can operate freely in the service of intellectual interest" (30). Because the sublimations of this "rarest" curiosity are, according to Leo Bersani, "extensions of . . . sexual desires rather than repressive substitutes or symptoms of those desires" ("Sexuality" 37), they are free to dispense with "fantasies of satisfaction . . . [and] the recurrent proclamations of a permanent state of nondesiring stillness" (White 109).

Freud's discussion of the fate of the instinct of curiosity can illuminate Alice's willful extinction of curiosity, William's penchant for brooding, and Henry's commitment to vagrant curiosity. The "neurotic inhibition" that marks those of stunted curiosity has some resemblance to Alice, especially given Freud's claim that "the intellectual weakness which has been acquired in this way gives an effective impetus to the outbreak of a neurotic illness" (29). She had suffered one of her worst attacks of hysteria in 1878, when her father's commitment to curiosity as freedom of thought and action inspired her to explore the possibility of suicide. In response to her asking whether suicide was a sin, the elder James granted her "full permission to end her life whenever she pleased" (qtd. Yeazell 15). Though Alice's question, notes Yeazell, "has posed an obscure challenge, Henry Sr. implicitly refuses to be drawn into battle. The daughter speaks of killing herself to assert her freedom, but suicide is a breaking of bonds only if there are felt bonds to break" (16). One could add that in this episode curiosity became definitively entwined for Alice with parental indifference, with the absence of bonds or of boundedness—in short, the "formless vague" vulnerability she loathed. To banish the formless, limitless detachment of curiosity and to repress the failure of her effort to elicit parental love, she erected her "hard core" of selfhood.

The second type of response to the ceasing of infantile curiosity is germane to William. His diary entry made sometime in 1868 suggests the link between brooding and the sexualizing of thought. After listening to a young woman he had found highly attractive play the piano, his "feelings came to a sort of crisis." He has an "unspeakable disgust" for his desultory life and longs for a "practical effect" on his will: "Oh God! an end to the idle idiotic sinking into *Vorstellungen* disproportionate to the object. Every good experience ought to be interpreted in practice." A few days later he translates his German phrase and elaborates on his mood: "In other words ideas disproportionate to any practical application—such for instance are emotions of a loving kind indulged in where one cannot expect to gain exclusive possession of the loved person" (qtd. Myers 583–84). In his frustrations, generated by his sexual reverie, James's anger evidently spills over into a hatred of ideas disproportionate "to any practical application." Having sexualized thinking itself, he seeks escape from the desire for mastery ("exclusive possession of the loved person") in a release from thought into action. Eventually his brooding will be alleviated, if not eradicated, by creating a philosophy whose raison d'être is to accomplish this release into the "fluency" of "unimpeded action" uncontaminated by "reflection." In this light radical pluralism is a fantasy of satisfaction and the arrest of desire.

The suggestion that Henry James partakes of the "rarest and most perfect" kind of sublimation finds support when we recall that Freud discusses curiosity in the context of an analysis of Leonardo, whose "overpowerful instinct for research and the atrophy of his sexual life (which was restricted to what is called ideal [sublimated] homosexuality)" make him a model of "perfect" sublimation (Freud 30). The imbalance in Leonardo between curiosity and active sexuality resembles Henry's psychic economy. Like Leonardo's, the novelist's early childhood was marked by an intensity of scopic activity. To borrow Freud's words, "The instinct to look and the instinct to know were those most strongly excited by the impressions of his early childhood" (82). Thus, most of the needs of James's sexual instinct could be sublimated in unbounded curiosity and thereby evade repression if not a (most likely) nonphysical sexual life.

Especially after 1900 this sexual life was conducted in his intense (mostly epistolary) homoerotic friendships with three young men: Hugh Walpole, Jocelyn Persse, and Hendrik Andersen. "He was curious about everything, he knew everything," noted Walpole in a reminiscence of James, whom he described as avid for "every detail, the full account of every adventure." Indeed, the insatiably curious Henry once complained: "I could have done even with more detail—as when you say 'Such parties!' I want so to hear exactly what parties they are" (qtd. Edel *The Master* 407–9). To Persse Henry James once wrote that he admired his facility in moving from one "promiscuous social exercise to another . . . so that even while I crouch in my corner, I get through you . . . the vibration of adventure" (*Letters* 4: 284). But this vibration should not be minimized as merely vicarious, a judgment that misses the near hallucinatory force of James's power of sublimation to express desire. Attending to this energy of libidinal sublimation as it ignites James's imagination of desire helps to revise our initial impression that thwarted, repressed passion defines the aging novelist's relation to his three beloved acolytes.[14]

But even successful sublimation, as Freud notes, remains "to some extent compulsive," a quality evident not only in Henry's relation to Hugh Walpole but also in his relation to "aridities"—the hours of strolling that William denounced and Henry cherished. For Henry such "aridities" were "half a terror and half an impossibility" (*Autobiography* 171). We have seen how his ceaseless converting made them impossible. But "aridities" are also a "terror" because what remains ineradicable in the act of perceiving is the possibility that "the cluster of appearances can *have* no sense" (*Scene* 273). When this occurs, says Henry, one begins "to go to pieces," since the "prime business" of the "painter of life" is "always to *make* a sense" and make connections: for the "restless analyst there is no such thing as an unrelated fact, no such thing as a break in the chain of relations" (273, 312). Although to represent "incoherence" (the "break in the chain") "as baffling" is "the last thing" permitted, the artist may "portray it, in all richness, *for* incoherence" (273). Henry's curiosity, then, is not without a moment of defensiveness manifested in a restlessness reminiscent of William's impatience. But William's defensiveness prompts his rejection of radical curiosity, and the incoherence it risks discovering, for the "fluency" of rationality.[15] In contrast, Henry converts his compulsion to "*make* a sense" into a productive attentiveness that enables him to represent rather than simply fear incoherence. Instead of remaining attached to an original motive of mastery or a search for fluent peace, Henry's sublimation of curiosity accepts hazard as a condition of its being: the "spectre of impotence . . . dogs the footsteps of perception" (307).

In sum, James's psyche is structured not by a dialectic of repression but of sublimation; his "rare curiosity" embodies the "rarest sublimation"—that which appropriates and elaborates sexual desires rather than renouncing them. Like Freud's Leonardo, Henry was not forced "to develop substitutive structures of a costly and harmful kind" (Freud 82). The novelist implicitly affirms this when he describes himself as simultaneously "throwing himself back upon substitutes" and as "so haunted . . . with visions of life . . . that the said substitutes . . . were in themselves really a revel of spirit and thought" (*Autobiography* 171). In finding "substitutes" like "wondering and dawdling and gaping" in themselves a "medium so dense," he empties the opposition between primary and secondary, collapsing one into the other. James also conceives of art as a power in and of itself "that *makes* life." He knows "no substitute whatever for the force and beauty of its process" (*Letters* 4: 770). In short, James rejects "depth models" or such binary modes of thinking as inside/outside, essence/appearance, or authenticity/inauthenticity. Replacing these oppositions, and the metaphysics that anchor them, is James's commitment to practice, particularly the practices of curiosity and representation, each a "variable process" in a world where "relations stop nowhere" (*Art* 5, 9).

In *Leonardo da Vinci* Freud implicitly rejects a "depth model" of sublimation by treating it as a power in itself rather than merely a kind of repression. But Freud seems uneasy with this insight and at times retreats from it into a defensive reliance on binary patterns. In this regard Freud recalls William James, a parallel that extends to the fact that both men are defensive about the same thing—interminable curiosity.[16] A number of recent commentators have noted Freud's ambivalence toward Leonardo, an attitude embodied in his book's dualistic premise that a conflict existed between Leonardo as artist and investigator. The investigator, in Freud's view, "made severe encroachments" on the artist, to the point where Leonardo "painted less and less, left what he had begun for the most part unfinished and cared little about the ultimate fate of his works" (14, 16). Indeed, Leonardo is so under the sway of curiosity that investigating has "taken the place of" acting, creating, and loving, thus thwarting a "possible transformation of the instinct to investigate back into an enjoyment of life" (25). Curiosity, Freud implies, can only be a regressive substitute for primary activity. Such a view conflicts with Freud's conception of the "rarest" sublimation that Leonardo embodies.

Leonardo's curiosity, says Freud, changed the "nature of his mental activity," so that when he attempted to resume painting he was most interested in the problems it presented: "[B]ehind the first one he saw countless other problems arising, just as he used to in his endless and inexhaustible investigations of nature. He was no longer able to limit his demands, to see the work in isolation and to tear it from the wide context to which he knew it belonged" (27). Hence resulted his inability to complete his artistic practice. What Freud ascribes to Leonardo here is a diminished faculty of attention, the distraction of a dispersed curiosity that cannot be harnessed for practice. Haunted by "a possible other than the actual," Freud's Leonardo in effect suffers "wonder-sickness." William James's rhetoric is apt because he shares with Freud a discomfort with unbridled curiosity and finds it a threat to practice. Both men conceive of unfocused curiosity as breeding a disturbing "wealth of possibilities between which a decision can only be reached with hesitation" (Freud 18). Blumenberg concludes his analysis of "the trial of theoretic curiosity" with a brief account of Freud's essay on Leonardo as containing or renewing "something of the old conflict between pure theory and the practice that promotes salvation. Theoretical curiosity is already a regression of the highest sublimation . . . in the aesthetic work. . . . Curiosity is an escape from the failure of full maturity." Freud's hierarchy, which places artist above investigator and completed action above deferred action, clearly manifests this "old conflict," which devalues theoretical curiosity at the expense of practice. As Blumenberg defines the dichotomy, "the work is finite, theory infinite—the detour to practice by way of theory leaves the work in the lurch, as a fragment" (451).

Freud's defensiveness has been described as the source of a "querulous tone" that "scolds" Leonardo for combining genius with inactivity and indifference. According to Bersani, this irritation expresses Freud's reluctance "to accept the psychic and social consequences of the sexual and ontological floating" resulting from his view of curiosity as sublimated libidinal energy that escapes repression (*Freudian* 45). Freud's unease with the radical mode of being he ascribes to Leonardo echoes the reaction of Leonardo's contemporaries, many of whom found disturbingly capricious his "frittering away" of time in curiosity instead of "industriously painting to order and becoming rich" (Freud 15). Given his unrelenting curiosity and his absence of an active sexual life, Leonardo "remained like a child for the whole of his life.... Even as an adult he continued to play, and this was another reason why he often appeared uncanny and incomprehensible to his contemporaries" (77).[17] Encouraging this bewilderment was Leonardo's fiercely independent judgment and his disrespect for tradition. The latter originated in the unlimited nature of his infantile sexual research, a result of the absence of a father's inhibiting presence. Leonardo's unflappable confidence in his own observation of nature, says Freud, repeats "in the highest sublimation attainable by man" the view of the "little boy as he gazed in wonder on the world." Leonardo's repudiation of authority marks him as the "first modern natural scientist" (72).

Eight years after Freud's remark, the first modern American novelist was also characterized as an enemy of the tyranny of tradition and "all sorts of intangible bondage." Describing Henry James in 1918, Ezra Pound found that his "hatred of tyrannies was as great a motive as any we can ascribe to Galileo or Leonardo" (311). We have seen that one of the tyrannies James hated was monadic subjectivity. His unwillingness to submit to its repressions made him, like Leonardo, "uncanny and incomprehensible" to his contemporaries and to his own family. This attitude toward James grew despite the fact that he did not suffer Leonardo's conflict between curiosity and production. Regardless of the abundant fruits of his artistic activity, "a certain inactivity and indifference seemed obvious" in him, as it did in Leonardo. In a society of energetic aggressiveness, each "was notable for his quiet peaceableness" and gentleness (Freud 18–19). "Nice and simple and amiable" is how William described "very powerless-feeling Harry" in 1889, an assessment William likely knew was superficial, given his subsequent remark, in 1902, that Henry "and I are so utterly different in all our observances and springs of action, that we can't rightly judge each other" (*Letters* 2: 169). William's characterization of Henry as "powerless-feeling" is blind to, or seeks to repress, the powerful challenge his brother presents to the very notion of what constitutes "purposive and virile" subjectivity and freedom of will. Implicit in Henry James, and explicit in Nietzsche and Foucault, is the belief that the subject "is an artificial reality imposed on material not intended to receive it." In this perspective, freedom is "not reducible to the freedom of subjects; it is at least partly the release of that which does not fit into the molds of subjectivity and normalization" (Connolly, "Taylor" 371).

Curiosity represents the "release" that does not fit; neither a symptom of repression nor a substitute for action, its libidinal energy escapes the tyranny of metaphysical dualisms. James's embrace of curiosity as conduct and sensibility, mastery and speculation, is apparent in the preface to *The American*

Scene, where the returning expatriate vows to "vibrate with more curiosity . . . than the pilgrim with the longest list of questions." James's curiosity is always a "double consciousness" of the sort he ascribes to Strether in the opening pages of *The Ambassadors*: "There was detachment in his zeal and curiosity in his indifference" (18). Curiosity, then, is necessarily "something that offends in us some of our long-standing distinctions," as Paul Valéry wrote of Leonardo in 1929. In words that apply with equal force to Henry James, Valéry argues that, "compared with what we are used to seeing, Leonardo appears to be a sort of monster, a centaur or a chimera because of the hybrid species he represents to minds too intent on dividing our natures." It is Valéry in the modern age who celebrates the scandal of Leonardo's "generalized curiosity," his shattering of received ideas, and his demand for "a reconsideration of our intellectual habits and something like a rebirth of awareness in the midst of ideas we inherited" (146).

A reconsideration of Henry James might begin by recognizing his art as a "process" of "force," for he is above all a believer in "the religion of doing." He defines this phrase in an important passage near the end of his final preface:

> [T]he whole conduct of life consists of things done, which do other things in their turn, just so our behavior and its fruits are essentially one and continuous . . . and so, among our innumerable acts, are no arbitrary, no senseless separations. . . . To "put" things is very exactly and responsibly and interminably to do them. Our expression of them . . . belong[s] as nearly to our conduct and our life as every other feature of our freedom. (*Art* 347)

This passage better enables us to understand James's famous remark to his brother, after reading *Pragmatism*, that "I was lost in wonder of the extent to which all my life I have . . . unconsciously pragmatised" (qtd. Perry 1: 428). Free to be both "lost in wonder" and interminable doing, Henry's pragmatism avoids being rooted in William's defensive dualisms, in "arbitrary . . . separations" like action and speculation, "behavior and its fruits."

This double sense—embracing William's thought but refusing its defensive gestures—is captured in one of Henry's famous letters to his brother. Responding to William's complaint about the "interminable elaboration" of *The Golden Bowl*, Henry stresses that more than a mere difference of literary taste is at stake in William's critique: "I'm always sorry when I hear your [*sic*] reading anything of mine, and always hope you won't—you seem to me so constitutionally unable to 'enjoy' it" (qtd. Perry 1: 425). Like the "melting" of saints' "confining selfhood," from which William's "constitution" shuts him out, Henry's "interminable" novels refuse "absolute straightness" and produce an analogous queasiness that exceeds the literary. Not only are the plots of the novels, in William's words, redolent with "twilight" and "mustiness," but their lack of "decisiveness in the action" recalls Henry's youthful posture of "dawdling" and straying curiosity (424). While recognizing that William's rigidity "constitutionally" bars him from his brother's style of being and writing, Henry affirms his enthusiasm for pragmatism's rhetoric of process and indeterminacy: "And yet I can read *you* with rapture. . . . Philosophically, in short, I am 'with' you" (425). This praise is more than a "lovely turnabout," as one critic calls it (Hocks 21). In a single letter Henry reveals and responds to William's dialectic of repression—his philosophical advocacy of what constitutionally unnerves him.

However unnerved, William in another letter nearly equals Henry's nuanced eye for fraternal paradoxes. Having just read *The American Scene*, William begins by declaring that "the *core* of literature is solid," adding that what Henry has produced is "but perfume and simulacrum." Yet in representing the "bare perfume of things" in "gleams and innuendoes," he somehow manages to "keep [his] method going" with "verve and animal spirits." For a flickering moment William grants Henry some of the virility he usually makes wholly his preserve. But no sooner has this been granted than it is withdrawn, as William continues "pouring a bath" of his "own subjectivity over" Henry. In short, his usual defenses take over. While saluting Henry's energy as "marvelous," William also finds his method "perverse," for Henry's "complication" of "verbal insinuations" will surely cause this "crowded and hurried reading age" to quickly lose patience with what requires "such close attention." He insists that "19 out of 20 worthy readers grow intolerant. . . . 'Say it *out*, for God's sake,' they cry." How deeply characteristic are these "belchings," as William calls them, of his "own crabbed organism." Exposed here are the fascination, impatience, intolerance, and admiration that perennially marked William's ambivalence in the face of Henry's exasperating, unrepentant curiosity. The workings of his "perverse" curiosity helped make Henry, in William's unwittingly apt phrase, "the curiosity of literature" (qtd. Matthiessen, *Family* 340–42).

William's misprision of Henry's curious mode of being should not be regarded as merely expressive of fraternal anxieties or rivalries but as culturally emblematic and prophetic. William's certain blindness to Henry's "rare curiosity" prefigured what would become a dominant response to the novelist within a decade after his death in 1916. With only rare exceptions, both those who sought to canonize him and those who lambasted him corroborated William James's account of Henry as basically powerless, absorbed in passive contemplation and aesthetic reverie. Indeed, when the progressive historian Charles Beard attacked Henry James in the 1930s, he explicitly invoked the aid of William James. So "vague and so intricate" was Henry's style, remarked Beard, that "even his brother the pragmatist philosopher" was driven to "explode in a letter 'Say it *out*, for God's sake' " (441). William's impatience had become Beard's, as it would be shared by many others.

As the next chapter will demonstrate, a generation of thinkers in the intensely politicized thirties and forties would exhibit an anxious perplexity and little appreciation for a novelist of the "hybrid species" who somehow conjoined the sensitive aesthete and subtle savage. Instead of confronting and understanding this challenging mutant, critics tended to reduce James to "the great *genteel* classic, embodying better than any other single man the principles of Anglo-Saxon 'idealism,' " as Wyndham Lewis declared in 1934 (115). Thus was James "tamed, and chained as a classic," a process of disciplinary action known as canonization.[18] James's entry into the canon can be read as a twentieth-century version of the trial of curiosity. This ordeal of prohibition produced a domesticated Henry James, robbed of the rare curiosity that propelled his adventure across the American scene in 1904. In order to set the stage for recapturing Henry James the cultural analyst of modernity (discussed in chapter 4), we must first examine the cultural ritual of containment that excluded his devotion to a pragmatic religion of doing.

3

"On a Certain Blindness":
Henry James and the Politics
of Cultural Response

"I hate American simplicity. I glory in the piling up of complications of every sort. If I could pronounce the name of James in any different or more elaborate way I should be in favor of doing so" (*Letters* 4: xxxi). The touch of bravado in James's avowal to his niece reminds us of his delight in complexity itself as a source of the "fun" to which art "all comes back to" (*Art* 345). At other times James spoke of being "accursedly born to touch nothing save to complicate it." James's passion for difficulty—the only thing "at bottom . . . that interests me"—is obvious to any reader. Less clear is what his commitment to "complications of every sort" means in a Protestant culture of "simplicity," one that "affords little room for the cultivation of ambiguity," as sociologist Donald Levine has observed. Recently he has argued that although a "flight from ambiguity characterizes the culture of most modern societies . . . in the United States this tendency has been manifest to an exceptional degree" (37).

The trial of curiosity in the nineteenth century represented one instance of this flight, as we saw in William James's need to extricate himself from the labyrinth of "wonder-sickness" by performing concrete deeds. Yet the American trial of curiosity neither begins nor ends with Jamesian pragmatism.[1] It starts with the taboos of Calvinism and Puritanism, which embroiled curiosity and its cognates in an ordeal whose repercussions are audible in William's pragmatism and a variety of literary discourses in the twentieth century.[2] These include literary nationalism, literary progressivism, and literary populism—all of which have figured prominently in the cultural debate over Henry James. In other words, the controversy that has characterized James's critical reception up to the present day has been shaped at its deepest, unspoken levels by a flight from the ambiguity of "rare curiosity" that Henry embodies in the face of Puritan and modern strictures. For over sixty years

both his detractors and defenders have often used James for their own polemical purposes, thus keeping debate at a polarized, narrow level. Yet to
make this claim fails to take us very far. For as critics have been eagerly
reminding us, the making of a literary reputation is inherently an intensely
contested political struggle that produces a decidedly biased account of the
author.

James's own reputation illustrates the collision between two prestigious
ideologies: modernity, which represses ambiguity, and literary modernism,
which valorizes it. Because of political and historical circumstances (some of
which will be discussed shortly) American literary intellectuals have tended
to conceive of modernism as an enclave of resistance to modernity. James
has often been enlisted as a canonical modernist upholding an idealist dichotomy that opposes art to life. Thus it has been easy to assimilate him to
antimodernist modernism and to ignore how, in significant ways, his stance
actually belies this tradition.

The present chapter does not present a history of twentieth-century critical
response to James but rather attempts to explain how and why his immanent
orientation and rare curiosity have been largely ignored. I trace this blindness—from which William James was the first to suffer—by selecting certain
important critical encounters where political pressures helped shape strategically partial portraits of Henry James. To offer an alternative to this image
of James created by Van Wyck Brooks, F. O. Matthiessen, and Lionel
Trilling, among others, I examine neopragmatist and immanent cultural
perspectives (exemplified, respectively, by Richard Rorty and Theodor
Adorno), both of which are more attuned to James's understanding of modernity. His understanding is rooted in an uneasy relationship to the Puritanism that had banned the indeterminacies of theatricality (vagrant
curiosity's correlative mode) and had historically conditioned Americans to
obey modernity's disciplinary demands. In the mid nineteenth century,
James found the "Puritan curse" only "half-buried" (*Autobiography* 447).

I

Max Weber's famous definition of modernity as the "disenchantment of the
world" connects modernity with aversion to ambiguity. The instrument of
disenchantment is bureaucracy, which above all else prizes "precision, speed,
unambiguity . . . unity, strict subordination, reduction of friction" (*From Max
Weber* 214). "Purely objective considerations" become the norm for con-
ducting business, which demands obedience to "calculable rules 'without
regard for persons.' " This last phrase, says Weber, is also the "watchword"
of the marketplace (215). In this rationalized, modern world, nature is no
longer the repository of cosmic balance and supernatural meaning but is
disenchanted, transformed into raw material for the use of science and technology. Modern man's reliance on instrumental reason, which habitually
separates subject from object, encourages the domination of external and
inner nature. But, as Charles Taylor argues, an instrumental stance toward

nature "is important for more than its results. It is important itself, because it affirms the autonomy and the freedom from illusion of the one who takes it" (266). Autonomy and instrumentality, in short, are the correlative qualities constituting modern subjectivity in a liberal, democratic social order. The modern subject is a product of the Enlightenment program to liberate "men from fear and to establish their sovereignty." This is accomplished through "the dissolution of myths and the substitution of knowledge for fancy" (Adorno, *Dialectic* 3).[3]

In this context modernism represents a return of the repressed. Much of the ferment of experimental literary, artistic, and intellectual activity that occurred roughly from 1875 to 1925 erupted in protest against the bureaucratic dominance of abstraction, rational cognition, and instrumentality that had disambiguated modern life in obedience to the Enlightenment (or Baconian) imperative of efficiency. Thus modernism insists on an obdurate difficulty expressed in formal innovation that refuses the familiar comforts of realist representation. Instead, defamiliarization—a making new by estranging the familiar—characterizes modernism's project to reunify human sensibility, dissociated by the hegemony of positivist science. Paradoxically, the healing of the breach between thought and feeling is achieved through deliberate shock tactics of dissonance—what Brecht called alienation effects.[4] Dissonance is a precious source of vitality in a world that Henry James, writing in 1907, pictures as a "great gray wash . . . causing color and outline to effectually run together" (*Scene* 455). Although a "gray" "sterility of aspect" is only part of the American scene, James (like Weber) finds it symptomatic of the loss of friction that modern bureaucracy imposes through the "jealous cultivation of the common mean . . . the reduction of everything to an average of decent suitability, the gospel of precaution against the dangerous tendency latent in many things to become too good for their context" (442).

Latent tendencies capable of complicating the unitary identity of things and people threaten the hegemony of the "hotel-spirit," which requires malleable "victims . . . trusting it so blandly and inviting it" to govern them (441). This spirit of identity, which for James is the spirit of modernity incarnate, exudes what Roberto Unger (in discussing the epistemology of liberalism) has described as "confidence in the primacy of the simple. . . . The complex, on the contrary, is always derivative and contrived. Hence simplicity is associated with naturalness and concreteness; complexity with abstraction and artificiality" (*Knowledge* 47). America's "universal organizing passion," remarks James, paints the country "with a big brush . . . steeped in crude universal white," shrinking to the negligible "gradations, transitions, differences of any sort." All are funneled into one "vast simplified scheme" (*Scene* 305). How small, James notes, is the "resistance in American air, to any force that does simplify" (305).

American susceptibility to simplicity partly derives from Puritanism's utilitarian attention to the empirical. Visiting Harvard in 1904, James was not surprised to find the "Puritan residuum" sponsoring education for business, "for a commercial, an organizing energy": "Harvard was still caring for that more than for anything else"(241). The "once capacious" literary tradition of "the Age of Emerson" is now an "empty cornucopia." Puritanism's home ground had never filled James with enthusiasm; indeed, he found New England "a danger after all escaped." But to this day the New York–born novelist is routinely misidentified as a New Englander, probably because his father was a friend of Emerson and the James family moved to Boston when Henry was in his early twenties.[5] The matter of regional affiliation may appear slight, but it was important to James. As if to memorialize his connection with his home ground, he entitled his oeuvre the New York Edition. James perceived that New England, the home of transcendental moral idealism, was a "danger" to his restless, urban identity. "Long would it take to tell why it figured" so, he notes, but a clue is contained in his account of a visit to a Boston theater. The "provincial" Boston stage left James's "uncanny appetite" for theater unsatisfied: "One would have only had to scratch a little below the surface of the affair to come upon the half-buried Puritan curse not so very long before devoted to such perversities" (*Autobiography* 447). The curse, James senses, is "still in the air" and accounts for the "want of self-respect in the total exhibition."

It was inevitable that New England culture, burdened by the "Puritan curse," that inveterate censor of vagrant curiosity, would not flourish beyond its final efflorescence in the Age of Emerson. In 1898 James remarked that "Puritan culture both used and exhausted its opportunity" (*Literary* 1: 654); hence the paltriness of the "Puritan residuum" he observed in 1904. The antitheatrical prejudice of the Puritans is a source of the bland, "homogenous" culture of New England, a world James is in "without being of it."[6] He is both in and of what he calls "New York heterogeneity," the urban center of hotels and theaters, two of his favorite boyhood haunts. New York's "heterogeneity" encourages theatricalized, stylized self-representation that escapes the "monotonous" "depths of rusticity" that New England personifies for James.

Boston and New York's opposed attitudes toward theatricality suggest that Puritan distaste coexists with America's notorious love of masking. "When American life is most American," Ralph Ellison has remarked, "it is apt to be most theatrical" (54). From Ben Franklin to the Boston tea party, from Huckleberry Finn, Jay Gatsby, and their countless fictional progeny to Ronald Reagan's simulacral reign, masquerade has been inscribed as Americans' second nature. And although bourgeois individualism, with its Puritan preference for centered, stable "prime identity" (to borrow Henry James's phrase) would seem inimical to theatricality, they actually have been easily reconciled. One explanation is that liberal individualism tolerates theatricality provided that "somewhere under all the roles there is Me, the poor old ultimate actuality." This is how Lionel Trilling describes the "insistent claims of the own self" (*Sincerity* 10). "When all the roles have been played," says Trilling, this core self "would like to ... settle down with his own original actual self." In William James's account of the social self there is a similar acceptance of multiple social roles anchored to an "original" self, a "central nucleus," to use William's phrase. But Henry James's sense of theatricality is not really assimilable to William James's or Trilling's conception of social roles, for Henry is less concerned with role playing organized by a centered self than with putting in question the notion of this anchoring self. Because this core self, what Henry James calls "prime identity," begins and ends "with itself" and has "no connections and suggests none," it remains static and homogenous. In contrast, a heterogeneous, theatrical self "bristles" with the mobility and impurity of internal difference, of something not wholly itself but infiltrated by "a different mixture altogether" (*Autobiography* 452).[7]

For the Puritans theatricality mixes art and life, creating the kind of adulteration or ambiguity that a social order of fixed essences is most eager to repress. Hence a "curse" is imposed upon those who would transgress boundaries. James suggests the cost of insisting on "different mixtures" when he recalls the presence in New England of "a certain young New Yorker, an outsider," a figure of "heterogeneity" in his un-Bostonian otherness, his "civility and complexity." What is intriguing about this unnamed young man is that he manages to break New England's placid surface not despite but because he insists on his difference. The lesson of the New Yorker who shone "in the high light of public favor" is that "variation or opposition sufficiently embodied, the line of divergence sharply enough drawn, always achieves some triumph by the fact of its emphasis, by its putting itself through at any cost, any cost in particular of ridicule" (451). Having experienced public humiliation in the *Guy Domville* fiasco of 1895, James clearly identifies with this lone New Yorker's triumph at the risk of ridicule.

By 1904 James was again prepared to pay the price as he vowed to go "to the stake" for his impressions. This embattled stance anticipates James's equivocal cultural status throughout the twentieth century as a figure whose triumph is not without a certain ridicule. To describe James's status as equivocal may at first seem strange, given the eminence of his literary reputation. But his cultural status, his larger moral authority as a "figure," is another matter. This is the same word James employs in commemorating his boyhood idol, the painter John La Farge: "I think of him as one of the very small number of truly extraordinary men whom I've known. He was that rare thing, a *figure*—which innumerable eminent and endowed men . . . haven't been" (*Letters* 4: 566). La Farge's "rare and distinguished personality," the "interest and fascination of his wondrous intelligence," was matched by no one else in James's adolescence save William James's "inexhaustible authority."

While La Farge's stature was always confined to an artistic elite, William James has steadily remained both an eminent thinker and an exemplary cultural "figure." He is "truly a hero . . . a captivating and splendid spirit," in Elizabeth Hardwick's words (21). Henry James's reputation lacks the amplitude of being rooted in intellectual, moral, and personal power. His difficult personality makes this understandable. In 1889, in a mood of affectionate befuddlement, William described Henry as being "like some marine crustacean" who "lives hidden in the midst of his strange heavy alien manners and customs. . . . He's really, I won't say a Yankee, but a native of the James family, and has no other country" (qtd. Matthiessen, *Family* 303). The comic charm of this famous remark can obscure the absurd, slightly grotesque portrait it paints: at home neither in Europe nor America, Henry carried his expatriatism within, masking it in "anglicisms" and "alien manners" that William excused as "protective resemblances." William here shrewdly points to a mimetic quality in Henry's self-representation—his assimilation to his surroundings. But William leaves unquestioned his atomistic assumption that his brother has an inner core protected by an outer shell. Yet this assumption is precisely what Henry's mimetic self, with its outward projection that collapses boundaries, contests.

To those not kin to or intimate with the James family, William's benign assessment of the oddity of Henry's self-representation could easily be overlooked. Indeed, Henry's mimetic assimilations, in tandem with his expatriatism, have tended to be perceived as a kind of affront, a perverse dissolving of the props of stable personal and national identity. Americans found it hard to forgive James's self-exile upon his return in 1904; one acute observer, H. G. Dwight, pointed to the "resentment" that James could arouse in his countrymen (qtd. Gard, 444). Twenty years later, "intense resentment" of the novelist sparked Van Wyck Brooks's hostility (Wilson, *Shores* 226). Paradoxically, the insult James embodies is exacerbated by the very abjectness of his crustacean ways. We can speculate that not only was his exile read as contemptuous rejection but his strange social presence was interpreted as contempt for and freedom from conventional masculine roles.[8] Whatever the actual psychodynamics of cultural resentment, James's expatriatism was to render him a polemical cultural figure; his artistic achievement was far less the object of contention. This imbalance was noted as early as 1920, just four years after James's death. His old friend William Dean Howells remarked that although the public had long acknowledged James as one of the country's few literary geniuses, "in fact, America was never kind" to him. "It was rude and harsh, unworthily and stupidly so" (qtd. Gard 539). Because he died soon after this statement, Howells never knew how prescient was his remark.

II

By 1925 Van Wyck Brooks, inspired by a vaulting literary nationalism, elected to pivot upon Henry James and his "deranged set of values." The issue was the one William had innocently raised in 1889: to what country did Henry James belong? William's fond familial answer would hardly do for Brooks. Unable to label him simply a Yankee, Brooks arraigned Henry as a culture-addicted aristocrat adrift in Europe's "museum culture." Floating in a "void" of aestheticized reverie, James had betrayed America for Europe, condemning himself to "enchanted exile," spinning out "the confused reveries of an invalid child" (131). Brooks's aggressive nationalism represented a retreat from his more subtle earlier position, formed under the influence of his friend Randolph Bourne. In the years before his death in 1918, Bourne had helped Brooks shape his important book, *America's Coming of Age*, which sought to reorient the nation's cultural life in the direction of a cosmopolitan urban intellectual class. But by 1925 Brooks's program had been reduced to a strident effort to nurture a vital native culture founded on passionate moral commitment and firm masculine values rooted in "the reality of the real." This reality is what Henry James, the "perpetually shocked" "Puritan child" could not, according to Brooks, "quite believe in" (80, 147). As the sworn enemy of aestheticism, which he found both in the genteel tradition and in modernism, Brooks found James doubly damned.

Today it is easy to smile at Brooks's philistinism, with its smug belief in its privileged access to the "real."[9] Yet his image of James was not merely the isolated outcry of a single voice. Brooks's friend Lewis Mumford repeated a condensed version of the former's attack, the following year, in *The Golden Day*, and V. L. Parrington and Charles Beard—two of the most influential leftist progressive historians of the thirties—went on to provide their own renderings of Brooks's indictment, as did the Marxist critic Granville Hicks. Beard rounds out the class dimension in Brooks's image of James: "The grandson of a millionaire, a whole generation removed from the odors of the shop, and granted by good fortune a luxurious leisure, James steered his way into a more rarefied atmosphere" (441). For sixty years Brooks's portrait of the novelist has not merely endured but flourished, inspiring embellishments expressed in taunting invective (Geismar, Habegger) and Marxist terminology (Eagleton, Jameson).[10] Geismar's hysterical book-length diatribe of 1965, appropriately dedicated to Brooks, is perhaps the *locus classicus* of the anti-Jamesian genre, unmatched in its indefatigable effort to prove the "simple truth" of its very simple thesis—that Henry James "knew nothing at all about the life of his time; or the barest minimum that a writer can know—and he cared less" (7). Despite its minority status, the progressivist, Marxist critique has been continually invigorated through its competition with an antagonistic, parallel countereffort—high modernism and liberal humanism's eminently successful canonization of Henry James. The Jacobites battle anti-Jacobites in a debate as durable as it is narrow, dualistic, and repetitive.

In the thirties F. Scott Fitzgerald, Edmund Wilson, and Richard Blackmur, among others, joined Pound and Eliot, James's distinguished successors in cosmopolitan expatriatism, in declaring their veneration of the Master. But the modernist defense hardly made James immune to political attack. For in the Stalinized atmosphere of the decade, as Western allies consolidated with Russia against Germany, many American intellectuals had become increasingly opposed to high culture's elitist emphasis on formal innovation. With the Popular Front trumpeting its best-known slogan ("Communism is twentieth-century Americanism"), radical politics infiltrated the middle class. The ensuing cultural climate regarded the democratic affirmation of populist and proletarian social realism as a sublime aesthetic achievement; Faulkner and Joyce were set aside for *The Grapes of Wrath*, which was hailed as a masterpiece.[11] Dwight Macdonald summarized the cultural values of Stalinism as founded on the following set of "false dichotomies: 'form' vs. 'content,' 'pessimism' vs. 'optimism,' 'intellect' vs. 'life,' 'destructive' vs. 'constructive,' 'esthete' vs. 'humanity' " (212). Since the second term in each pair was the value every artist should strive to attain, by these standards James clearly was a failure. The Parrington/Beard/Hicks image of James as fastidious, effeminate, "shut up within his own skull pan," in flight from life and "in love with culture," carried the warning label: "It is not well for the artist to turn cosmopolitan, for the flavor of the fruit comes from the soil and sunshine of its native fields" (Parrington 240–41). Parrington's influential verdict confirmed the truth of H. G. Dwight's remark about James's status in the eyes of Americans: "They can forgive almost any of his shortcomings before they can forgive his exile" (qtd. Gard 447).

The cosmopolitan culture of high modernism was on the defensive throughout the thirties, increasingly becoming a minority presence. But with the Nazi–Soviet pact of 1939, leftist politics suffered a sharp loss in prestige, and most intellectuals saw "the United States—whatever its faults—as the final repository of their hopes and ambitions." And this realignment survived the resurgence in America of Stalinist sympathy when Hitler betrayed Russia in 1941 (Pells 361). The changed political atmosphere encouraged the revival of high modernism by a self-consciously cosmopolitan intelligentsia—a group of anti-Stalinist intellectuals associated with *Partisan Review* and Columbia University. The journal, reborn in 1938, sought to marry Marxism and modernism and thereby promote an experimental avant-garde committed to a radical critique of liberal, middlebrow culture. Defining themselves against the nationalism of Brooks, the populism of Parrington and Beard, and the "degraded form" of Marxism called Stalinism, the New York intellectuals, as they became known, sought to create an independent Left that would rely on Marxist critique without adhering to the Soviet party line. Evident from the start was the precarious quality of their political position, its potential for becoming a depoliticized cultural Marxism.[12]

A major plank in the platform of this reborn urban modernism was the revival of Henry James's reputation. At Columbia F. W. Dupee, Quentin Anderson, and Lionel Trilling contributed to this effort, as did Philip Rahv, the coeditor of *Partisan Review*. Dupee, for instance, assembled an important collection of essays devoted to returning James to the canon. In a not entirely unrelated act, Dupee published "The Americanism of Van Wyck Brooks," which lambasted Brooks for betraying Bourne's (and his own) early vision of a "trans-national" intellectual and for promulgating a bellicose, nostalgic, middlebrow literary nationalism. Soon after Dupee, Dwight Macdonald found Brooks drifting toward the coarse dichotomies of Stalinist cultural values (Macdonald 211–12). The battle lines had been firmly drawn.

Ironically, Van Wyck Brooks had anticipated the defense of James that the New York intellectuals would undertake. The one merit Brooks had granted James was his challenge to "herd instinct." James was the first American novelist "to present the plight of the highly personalized human being in the primitive community. . . . He succeeds in presenting the struggle for the rights of personality" (104). From Brooks's viewpoint, James's humanism was severely compromised by his preference for Europe, which Brooks viewed as a "void." But in the forties the New York intellectuals, a number of whom were the children of Jewish immigrants, could readily identify with James's cultural exile. Yet if a shared sense of deracination drew them to James, he most appealed to them as an apostle of what might redeem alienation—personal relations. His densely textured novels offered a refuge from the reality of discontinuity and upheaval caused by immigration and global warfare, and from the philistinism of an ever more strident mass culture.

In 1947 F. O. Matthiessen explicitly referred to James as a "refuge . . . in our time of intense outwardness." "In the face of a breakdown of standards far more ruthless than anything he witnessed," declared Matthiessen, James "takes his readers away from sensationalism and violence to a realm where they must contemplate ethical issues, and he revives an awareness of the value of a far-distant kind of humane freedom" (*Family* 679). With a book on James (1944), an annotated anthology on the James family (1947), an edition of James's notebooks (1947), and an anthology of his American fiction (1948), Matthiessen did as much as anyone to refute what he called "Brooks's whole thesis of flight, frustration, and decline," and to reinstate James as a major figure (*Major* xiii). But Matthiessen was far less happy with James's (alleged) refuge than were the New York intellectuals. What is fascinating is Matthiessen's ambivalence about the author on whose behalf he undertook such extensive critical, scholarly, and textual labors.

Matthiessen's self-described pro-Soviet, Christian Socialist politics shaped his unease with what he regarded as Henry James's unbridled individualism. Such an atomistic creed was anathema to Matthiessen, whose deepest sympathies among the James family were with James senior, whom he called a genuine Christian "equalitarian democrat." William was more a Christian than a democrat, while Henry "was neither one nor the other." Matthiessen's books on Henry James and the James family both end with tributes to the family patriarch, who alone knew that "the ripest freedom comes through participation in society and not apart from it," and "finds its completion through fraternity, in solidarity" (*Family* 684). Acknowledging that the elder James's Swedenborgianism is far less "serviceable to us" than Henry's representation of "humane freedom," Matthiessen ends his critical study by suggesting that James's novels "may be validly translated into terms of social consciousness." The terms Matthiessen has in mind are a "synthesis" of Christianity and democracy that "recognizes anew man's radical imperfection," and that "men must be equal in their social opportunities." To achieve these goals, Matthiessen concludes, "many of James's values are, oddly enough, not at all remote" (*Major* 151). Thus James, who created "novels of intelligence rather than of full consciousness" because of his passive spectatorship, awaits translation into social terms (23). Until then "the world portrayed in his novels is of substantial value to us in recharting our own world, if only by providing us with a target to shoot against" (150). Apart from its more sophisticated understanding of the aesthetics of Jamesian fiction, Matthiessen's view of the novelist as a handy target is, finally, not very different from those of Brooks and Parrington.[13]

When Matthiessen examined James's response to the immigrants of the Lower East Side, he saw only contempt and incipient racism. And when he praised James's curiosity (he never lost his "boyhood curiosity. . . . He was to the end the absorbed spectator"), he saw it merely as a means by which James helped make concrete his limited, if ethically sensitive, art (*Major* 149). Matthiessen's politics, so contemptuous of the society of "liberalism and laissez-faire" in which the James brothers were raised, encouraged him to reduce Henry James to the level of a gifted bourgeois aesthete unable or unwilling to risk "participation in society" (*Family* 673, 684). James's "kind of detachment" leads to "aesthetic contemplation as the primary mode of experience." His curiosity, for Matthiessen, seems to exist in a void, empty of all productive consequences save opposition to abstraction. Matthiessen's conventional understanding of the aesthetic prevented him from grasping the capacity of "infinite curiosity" to be "plastic and inflammable" in its receptivity and mobility (James, *Literary* 1: 98). By reducing James to an artistically brilliant but shallow novelist essentially detached from social reality, Matthiessen proved as blind as Brooks to "the multiform devotion which gave James's career the appearance of a consecration" (Kazin 217).

Alfred Kazin's phrase is quoted from his seminal work, *On Native Grounds* (1942), which describes the crucial form of James's devotion: "James had burned his curiosity into the secret innermost core of everything he touched. *That* was James's success." Jamesian curiosity, wrote Kazin, possessed a quality of "defiance," "iron confidence," and "indefinable exultation" (217–18, 33).[14] Oblivious to the energy generated by what Henry James called "perception at the pitch of passion," Matthiessen and Brooks recall William James's blindness to his brother's rare curiosity. Matthiessen restricts it to Henry's boyhood spectatorship, a judgment that softens Brooks's harsher verdict, which dubs James an "invalid child," a "shocked little boy." Geismar reiterates this emphasis in calling James's a "fascinating case of arrested development" (435). This theme is repeated in Alfred Habegger's 1982 study in his chapter entitled "The Boy Who Could Not Become a Man," which states that "one of the basic givens in Henry James's life was a deep and humiliating anguish at his failure ever to become a proper man" (267). Rather than simply being fatuous, the repeated effort to infantilize James represents a defensive response to the unsettling mimetic aspect of his self-representation, which is discussed in chapter 7.

The James-as-child motif can be said to originate with William James's description of his brother as "at bottom very powerless-feeling Harry . . . full of dutifulness and affection for all gentle things" (Matthiessen, *Family* 303). As we saw in chapter 2, William's belief in his brother as "powerless . . . dear

innocent old Harry" strategically deflected the possibility of Henry as active
in multiform ways. That Henry's burning curiosity served as the motor of
his aesthetic practice never occurred to William, given his limited notion
both of Henry and of the aesthetic. Brooks, Matthiessen, and William James
all have difficulty seeing the aesthetic as anything other than passive contemplation, a mode of existence that inevitably arouses disgust in William
James: "There is no more contemptible type of character than the nerveless
sentimentalist and dreamer who spends his life in a weltering sea of sensibility
and emotion, but who never does a manly concrete deed" (*Principles* 129).
It is difficult not to detect in this description a caricature of Henry or, at
least, the sensitive young men about whom he wrote. William's unshakable
dualism of doing versus being blinds him to the possibility of the former
taking a variety of forms beyond the "manly concrete deed." William would
have been baffled by Henry's remark that the life of the critic is "heroic for
it is immensely vicarious . . . and the [critic's] sense of effort is easily lost in
the enthusiasm of curiosity" (*Literary* 1: 99). Matthiessen and Brooks would
have been equally puzzled. For the latter the manly deed that redeemed
aesthetic passivity was commitment to American cultural activism rather than
European decadence. For Matthiessen, the manly deed that translated aesthetic into social consciousness was devotion to the Popular Front's effort
to create universal equality.

"Noble feelings and immature longings" was how *The Nation* judged Matthiessen's politics. In *Partisan Review* Irving Howe denounced him as a
sentimental fellow traveler. Many New York intellectuals concurred, finding
his sentimentalism typical of genteel Harvard leftism. According to Rufus
Mathewson, a faculty member, "Columbia, on the other hand, was much
closer to the grimy center of things. . . . New York's intellectuals had a much
clearer view of the ugly side of the Soviet experience" (qtd. O'Neill 179,
176). Kazin's anti-Stalinism (nurtured at City College and Columbia) had
little patience for what he called Matthiessen's "literary and political pieties"
(177). Kazin's own approach to literary criticism, modeled on Edmund Wilson's, exemplified the double emphasis of the New York intellectuals. Instead of choosing between the "twin fanaticisms"—"the fatal either/or in
modern criticism"—of sociological or aesthetic criticism, Kazin sought "a
felicitous blending of the two" (348).

Less content than Kazin to be only a literary critic, and modeling himself
more on Matthew Arnold than Edmund Wilson, Lionel Trilling sought the
role of cultural and moral arbiter, a "figure" in Henry James's sense of the
word. Trilling's concern, according to William Barrett, was the "sensibility,
capacities of response, and general intelligence about literature" of the liberal
democratic bourgeoisie as it adjusted to a world that had survived the trauma
of Stalinism and nazism (169). In this postwar climate Trilling felt there was
an urgent need for the moral sobriety and maturity of writers of domestic
realism and refined sensibility—Arnold, Forster, Austen, Keats, Howells,
and James—rather than for the artistic, political, and moral extremism of the
modernist avant-garde. Not surprisingly, as early as the fifties Trilling was

being accused (by Delmore Schwartz) of having revived the genteel tradition.[15] But from Trilling's perspective American literary and aesthetic taste
had coarsened under Stalinist domination; one antidote he proposed was to
promote culture heroes rich in the aesthetic and moral complexity of the
great European realists. In 1945 the Stalinist critic Malcolm Cowley explained the change in literary values as "a reaction against historical or genetic
criticism of any type," particularly Marxism. The works most likely to be
praised, according to Cowley, "are those most widely removed from any
social movement and least contaminated with ideas. . . . Henry James is the
great example in this country of the 'pure' novelist" (122).

Although we will see that Trilling's sponsorship of Henry James rejected
Cowley's stereotype, the latter's stress on James's purity reflected the prevailing image of the novelist at the time. One source of this image—which
proved to be as durable with postwar liberals as with leftists—is found in
Philip Rahv's 1943 essay "Attitudes Toward Henry James." Like the present
chapter, Rahv's essay surveys the available accounts of James and finds both
his detractors and defenders wanting. Indeed, Rahv's premise that "Henry
James is at once the most and least appreciated figure in American writing"
might have served as my own motto (95). What Rahv intends (if not accom-
plishes) is to promote Henry James as a master modernist, a figure compatible
with neither the "sundry moralizers and nationalists who belittle James" nor
the cultists,

> who go to the other extreme in presenting him as a kind of culture hero, an
> ideal master whose perfection of form is equaled by his moral insight and staunch
> allegiance to "tradition." This image is no doubt of consolatory value to some
> high-minded literary men. It contributes, however, to the misunderstanding of
> James, in that it is so impeccable, one might say transcendent, that it all but
> eliminates the contradictions in him. (100)

Contradiction is the hallmark of modernism for Rahv and his *Partisan Review*
colleagues: "It is above all the creativity, the depth and quality of the
contradictions that a writer unites within himself, that gives us the truest
measure of his achievement." James's chief contradiction, says Rahv, is a
simultaneous search for and withdrawal from experience, "or rather a dread
of approaching it in its natural state"(101).

But the penultimate word in this last phrase undermines the alleged contradiction. Rahv ignores the possibility that James's "dread" expresses not
prudishness but understanding of the "natural state" as a cultural construct
that supports, for instance, the bias against the "unnatural" ambiguity of
theatricality. By the end of his essay Rahv expands James's alleged dread
of the natural into a dread of history, which the novelist enshrines as a
"supreme ideal," a "strictly private possession." Rahv leaves us with a James
richer in solipsism than in contradiction:

> It is true that on the whole James's sense of history is restricted by the point
> of view of the "passionate pilgrim" who comes to rest in the shade of civilization.

Above all, he comes to enrich his personality. Thus there is produced the
Jamesian conception of history as a static yet irreproachable standard, a beautiful
display, a treasured background, whose function is at once to adorn and lend
perspective to his well-nigh metaphysical probing of personal relations . . . and
his consistency in this respect implies an antihistorical attitude. (102)

The irony is egregious: by constructing a James as impeccably transcendent
as any leftist or cultist could fashion, Rahv skews his effort to "save" James
for modernism. Although overlapping with Rahv at some points, Trilling's
reading of James is far more astute.

III

Trilling's James is a nuanced observer of social manners who is also skeptical
of the seductive simplifications of political ideology. Thus the novelist was
equipped to serve as a central ally in Trilling's successful and influential
campaign to rescue the liberal imagination from populists, progressives, and
especially Stalinists. What Trilling found so poisonous about the ideology
of Stalinism was its hostility to contradiction. Its main tenet, as he noted in
a retrospective essay, "was the belief that the Soviet Union had resolved all
social and political contradictions and was well on the way toward realizing
the highest possibilities of human life" (*Last* 140). The paradox of Stalinism
was that it was a political ideology devoted to destroying politics. As Trilling
explains, "It must sometimes seem that their only political purpose was to
express their disgust with politics and make an end of it once and for all.
. . . [They hoped] to usher in a social order in which rational authority would
prevail" (200). This "negation of the political life," said Trilling, "was one
aspect of an ever more imperious refusal to consent to the conditioned nature
of human existence." Trilling sought to end this extremism by returning
the Enlightenment's "great primal act of imagination" to the center of cultural life (*Liberal* xii). A "liberal critic of liberalism," as Mark Krupnick has
called him, Trilling described his agenda in the famous preface to *The Liberal
Imagination*:

> The job of criticism would seem to be, then, to recall liberalism to its first
> essential imagination of variousness and possibility, which implies the awareness
> of complexity and difficulty. To the carrying out of the job of criticizing the
> liberal imagination, literature has a unique relevance, not merely because so
> much of modern literature has explicitly directed itself upon politics, but more
> importantly because literature is the human activity that takes the fullest and
> most precise account of variousness, possibility, complexity, and difficulty. (xiii)

Henry James, the hero of ambiguity, played a pivotal role in Trilling's
effort to redefine "reality in America," the title of the opening essay of *The
Liberal Imagination*. American reality, Trilling implied, should no longer be
defined by an intellectually bankrupt liberalism that had elevated Dreiser
and mocked James. Rather, a postprogressivist liberalism required a Jamesian

standard of complexity and depth. What remained unclear in Trilling's account was the content and context of this much-honored quality of complexity.

Trilling demonstrates James's centrality to the liberal mind in "The Princess Casamassima," a key essay in *The Liberal Imagination* and often judged a masterpiece in Trilling's oeuvre. Implicitly dissenting from Rahv's "antihistorical" James, Trilling finds that the novel's "moral realism . . . yields a kind of social and political knowledge which is hard to come by" (85). Directly rebutting the standard leftist complaint that the novel is a "capital example of James's impotence in matters sociological," Trilling shows that "quite the opposite is so. . . . *The Princess Casamassima* is a brilliantly precise representation of social actuality. . . . There is not a political event [in it] which is not confirmed by multitudinous records" (71, 64). Ultimately, however, it is not the materiality of James's "moral realism" that is most compelling to Trilling. Rather, he is gripped by the doomed effort of James's hero, Hyacinth, to extricate himself from radical politics and to affirm the value of high culture. Hyacinth's struggle, which ends in suicide, speaks to Trilling's own aesthetic idealism, which coexisted uneasily with his commitment to the conditioned and contingent. Hyacinth's fatal pursuit of aesthetic transcendence makes the novel "an incomparable representation of the spiritual circumstances of our civilization" (88). This statement is the closest Trilling comes to making explicit what a number of readers have argued—that he reads the novel as a political allegory in which an Arnoldian apostle of high culture is sacrificed to the machinations of Stalinist fellow travelers.

Mark Krupnick, one of Trilling's best critics, goes so far as to claim that Trilling "uses Hyacinth's story to forge his autobiographical myth. Hyacinth becomes a version of Trilling's own idealized self as a hero of culture." The "spiritual circumstances" that Trilling alludes to "were essentially Trilling's own in the mid-forties: the struggle between the rival claims of social justice and the glory of high civilization, the conflict between mass democratic values and art" (71). In short, Trilling's celebration of Hyacinth's idealism reveals what Krupnick calls Trilling's "own ambivalence" about politics. A way of addressing Krupnick's claims is to note that, in one sense, Trilling's autobiographical allegorizing is appropriate since it mimes the novel's depiction of the self as derived from an assemblage of cultural texts. Hyacinth is a hero unable to escape an obsession with the "romantic innuendoes" of his origins because he constructs his self by internalizing the mythic romances of the popular press to which he was addicted as a child. Thus, he cannot help but become the unwitting allegorist of his own life, which he fashions into a naturalistic tragedy of blood as fate. Hyacinth's self-allegorizing invites our own. James makes us experience how life is not a transparent given but, as Erving Goffman says, is "itself something shot through with various framings" (10), itself dependent on the production of narratives derived from cultural imagery. Because Trilling misses James's thematic use of allegory as constitutive of identity, he also misses the novel's ironic portrayal of

Hyacinth staging his own literary spectacle of self-sacrifice. Trilling takes Hyacinth as earnestly as James's hero takes himself.

Yet the integrity of Trilling's essay resides in its refusal to project onto James either his (Trilling's) own self-narrative of political frustration or Hyacinth's aesthetic idealism. Trilling insists on seeing James's moral realism as rooted in a precise historical imagination. Unfortunately, Krupnick is not as careful as Trilling in making distinctions between James and his characters. For Krupnick, James and Hyacinth share Trilling's "ambivalence" about politics, and all three transform history into the "object of an aesthetic passion" that affirms "disinterested aesthetic contemplation at the expense of the active will" (72). This statement is doubtless true of Hyacinth and often true of Trilling, but it is inadequate with respect both to James's conception of the aesthetic as practice and to subjectivity as culturally constructed.[16]

Given the materialist bent of his aesthetic idealism, Trilling embodies unresolvable ambivalences. Herein resides his importance as an eloquent representative of his own cultural epoch. As part of their revulsion against— indeed, traumatization by—Stalinism, intellectuals of Trilling's generation were variously drawn to art as a haven of formal beauty and internal complexity free of the vulgarity of politics. But Trilling, for one, was hardly content with this idealism; he never stopped pondering how art and politics were entangled, even as he sought to release art from this burden. If and when literature and politics were brought together, as in Trilling's famous juxtaposition of James and Dreiser, they remained static entities, suspicious of one another: "With that juxtaposition we are immediately at the dark and bloody crossroads where literature and politics meet. One does not go there gladly" (*Liberal* 8). The apocalyptic imagery suggests the trauma of having to bring together what he wishes to keep separate. Clearly, Trilling's desire somehow to divert art from the "bloody crossroads" was a response to a situation in which the political had become virtually synonymous with the paralysis of thought.

Quentin Anderson, Trilling's Columbia University colleague, is explicit about the political pressures that tailored Henry James to the portrait of him that Rahv had sketched: antihistorical apostle of personal relations. In a forthright essay of 1983, Anderson locates the basis of what he calls "James's cultural office" in the 1950s in Emerson's belief in the "infinitude of the private man." Entwined, says Anderson, with this Emersonian view of James is Stalinism. For many intellectuals "the Stalinism born of the Depression was not so much a politics as a desperate grab for a picture of the world that would satisfy the Emersonian demand for a complete imaginative possession of things" ("Office" 199). From the hindsight of 1983 Anderson can at last perceive that this image of James expressed a collective self-delusion: "In the 1950s, when Americans embraced Henry James as the very figure of the artist, they were unable to see that they were also granting themselves a holiday from the constraints of society and history. . . . What they got was a celebration of the power of individual vision" (208). Anderson sums up what

James meant to the New York intellectuals: "The experience of reading James was being substituted for emotional returns not available in a world fragmented by Hitler and Stalin. James offered us . . . liberation from a crippling social scene, yet it [his work] was suffused with complication and intensity" (198). Thus, the fate of ambiguity in American intellectual life reached a curious turn. In response to the political flight from ambiguity embodied in Stalinism, complexity was fetishized as the supreme value. Reduced to the static, complexity became part of the flight from ambiguity it was originally meant to oppose.

Complexity is similarly reified by another of Trilling's Columbia colleagues. At the conclusion of his *Progressive Historians: Turner, Beard, Parrington*, Richard Hofstadter praises the "rediscovery of complexity in American history" as a welcome relief from the "Progressive scheme of polarized conflict" (442). But he also confesses to uneasiness with this new emphasis: "The great fear" in our "continual rediscovery" of complexity is the possibility of "political immobility." But this is not necessarily the case "since a keen sense of history begets a feeling of social responsibility." Yet, asserts Hofstadter, "history does seem inconsistent with the coarser rallying cries of politics. Hence I suppose we may expect that the very idea of complexity will itself come under fire once again, and that it will become important for a whole generation to argue that most things in life and in history are not complex but really quite simple" (466). However, Hofstadter concludes optimistically, affirming his belief in history's refusal to gratify demands for simplicity. But his suggestion of an endless, polarized struggle between complexity and simplicity is a haunting insight. For imprisonment in sterile binaries describes not simply the limitations of liberal progressive thinkers but also those of their critics, including Hofstadter.

He, like Trilling, is a liberal critic of liberalism, a celebrant of the "imagination of complication." Both men helped emancipate American intellectual life from the parochialism of the progressivist nostalgia for the purity of moral absolutism and neat polarities: democracy versus capitalism; farming class versus professional class; property versus paper money; production versus speculation.[17] But the liberal critique of liberalism tended to replace old dualisms with new ones. Trilling (uneasily) opposed art and politics, whereas Hofstadter opposed history and politics. The binary mode of thought remained intact. For both men, as for many other postwar intellectuals, complexity itself became a "veritable cult," as Peter Novick has noted (324). By absolutizing complexity, Trilling's dialectic "functions almost counter-dialectically, as a tool for a kind of stasis. . . . He values negation for the sake of negation and contradiction for the sake of contradiction."[18] Sacrificed was the possibility of complexity becoming a source of critical power that could promote a hermeneutics of suspicion capable of interrogating not only the premises of one's own discourse but also of political and cultural constructs, including liberal individualism. Hofstadter and Trilling leave undisturbed the root dualism of classical liberalism (progressive and revisionary) that posits the individual as predating society. This belief, also upheld by William

James, is seemingly immune to critique, for it comprises the basic understanding of modern identity: the sovereignty of what Trilling called one's
"own original, actual self."[19]

What this belief conceals, of course, is that the community does not simply
interact causally with the individual but is constitutive of him: "A human
being alone is an impossibility," stresses Charles Taylor. However familiar
these claims, they are "constantly being lost from sight because of the ascendancy of the modern identity" and its compulsive autonomy. "However
tightly the dependence [between man and community] is conceived, it is
seen in causal terms, and not as touching our very identity. Bringing this
back into view is therefore a perpetually necessary philosophical task . . . in
order to purge our key normative notions—freedom, justice, rights—of their
atomist distortions" (8).[20]

This distortion is enshrined in the idealism of the genteel tradition. By
the early 1960s Trilling, the son of Jewish immigrants, had in effect modernized this tradition, stripping it of nativist and social phobias and its arrogant
sense of class privilege while remaining within its logic. This is clear from
Trilling's effort, in the 1960s, to situate aesthetic experience "beyond culture." Trilling's famous phrase signaled revisions within his own earlier
postwar emphasis on the conditioned. He now stressed the literary intellectual's refusal of bourgeois values and embrace of modernism's iconoclastic
detachment. In his introduction to *Beyond Culture*, Trilling acknowledges
that if all implications of the word "culture" are "insisted on," the phrase
"beyond culture . . . can be said to make nonsense"; since culture gives one
"categories and habits of speech . . . no aberration can effect a real separation." But for Trilling this fact "can have only a mere formal reality." In
the modern world the "belief that it is possible to stand beyond culture in
some decisive way is commonly and easily held." Encouraging this belief is
modernism's subversive strategy of

> detaching the reader from the habits of thought and feeling that the larger
> culture imposes, of giving him a ground and vantage point from which to judge
> and condemn. . . . It is a belief still pre-eminently honored that a primary func-
> tion of art and thought is to liberate the individual from the tyranny of his
> culture in the environmental sense and to permit him to stand beyond it in an
> autonomy of perception and judgment. (*Beyond* xiii)[21]

This stands as the credo of the liberal "imagination of complication," a
sensibility that, in the postwar era, became virtually synonymous with being
an American public literary intellectual. Because it reflects Henry James's own
high valuation of nuanced, responsive consciousness, this weltanschauung
helped restore the novelist's stature. But the compatibility between aesthetic
idealism and James's commitment to representing consciousness goes only
so far. One reason it breaks down is because James does not conceive of
consciousness as somehow immune from the tyranny of culture and history.

Indeed, he finds the rarest consciousness in his "most exposed and assaulted figures," those who have the "precious liability to fall into traps" (*Art* 66, 64). Although a number of his characters seek immunity from the traps and assaults of history, their quest is usually revealed as quixotic. For the attempt to go beyond culture is less an act of emancipation than obedience to the seductive myth that untrammeled freedom is the American birthright.

IV

Henry James's late cultural thought moves beyond the ahistorical ideology of monadic individualism, with its grounding in binary logic and its promotion of a selfhood devoted to inner and outer control. His project can begin to be understood by applying to James himself a crucial passage from the prefaces about writers of genius: "The interest of his genius is greatest," he says, "when he commits himself in both directions; not quite at the same time or to the same effect . . . but by some need of performing his whole possible revolution, by the law of some rich passion in him for extremes." Among writers who possess the "largest responding imagination before the human scene," the "current" of their genius is "extraordinarily rich and mixed" as it washes us with both "the near and familiar and the tonic shock . . . of the far and strange" (*Art* 31). James's immediate concerns here are realism and romance, but the words reverberate beyond this context to suggest his equation of genius with passion, agonism, contradiction, and mobility, with the radical heterogeneity of mutually conflicting impulses that at once incite and doom efforts at resolution. Implicit, too, in this urge to move "in both directions" is the androgynous texture of genius, its rejection of polarities. In sum, genius possesses a dialectical imagination that, in another preface, James visualizes as a "perpetually simmering cauldron," for "we can surely account for nothing in the novelist's work that hasn't passed through the crucible of his imagination" (230).

Igniting this fiery process is the pressure of dialectical reversal whereby the crucible of the imagination "destroys" "prime identity" to produce "a new and richer saturation." This famous image of the artistic process, a kind of Jamesian version of what Hegel calls negating the negation (the overcoming of opposites), leaves ambiguous the final term of the process. All James says about what passes through the "crucible" is that it achieves a "final savour. . . . Thus it has become a different and . . . better thing" (230). By omitting from his simmering process a synthetic, harmonizing moment producing an absolute (as in Hegel), James emphasizes instead the production of difference generated by the dissolving of identity. Difference is what makes for a "richer saturation" of an ongoing process that avoids closure. This elaborate metaphor of the crucible is hardly exhausted by its immediate purpose of defending the artist's right to alter the identities of "real persons." More generally, James's crucible directs attention to his suspicion (shared by Hegel) of the very concept of individual identity as impoverished unless it is nourished by dialectical mediation. Correlative with James's critique of "prime identity" is skepticism of the idealist goal of an autonomous self standing beyond culture. More congenial than aesthetic idealism to James's immanent stance is the recent example of Richard Rorty's neopragmatism. Rorty's "postmodernist bourgeois liberalism" finds Trilling's literary culture an instance of the Romanticism that survives as the "principal legacy of metaphysical idealism." What is metaphysical about Trilling's view—he being one of a number of figures, including Emerson, that Rorty associates with this perspective—is that it requires the futile "search for an Archimedean point from which to survey culture" (*Consequences* 150). This admonition has become so familiar that it can stand as a motto of our postmodern culture of immanence, which seeks to "de-divinize the world" and "treat everything—our language, our conscience, our community—as a product of time and chance" (*Contingency* 21–22). To try and transcend one's culture for absolute knowledge, for "truth as correspondence to reality," strikes the postmodernist as "the impossible attempt to step outside our skins . . . and compare ourselves with something absolute" (*Consequences* xix). The "Platonic urge" to transcend "the finitude of one's time and place" animates not only Trilling's quest to go "beyond culture" but also informs the desire for "meta-narrative transcendence" found in Marxism and other totalizing discourses. Quoting Jean-François Lyotard, Rorty understands postmodernism as refusing modernism's "explicit appeal to some grand narrative."[22] Sharing William James's equation of the grand with the dangerous, Rorty hopes that culture can be "poeticized" rather than rationalized or scientized as the Enlightenment sought to do (*Contingency* 53). Thus postmodernism and pragmatism both renounce the pursuit of epistemological grounds and instead seek only to offer new forms of intellectual life, more varied and revisable cultural artifacts.

Rorty's renovated bourgeois liberalism notoriously abjures the possibility of critique, for he associates it with theory's illusory attempt to stand outside practice. According to his logic, to abolish a space beyond culture leaves no ground for critique, which becomes merely a name for transcendental yearning.[23] Instead of critique, Rorty sees a "generic trait" of the postmodern intellectual as the fashioning of "redescriptions"—the making of a "final vocabulary" that justifies one's life and world (90). His exemplary agent of redescription is the ironist, a historicist and antiessentialist whose "final vocabulary" is indifferent to a need for an ultimate common truth or goal (74). According to Rorty, ironists arouse a "*special* resentment" because, unlike Marxists, they make no guarantees that their redescriptions empower. "Chances of freedom" for the ironist "depend on historical contingencies" and not on the "right redescription" (90).

Few ironists have aroused more resentment than Adorno. Although he would admire Rorty's refusal to be tempted to seek a space outside or beyond culture, Adorno does not believe that a commitment to immanence necessitates renouncing critique. Indeed, Adorno calls his practice immanent critique and grounds it in the contradictions that Trilling fetishizes and Rorty genially accepts as potentially revisable. Like Rorty's redescription, Adorno's immanent stance is less a stable standpoint or resolution than inherently precarious and tentative: "Immanent criticism cannot take comfort in its own idea. It can neither be vain enough to believe that it can liberate the mind directly by immersing itself in it, nor naive enough to believe that unflinching immersion in the object will inevitably lead to truth" (*Prisms* 33). In his essay "Cultural Criticism and Society," Adorno differentiates among bourgeois, transcendent, and immanent critique, or, in political terms, among liberal, Marxist, and Frankfurt Critical Theory. Adorno, like Rorty, finds that the first two assume an external standpoint from which to judge culture and society. Each assumption involves a different kind of fetishizing. The liberal position reifies culture by conceiving of it as a "form of property which is stable and independent of stock-market fluctuations. This idea of culture asserts its distance from the system in order . . . to offer universal security in the middle of a universal dynamic" (22).[24] Such security, says Adorno, depends on "isolated categories such as mind, life and the individual." On the other hand, the transcendent or Marxist critic reduces culture to an "abstract utopia" at the cost of insensitivity to the particular. "Cut off from experience of the object" by its metanarrative obligations, Marxist critique tends to depend on the "prescribed label" and "mechanically functioning categories" that divide the world into black and white. Such regimentation encourages "the very domination against which concepts were once conceived" (33). This Marxist structure of polarity produces

> the constant search for the Other, that is, for the uncontaminated element outside the totality that might serve as the fulcrum for its holistic transcendence. . . . Various candidates have been proposed for the role . . . e.g., avant-garde art, the sexual instincts, the third world, women, homosexuals. All . . . are theoretically homologous in that they serve the same necessary function of providing a supposed Archimedean point. (Whitebook 158)

One way Adorno avoids this search for an outside is to resist favoring the immanent over the liberal and transcendent methods.[25] Indeed, what enables immanent critique is a transcendental (as distinct from the transcendent) "moment" that Adorno associates with bourgeois liberalism. Adorno remarks that "without consciousness transcending the immanence of culture [its position within the social whole], immanent criticism itself would be inconceivable: the spontaneous movement of the object can be followed only by someone who is not entirely engulfed by it" (*Prisms* 29). The *transcendental* moment within immanent critique exposes the antinomies of the object, whereas a *transcendent* standpoint remains outside, "cut off from experience of the object" (33). Instead of mirroring or escaping the distortions of present social circumstances, the transcendental moment uncovers a discrepancy, a nonidentity, between a concept and its social actuality—for instance, the ideal of freedom and the fact of nonfreedom. This gap between ideal and actual, a gap otherwise hidden in a seamless social totality, can serve as a basis of immanent critique.[26]

By refusing to resolve paradoxes or dissolve difference into identity, Henry James avoids submitting to an ideology of harmonious totality—be it organic form or what he calls progressivism's "American identity" (*Scene* 129)—that posits the "semblance of unity and wholeness in the world" (*Prisms* 31). Instead, James's strategy resembles Adorno's effort to express the idea of harmony "negatively by embodying the contradictions, pure and uncompromised," within a work's "innermost structure" (*Prisms* 32). In his experiences in New York in 1904, James manages to sustain the precarious contradictions of immanent critique that require one to be simultaneously engulfed and detached. He calls himself the "victim of his interest" in the city, but he is also able to narrate his own entrapment. This logic (explored in chapter 6) can be adumbrated here by citing a minor, if telling, moment. Feeling baffled by his unexpected tenderness toward New York, James explores his ambivalence by contriving an interior dialogue in which he has "the voice of the air" impute to him an image of the town as a "bad, bold beauty . . . to whom everything is always forgiven." Then James imagines "the voice of the air" imputing to him a challenge that, in turn, the voice will correct: "On what ground 'forgiven'? of course you [James] ask; but note that you ask it while you're in the very act of forgiving" (*Scene* 109). In this convoluted dialogue, of which I have quoted only a small part, James dramatizes his failed attempt to stand apart and clarify his feeling about New York. Instead of finding an external vantage point from which to speculate, James is badgered by the air of New York into admitting his entanglement with the "bold beauty." Paradoxically, here James display the intricacies of self-consciousness, only to reveal the limits of self-reflection. Rather than definitively clarifying and liberating, self-reflection cannot banish contradiction; James must remain vulnerable on the unsteady "grounds of [his] perversity" (108).[27]

At once "beguiled" and exasperated, James is perpetually off balance and thereby open to New York's spontaneous movements without becoming enthralled by them. He is free to experience the particular because his "surrender" to it is neither total nor programmatic but rather "unsettled," riven by ambivalence that at times causes him to "tumble back . . . in appalled reaction" (86). James's uneasy commitment to heterogeneity sets him at odds with many of the obligations and assumptions honored by the social class in which he moves. Thus, rather than upholding the patrician elite as a kind of uncontaminated "other" in privileged possession of cultural and moral capital, Henry embarks on a ritual of self-contamination in New York that appropriately begins with his elaborate declaration of public exposure. Rather than confining himself to the genteel areas of New York City, James redraws the map to include Ellis Island, Central Park, the Bowery, and the Lower East Side.

James's cultural project takes for granted, and is launched from inside, what he (and later Randolph Bourne) calls the "inexorable"—man's confinement in what has created him: social and cultural conventions, practices, representations, and institutions. James is confident these constructions can be renovated—"nothing here is grimly ultimate"—but he is skeptical of attempts to escape history, whether through class revolt (as in Marx) or by becoming a god in nature (as in Emerson), or by returning to the flux (as in Henri Bergson and William James), to cite three such strategies (*Literary* 1: 693). In the extremity of their response, these oppositional stances are heroic hymns to man's Promethean powers, a grandeur absent in immanent critique. Yet, as Adorno notes, although "the transcendent method, which aims at totality, seems more radical than the immanent method, which presupposes the questionable whole," the former method is as "fictitious as only the construction of abstract utopias can be" (*Prisms* 31).

In America the equation of critique and Promethean heroism is so naturalized that immanent critique has been virtually invisible. We tend to conceive of cultural critique as draped in the flamboyant colors of alienation or elitism—be it patrician disdain, populist resentment, sixties counterculture, or modernism's arsenal of strategies to "*épater le bourgeois*" (dadaist mockery, avant-garde hermeticism, or proletarian social realism).[28] Radical curiosity has suffered a repression analogous to immanent critique because of a similar set of unexamined assumptions about the inviolable integrity of the self.

Immanent critique is compatible with Walter Benn Michaels's much-debated neopragmatist suspicion of cultural criticism's traditional opening move of "transcending your origins in order to evaluate them" (18). Such transcendence would leave one with only theological terms of evaluation. Michaels concludes that "the only relation literature as such has to culture as such is that it is part of it" (18, 27). In short, it is futile to imagine it possible to be outside one's culture and thereby have an attitude toward it. But if immanent critique concurs with this anti-theoretic effort to reject the idealist assumptions of oppositional criticism, it diverges from Michaels's ascetic refusal (shared by Rorty) to transform the acknowledgement of embeddedness into "heightened perception" of a culture's antinomic structure—what Adorno calls "the irreconcilability of the object's moments." Immanent critique "pursues the logic of its aporias, the insolubility of the task itself" (*Prisms* 32). This is its form of hope, its way of not "renouncing the idea of potentiality" (92).[29]

Potentiality involves "making the possible real," which implies a move from epistemology—questions of self-reflection and consciousness—to practice (94). Immanent critique encourages this move by insisting on the limits of self-reflection (limits Henry James discovered in New York): "Even the most radical reflection of the mind . . . remains only reflection, without altering . . . existence" (32). Adorno's point is to discourage idealism's fetishizing of the mind as sovereignly self-sufficient by confronting it with its own impotence before the intractability of social contradictions. "Immanent criticism holds in evidence the fact that the mind has always been under a spell. On its own it is unable to resolve the contradictions under which it labors" (32). With mind and epistemology dethroned and the potential to alter existence found to be a collective social project, immanent critique, like Deweyan pragmatism (as we shall see), focuses its energy on the insoluble task of cultural inquiry. Thus immersion and embodiment rather than self-reflection are its exemplary values, its form of social hope.

The importance for Henry James of exemplary immersion is evident in his famous praise of "saturation": "The great thing is to be *saturated* with something . . . and I chose the form of my saturation," he declared to William in 1888, who had accused him of being "hollowed out inside" (*Letters* 3: 244). In 1904 saturation takes the form of nonidentity, of refusing to stay within genteel boundaries or to resolve the tension of subject and object, stranger and native, detachment and entanglement. Only then can he perform his "whole possible revolution" and thereby embody the heterogeneity worthy of serving as a paradigm of cultural renovation. This paradigm, to summarize, promotes "slack in the institutional order," a concept formulated by William Connolly that serves as a "counterpoint to the idea of disciplinary control." Slack describes "an order that can afford to relax the reins of social control" and permit "a rather broad range of behavior to *be*, only lightly touched by the pressure of normative standards" (*Politics* 113–14). In political terms, James's heterogeneity translates into something resembling an expressivist pluralism that disperses power and rigid identification with one role or place and replaces them with a dynamic of shifting involvements that resists finitude and definition while breeding possibility and spontaneity.[30]

V

Both sides of the leftist–liberal struggle over the novelist ignore the historicist critical practice that animates James's late nonfiction. This myopia generates some striking ironies. Leftist contempt blinds these critics to what should be a source of affinity—James's critique of bourgeois, genteel culture. Liberal celebration blinds the other camp to one target of James's critique—their own idealist pretensions of possessing an emancipated consciousness. One would think that the current critical moment, with its suspicion of liberal humanism, would at least recognize Henry James's immanent stance as having the virtue of a bracing skepticism. But too often critics who employ Marxist and deconstructive rhetorics of suspicion use the insights of contemporary theory against James, who is made to embody all the bourgeois befuddlement and romantic naivete that deconstruction has been designed to "cure." James, in short, is treated like Isabel Archer. Thus, a recent work describes itself as "employing aspects of poststructuralist and Marxist methodologies . . . [so as to] demonstrate that James possessed an awareness and lucidity about himself yet was also deluded and mystified, trapped within his own artistic coils." This statement appears on the second page. It does not take too long for the reader to discover that in this book James's "awareness and lucidity" are nugatory, and his capacity for delusion and mystification unlimited. The James who appears in these pages desires a "psychic wholeness, a unity of experience. . . . [He] longs for a recreation or approximation of a past plenitude . . . [and] has nostalgic memories of the homogenous society of his youth. . . . He too is ahistorical, for he rejects the present and future" (Przybylowicz 247). Predictably, "James would not even be satisfied with maintaining class distinctions but would really prefer the actual negation and destruction of otherness. He would like the immigrants to disappear magically, so that everyone would be a mirror image of himself" (262). This indictment is merely Parrington and Brooks newly inflected. Previously the dupe of nationalism, agrarian populism, and Marxism, James is now the dupe of deconstruction. The repetitiveness of the indictment is matched only by its circularity. James is praised by liberals for fleeing from modern life yet damned for it by leftists. Yet this judgment is rooted in its own retreat, a flight from ambiguity manifested as stubborn blindness to what remains audacious in James's cultural criticism—the dialectical pressure he exerts upon cardinal bourgeois values of control, mastery, detachment, and autonomy.[31]

The failure of skeptical discourses like Marxism and deconstruction to perceive immanent critique points to a "stunted reflexivity" (to borrow Alvin Gouldner's phrase) rooted in an inability to acknowledge investments in some of the very values they seek to deconstruct, particularly mastery and containment.[32] This desire to banish rivals and promote Marxism as the ultimate cure (an arrogance that afflicts Freudianism as well, as Fredric Jameson has noted) creates a blindness confined not merely to literary Marxists. It also accounts for what Gouldner calls "the blunting of Marxism's own demystifying edge and for the corresponding growth in its own role as social mystifier" (*Dialectic* xii). Gouldner's major project in political theory, begun in 1976, was to demystify Marxism immanently by "grounding" his effort "in certain Marxist assumptions," particularly its emphasis on the reflexivity of ideology critique—"the capacity to make problematic what had hitherto been treated as given" (49). He calls his position "critical theory, the systematic self-reflection of critique" (293). Gouldner justifies his "nonnormal or reflexive Marxism" by assuming that "Marxism today—as a real historical movement—has not produced the human liberation it had promised." Instead, it has helped to produce "grotesque political monstrosities such as Stalinism. The need to conceal Marxism's own partial implication in the political and human catastrophe of Stalinism is one central source of Marxism's contribution to social *mystification*" (xii).

The importance for Gouldner of Stalinism as a stimulus to constructing his own position recalls the situation Trilling and his colleagues had faced thirty years earlier. In the face of Stalinism Trilling emphasized complexity, whereas Gouldner stresses reflexivity. The difference is that Gouldner realizes that his critical theory "*may* express the limited reflexivity of any ideology so that its grounding, too, is a grounding in *ideology*" (293). In contrast, ideology was precisely what Trilling and his generation sought to end, in Daniel Bell's famous phrase. Trilling's "liberal imagination" was founded on a return to a Platonic liberalism—its "primal imagination." This recovery of purity easily became, at least tacitly, a claim of moral elitism and superiority, a stance summed up in the word "detachment." It is precisely such a stance that Gouldner's critical theory is designed to reveal as epistemologically and

politically naive. One is tempted to attribute the greater flexibility of Gouldner's position to the experience of the thirty years intervening between his
and Trilling's initial project. But this explanation would be misleading because Gouldner's basic tenets—even the phrase "critical theory"—are deeply
influenced by the Frankfurt School, whose major works were written in the
forties. As émigrés from Nazi Germany in 1934, they were given a building
at Trilling's Columbia University campus. Max Horkheimer, since 1930 the
director of the Institute of Social Research (the Frankfurt School's official
name), along with Adorno, Herbert Marcuse, and Leo Lowenthal, formed
the nucleus of the group that stayed at Columbia until 1941. It was there
that Gouldner worked with them and was marked by "a lasting, if hybridized
influence" (*Dialectic* 22).

The common ground shared by the *Partisan Review*–Columbia circle and
the Frankfurt intellectuals was substantial. Not only were both groups committed to cosmopolitan "awareness of complexity and difficulty" (to use
Trilling's phrase) as the premise for social and cultural critique, but the main
target of critique was an aridly rationalist liberalism. Trilling could have been
speaking for the Frankfurt School when he decried the "tendencies of liberalism to simplify" as a result of its uncritical reliance on utilitarian rationality, what he called its "organizational impulse," which depends on "agencies
and bureaus and technicians" (*Liberal* xi–xii). Because this rationalizing impulse had become rampant in the twentieth century, Trilling expressed
concern that "the lively sense of contingency and possibility," the precious
"exceptions to the rule" of social control, would be devoured or coerced
(xii). The Frankfurt School was equally anxious that bureaucratic rationality
might obliterate exceptions, the unclassified residue.

Given these shared concerns, what is most remarkable about the relationship between the New York liberal intellectuals and the Frankfurt School
is its virtual nonexistence. A lack of sympathetic interaction existed despite
physical proximity. One possible way to explain this impasse is that the
Frankfurt School's indictment of the liberal imagination was so radical that
it implicitly challenged the essential premise of Trilling's project—the absolute difference between classical liberalism and Stalinism. With shocking,
deliberate perversity, Frankfurt Critical Theory found the seeds of Stalinism—and modern totalitarianism in general—in the Enlightenment values
of instrumental reason, sovereign selfhood, and mastery of nature, all central
tenets of both classical liberalism and modern identity. From the perspective
of the Frankfurt School, these values and beliefs encouraged identity thinking and repressed mimetic receptivity, thus impoverishing the very selfhood
that the Enlightenment intended to empower. In this light, Trilling's belief
in the detachment of the intellectual, if upheld undialectically, is merely
correlative of a naive and abstract autonomy.

The closest semblance of a dialogue between the Frankfurt School and
the Columbia liberals was a monologue or, more precisely, a diatribe delivered by Max Horkheimer in a series of public lectures held at Columbia in
1944 and later published under the title *Eclipse of Reason*. In the midst of

the trauma of Auschwitz, Horkheimer called on philosophy to serve as "mankind's memory and conscience" as it sought to preserve precarious pockets of spontaneous humanity—what Trilling would later call "the lively sense of contingency and possibility." What was polemical about Horkheimer's stance was his identification of the devouring spectre of instrumental reason not simply with fascism or unharnessed positivism but with the American pragmatism of Peirce, William James, and particularly Dewey. It was Dewey, a professor emeritus at Columbia and one of the seminal presences in American cultural life, whom Horkheimer singled out as the source of the "most radical and consistent form of pragmatism" (48). According to Horkheimer, Dewey espoused a dangerously naive scientism ready to ignore blithely the Holocaust. To say the least, Horkheimer's stunningly tactless (geographically speaking) oration did not encourage intellectual exchange with his American audience. This misfortune is deepened by yet another. Horkheimer had distorted and simplified pragmatism—and Dewey in particular—thus creating a rift that has reified into a general assumption among historians that pragmatism and critical theory are irreconcilable.[33] So firm is this assumption that Adorno's correction of Frankfurt myopia twenty years later remains virtually ignored.

Yet Adorno's late recognition of his kinship with Dewey laid the groundwork upon which to reconstruct intellectual history, to fill a resonant void in mid twentieth-century cultural thought. But linking Dewey to Adorno is only part of what emerges from pursuing affinities latent in the simultaneous presence, in the same place, of the American liberal critique of liberalism and the German antiliberal critique of liberalism. This intersection brings a third figure into play—Henry James. For although the American critique elevated him to renewed prestige, in retrospect it was the German critique that was more congenial and responsive to his dialectical imagination. This irony has richly suggestive implications. By pursuing them within the reconfigured intellectual landscape just sketched, the next two chapters will disclose the Henry James that canonization has obscured.

4

"The Religion of Doing": Breaking the Aura of Henry James

I take the opening pages of *The American Scene* as a kind of Proustian teacup: from them springs into being a Henry James who will be at the center of our attention, a "restored absentee" risking "exposure" and a "certain reckessness." Upon his record of impressions he resolves "to stand naked and unashamed," even willing to "go to the stake for them." Like some voluntary Hester Prynne on the scaffold or some Whitman tramping a perpetual journey, this Henry James stages his own spectacle of public vulnerability. He relishes walking the teeming streets of New York, riding the "densely-packed street-cars," feeling "the whole quality and *allure*... of the pushing male crowd," mingling with the "polyglot" vistors to Central Park and the "great swarming" life of the "New Jerusalem" on the Lower East Side (*Scene* 126, 83, 177, 131).

Receding from view is the impeccably Olympian formalist and aesthetic idealist who, like his characters, turns his back on an impossibly vulgar modern world to cultivate what critics were once fond of calling redemptive consciousness. This is the James that R. P. Blackmur installed in the modernist pantheon as "the novelist of the free spirit, the liberated intelligence," and the "ideal vision" (xlvi, xxiii). Blackmur's description is taken from his influential 1934 essay on the prefaces, which first appeared in the special James issue he edited for *Hound and Horn*. This occasion conveniently marks James's official canonization.[1]

The canonized Henry James has been, and remains, one of the most prestigious, indeed, sacred cultural icons on the altar of American high culture. And there is an undeniable and significant measure of truth in the official portrait. The problem is that it purports to be a definitive, fixed image of an author who was always skeptical of the static, whose restless mind's most characteristic movement is an immanent one that conceives of the way out as the way through. A cramped aura of sanctity has grown up around what might be called James's cultural presence. "Aura" is meant here in Walter Benjamin's sense of a fetishized cultural artifact "that exerts an irrational, and thus incontrovertible power... within a culture which lends it a sacrosanct inviolability" (Jennings 169).[2] The Jamesian aura diminishes the novelist by repressing some of the deepest impulses of his art and life. In short, James the cultural icon lacks even a suggestion of the author of *The American Scene*. This work played a pivotal role in creating what James called his "general renovation" of 1904, the year which sparked his late recrudescence of revisionary energy that produced the prefaces and the autobiography.[3]

One aim of the present chapter is to show how James's dispersed curiosity about America implicitly challenges the compulsion to identity. But the larger aim is to show how this personal project both echoes and anticipates the concerns of American and European cultural criticism. Tracing these connections will enable us to appreciate *The American Scene* as crucial rather than outré, as prescient rather than nostalgic, and as conversant and conversing with one of the major intellectual debates of its era and beyond: the philosophical opposition to identity logic. In the first third of the twentieth century this opposition was international in scope: William James, Dewey, Bergson, Simmel, Benjamin, and Adorno were among those who challenged its coerciveness. Henry James's participation in this critique can be glimpsed by returning to his germinal belief in the genius's "need of performing the whole possible revolution." Implicit in this movement in "both directions" is a commitment to the power and value of the irreconcilable and the uncontrollable in human experience, the genius's special affinity for what defies classification. Henry shares this allegiance with William, who conceives of experience as "unfinished and growing," resisting synthesis and absolutes. Seeking to save the fragile particular from absorption, William James's pluralism opposed Hegelian idealism, as did the succeeding generation of pragmatists (Dewey and Mead) and continental thinkers (Benjamin and Adorno).

This general concern to preserve particularity can serve as a basis for constructing new configurations reflecting a skepticism of the traditional political labels usually assigned to thinkers such as Dewey, Adorno, and Henry James himself. Each is more recalcitrant to such categories as bourgeois apologist (Dewey and James) or romantic anticapitalist (Adorno) than is often supposed by both leftist critics and liberal admirers. Indeed, these three figures encourage our suspicion of categories by their focus on the very act of classification as one of the defining ideological gestures in establishing what Foucault calls a culture's "regime of truth" (*Power/Knowledge* 133). Yet I do not wish to imply that a "hermeneutics of suspicion" (to borrow Ricoeur's famous phrase) is all that unites Henry James, Dewey, and Adorno (32). Adorno's late commendation of Dewey's "wholly humane version" of pragmatism provides us with the term that best sums up their connection, for pragmatism suggests their emphasis on vulnerability, critique, experiment, risk, and revision. These qualities animate the aesthetic, which all three conceive of not as idealist contemplation but as practice indissolubly entangled in social experience.

Insistence on the value of tolerating and encouraging difference (the "nonidentical," in Adorno's phrase) may count as the one absolute these thinkers share. The comparative slant of the present study will respect the value of the nonidentical by not turning Henry James into an American Adorno or Benjamin, or into any other figure with whom he will be juxtaposed. To resist the temptation of identity requires that one respect the profound differences in historical, political, and cultural contexts, to say nothing of disparate personal temperaments. I will be arguing that to a significant and unsuspected degree—but certainly not completely—Henry James shares some of the concerns and strategies of these and other thinkers. To dwell on this common ground, I will also argue, permits us to see a James rich in the incongruities he prized.

I

James's late nonfiction represents experience unburdened by the cultural imperative of "prime identity" (*Art* 230). When the compulsion to identity is relaxed (if not removed), nonidentity thinking becomes a way to loosen emotional and sexual constrictions and abandon oneself to the shocks of experience. In a key moment in his final preface James provides a vivid instance of what nonidentity thinking involves when he compares the experience of revising his late and early work. Rereading his most recent fiction, he proceeds "without an effort or a struggle," for his "present attentions" and "original expression" sufficiently coincide (*Art* 335). But this comfortable harmony, which James characterizes as breeding docility and passivity, "throws into relief . . . the very different dance," the "quite other kind of consciousness," experienced when he comes to revise his earlier work. What proceeds from "*that* return" is a "frequent lapse of harmony between" his "present mode of motion" and his "original tracks." Given James's commitment to pursuing "inevitable deviation," the incalculable difference that no "system of observation" can control (as was noted in the first chapter), this "lapse of harmony" is something he cherishes rather than laments. For it turns the question of revision from the "prepared" and predictable to the improvisational, as James feels pleasure in "shaking off all shackles of theory." Unharnessed, he "unlearns the old pace" of identity and sufficiency and falls into another rhythm, one attuned to the "high spontaneity" of "deviations and differences" produced by the disparity between past and present. So compelling are these "deviations and differences" that they become, says James, "my very terms of cognition." This "very different dance" of nonidentity exhilarates by making rewriting "an infinitely interesting and amusing *act*," alive with all the perils and contingencies missing in "finished and dismissed work" (*Art* 335–37).

The dance of difference that James performs upon his "return" to his early fiction is also the "mode of motion" that propels his other late "return" to America. James re-sees his native land with a "quite other kind of consciousness" that takes disparities to be not merely the objects but the "very terms of cognition." More than a theme with a fixed reference in the immigrant, nonidentity in late James becomes a mode of thinking and acting that conceives of individualism, identity, and consciousness as historical categories open to change and revision in a nonpossessive direction. This emphasis on provisionality extends to James's hope that twentieth-century America can devise social arrangements and institutions that maximize tolerance and flexibility.

A sense of James's dynamism is latent in Irving Howe's remark that his attitude toward New York City in *The American Scene* is, "finally, complex beyond description, a shifting mixture of curiosity, admiration, disdain, withdrawal, respect, animus" ("Introduction" xii). This estimate at least implicitly takes seriously James's commitment to his "religion of doing," which demands a mode of being that has "never . . . seen or said all or . . . ceased to press forward" (*Art* 343). Given my admiration for Howe's stress on a "shifting mixture," my approach may seem the all too familiar one of celebrating Jamesian ambiguity in the venerable tradition of Trilling's liberal humanism and its cherishing of "complexity." As Eugene Goodheart has observed, "Complexity tends to be in a certain sense politically conservative, because in encompassing opposing points of view, the complex perspective yields contemplation, not action" (10). But my invoking of complexity actually seeks to place James in a more radical cultural context. That he belongs there is implicit from the outset of *The American Scene*, where Goodheart's dualism of action and contemplation is dissolved into James's oxymoronic identity as "restless analyst." This self-descriptive epithet, which he uses throughout the book, is itself a phrase that challenges the conventional oppositions of activity and passivity, the hazardous and assured, and promotes interaction rather than hierarchy. Because his selfhood lacks impermeability and fixity—qualities central to the ideology of atomized individualism— James is saturated by incessant waves of "tonic shock" (*Art* 31). Rather than being distanced in static contemplation, James actively solicits and corporeally experiences shock as the imprint of the material pressure of historical change and the recovery of "extremest youth" (*Scene* 1). Indeed, on the first page of *The American Scene* James is assaulted by "instant vibrations" of curiosity prompted "at every turn, in sights, sounds, smells, even in the chaos of confusion and change" (1). This noncognitive, nonconceptual stratum of experience, charged with the primal, childlike avidity of insatiable curiosity ("I want to see everything," he wrote in anticipation of his trip), is the level at which James will most intensely live throughout his journey (qtd. Matthiessen, *Family* 310).

James finds this stratum liberating, at times even vertiginous, as when he is nearly overwhelmed by the sight of a "dense" New York crowd. In a remarkable passage James seems to surrender to a kind of homoerotic moment of fusion: "The assault of the turbid air seemed all one with the look, the tramp, the whole quality and *allure* . . . of the pushing male crowd, moving in its dense mass—with the confusion carried to chaos for any intelligence, any perception; a welter of objects and sounds in which relief, detachment, dignity, meaning, perished utterly and lost all rights" (*Scene* 83)

Finding his cognitive capacities routed, James leaves uncertain just where he is in relation to the alluring crowd, whether in its midst or at the fringe. But this very obscurity amply conveys his exhilarated sense of disorientation and absorption. Swept up in the chaos, whether he is situated near or afar, James seems carried along by the sheer energy of the moving, "dense mass" whose "grim, pushing, trudging silences" are the sound "of the universal will to move—to move, move, move, as an end in itself, an appetite at any price" (84). This nearly self-shattering experience ignited by the "male crowd" is a heightened instance of what has assaulted him from the start: a bombardment of stimuli, "leaving no touch of experience irrelevant" (3).[4] Immediately upon disembarking, impressions have flooded and exhilarated him: "The subject was everywhere. . . . It was thrilling, really, to find one's self in presence of a theme to which everything directly contributed . . . so far as feeling it went." James desires the "touch of experience" as he feels a "perpetual sense of precipitation" that banishes any notion of the irrelevant (3).

This freely confessed desire suggests why James would soon be found tenderly reciting Whitman's verses to Edith Wharton when he visited her in Lenox, Massachusetts. More than thirty years earlier the novelist had snidely dismissed the poet, but upon his return to New York in 1904, and in his memoirs, James would tacitly and explicitly invoke Whitman as providing some of the texture and precedent for his own project of exposure. Both men found urban tumult arousing. Not only does James speak of the "*allure*" of the "pushing male crowd," but its compelling energy, he declares, is "all one with every other element and note as well, all the signs of the heaped industrial battle-field" (84). Democracy, unleashed to its maximum imperial power by modernity, is "pushing and breaking the ice like an Arctic explorer." Like Whitman, James "shakes . . . to the depths of his being" in excitement and desire to experience "this will to move . . . as an end in itself, as an appetite at any price" (323, 85). Modernity and democracy are anything but inert abstractions to the novelist and poet. Both in describing his approaching trip and in representing his experiences in *The American Scene*, James consistently emphasizes embodiment, the physicality of his needs and desires, as if acknowledging the force of Whitman's words in "Crossing Brooklyn Ferry": "I too had receiv'd identity by my body, / That I was I knew was of my body, and what I should be I knew / I should be of my body."

To call James's return a "project of exposure" is somewhat oxymoronic since it mingles intentionality and spontaneity. But it was precisely this mixture that proved crucial in his decision to travel home. William had warned him that he would likely find America too loud and vulgar, and that it "might yield . . . little besides painful shocks." Yet Henry insisted that it was "absolutely *for* . . . the Shocks in general . . . that I nurse my infatuation."

Henry's "craving for millions of just such shocks," as a corrected William phrased it, represented a conscious attempt to cast off the burden of deliberation and to be "led on and on," subject at all times to the "hazard of *flânerie*" (qtd. Matthiessen, *Family* 310–11; *Scene* 189). His project simultaneously manages to accept the obligation of order and selection (what he calls the "treating," not the "feeling," of impressions) and to devise a way to resist the potentially coercive rationality of the ordering impulse. He honors this double obligation by improvising a literary form that embodies the waywardness of his experience. Henry conceives "treating" and "feeling," not in opposition to one another but as complementary, as phases (rather than competitors) in an encounter that from the start overwhelms the ordering impulse and forces him to redefine the meaning of "decent form." Measured and harmonious—decent—form is imperiled as early as the third page when James admits that impressions "were not for the present . . . to be kept at bay." There will be "more of them heaped up than would prove usable, a greater quantity of vision, possibly, than might fit into decent form." Faced with this contingency, James's response is the opposite of fastidious and economical. Here "wisdom," he says, means putting in "as much as possible of one's recklessness while it was fresh." This decision to represent excess by making "the largest surrender to impressions" results in a radically digressive, improvisational form (3–4).

Hints of such a surrender are evident in a letter from James to William Dean Howells regarding his imminent trip to America:

> I am hungry for Material whatever I may be moved to do with it. . . . There will not be an inch or an ounce of it unlikely to prove grist to my intellectual and "artistic" mill. . . . After my immensely long absence, I am not quite in a position to answer in advance for the quantity and quality, the exact form and color, of my "reaction" in presence of the native phenomena. . . . You speak of one's possible "hates" and "loves"—that is aversions and tendernesses—in the dire confrontation [of going to America], but I seem to feel . . . that I proceed but scantly . . . by those particular categories and rebounds; in short, that, somehow, such fine primitive passions *lose* themselves for me in the act of contemplation. (*Letters*, Lubbock 2: 9)

In conceiving of contemplation as action, James at a stroke abolishes classical epistemology's spectator theory of knowledge,[5] which posits a static mind passively receiving sense data. And he avoids a priori categories of hate and love that predetermine "exact form." His incessantly grinding "artistic mill" is not a reductive instrument of assimilation because what intrigues James is the very act of grinding, without a predictable product or end in sight. He relishes the prospect of having his hunger feed upon the enormous reservoir of "Material" that America will offer up. Seeking to feed without answering in advance, James stresses that it is not knowledge he wants so much as noncognitive immersion in movement itself: "What I am conscious of as a great personal desire is some such energy of direct *action*" (9). James in effect reiterates to Howells what he told William—that his American journey "should represent the poetry of motion, the one big taste of travel not supremely missed." But this Strether-like desire to catch the train before it's too late ("for once in my life not to fail to be on the spot") is virtually inseparable from James's other motive. The "poetry of motion," he explains to his brother, "would carry with it also the possibilities of the prose of *production*"—the making of a marketable commodity. "My primary idea in the matter is absolutely economic," he declared of his imminent trip (qtd. Matthiessen, *Family* 310). Accordingly, Henry's first host in America was his publisher, Colonel George Harvey of Harper and Brothers. Yet most significant is how entwined for James are financial and psychic economies, production and motion, instrumentality and improvisation. With each element jostling against the other, this complex of motives releases a maximum of energy.

James's flexibility and suppleness of approach to his subject, his desire to let his literary form be shaped by experience rather than by fixed, preordained goals, and his refusal to equate experience solely with cognition were all likely reasons why William James found *The American Scene* full of "animal spirit" and "in its peculiar way . . . *supremely great*" (qtd. Matthiessen, *Family* 341). For Henry's stance approximates his brother's pragmatism. Open to what William calls "the blooming, buzzing confusion" of primordial experience, Henry sets aside conventions of control as he lets the world of objects take the lead and relaxes (without banishing) the possessive, instrumental thrust of imperial subjectivity. On one level he does just the opposite by audaciously emptying the scene of all individuals but himself. "In *The American Scene*," notes Sharon Cameron, "others are gotten out of the way" and James "dominates with impunity the entirety" of the book (29). But what needs to be added is that he topples his imperialism from within. Henry banishes others not so he can wallow in serene autonomy. Rather, by "some rich passion in him for extremes" he clears the stage to magnify the impossibility of consciousness regnant (*Art* 31). Instead of dominating, he is invaded by the external world, including the very air itself, deliriously coming to life.

The desire to experience contemplation as action galvanizes James's return to America and initiates the spectacle of exposure that becomes the master theme linking the late James texts I explore. What makes *The American Scene* pivotal is that the "restless analyst" enacts with compelling actuality many of the central preoccupations of the ghostlier but no less haunting personages of these years: the fictional Lambert Strether; the small boy, son, and brother of the autobiography; and the revisionary narrator of the prefaces. An energy of curiosity and revision animates these works and their shared descent into memory, as they open what James calls "the cabinet of intimate reference." That his trip will tap deep references is evident from a remark made in 1903. James notes that "the actual bristling . . . U.S.A. have the merit and the precious property that they meet and fit into my (creative) preoccupations" (qtd. Matthiessen, *Family* 310). This statement, as suggestive as it is cryptic, may possibly be illuminated by a late remark in *The*

American Scene: "You are not final . . . you are perpetually provisional," is how James characterizes his "bristling" native land at the end of his journey, a judgment that crystallizes his late discovery of revision as the matrix of writing, identity, and nationhood.

James's recognition of American provisionality also represents a seminal moment of self-recognition. Whereas Emerson believed that American experience is comprised of two parties—hope and memory—James's parties might be labeled the revisionists and the "actual nonrevisionists." The latter he describes as having "their lot serene and their peace, above all, equally protected and undisturbed" (*Art* 343). James's re-vision of his native country, his life history and lifework, clearly situates him in the revisionist camp— those unserene, unprotected, and disturbed figures committed to the "active sense of life" (340). Preceding James in his 1904 discovery of revision was the aging Lambert Strether. A year before his creator, Strether quite unexpectedly found his self open to remaking and renewal.

II

Whether written in the mode of cultural analysis, fiction, aesthetics, or family chronicle, James's cluster of works comprises the textual site or arena wherein he "performs his whole possible revolution" (*Art* 31). This performance is a prolonged act of divestiture that dissolves, as if in slow motion, his persona of Master and reconstructs it by initiating an inquiry into "the mystery of human subjectivity in general," to borrow a phrase from Melville's *The Confidence-Man*.[6] James's inquiry focuses upon the nature of mastery and authority in late nineteenth- and early twentieth-century America and proceeds on at least three interrelated levels broadly designated aesthetic, cultural, and psychological.

As the quotation from Melville's work suggests, Henry James's project finds one source of momentum in the antinomian, interrogative energies of the American Renaissance, which in turn inspired the pragmatism of William James and John Dewey, both loyal admirers of Emerson.[7] Emerson's words from "Circles" express the common ground both movements traverse: "Nothing is secure but life, transition, the energizing spirit. . . . No truth is so sublime but it may be trivial tomorrow in the light of new thoughts. People wish to be settled; only as far as they are unsettled is there any help for them" (413). By stripping himself of the props of the familiar, Henry James does not hope to recover Emerson's "original relation to the universe" but rather to reenact his "abandonment" of "propriety." The task of abandonment is articulated, with distinctive inflections, in the thought of both Jameses and in William's pragmatist successor, John Dewey, whose notion of inquiry is particularly pertinent. For Dewey's description of what is at stake in this quest also describes Henry James's own unsettling act of cultural inquiry, what he calls his "recklessness" of "surrender" and what I have described as his spectacle of exposure.

"Involved in all inquiry and discovery," says Dewey, is "surrender of what is possessed, disowning of what supports one in secure ease. . . . For to arrive at new truth and vision is to alter. The old self is put off and the new self is only forming, and the form it finally takes will depend upon the unforeseeable result of an adventure" (*Experience* 201). This transitional selfhood, "in process of making" rather than "ready-made" (*Human* 130), is apparent from the very beginning of *The American Scene*, where James seems to prefer hovering between identities: "If I had had time to become almost as 'fresh' as an inquiring stranger, I had not. . . had enough to cease to be, or at least to feel, as acute as an initiated native" (1).[8] Instead of feeling distressed or weakened by his liminal status, he finds it a "great advantage" because his very fluidity of self maximizes receptivity, permitting him to "vibrate with more curiosity." In effect, the ease with which James inhabits this transitional phase necessitates a revision of Dewey's conception, which stresses the privacy and incommunicability attending this stage: "When an old essence or meaning is in process of dissolution and a new one has not taken shape . . . the intervening existence is too fluid and formless for publication, even to oneself. Its very existence is ceaseless transformation" (*Experience* 181).

James manages to capture something of this fluidity in his strategically marginal self or, more precisely, his self of the "margin," a realm comprised of "immense fluidity" (*Scene* 401). The margin is a crucial concept in *The American Scene*, linking James's mimetic self-representation and his portrayal of America's national identity. As the volatile space of potential and possibility, the margin is so vast that it leaves "the total of American life . . . huddled as for very fear of the fathomless depth of water, the too formidable future." A zone of uncertainty, the margin is a veritable quicksand engulfing all pretensions to mastery, control, and stable identity. Standing for neither a "possible greater good" nor "greater evil," the margin is the irreducible fact of "the mere looming mass of the *more*, the more and more to come. And as yet nothing makes definite the probable preponderance of particular forms of the more" (401). The repetitions and alliterations of this passage suggest language stalling and sputtering, struggling to articulate what refuses to be articulated. Indeed, James admits that "an inevitable failure to conclude" dogs his efforts to define and fix America's "margin." Its formlessness resists any definition more specific than "looming mass" or "immense fluidity."

The Jamesian margin recalls the contingent form of Deweyan inquiry. Both, in Dewey's phrase, "depend upon the unforeseeable result of an adventure." This last word connects the adventure of James's journey to what he calls America's "whole spectacle," the "great adventure of a society reaching out in the apparent void for the amenities." And this "adventurous fight, carried on from scene to scene, with fluctuations and variations," describes, says James, "the very *donnée*" of his book (12). Yet the Jamesian donnée is really a twofold one, for a twin adventure animates *The American Scene* from the start: the turbulent movements of the American spectacle are refracted in the "odd, inward rhythm" of James's own "fluidity of appreciation." He visualizes this fluidity as a "warm wave" permitting him to be "floated" (3).

Like Strether's adventure a year earlier, James's 1904 experience of dispossession and disowning begins with a primal ritual of disembarking at a dreary harbor after a long sea journey—one at Hoboken, New Jersey, the other at Liverpool, England. James describes himself "emerging from the comparatively assured order of the great berth of the ship" (1). With the pun on "great berth" he initiates a long process of growth, as if he had just been "struck from the float forever held in solution," ejected from the snug security of prenatal oneness. These words by Whitman, who speaks of the "float" in "Crossing Brooklyn Ferry," recall James's own sense of being floated by sensations. He feels imbued with the vulnerability of a child innocent of language and the cognitive grids and categories that fix experience even as they render it intelligible. Indeed, legibility is precisely what James, as usual, seeks to make problematic. "Forgive the fierce legibility," he once apologized to a recipient of his typed letter. Taking pleasure in the "chaos of confusion and change" that attends his arrival, James notes that "recognition became more interesting and more amusing in proportion as it became more difficult, like the spelling out of foreign sentences of which one knows but half the words" (1). This simile connects James's pleasure in difficulty with experiencing language in its materiality, freed (at least partially) from the bondage of meaning. Later James will describe the indeterminacy of the nation's future as "belonging to no known language" and thus expressible only onomatopoetically, as "something . . . *abracadabrant*" (121–22).

To enjoy the freedom of the "*il*legible word" is also to enjoy an illegible identity, as Strether discovers. "His very gropings would figure among his most interesting motions," says James of Strether's Parisian explorations, a remark that also applies to his own American gropings (*Ambassadors* 9). Before too long Strether gains sufficient "momentum" to "toddle alone," and delights in what he calls his "surrender . . . to youth," an echo of his creator's "surrender to impressions" (190). The escapes of James and Strether from the ossification of adulthood partake of the antimodernist romantic cult of the child, which implicitly affirms the value of irrational or prerational "pure experience" as a protest against the stifling abstraction of modern existence. Although James, as we will see, significantly qualifies this protest, to some extent his and Strether's unexpected liberation coincides with the most important philosophical movement of the day—the philosophy of life (*Lebensphilosophie*).

Life philosophy indicted the reigning philosophical discourses that had legitimated the sterility of modernity: the arid instrumentalism of contemporary social science, rationalism, and positivism. This reaction against scientism, if not the scientific method, grew into an international chorus: at various times Nietzsche, Bergson, Husserl, and William James were among its strongest voices, and the will to power, intuitionism, phenomenology, and radical empiricism were some of its best-known philosophical doctrines.

Impressionism might be considered its counterpart in aesthetics. Originating in German Romanticism's critique of Enlightenment scientism, which placed concepts, laws, and ideas at the service of the instrumental domination of nature, *Lebensphilosophie* celebrated creativity, dynamism, immediacy, and youth. "This metaphysics," writes Herbert Schnadelbach, "of the pre-rational, the a-rational, the anti-rational called in question the whole of Western rationalism and compelled it to prove its legitimacy" (142).[9]

Lebensphilosophie has been called part of the "purification program" that characterized artistic and philosophical modernism in the opening decades of the twentieth century. Modernism attempted to "once and for all cut through the veils of mediation and history" and reach what Husserl called "the things themselves" (Rochberg 236, 240). To arrive at the things themselves was also the goal of the most influential proponent of life—Henri Bergson. Only intuition, not abstract understanding, gives us access to the vital flux of raw reality. He shared this belief with his friend William James, whose "stream of consciousness" is correlative with Bergson's "internal stream" ("la durée réelle"). "You set things straight at a single stroke by your fundamental conception of the continuously creative nature of reality," James told Bergson, who returned the compliment: "You convey the idea, above all the feeling, of that supple and flexible philosophy which is destined to take the place of intellectualism.... When you say that 'for rationalism reality is ready-made and complete from all eternity, while for pragmatism it is still in the making,' you provide the very formula for the metaphysics to which I am convinced we shall come" (qtd. Perry 2: 619, 621). The enemy for both Bergson and James was what the latter called "vicious intellectualism," which sacrificed the flux of experience to the stability of concepts. Intellectualism's prestige was particularly high in America's Puritan culture, which had bred a hypertrophy of rationalism nurtured by the dichotomizing logic of Cartesian idealism and Enlightenment scientism. Although William was not exempt from these cultural influences, in *A Pluralistic Universe* (1909) he rapturously celebrates Bergson, issues a powerful attack against intellectualism, and offers his antidote of radical pluralism.

Henry James read his brother's book "with enchantment, with pride, and almost with comprehension" (qtd. Matthiessen, *Family* 344). Although Henry leaves unsaid what particularly enchanted him, William's plea that we should "fall back on raw unverbalized life as more of a revealer" of life than concepts would probably have touched a responsive chord in the novelist (*Pluralistic* 121). William describes this falling back as the "putting off [of] our proud maturity of mind and becoming again as foolish little children in the eyes of reason." Yet despite Henry's sympathy for such a statement, and its undeniable relevance to his own "creative preoccupations," it is unlikely that William's celebration of the child would have escaped unscathed his brother's ironic gaze. Henry would have smiled at William's statement, as he had at similar sentiments expressed by Emerson, William's predecessor in this American tradition of authenticity. Responding to Emerson's absolutizing of "sincerity and independence and spontaneity," Henry found it one of a "great many other things which it would be still easier to present in a ridiculous light" (*Literary* 1:382). In sum, Henry was likely to be left uneasy by the romantic individualism of William's pragmatism and radical empiricism.

Henry James might have described his quarrel with this mode of individualism (and its correlative subjectivism) as a failure to "perform the whole possible revolution," since it remains fixed in a static, subject–object dualism. Although William's radical empiricism depicted pure experience as prior to this split and reality as continuously flowing and relational, his social viewpoint was that of an unreconstructed Emersonian individualist.[10] In contrast, in his book on Hawthorne (1879) Henry deftly exposed how Emersonianism functioned sociologically and ideologically: "The doctrine of the supremacy of the individual to himself, of his originality, and, as regards his own character, *unique* quality, must have had a great charm for people living in a society in which introspection, thanks to the want of other entertainment, played almost the part of a social resource" (383). In what is only an apparent paradox, the revered father of the modern novel of "liberated" consciousness, one of the glorious achievements of bourgeois aesthetics, never mystified the "supremacy of the individual" into a natural birthright. The paradox dissolves once we invoke the infrequently made distinction between James's technique of *central* consciousness and the ideology of individualism's belief in *centered* consciousness, what Henry calls "prime identity." James employed the technique less to legitimate and authorize centered subjectivity than to reveal its compromised status and obliviousness to its own solipsism. By neglecting this distinction Fredric Jameson is able to relegate "Jamesian point of view" to a bourgeois "containment strategy" that functions as a "powerful ideological instrument in the perpetuation of an increasingly subjectivized and psychologized world" (*Political* 221). The distinction between central and centered is the source of an ineradicable gap in James's work between form and subject, intention and achievement. He finds this disjunction fertile and returns to it often in his prefaces.

They offer not a serene retrospect of James's organic artistry but instead announce his acceptance of makeshift compromises rather than any fully achieved formal harmony. The prefaces anticipate what Adorno would later teach—that form, not subject matter, is art's vehicle of critique. "What makes works of art socially significant is content that articulates itself in formal structures." The "unresolved antagonisms of reality reappear in art in the guise of immanent problems of artistic form," says Adorno, and "the aesthetic tensions manifesting themselves in works of art" express social actuality, which, for James as well, is an "antagonistic totality . . . a whole which is made up of contradictions" (*Aesthetic* 327, 8, 446). *The American Scene* is James's most direct confrontation with the fractured totality of modern civilization; his foregrounding of the difficulty in fashioning a "decent form" for his impressions becomes one way of representing the bewildering impact of modern America. A consequence of James's emphasis on formal mediation is that his social and cultural critique is most often *embodied* rather than discursively articulated.

His novels also register social and cultural contradictions by articulating these antagonisms technically, through the mediation of artistic form, which is structured by the aporia between centered and central consciousness. For instance, Isabel Archer assumes fully the role of central reflector only after the seed of her husband's deceit begins to flower in the famous "vigil" scene in chapter 42. Thus, her structural centrality coincides (negatively) with her dawning sense that her centered consciousness is actually decentered, that she has been a mere tool of her husband and his lover. Just as James's form pushes her center stage, Isabel's proud belief in her pristine autonomy and mastery starts crumbling; as she feels "haunted with terrors" and "assailed by visions" (355, 364).[11] This aesthetic tension, which expresses James's understanding of the contradictions of Emersonian individualism—its manufacture of an autonomy at once illusory and powerful—has been all but obliterated in the traditional image of James the aesthetic organicist and idealist. James as cultural icon is, predictably, regarded as a loyal advocate of the Emersonian tradition of inviolable individualism.[12]

James's 1879 remarks on Emerson regarding the "doctrine of the supremacy of the individual" reveal his skepticism of any claim that grants the individual a privileged status grounded in natural or intrinsic truth. This status, for James, is not ontological but historical and cultural, and is therefore subject to change. James's historicism leaves him free of nostalgia for Emersonianism when he visits twentieth-century America and encounters disconcertingly new kinds of subjectivity. What he discovers is a lag between the still flourishing ideology of self-reliance and the reality of vast and intricate mechanisms of social control, the "hotel-spirit" that produces an "institutionalized individualism" (to borrow Talcott Parsons's phrase). James is fascinated by the transmogrification of Emersonianism into a mocking parody of self-reliance that turns human subjects into "puppets" who "think of themselves as delightfully free and easy" (*Scene* 107).

One point this excursus on the Jameses and Emersonian individualism is meant to suggest is the complicated nature of Henry's relation to William's philosophy. Henry's own pragmatist sensibility and his fraternal pride in and enthusiasm for William's work can easily make it appear that he shares William's subjective pragmatism. Yet, as we saw in chapter 2, Henry's own views reflected decisive temperamental and philosophical differences with William's philosophy. A careful reading of Henry's epistolary responses reveals his concern to distance himself even as he lavishes praise on his brother's pragmatism. In the same letter, quoted earlier, concerning *A Pluralistic Universe*, Henry subtly expresses support of and divergence from William: "As an artist and a 'creator' I can catch on, hold on, to pragmatism and can work in the light of it and apply it" (qtd. Matthiessen, *Family* 344). This eminently pragmatic response shows how careful Henry was to establish his relationship to pragmatism as one of application rather than simple endorsement. Indeed, in another 1909 letter to William, Henry praises pragmatism as an "assimilable philosophy," possessed of "the most extraordinary suggestiveness and force of application and inspiration" (Lubbock 2: 141). Henry's application historicizes William's thought, moving it away from a tendency toward dualistic rigidity—which pitted conduct against sensibility, man against society—and toward a dialectical fluency alive to creative, experimental action produced by socially constituted agents. This revision is also the direction taken by William's successors, Dewey and Mead. As early as 1903 Dewey had objected to what he called the "control side" of Jamesian pragmatism, "its seeming over-utilitarianism," which scants the "aesthetic function in knowledge . . . the liberation side" (qtd. Perry 2: 526).[13]

III

In distancing himself from William's subjectivism, Henry anticipates a significant reaction against pragmatism and *Lebensphilosophie* in general that began in the 1920s. It is observable in Dewey's important work *Experience and Nature* (1925), which both continues William James's critique of intellectualism (the proposition that "all experience is a mode of knowing") but tacitly rejects its irrational worship of flux for its own sake.[14] "The assumption of 'intellectualism,' " says Dewey, "goes contrary to the facts of what is primarily experienced. For things are objects to be treated, used, acted upon and with, enjoyed and endured, even more than things to be known. They are things *had* before they are things cognized" (*Experience* 21). William James would have concurred that the noncognitive is the ground of the cognitive. But by the end of *A Pluralistic Universe* James seems to abandon one (cognitive) for the other (noncognitive). He ends up not merely "putting off his proud maturity" but urging us leave adult discourse altogether: "I must deafen you to talk." Only then can one "return to life" (*Pluralistic* 131).

William James's regression here can be explained in Deweyan terms as a consequence of his failure to abide by the distinction between "primitive" and "cultivated naivete" (*Experience* 35). In words that can be read as an implicit corrective to William James, Dewey describes his own brand of empiricism as a

kind of intellectual disrobing. We cannot permanently divest ourselves of the intellectual habits we take on and wear when we assimilate the culture of our own time and place. But intelligent furthering of culture demands that we take some of them off, that we inspect them critically to see what they are made of and what wearing them does to us. We cannot achieve recovery of primitive naivete. But there is attainable a cultivated naivete of eye, ear, and thought. (35)

Dewey's distinction not only distances him from William James but also serves to pinpoint Henry's difference from his brother. A self-described "subtle savage," Henry recovers a "cultivated naivete."

What makes Dewey's act of "disrobing" comparable to Henry James's

spectacle of exposure is their shared critique of constitutive subjectivity.[15]
Like Henry James, Dewey rejects individuality conceived of as "original,
eternal, and absolute" in the manner of the transcendentalists. Rather, subjective mind is neither "an aberration," as positivism believes, nor an "independent creative source," as classical liberalism believes, but "an agency
of novel reconstruction" occupying an "intermediate position" and always
situated within a process of inquiry and modification (*Experience* 178, 181).
Subject and object are not opposed entities but rather "phases" or "factors."
The objective is oriented toward "final and eventual consummation," while
the subjective "takes the immediate initiative in remaking problematic situations" (196). This understanding has the signal virtue for Dewey of conceiving the subject as "historic, intermediate, temporally relative and
instrumental" (185). In contrast, "subjectivism as an 'ism' converts" what
is fluid into an entity, into "something absolute and fixed; while pure 'objectivism' is a doctrine of fatalism" (196).

Dewey's critique and reconstruction of subjectivism represents an intrigu-
ingly heterogeneous strategy that performs, in Henry James's phrase, a whole
revolution: it retains life philosophy's valorization of dynamism and rejection
of stasis without veering into the subjectivism of Bergson (whom Dewey
sharply critiques) or of William James's pluralism. Dewey's stress on the
subject's embeddedness in a preexisting object world emphasizes the primacy of interaction—"the one unescapable trait of every human concern."
Dewey's concept of the subject, then, does not congeal into a species of
naturalism or determinism, be it positivism, classical liberalism, or Marxism
(197). These ideologies, argues Dewey, are infected by system, by "fixed
conceptual principles" (seen, for instance, in political economy's belief in
the "natural laws" of laissez-faire capitalism) that obstruct the effort of inquiry to treat concepts as tentative, continually revisable hypotheses.

Thus Dewey, like Henry James, remains strongly in tune with William
James's spirit of skepticism toward conventional notions of mastery—the
pretensions of such philosophic systems as Comtean positivism or Hegelian
idealism—that profess to totalize and unify all reality. "Totality, order, unity,
rationality," says Dewey, are mere "eulogistic predicates," which, when
"used to describe the foundations and proper conclusions of a philosophic
system," can artifically simplify existence (*Experience* 27).

When Henry James confronted the novelistic equivalent of such overarching ambition—Balzac's "Comédie Humaine"—he reacted with pragmatic suspicion. In 1875 he described Balzac's immense fictional edifice
as a

complete social system . . . on the imaginative line very much what Comte's
"Positive Philosophy" is on the scientific. These great enterprises are equally
characteristic of the French passion for completeness, for symmetry, for making
a system as neat as an epigram—of its intolerance of the indefinite, the unformulated. The French mind likes better to squeeze things into a formula that
mutilates them, if need be, than to leave them in the frigid vague. (*Literary*
2: 41)[16]

To the positivistic spirit of the French James opposes "us of English speech," who find "the civilization of the nineteenth century . . . so multitudinous, so complex, so far-spreading . . . it has such misty edges and far reverberations— that the imagination, oppressed and overwhelmed, shrinks from any attempt to grasp it as a whole" (41). According to the canonical image of James, not only did he eventually overcome his awe before this French challenge but he became a kind of Anglo-American version of the Comtean spirit, preoccupied with symmetry, organic wholeness, and building an ultimate monument that was to be his own bid for Balzacian grandeur. This edifice was the New York Edition, replete with a synthesis of the aesthetic wisdom of a lifetime contained in the prefaces. But, once again, James's "rich passion for extremes" demands a more complex explanation than canonical wisdom affords. James's ambition is indeed Balzacian, and he does solicit the aura of cultural sanctity that the monumental New York Edition embodies. Yet he builds his monument on shaky ground: "The tracks of my original passage," notes James in his final preface, are of such "shifting and uneven character" (*Art* 341). This statement reminds us not to confuse ambition and achievement. For James is also a parody of grand authority: the Balzacian march of his "original passage" soon slackens on the way to its goal and the New York Edition becomes anything but neatly systematic. The deliberate clash of intention and execution shatters James's imperial pretensions and generates a contradictory, unstable authorial identity that the magisterial, honorific Master represses. The Master's most ironic lesson is of the unavoidably compromised nature of mastery.

Henry James's emphasis, in 1875, on the imagination shrinking, "oppressed and overwhelmed," is a resonant chord in the context of an incipient modernity because it sounds the theme of the abject, vulnerable self confronting a masterful and powerful "passion for completeness" simultaneously embodied in totalizing literary projects, positivistic science, and bureaucratic rationality. Clearly, Balzac and Comte challenge the individual to redefine what counts as mastery. It will have to be reconstructed in a modern world where the frail, the damaged, and the particular ("the indefinite, the unformulated"), left without transcendental grounds of meaning, seem at the mercy of devouring, universal systems. In the seventy-five years since James's remarks on Balzac, the philosophical and aesthetic critique of systems and totality (antifoundationalism) generated an ensemble of diverse practices that sought to make potent the individual's socially constructed impotence. This ensemble has come to be known as modernism.[17]

Those who shrink from the totalizing impulse, like Henry and William James, tend to flaunt their abjectness as one possible strategy in attempting to redefine mastery. Thus the Master of the novel describes himself in his autobiography as appearing like a "dunce" as a youth. And age doesn't ameliorate matters. He remains envious and inept, embarrassed and withdrawn—and most of all "vague." Why Henry James foregrounds these qualities and how vagueness becomes "a positive saving virtue" will be discussed in chapter 7 (8, 412). We have noted William's insouciance about shedding his "proud maturity of mind." He turns his attention to the tension-racked urban bourgeois body and champions the "strenuous life": a return to nature through physical activity. Physical conditioning is imperative, says William, for the pragmatist and pluralist world demands a "certain ultimate hardihood, a certain willingness to live without assurances or guarantees. . . . [This] world is always vulnerable, for some part may go astray" (*Pragmatism* 290). William delights in contrasting the supple, carefree, "radical pragmatist" with the genteel academy's doctrinaire rationalist, who disdains "this real world of sweat and dirt" (40). To rationalists the pragmatic world "would not be *respectable*, philosophically. It is a trunk without a tag, a dog without a collar, in the eyes of most professors of philosophy" (125). William's self-inflicted marginalization, his pleasure in offending the academic orthodoxy, provided an undeniable source of energy for his work. Feeling perennially embattled, he spurred himself on to battle the philosophical fathers, attacking Hegel, the master of universal system and synthesis, with particular zeal.

Like many modern thinkers, William James in effect tries to save Hegel from himself by retaining the Hegelian method without adopting his system. Friedrich Engels was an early practitioner of this strategic approach, which dwells on the tension between Hegel's system and method. Engels found the former dogmatic in its vision of harmonious reconciliation of subject and object, universal and particular. But he discovered in the dialectical method, with its suspicion of all autonomous entities, a tool that liquidates fixed beliefs. William James's version of this tension is to praise Hegel's "vision" but regret his "technique" (*Pluralistic* 44). Hegel is an empiricist who refused to remain one because of a "perverse preference for the use of technical and logical jargon." James credits Hegel the empiricist with a "revolutionary performance," the vision that "concepts are not . . . the static, self-contained things that previous logicians had supposed, but were germinative and passed beyond themselves into each other" (46). Instead of substituting concepts for real things, as in the "ordinary logic" of identity, "in which, since Aristotle, all Europe had been brought up," Hegel's dialectical logic shows that "real things are not merely their own bare selves" but are "also their own others" (46, 67). Unfortunately, according to James, Hegel "aimed at being something far greater than an empirical reporter," something more authoritative than a "naively observant man" in the Jamesian "happy-go-lucky" mode (44, 49). Hegel had to believe his own system to be "a product of eternal reason" and logic, "with its suggestions of coercive necessity" (46). The result was that his dialectical logic was swallowed up by the identity principle embodied in "Absolute Spirit." The trouble with absolute idealism, according to James's fellow pragmatist, George Herbert Mead, is that it denies that "our life is an adventure. There can be nothing novel in the absolute. . . . All that is to take place has already taken place in the absolute" (*Movements* 508). Jamesian pluralism seeks to preserve what is vital in Hegel— his dialectical vision, his stress on the concrete and on becoming—and to dispense with the static absolutism that absorbs the particular into a total universal system.

But William James neglects the lesson of Hegel's dialectical logic for man in society. In James's quest for the "immediate experience of life," a quest that forsakes his pragmatism's suspicion of metaphysics, he jettisons Hegel's emphasis on the power of psychological, cultural, and historical mediations to constitute the individual and enmesh him in a web of dependent relations. Abandoning the primacy of mediation, of social bonds, James leaves their examination to other, less individualistic pragmatists like Dewey. Always more Hegelian in outlook than James, Dewey was also the more consistent pragmatist in his devotion to the primacy of the contextual.

IV

William James was not the only thinker to abandon an earlier philosophy for the lure of an irrationalist metaphysics. An even more dramatic instance of a late surrender to the flux was that of Georg Simmel. For most of his career he was a quintessentially urban intellectual and dedicated flaneur residing in late nineteenth-century Berlin. Simmel's best-known works of cultural criticism are his microanalyses of the materiality and phenomenology of urban life contained in *The Philosophy of Money* (1900) and in his studies of fashion, sociability, and theatricality. These investigations of modernist modes of representation were brilliantly synthesized in his famous essay on "The Metropolis and Mental Life," a pioneering study of how urban experience forms and deforms subjectivity. Like Henry James, who bears striking affinities with his German contemporary, Simmel believes in the primacy of form and representation as constraints that give meaning to human conduct. Simmel conceives of freedom neither as emancipation nor transcendence but as "the articulation of the self in the medium of things" (*Philosophy* 321). That the immediacy and uniqueness of subjective expression must always be mediated and estranged through an external, objective medium is for Simmel the irresolvable "tragedy of culture." The tragedy is mitigated, and sources of fulfillment are possible, so long as "creative tension" and "reciprocal cultivation" exist between objective and subjective culture. But this dialectic is imperiled by the increasing rationalization of modern life, which generates polarities of extreme subjectivism and objectivism (Rochberg 217).

The Philosophy of Money has recently been described as Simmel's "attempt to teach [his] contemporaries to be at home with their money-ridden society" (Liebersohn 133). Simmel finds pockets of freedom, "islands of subjectivity," amid the growing tyranny of what he calls "objective culture" (*Philosophy* 469). Clothing, jewelry, property, fashion, and coquetry are not to be liquidated in a purification rite but accepted as pleasurable "extensions of the personality" into external objects and modes of representation. "Personality expresses, reveals, and expands itself in possession" (322). Of all possessions, money is the most versatile because it is the most empty: "It adjusts with equal ease to every form and every purpose that the will wishes to imprint it with. . . . Money grants to the self the most complete freedom to express itself in an object" (324–25). Not surprisingly, Simmel's absorption

in fragmented, material detail, his cultivation of inwardness, and his understanding of distance and objectification as liberating rather than merely
alienating have led to accusations of aestheticism. Whereas a Marxist criticism
seeks to end the fragmentation of modern life by restoring wholeness in
community (the program of Simmel's student, Georg Lukács), Simmel resists
this quest for *Gemeinschaft*.[18]

But this Simmel, impeccable cosmopolite "without regret for *Gemeinschaft*
lost," represents only part of Simmel (Liebersohn 127). As Harry Liebersohn
has recently shown, "Simmel's commitment to modernity conflicted with a
will to utopian transcendence of it." Hostile to *Gemeinschaft* until World War
I, in 1914 Simmel expressed his "deep-seated longing to throw off the burden
of modernity's objective culture and experience a new authenticity. . . . All
the carefully balanced antinomies of modernity suddenly collapsed." Simmel
experienced "a sense of collective oneness previously denied to him" and
embraced *Lebensphilosophie* (157). Once the master of concrete detail and
particularity, Simmel now drowned in the flux of life, only to be reborn as
the "German Bergson," as he came to be known. William James thought
him an ally,[19] and with good reason: Simmel's late work sounds eminently
compatible with *A Pluralistic Universe* (Green 106; Perry 2: 580). Simmel
speaks of the "essence of life as the transcendence of itself. In *one* act, it
creates something more than the vital stream itself. . . . This function ac-
tualizes as *one* life what is then split through feelings, destinies and concep-
tualizations" (*Individuality* 367–68). In Simmel's hymn to oneness and lament
over concepts, tension is forfeited. Adorno's pungent aphorism about Bergson
could serve as an epitaph for Simmel and *Lebensphilosophie*: "The dialectical
salt was washed away in an undifferentiated tide of life" (*Negative* 8).[20]

Simmel left a divided legacy to the younger generation of German social
critics, which included Walter Benjamin, Theodor Adorno, Georg Lukács,
and Ernst Bloch. Lukács's early book *Soul and Form* (1911) was inspired by
Simmel the philosopher of life. But what Lukács saw as the negative example
of Simmel's cultural criticism also had a powerful impact. He called his
teacher's urban analyses the work of a great "impressionist," a "philosophical
Monet," but felt they lacked a constructive, synthetic vision. For Lukács
both impressionism and Simmel possessed "the capacity to see the smallest
and most inessential phenomenon of everyday life" and to "reveal an eternal
constellation of philosophical meaning." According to Lukács, "every great
impressionistic movement is nothing other than the protest of life against
the forms which solidify too much in it."[21] But impressionism in effect
becomes frozen in protest and negativism and is best regarded, says Lukács,
as "transitional phenomena," the "preliminary of a new classical period."
For Lukács, the Marxist Hegelian, this epoch would be defined by a positive
vision of organic homogeneity that would transcend the modern world's
fragmentation and multiplicity.

Adorno and Benjamin, Simmel's successors in the German tradition of
urban modernist cultural critique, nearly inverted Lukács's response to Simmel. They valued his work for not imposing a political program that might

have deflected him from intense scrutiny of the nuances of alienated urban experience. To some degree these differing responses to Simmel reflected varying degrees of belief in communism as a political organization capable of elevating the proletariat to the subject–object of history, to repeat Lukács's famous phrase. Lukács fervently embraced the Hungarian Communist party in 1918. Benjamin intermittently supported Soviet communism from about 1928 until 1938, two years before his suicide. Adorno consistently rejected party affiliation, preferring to use Marxism as dialectical critique. While the divergence in the political commitments of Benjamin and Adorno led to tensions in their friendship, an important core of shared intellectual aims united them until the mid 1930s.[22] In their self-consciously modernist excursions into German philosophy and sociology, Benjamin and Adorno sought to cut against the grain of traditional biases and habits afflicting both traditions, such as the endemic dualisms of German sociology that also afflicted the English social organicist tradition of Edmund Burke, Samuel Taylor Coleridge, Matthew Arnold, and George Eliot.[23] As one recent commentator has noted,

> Sociology came to be structured around a series of contrasts that identified premodern aspects of social order; these contrasts were the classic divisions between *Gemeinschaft* and *Gesellschaft*, status and contract, mechanical and organic society. . . . These contrasts typically indicated a critical or at least ambivalent attitude towards modern society by identifying a pre-modern source of authority, authenticity or stability as the point for a critique of contemporary development. Sociology, then, could be said to be a nostalgic science of society, since implicitly it is forced to identify with the past as a source of values. (Turner 236)

While neither Benjamin nor Adorno is entirely immune to the lure of nostalgia (indeed, they have been accused of succumbing to it), this moment of regression is far outweighed by their commitment to anatomizing modernity on its own terms rather than lamenting the allegedly unalienated past. Thus, their cultural critique joins with Max Weber's in advancing beyond the traditional Germanic idealist orientation.

Like Weber, Benjamin and Adorno confess their profound ambivalence toward modernity but use this admission creatively, rather than regressively, as a means of mapping contradictions and not dissolving them. Like Weber, in Karl Löwith's words, Adorno and Benjamin "affirm the productivity of contradiction." In this affirmation all three are unlike Marx, "who remained a Hegelian not least in his wish fundamentally to resolve the contradictions in bourgeois society." Weber seeks a space for individual freedom created not by means of aesthetic, idealist withdrawal but by "ostentatiously and deliberately placing himself within this world, in order to oppose it from the inside by 'renunciatory action' " (56–57). While the tenor and content of these renunciations differ in each case, Benjamin and Adorno join Weber in this immanent stance. Yet the Marxist Benjamin's devotion to immanence is more methodological than political.

Given their immanent orientation, it is understandable that Benjamin and Adorno preferred Simmel's attentiveness to urban life rather than his late-blooming vitalism, with its transcendence of society. Adorno praised Simmel's "return to concrete objects," for concreteness was one antidote to the hegemony of abstract system rampant in a modern world where contradiction and fragmentation were the norm (qtd. Buck-Morss, *Origin* 74, 242). This condition rendered futile philosophy's traditional effort—the "Cartesian demand" that reality be studied as absolute and rational totality (Adorno, "Actuality" 132). In his position paper of 1931 entitled "The Actuality of Philosophy," which was written under Benjamin's direct influence, Adorno stated that if philosophy is to survive, it "must give up the great problems, the size of which once helped to guarantee the totality." To preserve the nonidentical, the particular, was the task of dialectical thinking. Today, noted Adorno, "between the wide meshes of big questions, interpretation slips away" (127). To recover interpretation is to recover what slips between the big issues—minute particulars. Therefore "interpretation succeeds only through a juxtaposition of the smallest elements" (127). Like Simmel, who constructs a constellation of detail, Adorno (borrowing Benjamin's idea) also sanctions "the manipulation of conceptual material" in the "trial arrangement of constellation" (131). But there is a crucial difference. As Lukács noted, Simmel's constellations were "eternal," whereas Benjamin and Adorno root particulars in historical actuality, and their constellations represent a rescue of that which has been imprisoned in an ideological totality.

Benjamin describes his critical method as proceeding "eccentrically and by leaps . . . to rip out of context and to quote that which remained inconsequential and buried, because it had helped the powerful but little" (qtd. Jennings 26). In Benjamin's famous words, his project involves "brushing history against the grain." He practices the "mortification" of works of art so as to explode the accretions of myth that continue to promulgate (through advertisements and commodities) the illusion of human freedom and hide the reality of the individual's political impotence. His vantage point is the marginal, shifting one embodied in the city stroller, the flaneur, whose prototype is Baudelaire, the subject of some of Benjamin's best-known essays. Baudelaire is exemplary in his willingness to dwell in rather than resist the disorienting urban world, where "nature itself takes on the character of a commodity." The flaneur is a figure of wandering curiosity and of indeterminacy; an 1866 French description of *flânerie* calls it "that eminently Parisian compromise between laziness and activity" (qtd. Clark 42). Like that other flaneur, the "restless analyst" Henry James, the identity of Benjamin's flaneur resists stability, existing in an intermediate role, lingering on the threshold of the city and the bourgeoisie: "Neither has yet engulfed him," says Benjamin, for "in neither is he at home. He seeks refuge in the crowd" (*Reflections* 156). At the decentered center of the cultural thought of Adorno and Benjamin is the fragment, be it the concrete particulars accidentally glimpsed in the streets of Berlin and Paris, or the essay as a form embodying "the risk of experimentation" (Adorno, "Actuality" 132).

Both pragmatism and Critical Theory (as Adorno's thought was called after 1937) are "philosophies directed against philosophy" (Adorno, *Prisms* 235). The antifoundationalist premise of both schools is that "the text which philosophy has to read is incomplete, contradictory and fragmentary" not because of subjective distortion but as a result of "irreducible reality break[ing] in ... concretely-historically" ("Actuality" 126). The historical reality Adorno and Benjamin have in mind is the phantasmagoric one produced in and by a capitalist world structured by the commodity, which promotes in the consumer a ceaseless, cyclical rhythm of desire, seduction, and boredom. Interrogating the cultural and psychological effects of capitalism upon the human subject, Critical Theory works within a Marxist framework of dialectical materialism. But by the late thirties Adorno and Benjamin had rejected Marxism's necessitarianism, finding its preordained laws to be a form of identity thinking. Nonidentity can be said to inhere in Critical Theory, for it thrives on an internal contradiction that strips theory of its defining identity—the metaphysical props of certainty and logical necessity. The historical significance of Critical Theory, as Horkheimer stresses, "is not self-evident; it rather depends on men speaking and acting in such a way as to justify it. It is not a finished and fixed historical creation" (*Critical* 220).

This eminently pragmatist stance of openness recalls Dewey's similar critique of Marxism, made in 1939, two years after Horkheimer's statement. Dewey found Marxism a "dated" product of nineteenth-century science's emphasis on necessity and a "single all-comprehensive law" of economic determinism (*Later Works* 13: 125).[24] Unlike the Frankfurt circle, Dewey's pragmatic social critique grants Marxist methodology no special privilege in analyzing twentieth-century capitalism, which he called the "serious and fundamental defect" of our civilization. "Corporate organization," says Dewey, exists where "the control of the means of production by the few ... operates as a standing agency of coercion of the many" (qtd. McDermott 648). Instead of Marxism, Dewey advocated what he called a radical liberalism (socialism) premised on "the necessity of thorough-going changes in the set-up of institutions" (647).[25]

Only "with the disintegration of all security within great philosophy," as Adorno put it in 1931, can "experiment make its entry" ("Actuality" 133). Experiment is also the pragmatic watchword, the mode Dewey calls inquiry. In both its German and American modes, it requires a balancing act between the irrationalism of *Lebensphilosophie* and its opposite, the phenomenalism of positivism. By avoiding the security of these extremes, experiment achieves a cultivated rather than a primitive naivete, a word used by Adorno as well as Dewey. One form this takes is the fashioning of strategies derived from the very marginality that threatens to engulf these precarious experiments. Both the German and American projects are drawn to "unintentional reality," everything, says Adorno, that "has slipped through the conventional conceptual net or to things which have been esteemed too trivial by the prevailing spirit" (*Prisms* 240). The rejection of mastery found in Dewey's willed vulnerability, his disrobing, is conspicuous as well in Adorno and Benjamin. For instance, Benjamin flaunts abjectness in his antisubjectivism, expressed in his loyalty to things and knowledge rather than to inwardness, and in his desire to fashion a work entirely of quotations that would "eliminate all overt commentary." A less ascetic aspect of Benjamin's absorption in things, notes Adorno, is the "moment of naivete" in his thought, which enabled it "to free itself of all impulse to classify" (231). This naivete is synonymous with the faculty of spontaneous response, a precious component of aesthetic consciousness.

The effort to renounce the impulse to classify is precisely the same one Dewey makes in 1925. His own experiment in willed naivete exposes traditional philosophy's urge to classify as based on a fear of the spontaneous or contingent, found in "struggle, conflict and error." What Dewey calls the "left over" and Adorno the "remainder" comprise what has been barred "by definition from full reality" (Dewey, *Experience* 48). " 'Reality' becomes what we wish existence to be." According to Dewey, "The genteel tradition [from Aristotle onward] has relegated the uncertain and unfinished to an invidious state of unreal being, while they have systematically exalted the assured and complete to the rank of true Being" (47). Dewey's effort to reinstate the contingent, the "left over," the hazardous, and the changing is one reason that Adorno would praise him as a "truly emancipated thinker" (*Aesthetic* 460).[26] Dewey's critique of the philosophical tradition in a sense extends the logic of William James's campaign on behalf of "wild facts, with no stall or pigeon hole . . . which threaten to break up the accepted system." William admires this "unclassified residuum" (which positivist science treated with contempt) and equates it with the interests of genius. "Only the born geniuses let themselves be worried and fascinated by these outstanding exceptions. . . . [They] are always getting confounded and troubled by insignificant things" that lie beyond the narrow range of "cosmopolitan culture" (*Will* 223–24). But for all his love of uncontrolled, recalcitrant facts, William nevertheless is intent upon bringing them "within the fold." Only then, he says, is "peace attained" (223). The "control side" in Jamesian pragmatism that Dewey had detected is an impulse evident in William's a priori need for the peace of classification, a need that coexists uneasily with his praise of the defiant.

Perhaps the most oppressive a priori principle—in the view of Dewey, Benjamin, and Adorno—was not the imperative to classify or control but the correlative belief in constitutive subjectivity. What Adorno says of Benjamin describes himself, Henry James, and Dewey: "From the very start his thought protested against the false claim that man and the human mind are self-constitutive and that an absolute originates in them" (*Prisms* 235). Only Benjamin went so far as to cancel the subject, a move that Adorno found a source of "terror" in his friend's thought. But all of them, to varying degrees, gave up the "control side" that provided the illusion of autonomous mastery. Indeed, for Benjamin truth is not discovered by subjectivity; rather, "truth is the death of intention" (*Origin* 36). This reduction of control and intention, seemingly a pivotal surrender of power, is actually the fulcrum facilitating immersion in the overflowing, thick materiality of the modern world. "Overflowing" and "thick" are favorite terms of William James to describe the "primitive flux" to which he urges us to return. But despite their refusal to make this return, these thinkers found a way to experience and impart what William James also sought—the visceral, nonconceptual texture of experience. In several eloquent sentences about Benjamin, Adorno suggests the precarious dialectic that orients his own thinking and that of Dewey and Henry James:

> Benjamin's thought is not content with intentions. The thoughts press close to its objects, seek to touch it, smell it, taste it and so thereby transform itself. Through this secondary sensuousness, they hope to penetrate down to the veins of gold which no classificatory procedure can reach, and at the same time avoid succumbing to the contingency of blind intuition. . . . He charged [the concept] with accomplishing what is otherwise reserved for nonconceptual experience. He strove to give thought the density of experience without having it therefore lose any of its stringency. (*Prisms* 240)

Density and stringency, or what Henry James calls intensity and economy, are found not by questing for the unmediated—a "searching behind the phenomenal world for a world in itself," in Adorno's phrase—or by seeking for "the true shape of reality" as William James described his goal. Instead, the tensions of secondary sensuousness, of cultivated naivete, breed a "mingled" texture. For all his renown as a psychological novelist, Henry James conceives of the representation of consciousness not as a descent into psychic depths in search of truth but as a dissolving of the stable oppositions—depth and surface, inside and outside—that define selfhood as a discrete and intelligible entity. Thus, his most lucid central reflectors—Maggie Verver and Strether, for instance—have the most permeable, empathic selves: "I seem to have a life only for other people," typifies Strether's sense of his fluid nonidentity (*Ambassadors* 160). The border between inner and outer experience, like that of self and other, is continually blurred in James's late works. This blurring is everywhere on display in the course of James's trip to America, where he enters into conversation with things, including commodities in "shop-fronts" and "the voice of the streets" of New York. He even stages conversations between buildings. In explaining the logic that breeds such a heightened sense of objects, James sounds remarkably like Benjamin: "To be at all critically . . . [or] analytically minded . . . is to be subject to the superstition that objects and places . . . must have a sense of their own, a mystic meaning proper to themselves to give out: to give out, that is, to the participant at once so interested and so detached" (*Scene* 273). Like Benjamin and his beloved Proust, here James joins with both in submitting to the mystic spell or aura of objects and places. These are imbued with a "wealth of meaning" elicited only by the participant able to remain precariously poised between desire and distance (136).[27]

By submitting the aura of Henry James, the cultural icon, to corrosive critique, I have followed not only Benjamin, with his desire to have texts undergo "mortification," but James as well. For what is one meaning of his American journey, that ordeal propelled by hunger for movement and shock, if not his own effort to destroy the aura of Henry James?[28]

James's communion with objects and his willingness to let them guide his perambulations align him with Benjamin and Adorno's efforts to construct from modern urban experience "authentically materialist knowledge" (Adorno, "Actuality" 127). The task of chapter 6 is to demonstrate that significant new dimensions of *The American Scene* are revealed when it is read against Adorno and Benjamin's materialist cultural critique.[29] Chapter 5 pursues the reconfiguration of intellectual history that this chapter has begun by exploring further the interaction of Dewey, William James, Henry James, and Adorno. The context will be broadened to illuminate a diverse range of responses to the fate of curiosity amid the challenges of modernity.

5

Abolishing the Logic of Identity: Contexts and Consequences

When pressed for a "brief nickname" to describe his philosophy, William James usually offered "radical empiricism." In 1896 he declared that a radical empiricist is anyone who believes that pluralism is the "permanent form of the world": "For him the crudity of experience remains an eternal element thereof" (*Will* 6). The radical empiricist seeks to preserve this crudity from the assaults of "professionalism and pedantry" with their monistic, absolutist doctrines intolerant of what James calls the "ever not quite" (qtd. Perry 2: 630; *Will* 6). In this battle James gained crucial support from Henri Bergson's *Creative Evolution* (1907): "We are fighting the same fight," James excitedly wrote him. Two years later, in *A Pluralistic Universe*, James announced a breakthrough:

> I have finally found myself compelled to *give up the logic* [of identity] fairly, squarely, and irrevocably. It has an imperishable use in human life, but that use is not to make us theoretically acquainted with the essential nature of reality. . . . Reality, life, experience, concreteness, immediacy, use what word you will, exceeds our logic, overflows and surrounds it. . . . I prefer bluntly to call reality if not irrational then at least non-rational in its constitution. (*Pluralistic* 96–97)

According to Gerald Myers, James's "public renunciation of the logic of identity seems to have been accompanied by a feeling of liberation or exhilaration, as if a dramatic discovery had been made" (338).[1] But, as we shall see, his effort to reach reality's essential nature was hampered by paradoxes that pushed James's pluralism in the opposite direction of his original intentions.

The present chapter seeks to explore the contexts and consequences of William James's effort to give up the logic of identity. The most immediate context relates James's renunciation to his growing estrangement from late nineteenth-century American advocates of social control, professionalization, and academic entrepreneurship. His radical empiricism seems to function like a kind of philosophical rationalization of his emotional and intellectual disengagement from modernity in general. The larger context extends outward to situate James's radical empiricism—his American brand of *Lebensphilosophie*—in a constellation of American and European thought that simultaneously acknowledges the worth of James's (and Bergson's) project but resists its effort to escape social reality.

Radical empiricism both derives and veers from pragmatism. As inherited from Charles S. Peirce, the pragmatism of James, Dewey, and Mead seeks to challenge Cartesian rationalism's dichotomous logic and give the human self access to less repressive modes of thinking that would break with "the modern dominance of epistemology over ontology, 'knowing' over 'having' or 'feeling' " (Rochberg x, 39). James's empiricism clearly participates in this effort, yet the emphasis of his form of pragmatism on context and social embeddedness seems at odds with radical empiricism's "Bergsonian nostalgia for the rich, whooshy, sensuous flux we bathed in before conceptual thought started to dry us out" (Rorty, rev. of Barzun 33).[2] Dewey and Mead sought to escape this nostalgia by finding in the continually revised, self-correcting hypotheses of science a model for creative human inquiry that would achieve much of the dynamism of life philosophy without having to immerse oneself in the irrational flux.

Sharing a concern to overthrow the abstract sterility of Western rationalism, Adorno sympathized with Bergson's project. But, like the post-Jamesian pragmatists, he sought to avoid capitulating to irrationalism. Without taking science as an alternative model, Adorno leveled a sustained, relentless attack against identity logic and the bourgeois capitalist social order that enthrones it. His "brutal transitions from the socio-historical to the philosophical level" reveal that "the concept's power to master non-conceptual heterogeneous material . . . merely prolongs, on the level of thought, domination on the social level" (Tertulian 91). With this explicit entwinement of philosophical and social critique, largely conducted utilizing Marxist categories, Adorno can be said to radicalize the pragmatist attack on abstract reason (intellectualism).[3] This mode of reason is at best indifferent to particularity, at worst violently hostile to it. Yet Adorno discerns pledges of otherness and difference that manage to survive in "residues of freedom and tendencies toward true humanism" (*Dialectic* x).

To preserve these tendencies and residues, Adorno practices dialectical (or nonidentical) cognition, which functions by multiplying difference while preserving resemblances rather than assimilating them through identification.[4] Analogy and similitude (as opposed to conceptual definition) characterize this kind of mimetic cognition. It attempts to use concepts nonconceptually, not as instruments that circumscribe but as tentative acts of expression that suggest rather than fix meaning. In turn, this dialectical or mimetic cognition serves Adorno as a model both for renovated human conduct (which he calls aesthetic or mimetic) and for the social and political arrangements that would encourage such conduct. Mimetic behavior also constitutes the promise of happiness embodied in modern art.[5]

Adorno's multiperspectival vantage point, which explores links among experience, conduct (individual and social), and art, recalls Dewey's complex of interests, an affinity Adorno acknowledges. Tracing their affinity leads to Henry James and his own fascination, in his late work, with how the energies of art and life, the aesthetic and the social, overlap and interfuse to produce new modes of experience, practice, and social organization. All three thinkers (along with Mead) attempt to resist the repressions and closure of identity by conceiving of the very structure of selfhood as founded on otherness. Without surrendering to the illusions of immediacy found in primitive flux, Adorno, Henry James, and Dewey are devoted to maximizing a sense of spontaneity, fallibility, restlessness, and ferment in the practice of thinking and writing.[6] Only then can a "sphere beyond control, a sphere tabooed by conceptuality," emerge (Adorno, *Negative* 14).

The Adorno that emerges after being juxtaposed with Henry James and Dewey is not the gloomy virtuoso of sterile, self-lacerating negativity but an Adorno devoted to what he calls "the playful element in philosophy," which serves as a "corrective to the total rule of method" (14). This infrequently recognized Adorno wrote two crowning late works, *Negative Dialectics* and *Aesthetic Theory*, that fulfill his promise—made twenty years earlier in the opening pages of *Dialectic of Enlightenment*—"to prepare the way for a positive concept of Enlightenment which will release it from entanglement in blind domination" (ix). The mimetic and the nonidentical are gestures toward this release.[7]

I

William James's renunciation of identity logic radically reoriented what Western rationalism had defined as fully human and masterful. Pluralism begins by questioning the absolute value we have traditionally accorded man's conceptual abilities. Intellectualism, notes James, "has its source in the faculty which gives us our chief superiority to the brutes, our power, namely, of translating the crude flux of our merely feeling-experience into a conceptual order" (*Pluralistic* 98–99). This "sublimest of our human perogatives" grew debased and intellectualism turned "vicious," says James, when "Socrates and Plato taught that what a thing really is, is told us by its definition. Ever since Socrates we have been told that reality consists of essences, not of appearances" (99). James's antidote—"to think in non-conceptual terms"—involves surrendering not only maturity but dignity and propriety: "It is too much like looking downwards and not up. Philosophy, you will say, doesn't lie flat on its belly . . . in the very thick of its sand and gravel . . . never getting a peep at anything from above. Philosophy is essentially the vision of things from above" (125).

The boldness of James's Nietzschean transvaluation of values is compromised by a latent paradox evident in his remark that, however difficult "such a revolution is, there is no other way, I believe, to the possession of reality" (121). This last phrase contradicts James's previous characterizations of reality as embodying excess, overflow, and fluidity. In his desire to take "possession," James appears to reify reality into a graspable essence. The same congealing is evident in his effort to look behind "the more primitive flux of the sensational life for reality's true shape" (127). His metaphysics here partakes of the "vicious" intellectualism his pluralism is meant to defeat and *Pragmatism* opposed. There he warned that we can never grasp reality but only "some substitute for it which previous thinking has peptonized and cooked for our consumption" (119). Evidently James's transvaluation stops short of interrogating his own pursuit of "reality," a pursuit sparked by the same impulse to master and dominate that animates traditional philosophical discourse. Dewey acutely saw how the effort to liquidate reality could easily turn into its opposite. In Bergson's reverence of flux Dewey found an intense "craving for the sure and fixed." To deify change, as Bergson does (and James), "sidesteps the painful, toilsome labor of understanding and of control which change sets us, by glorifying it for its own sake. Flux is made something to revere. . . . It is not, as it is in experience, a call to effort, a challenge to investigation, a potential doom of disaster and death" (*Experience* 46).

James tends to ignore the paradox presiding over his quest for the real because he believes paradox is inconceivable in the realm of pure experience. "Experience in its immediacy seems perfectly fluent, . . . self-luminous and suggests no paradoxes. Its difficulties are disappointments and uncertainties. They are not intellectual contradictions" (*Radical* 45). Though he bans paradox from the pluralistic universe, James finds a place for it in his account of the decline of concepts into "vicious intellectualism." The decline "is but the old story, of a useful practice first becoming a method, then a habit, and finally a tyranny that defeats the end it was used for" (*Pluralistic* 98–99). The reversal from usefulness to tyranny is the insidious process that James's pluralism believes it has detected and resolved. Yet James's own thought seems plagued by this reversal, whereby opposing terms migrate into an identity and seeming liberation becomes another kind of enslavement. With uncanny irony what James represses returns: his refusal of paradox breeds paradox everywhere in his late thought and hobbles his strenuous effort to provide a philosophical defense of the individual's sanctity in the modern world.

Herbert Marcuse has noted profound, if unacknowledged, anxiety among philosophers of individualism (including James) at the end of the previous century. Marcuse reminds us how decisively individualism's liberating doctrine of autonomy was transformed by the rationalizing imperatives of modernity. What began as a "critical oppositional attitude" was absorbed by market demands for efficiency and uniformity. Marcuse continues:

Philosophic justifications of individualism took on more and more the overtones of resignation. Toward the end of the nineteenth century the idea of the individual became increasingly ambiguous: it combined insistence on free social performance and competitive efficiency with glorification of smallness, privacy and self-limitation. The rights and liberties of the individual in society were interpreted as the rights and liberties of privacy and withdrawal from society. William James [possessed a] hatred of "bigness and greatness in all their forms. . . . The smaller and more intimate is the truer, the man more than the home, the home more than the state or the church." The counter-position of individual and society, originally meant to provide the ground for a militant reformation of society in the interest of the individual, comes to prepare and justify the individual's withdrawal from society. The free and self-reliant "soul," which originally nourished the individual's critique of external authority, now becomes a refuge from external authority. ("Social" 157)[8]

In light of Marcuse's view, we can read James's antiintellectual celebration of "pure experience" as an anxious retreat from the modern industrial order, with its imperialist designs of social and managerial control. His optimism about flux "is only the reverse side of pessimism about actualities," as Dewey wrote of Bergson (*Human* 69).

Jamesian pluralism can be regarded as part of "a general containment strategy of a late nineteenth-century bourgeoisie suffering from the after-effects of reification." As the "fiction of the individual subject becomes ever more difficult to sustain, more desperate myths of the self are generated." This analysis is part of Fredric Jameson's portrayal of Henry James (*Political* 221). While mistaken about Henry, Jameson's words are considerably more apt when applied to William James. Given William's characteristic bravado and eloquence, his desperation is not immediately obvious. But even Gerald Myers's unsuspicious account of James's sense of triumph hints at an unsettled mood below the surface. The decision to give up the logic of identity involved a belief that "the only recourse" was to return to Bergsonian intuitionism "and to stop attempting coherent reports of the details of reality . . . even though James had striven for many years to cast the pure experience hypothesis in as rational a mold as possible. Even if he had preserved this rationality, he might have retained his conviction that what is intuitive defies adequate conceptualization . . . because this conviction does not require an irrational metaphysics" (338). In short, despite the availability of more moderate options, James insisted on embracing irrationalism and metaphysics, positions his pragmatism had abjured.

Given his abandonment of beliefs he had previously upheld, James's pluralism seems as much like capitulation as triumph. Mingling with his sense of freedom are echoes of what Marcuse calls "smallness," "self-limitation," "withdrawal," and "refuge" evident in pluralism's stance of being "flat on its belly . . . never getting a peep at anything from above." An undercurrent of the abject and stunted would seem difficult to ignore. A besieged, defensive quality is also apparent in James's social and political views. They are predicated on his acute unease with power, which he associates with bigness: "The bigger the unit you deal with, the hollower, the more brutal, the more mendacious is the life displayed." Adamantly opposed to America's

imperialist aggressions in the Philippines and in the Spanish-American war,
James declared: "Damn great Empires! including that of the Absolute. . . .
Give me individuals and their sphere of activity." This remark implicitly
links his philosophical and political views. Both uphold individualism as a
refuge against "those old-fashioned animal ambitions for mastery . . . which
seem now to be sweeping away the world." Leaving his own ambitions
unacknowledged, James restricts the desire for mastery to imperialist philosophy and foreign policy (qtd. Perry 2: 315).[9] Pluralism radically narrows
our sphere of activity by stripping us of the tools of intellectual experience,
relieving us of language, the instrument of intersubjectivity, and deracinating
us to float in the flux.

II

William James's return to origins, his "descendental" embrace of the "sand
and gravel," represents a flight not only from his professed opponent—the
idealism of Hegelian systematizing. He is responding to another, unspoken,
but more ominous source: the growth of a professionally administered social
order. The coercive character of modernity is reflected in the ascendancy of
social control as the governing concern of the social sciences in the opening
decade of the twentieth century. By 1909 it was not only academic philosophy
that was "essentially the vision of things from above," not only philosophy
that stressed "categories and their rules, their order and necessity," and took
"the superior point of view of the architect" (*Pluralistic* 125). Scientific management was equally enamored of the superior point of view. Its motto
declared: "In the past the man has been first; in the future the system must
be first" (7). So wrote Frederick Taylor, the founder of efficiency management, two years after James envisioned his pluralistic universe.

The Jamesian pluralist diving back into the flux seems as far from Taylorized
efficiency as possible. This opposition is affirmed when we recall that James's
individualism extended to disgust for what he called modern civilization's
insistence on "herding and branding, licensing and degree-giving, authorizing and appointing, . . . regulating and administering by system the lives
of human beings" (qtd. Perry 2: 267). Yet the "passive and receptive listening" that James recommends, his celebration of an existence that has
abandoned concepts for "raw, unverbalized life," could also describe a state
of helplessness. Emptied of subjectivity, one is reduced to an object vulnerable to manipulation. Such is Taylorism's aim: the worker hands over his
mind to a new institution—scientific management (Sohn-Rethel 157). The
affinity of radical empiricism for its opposite is evident in phenomenalism,
which equates the real with immediacy, as do both James's "ultra-crude
empiricism" and positivism, a creed that James usually denounced as scientism. James's antiintellectualism, a commitment to saving the subject from
scientific abstraction, risks imprisoning him within it. In short, James's return
to the flux provides no *inherent* liberation from an administered world. This
point is borne out by the fact that at the time of his death he was hailed as

a patron saint of the efficiency movement. James's critique of intellectualism can lead just as easily to social control as to his cherished anarchy of a "tramp and vagrant world adrift" (*Pragmatism* 125).

This reversibility is vividly underscored when we turn to someone who embodied much of what James abhorred—Edward Alsworth Ross, author of the seminal *Social Control* (1901), the first text devoted to developing apparatuses of efficient social management. As a pioneer of positivist sociology, Ross inaugurated a reorientation in that fledgling field from humanitarian to managerial concerns. But what is of particular concern here is the autobiographical account of his philosophical crisis while still a young man living in Berlin in 1888. It is remarkably congruent with James's own youthful struggles a generation earlier (partly enacted in Berlin and Dresden) in the labyrinth of speculative thought. A prolonged diet of Kant, Hegel, and Schopenhauer results in a "fierce Sturm und Drang" that leaves Ross "in the depths," contemplating suicide. Renouncing "pessimism not for being false, but for being unendurable," Ross works himself "nearly free of the spell of philosophy" in a way that recalls James's moves toward stability. Both men turn from thought to action, from philosophy to science. In 1872 James rejoices in his new job as a physiology instructor, for biology diverts him "from those introspective studies which had bred a sort of philosophical hypochondria" (qtd. Perry 1: 328). Sounding like a Jamesian pluralist, Ross finds an antidote to his own "philosophical hypochondria": "Thinking is an evil of a very positive kind and I banish it. The texture of a happy life is woven of . . . abandonment for the moment . . . of self-willed acts. Where reflection . . . can only disturb the joy and harmony of the moment, I repress it" (*Seventy* 28, 30).

But, having rejected reflection, Ross draws different conclusions than James. Poetry, not science, is the surprising consequence of his embrace of pure experience: "This refusal to reflect makes possible the complete surrender to the object and the moment which makes possible the poet. Hence I am now finding my highest satisfaction in poetry" (30). Poetry comes to represent a necessary part of Ross's "slow but constant" journey toward sociology. He sets his literary aspirations aside without regret because he is not really abandoning them but simply shifting to that other mode of complete surrender found in science. Thus, in a few months poetry yields painlessly to positivism (a creed somewhat less hostile toward subjectivity than objectivism). For the rest of his life Ross devotes himself to the singleminded pursuit of social organization. "I had become a positivist, giving up all attempt to ascertain the cause or 'ground of being' of things: I have confidence only in that philosophy which begins by renouncing philosophy. Philosophy is an inquiry into the causes of things. . . . This is an idle question leading to nothing but failure and despair" (32). William James, who describes his method as turning away from "a lot of inveterate habits dear to professional philosophers," could not have agreed more enthusiastically (*Pragmatism* 31). But James calls his philosophical antiphilosophy pragmatism and opposes it to positivism's fetishizing of fact and predictability.

The dread both Ross and James feel toward philosophical speculation is rooted in painful experiences concerning the fragility and instability of human reason. Early in his autobiography Ross confesses his lifelong "horror of the subjective," a revulsion prompted by seeing two close relatives suddenly stricken by "delusional insanity" (*Seventy* 7). The horror is clearly evident in *Social Control*, which is premised on the conviction that controls are imperative since "there is an unreclaimed jungle in man.... There are unpleasant, slimy things lurking in the . . . undergrowth of the human soul" (196). In his own brush with man's "unreclaimed jungle" when he confronted an epileptic patient and his "greenish skin," James felt himself become "a mass of quivering fear." Since introspection always involves risking such repulsive encounters, our actions and will must perpetually guard against prolonged reflection.[10]

After renouncing philosophy and poetry, Ross celebrates the "positive contrasts that make life seem solid and real" and craves "clear outlines" and "firm colors" (*Seventy* 33). He memorializes his "solid and real" life in an autobiography that concludes with a chart, entitled "Edward Alsworth Ross Anthropometric Data," assembled by a professor of physical anthropology. The anthropologist, evidently enlisted to ensure neutrality, lists twenty-six different measurements and indexes ("breadth of forehead," "total height of face," "hip breadth," and so on) and then analyzes the data: "Dr. Ross is exceptionally tall, not only in comparison with the general run of mankind, but also when compared with the tallest members of the white race" (333). With this appended data, Ross re-presents his germinal decision involving "complete surrender to the object." He ends his life history, his most sustained and flagrant act of subjectivity, by submitting to the procedures of social control. In effect, he rehearses his Berlin pursuit of vocation: poet effortlessly turns into positivist, as Ross dissolves into the data of scientific measurement.

If James and Ross christen their careers with a remarkably similar purgative ritual that banishes speculation for action, what follows this common initiation is, of course, quite different. Ross will become the foremost proponent of "regulation . . . the rigid, confining crust which forms upon a society" in order to guard against its sworn enemy—"an era of individualism" (*Social* 406). His obsession with control was expressed both in his social psychology and in his political attitudes. Ross has been called "sociology's most demagogic champion of a Teutonic America," promulgating for most of his long life a particularly virulent brand of midwestern populism that preached a Nordic supremacist doctrine hostile to Jews, blacks, Catholics, and Asians (Vidich and Lyman 156). His antithesis in this regard is William James, who consistently defended the alien and promoted tolerance, attitudes that helped make him a hero of the young intellectuals of 1910. But it would be wrong to consign Ross to the dustbin of the history of sociology and provincial nativism. Although a positivist, he was not an objectivist like many in the field of social control (Luther Bernard, for example). Because Ross does not eliminate subjectivity, he is able to grant the subject's necessary mediation by the object.[11] In contrast, James is often hostile to external control, indeed, to mediation in general, be it concepts or social institutions. Ironically, the more James seeks to expunge mediation, the more his subjectivism comes to resemble the mirror image of its opposite—objectivism. Thus James proves less astute a social analyst than Ross.

Whereas James's radical empiricism equates freedom with the nonconceptual flux that opposes the social, Ross intuits that subject and object, poetry and science, reciprocally interact (even if he ultimately privileges the second term in each pair). Hence nothing human can escape the bonds of sociality, even modernist aestheticism. In *Social Control* Ross contends that however disruptive the "decadent" "anti-social individualism" of the modern artist (he quotes Flaubert's "I abominate everything that is compulsory, every law, all government"), art's inherent capacity to arouse sympathy "conciliates the individual with society . . . calls forth fellow feeling and knits anew the ever-ravelling social thread." Ross continues: "Despise the multitude as he may, the artist levels his appeal at our sympathies" and thus arouses a socializing impulse (257, 269).

If Ross reveals the social content of aestheticism, James fails to interrogate the idealist grounds of his own Flaubertian belief in the sanctity of the intellectual as an oppositional force. In his famous definition of *"Les Intellectuels"* James declares: "We stand for ideal interests solely, for we have no corporate selfishness and wield no powers of corruption" (qtd. Matthiessen, *Family* 635). Ross's homologous concept of the "mandarinate" implies no such righteous power of opposition. With prophetic accuracy he virtually predicts the increasing influence of the "public" intellectual (Dewey, Walter Lippmann, Herbert Croly, and their progeny): "The mandarinate will infallibly draw to itself a greater and greater share of public power" (*Social* 88). In sum, Ross's understanding of dialectical mediation nurtures his sociological perspective, while James's individualist viewpoint (to borrow Ross's vocabulary) is "pre-sociological": he assumes that individuals make institutions and government, "but that these in turn do not make the soul of individuals." A sociological view, says Ross, "sees social progress as a double and interacting development" among individuals, society, and government (*Seventy* 178).[12]

That individualism is a historically conditioned ideology never seems to occur to James, despite his pragmatic rejection of universal, timeless truths (a rejection also expressed in "On a Certain Blindness"). His pluralistic belief that "the essence of life is its continuously changing character" would seem to admit history. But James's is a statement about metaphysics rather than an insight into the fact that bureaucracy and standardization not only devalue individual needs but produce new forms of subjectivity. While deeply aware of this devaluation, James responds by redoubling his efforts to defend the individual as a sovereign entity. However morally admirable his defense of the will to believe, James's rugged individualism had become a "ragged individualism" by the close of the nineteenth century.

The above phrase was coined by Dewey in 1930. He seems implicitly to dissent from William James's views and points to his own efforts to delineate forms of individualism, both old and new. As if addressing James, Dewey opposes those who would treat "individualism as if it were something static, having a uniform content."[13] Such a view "ignores the fact that the mental and moral structure of individuals, the pattern of their desires and purposes, change with every great change in social constitution." Opposing the corporate to the individual breeds confusion because this dichotomy suggests that "the individual, by exercising restraint, can remain aloof from technological progress." But for Dewey "the urging of some inner restraint through the exercise of the higher personal will . . . is itself only a futile echo of just the old individualism that has so completely broken down" (*Individualism* 81–82, 68). To believe that industry is "outside of human life" and values rather than within them, says Dewey, is to rest in "the genteel tradition," which refuses to face this fact (158). If we tease out the implications of Dewey's disparagement of the power of personal will, with its illusory sense of autonomy, it seems that he is aligning William James with a genteel worldview, a judgment that Santayana shares.

In deflating rugged individualism, Dewey does not seek passivity and conformity. Social integration, he believes, will release individuality "for creative effort" (142). Though he does not mention James, Dewey roots his belief in a Jamesian emphasis on process. Individuality, rather than self-sufficiency, is a "potentiality, a capacity of development," and "develops into shape and form only through interaction with actual conditions" (168). Thus Dewey does not reject Jamesian individualism but rather socializes it by using its own stress on change to return it from the timeless flux to the reality of corporate America.

Dewey's understanding of individualism as a political, historical construction contrasts with James's neglect of the embedded, a neglect that encouraged his disregard for the political consequences of his thought. This lack of reflexivity may partly account for the fact that his ideas tended to be easily appropriated by his opponents (behaviorists and materialists in psychology, efficiency experts and social-control thinkers in sociology). The historian James Gilbert, among others, has noted this paradox. James, he says, laments "the crisis of individualism," of which "he was also a cause." Gilbert is speaking of James's functionalist psychology and its assault on German idealism and British empiricism, two of the cornerstones of American liberal individualism. "James helped to weaken traditional philosophic individualism at the same time that he attempted to reconstruct it upon the base of a firmer, modern psychology." But his less democratic and liberal followers transformed Jamesian functionalism "into the dogmas of behaviorism, mental testing, and materialist definitions of mind" (182, 193). James's sponsorship of and contempt for the mind-cure movement of Protestant positive thinking is another instance of his conflicting impulses (as we shall see in chapter 9).

James's entanglement with the intellectual doctrines he opposes seems to reflect contradictions in his own psychic economy. Bruce Kuklick is not alone in noting that "more than anything else James's temperament explained his point of view" (311). In chapter 2 we saw his temperament assailed by conflicting impulses—a love and terror of both anarchy and efficiency. These ambivalences are expressed by what I earlier termed a double rhetoric that often makes James's thought appear to be at odds with itself. To keep from relapsing into the depressions of his twenties, James tended to compart-mentalize and repress these ambivalences rather than explore them. Gerald Myers notes his consistent avoidance of sustained introspection (48). One result of this psychic self-preservation is a taboo on dialectical understanding. This interdiction stunts not only James's self-insight but also his political understanding, confining it to simplistic oppositions: "Surely the individual is the more fundamental phenomenon, and the social institution... is but secondary and ministerial.... System... does violence whenever it lays its hands upon us" (*Memories* 102–3). The poverty of sociological understanding in this statement is striking. In the era of Marx, Weber, Nietzsche, Freud, Durkheim, and Mead, James seems oblivious to the fact that one can no longer separate man and society, that the violence of control is not externally imposed (that is, something one can choose to escape) but rather internalized as the condition of social life.[14]

As was suggested earlier, James's myopia is not merely a case of intellectual blindness. Rather, it is grounded in psychic needs. To maintain his mental balance James in effect surrendered to the circularity produced by the con-flicting motives of his two late philosophies. While his pragmatism turned him "towards facts, towards action, and towards power" in the modern world, his pluralism moved him back to a primitive realm of stasis and transparency, a realm "before reflection shatter[ed] our instinctive world for us." Here resided what he called "perfectly fluent," immediate experience and the "active sense of living" (*Radical* 45). His dualisms derive from this self-canceling double movement. Dewey had noted how dualistic thinking had its "origin, fundamentally, in fear of what life may bring forth. They [op-positions] are marks of contraction and withdrawal" (qtd. McDermott 543). This lockstep movement is also a source of the loneliness behind the bustling activity and optimism that astute observers noted in James. John Jay Chap-man described his meeting with him: "You felt that he had just stepped out of his sadness in order to meet you and was to go back into it the moment you left him" (206). And Santayana, always acutely aware of James's para-doxes, found that his Harvard colleague's energetic "American sense of being just born into a world to be rediscovered" was only part of the story. James "was really far from free, held back by old instincts, subject to old delusions, restless, spasmodic, self-interrupted: as if some impetuous bird kept flying aloft, but always stopped in mid-air, pulled back with a jerk by an invisible wire tethering him to a peg in the ground" (*Persons* 401).

Santayana's vivid image suggests the conflicts and frustrations that would lead James to will into being an innocence capable of the Emersonian re-discovery of an "original relation to the universe" (Emerson 7). Although James wanted to "let redemption take the place of innocence" as the measure of a philosophy's "human success," a willed innocence remains conspicuous in his later thought: "The way of escape from evil," he declared in *Pragmatism*, "is by dropping it out altogether, throwing it overboard and getting beyond it" (124). That James's effort to attain a redemptive pluralism was politically and morally innocent was apparent to Santayana, who "trusted James's heart" but "didn't respect his judgment" (401). In his memoirs Santayana observes that although James was both "a physician and a pragmatist," his "over-ruling tradition" was "literary and theological" (404). James was predictably outraged when America seized the Philippines and "felt that he had lost his country." Santayana attributes this reaction to James's "romanticism," which "held a false moralistic view of history, attributing events to the conscious motives and free will of individuals" rather than to the vested interests of empire building (403). Santayana would likely concur with Marcuse's remark that Jamesian individualism becomes less a critique of than a "refuge from external authority" ("Social" 157).

III

The external authority of social control presented itself to James not as abstract doctrine but in the formidable figure of his insatiably ambitious Harvard colleague Hugo Münsterberg, a pioneer inventor of social-management apparatuses. In 1892, seeking release from teaching psychology to pursue philosophy, James had brought Münsterberg from his native Germany to direct the Harvard Psychological Laboratory. But by the end of the decade Münsterberg, too, had grown dissatisfied with purely experimental psychological research. Thus he joined James in the philosophy department and, like James, sought an increasingly larger public audience. He quickly became a masterful academic entrepreneur thanks to his copious writing and tireless self-promoting. Münsterberg's work was dedicated to the disciplining and organizing of an emerging mass society of industrial capitalism. He addressed himself to a variety of social and cultural problems: personnel management (he virtually invented psychological vocational testing); scientific testing to determine the reliability of eyewitnesses in criminal trials; unification of German–American international relations (a failed effort that ended up hastening his death in 1916); film as an instrument of psychological control; the professionalization and centralizing of the social sciences; advertising; and the education of children. This list fails to exhaust his areas of expertise, or self-anointed expertise, as critics charged. Continually embroiled in controversy and publicity efforts, Münsterberg aroused the wrath of many of his Harvard colleagues, who found his forays into applied psychology and his fetishizing of expertise vulgar and self-serving.

Whereas Münsterberg's megalomania convinced him of his authority in every field he entered, James seemed to flee from authority, even though he had struggled for twelve years to write the book that would earn him the mantle of father of American psychology. As a recent biographer has noted, "After completing his landmark book, [in 1890] James largely rejected the professional scientific authority that he had tried so hard to develop in the late seventies and eighties. He took steps to free himself from the institutional responsibilities his scientific pioneering had engendered. . . . James's first step in loosening the professional coil" was to hire Münsterberg (Bjork 173–74). These facts make James's relationship to Münsterberg a unique window through which to observe close up James's acute unease with both scientific and institutional authority and the larger matrix they serve—modernity itself. Münsterberg was a pivotal figure in James's divestiture of power. Yet this renunciation was marked by James's ambivalence toward both the German émigré's obsession with authority and his own surrender of it. This double ambivalence pervades his dealings with Münsterberg and eventually prompted James to deflect it by devising various psychological strategies.

By 1900 no one seemed more distressed about the reach of Münsterberg's ambitions than his former champion.[15] In that year James mocked the glib systematizing of Münsterberg's major philosophical work on the epistemological foundations of psychology, describing it as an "exquisite example of Münsterberg's fluent ingenuity along unreal lines of artificial obstruction. . . . How Münsterberg must have been pleased when this self-extrication from a self-imposed difficulty was safely invented" (qtd. Perry 2: 150). But James leveled a more serious charge that would establish the terms of their increasingly uneasy relationship: "Shall the direct dealings of our minds with life . . . passively consent to be first falsified and mutilated and then handed over to certain professionals called psycho-physicists, who claim to be the only persons licensed to give any account?" (qtd. Perry 2: 151). His relations with Münsterberg from 1904 onward reveal James's vaunted tolerance strained to and beyond the breaking point, providing a glimpse of the tensions and repressions that James's escape from authority and history were built upon.

Münsterberg reveals that James's tolerance, however genuine, also operates in his psychic economy as a nearly compulsive benignity that serves to displace his anxiety about totalizing forces to a level safely abstracted from political actuality. This is not to say that James fails to admit the reality of social control and to state firmly his differences with Münsterberg. But by habitually naturalizing these differences James avoids what could potentially be a source of reflexive insight into the precarious status of his own philosophy of individualism. This naturalizing process is evident in a letter James wrote to Münsterberg in 1906:

Were it not for my fixed belief that the world is wide enough to sustain and nourish without harm many different types of thinking, I believe that the wide difference between your . . . philosophizing and mine would give me a despairing feeling. I am satisfied with a free, wild nature; you seem to me to cherish and pursue an Italian garden, where all things are kept in separate compartments, and one must follow straight-ruled walks. . . . But emphases and tempers are only the colors the world is painted in. . . . I don't wish to inflict polemic upon you. The world is wide enough! Do your best; and I'll do my best. (qtd. Perry 2: 471)

Granting James's characteristic graciousness and respect for difference, we can note here that the enforced blandness of his tone barely suppresses the "despairing feeling" he denies experiencing. What stands between James and despair is a "fixed belief"—twice repeated—that "the world is wide enough" to contain what he would like to believe is simply a dispute about wild versus manicured nature. In a notebook entry he remarked: "I want a world of anarchy, Münsterberg one of bureaucracy, and each appeals to 'nature' to back him up. Nature partly helps and partly resists each of us" (qtd. Perry 2: 700). In naturalizing the "wide difference" between their philosophies, James staves off potential despair by draining their conflict of social and political content. By refusing to admit to qualitative differences, James frames his disagreement with Münsterberg as merely a matter of different "emphases and tempers" rather than a clash between irreconcilable moral and political visions.

As an apostle of value-free science, Münsterberg would obviously welcome a camouflaging rhetoric of nature.[16] His reply to James invokes a similar subterfuge as he drapes his bureaucratic dissent in nature's colors: "Yes, the world of immediate experience is to me also a wild nature," he says, "but I think our life's duty makes us gardeners, makes us . . . unweed the weeds of sin and error and ugliness; and when we finally come to think over what kind of flowers were left as valuable, we bring together those which are similar" (qtd. Perry 2: 472). Like Doctor Rappaccini's Italian garden, Doctor Münsterberg's barbered foliage is redolent of an ominous homogeneity.

By the turn of the century James's immediate world, the Harvard philosophy department, was feeling the effects of Münsterberg's appetite for control and management. In 1901 the latter, now chairman of the department, began his four-year campaign to raise funds in order to house the philosophy department in a building of its own, to be called Emerson Hall. James, a notorious opponent of academic careerism, responded to Münsterberg's brochure for funding the Emerson Hall project: "Your jolly epistle . . . gives me a sense of the amount of life from which I've been cut off. I admire the talent with which the circulars are written;—like the elephant's trunk which uproots a tree or picks up a pin, your brain produces *Grundzüge der Psychologie* and the paragraph on Emerson Hall with equal ease! Return thanks to God for such an organ!" (qtd. Perry 2: 270). Along with the "Ph.D. Octopus" that James inveighed against in 1903, the Münsterberg trunk belongs in James's gallery of predatory academic grotesques. It is not hard to detect a note of unease in James's praise of his colleague's elephantine skills. James expressed dislike more directly in his opposition to the Emerson Hall project: "Philosophy, of all subjects, can dispense with material wealth, and we seem to be getting along very well as it is. . . . I am not sure that I shouldn't be personally a little ashamed of a philosophy hall, but of course I shall express no sentiments in public" (270). James internalized his irritation toward his colleague. But when the building was dedicated four years later, James released his self-confessed shame. That day, the centenary of Emerson's birth, Münsterberg's five speeches in the space of an hour drew James's wrath, and he complained bitterly to Harvard's president, Charles William Eliot, and to Münsterberg himself that it was wrong for a German to play so conspicuous a role in an American ceremony (Hale 102). Eliot mollified James by agreeing that Münsterberg's "German way of doing things... grated on the ears of all the Yankees." But he added that "when you recommended Münsterberg for an appointment here you must have expected that he would be different from us" (qtd. Hale 103). A wounded Münsterberg resigned his chairmanship ("a born American ought to take my place at once," he wrote Eliot), and an apology from James superficially patched things up. But the German later informed Eliot that James's attack "changed totally my feelings toward this community" (qtd. Keller 42).

How do we explain James's uncharacteristic intolerance and his lapse into nativism? Apart from the episode's manifest content—irritation at Münsterberg's egomania—the sharpness of James's attack may have been in response to a less obvious disturbance. The day of the Emerson Hall dedication, Münsterberg's indiscriminately acquisitive trunk had appropriated the name of James's hero, his great predecessor in the fight against institutional authority. In witnessing Münsterberg's attempt to turn Emerson's centenary into an occasion for the spreading tentacles of the "Ph.D. Octopus" to conquer new territory, James's earlier feeling of being "ashamed" probably revived. Perhaps he saw Münsterberg's imperial overreaching as evidence of his own failure to protect his beloved Emerson against the aggressively phallic depredations of elephant and octopus. James sought to displace his own sense of impotence ("the amount of life from which I've been cut off") by attacking Münsterberg as an alien invader, an intrusive German who outrageously aligned himself with the father of American individualism—precisely the value Münsterberg's applied psychology sought to discipline.

Not only are Münsterberg's career ambitions boundless, but his efforts to rationalize society invade the psychic boundaries of the individual. Like Edward Ross's, his form of social management aims not at physical, external coercion but at internal domination through "suggestion," that key term of social control. "Superior methods of control," declared Ross in 1901, "are inward. . . . The best guarantee of a stable control from within is something that reaches at once feeling, reason, and will." A "good disciplinary agent" will "lure . . . instead of drive man. . . . The moulding of his will by social suggestion . . . if skillfully done, do[es] not arouse the insurgent spirit" (*Social* 429, 419). One year earlier, in an essay on "School Reform," Münsterberg asked: "Is not all the meaning of good education . . . to suppress the lower instincts, to reinforce the higher; above all, to awake new desires, to build up new interests, to create new instincts?" (qtd. Hale 64). What Münsterberg's "reform" seemed to come down to was something very familiar—habit formation. James's *Principles of Psychology* had, of course, called habit the very basis of the will's capacity to create order and efficiency, and society's "most precious conservative agent." But James also viewed habit as a tool of self-empowerment, a quality needed and tested in a pluralistic universe of incessant challenge and risk. In contrast, Münsterberg, Ross, and behaviorists like J. B. Watson, inspired by James's functionalist view of mind, conceived of habit as the means of replacing autonomy with duty and conditioning rather than strengthening the ego. Thus duty would be imposed from outside by various experts ("the gardeners") in social engineering, who would "link the will of the child to the historic will of society as a whole." For Münsterberg "independence meant only the ability to do what one ought to do without external compulsion" (qtd. Hale 65–66).

Münsterberg's counterpart in sociology, the objectivist Luther Lee Bernard, concludes his *Transition to an Objective Standard of Social Control* (1911) by assessing the status of the claims of the individual in a world ruled by "truly scientific control":

> The counter plea of "interference with individual liberty" should have no weight in court, for individuals have no liberties in opposition to a scientifically controlled society but find all their legitimate freedom in conformity to and furtherance of such social functioning. . . . The chief opposition to such effective social control comes from the old subjectivistic, individualistic and hedonic [*sic*] dogma of personal liberty. (95–96)

Stripped of Dewey's concern for individual growth, Bernard's logic bluntly demolishes the foundation of classical liberalism—its belief in the sovereignty of the individual. Freedom shrinks to conformity and "the dogma of personal liberty" becomes a quaint remnant of an earlier, wider world. Given this reorientation of the social sciences, it is no wonder that James feels the need to ward off despair with a "fixed belief that the world is wide enough."

By colonizing the self's agency, Bernard and Münsterberg in effect extend to its logical conclusion Dewey's belief that the "revolution" of the modern spirit consists of a shift from man accepting and submitting to nature to man controlling nature (*Quest* 100). Exploiting the ambiguities in the word "control" as used by Dewey and other progressives, social-control theorists interpreted the word in a closed, repressive sense, whereas Dewey associated control with openness to future action. Yet, as critics of Dewey (for example, C. Wright Mills and, more recently, Jeffrey Lustig) have argued, Dewey's social thought can be disturbingly ambiguous—even naive—about its actual political consequences and implications.[17] Instead of helping to encourage individual and communal growth, some say, Dewey's emphasis on instrumental reason and science as a model of inquiry shows he favors "adjustment to the iron cages of advanced industrial society" (Lavine 17).[18]

Dewey's belief that social adjustment and integration involve transferring the instrumentalism of the scientific method to the "wider field of human life" can have a darker side (*Quest* 273). For behind this goal lurks Dewey's Münsterbergian belief that the inner man is the jungle which can be subdued to order only as the forces of organization at work in externals are reflected in corresponding patterns of thought, imagination and emotion. The sick cannot heal themselves by means of their disease and disintegrated individuals can achieve unity only as the dominant energies of community life are incorporated to form their minds. (*Individualism* 65)

As with E. A. Ross and William James, Dewey's emphasis on control is here motivated by fears of man's inner jungle suddenly erupting. Dewey's criteria of unity and harmony are designed to enforce an identity between corporate America and citizens incorporated by domestic, communal norms. To conceive of government's responsibility as the subduing of man's inner life, so as to synchronize external and internal, is a goal ominous in its implications and at cross-purposes with the creativity and freedom Dewey seeks to unleash.

If in hindsight the early twentieth century's enthusiasm for social control seems disturbing in its lack of concern over the manipulation and imposition implied in the word "control," a historian of the period reminds us that "in the relatively more innocent atmosphere of the years before the first world war, social control appeared less threatening" (D. Ross 162). Edward Ross, for instance, believed that American society possessed an innate receptivity to control. Unlike Europe, "we Americans . . . have steadily sought the light of fact and reason, and shunned the fog" of European romanticism, which in the nineteenth century nearly crippled man in the "half light" of "sentimentalism and idealism" (*Social* 301). For Ross the beacon of fact and reason was the Enlightenment. "Favorable conditions here," he claimed, have made it "effective in influencing men." The Enlightenment would "always remain the foundation of a system of social control" (302).

Enthusiasm for the Enlightenment continues unabated in Dewey. Earlier we noted his admiration for Bacon. Inspiring Dewey's belief in the need for critical reconstruction of beliefs and institutions was Bacon's, Locke's, and Newton's "fervent faith in intelligence, progress, and humanity. . . . They merely sought to free intelligence from its impurities and make it sovereign" (qtd. McDermott 57). For Dewey "the method of democracy" must become one of "organized intelligence," which he defined as the ability to implement the experimental, scientific method bequeathed by Bacon. The modern age has realized "the prophetic vision of Francis Bacon of subjugation of the energies of nature through change in methods of inquiry." The result has been the release "of more productive energies in a bare hundred years than . . . in prior human history in its entirety" (qtd. McDermott 657, 654). Dewey made these statements in 1935. Ten years later the Holocaust of Nazi genocide prompted a radical revaluation of science's and technology's ability, in Dewey's confident words, to "release productive energies."

This revaluation of the heritage of the Enlightenment was a major concern of the Frankfurt School during the World War II. Two books in particular— Horkheimer's *Eclipse of Reason* (1947) and Adorno and Horkheimer's *Dialectic of Enlightenment* (1944)—delivered wholesale indictments both of the Enlightenment and its modern incarnation in American pragmatism. For Horkheimer and Adorno Bacon embodied the Enlightenment spirit of utilitarian experiment, which disdains idle curiosity, contemplation, and speculation and substitutes the "powerful machinery of organized research" (*Eclipse* 48–49). Pragmatism, according to Horkheimer, is Baconianism reborn, for it "tries to model all spheres of intellectual life after the techniques of the laboratory." Its emphasis on practical application reflects "with an almost disarming candor the spirit of the prevailing business culture, the very same attitude of 'being practical' as a counter to which philosophical meditation as such was conceived" (50, 52). The product of a society that has "no time to remember and meditate," pragmatism replaces truth with calculability, critique with adjustment, reason with instrumentality. Fungibility—universal interchangeability—is the law of the Enlightenment and its tool is abstraction: "Enlightenment behaves toward things as a dictator towards men. He knows them insofar as he can manipulate them" (*Dialectic* 9). Hidden in the zealously demythologizing energy of the Enlightenment, say Horkheimer and Adorno, lurks its opposite—mythic, primal fear of difference: "Enlightenment is mythic fear turned radical. . . . Nothing at all may remain outside, because the mere idea of outsideness is the very source of fear" (16). In sum, the Enlightenment is as "totalitarian as any system," for it defines nature as "that which is to be comprehended mathematically; even what cannot be made to agree, indissolubility and irrationality, is converted" (24).

As the exponent of "the most radical and consistent form of pragmatism," Dewey's enthusiasm for Bacon particularly incensed Horkheimer. What Dewey failed to understand was that science,

> like any existing creed . . . can be used to serve the most diabolical social forces. If Dewey means to say that scientific changes usually cause changes in the direction of a better social order, he misinterprets the interaction of economic, technical, political, and ideological forces. The death factories in Europe cast as much significant light on the relations between science and cultural progress as does the manufacture of stockings out of air. (*Eclipse* 75)

The implicit charge here is that pragmatism's difficulty in making qualitative distinctions is part of its deficient historical sense. According to Horkheimer, pragmatists "are liberal, tolerant, optimistic, and quite unable to deal with" the possibility that "truth might . . . turn out to be completely shocking to humanity at a given historical moment" (51).[19] But Horkheimer ignores (or was unaware of) the fact that in 1939 Dewey revised his "simple faith" in Enlightenment science, a faith he found "no longer possible to hold." In *Freedom and Culture* Dewey anticipates the Frankfurt School's concern with the destructive power of technology, particularly the "pseudo-individuality" produced by the mass media. At the mercy of the media's "power of organized propaganda," individuals are trained, says Dewey, to become "dependent on external stimuli" and develop an "appetite for the momentary 'thrills' " rather than for critical thinking (*Later Works* 13: 156, 94–97). The severity of the Frankfurt School's attack on pragmatism is not merely intemperate excess but a sign of a traumatic reaction to World War II. In the words of a recent historian, Horkheimer and Adorno viewed "modernity through the prism of Auschwitz. . . . [Their] clear intention was to suggest that Auschwitz presented the possible fate of the modern world as a whole. . . . Auschwitz was the Enlightenment's truth: reason as total domination" (Herf 234). What *Dialectic of Enlightenment* willfully neglects is the Enlightenment as a shaper of the tradition of political liberalism, democratic consensus, and public debate. Instead, the catastrophe of German modernity was equated with the entire Enlightenment. As Jeffrey Herf has remarked, "Germany did not suffer from too much reason, too much liberalism, too much Enlightenment, but rather from not enough of any of them" (234). Looking back on their book in 1969, Horkheimer and Adorno observed: "We would not now maintain without qualification every statement in the book: that would be irreconcilable with a theory which holds that the core of truth is historical, rather than an unchanging constant to be set against the movement of history" (*Dialectic* ix). The lopsided denunciation of pragmatism in *Eclipse of Reason* must also be judged in the bleak light of its historical moment, which encouraged the hysterical equation Dewey equals Bacon equals totalitarianism.[20] Recently Leo Lowenthal, the last surviving member of the Frankfurt School, has made a significant admission in saying that "the way in which we treated pragmatism . . . was simply superficial" (143).

This acknowledgment of misjudgment helped to initiate the recovery of affinities between pragmatism (both Deweyan and Jamesian) and Frankfurt Critical Theory that were all but obliterated in the war years. The process is beginning to occur. Writing of Horkheimer's dismissal of William James, David Marr remarks: "Philosophical combat sometimes involves antagonists who might have been intellectual allies under public circumstances different from those which have conditioned twentieth-century politics and thought" (93). This is a provocative remark, one that Marr does not really develop beyond mentioning that James and Horkheimer share a dislike of abstraction. Yet underscoring this dislike is a more important kinship: a shared rejection of identity logic's coercive use of concepts. This is easily overlooked, since Horkheimer accuses pragmatism of reducing concepts "to summaries . . . streamlined, labor-saving devices. It is as if thinking itself had been reduced to the level of industrial processes" (*Eclipse* 21). But he ignores how similar James's attack on "vicious intellectualism" is to his own. Indeed, James would have assented to much of the Frankfurt School's portrayal of the Enlightenment as accomplishing (in Max Weber's phrase) the "disenchantment of the world."

James's own critique of the arrogant determinisms of science and rationalism is congruent with the Frankfurt School's position. While advocating scientific method and inquiry, James scorned the pretensions of scientific knowledge. In a letter written in 1907 he complains: "Of all insufficient authorities as to the total nature of reality, give me the 'scientists' from Münsterberg" on down. "I know no narrower sect or club. . . . Their only authority at large is for *method*—and the pragmatic method enlarges and completes them there" (*Letters* 2: 270). James's pragmatic method, which insists on the tentativeness of knowledge, defends those (psychic researchers, for instance) marginalized by scientism's "professional conceit and bigotry," which is ruled by the ideal "of a closed and complete system" (*Will* 222).

James sought not only to recover particularity but also to encourage the individual's empathic receptivity, which would be open to the concrete. "By a stroke of intuitive sympathy with the thing," says James, we learn that "what really *exists* is not things made but things in the making," an emphasis recalling Emerson's definition of the scholar as man thinking, not man the thinker. Rather than insisting on an abstract, "closed-in system," the pluralist "only evokes and invites . . . so that we now join step with reality with a philosophical conscience never thoroughly set free before" (*Pluralistic* 117–18). The rejection of any system releases a noncoercive emphasis on process, sympathy, and tolerance. Vanquished is the guilt induced by traditional philosophy's disdain for "the detail of things" and the worship of "categories and their rules." Here is the fertile ground of reconciliation between the German and American projects.

IV

A half century after the death of William James (and twenty years after *Dialectic of Enlightenment*), Adorno began his philosophical summa, *Negative Dialectics*, with a salute to pragmatism and a near Jamesian denunciation of systematic philosophy and its attenuation of human affect. Like James, Adorno notes the great prestige of systems in the history of philosophy: "Compared with the systems, the opposition seems trivial. Systems elaborate things; they interpret the world while the others keep protesting that it can't be done. The others display resignation, denial, failure" (20). Adorno's targets are not only the idealistic systems of Hegel and Kant but the systematizing impulse itself, which he finds motivated by rage at difference, at what remains extraneous: "Great philosophy was accompanied by a paranoid zeal to tolerate nothing else . . . while the other kept retreating farther and farther from the pursuit. The slightest remnant of non-identity sufficed to deny an identity conceived as total" (22). Adorno characterizes this totalizing compulsion to extinguish what is not-I as a devouring hunger: "The system is belly turned mind, and rage is the mark of each and every idealism" (23). James's encounters with Münsterberg's trunk would have confirmed Adorno's point.[21]

Adorno seeks a means of rescuing for consideration that which systematic philosophy takes for granted: "The matters of true philosophical interest at this point in history are nonconceptuality, individuality, and particularity—things which, ever since Plato, used to be dismissed as transitory and insignificant." Philosophy's concern, says Adorno, should be precisely what it "downgrades as contingent, as a negligible quantity" (8). Clearly James and Adorno share a basic orientation: having dismantled system, both are (in James's words) "looking downwards and not up . . . in the very thick of experience," sympathetically gazing at details and abiding "with minutiae," says Adorno. "We are not to philosophize about concrete things . . . rather out of these things." Because of this "surrender to the specific object we are suspected of lacking an unequivocal position" (33). Refusing the definitive and embracing the equivocal, William James and Adorno both critique the identity principle and its fetishizing of concepts.

"To defend the irreducibility of non-conceptual material (of the real in its opacity) against the ravenous power of the concept" is what drives Adorno's project and also provides an apt summary of Jamesian pluralism (Tertulian 91). To challenge this power Adorno offers dialectical thinking, which "says no more, to begin with, than that objects do not go into their concepts without leaving a remainder, that they come to contradict the traditional norm of adequacy." Negative dialectic is the "consistent sense of nonidentity. . . . [It aims] to break the compulsion to achieve identity" (5, 157). But this aim demands allegiance to contradiction, for "the appearance of identity is inherent in thought itself. . . . To think is to identify. . . . We can see through the identity principle, but we cannot think without identifying" (5, 149). Rather than resolving this contradiction, Adorno dwells in it; a willed tension propels his thought.

Adorno's insistence on contradiction marks the beginning of his divergence not only from Jamesian pluralism but from any social theory (such as Dewey's) that posits integration as a social ideal. Adorno regards organicist ideologies of totality, harmony, or wholeness as perpetuating the identity principle. But he also perceives as "self-defeating" the "blunt prioritization of particularity, diversity, and non-identity," for it leads to worship of irrational flux, as evident in life philosophy (Dews, "Adorno" 42).[22]

Although he does not mention James, Adorno does discuss Bergson. While acknowledging that Bergson's pursuit of the nonconceptual inspires his own, Adorno finds that his disregard of contradiction vitiated his project. Speaking of Bergson's invention of "another type of cognition for nonconceptuality's sake"—his famous intuitive mode—Adorno regrets that "the dialectical salt was washed away in an undifferentiated tide of life; solidified reality was disposed of as subaltern." Thus Bergson, "the hater of the rigid general concept," established "a cult of irrational immediacy, of sovereign freedom in the midst of unfreedom" (*Negative* 8). Adorno's critique of Bergson is equally applicable to Jamesian pluralism. Like Bergson, William James's sense that his "philosophical conscience" had been "thoroughly set free" was purchased at the price of a disregard for social reality, with its contradictions and mystifications.

The self-defeating character of Bergson's and James's project is vividly illustrated here: their protest against identity logic reinstates it by positing a transparent world that James calls "self-luminous," without paradox. Because their project is founded on the repression of contradiction, their embrace of "sovereign freedom" is quickly paralyzed by contradiction. As Adorno writes, "Every cognition including Bergson's own needs the rationality he scorns. . . . Absolutized duration, pure becoming, the pure act— these would recoil in the same timelessness which Bergson chides in metaphysics since Plato and Aristotle. He did not mind that the thing he groped for, if it is not to remain a mirage, is visible solely with the equipment of cognition." Both James's and Bergson's attempt to break away from idealism linked them with their "positivistic arch-enemies" in a shared phenomenalism (9).

What is ironic about James's submission to the irrational is that he imagines it to be a great triumph. Reaching a height of rhetorical intensity near the end of his lecture on "The Continuity of Experience," he confesses to his audience: "As long as one continues *talking*, intellectualism remains in undisturbed possession of the field. The return to life can't come about by talking. It is an *act*; to make you return to life, I must set an example for your imitation, I must deafen you to talk. . . . I say no more. I must leave life to teach the lesson" (*Pluralistic* 131–32). Faced here with the contradiction of uttering the unutterable, James dramatically banishes it along with philosophical discourse itself. Rather than dwelling in contradiction and exploring its objective, historical roots, James instead repeats his inveterate move from the inaction of talking and thinking to the act of pure living, from wonder sickness to an illusory sense of "sovereign freedom" that is regressive in its return to a state of infantile simplicity and oneness.

Bergson's futile search for the nonconceptual will guide Adorno's own project, which draws strength from the antinomies his predecessor ignored:

> The plain contradictoriness of this [Bergsonian] challenge is that of philosophy itself. . . . Though doubtful as ever, a confidence that philosophy can make it after all—that the concept can transcend the concept . . . and thus reach the nonconceptual—is one of philosophy's inalienable features and part of the naivete that ails it. Otherwise it must capitulate, and the human mind with it. . . . The utopia of cognition would be the ability to unlock the nonconceptual domain with conceptual means—without reducing the one to the other. (*Negative* 9–10)

This ability is enacted in the construction of constellations (a mode of inquiry examined in the next chapter). Implicit in Adorno's aporetic logic here is the belief that "thinking is mediated by objectivity"—the subject must recognize the primacy of the object rather than attempt to dissolve it. The impulse to liquefy things inheres in the Marxist lament over reification. Implicitly challenging Lukács, Adorno declares: "The category of reification, which was inspired by the wishful image of unbroken subjective immediacy, no longer merits the key position accorded to it" (374). Adorno's materialism also clashes with Lukács's elevation of the proletariat as the subject/object of history. Such a position is rooted in the idealist "delusion that the transcendental subject is the Archimedean fixed point from which the world can be lifted out of its hinges" (181).

Indeed, *Negative Dialectics* draws its own initial impulse from the historical failure of Marxism to fulfill thesis eleven—the command that philosophy cease interpreting the world and begin changing it. With the collapse of Marxism in the catastrophe of Stalinism, and the Hegelian dream of attaining absolute spirit lost, what remains is critique from inside the system.[23] Rather than simply opposing mechanisms of oppression (like concepts or identity thinking), Adorno turns them against themselves, thereby cracking open and appropriating the latent power congealed in their objectifications. Thus he shows that immanent critique disrupts the compulsion to achieve identity not by rejecting identity but "by means of the energy stored up in that compulsion." Adorno's idiosyncratic—even posthumous—Marxism refuses to attribute contradiction to "faulty subjective thinking." Immanent critique shares the pragmatic urge to "unstiffen" theory (to borrow James's term) by moving from idealist abstraction to "facts and concreteness" (*Pragmatism* 38, 43). The trajectory of negative dialectics moves from a recognition that "the object of a mental experience is an antagonistic system in itself—antagonistic in reality" to the imperative that this "coercive state of reality, which idealism had projected into the region of the subject and the mind, must be retranslated from that region" (*Negative* 10). By insisting on the interaction of subject and object, Adorno hopes to remedy the deficiencies of *Lebensphilosophie*, which he believed went "too far in emphasizing subjectivity and inwardness" and thus "minimized the importance of action in the historical world" (Jay, *Dialectical* 51).

Adorno's retranslation, his emphasis on the objectivity of contradiction, is one way to socialize both William James's philosophical critique of identity logic and the subjectivism of his pluralism. When retranslated into the vocabulary of Critical Theory, James's philosophical sense of the "misuse of concepts," founded on one's "forgetting that concepts are only man-made," resembles reification in Adorno's sense of the word. Adorno calls reification a forgetting, and both his and James's logic recall Marx's description of commodity fetishism, where the objects of man's labor take on a life of their own (*Dialectic* 230). Another passage ripe for retranslation is James's Bergsonian demand to "turn your face towards sensation. . . . It violates our mental habits, being a kind of passive, receptive listening quite contrary to that effort to react noisily and verbally on everything, which is our usual intellectual pose" (*Pluralistic* 113). Adorno also revises reductive, predatory mental habits yet he does so without making receptive listening and conceptual precision an either/or alternative. He would be in full sympathy with James's suggestion here that nonconceptual experience involves a relaxation of control, a condition akin to the mimetic capacity. Indeed, Adorno says that Bergson's "intuitive mode of mental conduct" embodies "an archaic rudiment of mimetic reactions," for it involves "sympathy by which one places oneself within an object in order to coincide with what is unique in it and consequently inexpressible" (Bergson). Yet Bergson's sense of intuition remains abstract and proceeds "only desultorily" because it has "spurned rationality" (Adorno, *Negative* 8). To reinstate the mimetic as a mode of rational being in the world (and not just as a quality of artifacts) is one of the tasks Adorno shares with Henry James.

Adorno's retranslation transforms the Bergsonian/Jamesian recognition of the discrepancy between concept and reality into a tool of cultural analysis. For instance, Adorno regards freedom as a concept "that lags behind itself as soon as we apply it empirically. It is not what it says, then. But because it must always be also the concept of what it covers, it is to be confronted with what it covers. Such confrontation forces it to contradict itself" (151). The individual embodies another contradiction: he is "both more and less than his general definition." Thus individuality is best understood as "not yet" and therefore "bad wherever established. . . . Without exception men have yet to become themselves. By the concept of the self we should properly mean their potential, and this potential stands in polemical opposition to the reality of the self" (151, 278). Like Henry James's elected marginality, Adorno's sense of self is also perpetually provisional, dwelling in the margin of irreducible possibility, the "more to come."

To remain marginal, Adorno is careful neither to ignore nor dissolve the contradiction between the concept and reality of freedom and selfhood. To ignore contradiction is to be duped by it, as was Bergson (and William James) in proclaiming an illusory freedom. To attempt to resolve the contradiction in consciousness would only involve more concepts—"wretched cover concepts that will make the crucial differences vanish." Instead, one must realize that on one's own "one cannot eliminate the objective contradiction and its emanations." Instead of resolving them, "it is up to dialectical cognition to pursue the inadequacy of thought and thing, to experience it in the thing" (153). Microanalysis of cultural phenomena is the form this experience takes. It demands both intellectual and visceral responsiveness, founded on the fact that since man is ineluctably involved in the external world, there is no refuge from "concrete suffering as an embodied creature" (Dallmayr 65). One pursues a path toward the nonconceptual through bodily experience of the contradictory object. The "restless analyst" of *The American Scene* treads this path, which demands pragmatic fidelity to the contingencies of experience. "Our aim," declares Adorno, "is total self-relinquishment" (*Negative* 13). But if he were to achieve his aim, complete relinquishment would threaten to become the irrationality of a Jamesian or Bergsonian antiintellectualism. Thus Adorno must struggle against the very goal he sets for himself.

A willingness to remain in tension with one's goals characterizes the nearly utopian state Adorno names "reconciliation." It releases the nonidentical and is receptive "to the multiplicity of different things," which remain distant rather than assimilated by "philosophical imperialism" (6, 191). Yet, at the same time, different things are not fixed in static, atomistic isolation. Instead, their monadic crust is dissolved into the antihierarchical order of constellations, which generates a mimetic sense of relation to otherness. Mimetic or reconciling reason embodies a feeling of intimacy that also retains a sense of strangeness. In sum, Adorno conceives of reconciliation as resistance to stasis and harmony, to "the domination of what is always the same" (*Prisms* 92). In these terms he defines the form of hope embodied in negative dialectics as the pledge "not to come to rest in itself, as if it were total" (*Negative* 406).

V

Electing restlessness rather than rest accords with Adorno's belief that "philosophy can always go astray, which is the sole reason why it can go forward." He calls this antinomy a "ferment to an emphatic philosophy" akin to Dewey's "wholly humane version" of pragmatism (*Negative* 14). This acknowledgment of Dewey at the start of *Negative Dialectics* is a brief but pointed recognition of a predecessor in the effort to forego traditional philosophy's "quest for certainty" (in Dewey's famous phrase) and to reconceive of it as cultural inquiry, as an experimental "mode of conduct" that "shields no primacy, harbors no certainty" (34).

The Dewey whom Adorno finds congenial would not be the Dewey of *Individualism Old and New* but, more likely, of *Experience and Nature*. For this work recovers risk and vulnerability and begins with the claim that "philosophy is a critique of prejudices." What seems to be "fresh, naive" "life-experience" is "already overlaid and saturated" with interpretations and classifications—the "prejudices" of past generations (*Experience* 34). Philosophy's responsibility is to detect and "cast out" these prejudices: "Clarification and emancipation follow." This last phrase makes vivid the divergences in Adorno's and Dewey's critical trajectories. The unflappable optimism of the latter's trust in the efficacy of critique is matched by the pessimism of the former's skepticism that critique can have any efficacy. But these differences are less important than their shared reorientation of philosophy from metaphysics to critical practice, which historicizes modes of thought by exposing their naturalizing obfuscations.

As one of the most naturalized prejudices, subjectivism counts as a modern pathology that Dewey and Adorno are most concerned to examine. Because "it appears to be a datum, not an interpretative classification," subjectivism is misconceived as "eternal, original and absolute" (*Experience* 195, 185). This delusion, says Dewey, dooms the individual to a "blind solitariness" (198). "The subject's desperate self-exaltation," declares Adorno, "is its reaction to the experience of its impotence" (*Negative* 179–80). Liberal ideology "in practice has never yet endowed a subject with the unabridged autonomy accorded to it in theory. Hence the subject must feel guilty" (221). Both Dewey and Adorno stress that illusory omnipotence blinds us to the fact that "the trouble is with the conditions that condemn mankind to impotence and apathy and would yet be changeable by human action; it is not primarily with people and with the way conditions appear to people" (190). Adorno's eminently Deweyan statement focuses on conditions and action and serves as Adorno's pragmatist antidote to the idealizing tendencies of Marxist humanists. Their regressive lament over reification assumes that

consciousness is the problem and they yearn for a restoration of man's unalienated essence. In contrast, Adorno finds reification an "epiphenomenon."
Dewey and Adorno both reveal that traditional philosophy's bias toward
system suppresses the uncertain situation in which thought occurs. System
disguises the fact that "every existence is an event," and every act of thinking
involves "risks of waste, loss and error," according to Dewey. "No one can
guarantee where we shall come out." Because every thinker puts "some
portion of an apparently stable world in peril," thinking thus provides "the
ultimate evidence of genuine hazard, contingency, irregularity and indeter-
minateness in nature" (*Experience* 182, 60–61). In Dewey's opinion, the
indeterminacy of thinking and of experience are intimately aligned with
what he calls "the aesthetic function *in* knowledge" (qtd. Perry 2: 526).
Jamesian pragmatism's insufficient attention to the aesthetic—the "liberation
side" of pragmatism—is what Dewey (and implicitly Henry James) seeks to
rectify.

Adorno, too, makes the aesthetic inseparable from his effort to recover
the uncertain, refractory situation in which thought occurs. Thus Adorno
appeals to the pure materiality of music as an analogue: "Instead of reducing
philosophy to categories, one would in a sense have to compose it first." To
compose philosophy imbues it with the quality of an unstructured event or
act unfolding in the "sphere beyond control." Here "the open thought [has]
no protection against the risk of decline into randomness. . . . But the consistency of its performance, the density of its texture, helps the thought to
hit the mark" (*Negative* 35). To maintain tension, says Adorno, the "crux"
of philosophy must be "what happens in it, not a thesis or a position."[24]
The consequence is that philosophy, in essence, "is not expoundable. If it
were it would be superfluous; the fact that most of it can be expounded speaks
against it" (33–34). Adorno's commitment here to abandoning the quest for
certainty and his emphasis on event brings him close to William James's
imperative to cease talking and let life teach the lesson. Indeed, Adorno
expresses his desire to leave philosophy behind when he equates utopia with
"blind, somatic pleasure" (*Minima* 61). But he denies himself utopia for the
sake of utopia; such is the ascetic logic of his thinking, which is suspicious
of all closure.[25]

The value of risk and vulnerability constitutes the virtual premise of Adorno's aesthetic theory and the subject of his final book. "If aesthetics wants
to rise above empty chatter, it must expose itself, stepping out into the open
where there is no place to hide. This means aesthetics must give up that
sense of security which it had borrowed from the sciences. (Nobody realized
this more candidly than John Dewey)" (*Aesthetic* 484). Once again Adorno
seems inspired by Dewey's emphasis on contingency and hazard and by his
rejection, in the opening pages of *Art as Experience* (1934), of traditional
aesthetic theory's banishment of art to a "separate realm, where it is cut off
from that association with the materials and aims of every other form of
human effort" (3). Adorno's enlarging of the notion of mimesis beyond
artifacts to include behavior correlates with Dewey's demand that a "primary

task" of the aesthetician should be "to restore continuity between the refined and intensified forms of experience that are works of art and the everyday events, doings, and sufferings that are universally recognized to constitute experience" (*Art* 3). Adorno appears to diverge from Dewey in his situating of the mimetic in the archaic, instinctual reaches of the psyche—the inner "jungle" so feared by Dewey, Ross, and William James. As a return of what instrumental reason has mocked as useless, mimetic behavior represents "a receptacle for all that has been lopped off from and repressed in man by centuries of civilization" (*Aesthetic* 453).

But it is unfair to Dewey to suggest that he simply fears the "jungle" of noninstrumental impulse. There is another "moment" in Dewey that concurs with Adorno's valuation of the spontaneity alive in children. Dewey decries the "premature mechanization of impulsive activity after the fixed pattern of adult habits" and the "weight of adult custom," which encourages conformity while discouraging the child's "plasticity and originality" (*Human* 92–93). Adorno locates the "genesis of stupidity" in the "taboo" upon children's curiosity and questioning. The interdiction leaves scars: a "tiny area of insensitivity is apt to form at the spot where the urge was stifled. Such scars can lead to deformities. . . . And not only tabooed questioning but forbidden mimicry, forbidden tears, and forbidden rashness in play can leave such scars" (*Dialectic* 257). Adorno had encountered these scars in his study of the "authoritarian personality," whose intolerance of ambiguity contrasts with the open receptivity of mimetic behavior.[26]

For both Adorno and Dewey the behavior of unscarred, expressive, curious children offers an image of utopian community, a "promesse de bonheur" (the Frankfurt School phrase). Dewey finds in "the unformed activities of childhood and youth the possibilities of a better life for the community." We idealize childhood, for it "remains standing proof of a life wherein growth is normal not an anomaly, activity a delight not a task" (*Human* 94). In this world, says Adorno, where feeling and knowing are "not absolutely distinct," we glimpse behavior untouched by "the deadly dichotomization of emotion and thought." But this binary state, Adorno stresses, "is a historical result that can be undone," for it is a "distorted reflex" of the "division of labor" (*Aesthetic* 455). Yet its undoing, says Dewey, is not achieved by indulging in dreams of romantic freedom "in which *all* life is plastic to impulse, a continual source of improvised spontaneities and . . . [in which] we rebel against all organization" (*Human* 95). Only by "utilizing released impulse as an agent of steady reorganization of custom and institutions" can historical and social conditions of psychic division be modified (96). With this statement Dewey adroitly coordinates the aesthetic and the political; their interplay provides the basis for social and psychic change.

The release of impulses, whether found in mimetic behavior or children's play, defines art's purpose for Dewey. "Carelessness about useful occupations" describes part of this release, which Dewey sees as art's "indispensable moral function." Reading Adorno and Dewey together helps clarify their shared effort to make art a "spokesman for repressed nature" (Adorno, *Aes-*

thetic 348) and an agent that "releases energy in constructive forms" (Dewey, *Human* 153). In the final passage of *Art as Experience* (a book Horkheimer praised[27]) Dewey offers a utopian view of art fully in accord with the Frankfurt School perspective: "Art is a mode of prediction not found in charts and statistics, and it insinuates possibilities of human relations not to be found in rule and precept." Implicit in the skeptical Adorno and emphatic in the optimistic Dewey is the belief that the mimetic or uncoerced behavior found in children possesses a political and social potential to escape paralyzing dichotomies and glimpse "the possibilities of a better life for the community" (Dewey).

Adorno's adherence to possibility, to what he called residues or pledges of otherness "in the breaks that belie identity," should remind us of the inadequacy of the received wisdom that sees him as paralyzed by terminal despair. Instead, Adorno finds in the "sheer senselessness and blindness" of the course of the world precisely what "resists all attempts of a desperate consciousness to posit despair as an absolute." Rejecting Schopenhauer's absolutizing of despair, Adorno believes that "the world's course is not absolutely conclusive, nor is absolute despair; rather, despair is its conclusiveness" (*Negative* 404).

VI

The antidote to the despair of conclusiveness is the inconclusive, or what both Adorno and Henry James call the aesthetic. The surrender of security that Adorno urges upon aesthetics is everywhere the note sounded in James's prefaces. They are far from a record of difficulties avoided and problems solved, far from being the tranquil, magisterial summation from the Master of the novel as a formally perfected art form.[28] While it is true that James prizes a "deep-breathing economy and an organic form," organicism is not the essence of James's craft, as Percy Lubbock (and the generations of Jamesians he influenced) took it to be.[29] Rather, organic economy is an aesthetic ideal or potential perennially deferred and complicated by the conditions of artistic creation. Lubbock ignored that the "Angel, not to say . . . the Demon of Compromise" presides over the prefaces and is also the source of their master theme: the unbridgeable gap between original intentions and actual accomplishment (*Art* 298). Such a fissure engenders the energies of art while leaving it permanently open to the possibility of failure. This chronic insecurity demands the tentative stance that Peirce called fallibilism—the belief that every conceptual organization of experience is in principle potentially revisable. According to Adorno, not only have "perfect works of art rarely ever existed," but "the fact that no artist knows for sure if his work will amount to something" testifies to art's "exposed quality" (*Aesthetic* 485).

The hazards of exposure pervade James's aesthetics. He speaks of artistic creation in terms of "crisis" and "torment," arousing "terror" and "fear" as the writer perpetually improvises the imperfect "substitution" to replace his "original design" (*Art* 3–6, 297). Artistic creation viewed as a risky adventure is a conspicuous metaphor in the prefaces, which narrate what James calls "the thrilling ups and downs, the intricate ins and outs of the compositional problem" (319). James describes at least four of his greatest novels as "efforts so redolent of good intentions baffled by a treacherous vehicle, an expertness too retarded" (344). Since "inevitable deviation (from too fond an original vision)" abides in it, the aesthetic is a force at odds with the totalizing impulses of mastery, harmony, and unity (325). These impulses are neither central to James's craft nor irrelevant but rather in an incessant process of being challenged and refashioned in the "simmering cauldron" of artistic imagination.

James's aesthetic validates Adorno's claim that "dissonance is the truth about harmony." Noting the "antiharmonistic postures" of Michelangelo, Rembrandt, and Beethoven, Adorno finds their original allegiance to harmony supplanted by a recognition of its insufficiency: "Harmony is unattainable, given the strict criteria of what harmony is supposed to be. These criteria are met only when the aspect of unattainability is incorporated into the essence of art," as occurs in the mature style of the most eminent artists (*Aesthetic* 161). James's discovery of "treachery" in the straightest, most mature intentions incorporates this negative affirmation of harmony. Michelangelo is the "greatest of artists," says James, especially "considering how his imagination embarrassed and charmed and bewildered him." *Moses*, the sculptor's supreme achievement, is "so far from perfection, so finite, so full of errors, so broadly a target for criticism as it sits there." James finds its very imperfections a source of "vigor." Michelangelo's "willingness to let it stand" testifies to its "life, health, and movement" (*Letters* 1: 181). Far from being an apostle of organic form and formal unity, James defers "the ideal of perfection that all works of art must hanker after" (*Aesthetic* 80).

James would concur with Adorno that "crisis" (a word they both use) "is as old as the concept of art itself. The possibility and the greatness of art depend on how art handles this antinomy. Art cannot live up to its concept" (*Aesthetic* 80). Judged on Adorno's terms, James's handling of art's antinomic character—what the novelist calls its "cruel crisis"—is exemplary (*Art* 6). For instead of repressing or resolving the crisis of art's inherent nonidentity, James comes to regard it as an "eternal torment of interest" that generates the "variable process" of "doing" (8–9). For instance, James locates the "power" of the novel "as a literary form" in its ability "to appear more true to its character in proportion as it strains, or tends to burst, with a latent extravagance, its mould" (46). The responsible artist must not evade this refractory dynamism and the tense and tentative process of representation it demands. To take refuge in "conveniences" and "simplifications" cripples representation, arrests "art's law of motion" (*Aesthetic* 81). Rather than regretting this condition of crisis, James finds it a source of fun. "It all comes back to that," he says near the end of his last preface, "to my and your 'fun'—if we but allow the term its full extension." The full extension of fun involves acquiring the "confidence" to accept being caught in the "beautifully tangled" web of the artistic process.

The prefaces, like James's other major late works, are spectacles of exposure and curiosity that find pleasure ("fun") in releasing impulses and forsaking comforts of control. The Jamesian spectacle resonates, in short, with echoes of the mimetic world of childhood as conceived by Dewey and Adorno. But true to the logic of immanent critique, neither Adorno nor James portrays mimesis as a privileged term or essence. Analogous to the function of James's term "margin"—a concept by which he points to the nonconceptual, the fluid "more" that eludes the concept's grasp—mimesis is a protean and enigmatic concept that seeks to undermine the fixity of concepts. It thus resists any theorizing about itself. Hence Adorno imbues it with an "always-already" appearance, as Fredric Jameson remarks of the irreducibly "peculiar" status of mimesis. This "indispensable and indefinable" impulse is an ungrounded "foundational concept never defined nor argued but always alluded to, by name, as though it had preexisted" (*Late* 104, 238, 64).

The evasiveness built into mimesis and margin encourages Adorno and James to resist embedding them in the romantic and modernist mythology of art as an island of mimetic freedom, of pure margin, amid capitalist disenchantment. Instead, Adorno (explicitly) and James (implicitly) argue that art is at once a "refuge" for prerational, spontaneous, mimetic (or marginal) behavior and "also shares in rationality." Adorno refuses to make art an enclave of defiant (and socially impotent) irrationality, protesting an instrumental social reality. Using Max Weber's phrase, Adorno describes art as part of the disenchantment of the world and "inextricably entwined with rationalization." Art is a product of rationality—the constructing and imposing of a form—in dialectical interplay with mimesis: the expression of "nonconceptual affinity" with otherness. The irreconcilability of mimesis and rationality, insists Adorno, is precisely what "helps formulate art's law of motion; this dilemma must not be done away with. . . . It is literally because no art work can succeed that the powers of art are set free" (*Aesthetic* 81).[30]

Analogously, the rarity of Jamesian curiosity resides in its elusiveness, being neither purely theoretical nor solely instrumental. Instead, mimesis and curiosity survive in the modern world not as beacons of purity but as antinomic structures: "Aesthetic behavior is neither mimesis pure and simple nor the repression of mimesis" but rather a "process set in motion by mimesis, a process also in which mimesis itself survives through adaptation." This behavior involves the subjective capacity to have experience of the other by "assimilating itself to that other rather than trying to subdue it" (*Aesthetic* 455). Rather than a utopian alternative to reason, mimesis is an "ends-oriented reason" that simultaneously is "objectively practical because it forms and educates consciousness" (345). As the next chapter will show, mimetic reason builds constellations rather than categories and systems.

The reading of Adorno sketched in the preceding paragraphs runs counter to the influential critique of his former student, Jürgen Habermas. He depicts an Adorno possessed of a kind of heroic self-destruction who "surrendered to an uninhibited scepticism regarding reason," finding it irreparably infected by instrumentality and identity logic (*Discourse* 129). Adorno therefore deliberately refrains from giving mimesis conceptual content, preferring to keep it "the sheer opposite of reason, as impulse" (*Theory* 386). The consequence is that Adorno can "at most . . . circle around the idea" of mimesis and locate it solely in avant-garde works of modernism. But, says Habermas, he is unable or unwilling to integrate mimesis in an intersubjective social context or use it as a basis for social theory. Frozen in an "aporetic situation," with "no way out," Adorno must surrender to those who will undo his antinomies and dissolve his dialectics (*Discourse* 128). Such is the scenario of succession Habermas devises for himself and others of the second-generation Frankfurt School.[31]

Adorno's (alleged) aporia, which inspires Habermas, is analogous to the miscarriage of Marxism that produced *Negative Dialectics*. Habermas launches his theory of communicative action in the space of mimetic reconciliation—uncoerced intersubjectivity—that Adorno can (allegedly) evoke but not inhabit. In short, Habermas implicitly portrays Adorno as a romantic irrationalist, akin to a Bergson or a William James, who stubbornly pursues the nonconceptual at the cost of social critique. Adorno has reached an impasse endemic to a "paradigm of the philosophy of consciousness," of subject-centered reason. The solution is to switch to a "paradigm of linguistic philosophy—namely that of intersubjective understanding or communication" (*Theory* 390).[32] This change will unlock the rational content of Adorno's mimesis and, claims Habermas, reveal that there is "already a mimetic moment in everyday practices of communication and not merely in art." As a predecessor in this crucial paradigm shift, Habermas acknowledges George Herbert Mead as the first to conceive of the self not as substance but as an intersubjective process rooted in mimetic capacities of role-playing and empathic projection. For Mead imitation is neither a utopian nor aesthetic ideal; it is part of the self's ontology.

This Frankfurt embrace of pragmatism, embodied in Habermas's turn to Mead, is particularly resonant in the present context, which has sought to portray Adorno as the ally and not the antagonist of pragmatism in its post-Jamesian, Deweyan phase. But to follow Habermas's lead and oppose Adorno to Mead would blind us to the resemblances in their conceptions of self. Both Mead and Adorno not only insist on the pivotal importance of mimesis but share an emphasis on the self's nonidentity. Because Mead conceives of the self as already socialized and mediated, he portrays the "I" not as a solitary, transcendental ego but as one of two phases in a differential process that constitutes the self. The "Me" is the normative, communal moment of the self; it operates "in a certain sense [like] a censor," says Mead. The "I" gives "the sense of freedom, of initiative," and is "never entirely calculable" but "always something different from what the situation itself calls for" (*Mind* 210, 177–78). Although it is a source of novelty and indeterminacy, Mead's "I" is not unmediated. Instead, it is "the *immediate* phase of *mediation* rather than something outside or prior to the mediation process." To believe in an a priori, unmediated "I" merely upholds "the fiction of modern individualism" (Rochberg 38). The "I" and "Me" are perennially out of synch yet dependent on each other: "It is impossible for the knowing I to be congruent with the known I" (Joas 109). Thus, in Mead's view we are never fully aware of what we are, since we exist in a kind of perpetual disequilibrium of internal division.

Like his close friend Dewey, Mead carefully distanced himself from William James's individualism and found Bergson's vitalism symptomatic of the modern cult of subjectivism, which disdains conceptual analysis per se and worships spontaneous intuition. In words he might have applied to William James, Mead concluded that "Bergson's flight to irrationalism is unnecessary" (*Movements* 507).[33] Thus, there are ample grounds to resist Habermas's creative misprision of Adorno and to enlarge our frame of reference to include Mead in the company of Dewey and Adorno as representatives of the effort to socialize the Jamesian/Bergsonian abandonment of identity logic. All three demonstrate that the self's mimetic capacities express enlarged modes of rational behavior and "that individuation is possible only by way of socialization" (Habermas, *Theory* 391).

Henry James, Mead's contemporary, also starts from this premise: "Experience, as I see it, is our apprehension and our measure of what happens to us as social creatures" (*Art* 65). Thus the Jamesian self is perpetually negotiating an identity out of its interaction with various others. James's engagement with nonidentity is as fertile as Adorno's and contrasts with William James's less nuanced critique of identity logic, which dissolves in the flux of nature. Henry shares his brother's insight into how the refractory quality of experience is devoured by intellectual constructs, which impose a factitious order. Henry would also agree with William's claim that "when we conceptualize we cut out and fix and exclude everything but what we have fixed. A concept means *a that-and-no-other*." Believing that "only concepts are self-identical," William locates all dynamism in nature: "Nature is but a name for excess; every point in her opens out and runs into the more." But Henry refuses simply to exchange concept for flux and to embark on a futile quest for fluency and transparency—what William calls "reality's true shape" (*Pluralistic* 113, 129). Instead of exchanging culture for nature, Henry reclaims nature's excess, its "more," for culture. Rather than abandoning the concept, he invests it with the density and sensuous complexity that is otherwise reserved for nonconceptual experience. Thus Henry achieves what he calls "the thicker fusion," which William imagined to be solely nature's preserve (*Art* 207).

Although William James grants that we can "apprehend reality's thickness," evoking "it in imagination by sympathetically divining someone else's inner life," he insists that if we are really "curious about the inner nature of reality . . . we must turn our backs upon our winged concepts altogether, and bury ourselves in the thickness of those passing moments" (*Pluralistic* 112). Henry, however, neither limits himself to imaginative projection nor momentary burial. Instead he chooses a more difficult alternative, one that uses the material medium of language to represent the inner life's thickness.

"We want it clear," Henry says of representation, "but we also want it thick, and we get the thickness in the human consciousness that entertains and records, that amplifies and interprets it" (*Art* 256). What produces this texture are the "rash multiplications of the candid consciousness," which breed "impressions [that] could mutually conflict—which was exactly the interest of them" (213). He stylistically registers thickness by setting language in motion, creating a ferment of suggestiveness and indeterminacy. In their inevitably overdetermined acts of self-representation, James's characters embody unbridled multiplicity, which tends to burst the monadic shell of identity to which they are consigned by a culture of self-reliance. Rejecting an "economy of the self-possessed and masterful self," James "represents experience in uneconomical terms . . . that exceed the bounds of determination and resist the reductions of meaning necessary to masterful plots and masterful selves."[34] The refusal of mastery incites excess, making overflow a condition of the Jamesian self. That the self spills over into a multitude of "expressive things" and is known only through its mediations and representations is the substance of the lesson that Madame Merle seeks to impart to her young friend, the (at that time) oblivious Emersonian Isabel. Madame Merle's disclosure of spillage clashes with the deepest American cultural biases, a discordancy James builds into his "ado about Isabel Archer" by having the villain articulate the unsettling implications of his materialist vision of the fluid self.

Henry James is never more pragmatic than when he equates aesthetic experience with deviation, excess, and contingency. Acknowledging the "shifting and uneven character of the tracks" of his "original passage," he admits that he "couldn't at all, in general, forecast these chances and changes and proportions; they could show for what they were as they went . . . all of which means, obviously, that the whole thing was a *living* affair" (*Art* 342). James makes revision a genuinely "living affair" by practicing nonidentity thinking. Unlike commonsense habits or traditional thinking but like pragmatic fallibilism, this cognition "does not demand a frame of reference in which all things have their place" and "unframed thoughts are kept out." Instead, says Adorno, a "dialectics no longer 'glued' to identity" creates vertigo and the "shock of inconclusiveness" (*Negative* 31–33). This turbulence occurs when we experience the concept differentially, as "inwardly in motion . . . no longer purely itself; in Hegel's terminology it leads to its otherness without absorbing that otherness. It is defined by that which is outside it, because on its own it does not exhaust itself. As itself it is not itself alone" (157).

The experience of nonidentity, of gropingly discovering that the self is not itself alone but defined by what is outside it, describes the ordeal, for instance, of Isabel Archer, Lambert Strether, and Maggie Verver—and of Henry James himself, restlessly traversing his native land in 1904. These fictive and actual selves are in the process of revising the structure of repression that constitutes (in Adorno's phrase) the "anal deformations" of their bourgeois subjectivity. Henry James and his characters appropriate the en-

ergy congealed in the repressive will toward identity, unburdening themselves of its ascetic discipline and transgressing Enlightenment rationalism's
taboo against mimesis and vagrant curiosity. In part 2 we will discover what
cultural criticism, autobiography, and fiction look like when created by a
self no longer glued to identity but mimetically receptive to the vertiginous
texture of modernity.

II
THE CHALLENGE
OF MODERNITY

6

"Adventures of the Critical Spirit": Rereading *The American Scene*

One of the pleasures of *The American Scene* is witnessing James improvising the rhythms of his vagrant motions as he drifts, untethered. This willed vulnerability to contingency is founded on his devotion to what Wright Morris once called a unique "*presentness*" of perspective, "free from visions of the future and crippling commitments to the past" (214). Yet James's "presentness" is a result less of rigorous concentration than of its opposite—his willingness to digress from the present subject for a "desultory stroll, for speculation's sake" (*Scene* 183). For instance, after spending a few hours in Central Park enjoying the "polyglot" crowd, with their "variety of accents," James feels he has been given "exactly what [he] desired—a simplified attention and the power to rest for the time" in the sense that the aliens "were flourishing . . . in contentment" (182). Yet relaxing attention itself proves fertile: "It was by way of not worrying" that he finds, "chanced upon at a subsequent hour, all sorts of interesting and harmonious suggestions. These adventures of the critical spirit were such mere mild walks and talks as I almost blush to offer, on this reduced scale, as matter of history" (182). And James is off on another "train of association" of "boundless evocation." What he call his "*flânerie*" is true to the word's French meaning of a stroll without destination.

In sum, James's ability to remain anchored in the shifting present lies in his willingness to be distracted. Walter Benjamin found a gift for distraction fertile for breeding mimetic responsiveness, a capacity that makes the "sharp distinction" between doing and feeling "unreal" (James, *Art* 65). James enacts this blurring of distinctions when he fuses (as in the quotation cited earlier) the "critical spirit" with walking and talking, and strolling with speculating. The contemplative, critical James and the mobile, immersed James converge in the "restless analyst," whose feeling and doing interpen-

141

etrate, making him nearly as polyglot as the "mingled medium" he walks in (*Scene* 177). Divesting himself of the dichotomizing habits of an idealist culture, James practices a cultivated naivete. The quoted passage, with its pauses, accidents, and adventures offered as history on a reduced scale, suggests some of the texture of urban flânerie found in both James and Benjamin. Their shared practice of a peripatetic cultural analysis will be a major concern of this chapter.

Like Benjamin's attitude, James's open, mimetic stance embodies an alternative to what has been called "the modernist Cartesian pathology of autonomous subjectivism or autonomous objectivism," both of which breed tendencies of resentment and subjugation of otherness (Rochberg 62). Mimetic behavior thus represents what Adorno calls a "third possibility" beyond the idealist inflation of the subject or its positivistic reduction (*Negative* 166). In tracing James's mimetic responses, we will see that he comes close to achieving Benjamin's "intentionless state of being," which mimes its original object in a new modality called, variously, "exact fantasy" and "constellation." Rather than subsuming the object, James imitates it, thus crystallizing and preserving its otherness. In short, his perennial restlessness and distraction are not merely subjective but mimetic gestures, expressive responses linked to the qualities of the environment that elicit them.[1] James's decentered perambulations mimic some of the latent "heterogeneous, miscellaneous" qualities of 1904 America itself, with its "instinctive refusal to be brought to book," its "incoherence and volatility" of mood and "boundless incapacity for attention" of a sustained kind (*Scene* 171).

Given his assault on the dualisms of the "Cartesian pathology" and his embodiment of a "third" mode of being that eludes the categories and values by which American liberal individualism makes sense of experience, it was inevitable that James would create a problem for his contemporaries. This is not to say, of course, that the indeterminacy he creates is understood in the above terms. Rather, the term critics use to describe his mimetic receptivity is curiosity. To best appreciate his urban immersions and their resemblance to those of Benjamin, we will first look at how James's contemporaries responded to his rare curiosity.

I

By 1904 James was not only an anomaly to the reading public, but they also found him full of inordinate, even disquieting, curiosity about America. This theme surfaced in the wake of his American visit, as James's repatriation occasioned several extensive evaluations of his career. Curiosity as a leitmotif is central in the two most important critical retrospectives, those by H. G. Dwight (1907) and W. C. Brownell (1905). Both represent early attempts to place James in an American cultural context and, even more important, to recognize James as a troubling presence. "While readers expressed . . . the most varied degrees of bewilderment, exasperation, or ridicule, the most frequent point of agreement was that of uncertainty as to what, after all, to

make of Henry James" (qtd. Gard 439). Thus Dwight summarizes what he
calls "the flood of remark" called forth by James's return. Unlike many later
critics, James's contemporaries frankly confessed their unease rather than
defensively displacing it into an attack on his alleged gentility. Indeed, a
cause of James's unpopularity among his contemporaries is his ungenteel
excess of curiosity, a conclusion that both Dwight and Brownell reach.

The value of Dwight's essay is that he links the public's uncertainty about
James both to familiar sources—the "strangeness" of his style "for eyes
accustomed to the telegraphic brevity of the newspaper"—and to less obvious
cultural anxieties that James arouses. Not only does the novelist address an
American "public without leisure and a people . . . the least sensitive to the
movements of the inner life." There is also, says Dwight, "an unmannerly
levity about him, as of him who should go into great company whistling,
with his hands in his pockets. We relish the grand air better, and a proper
sense of one's responsibilities. . . . He does not obviously give you, as Mr.
Brownell puts it, a 'synthetic view of life seen from a certain centralizing
point of view' " (444). Instead of the grand air of a central synthesis, James
gives us an "endless chain of suggested improprieties . . . a tissue of hideous,
nameless complications," in the words of a scandalized reviewer of the then
recently published novel *The Golden Bowl* (435).

According to Brownell, curiosity diverts James from a morally responsible
synthesis. His work is "an unfolding, a laying bare, but not a putting together.
The imagination to which it is due is too tinctured with curiosity to be truly
constructive. . . . His curiosity is not merely impartial, but excessive" (411,
418). Comparing the novelist to the great French anatomist Cuvier "lecturing
on a single bone and reconstructing the entire skeleton from it," Brownell
finds James "a Cuvier absorbed in the fascinations of the single bone itself"
and thus perversely indifferent to the responsibility of reconstructing the
whole (397). The causes of James's uncertain cultural status begin to suggest
themselves. "He will not fit into any of our comfortable old pigeon holes"
(Dwight 444) because he seems to combine disparate, even antithetical,
identities: a "scientific aspect" and curiosity (Brownell) that simultaneously
mocks and unravels its authority by adopting a certain "levity" that refuses
both a "grand air" and, more important, the major responsibility of cultural
authority—to conclude, to reconstruct, to synthesize.

The result of James's visit, said Dwight, was to exacerbate the novelist's
"disagreeable effect" on the public—the "resentment he seems so curiously
capable of arousing" (447, 444). *The American Scene* perhaps revived memories
of his original expatriation, James's most notorious, arrogant refusal of synthesis and centrality. Dwight finds the public judgment of 1907 harsh and
unmerited, symptomatic of the "national jealousy" that James's stylistic
opacity and personal exile arouses. But the jealousy is understandable:
"Nothing could be more natural than such a feeling. . . . It is always inspired
by those who worship other gods than ours, who act from motives to which
we do not hold the clue" (447). Doubtless to most readers the motives that
guided James's unseemly interest in ghetto life remained unfathomable. And

this attention to one of the "less flattering points of the picture" of America offended "our passionate national sensitiveness" was how Dwight described the impact of *The American Scene* as a whole.

Indeed, this work seems to incorporate all the discordancies and perversities in James's long career. As summarized by Dwight, they include "the novelty of his subjects, the strangeness of his style, the minuteness of his analysis, the lightness with which he goes about serious things, the curiosity he displays toward things which it is our Anglo-Saxon instinct to avoid" (447). Taken as a whole, James's bewildering idiosyncrasies amount to a transgression of Anglo-Saxon propriety. Dwight seems on the verge of rendering an improbable yet warranted verdict—that the power of James's curiosity resides in its vulgarity. James's "unmannerly levity" and insouciance, Dwight goes on to declare, combined with his "undermining of the public morals" as a result of the "*succès de scandale*" of *The Golden Bowl*, makes him "as truly and typically American" as Whitman (448, 435). But this Whitmanesque James is the same person who (as Dwight had earlier reported) is routinely and "notoriously" dubbed "a woman's writer; no man was able to read him" (438).

Brownell emphasizes yet another paradox: a James whose passion for "cold-blooded" "scientific curiosity" and "cultivated indifference" has made him "ferociously egoistic . . . [and] ardently frigid" (418). Brownell's James moves from the self-effacement of objectivism to the self-importance of subjectivism. In Dwight's survey of public response, James is equally contradictory: genteel and precious in his "high-minded" appeal to a desiccated "parlor audience" of the "ultra-intellectual," yet provocatively modern and audacious in his unrestrained curiosity about adulterous sexuality and urban immigrants (438). Effeminate and genteel, scandalous and strenuous, James embodies an impenetrable "uncertainty," a word that strains to contain all the unsettling contradictions Dwight's essay discloses. In registering the unresolved tensions that make James a cultural problem, a strange hybrid, both Brownell and Dwight provide a valuable counter to the leveling of contradiction found in the congealed "aura" of Henry James the aesthetic idealist. This latter portrayal can be eerie in its sterility, as we saw in F. O. Matthiessen's depiction of James. Missing from Matthiessen's image of an impoverished James and from the "incomprehensible" James of Brownell is a sense of the fertility of James's curiosity.

In contrast, Dwight acutely grasps Jamesian curiosity as a source of power that aroused resentment and clashed with Anglo-Saxon conventions, a clash registered in Brownell's response to James. What makes this critic uneasy is that James seems under the sway of his disordered faculty of curiosity, which has prevented him from yielding "to the temptation to give the public what it wanted." The result is that James has elected to be an "original writer" while sacrificing being "a great one" (426). Brownell's judgment reflects his queasiness about a writer whom he would doubtless have loved to champion wholeheartedly, and whose New York Edition he supervised as a chief editor at Scribner's. Brownell has been described as one of the "gatekeepers for the Brownstone culture of New York." While politically liberal and opposed to the antidemocratic elitism of an E. L. Godkin, Brownell was culturally conservative, a dedicated Arnoldian upholding the responsibility of a cultured minority to maintain the highest standards (Bender 208). Modernist art and literature of the early twentieth century distressed him. In its rage for experiment it shared James's "lack of some unifying philosophy," which preferred originality to greatness. The title of his 1917 antimodernist diatribe laconically declared what the new age lacked: *Standards.*

With his concern for standards, it is highly unlikely that Brownell would have shared James's enthusiasm, in 1898, for "conditions hitherto almost unobserved"—the rise of a "huge American public" seeking "literature for the billion [which] will not be literature as we have hitherto known it at its best" (*Literary* 1: 652). What would have alarmed Brownell is precisely what excites James: the indeterminacy and fluidity of this "unique situation," prompting a redefinition of literature's identity, standards, and its public. Benjamin might describe the situation as the decline of auratic art (the unique artifact for an elite audience), which is concomitant with "the increasing significance of the masses in contemporary life" (*Illuminations* 223).[2] "The coming billion," declares James, "hang before us a wide picture of the opportunities, . . . presenting to the critic some of the strain and stress— those of suspense, of life, movement, change . . . that the critic likes most to encounter." The prospect of a situation where "more people than ever before buy and sell, and read and write, and run about . . . in the great common-schooled and newspapered democracy" presents, in James's view, "a delicious rest from the oppressive *a priori*" (*Literary* 1: 651–52).

James is not being vaguely fanciful in his use of this phrase. The "oppressive *a priori*" he delights in keeping at bay is summed up in Brownell's terse title. The particular standards James has in mind are those of the New England intellectual mandarinate, which reigned until their recent "breaking up" into a "huge American public." No longer is "New England, quite predominantly, almost exclusively, the literary voice, and dealing with little else than material supplied by herself" (654). Rather, James has a sharp sense of "how the Puritan culture both used and exhausted its opportunity" and is "a past already left long behind." Everywhere in modern life and letters James hears the "note of the difference" between the "combinations and proportions" of "the American world of today" and that of Emerson's time. Exhilarated by this difference, James sees the themes of modern life "yearning for their interpreter." He finds two subjects especially suggestive: the American businessman as "the epic hero" and the "special situation of women in an order of things where to be a woman at all . . . constitutes in itself a social position" (655). "Vast indeed is the variety of interest and curiosity" pervading the American scene.

James's enthusiasm for the indeterminate, open-ended quality of the present moment is particularly striking in the context of the patrician orthodoxy's disgust with modern cosmopolitan democratic culture. Some genteel intellectuals suavely disguise this disgust in "an absolute ease of mind about one's point of view, a thorough and never-failing intellectual wholeness," to borrow James's description of his consummately serene friend Charles Eliot Norton (*American* 124). Foregoing the genteel intellectual's "cramped posture" of smug aesthetic serenity for a "restless" curiosity that savors the bewilderment of "strain and stress," James seems closer to the younger generation of self-conscious modernists who declared "the futility of the Arnoldian ideal." These are the words of Randolph Bourne, a central figure in the revolt against the genteel tradition and a thinker with whom James shares genuine affinities. James's ardent cosmopolitanism was one reason Bourne admired him.[3] In his famous argument for a "trans-national America," Bourne refused to accept Anglo-Saxon hegemony (the "Anglo-Saxon was merely the first immigrant"), welcomed the multiplication of differences, and attacked an ideology of assimilation eager to have immigrants "melted down into the indistinguishable dough of Anglo-Saxonism" (*Will* 261).[4]

A less obvious and more significant point of convergence between Bourne and James is their effort to modify the force of the Puritan strain in the American character. Bourne hopes to ease the repressiveness of self-control and encourage a receptive, empathic subject modeled on the dynamism and energy of the "modern city" (148). This project can be correlated with the attitude of James and Bourne toward the alien: both men value variety and regard the subjugating power of the identity principle as a threat. Like James, Bourne wishes to tap sources of intelligence beyond abstract rationality without surrendering to irrationality. In good Deweyan fashion, the experimental is his mediating or third term: "In place, then, of the rational or the irrational life, we preach the experimental life" to contest "the rational ideal" (158). This ideal "has made directly for inflexibility of character, a deadening conservatism that is unable to adapt itself to situations, or make allowance for the changes and ironies of life" (157). A key term for Bourne, irony is a component of the "experimental life" and the ironist is the kind of urban intellectual he envisions.

Bourne describes the ironist as having "lost his egotism completely. He has rubbed out the line that separates his personality from the rest of the world. . . . He lives in a world of relations, and he must have a whole store of things to be related" (147–48). This view of the modern intellectual as weightless and permeable strikingly recalls the decentered self of the "restless analyst." As a student of Dewey, whom he would incisively critique in 1917, Bourne came to represent the kind of post–(William) Jamesian pragmatist whose response to modernity was, like Henry James's and Benjamin's, immanent, antisubjectivist, and materialist.[5] The premise behind the ensuing rereading of *The American Scene* is that James's text has more in common with Bourne's and Benjamin's early twentieth-century urban modernism than with the genteel lamentations of the late-Victorian cultural elite. Far from startling, this premise simply recovers the precanonical Henry James with whom his contemporaries grappled but later, more "sophisticated" readers ignored—the figure of baffling heterogeneity embodied in exorbitant curiosity.

II

James's admission, in the preface to *The American Scene*, that he is "incapable of information"—the stuff of "reports and statistics"—has a touch of the "unmannerly levity" that provoked his contemporaries and incited critics. It is the kind of statement pounced upon by those eager to dismiss him as an aesthete in solipsistic pursuit of mere impressions. Perhaps H. G. Wells first initiated this reading in his own report on his travels in America, *The Future in America*, which appeared the year before James's work. As Peter Conrad has stated, "Wells, after reading *The American Scene* [in installments], noted that James had novelistically confined himself to 'life and manners' and the evaluation of an 'ineffectual civilization.' The innuendo is that James has wished his own ineffectualness on America, decoratively describing the social fancies not the social and economic substance of the country" (133). A more recent James critic, after endorsing Conrad's view of Wells on James, finds the latter deliberately advertising a "tactic of evasion," a "disavowal of the actualities of history and power . . . in order to repress what is truly scandalous about his text . . . an underlying unity and discreet continuity" between art and power (Seltzer 103, 109).

The Wellsian and neo-Wellsian accounts together posit a frightened James evading history, politics, and science and embracing "social fancies" as a way of "disowning the shame of power" (Seltzer 139). Two alleged textual "smoking guns" help inspire this thesis: James's remark about his "artful evasion of the actual" and his confession of being "incapable" of information (*Scene* 87). Yet a closer look at the contexts of both remarks will provide a clear challenge to this image of a befuddled and ashamed James and will point the way to an alternate reading.

In the New York streets James pauses after having just been "shaken" by the sight of a procession of immigrants being processed at Ellis Island. He reflects on the occasional "excursions of memory . . . which ministered, at happy moments, to an artful evasion of the actual. There was no escape from the ubiquitous alien into the future, or even into the present; there was an escape but into the past" (*Scene* 87). But the escape is no sooner made than it is undermined. First, the past is but "absolutely comparative," for "it is all recent history enough, by the measure of the whole." What is more, it is full of "flaws and defacements" that ominously loom even as James wanders around his boyhood neighborhood near Washington Square. There he enjoys "felicities of the backward reach, which, however, had also its melancholy checks and snubs" (91). The sharpest snub occurs when James finds his place of birth "ruthlessly suppressed." "The effect for me," says a startled James, "was of having been amputated of half my history." The abrupt alienation not only ruptures James's "artful evasion of the actual" but also implicitly joins him with the very figure he sought relief from— "the ubiquitous alien."

The point of James's effort to escape is to demonstrate the impossibility of evasion rather than to oppose the actual to the aesthetic.[6] In revisiting

Washington Square, evasion becomes its opposite as James realizes that the "affirmed claim of the alien" is "not to be dodged." Indeed, he is at pains to specify that "we, not they, must make the surrender and accept the orientation" of the alien's right to share the "American consciousness."[7] Grandson of an immigrant, James, like all Americans, is flawed and defaced, haunted by a double "dispossession" inflicted not only by "extremely recent ... migrations" but also by "commercial democracy's" ceaseless rhythm of destruction and rebuilding. The tumult of urban life makes the "perpetually provisional" the oxymoronic condition of modernity (*Scene* 408).

If "evasion" turns out to be illusory, another mode of confronting New York is embodied in James's other alleged evasion—of "information"—which taps an even deeper (if not immediately apparent) source of engagement in urban life. "It should unfailingly be proved against me that my opportunity had found me incapable of information, incapable alike of receiving and of imparting it; for then, and then only, would it be clearly enough attested that I *had* cared and understood." To reduce the meaning of this admittedly puzzling statement to a confession of "ineffectualness" ignores the dialectical reversal James performs here. In suggesting that his incompetence at receiving and imparting information will be the very measure of his caring and understanding, James implies that there is a distinction between types of cognition: one founded on abstract, quantifiable conceptualization (information) and another based on the nonconceptual and concrete, which he associates with "representation" and which we have dubbed mimetic.

James calls abstract reason "ciphering," which he equates with the journalist's task of adding up "items and objects, signs and tokens" into a "careful sum" suitable for "warrants and documents." In 1904 journalists were busy muckraking, an activity based on fact collecting, a "home-grown utilitarian movement" founded on the authority of scientific expertise. Progressivism's rage for fact-finding commissions and bureaus of municipal research sought to impose "the hard, determinate verdict of social science" (Rodgers, *Contested* 188). This is not the verdict that the "restless analyst" seeks. Unlike the journalist, who "is nowhere, ever, without his items" of inert information, James lets his impressions fix themselves "by a wild logic" of their own, "subject to no definite chemical test, no mathematical proof whatever" (*Scene* 307–9). What his "wild logic" produces is "simply a bold drawn image"— a representation that eludes test and proof because it renders "the latent vividness of things" (307). This vividness attaches to "properties of the social air" so numerous and subtle that "newspapers, reports, surveys" are "powerless to 'handle' " them ("Preface"). But James can represent what escapes fact-clogged newspapers and "prodigious reports and statistics"—the "obstinate, the unconverted residuum" of particularity rapidly being swallowed by the "assimilative organism" of American democracy (124). What has nurtured his keen eye for "latent vividness," he declares, is a lifetime of concern "with the human subject, with the appreciation of life itself, and with the consequent question of literary representation" ("Preface"). Implicitly, then, James identifies representation as the preserve of discriminating care, sympathetic understanding and complexity. Thus, from the opening pages of *The American Scene* representation is dissociated from a specific ideology—the authority of utilitarian, abstract reason (embodied in the journalist's gathering of information) in a world dedicated to the Enlightenment ideal of progress.

America elicits from Wells the scientific socialist a hymn to "material progress." He defines it as the "constant substitution of larger, cleaner, more efficient possibilities, and more and more wholesale and far-sighted methods of organization for the dark, confused, untidy individualistic expedients of the Victorian time" (86). Wells's dichotomies tempt us to join him in placing James in the Victorian darkness of Luddite reaction and nostalgia. Because of James's need to perform the "whole revolution" and entertain all possibilities, he confronts the option of evading modernity. But we have seen that he discovers the emptiness of both evasion and its opposite—unquestioned trust in "methods of organization." Instead, James begins to adumbrate a third position, one that neither regresses to Victorian individualism nor embraces the fervent optimism of Wells's march of progress. One advantage of James's stance is that it permits inquiry (rather than mere celebration) into modernity's organizational imperative, what he calls America's "genius for organization." A triumph of *The American Scene* is James's prescient analysis of how modern bureaucratic power works, how the "hotel spirit" and "the thousand forms of this ubiquitous American force" make and impose their law (106). Discussion of the "amazing hotel world" will be reserved for chapter 10. Here I am concerned with examining James's method of cultural analysis in order to demonstrate how he fashions a representational technique far more complex and strategic than the typical judgment of impressionism or aestheticism suggests.

James's mode of representation is inseparable from his third position, which I previously defined as that of the immanent urban intellectual. Rather than promulgating the perspective of a particular party or class of "ideal interests solely," Henry James partly anticipates Bourne's plea that intellectuals practice more nuanced kinds of agency. In 1917 Bourne urges a "heightened energy" of hesitation, tentativeness, experiment, a willingness to "roam widely and ceaselessly" and avoid "premature crystallization" so as to keep "the intellectual waters constantly in motion" (317). In hoping to prevent "ice" from forming, Bourne here adumbrates a politics of nonidentity that echoes James's avoidance of the polarities of genteel nostalgia and liberal progressivism's cult of efficiency. We will see that in place of overt statement James's representational method embodies his mobile cultural critique.[8]

III

A decade after James, another inveterate walker in the city, Walter Benjamin, also began to devise a method of representation to resist the flood of information. As the paradigmatic source of information, newspapers encourage solitary experience and thus help erode a community of listeners nourished by narratives "passed on from mouth to mouth" in storytelling (*Illuminations* 84, 87). Benjamin announces in "The Storyteller" that "experience has fallen in value" as the "spirit of storytelling" fades and the "dissemination of information" flourishes. Transparent, "understandable in itself," requiring no interpretation, information's value "does not survive the moment in which it was new. It lives only at that moment" (89–90). It is correlative with speed, efficiency, and instrumentality. These modern values stand opposed to what Benjamin describes as the optimum stance for listening—"a state of relaxation which is becoming rarer and rarer" (91). To cite Benjamin's famous remark, "Boredom is the dream bird that hatches the egg of experience." Whereas the recipient of information, poised for action, ingests it as quickly as possible, the listener, relaxed to the point of boredom, takes the time to open himself up to external stimulation. But the pace of modern life makes relaxation hazardous. With its strangers, crowds, collisions, and traffic, urban experience is one of shock, as Benjamin would stress in his seminal (and less nostalgic) essay "On Some Motifs in Baudelaire."

Influenced by Georg Simmel, his predecessor in urban phenomenology, Benjamin here emphasizes the need for the city dweller to nurture "the protective eye," a vigilance of attention that, according to Simmel, camouflages itself in a blasé pose. A mask of indifference hides the fact that urban conditions have decisively attenuated one's capacity to relax and surrender— except in those willing to lower their defenses and risk shock. Baudelaire is exemplary in this regard. He "made it his business to parry the shocks, no matter where they might come from, with his spiritual and physical self" (163). Traumatophilia, the psychoanalytic term Benjamin uses to describe Baudelaire's trafficking in shock, depends on a forfeiture of efficiency; the more efficiently consciousness is "alert as a screen against stimuli . . . the less do these impressions enter experience" (163). Analogously, "the perpetual readiness of volitional, discursive memory . . . reduces the scope for the play of the imagination" (186).[9] Benjamin's implicit lesson is that the urban critic suspicious of the ideology of information and desiring to risk shock must find an alternative to the conventional instruments of authority—the discursive, the efficient, and the volitional. Benjamin embodies this alternative in his method of critical practice whose keynote is "representation as digression."

In the prologue to his first work, a study of German tragic drama conceived in 1916 and written in 1924, Benjamin delineates his position. He begins by seeking to correct the rationalist prejudice of traditional philosophy, which privileges system and abstraction. Benjamin stresses that the philosopher shares with the artist "the task of representation. There has been a tendency to place the philosopher too close to the scientist" (*Origin* 32). Benjamin urges adherence to philosophy as the "representation of truth and not as a guide to the acquisition of knowledge," which is the province of science and mathematics. Philosophy's model should be the treatise, which dispenses with the "coercive proof of mathematics" for the method of representation.

"Method is a digression. Representation as digression—such is the methodological nature of the treatise. The absence of an uninterrupted purposeful structure is its primary characteristic. Tirelessly the process of thinking makes new beginnings, returning in a roundabout way to its original object. This continual pausing for breath is the mode most proper to the process of contemplation" (28). The "irregular," dissonant rhythms of the urban flâneur are not hard to detect here, nor is the parallel with Henry James, whose image of representation as a "widening circle" demands that experience "pause from time to time . . . to measure . . . as many steps taken and obstacles mastered . . . as possible" (*Art* 3).

Benjamin might well have been encouraged by the opening move of James's cultural critique—his pointed refusal of information and embrace of representation. In another context—the first page of his first preface—James equated representation and digression as he imagined "the practice" of "representation" as "spreading in a widening, not in a narrowing circle" causing "experience" to "fear . . . losing its way" (*Art* 5). The transgressive energy of the practice of representation engenders the anxious need to measure and survey. Yet these needs are at best only temporarily satisfied because they are continually aroused by "the too-defiant scale of numerosity and quantity" embodied in both the "canvas of life" and in America's uncontrollable "will to grow" (*Scene* 121, 54). Throughout his prefaces and *The American Scene* James counsels acceptance of the limited, precarious powers of a cultural analyst or novelist to order experience. For both James and Benjamin, relaxing the will to dominate and surrendering to the accidents of digression constitute the mode of being and representation that allows the "latent vividness" of urban experience to flower. Hence both men practice "the art of being off center" (*Illuminations* 176).[10]

Indeed, the meandering peregrinations of the flâneur provide the model for Benjamin's release of philosophy from the tyranny of system and concept. "Systematic completeness" fails to encompass what digression uncovers: the "irreducible multiplicity" of urban life, where meaning resides in the peripheral and the aleatory. From this mingled texture Benjamin derives the critical form he calls constellation—the representation of "fragments of thought" by "immersion in the most minute details of subject matter" (*Origin* 34, 29). As the expression of nonidentity thinking, constellation uses concepts nonconceptually, that is, without giving the illusion of exhausting the thing conceived. Since human communication cannot dispense with concepts, they must be retained—but in a mediating role that provides the linguistic bridge between phenomena and representation (34). Because they are neither coercive concepts nor laws, constellations are without the instrumentality of knowledge. When "concepts enter into a constellation," says Adorno, they survive without delivering themselves "to abstraction as a supreme principle . . . because there is no step-by-step progression from the concepts to a more general cover concept. . . . The constellation illuminates the specific side of the object, the side which to a classifying procedure is either a matter of indifference or a burden" (*Negative* 162). In short, the constellation releases what Henry James had also sought—objects' "mystic meaning proper to themselves to give out." Comprised of what slips through the "conventional conceptual net," the constellation preserves the "residuum" deemed by the dominant ideology too marginal to be worthy of attention.

But the question of who constructs and selects constellations requires further exploration. To assume the presence of an originating subject is problematic because Benjamin and Adorno strongly reacted against the reduction of knowledge to subjective appropriation, which they equated with a Nietzschean will to power. As a corrective, constellations demand a delicate balance whereby the subject immerses itself in the particularity of the preexisting object (to avoid idealism) without extinguishing its own creative imagination (to avoid positivism). Adorno calls this tense interplay "exact fantasy"—"a dialectical concept which acknowledged the mutual mediation of subject and object without allowing either to get the upper hand" (Buck-Morss, *Origin* 86). Adorno describes exact fantasy as both active and passive, artistic and scientific; the subject's fantasy "rearranges" and transforms a "pre-given reality," yet it "abides strictly within the material which the sciences present to it, and reaches beyond them only in the smallest aspects of their arrangement" ("Actuality" 131). The subject, in effect, is a mediator (as in Dewey) who both mimics and modifies a preexisting text in the manner of a translator or conductor.

Henry James enacts a mediating role in presenting his own version of exact fantasy. At various times in his text he gives inanimate objects a voice. Rather than merely ingesting them into his consciousness, James heightens the palpability of their presence, their otherness, by his exuberant mimicry, which contrives conversations with buildings, streets, and commodities. His revision of constitutive subjectivity is also evident in his conception of representation. Like Benjamin, James equates it with unharnessed movement, whose source of control—an agent practicing representation—is disconcertingly absent. For Benjamin truth is not a function of an originating subject but rather "an intentionless state of being" (*Origin* 36). Analogously, Jamesian representation also seems intentionless, a whirlpool of energy that resists possession. He suggests this in his initial effort to define representation, which occurs in his first preface: "The art of representation bristles with questions the very terms of which are difficult to apply and to appreciate; but whatever makes it arduous makes it, for our refreshment, infinite, causes the practice of it, with experience, to spread round" (*Art* 3). "It" is bristling, infinite, arduous, and spreading, James tells us, but he leaves unnamed "whatever makes it" so. By occluding a source of intention, and by representing representation as if it is a locus of turbulent motion from which *derives* an anxious subject seeking to harness its power, James implies that the human subject is inferential.

James thereby avoids a subject–object dualism, a strategy that resembles pragmatic contextualism, in particular Dewey's careful exclusion of direct references to a subject when he defines inquiry as the "transformation of an indeterminate situation" (qtd. McDermott 227). By ignoring the personal mental states of individual inquirers, Dewey emphasizes the inherently un-settled nature of the situation and rejects what he calls the "spectator" view of classical (Cartesian) epistemology (Thayer 172, 442). In refusing to root inquiry in a doubting or anxious subject, Dewey, like Henry James, defines the individual as inseparable from the hazards of ongoing practice and its propensity for spreading in a widening circle. This view avoids the dualisms of monadic individualism.[11]

The *American Scene* repeatedly stresses the subject's contextual rather than originating status. James must accept that America's "too-defiant" growth makes "the impossibility ... of conclusions" a fact that prevents his impo-sition of definitive order and meaning (121). All James can do is consent to be "led on and on," fashioning a "reduced" history derived from evocations sparked by the "immediate crudity of what 'happens' " (182). An absence of complete control is also the "very essence of the novelist's process," which involves one being "unduly tempted and led on by 'developments' " (*Art* 4). "*The will to grow* was everywhere written large" in America, a motto that can also serve representation. Such dynamism renders the effort to order always belated and flawed. "Yet even here I fall short" is James's repeated refrain about his effort in *The American Scene* to represent "much too nu-merous" impressions. Loss of control inheres in James's worship of the "religion of doing," for he who is "always doing ... can scarce, by his own measure, ever have done." James's point is how easily "the religion of doing" gives way to the infinity of doing. The impossiblity of ending doing forces upon us the fact that "our noted behaviour ... perpetually escapes our con-trol" (*Art* 348). But the ineradicable indeterminacy of experience and be-havior, which makes substitution and compromise unavoidable, is also ameliorative. Thus James's "accepted vision" of America's "too-defiant scale of numerosity" is a fact he "can rest in at last, as an absolute luxury, con-verting it ... into *the* constant substitute for many luxuries that are absent" (*Scene* 121).

The luxury of being without "immediate need of conclusions" about America permits James to leave open the question of what defines the "Amer-ican character." What meaning, asks James, "can continue to attach to such a term as the 'American' character?—what type, as the result of such a ... hotch-potch of racial ingredients, is to be conceived as shaping itself?" (121). James's questions insist on honoring the dynamic reality of American hetero-geneity that is muffled by that fabled ideological instrument of pseudounity, the "American character," so dear to the identity logic of progressivism. His refusal of conclusions in favor of "the liberty of waiting to see" is neither a perverse whim nor proof of his incompetence at providing information (122). Rather, it enacts James's critique of the ideology of information. In rejecting conclusions he rejects all they imply—definitive, categorical judgment—the synthetic act of authoritative knowledge.[12] In place of conclusions, as we shall see, he devises "chains of relation."

Abandoning mastery and information, immersed in materiality, James finds himself strangely exhilarated: "He [the restless analyst] doesn't *know*, he can't *say*, before the facts. . . . The facts themselves loom, before the understanding, in too large a mass for a mere mouthful: it is as if the syllables were too numerous to make a legible word" (121). Here James appears so choked with facts—with sensory, empirical data rather than abstract information—that cognitive processes of understanding, knowing, and saying are overwhelmed. Thus he speaks of his "observation" at times "quickened well-nigh to madness . . . by every face and every accent that meets your eyes and ears" (120). So bewildering is American ethnic multiplicity that cognitive, conceptualizing powers are less effective than eyes and ears in establishing intimacy with the "American spectacle" and hearing its "Babel of tongues" hum (118). James likens the effect of the spectacle to opening a million "contingent doors and windows" (121). This openness invites not the evasions of conclusions but the entering into of sensuous contingency, the living of questions, not the answering of them.

Entering and living require "cultivated naivete of eye, ear, and thought." Dewey's project of cultural inquiry intersects with those of James and Benjamin. The latter had remarked that since truth is an intentionless state, "the proper approach to it" is "total immersion and absorption" (*Origin* 36). Immersion encourages a relaxation of the ego's defenses, an openness to otherness, a stance that James calls "the surrendered consciousness" (*Scene* 116). Surrender is part of "the process of shedding." James's phrase, which explicitly refers to immigrant assimilation, is equally pertinent as a description of his own project of vulnerability. His shedding of distance and a priori assumptions encourages the intimacy required for conveying "the sense and taste" of a "situation," as he noted in the preface to *The Princess Casamassima*.

A precedent for James's surrender to urban experience is found in the Roman peregrinations of William Wetmore Story, which formed the basis of the sculptor's popular guidebook to the city, *Roba di Roma* (1863). Unlike Story's pompous sculpture, his Roman book fills James with enthusiasm, for in it Story at last found the perfect vehicle for his "restless . . . curiosity," his "flexibility of attention" (James, *Story* 2: 170, 215). Rereading the volume in the course of writing his biography of Story, published the year before his American visit, James remembers "perfectly" his "consuming envy" at Story's "impregnation with the subject" (2: 131). Contributing to this intimacy are Story's uninhibited "rambles" over "roba," which in his preface he calls "everything—from rubbish and riff-raff to the most exquisite products of art and nature." Accordingly, *Roba di Roma* begins with Story's rhapsodic description of Roman dirt: "Its very dirt has a charm which the neatness of no other place ever had" (5). He devotes his longest chapter to the Jewish ghetto, a site that genteel guidebooks like Murray barely mentioned. After his first reading of *Roba di Roma* in the 1870s, James despaired that he could ever achieve Story's decidedly ungenteel "impregnation" with his "multitudinous subject," which embraces "practices, processes, states of feeling, no less than objects, treasures, relics, ruins" (2: 131). But a year after his reperusal of Story's book, James attempts his own American version of Story's urban ramblings up and down, high and low, over the "many things which wise and serious travellers have passed by as unworthy of their notice"(*Roba* 6). Possessed of some of Story's restless drive and curious eye for detail, James also has what Story's artistry usually lacked—the power of concentrated "insistence" (*Story* 2: 216). Insistence produces intimacy, the quality essential for creating "the logic of intensity" that animates vivid representation. This mimetic logic transforms feeling into a kind of doing and thereby imperils "simplification"—the propensity for sharply distinguishing "parts of any adventure" (*Art* 65–66). With its undoing of rigid separations, the "logic of intensity" is not confined to Jamesian aesthetic technique but also presides over his New York adventures.

IV

Shedding or surrendering describes James's strategy and becomes a subject in its own right for the restless analyst, especially as he walks the streets of New York, the city that "*most* plays into the surrendered consciousness." James frankly avows that he is susceptible to the allure of New York: "I like indeed to think of my relation to New York as . . . almost inexpressibly intimate" (*Scene* 117). And this feeling of intimacy breeds impressions filled with a sharp sense of "continuity . . . free from hard transitions." Thus it is not surprising that his return to the city where much of his youth was spent prompts several remarkable recognitions of resemblance as the mimetic faculty of childhood revives.

The subject of surrender or immersion first preoccupies James because of his recognition of the "equality of condition" created by the aliens "being at home . . . at the end of their few weeks or months. . . . and that *he* [James] was at home too, quite with the same intensity" (125). For the immigrant to be already "at home" in New York has required a rapid "process of shedding" of ethnic qualities which James likens to the washing out of color by the "immersion" of "bright-hued stuff" into a "tub of hot water." He not only regrets the washing out of the color of foreign identity but also the fact that the "water of the tub . . . more or less agreeably dyed with" the original brightness has not "rubbed off on . . . surrounding persons" (129). "Fellow-soakers in the terrible tank" seem immune to taking on "tint[s]" of alien color, but not James. Having recognized his "equality of condition" with the alien, he sees himself as one "fellow-soaker" citizen who is not immune. Rather, James proceeds to mimic his alien counterparts: their immersion prompts his own act of surrender, which is how he visualizes his "fascination in the study of the innumerable ways" in which the alien is at home in New York. The city "offers to such a study a well-nigh unlimited field," and James can hardly resist plunging in: "I seem to recall winter days, harsh, dusky, sloshy, winter afternoons, in the densely packed East-side street-cars, as an especially intimate surrender to it [his study of the alien]. . . . It took on that last disinterestedness which consists of one's getting away from one's subject by plunging into it, for sweet truth's sake, still deeper" (126). The dialectical logic of this passage is characteristic of James's need to perform the "whole revolution." Getting away by plunging in encapsulates James's "relation to his subject" throughout his travels. For James, as for Benjamin and Adorno, truth requires the subject's yielding to the alien object. Yet James's act of objective surrender not only mimics but also opposes the aliens' surrender, for his immersion seeks to preserve the color that they seek to shed.

But is not James's disappointment in the fading of alien color as much an aestheticizing of the immigrant as it is sympathetic surrender? In judging the alien by his own desire for heterogeneous objects, James seems nearly to blur the precarious line between identification and appropriation. Yet, in another turn of the dialectical screw, he corrects himself by recognizing the alien as subject—one who necessarily presents himself "to be plain" as a crucial "step in the evolution of the oncoming citizen." As an incipient citizen, the immigrant has reached "the stage of his no longer being for you—for any complacency of the romantic, or even verily of the fraternizing, sense in you—the foreigner of the quality . . . that he might have been *chez lui*" (127). Here James acknowledges that the alien must be honored as alien, as other, unassimilable to one's own needs. This is not to say that James dismisses as merely complacent nostalgia his protest on behalf of foreign color; indeed, resisting American homogeneity is part of what he feels constitutes responsible citizenship. With typical capaciousness, James seeks to respect various conflicting conceptions of citizenship—the alien's, his own, and even the official American one—for "in the happiest cases" the converted alien has acquired an American identity of "all apparent confidence and consistency" (129). The tension of these contending interests is above all what he seeks to represent.

Given James's devotion to heterogeneity, it is apt that the disinterested surrender that defines his dialectical stance is not an a priori first principle. Rather, he slowly gropes toward it on his "aimless strolls" in New York when he converses with the streets and the air. These exchanges permit him a "pausing for breath," in Benjamin's phrase, that renews his energy for intense scrutiny. During one such pause James examines his lingering defensiveness, his sense of critical detachment from much that he confronts. As he walks the streets, having just emerged from the "endless labyrinth of the Waldorf-Astoria," James ponders why the "vociferous and clamorous" city of monstrous skyscrapers can exert any charm at all and even manage "to let so much of its ugliness edge away unscathed from his analysis" (108). The "restless analyst" is beginning to recognize his compromised position: while professing to wield his analytical scalpel with aloof severity, he can't resist the pleasures of roaming around New York. He imagines the "voice" of the New York "air" challenging his pretensions to detached critique: "It's all very well to 'criticize,' but you distinctly take an interest and are the victim of your interest. . . . You can't escape from it, and don't you see that this, precisely, is what *makes* an adventure" (108). This rebuke jars James into recognizing that analytical detachment comprises only one part of his "relation to his subject." His "getting away" is inseparable from his plunging deeper; only interest can generate disinterestedness. Thus, the very act of walking in New York already testifies to his immersion. James makes his understanding explicit: "I defy even a master of morbid observation to perambulate New York unless he be interested . . . interest must be taken as a final fact" (110).[13] What he recognizes here, in effect, is that critique can only be an additive, not an immediate relation to a subject, to borrow Dewey's distinction (*Experience* 261). Before critique is possible, there is already a subject situated, immersed, interested, "weaving itself out of the flux of experience rather than out of eternal values," as Bourne remarks of urban consciousnes (*Will* 147). James captures this sense of the self's embeddedness, with its attendant risks and hazards, when he calls himself a "victim of [his] interest." By making interest a "final fact," James anchors critique to its social context and historical moment.

"You can't escape" becomes his watchword in New York and in the New York Edition. In his prefaces James insists that the artist "can never be responsible *enough*" and must seek the point of view that will give him "most instead of least to answer for" (*Art* 328). He locates this point in the "formidable foreground" where "the pressure of the present and the immediate" are most intense (*Scene* 130). New York strikes James as "all formidable foreground" because the "intensity of the material picture" leaves no space for the analyst to step back and speculate. When he finds speculation "irresistibly forced" upon him, James apologizes for indulging the impulse and describes it as irresponsible, mere "intellectual dalliance" (130). For speculation regarding "ultimate syntheses, ultimate combinations and possibilities" relies on "distance," which reduces experience to the mental and insulates the body from the bristling assault of "signs and sounds" (131).

James's stress on the primacy of interest as the basis of critique and his ban on theory resonate beyond *The American Scene* because they challenge genteel humanism's defining gesture. Inherited from Schiller's German idealism by way of Matthew Arnold, this tradition designated the aesthetic as a realm of freedom divorced from personal motives, affiliation, practice, and the turbulent arena of clashing interests found in the marketplace. This transcendent aesthetic space was the residence of culture.[14] Among its guardians were such masters of "morbid observation" as Henry Adams and E. L. Godkin. These two mainstays of the genteel tradition are relevant here for their striking divergence from James's dialectical response to modernity. Even a brief look at Godkin is enough to suggest the essential shallowness of the received opinion that classifies James as a distinguished representative of the cosmopolitan elite of self-styled "best men."[15]

It would be difficult to conceive of Godkin and Adams strolling through the turn-of-the-century streets of New York, viewing the swarms of immigrants with rapt attention. For both men lacked James's "interest" and his willingness to be its "victim." Instead, these antimodern modernists had "withdrawn from the city under the cover of culture" (Bender 194). This culture took them far away: Adams contemplated the medieval cult of the Virgin; Godkin, in his last book, absorbed himself in the prospects of Australian democracy. In different ways Adams and Godkin had withdrawn from what they felt to be the "unmitigated blackness" of modernity, to cite James's famous characterization of Adams's mood in 1915 (*Letters* 4: 705). The reasons for their disgust were everywhere. Like many members of their class, Adams and Godkin were fearful and contemptuous of the immigrant and the "dangerous classes" in general. Indeed, one historian has described the genteel elite as "overwhelmed by phantasmal fears" that undermined "their broad and tolerant view of human affairs" (Sproat 242). As a founder and editor of *The Nation* (where both Henry and William were first given an opportunity to publish) for over thirty years, Godkin's "purpose was not the extension of democracy but rather its purification" (Bender 183). *The Nation* stood with Harvard and Yale, said Charles Eliot Norton, "as almost the only solid barriers against the invasion of modern barbarism and vulgarity" (qtd. Bender 183).

A few years before his visit to America, Henry James reviewed Godkin's final work, *Unforeseen Tendencies of Democracy*, finding it impoverished and bitter. But since Godkin was an old friend, James's judgment is delicately rendered. He describes Godkin's conception of the political as lacking in "reference to the social conditions." This narrowness is a "pity," since "at so many points" these conditions—"whether for contradiction, confirmation, attenuation, or aggravation—[are] but another aspect of the political" (*Literary* 1: 690). Under the apparent blandness of James's remark is his acute implication that Godkin has fashioned an ahistorical, formalistic social theory that conveniently filters out the messy fact that "contradiction" and "aggravation" define contemporary "social conditions," where the "dangerous classes" agitate for equality in the land of equality. Godkin's work "becomes suggestive," says James, "in proportion as we read into it" what Godkin leaves out—the "interweavings" of political, social, and cultural phenomena. Because it insists on these "interweavings," which never leave the "social question too much in abeyance," *The American Scene* should be read as a response to Godkin, repairing his deficiencies and delving into subjects and places that most of the gentry class viewed with repugnance. By the time of James's 1904 visit, Godkin had been dead two years. But James's 1898 review was already an obituary for his old friend—and for the genteel worldview, from whose "grim despair" James dissents (690).

Closer to James's stance is a perspective, which he describes in his review of Godkin, "which both takes the democratic era unreservedly for granted and yet declines to take for granted that it has shown the whole ... of its hand." From this viewpoint, James finds the era "exciting" in "its inexorability and its great scale." He evokes these qualities in a suggestive image: "If ... we are imprisoned in it, the prison is probably so vast that we need not even meditate plans of escape" (690). The vast prison suggests the Jamesian dialectic of freedom and its opposite, an interplay absent in an analogous image—Emerson's prison metaphor: "I

do not wish to remove from my present prison to a prison a little larger.
I wish to break all prisons." Emerson's defiance makes James's view seem
decidedly passive. But the difference is less between passive and active
than a social critique that is idealist in its wish for radical transcendence
and a critique pragmatic and immanent in its insistence on the contextual.
Emerson might be described here as speaking "the language of false
escape," to borrow Adorno's phrase. Like James, Adorno is skeptical of
liberation from the "open-air prison which the world is becoming" (*Prisms*
31, 34). But this is not to suggest that their vision of society as a prison
is identical. The amount of global violence in the fifty years separating
the statements makes it utterly impossible for Adorno's prison to approx-
imate James's, and vice versa. Yet we can interpret their shared equation
of society and prison as a metaphor for the "irreducible reality" of external
constraint, of history as the realm of necessity. The consequence of this
irreducibility, according to Adorno, is that "thinking [must] prove itself
only dialectically, in historical concreteness" embodied in the arrangement
of constellations of seemingly trivial details ("Actuality" 132). In "inexpressibly intimate" New York, rife with links and affinities, with "fusion
. . . always going on," James is most stimulated to discover and arrange
constellations, to which we now turn (*Scene* 116).

"For the restless analyst, there is no such thing as an unrelated fact, no
such thing as a break in the chain of relations" (312). But James must pay
a "penalty" for his acute sense of relatedness, which gathers all impressions
together into what he calls a "total image" (422). Receiving "too many
impressions of too many things" makes inevitable the "anguish" of selection
and omission. In short, the "chain of relations" is constructed only after a
violent process of exclusion. The "total image" upon which multiple impressions hang together must be shattered in a process "like mutilation," for the
"history of any given impression" resides "often largely in others that have
led to it or accompanied it" (422). Rather than discontinuity and incoherence,
destruction of the totality of gathered impressions produces looser, less rigid
and coercive kinds of coherence and continuity.[16]

In New York James never ceases weaving his "chain," given the fact
that there "almost any odd stroll, or waste half-hour, or other promiscuous
passage" leaves one "tangled" in an excess of impressions (108). From
such chance encounters he lets representation take the impress of "roundabout" rhythms (200). The result of this relaxing of control is a skewing
of scale and harmony that amuses rather than distresses the Master of
artistic symmetry and formal perfection: "Wherever I turned . . . wherever
any aspect seemed to put forth a freshness, there I found myself saying that
this aspect was one's strongest impression. It is impossible . . . not to be
amused at the great immediate differences of scene and occasion that could
produce such a judgment" (194). His abandonment of hierarchy for a paratactic amplitude of "odd sharp notes" formally enacts James's judgment that
America's single-minded pursuit of "pecuniary gain" has suppressed heterogeneity, the "precious bitter-sweet of a sense of proportion" (428). Rather

than replicating a "raw" sterility, his own text will mime disequilibrium to reanimate a dynamic sense of proportion. Benjamin also focuses on apparently peripheral and marginalized details to avoid "the sort of forced contiguities and continuities prevalent in traditional history writing" (Jennings 50–51). Both he and James are committed to rendering microhistory, or what the latter calls the "roundabout processes of peaceful history, the very history that succeeds for our edification, in *not* consisting of battles and blood and tears" (*Scene* 200).[17]

James proclaims his commitment to empiricism when he notes his preference not for perspectives "that may be followed, more or less, at a distance" but for those that grant "revelations . . . only on the spot." To discover the way in which democratic institutions "determine and qualify manners, feelings, communications, modes of contact and conceptions of life" requires intimate scrutiny (55). James's sociological lens reveals some striking patterns of interplay between forms of representation, particularly architectural and social. In detecting these unsuspected continuities, he fashions various chains of relations encompassing different social classes and phenomena.

One of these chains encompasses bourgeois manners and modes. Gazing up at newly erected New York skyscrapers, James finds these "towers of glass" less aesthetic objects than shrines to the "economic idea." Because their raison d'être is "to bring in money," "window upon window" are crowded together, destroying any possibility of architectural "grace": "If quiet interspaces, always half the architectural battle, exist no more in such a structural scheme than quiet tones, blest-breathing spaces, occur, for the most part, in New York conversation, so the reason is, demonstrably, that the building can't afford them. (It is by very much the same law, one supposes, that New York conversation cannot afford stops)" (95). What James reveals here is capitalism's "genius for organization" imprinting its norm of efficiency upon disparate modes of representation—the conversations of New Yorkers and the city's skyscrapers. This pattern is articulated in several directions. For instance, James also finds loss of "interspaces" in styles of American interior design that merge "all functions" and thus discourage intimacy by eliminating "the room character" indispensable to conversation (167). James records a similar loss of "margin" when he looks at the facades of New Jersey villas, which project "the expensive as a power by itself . . . exerting itself in a void." One reason the mansions exude an impression of sterility is their lack of a "minimum of vagueness," of "mystery" and "saving complexity . . . as might be represented by a foot of garden wall or . . . interposing shade." With "privacy" denied representation, "there couldn't *be* any manners to speak of" (10).

These are local links in a "chain of relations" whose larger theme is the atrophying of experience or the shrinkage of "the margin," a subject that also concerns Benjamin and Adorno. The former ponders the ways in which the technological imperative of the "smooth functioning of the social mechanism" has "subjected the human sensorium to a complex kind of training"

(*Illuminations* 175). Benjamin mentions the shift from steady movements encouraging sociability to sharp, abrupt movements that isolate: the lighting of a match; the lifting of a telephone receiver; the darting, nervous eyes of the vigilant pedestrian (175). As if echoing James's reaction to the New Jersey mansions, Adorno asks: "What does it mean for the subject that there are no more casement windows to open, but only sliding frames to shove, no latches but turnable handles, no forecourt, no doorsteps before the street, no wall around the garden?" (*Minima* 40). This loss of what James calls "social and sensual margin, overflow and byplay" (*Scene* 45), engenders a concomitant impoverishment in the human subject; a loss of "hesitation, deliberation, civility," says Adorno, makes gestures "precise and brutal and with them men."[18]

James constructs this "chain of relations" from his excursions in a upper-bourgeois world whose vitality has withered in its zeal to maximize profit (*Scene* 11). American modernity's bias in favor of the immediate is evident in its devotion to the "short-cut," which dictates a quick detour around such impediments as history, manners, and representation itself. Impatience with mediation is manifested in intolerance toward the pleasures of "breathing space." Yet James is neither urging nor implying anything so nostalgic as a return to lazier premodern days. Indeed, he locates America's unique burden in its rootedness "in the present pure and simple, squaring itself between an absent future and an absent past as solidly as it can" (161). In his strolls James imagines hearing the great American cities expressing the trauma and anxiety of their attenuated, "compromised" historical position, one that has filled them with nervous swagger, bluff overconfidence, and "sham refinement." Speaking of New York, James insists that "the very sign of its energy is that it doesn't believe in itself." But all of this is cause for "pity" rather than contempt (110–13). James carefully avoids nostalgia by challenging America to begin redeeming its commitment to the actuality, not merely the concept, of urban democratic "hotch-potch."

For James democracy and modernity remain compelling but uncompleted projects that have amassed a "long list of the arrears" of the "undone" (463). Far from retreating from modernity, James wants a more varied modernity— less stable, less disciplined and disciplinary. In other words, James seeks a social order that will tap the energy of its own marginality; recall the Jamesian sense of margin as a reservoir of potential power that exists as an "immense fluidity" stimulating a "maximum of suggestion" (401). A marginal social order of "hotch-potch" or slack would modify the repressive controls of a totalizing system by generating the "friction" that occurs as a result of "having to reckon with a complexity of forces" rather than the reigning "sterility of aspect . . . where a single type has had the game . . . all in its hands" (427). The modernity James envisions is neither organized according to a class hierarchy nor modeled upon a genteel social code of neutral "respectability" or "positive bourgeois propriety." Indeed this propriety—"serenely, imperturbably, massively seated"—prompts James's "experimental deviation from the bourgeois" (455).

V

To propagate friction and deviation within his text James refuses to be limited to fashioning a chain of relations that clusters solely around the shrinking borders of the elite bourgeois. Concomitant with his arranging of this chain are his digressions into the marginal world of New York's other half, where he overrides "Anglo-Saxon" decorum to become entangled as a "victim of his interest" and curiosity. In the "New Jerusalem" he learns with his eyes and ears how to read the alien. In so doing he discovers crystals of "insidious continuity, the close inter-relation of observed phenomena" (*Scene* 424). The continuity he fashions is insidious both in the sense of running counter to an assimilationist rhetoric and in being found, for the most part, on a sub-terranean level—the *Lower* East Side. There dwell, in James's words, "myr-iads of fine fragments . . . living in the snippet" (132). The Jamesian chain of relations embodies (rather than explicitly states) a political meaning that resides in its implicit refusal of the phobic dichotomies propagated by the "best men" of the genteel elite in their efforts to distance "barbarian" immigrant invaders. The chain also serves as an alternative mode of repre-sentation to both the muckraking journalist's fetish for information and pro-gressivism's totalizing construct called the "American character." Describing as "criminal" the ideology of continuity that produces melting-pot rhetoric, James longs for a "split or chasm . . . for an unbridgeable abyss . . . !"—a desire that expresses the limits of his appetite for apocalypse (465).

Walter Benjamin also mutilates or mortifies (to use his term) totality and breaks apart continuity to express his criticism of totalizing bourgeois ide-ology. But whereas James's critique remains immanent, Benjamin's serves transcendental ends of violent, apocalyptic messianism. The goal of historical materialism, says Benjamin, is to "blast apart historical continuity."[19] James can hardly be said to possess either the depth of Benjamin's animus nor his political goals. But James's self-confessed "habit of finding a little of *all*" his "impressions reflected in any one of them" (*Scene* 116) has striking affinities with Benjamin's method, which the latter described as the effort at "dis-covering the crystal of the total process in the analysis of the small discrete moment" (qtd. Jennings 28). This shared commitment reflects the residual and paradoxical organicism in both their methods, an organicism in the service of exploding the continuity it seeks to discover. To find the "crystal of the total process" Benjamin and James insist on "the abandoning of deductive methods" for an "ever wider-ranging, an ever more intense reap-praisal of phenomena" (*Origin* 45).[20]

We can observe James's empirical, "roundabout" method at work in the "accident of a visit" he pays to a Bowery theater. This "adventure of rash observation" particularly amuses James for its disclosure of a seemingly minor but revelatory detail. Gazing at his fellow spectators—who are all immi-grants—he reflects: "There they all sat, the representatives of the races we have nothing 'in common' with, as naturally, as comfortably, as munchingly, as if the theatre was their constant practice—and, as regards the munching

... I was struck with the appearance of quality and cost in the various confections" (*Scene* 196). Once again the immigrant stirs James's imagination,
this time to dwell upon the impressive confections. The "cult of candy,"
writes James, "open[s] up for us ... a view ... to follow as far as it might
take us." It first takes us to James's reading of the candy as a "supreme
symbol of the *promoted* state of the aspirant to American conditions" not only
in the Bowery theater but " 'the people' over the land." Their casual munching of "solid and liquid sweets," which "form in other countries an expensive
and select dietary" available only to the affluent, is a "phenomenon" that
strikes James as "more significant of the economic and even the social situation of the masses than many a circumstance honored with more attention"
(197).

This last remark contains a hint of self-justification toward his "information"-hungry audience as James defends his perhaps inordinate interest in
seeming trivia. He is also justifying his neglect of conventional hierarchy
and scale in order to explore the question of candy. His analysis, which
continues for another three quarters of a page, registers a deliberate loss of
proportion that mimics the peculiar disproportion in the eating and spending
habits of the American urban poor, "in which so much purchasing power
can flow to the supposedly superfluous" (197). The American immigrants'
ability to afford numerous, elaborate, expensive sweets contrasts with their
counterparts "in other climes," who are known "by the wealth of their
songs." This difference "at first" testifies to "the diffused sense of material
ease" in America. But James's analysis of candy "and the "light [it] might
throw on manners and wages" doesn't end with a hymn to American prosperity. Such a conclusion would merely replicate the dominant ideology of
"democratic consistency" and its gospel of uplift (55). Instead, James probes
the infrastructure of this ideology to reveal the remarkable extent of its
managerial reach and finesse. He is fascinated by the invisible role that the
"most ubiquitous of all" American forces, "the genius for organization,"
plays in producing the immigrants' desire for candy. "Since the solicitation
of sugar couldn't be so hugely and artfully organized if the response were
not clearly proportionate," James asks himself: "How is the response itself
organized?" He answers this question later in the book when he describes
the ability of the "hotel-spirit" not only to satisfy American desires but also
to "create new and superior ones," as it converts the "great national ignorance" into "extraordinary appetites such as can be but expensively sated"
(440). (This prescient insight will be further explored in chapter 10.)

James's scrutiny of alien "munching" uncovers how far the public and
private spheres—"wages and manners ... market and home"—now inter-
penetrate. Capital has invaded both realms, a fact James reveals in noting
that in modern America "wages ... *are* largely manners." And the market
has colonized the home, transforming the realm of private appetites into
"boundless American material" to be "artfully organized" (107). James reveals candy consumption to be part of the "shedding process" by which the
alien is first rendered "neutral and colorless" and then rebuilt into a sugar-

addicted American consumer. Analogous to New York's frantic pace of destruction and renovation, the assimilative machinery destroys and reconstructs subjectivity in the interest of "the 'American' identity... acquiring ... confidence and consistency" (129). In sum, the coerciveness of the identity principle is the motor of social control, which galvanizes modernity's insatiable will to progress.

In the spirit of James's and Benjamin's passion for magnifying the apparently inconsequential, I have uprooted James's prolonged scrutiny of "the cult of candy" from its context as part of a "concatenation of interlinked appearances" clustering around alien self-representation (440). His visit to the Bowery theater follows James's wanderings in Central Park, where he takes in a "swarm of queer sounds, mostly not to be interpreted." Frederick Law Olmsted's design of Central Park deliberately encouraged a radical egalitarianism that struck many of the gentry, including Godkin, as an invitation to immigrant loitering and rowdyism (Godkin, *Problems* 125). In contrast, James finds "thrilling" the passage from "the discipline of the streets" to the "sweet *ingratiation* of the Park" (*Scene* 176–77). As if responding to upper-class anxiety about the park, James not only finds it "New York at its best" but adds that it puts one at ease about the "social question." What surprises and delights James is that despite (or because of) the "number of persons in circulation," he can somehow relax in the park's "many-smiling presence" (177). In the midst of a "polyglot Hebraic crowd of pedestrians," who have "none but the mildest action on the nerves," he observes the remarkably fastidious appearance of immigrant children and parents, particularly in regard to "the gleam of cared for teeth" and "the pride of varnished shoe" (179). "Two industries, at the most, seemed to rule the American Scene. The dentist and the shoe-dealer divided it between them" (180). The former will briefly concern us here.

Predictably, the large intake of sugar has made the dentist crucial. The importance in America of the "dental question" contrasts with European "indifference" and "systematic detachment from the chair of anguish" (180–81). But the dentist's function, James suggests, exceeds the hygienic and ultimately ministers to the accelerated class mobility that has made America barely legible as a social text. Until recently the cliché of "the 'common man' " had served a useful function as a baseline for measuring class status. But now the "common man and the common woman" are less stable entities than themselves figures confidently awaiting their imminent "social rise" (179). And the "cherished and tended teeth" of "common" Americans is one of their means for advertising "their promotion, their rise in the social scale" (179). Their "care and forethought" in "writing themselves on the facial page" testifies to the seriousness with which they cultivate the representation of a "ruthlessly pushed-up and promoted look worn by men, women, and children alike" (182, 178). Thanks to "far-shining dental gold," pleasing teeth ensure what James, using the idiom of the day, calls a " 'Californian' smile," a facial advertisement of prosperity residing in the mouth, if not in the bank (180).

The chain of relations James fashions in his attention to such things as teeth, shoes, and candy exemplifies his guiding belief that "things short in themselves might yet have such large dimensions of meaning" (440), a logic that also informs Benjamin's discovery of the "crystal of the total process" in the discrete. Like Benjamin's "representation as digression," which depends on an "absence of an uninterrupted purposeful structure" (*Origin* 28), James's restless analyses seek to "interpret unintentional reality" while proceeding at an "irregular rhythm." Thus James finds "mishaps and accidents . . . as contributive to judgment as the felicities" (*Scene* 410). In a typical "pausing for breath," James remarks: "I have strayed again from my starting point, and have again, I fear, succumbed to the danger of embroidering my small original proposition with too many, and scarce larger, derivatives" (182). This confession of "fear" is, of course, playfully disingenuous, for James knows perfectly well that his strolling continually obliterates any fixed "starting point" or "original proposition," and that his representations are founded on nothing if not his repeated succumbing to the embroidery of "derivative" observations. Or, more precisely, the original is redefined as the derivative. James suspends his will to originate, to order and master, preferring from the start to let impressions fall "into a train of association" (1). His leisurely, meandering sentences embody this train in motion, moving backward and forward, from the "vibrations" of "extreme youth" to the "mere looming mass" of the blank future, yet most intensely receptive, indeed, dependent on the vagaries and improvisations of present flâneries. In other words, the mimetic has begun to act itself out in the style and conduct of James's sentences.[21]

In describing his New York experiences, James devises a mode of representation that mimes urban phenomenology—the onrush of stimuli that makes the mind vibrate with associations. "For once quite agreeably baffled," James converts his very bafflement into openness as he empathizes and identifies, however uneasily, with much of what he encounters. Far from being merely an inward, psychological event, the receptivity of his mimetic selfhood projects outward to be embroidered with the rhythms and emblems of modernity. Hence his warm reaction to Central Park and his intimate response to Ellis Island and to the immigrant ghettos of New York. In all three locales "the main fact of life" is "overflow," the turbulent marginality that modernity at once solicits and contains (131). Population density is the immediate cause of overflow, but these spaces also overflow in their power to blur psychic boundaries and induce identification. The alien becomes an image of the "restored absentee," a recognition that acts as a catalyst in James's renovation. In short, James's alien contacts in New York function the way "natural correspondences" do for Benjamin—"stimulating and awakening the mimetic faculty in man" (*Reflections* 333).

James's overflowing self resembles Mead's view of identity as a variable process, capable of including within itself what Dewey calls "inconsistent selves and unharmonized dispositions" that defer the obligation of sincerity for the mobility of representation (*Human* 130). Bursting familiar moorings, such as genuineness or authenticity, James's fluid self exposes these bulwarks of liberal individualism as actually "nothing other than a defiant and obstinate insistence on the monadological form which social oppression imposes on man" (Adorno, *Minima* 154). Adorno's remark implies that forms other than the monadological can be constructed, an implication that adumbrates the premise of James's autobiography. In its most public mode, the Jamesian self is theatrical. The diversity of its role-playing, its appetite for the play of sociability, draws on radical curiosity's mimetic receptivity in order to challenge "the hold of a traditional conception of the singleness and simplicity" of the self (Dewey, *Human* 130).

James accommodates a normative and critical understanding of mimesis. He shares Mead's normative emphasis on the mimetic qualities inherent in the role-playing of everyday interaction. Theatricality is the condition of public behavior, in the sense that all relations in public require strategies of self-representation responsive to the constraints and expectations of social norms. But, unlike Mead, James finds theatricality, at a heightened pitch of mimetic receptivity, a rare and valuable cultural achievement, a critical challenge to bourgeois definitions of the authentically human. His two volumes of memoirs, to which we will now turn, memorialize this achievement. There James reenters the mimetic world of childhood, of released impulse, and conducts a sustained cultural and psychological inquiry into the origin and course of his alien being. At once relaxed to the point of blank dumbness and productive to the point of ceaseless crisis, the bewildering Jamesian self beckons the reader to enter into its "incurable perversity" and "ambiguous economy."

7

"At the Active Pitch": Mimetic Selfhood in James's Autobiography

In the New York of 1851 the Hudson River Railroad was in the course of being built. On the corner of Eighteenth Street was a mansion whose grounds were full of animal life, "browsing, pecking, and parading creatures" that seemed to belong to a world separate from the "riot of explosion" and hurtling fragments of rock attending the railroad's construction. On his way back home to Washington Square after visiting his tutor on Twenty-first Street, the eight-year-old Henry James would "dawdle and gape" at both scenes. The two "chance feasts" offered up by the "beguiling streets"—the thunderous construction and the tranquil animals—register the heterogeneity of a rural world in the process of becoming urban. James is rooted in this moment of transition, which is to say that the experience of being rooted is precisely what his daily life calls into question (*Autobiography* 15–16).

Surprise and incongruity make his "flâneries and contemplations" inexhaustibly rich, especially since his "visiting mind" comes to rest with neither the animals nor the railroad but in the difference they create. What he savors are the "vibrations" given off in the clash of rival claims of various orders of fascination, each beseeching him (16–17). James is fortunate in his historical moment because his immersion in a world of transition, joined with a temperamental inclination to "hang back," provide him with a rare opportunity to experience a society in the process of constructing what the anthropologist Pierre Bourdieu calls a "field of doxa"—the sum total of all that counts as self-evident, taken for granted, and natural. From this pure state of doxa we derive the more familiar word "orthodoxy," doxa's "imperfect substitute." James witnesses this creation of the self-evident because New York is in the course of being redefined as a world of railroads and explosions, of tearing down and building up, where browsing animals will be relegated to city zoos. This denaturing is inseparable from the construction of a new category of the natural. And it is occurring before James's eyes, affording him an intimate view of heterodoxy—"awareness and recognition of the possibility of different or antagonistic beliefs"—congealing into orthodoxy (Bourdieu 164). In the shifting, contested space of transition James nurtured his appetite for tension and strain.

His earliest memories reveal a child gripped by "the play of strong imaginative passion," which led him to practice "the art of missing or of failing, or of otherwise going astray" (*Autobiography* 454–55, 302). Yet this art of vagrancy is not an "absolute precept" that consigned him to permanent ineptitude. Rather, it was part of his restless, curious economy, which found varieties of application in seemingly negligible attitudes and emotions. It is the aim of this chapter to recover and foreground the heterodox audacity of his self-representation, which too often has been ignored by a critical orthodoxy that finds James guilty of idealizing the past. Instead of ignoring, minimizing, or explaining away the strangeness of his self-portrait, I propose to consider it as an experimental venture to enlarge the self's range of modalities, an effort that inevitably clashed with the orthodox biases of American culture.[1]

The best way to chart James's experiment is to follow his lead and stress the liminality of his boyhood, for there he first confronts the question of boundary that his autobiography will interrogate. William's preference for hard edges contrasts with Henry's willingness to revise the bounded self of "bourgeois circumspection." In representing a permeable self "fed by every contact and every apprehension," Henry makes his memoirs a seminal portrayal of mimetic behavior (242, 454). If the person, that entity of "unshakable unity" as Adorno claims, is a "historically tied knot that should be freely loosened and not perpetuated," in his autobiography James unties this knot (*Negative* 276).[2]

I

As we have seen repeatedly in this study, James's blurring of boundaries encourages us to cross a boundary of literary history and compare him to another New Yorker usually deemed antithetical to James. Four years after his boyhood perambulations, someone as addicted as James to observing the city's variousness published an aggressive celebration of heterodoxy. In "Song of Myself" Walt Whitman reanimates primal questions that the cultural orthodoxy prefers to think beyond question, particularly the matter of human form. Whitman asks:

> To be in any form, what is that?
> (Round and round we go, all of us, and ever come back thither,)
> If nothing lay more develop'd the quahaug in its callous shell were enough.
>
> Mine is no callous shell,
> I have instant conductors all over me whether I pass or stop,
> They seize every object and lead it harmlessly through me. (Sec. 27)

Fifty years after dismissing *Drum-Taps* as the discharging of the "undigested contents" of a "blotting book" upon the "lap of the public," James in his autobiography in effect repeats Whitman's questions: What does it mean for the self to have form? Must the self be limited to a single form or can it be various? The premise implicit in these questions is that "every established order tends to produce (to very different degrees and with very different means) the naturalization of its own arbitrariness" (Bourdieu 164). In confronting his audience with other possibilities of human form, James seeks to provoke them to reflect upon this conversion of the arbitrary into the natural.

In his old age James had come to reverse his estimate of Whitman. He now characterized him as "a great genius" to Edith Wharton as they read aloud his "Song of Myself." Perhaps James recognized that he and Whitman shared a desire to unsettle the question of identity, an impulse nurtured by witnessing the form and identity of New York undergoing redefinition. Having observed the "natural" as a social category, hence changeable and not preordained, James and Whitman interrogated the allegedly self-evident, the taken for granted. While their perspectives differ, we should recognize their shared project. Not only has their kinship been largely ignored, but their differences have been naturalized as a defining dichotomy of American literature: the contest of "paleface" against "redskin." Since 1939, when Philip Rahv pitted James against Whitman, this configuration has been taken for granted as canonical. Like all things canonical, it serves as a mechanism of containment that confines heterodox inquiry to the flagrantly deviant and eccentric Whitman, while Henry James the genteel patrician stands aloof. Santayana alone (as the next chapter will demonstrate) aligned James with Whitman as opponents of the genteel.

Whitman's refusal of the "callous shell" assaults what is virtually unquestioned in the ideology of individualism: the equation of identity and stability—the self as substantial, autonomous monad. This conception has roots deep in Western culture, going back to the Renaissance. As Norbert Elias has shown in his celebrated study, *The Civilizing Process*, it was then that the "image of man as *homo clausus*"—"the encapsulation of the self within itself"—became "self-evident, not open to discussion as a source of problems" (254). While Lockean empiricism and Humean skepticism kept discussion open in England, Elias observes "how persistent and how much taken for granted in the societies of modern Europe is the feeling of people that their own 'self', their 'true identity', is something locked away 'inside' them, severed from all other people and things 'outside' " (253).

De Tocqueville was the first to correlate the claustral image of humans with both Descartes and with the particular character of American social conditions. In a famous passage he argues that America is "one of the countries where the precepts of Descartes are least studied and are best applied. Nor is this surprising. . . . They follow his maxims because [their] social condition naturally disposes their minds to adopt them." The absence of social classes and inherited tradition, along with abundant opportunities for social mobility and the accumulation of wealth, all encourage the American to "shut himself up tightly within himself and insist upon judging the world from there" (4). In short, American conditions were ideal for naturalizing the image of *homo clausus* into an orthodoxy that encouraged what Bourdieu calls "institutionally organized and guaranteed misrecognition" (171). Ignored was the possibility that the windowless monad "is an artificial product of men which is characteristic of a particular stage in the development of their self-perception" (Elias 260).

The essentializing of the Cartesian self, the intellectual basis for the American orthodoxy of individualism, is assailable precisely because of this fact. For orthodoxy, as Bourdieu argues, aims at but never entirely succeeds in "restoring the primal state of innocence of doxa"—the transparency of self-evident natural order. As an "imperfect substitute" for doxa, orthodoxy exists only in opposition to heterodoxy—the existence of *"competing possibles"* (169). One such competing possible—Peirce's 1868 challenge to Cartesianism—inaugurated pragmatism. Flourishing contiguously with Peirce's epochal reorientation were local pockets of resistance.

The dedicated pursuit of competing possibles absorbed the James household. Monads of any kind, or what the elder James called the "idol of self-sufficiency," were the sworn enemy of the "converting" process, which branded as hopelessly literal anything that failed to encourage "ambiguity of view and of measure" (*Autobiography* 123). The literal, Henry James noted, "played in our education as small a part as it perhaps played in any." What reigned instead was the converting process embodied in the act of representation. The conversion of "mere actuality" into scenes, be it on the actual stage, in the theater of social life, or by "plying the pencil" in pictorial or dramatic composition, comprised the world of the young Henry and William. Echoing Alexander Pope, who as a child felt "dipt" in ink and "lisp'd in numbers," Henry confesses: "I thought, I lisped . . . I composed in scenes." The "reflected image hung everywhere about," saturating his childhood in representations. Being "addicted . . . to fictive evocation" seemed to James "absorbing and genuine . . . natural," whereas "mere actuality" possessed no special prestige. "My face was turned from the first to the idea of representation" (148–49).[3] In this "queer educative air" conversion was conceived of as an autotelic activity indifferent to obtaining the two prime orthodox values of "success" and "Virtue." Both were deemed irrelevant to the process. Conversion was also an activity free of the "inhumanity of Method" found in a "regular course of instruction" (124–25).

The suspicion of the monadic implied in the converting process leads to a skepticism about the very notion of boundary. Indeed, the title *A Small Boy and Others* raises the question of whether boundary must be defined as fixed and exclusionary. This work goes on to destabilize identities in order to reopen the question of how self and other are related. The possibility of conceiving of boundary less as a barrier and more as a locus of response and exchange will preoccupy James in his first volume of memoirs, whose title makes problematic the very notion of autobiography. For James leaves unclear whether he is telling his own life history or his brother's. The first sentence of *A Small Boy and Others* speaks of "the attempt to place together some particulars of the early life of William James and present him in his setting, his immediate native and domestic air." Evidently William is the "small boy" among "others" whom Henry will serve as biographer. However, this neat alignment is quickly blurred in the book's second sentence, where Henry declares: "I had been too near a witness of my brother's beginnings of life, and too close a participant, by affection, admiration and sympathy, in whatever touched and moved him, not to feel" possessed of a "greater quantity" of "history" "than I could hope to express." Henry, in short, overflows with memories not strictly his own because his history is "so fused and united and interlocked" with his brother's (4). With overflow as the defining condition of Henry's selfhood, the distinction between autobiography and biography is made problematic from the start.

James delights in the challenge of navigating the shifting ground between biography and autobiography, where at once "aspects began to multiply and images to swarm." In a mood reminiscent of his exhilaration at the torrent of impressions that washed over him at the outset of his American journey, James knocks "at the door of the past" and plunges into the "world of . . . childhood," as his "instant conductors" "seize every object." The seventy-year-old James has recaptured what Whitman also recovers: the avidity and insatiable curiosity of a child. Liberated from the "callous shell," James feels not just his own but also William's "small feet plant themselves afresh and artlessly stumble forward again," "our steps" discovering "the wonder of consciousness in everything" (4). But to argue that James's opening pages *recover* the mimetic openness of a "small boy" is imprecise. As the autobiography reveals, James never loses this perspective. Instead it inheres in what he becomes—a "man of imagination at the active pitch" (455).

While acknowledging the difficulty of discriminating between himself and William, Henry nevertheless vows that his depiction of self and other would "decline mutilation or refuse to be treated otherwise than handsomely" (3). But mutilation was, in effect, what Henry was accused of when William's son, Henry James III, complained to his uncle of the liberties taken in revising his father's letters. Henry had published, without comment, numerous passages of his brother's correspondence, which he later admitted he had retouched. In letters to his nephew he sought to justify his tamperings. First of all, the "ideal of documentary exactitude, verbatim . . . free of all living back imaginatively" was never "in the least" Henry's intention (*Letters* 4: 800). This would be as closed and conventional as the monadic subjectivity he disavows. Feeling so "interlocked" with William made the letters their mutual property: "Everything the letters meant affected me . . . as of *our* old world only, mine and his alone together." Therefore Henry felt free to revise so that William "should be more easily and engagingly readable." But Henry also admitted that in the "long ferment of an artistic process," he "lost the right reckoning, the measure of my *quantity* of amendment." He confessed to his nephew: "The sad thing is I think you're right in being offended" (801–4).

Yet the quantity of revisions was not his real mistake. Rather, Henry felt he erred "in thinking that with so literary, so compositional an obsession as my whole bookmaking impulse is governed by, any mere merciless transcript might have been possible to me. I have to the last point the instinct and the sense for fusions and interrelations, for framing and encircling . . . every part of my stuff in every other" (803). James's response to his nephew is important for the correlations it implicitly discloses: the novelist's "book-making impulse" makes problematic the possibility of a "mere . . . transcript," and his closeness to William makes problematic the bourgeois norm of identity as *homo clausus*. Indeed, the issue of identity is at the heart of his nephew's complaint: Henry James III implicitly assumes that his father's letters *are* his father's letters and legally his [the son's] property, since he is William's executor; therefore they permit no tampering. But Uncle Henry finds identity a sterile tautology, as impoverished as "documentary exactitude." Both are insufficiently imbued with otherness, with the "fusions and interrelations" that define both his compositional "obsession" and his relation to William. Modes of being and representation are deeply entwined in the autobiography, in which James splices together his love of stylized representation with the formation of his relational self.

The priority Henry grants "the represented thing (over the thing of accident, of mere actuality)" (150) challenges what Adorno calls "the highest concept of bourgeois morality—genuineness" (*Minima* 154). The correlate to the belief in "the supremacy of the original over the derived" is that man "should be wholly and entirely what he is." Genuineness, concludes Adorno, insists on the monadological, a kinship expressed, albeit inversely, in the autobiography, where James equates representation and intersubjectivity. Intimately connected in James's memoirs is his initial entry into the "house of representation" and his unabashed mimicry of his older brother. "Almost exclusively," James declares, life "was conditioned for me by my brother's nearness," a conditioning nowhere more intense than in the domain of representation, where William's facility at drawing "couldn't but act upon" Henry (4,149). James's portrayal of a small boy in a state of "friction" with others reveals what Adorno (and Mead) says "undeviating self-reflection" always exposes—that "even in the first conscious experiences of childhood . . . the impulses reflected upon are not quite 'genuine'. They always contain an element of imitation" (*Minima* 155). An ideology of the genuine suppresses precisely what James celebrates in *A Small Boy and Others*—that "the human is indissolubly linked with imitation: a human being only becomes human at all by imitating other human beings" (154).

"Anything that does not wish to wither should rather take on itself the stigma of the inauthentic" (154). James in effect heeds Adorno's warning by accepting his "brother's occupying a place in the world to which" he "couldn't at all aspire." That this counts as the "promptest" of his "very own" "first perceptions" is an emblematic irony: what James discloses as original, his "very own" perception, is already suffused with otherness. William is "already beforehand . . . already seated at his task" when Henry arrives, "when arriving at all, belatedly and ruefully." From the start, then, Henry's belatedness blurs his identity with the shadow of otherness. Significant is his equanimity about "hanging inveterately and woefully back." James concludes that "this relation alike to our interests and to each other seemed proper and preappointed" (7–8).

In deeming his belatedness "proper" James is within the logic of his preference for the "presenting again" inherent in re-presentation, its lack of priority, which strikes James as "natural." In short, belatedness defines James and his principal passion. In his memoir he joins his sense of hanging back with his love of the "represented thing." Sparking recall of his fledgling efforts at representation is a memory of William refusing his request to play and affirming his older "brother's privilege." Henry takes "refuge easily enough in the memory of" his own "pursuits." Yet, as before, what he claims as his "own" turns out to be derived: his pursuit of drawing—"I also plied the pencil"—imitates William "at seated play with his pencil." Far from seeking to conceal or leave implicit his blatant mimicry, James insists on it: "He [William] drew because he could, while I did so in the main only because he did." Drawing proved a "false scent," but an unavoidable and excusable mistake since, says James, "my brother's example really couldn't but act upon me—the scent was apparently so true for him" (149).

Henry's intersubjective sense of identity, in which he seems to share his self with his elder brother, aligns him with George Herbert Mead's account of identity as a process of mediation between self and other in which "the individual experiences himself as such, not directly, but only indirectly" by first becoming "an object to himself . . . by taking the attitudes of other individuals" (*Mind* 138). Role-playing permits one to anticipate the behavior of the other and mimic it internally on what Mead calls the "inner stage." In our imagination we represent his arguments "with his intonations and gestures and even perhaps with his facial expression." Mead concludes that "to be aware of another self as a self implies that we have played his role" ("Social" 377).[4] What Mead suggests here is that the inner life's "mechanism of introspection" is not inner at all but essentially social and thus theatrical. To become an object in order to become a subject encourages a respect for "thingness," for the materiality of external reality. The ability to anticipate the attitudes of others depends on mimicry, empathy, and distance, qualities that encourage one to esteem the value of objectivity and impersonality. But these attributes are held suspect by orthodox American individualism, whose watchword is Emerson's antimimetic directive to "insist on yourself; never imitate" (278). The self is strong in proportion as it resists imitation. So naturalized does this equation become that it acquires the status of a first principle of bourgeois selfhood. But to James's consciousness the "gratification nearest home was the imitative, the emulative" (150).

The notion of self as social construct has a genealogy of its own, and one branch of it moves back from Henry James and Mead to James senior and to the pivotal figure of C. S. Peirce, whose 1868 critique of Descartes inaugurated the challenge, the "competing possible" that orthodoxy engenders. Peirce argued that the self is not primary or given but derived, an inference resulting from self-correcting procedures of experimental inquiry. By contrast, Cartesian man, the "epistemological subject" of classical philosophy, says Norbert Elias, "gains knowledge of the world 'outside' him in a completely autonomous way. He does not need to learn, to take this knowledge from others." In his self-sufficient mastery of objects, the knowing subject "was never a child and seemingly came into the world an adult." If we accept this image of man, notes Elias, "there is no way out of the epistemological impasse. Thought steers helplessly back and forth between the Scylla of positivism and the Charybdis of apriorism" (248). To avoid these reifications, Peirce's pragmatism emphasizes the self as contingent, inseparable from the process of experimental inquiry and interpretation. A self prior to this process was meaningless to Peirce, as empty an abstraction as Cartesian man's self-sufficient immunity to error. Fallibilism redefines human inquiry, action, and selfhood as open and revisable events.

Peirce's pragmatist critique of individualism resonates with the antiindividualist stance of his dear friend, the elder James. Indeed, fallibilism was the keynote of James senior's educational theory. "Most appealing" to father, according to Henry, was the "kind of personal history" that should "fairly proceed by mistakes, mistakes more human, more associational . . . than straight and smug and declared felicities" (*Autobiography* 301). One value of mistakes was their encouragement of "*waste*," another key word in the James household. Into waste, the "whole side of the human scene usually held least interesting," James senior "could read . . . so much character and color and charm" (302). This transvaluation had the profoundest effect on his two eldest sons. Father's fondness for "waste" and "the art of missing and failing, or otherwise going astray," engulfed William in acedia. But Henry found that the process of converting waste made "life in those years" profit "greatly for animation and curiosity" (301). Henry combined mistakes, waste, and curiosity to create a nourishing matrix of options ("not absolute precepts," he insisted) that "enlarged not a little" his "field . . . and categories of appreciation and perception" (302).

Although "the imitative, the emulative" was the "gratification nearest home," it also encouraged mimetic rivalry. We have noted that Henry drew only because William did. They both made "the most of every image within view," but, adds Henry, "*I doubt if he made more than I even then did*, though earlier able to account for what he made" (150; emphasis added). Henry's rare admission of superior ability disrupts his carefully maintained role of idler in awe of William the master and also suggests the double register of mimesis: it is a means of instrumentality and adaptation as well as the opposite qualities of spontaneity and impulse. Henry's hanging back in mimicry not only led him to become skeptical of monadic forms of being but also helped develop his skill for representation, which he easily converted into a career by the age of twenty-two. Finding and abiding with a career was no small achievement in a household where "the act of choice—choice as to the 'career' for example"—was discouraged, given Henry senior's love of waste and mistake. He held open the door "for experiment," but when "any very earnest proposition in particular" was mentioned, the door had a "tendency to close" (302).

That Henry escaped this double bind and made the "choice" more easily and earlier than William is all but impossible to discern from the autobiography's insistent focus on William's priority. Even more telling is Henry's avoidance of the fact that mimicry was reciprocal: William copied Henry as flagrantly as Henry copied William, though at a later stage in their development. This reciprocity has come to light in Howard Feinstein's study, which demonstrates that the James household was pervaded by mimesis in both its impulsive and instrumental moments. Horkheimer had earlier noted the paradoxical quality of mimesis. In *Eclipse of Reason* he had written that mimicry is both "the oldest biological means of survival" (one can evade death by playing dead) and the expression of spontaneous openness to others inevitably discouraged by imperatives of survival. Mimesis begins with the infant's whole body as "an organ of mimetic expression." The chief way the infant learns is by unconsciously imitating everybody and everything. "Only in the later phases of childhood is this unconscious imitation" curbed and directed toward a definite, rational goal. According to Horkheimer, "Civilization starts with, but must eventually transcend and transvaluate, man's native mimetic impulses. Cultural progress as a whole, as well as individual education, . . . consists largely in converting mimetic into rational attitudes" (*Eclipse* 114–15).

Whereas Henry managed to entwine the mimetic and the rational, play and work, William could not. As the eldest son and prime instrument of his father's diffuse ambitions, William probably found his mimetic proclivities instrumentalized very early. Until the age of thirty he remained trapped in a web of rivalrous imitation with his manipulative, competitive father. One consequence was William's abiding psychic rigidity, a distaste for admixture in any context. His defensiveness was exacerbated by his mother, whom William consistently—and correctly—sensed was basically unempathic toward him despite her much-celebrated posture of selflessness.[5] Henry was and remained her favorite child. The psychodynamics of their relationship will concern us in the next chapter, which examines Henry's remarkably different pattern of Oedipal development.

William had the unique burden of imitating both Henry and their bewildering father, who repeatedly encouraged and then discouraged him from various careers, including art, science, and philosophy. Apparently realizing the anarchic quality in his father's disdain for choice, Henry "didn't expose himself, as William had done, to a direct confrontation with his father over art. Perhaps he had learned from his brother's failure" (Feinstein 225). To escape their overbearing father, both sons learned to practice what Feinstein calls "the manipulative politics of invalidism," a feigning or exaggeration of ill health that became both the excuse to travel abroad and the locus of their reciprocal mimesis (196). Feinstein shows that William's imitation of Henry focused not only on his enviable backache (that "delightful disease . . . which has long made Harry so interesting," according to William) but also included copying Henry's book-reviewing activity. William started submitting reviews to *The Nation* soon after Henry's began appearing in Godkin's journal. Exchanging roles and becoming the mimic and not the mimed, the envious instead of the envied, could not have comported well with William's Emersonian standards of self-reliance.

Presenting a configuration that completely reverses the typical pattern of Henry's autobiography, Feinstein reveals the spectacle of William scrambling "to keep pace with Henry, and obscure the separation the younger brother was patiently trying to effect" (228). Whereas the intense bond between William and his father "hamstrung William's effort to individuate, to establish a psychologically separate self," Henry "knew what he wanted far better than William. . . . He alone would attain the goal that once seemed their shared destiny" (223, 229).

Apparently less liberating than inhibiting was William's "keen awareness of the risks of psychological fusion . . . the disastrous psychological consequences of the failure to recognize and affirm the boundaries between persons" (Feinstein 138). William is so alert to the dangers of fusion precisely because he has not escaped them; he is absorbed in obeying his mercurial father. William's yearning for boundaries, according to Feinstein, extended to his aesthetic preferences: he admired the clean lines of Pre-Raphaelite art, which gave paintings a "characteristic hard edge, creating a visual world of shapes with impermeable boundaries." This preference later informed his psychological theories, which emphasize "the hardness of edge that divides human experience as decisively as lead separates the fragments of stained glass" (109). William's predilection for hard edges can be seen as the sublimated expression of the defense he sought against an invasive father who doted on his brilliant firstborn.

Thanks to his being born second, Henry was spared both the need for hard edges and William's doomed pursuit of his father's crippling ideal of being "something free and uncommitted." In the midst of the elder James's compulsive experiments in remaining uncommitted, Henry found an opportunity to "pick up, and to the effect not a bit of starving but quite of filling" himself, the "crumbs" of William's "feast" (*Autobiography* 246). Statements like this tend to provoke accusations from critics of Henry's abject passivity, of his failure to "become a man." A recent account finds William to be "the worst older brother imaginable, so energetic and universally competent that Henry gave up ever trying to equal him. . . . The older brother's robust ability sent Henry retreating back into himself" (Habegger 260). Thanks to Feinstein's work, we now know the inadequacy of this conventional wisdom. Not only did William turn to Henry as a model, but Henry at times found his brother's protean abilities inspiring. Far from simply "retreating" into himself, Henry was also stimulated to "live, by the imagination, in William's so adaptive skin." According to Henry, "To see that he [William] was adaptive, was initiated, . . . was my measure of content." Living in William's skin was nearly ideal for cultivating a vicarious "freedom of fancy" that nurtured Henry's mimetic gifts (*Autobiography* 247).[6]

But neither the pleasures of fraternal love nor imaginative liberty fully account for what Henry calls "a sort of ecstasy of resignation" (246). His repeated and unabashed expression of this "ecstasy" strikes a willfully discordant note in a Protestant culture that would obviously look askance at such a confession, especially from a man. To find joy in "resignation" is to risk the charge of "sissy."[7] Henry seems almost to invite such scorn by displaying so lavishly his awe of William and his own ineptitude. Yet this self-representation carefully hid the more flattering fact that Henry served as a pivotal model for William. Rather than idealization being the autobiography's motivating impulse and orientation, as many have charged, it seems more accurate to speak of Henry James's deliberate de-idealization of himself. In short, we are faced with the question of why he foregrounds his radically mimetic behavior, which violates Victorian codes of masculinity. The logic that leads Henry to stress his "ecstasy of resignation" resembles Whitman's when he responds to the child's question in "Song of Myself" by saying: "I do not know what it [the grass] is any more than he" (sec. 6). Whitman's inability to answer reflects a refusal to accept hierarchy and authority, and an insistence on sharing the child's interrogative stance, which challenges the taken-for-granted. In James's song of himself he also becomes a small boy among others, flaunting his mimicry and spectatorship to make problematic what is self-evident—the assumption that the monadic is the one answer to the question: "To be in any form, what is that?" In "On a Certain Blindness" William had recognized and acclaimed other forms of being, but he left undisturbed the root assumption of insulation. His brother's memoirs disturbed this assumption, as we shall shortly see.[8]

II

Henry James's memoirs enact a curious spectacle: the internationally acclaimed Master of the novel unraveling his mastery, displaying himself as a "dunce," a "fool" grateful for his brother's crumbs. By making his point of view that of a marginal, mimetic self, James practices a strategy of defamiliarization that deliberately estranges his audience's expectations and orthodoxies.[9] James celebrates vagueness, envy, belatedness, and imitation, qualities conventionally believed to be destructive of the self's integrity. But it is precisely the assumption that the self possesses integrity—a closed, unified stability—that is called into question. The countermodel he offers— a curious, "gaping" self perpetually in "crisis," vibrating to external stimuli— recalls Whitman, but without the poet's immunity from embarrassment. Rather, James seems to cherish embarrassment as a dissonance constitutive of his fallibilistic selfhood. In all of James's self-portrayals—the belated young flâneur, the hapless law student, the failed Civil War recruit, the successful author—embarrassment abides. Paradoxically, James is quite unembarrassed about revealing it.

What makes "endless crisis" inherently embarrassing is the loss of control it entails. This loss makes him a "victim," for he is enthralled by "imaginative passion," which causes "at every step some rich precipitation." When it is "fed by every contact and every apprehension," passion at such a pitch is "strong enough to *be* . . . the very interest of life" and "constitutes in itself an endless crisis" (454). As hostage of this passion, James resembles no one so much as Whitman "quivering . . . to a new identity," betrayed by his "instant conductors" ("Song of Myself," sec. 28). Although James's passion is libidinally sublimated, it remains as pressing and refractory as Whitman's bodily passion of desire.[10] Indeed, James's late-blooming appreciation of Whitman serves to underline their shared sense of passion as devouring. James made his hypertactility explicit in a letter to Morton Fullerton that has recently been published. Thanking him for "your more than touching, your penetrating, letter," James goes on to declare: "I have told you before that the imposition of hands in a certain tender way 'finishes' me, simply. . . . I can only gasp—gently and thank you. You do with me what you will" (*Selected Letters* 325). James's orgasmic response recalls Whitman's declaration that "[t]o touch" his "person to some one else's is about as much as" he "can stand." His "stiffening limbs" become "traitors" that announce his helpless arousal by the "villain touch!" But desire does not impel the poet toward union with another. Rather, it isolates and confines him to his own body: "My flesh and blood playing out lightning to strike what is hardly different from myself" (sec. 28).

This paradox—Whitman's openness leaves him closed to any relation but his solitary autoeroticism—also structures James's experience of otherness. To achieve a pitch of receptivity wherein one feeds on "every motion and every act" demands what might be described (oxymoronically) as inviolable openness, a condition precluding the closure implied in a commitment to relationship or even active sexuality. James imparts a sense of autogenesis when he ponders where in the world he will find a model for his "man of imagination." His model turns up in a

> shape almost too familiar at first for recognition. . . . He had been with me all
> the while, and only too obscurely and too intimately. . . . I had, in a word, to
> draw him forth from within rather than meet him in the world before me, the
> more convenient sphere of the objective, and to make him objective, in short,
> had to turn nothing less than myself inside out. What was I thus, within and
> essentially, what had I ever been and could I ever be but a man of imagination
> at the active pitch? (*Autobiography* 455)

In this staging of self-birth, James turns himself "inside out," becoming subject and object of his passion, or rather "subject and victim." James's aside—"It wasn't what I should have preferred, yet it was after all the example I knew best and should feel most at home with"—immediately following the passage just cited, acquires poignancy in this context as a confession of solitariness, a quality he shares with Whitman. For both, a self stripped of a claustral, "callous shell" is no longer an entity but a process that performs a "whole possible revolution," including a moment (or phase) of isolation that, in the inexhaustibly "rich precipitation" of experience, is continually dissolved, recovered, and dissolved again.

This dialectic reveals the striking antinomy that structures James's psychic economy: its mimetic receptivity is born of and sustained by loneliness. "This loneliness . . . what is it still but the deepest thing about one? Deeper about me, at any rate, than anything else: deeper than my 'genius,' deeper than my 'discipline,' deeper than my pride, deeper, above all, than the deep countermining of art" (*Letters* 4: 170). In this famous declaration (to Morton Fullerton in 1900) James suggests that his loneliness is deeper than genius, discipline, pride, and art not in the sense of overshadowing and impoverishing them but as being the richest (deepest) soil of his being, from which all else in him springs. If, on the most obvious level, James's "essential loneliness" is the barrenness of celibate bachelorhood, on a less obvious and more important level it is also the fertility of "a man of imagination at the active pitch." He did not overcome loneliness to become such a man; rather, it helped make him so. Loneliness is less a fixed quality of being that condemns him to sterile isolation than a field of potentiality and dynamic relation, analogous to the ineradicable, pulsating "margin" that James sees as the one constant in American life. Thus, there is little of the melancholy or wistful in James's hymn to loneliness; indeed, he trusts it will give his friend Fullerton a "lift!"

Regrettably, James's loneliness and embarrassment have been interpreted all too literally as merely neurotic symptoms, as defects or shortcomings. Critics have ignored their more significant meanings as forms of creative vitality that challenge conventional categories and values. One reason James insists upon and even heightens the tension of embarrassment is to dramatize the acute unease, the self-contempt, that inevitably results when the monadic is surmounted in a culture that fetishizes autonomy. Humiliation and self-contempt are one moment in James's self-representation, the moment founded on the internalization of the culture's ideology. This identification with the aggressor, a primal element of mimetic behavior, functions as a "protective inoculation" that permits James to discover the power in embarrassment's negative energy.[11]

The internal dissonance that James's dialectical self insists on mimics, to some degree, the quintessential urban experience of shock. The "vibrations" from the "beguiling streets" that assault James are felt by other walkers in the modern city, including Baudelaire, Simmel, and Benjamin. Like Benjamin's flâneur, James's response to modernity is simultaneously one of immersion and "hanging back," an uneasy position that Simmel was the first to identify as the basis of a uniquely urban subjectivity. Simmel's remarks on the "stranger," which were published in 1908, directly influenced Benjamin and are strikingly congruent with James's self-representation as a "restless analyst." The formal position of the stranger is reducible neither to a marginal figure nor a wanderer. Rather, a stranger embodies "a specific form of interaction" that is a "synthesis of nearness and remoteness." Above all, the stranger possesses an "objectivity" that "does not signify mere detachment and nonparticipation, but is a distinct structure composed of remoteness and nearness, indifference and involvement" (*Individuality* 145). The stranger is a resonant figure because he dissolves univocal definitions and embodies the kind of "double consciousness" found in James's and Strether's radical curiosity.

James's "way of taking life," in which "pedestrian gaping" was his "sole and single form of athletics," recalls the dialectical stance of Simmel's stranger (*Autobiography* 113). Both positions reveal how entangled are active and passive elements, especially in those "in whom contemplation takes so much the place of action" (17). In making contemplation a kind of action, in conceiving of "taking in" as "immersion" in the "material pressure of things," and in feeling "anything with force" as an "act or event of life" (569), James's form of nonparticipation becomes "a positive and definite kind of participation," as Simmel describes the stranger.[12] In sum, nonparticipation is not a refusal of action and submission to passivity but commitment to a particular mode of practice called "discrimination." Discrimination is Adorno's term for the mimetic capacity to experience otherness. As an ideal, discrimination provides "a haven for the mimetic element of knowledge." But in the secularized Enlightenment world discrimination has become the process whereby "the mimetic element in turn blends with the rational one" (*Negative* 42, 45). Those with an eye for nuance, says Adorno, practice nonidentity thinking because they can "distinguish even the infinitesimal, that which escapes the concept; discrimination alone gets down to the infinitesimal" (45).

Under the gaze of James's discriminating eye, what escapes the concept begins to flower: vagueness becomes a "virtue" rather than "mere inaction"; blankness becomes "inclusively blank . . . rather than poorly, and meanly, and emptily" blank; blackness becomes "*rich* blackness" rather than "mere mean" blackness (*Autobiography* 412, 234, 242). In short, James experiences vagueness, blankness, and blackness—and loneliness and embarrassment—as nonidentical. This process, it will be recalled, involves setting the concept "inwardly in motion" so it is "no longer purely itself." By defamiliarizing these concepts, all of which usually signify negation, sterility, and poverty, James releases their stored-up energy, which was hitherto repressed as terms of opprobrium in the culture. Thus emerges what Adorno calls "the 'more' which the concept is equally desirous and incapable of being" (*Negative* 162). The new meanings James releases clear a space for his sense of difference (nonidentity) to grow, since vagueness and blankness, as we shall see, are words he uses in self-description. Discrimination, then, is not an elitist mechanism of exclusion but an instrument of individual and cultural replenishment that propagates the "more"—what James calls the "margin." Mining its fluid potential mitigates the conceptual and emotional impoverishment inflicted by the cultural bias of the identity principle. Discrimination enlarges possibilities of perception and hence of experience. Because discrimination rejects the fixity of identity logic, those possessed of exceptional discrimination, like James, continually experience what Adorno calls the vertiginous "shock of inconclusiveness" (*Negative* 33). In this impassioned world of the "man of imagination" neither subject nor object dominates; rather, each mediates for the other. Discrimination is a complex dynamic because it involves not only "the experience of the object turned into a form of subjective reaction." These reactions, in turn, require "ceaseless objective correction," which occurs "in self-reflection, in the ferment of mental experience" (45, 47). Ferment, the term James also uses to describe the "artistic process," is produced by the interplay of the mimetic and rational, subjective reaction and objective correction. This self-revising energy viscerally registers and feeds upon the pressure of external events. This materialist orientation of the Jamesian self is clarified when we compare it to what Walter Pater, in the "Conclusion" to *The Renaissance*, calls that "strange perpetual weaving and unweaving" that characterizes modern identity. Although James shares this instability, his weavings are created by an openness to external contact, whereas Pater's result from "the individual in his isolation." Experience, says Pater, "already reduced to a swarm of impressions, is ringed round for each one of us by that thick wall of personality through which no real voice has ever pierced" (60). But in those who are unprotected by this "thick wall," whose "personality" possesses merely a thin membrane of "vagueness," the "swarm of impressions" is heightened to fever pitch.

This turbulent James coexists with the more familiar Master of impeccable detachment and magisterial self-assurance, "weaving," in Ezra Pound's words, "an endless sentence." Whether intentionally or not, Pound hints at what the clash of the impeccable and the turbulent produce: the faintly absurd quality rarely absent from James's deportment. Lurking in the exquisitely "done" texture of his social representation is its dialectical shadow of embarrassment. This dissonant, self-parodying element is evident in his scientific detachment, which, according to Brownell, ultimately became excessive—too tinctured with curiosity to be truly constructive" (qtd. Gard 411). And dissonance, as we have seen, inheres in the prefaces, creating ambivalences and perversities that constitute their most compelling drama. James's grueling effort at codifying a poetics of fiction becomes a mockery of its intended task as the "demon of compromise" and fallibility stalks his pages. The prefaces represent the making of fiction as a field of combat, a state of virtually perpetual crisis.

That James conceived of his selfhood as an analogous site of tension is evident from the account of his first extended visit to London. Here we witness a self vulnerable to "extreme embarrassment," even as his literary mastery began to be proclaimed to the world. Immersed in a new culture, James characteristically relishes dissonance: "I was . . . in the midst of . . . perversities, idiosyncrasies, incalculabilities, delightful all as densities at first insoluble, delightful even, indeed, as so much mere bewilderment and shock" (*Autobiography* 558). One instance of bewilderment that is closer to humiliation than to delight occurs when a group of Englishmen attempts to engage the young American author in conversation: "Vivid has remained to me," notes James, "as the best of my bewilderment, the strangeness of finding that I could be of interest to *them*. . . . My identity for myself was *all* in my sensibility to their own exhibition, with not a scrap left over for a personal show" (559). Thus James is left with "an abject acceptance of the air of imbecility." Instead of being "quite forward and informing and affirmative" to the Englishmen's "attentions," his self-representation is vague, remaining "vivid" only in its "strangeness." The appearance of "imbecility" is all that is left after James's mirroring of otherness empties him of subjectivity and makes him seem a passive object. His attentiveness to the others' "exhibition" reaches such intensity that sociability is ruptured.

Paradoxically, this failure of sociability occurs because of James's extreme commitment to the self as social process. The London incident reveals the inherent volatility of this process, a quality also implicit in Mead's sense that the self is not something that preexists and then enters into relations but is, "so to speak, an eddy in the social current and so still part of the current. It is a process in which the individual is continually adjusting himself in advance to the situation to which he belongs" (*Mind* 182). A plausible inference would be that individuation is not a stable but a precarious achievement that is always at risk of dissolving back into the "social current." This dissolution would end the vital interplay between self and other. Interplay is lost in the incident with the Englishmen, for James becomes so absorbed in "taking the attitudes of others" (Mead's phrase) that he becomes fixed in objecthood and is unable to achieve the next stage in the dialectic— "becoming a subject to himself" (138).

The self conceived as intersubjective process rather than as insulated entity is at once more fluid and various ("a multiple personality is in a certain sense normal," according to Mead) but also more susceptible to disorientation (142). The process of "continually adjusting" and "taking the attitudes" of others risks disseminating one's subjectivity to the point of leaving "not a scrap . . . for a personal show." But for James the gains of mimetic selfhood outweigh the risks—indeed, the gain is risk. Even the incident just discussed, which James calls "the proved humiliation of my impotence," points to his capacity to experience otherness (*Autobiography* 559). But in this instance "self-relinquishment" is carried too far, and bewilderment and shock are more alienating than exhilarating.

III

The excitement and danger of shock become most acute for James, and his subjectivity seems most in crisis, when the nation itself undergoes a trauma of identity.[13] At the outbreak of the Civil War, the perennial embarrassment of "hanging back" is heightened when James suffers a physical injury while helping to put out a fire. But he works his injury for all it is worth, affirming his mimetic mode of being as it is put to its severest test. The war had the immediate effect of renewing the inevitable bourgeois demand for identity, what James calls the "conventional maximum" of decisive masculine assertion. Some "publicly brandished" flag of engagement in public life was in order. "I must have come as near as possible to brandishing none whatever," James admits. But he does finally raise the unconventional minimum "standard" of public identity, which he visualizes as an "emblazoned morsel" (*Autobiography* 411). This morsel is his enrollment in Harvard Law School, to which he proceeded "on the very vaguest grounds that probably ever determined a residence there." The "Law School Experiment" is a commitment to a kind of vagueness that the tumultuous moment demands: "Just staying home when everyone was on the move couldn't in any degree show the right mark; to be properly and perfectly vague one had to be vague *about* something; mere inaction quite lacked the note—it was nothing but definite and dull" (412).

What he soon becomes brilliantly vague about is the "obscure hurt" he suffered at the outbreak of the war, as he attempted, along with a group of other men, to extinguish a "shabby conflagration." This most notorious incident in James's biography is usually read as a climactic humiliation, a symbolic or literal castration that permanently stigmatized him for life. James's "obscure hurt" made enlistment impossible, and his reticence concerning this "private catastrophe" has fostered the suspicion that it was a "trumped up" lameness, an excuse to avoid the combat his two younger brothers heroically participated in. James's reminiscences, says Daniel Aaron, "are often suspiciously blurred, as if he were trying to screen the story of his nonparticipation behind a fog of words" (*Unwritten* 107). Leon Edel speaks of James's effort to "becloud the whole question of his nonparticipation" with "vagueness and circumlocution" (*Untried* 175). But these accusations of evasion ignore James's insistent dwelling on his embarrassing accident, a fact that includes the humiliating verdict of a "great surgeon" to whom he went for medical consultation: the doctor found "nothing" (*Autobiography* 417). The "obscure hurt" is an apt emblem for an identity that has been obscure since his "bewildered and brooding years" as a small boy. This apparent nullity of self is now made a matter of public record by "so high an authority" as the surgeon. Yet James's nonidentity, which is understandably invisible to the authorities, becomes his "*modus vivendi*," which, immigrantlike, thrives on dislocation (he had lived in London, Geneva, Paris, and New York) and in feeling "singularly alien" in the "presence of matters normally, entirely, consistently American" (307, 418). The famous moment of embarrassing injury can be viewed as consecrating his estrangement from "prime" American identity as he is "jammed into the acute angle between two high fences." Pinned in a stance of in-betweenness, he is at a "dire disadvantage of position" physically but at an acute advantage for developing his powers of sympathetic identification (415).

Regarding James's mishap, Paul John Eakin has argued that his experience

of "an apparently disabling injury is an enabling event." Helping to put out
the fire was

> principally a psychological event in which the young man earned for himself
> the right to be what he had always been, one of life's noncombatants; and he
> did so, paradoxically, in the most heroic terms available to him at the time,
> those of the Civil War. . . . Henry rose to the occasion . . . and in so doing made
> himself the cause of his inveterate and increasingly problematic passivity. (247)

In terms of my argument, I would revise Eakin's astute reading to suggest
that James's injury, and the war in general, enabled him to transform his
"passivity" into an active assertion of mimetic selfhood. "By a turn of fortune's hand," James's wounding becomes the public sign, the raised "flag"
of his open, gaping self, which is "bristling with embarrassments" (414).
This bristling functions as "instant conductors" of empathic power that create
a sense of "fusion" with others wounded in action and with the "huge
comprehensive ache" his country suffers. "From the very first" hour of his
injury, James feels a "queer fusion or confusion" between the painful "passage of personal history" and the "great public convulsion" of incipient civil
war (414–15).

His "physical mishap" establishes a "sort of tragic fellowship" with the
bleeding "social body," a blurring of boundaries that becomes the keynote
of this time of crisis. The "twenty minutes" in which occurs the "horrid
even if an obscure hurt" enables James "to establish a relation to everything
occurring round" him, "not only for the next four years, but for long after-
ward." What is initially an "embarrassment" becomes what James calls an
"interest," a "painful one" but "inexhaustible," since "the whole enveloping tonic atmosphere [was a] force promoting its growth." The atmosphere
of war is a "tonic" and promotes the "interest" of his wound because the
nation has become wounded, its self-identical homogeneity now "a body
rent with a thousand wounds" (415). The "hurrying troops, the transfigured
scene, formed a cover for every sort of intensity, made tension itself in fact
contagious" (416). The outbreak of contagion erodes differences and distinctions. Thus the "endless crisis" that defines James's mimetic self now
also describes the torn "social body." The nation's homogenized identity
must be opened to the enfranchisement of other races, an "ingurgitation"
of the alien that began with the Emancipation Proclamation of 1863 and
continued with the great influx of immigrants throughout the later part of the
nineteenth century.

Under "cover" of crisis, James transforms his injury into a "*modus vivendi*
workable" for a lifetime. Rather than growing out of his vagueness, his
nonidentity, he uses it for all it is worth: "Could I but work that force [of
vagueness] as an ideal I felt it must see me through" (412).[14] The power of
this "ideal" resides in a primal source: the "dawning sense of freedom"
nourished by the "untamed impulse that precedes the ego." James's "ecstasy
of resignation" remains imbued with "the memory of the archaic impulse

not yet steered by any solid I" (Adorno, *Negative* 221). As Adorno has re-marked: "Not to be oneself is a piece of . . . utopia" (qtd. Huyssen 20).[15] But James and Adorno both insist that casting "off the facade of identity" can never be absolute because to reject identity requires the very strength— the "character or will"—that one owes to identity. Defining his lifelong philosophical task as the effort "to use the strength of the subject to break through the fallacy of constitutive subjectivity," Adorno describes a logic that also orients James's immanent critique of monadic subjectivity (*Negative* xx).[16]

In his autobiography James foregrounds both the "strain of holding the I together" and the suspension of this obligation. The holding and the loos-ening of the I produce an oscillating rhythm: at extreme moments his "gap-ing" leaves him without a "scrap of identity" and he appears to be an "imbecile." At other times "vagueness" becomes a "cover for every sort of intensity." As James grew into manhood, the gaping and the vagueness of his mimetic behavior found its most "workable" public mode in theatricality, self-representation that mitigates the reification of identity by letting the contingencies of social interaction continually shape and reshape it.

IV

As James's own selfhood and that of some of his most important characters (Miriam Rooth in *The Tragic Muse*, Ralph Touchett, Lambert Strether, Mag-gie Verver) suggest, theatricality is a valuable cultural achievement, for it modifies the demand for authenticity. With its stylized self-representation, which dismisses sincerity as an aim, theatricality is "rid of the compulsive character of identity" and its insistence on the continuous, unmediated, and transparent (Adorno, *Negative* 299). But Jamesian theatricality does not liq-uidate identity for illegible, unrestrained free play. Instead, its energy derives from maintaining the interplay of both moments of mimesis: its empathic, spontaneous improvisations and its rationalized, strategic defenses and masks. In short, theatricality embodies an immanent critique of the identical and purposive self without being able to overcome that self.[17]

James's belief in the primacy of theatricality destabilizes idealist dichot-omies: one opposes life to art and another gives priority to subjective expres-sion over impersonal form. The antinomic structure of the Jamesian theatrical self is founded on what Adorno, in his analysis of tact, calls the impossibility of reconciling "the unauthorized claims of convention and the unruly ones of the individual" (*Minima* 36). This irreducible tension of object and subject defines and propels theatricality, as Simmel emphasizes in his fragment entitled "On the Theory of Theatrical Performance." James shares Simmel's belief that "man can very seldom determine his form of behavior purely out of his innermost self." But neither Simmel nor James laments this depen-dence on "some pre-determined guise" or "pre-existing form" (308). The priority of forms is an opportunity to use them imaginatively, a capacity that makes us "all in varying degrees poets and painters" (309). Theatricality, says Simmel, is a "creative response," what James calls a making of "interest" out of "clumsy Life" (*Art* 121).

When this making is achieved by a "consciousness that was to be nothing if not mixed and a curiosity that was to be nothing if not restless," perception or "taking in" becomes a "precious fine art" that invests "mere actuality" with "mystery, dignity and distinction" (*Autobiography* 95, 150). Thus "taking in" an ordinary French street scene—as baker, oyster lady, and wood merchant sell their wares—converts it into a "vivid exhibition," a domestic tableau full of "aesthetic ingenuity," its "life and manners" "pointedly and harmoniously expressed" (190). For James art is not passive contemplation but a mode of practice "inherently and immediately enjoyable," to quote Dewey's phrase from *Art as Experience*. Embedded in the daily processes of living, art is an activity of cognition producing scenes and images that, in turn, may become materially and formally embodied in artifacts, the difference being one of degree and not kind. Simmel emphasizes this continuity when discussing the theatricality of social life:

> We are all in varying degrees poets and painters. . . . Our eyes pick out bits and pieces everywhere, impose some coherence on them, and deal with them as finished, completed objects. . . . In short, in perception, we make use of the self-same function, which liberated from practical affairs and integrated into a complete entity on its own, exists in terms of the art of painting. ("Theory" 309)

There is "considerable artistry inherent in our normal behavior," writes Martin Price, and "the intensification and direction it gains in a work of art does not obliterate the continuity of art and life" (266).

The young Henry James confronted this continuity repeatedly in Europe. "Exhibitions, illustrations abounded in Paris and London," making his "bent for gaping" at and drawing pictures and scenes "quite normal." As he daubed in London and Paris, Henry was struck by the fact that "everyone else" did it too. "The quite normal character" of making representations topples art from its privileged high-culture position: "In Europe we knew there was Art, just as there were soldiers and lodgings and concierges and little boys in the streets" (*Autobiography* 150). The sentence ends with "hot rolls" and "iced water," as it anchors art in the paratactic heterogeneity of James's experiences. For William and Henry the most intimate fact of daily life, as they wandered the streets of New York and the great world capitals on their first trip abroad, was the easy way that art and life, public and private, self and other intersected while preserving their differences. For instance, the young Henry reported being "with precocious passion 'at home' among the theatres" (59). Because hotels frequently served as residences for the family, home itself was often a kind of theater, one where the "social scene" was staged. No wonder James declared that "life in general, all round us, was perceptibly more theatrical" than the "experience of the theatre" (200). As a self-proclaimed "hotel-child," James enjoyed blurring the boundaries of public and private: "So entrancing an interest did I feel at the time to *be* an hotel-child . . . so little would I have exchanged my lot with any small person more privately bred" (19).

The hotel's charms were numerous for James, especially its power to act as a frame in organizing public life and manners into a spectacle. He relished the splendid variousness of the show: "There, incomparably, was the chance to dawdle and gape; there were human appearances in endless variety and on the exhibition stage of a piazza that my gape measured as by miles; it was even as if I had become positively conscious that the social scene so peopled would pretty well always say more to me than anything else" (20). At once immersed and detached in his gaping expansiveness, the publically bred "hotel-child" escaped the bourgeois bias for a privatized mode of living. Instead, he could enjoy a relationship with society as something objective, outside himself, a stance that nurtured his powers of discrimination and increased his capacity to experience the object.

James's lived experience of the mimetic continuity of art and life is usually ignored because of his reputation as an archformalist who segregates art and life. A year before his death, James had the opportunity to confront directly the charge of formalism when H. G. Wells challenged his (alleged) aesthetic idealism. In effect, Wells prompted James to write a coda to his autobiography's meditation on art and life. Although this famous exchange of letters with Wells is often quoted, its value in defining James's particular kind of formalism has not been properly understood. Summing up their disagreement retrospectively, Wells asserted: "We were at cross purposes based on very fundamental differences. . . . From his point of view there were not so much 'novels' as The Novel, and it was a very high and important achievement. He thought of it as an Art Form and of novelists as artists of a very special and exalted type" (Edel and Ray 216). Earlier (1915) Wells had addressed James: "To you literature, like painting, is an end, to me literature, like architecture, is a means, it has a use" (264). In his famous reply James rejected these distinctions:

> I . . . hold your distinction between a form that is (like) painting and form that is (like) architecture for wholly null and void. There is no sense in which architecture is aesthetically "for use" that doesn't leave any other art whatever exactly as much so. . . . It is art that *makes* life, makes interest, makes importance, for our consideration and application of these things, and I know of no substitute whatever for the force and beauty of its process. (267)

James's rejection of the conventional dichotomy between art and life initially puzzled Wells. But he eventually glossed the statement correctly: "When you say '[I]t is art that *makes* life, makes interest, makes importance,' I can only read sense into it by assuming that you are using 'art' for every conscious human activity. I use the word for a research and attainment that is technical and special" (267).

Wells's final words are unintentionally ironic. By the debate's end he appears to have switched sides with James, for now it is Wells who limits art to the "technical and special," the exclusionary move of all traditional formalism. The debate leaves Wells in the position he despises—that of formalist—while James advocates what Wells believed was his own viewpoint: art as an activity for use. By revealing the reversibility of his and Wells's claims, James renders the disagreement "null and void." James collapses the terms of the debate not by abandoning formalism but by extending it to the point where art includes "every conscious human activity." Art "makes life" by imposing form upon unshapely, "clumsy life." By showing that a formalist or aestheticizing impulse inheres in all conscious human action, James becomes a formalist in a sense opposite the conventional one, which separates life and art.[18] He refuses to oppose them categorically because his pragmatic "religion of doing" discourages "arbitrary" and "senseless" separations in the belief that "our behavior and its fruits are essentially one and continuous and persistent and unquenchable" (*Art* 347).

Both his debate with Wells and the depiction of mimetic selfhood in his memoirs deserve to be read in a broader context than mere retrospective, idealized self-justification. James himself provides the terms of this wider context when, in a preface, he speaks of a "high, and helpful public and . . . civic use of the imagination." Regrettably, critics have failed to take seriously James's civic ambition, which "implies and projects the possible other case, the case rich and edifying where the actuality is pretentious and vain" (223). They attend solely to James's immediate concern to defend the "supersubtle" characters of his short stories of artists and writers, whose fineness of sensibility "protest[s] against the rule of the cheap and easy" in contemporary life. When challenged by readers, who insist that "the life about us for the last thirty years refuses warrant for these examples," James replies: "so much the worse for that life" (222). In this "ironic spirit" he justifies his "campaign . . . on behalf of the something better." This campaign is idealized, he admits, since it relies on "*signal* specimens" that possess "immunity from the general infection" of life's "stupidity and vulgarity and hypocrisy" (223). Faced with the possibility that "we have been, nationally, so to speak, graced with no instance of recorded sensibility fine enough to react against these things," James resolves to "baffle any such calamity" by *creating* "the record" of the "honorable, the producible case" (222–23).

This resolve is expressed in stories of the literary life James published in the late 1880s and 1890s. But at this point his campaign is only in its idealist phase. Not until the revisionary energies of his late nonfiction does he create a new matrix in which his efforts find their historicist and pragmatic consummation. James's resolve to challenge the blandness of contemporary life is revived and quickened by his visit to America, where his distress at the absence of "other presences, other figures and characters, . . . other professions, . . . other interests, exemplars of other possibilities" inspires his civic effort of responsible citizenship (*Scene* 427–28). In writing the prefaces following his return to England James renewed his desire to recover the friction of otherness, a project he described not only as a "civic use of the imagination" but undertaken also "in the interest of civilization" (*Art* 222). Several years later James found an arena both intimate and public for promulgating the record of "other possibilities." This time the record he created was not that of idealized "*signal* specimens" immune to the "general infection" but a small boy, brother, and son shaped by the "friction" of urban tumult colliding with "strong imaginative passion." The pragmatic fallibilism of *The American Scene* and the prefaces also shapes his autobiography, dissolving the idealism of James's earlier characters and making his "civic" commitment "rich and edifying." The content of this commitment is a representation of mimetic subjectivity, the repressed other of bourgeois individualism.

James's civic campaign in his autobiography is an enlarging, not an elitist, act of discrimination. It seeks to bridge what Dewey calls the "chasm between ordinary and esthetic experience" that has been "accepted as if it were normal," as if the aesthetic possessed a private, "merely contemplative character" (*Art* 10). James's deidealization of art runs counter to a prestigious bias of modern thought inherited from the Greek distinction between theory and practice. This opposition, says Dewey, divorced practice "from insight, imagination from executive doing, . . . emotion from thought and doing." Exemplifying the Deweyan pragmatic tradition, James's "religion of doing" abolishes art's confinement to the realm of theory where a contemplative subject surveys the world. James would doubtless concur with Dewey that science is an art, that art is practice, and that "the only distinction worth drawing is not between practice and theory" but between those modes of practice that are immediately enjoyable and those which are not (*Experience* 290). Dewey's distinction resembles James's; we need only recall that his "religion" and his "scientific curiosity" (as Brownell described it) evolved from his "far from showy practice of wondering and dawdling," which he was "to enjoy more than anything" (*Autobiography* 17). His "New York *flâneries* and contemplations" nurtured his "visting mind"—"the only form of riot or revel" James would ever know (16).

James's "religion of doing" sponsors new forms of doing and being whose aim is to restore our capacity to see, hear, touch, and feel as "live creatures," a capacity that the "institutional life of mankind" has "narrowed and dulled." Dewey's words suggest the affinities between James's project and Dewey's in *Art as Experience*. In recovering "the continuity of esthetic experience with normal processes of living," we grasp experience as "art in germ," for "experience in the degree in which it *is* experience is heightened vitality. Instead of signifying being shut up within one's own private feelings and sensations, it signifies active and alert commerce in the world; at its height it signifies complete interpenetration of self and the world of objects and events"(19).[19] Dewey's words aptly describe James's antisubjectivist self-representation in his memoirs, where he reveals the hazards and pleasures of interpenetration. His stance of reciprocity, of being fed and feeding, yields to the object, doing justice to its qualitative texture by giving it a "richer saturation." Jamesian discrimination, comprised of the interplay between subject and object (without one dominating the other), values distance as that which nurtures intimacy: "Retention of strangeness is the only antidote to estrangement" (Adorno, *Minima* 94). This dialectic is dramatized in James's wartime visit to Portsmouth Grove. Here his capacity for sympathy, a capacity nourished by the war, is vividly enacted and his unexpressed kinship with Whitman is finally made explicit.

James's visit to a "vast gathering of invalid and convalescent troops" is one of those "certain single hours" that survive in the "museum of the soul's curiosities . . . the cabinet of intimate reference" (*Autobiography* 422). The afternoon is sacred because it is his "nearest approach to a 'contact' with the active drama" of war. During his visit James establishes a "relation" as he dissolves the soldiers' stoic reserve into a "rich communicative confidence," drawing "from each his troubled tale." James's memory of the visit inevitably reminds him of Whitman's more celebrated ministrations to Civil War troops. James delights in having "coincided" with "dear old Walt." Although, says James, "I ministered much more summarily . . . I can scarce have brought to the occasion . . . less of the consecrating sentiment than he" (424). James goes on to compare their differing kinds of intimacy. While the poet's "ground of appeal" is the "familiar note and shared sound" of the "common Americanism of his hospital friends" and himself, James's intimacy is founded on "quite another logic." His relation to the troops can never be Whitman's because James himself is both a convalescent nursing his wound as well as a returned expatriate (his family had returned from Europe a few years earlier) who is only now acclimating, if not assimilating, himself to America as a result of the war. These two facts make impossible the familiarity and fund of shared experience that binds Whitman to the troops. But it is precisely the fact that the "common Americanism" shared by James and the soldiers "disclosed freshness and strangeness, working . . . over such gulfs of dissociation," that enables James to empathize so deeply. Not despite but because of the "gulfs" between them James is impelled to "reach across to *their*, these hospital friends', side of the matter."[20]

Looking back on this incident after fifty years, James is dismayed to discover that in modern (1913) America these "gulfs" have been all but closed due to "our national theory of absorption, assimilation, and conversion" (425). James is referring to "democratic consistency," the "assimilative force" that molds aliens into homogenous citizens (*Scene* 55). He regrets this process because the "national theory" of "absorption" is endangering, if not destroying, the possibility of what, for James, is the richest kind of intimacy: a relation that retains "freshness and strangeness" to stimulate the imagination's expansive reaching across to the other.[21]

What James seeks to nurture in modern life is the simultaneous "nearness and remoteness" of dialectical cognition, which recalls the creative tension of the stranger's stance as defined by Simmel. For Simmel the Jew is a "classic example" of the stranger, and his understanding of this social type was no doubt rooted in his status as an assimilated Jew living in Berlin. There, as in Paris, "they were supposed to be Jews, but not be like Jews." Thus Simmel's experience of nonidentity was acute and direct. This sense of difference, claims Jürgen Habermas, also explains the Jewish affinity for sociology. Because "the Jew's experience of society as something one runs up against was so insistent . . . they carried along a sociological view, so to speak, from their doorsteps." Similarly, their alien status made them "sensitive to the role character of human existence in general" (*Profiles* 35).

James's expatriatism proclaims his nonidentity and alien stance. He conceived of his expatriatism as a deliberate transgressing of boundaries: "I aspire to write in such a way that it would be impossible . . . to say whether I am at a given moment an American writing about England or an Englishman writing about America . . . and so far from being ashamed of such an ambiguity I should be exceedingly proud of it, for it would be highly civilized" (*Letters* 1: 142). This cultivation of dissonance, while recalling the German urban modernists, also inspired an American tradition of critical cosmopolitanism that included Randolph Bourne and George Santayana. A onetime student of Simmel's in Berlin, Santayana fashioned an expatriatism that is perhaps the most elaborately calculated estrangement in American intellectual history. Claiming the world as his host—"I was a temporary guest in his busy and animated establishment"—Santayana made explicit the nexus of cosmopolitanism, discrimination, and antisubjectivism that linked the German and American traditions: "The feeling of being a stranger and exile by nature as well as by accident . . . opened" a mobility of "speculation" as a "travelling Spirit" that permitted him to avoid being fatally infected by the modern world's "long fever [of] . . . subjectivism, egotism, conceit of mind" (*Persons* 539, 546–47).

The tradition of cosmopolitan nonidentity in both Germany and America gains even greater clarity when juxtaposed with a rival tradition derived from *Lebensphilosophie*—the existentialist cult of inwardness associated with Heidegger. In his famous polemic against the "jargon of authenticity," Adorno describes the "hardened inwardness of today [that] idolizes its own purity . . . and retreats from the empirical content of subjectivity" as "the ego posits itself as higher than the world" (*Jargon* 73–74). This privatized, monadic self of authenticity somehow imagines "it has a starting point somewhere outside" the "universally mediated world," where even primary human experience is "culturally preformed" (99). Starting with Heidegger's dislike of "cultural mediations," Adorno spins a web of associations: unease with "the experience of something derived" extends to a distrust of culture itself, of cultural critics (who immerse themselves in objects), and of the city, the site of modern culture. In its self-sufficient inwardness, the cult of authenticity delimits philosophy to ontology—the "chemically pure . . . inquiry into an unruined essence" (98).

Inauthenticity begins with "interestedness," which is linked to surrender to the marketplace, "the world of exchange and wares" (96). Antithetical to the restful, inward contentment of authentic being, interestedness also signifies the stirrings of "emancipated consciousness." The motor of interestedness is "curiosity," and, according to Adorno, Heidegger "equates emancipated consciousness with curiosity. His hatred of curiosity is allied to his hatred towards mobility; both are even hammered into the mind by the ripe old saying: stay in the country and earn your living honestly" (110). The curious self of the urban market experiences "dispersion, which is the consequence of the consumer habit," viewed by Heidegger as "original evil" (71). Dispersion violates the "mineness" of authentic selfhood, the pure identity that conceives "subjectivity as a possession of itself" (115).

Not unexpectedly, the mobile, urban, dispersed curiosity of inauthenticity was associated with the Jew. Simmel's fascination with the object world of cultural mediations violated "a taboo of traditional philosophy" against cultural criticism. According to Adorno, because Simmel's cultural analysis favors the concrete rather than the fundamental and pure themes of "occidental metaphysics," it incurred the wrath of a German academic climate where "authentic" values held sway (98). The Heideggerian tradition of authenticity (or, more precisely, Adorno's polemical portrayal of it) is strikingly relevant. Its set of values possesses a more than passing resemblance to those of the late nineteenth-century genteel American patricians. Unifying both is an antiurbanism that believes in privileged access to a realm of pure, disinterested inwardness, a refuge from the vulgarities of interestedness.[22] Born into and formed by this elite, James and Santayana also emerged from it to become distinguished representatives of cosmopolitan inauthenticity and nonidentity. As the next chapter will demonstrate, these qualities form the fertile matrix from which both men interrogated the rigid genteel psyche.

8

Lifting the Yoke of the Genteel: Henry James, George Santayana, and Howard Sturgis

William and Henry James "were as tightly swaddled in the genteel tradition as any infant geniuses could be, for they were born in . . . a Swedenborgian household. Yet they burst those bands almost entirely. The ways in which the two brothers freed themselves, however, are interestingly different." George Santayana's famous statement in his seminal essay of 1911 points to one of this chapter's concerns: the impact of the late Victorian genteel "yoke" of propriety and repression upon the two eldest James brothers. They were raised in a household that seemed to embody both a sterile transcendental idealism and an energetic flouting of bourgeois conventions. This dual heritage is only one of several paradoxes that characterize William and Henry's relation to the genteel tradition. Thus, the "almost" in Santayana's claim regarding their bursting of genteel bands should remind us that compromise inheres in their revolt. The James brothers, like Santayana, were by birth or position part of the bourgeois aristocracy and enjoyed its privileges. They "sometimes sipped the rim of the plutocratic cup," to borrow Santayana's description of his own life (*Persons* 541).

Santayana's own effort to free himself almost entirely from the genteel Protestant tradition that his Spanish Catholicism and materialism held in unbridled contempt is also a concern of this chapter. Santayana's defiant, often chilly asceticism (a *déraciné*, he asserted, "cannot be replanted and should never propagate his kind") presents a very different emotional temper than Henry James's passionate receptivity (362). The philosopher's memoirs provide a fascinating self-portrait of a man at once an outsider and an intimate of the rituals of Boston's elite society. His double status inevitably recalls his most distinguished predecessor in cosmopolitan expatriatism. But bringing together Henry James and Santayana invites inclusion of an additional figure—Howard Sturgis, the philosopher's cousin, scion of the prominent

Boston banking family living in London. "To the startled eyes of new-comers," reported Sturgis's friend Edith Wharton, he appeared the "strang-est of men" (Wharton 225). "Host and hostess in one," according to Santayana, Sturgis was an openly effeminate man of leisure, a novelist, and perhaps best known today as one of Henry James's closest friends after 1900.

All three men were restive under the constraints imposed not only by genteel conventions, both moral and cultural, but also by their alleged an-tithesis—the gospel of anti-intellectual "aggressive enterprise" that Santa-yana dubbed "Americanism." Both genteel decorum and industrious Americanism share an ethic of compulsive heterosexuality that Santayana, James, and Sturgis challenged, each in his own fashion. For all three men the genteel was not merely the bias of an elite class toward aesthetic idealism but a "yoke," a "tyrant from cradle to the grave," in Santayana's words, which disciplined body and psyche. The latter internalized prohibitions and compulsions, the mode of social control extolled by Hugo Münsterberg and Edward Ross. Thus the genteel is an ideology that intimately links cultural and sexual politics.

Like James in *The American Scene* (echoing de Tocqueville, Mill, and Baudelaire), Santayana found a "levelling tendency" endemic to the Amer-ican democratic spirit (*Character* 208). Both men were concerned less with the Brahmin fear of the erosion of class distinction than with the impover-ishment of human affect and "impulsive sentiment." The engine of this imperative of control, says Santayana, was "Americanism," which began as a tradition that "at first was itself revolutionary." Yet by the last quarter of the nineteenth century, it had ground itself into orthodoxy, producing "a soul that would impose itself on human nature, and remake all human souls in its own image" (qtd. Lyon 214). The image was one of "absorption in work—a work controlled and directed by the momentum and equilibrium of its total movement." Eluding this totalizing force, this "crushing routine," are those not in business, such as "the invalids, the ladies, the fops." Yet these marginal figures are nonetheless "prevented from doing anything else with success or a good conscience," for the "national orthodoxy" of work and progress makes "even what is best in American life compulsory" (*Char-acter* 210). But this hegemony is not monolithic. Modifying it is the fact that American life "*is* free as a whole because it is mobile," and "American orthodoxy, though imperious, is not unyielding" (213). In twentieth-century America Santayana discerned "mitigations of Americanism" that reflected a "certain hesitation in the main current itself, carrying the nation towards actions and sentiments not altogether congruous with experimental progress" (qtd. Lyon 207).

The bachelor expatriates—Santayana, Sturgis, and Henry James—dwell in this uncertain realm of incongruity, crafting self-representations in life and in autobiography that are both cosmopolitan and marginal, powerful and parodic. They combine elements of the invalid, lady, and fop to create new forms of sexual identity, new configurations of mastery and passivity, femininity and masculinity. In short, the androgynous becomes an alternative model of behavior.

In effect, sponsoring or mediating James's and Santayana's recovery of androgyny is Whitman, the great mother of poets, who renovates the claustral self and expansively embraces polymorphous sexuality. By 1904 James had rediscovered Whitman; present at that memorable evening at Edith Wharton's home was Howard Sturgis, a most appropriate audience.[1] Fourteen years earlier Santayana had begun the first of many encounters with the poet: "He produces a new effect, he gives you a new sensation," Santayana remarks of Whitman's genius for "the widening of your sympathies, your reconciliation with nature" (qtd. Lyon 285, 290).[2] The entwining of sympathy and nature (inner and outer) underlies Santayana's understanding of both self and philosophy. A "comprehensiveness in sympathy" will be the cornerstone of his philosophy of naturalism, which esteems "proportion and relativity . . . charity, humility and humour" in contrast to the "ethical absolutism" of "self-inhibited puritans" (138, 148). His is an androgynous perspective able to "see both sides and take neither, in order, ideally, to embrace both, to sing both, and love the different forms that the good and the beautiful wear to different creatures" (*Persons* 155).

Santayana's novel *The Last Puritan* (1936) memorializes the collision between constricted Puritans, imprisoned in "spiritual self-reliance," and the worldly sympathy of those "brilliant slaves of their circumstances" who revel in animal impulse (509). In that work the androgynous Mario, also known as Vanny, "half Italian and half American," emerges as the novel's moral center for, unlike his cousin, Oliver Alden, the novel's doomed Emersonian hero, he accepts that "we are frankly animal" and must not "disown the living forces of nature" (600). Mario attributes his easy acceptance of his varied nature (manifested in his "extreme manliness" and "exotic" brand of "coquetry") to having been his "mother's darling" (7). She teaches him, virtually from birth, that the "sense of power," art, and love are embodied in the feminine. Mario is a particularly resonant figure in the present context because he is partly modeled on Howard Sturgis, whose own novel *Belchamber* (1903) influenced Santayana's. *Belchamber*'s effeminate titular hero has a capacious sympathy that finds its deepest fulfillment in mothering another man's infant son.

It is significant that for James and Santayana the representation of androgyny involves the staging (in memoir and novel, respectively) of a particular primal scene: the son's early identification with his mother. In his own life Sturgis was celebrated by both Santayana and James for his maternal presence, embodied in his never absent workbasket of embroidery. Like the knitting of James's own mother, Sturgis's work is the emblem of his nurturing sympathy. Possessed of a "dramatic fertility in his own person," as Santayana described his cousin's mimetic, androgynous self, Sturgis brings the logic of mimetic behavior to its inevitable, absurdist conclusion (*Persons* 359).

Santayana, Sturgis, and James embody various degrees and strategies of

sexual experimentation. Sturgis's flamboyant effeminacy, Santayana's fastidious, immaculate asexuality, and Henry's passionate sublimations represent
three efforts to mitigate the nervous repressions of the genteel and the rigidity
of pragmatic Americanism. Before pursuing these issues, I will set James
among some other genteel figures for the purpose of instructive contrast.

I

By the second decade of the twentieth century the genteel had become an
epithet employed to disparage a variety of sins of the Victorian fathers. But
prior to this revolt, the word's political and cultural associations were a badge
of honor in the highest American intellectual circles. E. L. Godkin, the man
whose legacy William James described as the "towering influence in all
thought concerning public affairs," was a self-proclaimed "mugwump" (qtd.
Perry 2: 294). This label included "men of cultivation . . . known to the
masses as . . . dissatisfied, querulous people, who complain of everybody and
cannot submit to party discipline. But they are the only critics who do not
criticize in the interest of party, but simply in that of good government"
(Godkin, *Problems* 212). Along with lofty disinterestedness, the other supreme fiction of the genteel patrician class was that natural laws were the
foundation of laissez-faire economics. By adhering to John Stuart Mill's economic liberalism, the Mugwumps conveniently put Nature wholly on their
side. With Nature undergirding their authority, the gentry could, with a clear
conscience, advance "their own interest, as a class and as intellectuals, while
denying the legitimacy of any other interest" (Bender 189).

In loyal, Godkinian tones William James insisted that "the mission of the
educated intellect in society . . . reestablishes . . . the normal perspective of
interests, and keeps things in their proper places in the scale of values." In
James's view, intellectuals should be a source of "incessant criticizing" and
"blow cold upon the hot excitement, and hot upon the cold motive." This
attitude, he confessed, "sometimes wears a priggish expression and is generally unpopular and distasteful" (qtd. Perry 2: 298). Thus, "living Mugwumps" have a lonely road to travel. Often, says James, "their only audience
is posterity" (299). A Protestant sense of solitary calling characterizes James's
"mission," which retains something of what Santayana, in his analysis of the
genteel tradition, called the "agonized conscience." This inheritance from
Calvinism views "life in sharp and violent chiaroscuro, all pure righteousness
and black abominations, and exaggerating the consequences of both" (qtd.
Lyon 38–39).

The Manichean moralizing that Santayana implies is a feature of genteel
social thought recalls Henry James's estimate of Charles Eliot Norton's "intellectual and aesthetic 'missionary' labor." Norton's frequent travels in Italy
nurtured a lifelong love of Dante, who would be his principal scholarly
subject. Yet, "as a good New Englander," Norton was "never . . . without
certain firm and, where they had to be, invidious discriminations" that made
him "incapable of doubting" America's finer moral tone (*American* 122).

Indeed, a zeal for moral labeling marked his career: "With admirable urbanity of form and uncompromising straightness of attack, the Professor of the History of the Fine Arts at Harvard for a quarter of a century" spared no effort to "brand the ugly and the vulgar and the inferior wherever he found them" (124). James visualizes Norton's moralism as a lifelong effort to "try and lose himself in the labyrinth of delight while keeping tight hold of the clue of duty, tangled even a little in his feet" (127).

Some thirty years prior to this assessment, Henry had experienced first-hand Norton's relentless "aesthetic crusade." Writing from Paris to William in 1872, Henry remarked: "The Nortons are excellent, but I feel less and less at home with them, owing to a high moral *je ne sais quoi* which passes quite above my head. . . . Charles . . . takes art altogether too hard for me to follow him,—if not in his likings, at least in his dislikes. I daily pray *not* to grow in discrimination, and to be suffered to aim at superficial pleasure. Otherwise, I shudder to think of my mind ten years hence" (qtd. Perry 1: 328). Sounding here like Oscar Wilde celebrating those who judge by appearances, James did not grow in terms of Norton's lofty style of discrimination. Instead, he practiced an inclusive, not an exclusionary, form of discrimination.

Norton conceives of the aesthetic as serene contemplation, a view that functions as part of a larger cultural strategy implemented by a Victorian, Protestant leisure class. Certain members of this class are ambivalently drawn to European Catholic culture as offering aesthetic release from the "rigid male ideals" of the American bourgeois aristocracy. Jackson Lears has described the aim of this alternative as "loosening rigid character ideals and creating more fluid possibilities for self-definition" (*No Place* 219). Although it would initially seem that Henry James's achievement of a looser, more open mode of subjectivity fits this cultural pattern, such a conclusion ignores significant differences that emerge when we juxtapose the efforts of James and Norton to seek "a wider selfhood."

This last phrase is taken from Lears's discussion of Norton's attempts to escape the strictures of Victorian morality. According to Lears, Norton "identified Catholic Europe with 'feminine' values of repose, contemplation, emotional dependence," which he then sublimated "into some form of accommodation with the dominant culture." Because Norton "could not accept as a model the self-absorbed aesthete," he could turn to "aesthetic contemplation" only by "preserving an ethic of suffering" that "blocked his retreat to the debased mode of passive aestheticism" (219, 247). "On the whole," writes Lears, "Norton adjusted to modern ego ideals, sublimating his 'feminine' impulses in socially acceptable forms" (242, 246). While not mentioning James, Lears's reading accords with the novelist's portrait of Norton as a "quite anomalous" Puritan aesthete forever stalled before the labyrinth of delight. Unable to "lose himself" in the "labyrinth" of free curiosity, Norton's need to control and accommodate results in his cult of stoic masculinity. Norton seems trapped in a guilty relation to the aesthetic, which, in the accounts of Lears and Henry James, he associates only with the contemplative, indolent, and effeminate aesthete, an image implicitly rooted in a conception of the feminine as solely the repository of passivity and dependence. Perhaps one reason Norton makes this equation is that it leaves open a place for his own intervention: he supplies the weak, feminized, European aesthetic with the stern American Victorian moral fiber that safely renders it a prime attribute of the discriminating gentleman's "moral conscience."

His fellow Mugwump William James conceived the aesthetic in such a way as to make unnecessary the injection of moral fiber. For William the aesthetic and the ascetic have a natural affinity: he equates the saint's "craving for moral consistency and purity," his need for autonomy and withdrawal from life, with "that law which impels the artist to achieve harmony in his composition by simply dropping out whatever jars, or suggests a discord" (*Varieties* 296). Knowing what to omit, says William, is crucial to "character" in life and literature. Henry, as we have seen, expressed an ambivalent attitude toward omission and discord, tending to nurture the latter at the expense of the former. Doubtless William would find this ratio as perverse as Henry's attraction to vagrant curiosity.

If Norton and William James feared the pleasures of vagrant curiosity, another Brahmin, William Wetmore Story, was virtually helpless to resist them. As Henry James commented in his biography of the sculptor, he "had not . . . enough indifferences." James felt prompted "to commiserate his [Story's] flexibility of attention," for although Story's disposition to "flit rather than to rest" gave him pleasure, it also impaired his artistic concentration (*Story* 2: 226, 215). He possessed Henry James's receptivity but lacked his discipline. In Rome, Story's capacious appetite for "active diversions . . . tempted him perpetually," and his unapologetic hedonism mocked Bostonian decorum. The transplanted Brahmin aristocrat described the genteel society of his birth as having "little blood and few sensual temptations" (1: 299). Before the final move abroad, and with an American career still possible, Story's was an "alienated mind," remarks James, who doubtless sympathized with the sculptor's response to New England. James might have been speaking about himself when he described Story's relationship to Boston: "Its very virtues irritated him, so that its ability to be strenuous without passion, its cultivation of its serenity . . . must have acted as a tacit reproach" (1: 304).

That James identified too closely with the expatriate sculptor was more or less what Henry Adams charged after "devouring" the Story biography. Adams's epistolary response and James's reply open a revealing window upon the latter's relationship to the genteel tradition. The "painful truth," writes Adams, is that "you have written not Story's life, but your own and mine,— pure autobiography"(524). As Adams admits here, he also identifies with Story, whom he finds emblematic of all "my New England generation. . . . [We] were in actual fact only one mind." He labels this single-mind "type bourgeois-bostonien." With characteristic self-contempt, he indicts it for an essential provincialism. In a verdict that would have delighted Santayana, Adams describes his generation as one of shallow, "improvised Europeans" full of "self-distrust . . . [and] nervous self-consciousness." This Harvard Unitarian mind—he names Emerson, Story, James, Lowell, Sumner, Alcott, "and all the rest"—"knew nothing" of the world. James has now painfully exposed this. "You strip us, gently and kindly, like a surgeon," says Adams, "and I feel your knife in my ribs" (524).

Adams's remarkable response requires some disentangling, for while its sweeping indictment portends unflinching honesty, his tone actually conceals a deeper source of displeasure. A certain note of desperation lurks in Adams's exaggerated rhetoric of identity here and elsewhere. (Upon the death of William James, Adams wrote Henry that their three lives "have made more or less of a unity" [406].) This fear melts all differences into a single-mind "type bourgeois-bostonien." The problem with this "uniform" label is its obvious inadequacy regarding the unprovincial expatriates James and Story, the only two on Adams's list who actually thrived in Europe. As James's biography makes clear, Story is certainly bourgeois, but he is far more bohemian than Bostonian in his tastes, psyche, and appearance.[3] His bohemianism—particularly his insatiable curiosity about everything Roman, "from rubbish and riff-raff" on up, including his admiration for the Jewish ghetto—is what James admires in Story and marks the sculptor's divergence from Adams's typecasting. In short, Adams's deeper source of irritation likely derives from the affinities James and Story share, affinities that rupture "bourgeois-bostonien" identity.

None of this is articulated directly; it peers out from James's reply, which adroitly separates himself and Story from Adams. Rather than being puzzled by or sympathetic to Adams's pain, James offers no apologies for stabbing him. Instead, James remarks that he "can see" a "kind of *inevitableness*" in "the whole business" of Story "having made" Adams "squirm" (*Letters* 4: 289). But James does not squirm. Writing Story's life, he tells Adams, put "me to conclusions less grim . . . than in your case." Perhaps James sees Adams's squirming as inevitable because James understands that the "whole business" of Story includes not only his happy expatriatism and bohemian freedom but, most troubling, a philo-Semitism abhorrent to Adams's staunch anti-Semitism. This "whole business" was what James admired and, to some degree, identified with. Sensing this, and feeling disgusted by it, Adams dissolves the special affinity between Story and James into an all-embracing single "type" that welds them to Adams. But Adams's assimilative strategy (which anticipates the efforts of generations of critics to yoke James and Adams together as exemplary of "type bourgeois-bostonien") is a defensive move that cannot deflect the difference that James's biography implicitly insists on, a difference underscored by the violent tone characterizing their exchange of letters.[4] By making Adams squirm—and even politely stabbing him—the "whole business" of Story inadvertently became a way for James to dramatize divergence from the "New England generation . . . 1820–1870" (Adams 524).

One reason Henry James carefully avoided making his career a "New England adventure" was that "the New England air was no natural conductor

of any appeal to an aesthetic aim." This derived from the unresolved ambivalence of the New England mentality regarding the aesthetic, which it
both spurned—as passively feminine or perverse—and craved as a pleasurable loosening or dispersion of self. Such a view fails to encompass James's
grasp of the aesthetic as energetic practice involving moments of passive
dispersion. Abandoning New England frigidity, James entered the "labyrinth
of delight" at whose entrance Norton remained immobilized (*American* 121,
127). But in entering this strange and shifting ground of expatriatism and
nonidentity, James did not escape the genteel label. Instead, he was seen
by many as merely embracing another version of it. Van Wyck Brooks, for
example, regarded him as "the personification of 'feminized' European aestheticism" (Lears 256).[5]

Versions of this charge have also been leveled at Santayana. For instance,
his Harvard colleague William James called him "a spectator rather than an
actor by temperament" but respected him despite this "element of weakness" (qtd. Perry 2: 270). The alleged passivity and weakness of Henry
James and Santayana (when judged by the standards of William's muscular
pragmatism) are more accurately regarded as expressing their effort to diffuse
traditional gender polarities that define the masculine as the repudiation of
the feminine and the embracing (indeed, the fetishizing) of a rigid autonomy.
Henry James and Santayana find an antidote to this pattern in an androgynous
mixing of genders that incorporates otherness into the self, a process originating in the flexible gender identifications that occur in the pre-Oedipal
phase. In the case of both men, androgyny is more a dimension of sensibility
and psychic economy than of actual behavior. As we shall see, Santayana's
androgyny is, ultimately, an ideal celebrated in his philosophy and his fiction,
while James's androgyny is a facet of his libidinally sublimated curiosity.

Androgyny also figures in James's aesthetic and social thinking. He conceives of artistic practice as inherently androgynous, for at the highest pitch
of intensity it erodes the distinction between doing and feeling, male and
female. For instance, Shakespeare's "disciplined passion of curiosity," which
"flowers . . . into the freshness of each of" his characters, possesses an empathic pliability that James associates with the feminine genius (*Literary* 1:
1212). James is ambivalent regarding this feminine suppleness; he both
celebrates it and finds it disconcerting. He once warned against the "fatal
gift of fluency" as an endemic hazard among women novelists. Though he
remained ambivalent about aesthetic androgyny, by the turn of the century
James had gradually become an advocate of androgyny as a social ideal for
women. In light of this ideal, his skepticism toward the separatist feminism
of *The Bostonians* is understandable. This separatist movement practiced a
politics of identity by polarizing the sexes and enforcing the rigid cultural
divisions that were such a dismal feature of the American scene (a subject
explored in chapter 10). By 1914 James welcomed women's "effective annexation of the male identity" as the "consummation awaiting us" and
applauded their "repudiation of the *distinctive*," by which he meant the
rejection of fixed gender roles (2: 780–81). This "shift of the emphasis from

the idea of woman's weakness to the idea of her strength" constituted a salutary "new evolution and transformation" in female identity. To serve as the patron saint of this evolution James nominated the once scandalous bohemian George Sand. The idol of an earlier generation of radical American thinkers, including Margaret Fuller, Sand's most "abiding value will probably be in her having given her sex . . . the real standard and measure of change" (774). Sand's mimetic experiments in androgyny, which reveal gender as artifice, reject enslavement in the cultural prison of femininity, which had been the site of "immemorial disabilities" (780). Not only could she "figure as a man of the mere carnival or pantomime variety" but, more important, she dealt with life "exactly as if she had been a man." Her bold annexation of male identity, which provides "richness" to the masculine, is precisely the "challenge" that women should emulate instead of looking to the "challenge of the 'average' male" for inspiration (774). While admiring and recommending Sand's "repudiation of the distinctive"—of static, invidious gender distinctions—James envisioned the "new evolution" as proceeding in one direction only: female appropriation of the masculine. It is not "probable," he remarks, that men will be drawn "over to the feminine type," though earlier, in *The American Scene*, he had been more optimistic (780). Yet James's own psyche was feminized thanks to an early identification with his mother and the presence of a de-Oedipalized father— one who did not embody prohibitive law.[6] Instead, the elder James encouraged rather than repressed Henry's curiosity. By studying his relationship with his parents, we can better understand Henry James's ambiguous attitude toward the genteel tradition's social, intellectual, and sexual norms.

II

James senior was perhaps closest to his son in managing to avoid accommodating his behavior to patrician ideals of duty and becoming "actively inert in his own behalf." He was the most immediate influence upon Henry's permeable "gaping" self, which made self-abnegation a kind of self-assertion. Father passed on to son two other cardinal values: vagueness and inertia. But Henry transformed them to suit his own creative purposes rather than leaving them to float ineffectually in an idealist realm characterized by "freedom from pressure" and "serenity of synthesis"—keynotes of the James household (*Autobiography* 336, 363). Henry found his father's freedom from the pressures of commitment to a particular profession, college, church, country, or homestead enjoyable yet "positively embarrassing" and even "tasteless and . . . humiliating" in a culture where "business alone was respectable" (278). Susceptibility to embarrassment became both a crucial difference between father and son and constitutive of the novelist's developing sense of identity, as embedded in "social and material crowdedness" replete with norms and ideals (338).

As his memoirs make clear, Henry James came to know intimately the severe social and philosophical limitations of idealist or transcendent critique,

with its contempt for "vulgar visibility." He merely had to listen to his
father, whose purity of faith was "fed so little by any sense of things as they
were or are" (362, 370). Instead, James senior was absorbed in the tranquil
rhythms of his writings, "with their so easy glide from . . . analytic play, in
the outward sphere, to serenity of synthesis and confidence and high joy in
the inward" (363). "Serenity of synthesis," which his father believed would
"bridge the chasms, straighten the distortions, rectify the relations," would
never do for his son, who sought the burden of mutually conflicting impressions
(371). Frustrated by the lightness of his father's being, which slipped free
"from pressure," Henry felt "a shade of irritation" at the elder James's
"implied snub" of his love of crowdedness. The novelist celebrated "variety,
variety, *that* sweet ideal, *that* straight contradiction of any dialectic, hummed
for me all the while as a direct, if perverse, . . . effect of the parental concentration" (344). Henry rejected not merely the inward center of peace but
the very notion of telos by reveling in variety: "I heard it [the "hum" of
variety], felt it, saw it, both shamefully enjoyed and shamefully denied it
as form" (344).

An Oedipal dimension can be detected in this enjoyable secret shame
which flouts "parental concentration," and it is clearer still in James's admission that "I owed thus supremely to my mother that I could . . . muddle out
some sense of my own preoccupation." "Under" the "singular softness" of
his mother's nourishing recognition, the young Henry could find comfort
from the elder Henry's "implied snub" and gain the confidence to pursue
"variety" as the potent "contradiction" of his father's "dialectic." The Oedipal overtones suggest the deep emotional investment involved in this clash
of dialectics. By revising the radical idealism of his father's life and thought,
Henry wished to prolong the moment of "analytic play," deferring reconciliation in "inward" "synthesis" so as to promote tension between subject
and object, identity and nonidentity, femininity and masculinity.

In psychoanalytic terms,[7] James's cultivation of tension can be said to
express his revision of the supposedly normal resolution of the Oedipal
scenario, which involves the male child's flight from the mother and identification with the father. While identifying with James senior's contempla-
tiveness and iconoclasm, Henry rejects his near indifference to otherness.
This solipsistic serenity in effect de-Oedipalizes the elder James, for his
avoidance of pressure makes it difficult for Henry to develop the emotional
friction necessary to produce the cathectic charge of Oedipal identification.
Henry's relationship to his mother encourages difference (rather than paternal
indifference); with her he establishes mutual recognition. In the James
household he is known as her perennial darling and "angel." One effect that
this cross-identification breeds in Henry is the precious sense of difference,
of identity as the recognition of otherness rather than (as in the Oedipal
construct) the confirmation of sameness. As he oscillates between mother
and father, Henry's flexibility of gender identification permits him to prolong
this bisexual pre-Oedipal phase. Correlative with his relish for variety and
tension is James's divergence from the conventional scenario of heterosexual

entitlement, which posits as essential the devaluing of the mother and rejection of the feminine to ensure the attainment of masculine identity.
James unobtrusively weaves into his autobiography the play of reciprocal
attunement to his mother. It occurs as the oppressiveness of his father's
"narrowness of exclusion" becomes most acute—when James senior reads
his philosophical "papers" to a captive audience consisting of his wife and,
occasionally, Henry. In retrospect, the novelist finds "touching" this "brief
illusion of publicity" granted his father. But such occasions might have
proved suffocating to Henry had not his mother ventilated them by means
of her profound and intricate act of listening, which expressed her genius
for what her son called "complete availability." James writes, "I see our
mother listen, at her work, to the full music of the 'papers.' " In this subtly
evoked primal scene of parental reading and listening, the "full music" that
the mother is able to hear includes her son's "irritation," his "suffer[ing]
. . . under the impression" of his father's obtuse "style." Her recognition of
Henry assuages his anxiety, permitting him to "muddle out some sense" of
his own difference, which is threatened by the presence of the droning father
(343–44). How different is William's classically Oedipal relationship to his
parents.

Henry describes his mother's "selflessness" as "consistently and unabatedly
active," a quality that distinguishes her self-abnegation from that of the
Victorian angel-in-the-house, who is emptied of all subjectivity save that of
the instinct for self-sacrificial nurturance (343). Indeed, her son implies that
she possesses something of the chameleon poet's negative capability: "She
was he [father], *was* each of us," notes Henry of her "gathered life in us."
This recalls the empowering self-abnegation of Henry's self-representation.
The same hazards are risked by mother and son. Henry's penchant for
absorption in otherness at times leaves him "with not a scrap . . . for a personal
show." Analogously, he wonders how his mother can have "anything ever
left *acutely* to offer," such as a "special show" of a "personal claim."[8] Henry's
diffuse, feminized identity mimics his mother's relational self ("she was . . .
our possibility of *any* relation"), which provides an alternative to his father's
insulated autonomy.[9]

Henry also expresses his difference from the elder James by exulting in
the impact of the "material pressure of things." Finding pleasure in materiality and embeddedness becomes one way of resisting his father's ascetic
abstractions (569). Another way is Henry's willed vulnerability to embarrassment, which serves as an index of "friction" and thus a source of the
"pressure" James values in the face of his father's (at times) infuriating
tranquility. Yet Henry manages to derive sustenance from the elder James's
tenacious commitment to vagueness and inertia by "work[ing them] for all
[they] were worth" and converting them to his own creative purposes (279).
By his mid twenties Henry has rejected the "serene synthesis" that was the
emblem of his father's flaccid, genteel idealism, having come to "feel . . .
confidence in the positive saving virtue of vagueness" itself (412). For his
vagueness is not his father's. Its signal virtue is not immunity but precar-

iousness rooted in receptivity to "possibilities." To cultivate possibilities, to "watch and protect the germs," is to form a "consciousness . . . [that has] after all its own intensity" (280). Thus James will reject the serene synthesis of marriage, preferring to mimic his mother's gift for hearing the "full music," for achieving sympathetic, multiple engagement. The force of his mother's "complete availability" is preserved in his own bachelorhood, that mode of perennial vagueness or deferral of sexual identity that would be simplified if labeled "homosexual" or anything other than indeterminate. Certainly his desires and pleasures are homoerotic, but he keeps his body to himself.

The result is a sexuality akin to what Santayana calls "perfect love," a condition of willful, transformative self-negation that entails "the total abdication of physical, social or egotistical claims." This negation is engendering, for with abdication "great passion becomes worship . . . becomes wholly aesthetic, pure joy in beauty and charm." The passion of this "sublimated" love, says Santayana, "does not become bloodless, or free from bodily trepidation. . . . It is essentially the spiritual claim of a carnal fire that has turned all its fuel into light. The psyche is not thereby atrophied; on the contrary, the range of its reactions has been enlarged. It has learned to vibrate harmoniously to many things at once" (*Persons* 429). As well as any words can, Santayana's remarkably Jamesian evocation of libidinal sublimation reproduces the texture of the novelist's capacious affective life, his passionate curiosity and saturation in human experience. In particular, it evokes his rapturous feelings of ardor for his beloved men: Andersen, Walpole, Fullerton, and Persse.

That the abjuring of physical possession engenders such intensity of feeling in James suggests that there was most likely no beast in his closet raging to emerge, no (or little) sexual frustration or repression that inflicted an emotional frigidity upon his psyche. Here, as we will see, he stands in contrast to Santayana. On the other hand, it is certain that he understood such frigidity, identified with it, and surmounted it. This is clear from his portrait of John Marcher in "The Beast in the Jungle." Marcher's inert solipsism, with its extinction of curiosity, is less a self-portrait than a projection of what James might have become had he not practiced his "religion of doing." Under this pragmatic aegis, he committed "himself in both directions," enacting in art and life his own version of the androgynous ideal, latent in his conception of genius, as the "rich passion" to perform the "whole possible revolution" (*Art* 31).[10] That such an ideal was at best marginal in America is implicit in James's contrast of his vague self with the fixed self of business and its mandatory routine: "To attend strictly to business was to be invariably *there*, on a certain spot in a certain place" (*Autobiography* 305). Business can function as a metaphor for the generally congealed status of the American male, whose submission to compulsory heterosexuality results in psychic desiccation, a major theme of *The Ambassadors* and the subject of the next chapter. James's (androgynous) vagueness eventuates in his expatriatism, which is another form of bachelorhood. If this strategic indeterminacy can be said to resist the (heterosexual) routine of American business, it is also traversed by it. Thus he situates his vagueness "on a mere margin, the margin of business." Yet for James the tension of marginality provides a salutary pressure, stimulating the "consciousness" of "possibilities" (279).

III

Santayana was less sanguine; those who escape the "crushing routine," the "levelling tendency" of the "gospel" of business, are made to feel like "traitor[s]" and "soulless outcast[s]." The self-contempt of those on the "margin of business" comes from having internalized the "overpowering compulsions" of American life, which not only obstruct freedom but colonize the American psyche (*Character* 211). "Compulsions" are far more "galling" and pernicious than "prohibitions," says Santayana, because "what is exacted cuts deeper; it creates habits which overlay nature, and every faculty is atrophied that does not conform with them" (210). In short, the triumph of the American spirit's "insolent claim to monopoly" over external nature now extends to the coercion of man's inner nature. The hubris and compulsions of this insatiable will to control constitute main targets in Santayana's prolonged, near obsessive campaign against the genteel. It was far from merely a philosophical critique. His inquiry was virtually inseparable from his personal sense of suffocation, which could find release only in resigning from Harvard, abandoning America, and assuming the life of a perpetual stranger.

Under Santayana's withering, virtually wholesale indictment, subjectivism, idealism, moralism, transcendentalism, egotism, pragmatism, absolutism, and the New Humanism are arraigned as modes of the genteel tradition in philosophy. In his eyes they are all guilty of the intellectual defect he identified as the "dominance of the foreground." This obtains when "some local perspective or some casual interest is set up in the place of universal nature or behind it, or before it, so that all the rest of nature is reputed to be intrinsically remote or dubious or merely ideal" (qtd. Lyon 115).[11] This mistaking of the local for the universal, in Santayana's view, is not only the source of metaphysics but of humanism. The latter doctrine has driven man to repudiate arrogantly his "animal status" for the "Satanic dream that we are creators and not creatures" (202). In contrast, Santayana's self-described "hard non-humanistic naturalism" venerates the greatness of nature after the manner of "the old Ionians or the Stoics or Spinoza," who despised the foreground and "sunk speechless before the infinite."[12] Since then there have been few modern figures—Whitman is an exception—inclined to reacquaint man with his relativity, both natural and historical.

The poet's animal stoicism and "faculty of appreciation" represent one of the rare antidotes to the hegemony of the genteel tradition, with its "agonized conscience" and "moral absolutism" intent on sweeping "everything foreign from the face of the earth" (138). Santayana prizes the poet's insistence on our animal status and quotes with admiration Whitman's desire to live with the animals, for "they do not sweat and whine about their condition . . . and weep for their sins" (289). Despite his "vague pantheism," there is in Whitman a vital and "profound piety that recognizes the life of everything in nature, and spares it, and worships its intrinsic worth" without judgment, without assimilation to our particular interests. This natural piety, "more primitive and general than any social aspirations," is for Santayana the poet's "ultimate appeal" (289). Along with Whitman's "sympathy and receptivity," Henry James's rejection of subjectivism and the fixed, closed self of bourgeois routine doubtless held exceptional personal appeal to Santayana, the perpetual stranger of "complex allegiances."

Not surprisingly, Santayana felt a far greater affinity for Henry James than for his Harvard colleague William James. So lovable and natural, William "was at times the dupe of his desire to be appreciative. . . . He was too impulsive for exact sympathy; too subjective, too romantic, to be just" (*Character* 94).[13] After his first and only meeting with Henry James, Santayana noted:

> In that one interview he made me feel more at home, and better understood, than his brother William ever had done in the long years of our acquaintance. Henry was calm, he liked to see things as they are, and be free afterwards to imagine how they might have been. We talked about different countries as places of residence. He was of course subtle and bland, appreciative of all points of view, and amused at their limitations. (*Persons* 287)

In distinguishing Henry James's response to the genteel from William's, Santayana observes that "to understand oneself is the classic form of consolation; to elude oneself is the romantic." The novelist's "understanding," Santayana suggests, proceeds immanently: he overcomes the genteel by immersing himself in it, somewhat like the humorists Santayana describes, who keep the "savour" of their wit by only "half-escaping" the tradition. Henry's sensibility is enriched by rejecting the genteel delusion of transcendental liberation. Such "systematic subjectivism" is really only a snare that returns the solitary ego to its dream of infinitude (qtd. Lyon 41). Instead, Henry converts his entanglement in the genteel into a broader view. He is able to adopt "the point of view of the outer world" (i.e., a naturalist vantage) and thereby achieves a historical awareness that views the genteel American tradition simply as a "curious habit of mind . . . to be compared with other habits of mind." In this way, the way of understanding, James turns the genteel "into a subject matter for analysis" (48). Thus characters in his fiction suffer calamities by believing in the "universal jurisdiction" of certain ethical and moral values.

Santayana freely grants that William James's romanticism, the chief source of which "was his personal spontaneity . . . and his personal vitality," gave a "rude shock" to the genteel. William "kept his mind and heart wide open to all that might seem, to polite minds, odd, personal or visionary" (49). Yet William's "radically empirical and radically romantic" philosophy had inadvertently "broken the spell of the genteel tradition," only to continue "it into its opposite." A paradox, Santayana implies, inheres in one's relation to the genteel: to escape it wholly, by romantic rejection, is to risk "continuing it" because the basis of rejection is merely avoidance—an eluding of one's own finite nature, which ultimately becomes an eluding of history. This avoidance triggers the haunting, ironic circularity of subjectivism: not only does William James's romantic celebration of free will unwittingly universalize the values of liberal Protestantism, but his "radically romantic" empiricism returns to the flux, to "the beginning of the world," since it is the "philosophy of those who as yet had had little experience" and act as if unfettered. Yet this is precisely what makes his "way of thinking and feeling" representative "in a measure [of] the whole ultra-modern, radical world." For modernity perceives the universe as "wild and young, and not to be harnessed by the logic of any school." What Santayana suggests is that William's irrationalism (like Bergson's) remains inspiring, for it mirrors modernity's disregard for the past (48–49, 52).

In this culture of subjectivism, says Santayana, the ability to face nature and history directly requires courage. His naturalism makes consciousness epiphenomenal and demands that one identify with one's body, since "no discoverable mind can ever have existed except in a body" (*Persons* 417). The light of the spirit is always "kindled by something else. . . . It is kindled in an animal psyche, in a living perishable heart; and it falls on the world in which that heart and that psyche have been formed, and is deeply dyed in their particular passions" (171). A fascinating aspect of Santayana's autobiography is its own tension between the claims of the spirit and nature. The above passage, for example, with its lyrical yet chastely abstract and decontextualized celebration of sensuality and physical pleasures, finds itself in the barely articulated context of Santayana's personal situation: the personal ordeal of an "animal psyche" absorbed in numerous homoerotic friendships while stranded at the dead center of genteel Boston society.

The times demanded a mandatory heterosexuality, especially for Harvard professors, and Santayana, as one of the few unmarried faculty members, was already arousing suspicion in that quarter. In a private memo President Charles Eliot confessed to "doubts and fears about a man so abnormal as Dr. Santayana . . . [a] withdrawn, contemplative man who takes no part in the everyday work of the institution, or of the world" (qtd. McCormick 97). Although his colleagues rallied around him and granted him tenure in 1897, Santayana experienced no sense of liberation. He described the next fifteen years as a "somnambulistic period" in which he lived as if an automaton (*Persons* 352).[14] The years he spent living a closeted life in Cambridge amid the "compulsions" of "Americanism" cut deep, denying him a sense of fulfillment of his natural preferences in a world that, for the materialist, "stimulates and feeds from every quarter the concupiscence of the flesh, the concupiscence of the eye." Bombarded by such temptation, "what can the poor rush-light of spirit . . . do to clarify them?" (422).

Santayana's clarification eventually came in the form of renunciation—not of the spirit but of the nagging claims of the body. He learned to possess things and persons in the mind, for "to possess them physically or legally is a burden and a snare" (428). Maintaining allegiances but surrendering possessions, Santayana described himself as "driven from the temporal to the eternal" (426). Bolstered by this psychic and sexual renunciation (reminiscent, in some ways, of William James's willed act of self-making) and the recent windfall of an inheritance, Santayana submitted his resignation from Harvard in 1911, effective the following year. Thus, at the age of forty-eight he ended a twenty-three-year career as a professor in the nation's preeminent department of philosophy.

He was to spend his remaining forty years in Europe, never once returning to America. England, France, and Italy would be the scene of his temporary, makeshift residences, usually consisting of one or two rooms in a hotel. During his last ten years, he lived in a small room with a narrow bed in the Hospital of the Blue Nuns in Rome. "Five valises and nine cases of books and papers" made up the sum of his worldly possessions (75). As he explained, "Materially I might be the most insignificant of worms; spiritually I should be the spectator of all times and all existence." He had thus made good on his "platonic transition . . . from the many to the one, from the existent but transitory to the ideal and eternal" (423). The stark trajectory of his material life is not simply that of an evaporation into disembodied spirit. The compelling literalness of Santayana's renunciation of the material world is a clue to its fertility; it unleashed in him a ferment of creativity, of imaginative engagement, because it passionately adhered to nature's merciless discipline.

With consummate dramatic timing, Santayana staged the embrace of his host, the world, and his abandonment of the foreground of America precisely at the conclusion of his valedictory: "The Genteel Tradition in American Philosophy." In August 1911, the year he resigned, he delivered this address in Berkeley, California. The setting was crucial, for at the conclusion of his speech he turned to the sierras and forests that surrounded him, extolling their "non-human beauty," which "give[s] no sign of any deliberate morality seated in the world." It is the "yoke of this genteel tradition itself that these primeval solitudes lift from your shoulders" (qtd. Lyon 55–56). In the final moments of his soaring peroration to the mountains of northern California, Santayana delineates what man can achieve once the yoke of anthropocentrism is lifted. His sketch of "unregenerate natural man" blossoming in plain sight of nature's ineffable "variety" is worth scrutinizing, for it crystallizes a number of themes that resonate in this chapter, themes that his later work would explore once it had emerged from the shackles of the genteel (134, 55).

Earlier in the speech Santayana singles out the James brothers' notable efforts to escape the genteel. But Whitman remains the one American writer to have left it "entirely behind" (47). The echoes of his unique achievement silently but powerfully suffuse Santayana's closing hymn to nature. If nature's ferment of differences is smothered by genteel idealism, Whitman is the renegade who has given voice to its unspeakable variety and "non-censorious infinity." Years earlier Santayana had heard "the voice of nature" in Whitman's images of "frankness and beauty" and had found that in reading the poet one was "returning to nature" (286, 298). Now Whitman's unnerving "impartiality," expressed in his loosely structured verse, mimes nature's absence of intention, responsibility, or plan (290, 55). Such seeming chaos naturally makes Whitman "an unpalatable person" for "educated Americans," who fear that Europeans will mistake his gross sensuality and "formlessness" as "representative of their culture" (47). Ironically, although Whitman is indeed unrepresentative of genteel American culture, "foreigners" find him both "representative and original." For the poet gives voice to the "inarticulate principles" latent in democracy. To foreign eyes Whitman's great achievement is to have carried democracy "into psychology and morals." His "refusal to discriminate" is no mere poetic idiosyncrasy but a means of renovating the rigidly stratified genteel psyche and its tight control on "sights, moods and emotions." In Whitman's verse they are "declared to be all free and equal," with each "given one vote."

In 1911, enlisting "foreign" opinion in extolling Whitman's construction of a democratic subjectivity reflects a particular cultural and sexual politics that Santayana is careful both to express and keep tacit. Thanks to the efforts of John Addington Symonds and Edward Carpenter, Whitman "functioned as a badge of homosexual recognition" in England and was a "step in the consciousness and self-formation of many members of that new Victorian class, the bourgeois homosexual."[15] But unveiling this tacit dimension should not imply that Santayana's address contains an exclusively homosexual subtext. Rather, his penultimate plea—"let us therefore be frankly human"— should be understood as a demand for a postgenteel psyche open to a range of sexual "sights, moods and emotions." According to a Whitmanian democratic selfhood, heterosexuality and homosexuality will each be given one vote; neither will be privileged. Attunement to a variety of possibilities and options will replace the absolutisms that sanction gender polarities as if they were wholly natural.

The power of the maternal is everywhere implicit at the conclusion of Santayana's address on the genteel. His subtext claims that by lifting the genteel yoke we can be reunited with the mother that was repressed and repudiated in the Oedipal scenario. What can be called the pre-Oedipal texture of Santayana's hymn to nature accounts for much of his passionate eloquence. He brings the pre-Oedipal undertone to full voice by speaking through Whitman. For the recovery of the mother is virtually synonymous with reunion with Whitman, the great mother of poets. Both mothers are androgynous, imbued with a "relativity of morals." Their multiplicity bespeaks the "variety, the unspeakable variety, of possible life." Their recovery inspires man to dissolve the monadic autonomy of masculinity for a flexible identification with both sexes. Nature, says Santayana, teaches that "your natural dignity and joy" is in "representing many things, without being them" (55–56). Yet if the child's polymorphous proclivities seem set free under the watchful eye of Mother Nature, this is not to say that Santayana is to be confused with Emerson or Whitman or Marcuse. His "hard, nonhumanistic naturalism" saves him from such romanticism. Thus, he portrays man not as a fallen god needing or reclaiming redivinization but as a profoundly humbled soul whose "forced sense of [his] own importance" is suspended once he grants nature's primacy. Indeed, nature admonishes us that what one can do "avails little materially, and in the end nothing." Nature, in short, metes out injury to the child's narcissism, its imperial pretensions to becoming a transparent eyeball. For all her beneficence, Mother Nature remains a "non-human beauty."

Santayana's own mother had something of this beauty. With her he discovered no pre-Oedipal freedom. Instead, he admired her "philosophic conformity with fate," while always regarding her as a "rather hostile power." He completes her portrait:

> In her apparent passivity she retained absolute authority in matters of discipline and money. She was not meddlesome, she left us for long stretches of time to do as we liked; but then suddenly the sword would fall, pitiless, cold and surgically sterilising, to cut off our tenderest tentacles for our own good. I could shrug my shoulders at this high control. . . . I could even sympathise with my mother's intelligent firmness . . . but the others [his brothers and sisters] suffered. (*Persons* 248–49)

Santayana goes on to call his calmly castrating mother "heroic." He not only sympathizes with but actively admires her rather than his deaf, embittered father, who, "unlike my mother, was not brave" (17). "In me, my mother saw and dreaded an equal . . . an equal to her in independence of will." Only "the others," with their "incapacity to resist contagion," suffered her lacerating control (249).

One interpretation that this remarkable passage provokes is Santayana's counterphobic identification with the phallic mother. Though this reverses the typical Oedipal configuration, polarization still abides as he appears to give up his emasculated father and to internalize his mother as the image of just but merciless Nature, ever ready to punish those who are needy or dependent. But in becoming his mother's equal in "non-human" immunity from merely human suffering, a price was paid in the paralysis of affect. Even in old age, returning at last to the feminine, the bosom of Rome, "mother and head" of his "moral world," where he composed his memoirs, Santayana expressed no anger, sorrow, or pity for his mother or himself (467). Only "the others" suffered. Only they "demanded a sympathy that they never found" (249). His ban on self-expression may have partaken of the "somnambulism" that helped him withstand his later years at Harvard. Evidently this condition became as much a prison as a survival strategy. The prison's name is invulnerability, the perennial instrument of masculine entitlement in its rejection of the feminine. Ironically, Santayana's commitment to an androgynous nature was ultimately restricted to the philosophical; in his own psyche, as he grew older, the masculine compulsion for indomitable mastery came to rule.

IV

The maternal sympathy denied Santayana he found in his cousin Howard Sturgis. So rich was his affective capacity and responsiveness that Santayana called him a "universal mother." To understand the mix of admiration and unease in Santayana's response to his uncanny, androgynous cousin, we need to recall the Freudian structure of the uncanny as the return of the repressed. Santayana's ambivalence would seem preordained, given that Howard had been coddled as his mother's "last and permanent baby" (358). Sturgis's "inimitable honest mixture of effeminacy and courage, sensibility and wit, mockery and devoted love" (514) becomes, as we shall see, a striking cultural achievement in its comic play upon the genteel code. But first we should examine how he inadvertently reveals the closeted emotional and sexual life behind Santayana's fastidiously preserved aloofness.

The portrait of Sturgis in Santayana's memoirs is made indelible by certain details, fragrances of a lost but still cherished maternal paradise that will recur in his portrayal of Mario Van Der Weyer in *The Last Puritan*. What intrigues Santayana is that Mrs. Sturgis's "boudoir became Howard's nursery and his playroom. As if by miracle, for he was wonderfully imitative, he became, save for the accident of sex, which was not yet a serious encumbrance, a perfect young lady of the Victorian type" (358). Not only did he learn to sew and embroider (all his life "his work-basket stood by his low chair") but his mimicry became a "sort of involuntary caricature." While "crossing a muddy road he would pick up the edge" of his coat "as the ladies in those days picked up their trailing skirts." Santayana finds Howard's effeminacy unsettling and explains it as a compulsion, perhaps even a case of hypnotic automatism. His cousin's "grotesque exaggerations" seem symptomatic of a "fixation . . . to his mother" (359). Yet at the same time Santayana commends Sturgis's "remarkable courage" in entering and surviving Eton with his effeminacy intact, his nature unyielding to social pressures. Howard's brothers had sent him there as a "last desperate measure . . . to cure him of his girlishness" (359). What evidently helped him persevere at Eton was his mother's staunch support of his girlishness: "Would it have been *right* to correct dear little sweet Howard for girlishness when girlishness wasn't *morally wrong?*" Santayana's tone here is complex, a mixture of admiration at Howard's fidelity to his nature and mockery (disguising jealousy) of the indulgent mother who thought her son "sweeter as he was" and thus desisted from correcting him (359–60).

Howard was to remain uncorrected, a "permanent baby" who preserved his girlishness by virtue of a heroically sustained act of mimesis: he became a man's impersonation of a perfectly genteel lady—or, more precisely, mother.[16] As "host and hostess in one," Howard held court at his Windsor estate, Queen's Acre, with his companion, William Smith, appropriately nicknamed "the Babe." Howard could be found "in a soft nest of cushions, of wit, and of tenderness, surrounded by a menagerie of outcast dogs, a swarm of friends and relations, and all the luxuries of life." Thus is he

described in the prologue to *The Last Puritan*, as he will be a second time—
six hundred pages later—in the epilogue. He is enshrined as one of the
novel's presiding spirits, a tutelary deity inspiring Santayana's invention of
his moral hero, Mario.

One of the "swarm of friends" at Queen's Acre was Henry James, who
dubbed it a "sybaritic sea." Like Santayana, he, too, admired their mutual
friend's maternal care and hospitality, which, at different times, proffered
invitations to both James and Santayana to take up permanent residence
with him and "the Babe." In 1912 James graciously declined: "What an
angel of bounty you are, and what handsome advantage is taken of it! I shall
not add by a touch, dearest Howard, to that handsomeness" (*Selected Letters*
396). Santayana declined less graciously in 1920, the year of Howard's death.
"Old, desolate, ill and hard up," Howard proposed (at least in Santayana's
ungenerous account) that Santayana come and live as a "paying guest." To
a "suggestion that might have enticed me twenty-five years earlier" Santayana remained cold and cruel, permitting himself several pages of self-
confessed "heartlessness" aimed at his cousin. In fact, Santayana almost
gloated over the pathetic ruin that Howard had become in his cancerous and
impoverished condition. A "thick mist of sadness" had set in at now-
dilapidated Queen's Acre and Howard was "living in the past," his sentimentality an inadequate substitute for the "genuine British stamina" that
would have kept him "jolly in old age" (510). Apparently his inveterate
girlishness ultimately proved his undoing.

As if partly aware of his homophobic reaction, Santayana granted that his
attitude toward his suffering cousin was "inhuman." But he attributed his
coldness to "sympathy with nature . . . not any aggressive selfishness" or
competitiveness (512). In this very denial is a clue to the source of Santayana's
ambivalence toward Howard. In a sense Santayana competed with him for
access to nature's vast sympathy. However, this was a rivalry that Santayana
could not win; Howard was the "universal mother" of sympathetic imagination and the very embodiment of fidelity to, and joy in, one's "native way
of living" (511). Earlier Santayana had admired this ease of acceptance. But
his admiration always partook of envy, which fully emerges in the gleeful
cruelty contained in his description of his cousin's final days. What Santayana
probably envied was not only Howard's utter ease with his mixed nature but
also his unrenounced intimacy with Mother Nature, exemplified in his own
mother's serene confidence and pride in her son's "rare" nature. No "surgically sterilising" maternal sword fell on Howard, no yoke of propriety
imposed a fetish of masculine self-sufficiency.

Santayana's compulsive autonomy, the expression of his closeted femininity and androgyny, stands in contrast to Howard Sturgis. One way to
frame their difference is that Howard is richly endowed (as Santayana
notes) with the "free spirit of comedy" (510) that the philosopher himself
celebrates in his *Soliloquies in England*, a work completed in the decade
following his exile from America. This spirit is intimately aligned with
what "non-human" nature teaches man—that his inner nature is to "rep-

resent many things, without being them" (qtd. Lyon 56). Howard's mimetic powers of representation are embodied in multiple modes: his fiction, his own mimicry of a Victorian lady, and his imitations of friends, which Santayana described as "works of art, taking off not only voice and manner to perfection, but supplying diction and sentiments to suit" (*Persons* 510). Henry James was said to be one of his masterpieces. "Sparks of this free spirit of comedy flew constantly from Howard in his youth," and in this sense he became his own greatest work of art. To live in the spirit of comedy is to make one's soul as "plastic and volatile . . . [as] the general flux of nature" (*Soliloquies* 139).

Existence is "comic inherently" because it "involves changes and happenings" and "incongruity, a consequence of change." The comic spirit embodies and expresses inadmissible knowledge—that "this world is contingency and absurdity incarnate, the oddest of possibilities masquerading momentarily as a fact. . . . To be irrational and unintelligible is the character proper to existence" (140). Metaphysicians, tragedians, literalists—"all the solemn sages" of custom and convention—passionately oppose the comic spirit.[17] The "Censor" is the collective name Santayana gives to these moralists who have "habitually aimed at suppression" (134, 153). As a new incarnation of an earlier foe—the genteel—the Censor is all the more insidious because he attacks from the inside: "The latest psychology" calls the Censor the super-ego, "an important official of the inner man." By "locking up our unseemly passions in solitary dungeons, the Censor composes a conventional personage that we may decently present to the world." This zealous propagandist of self-regulation puts the inner man in "harness"; he is "groomed and reined in like a pony" (154–55).[18]

Santayana's delineation of the comic spirit allows us to describe more precisely Howard Sturgis's achievement. First, his liberation from propriety and convention is thoroughly immanent in its parodic inflation of the genteel Victorian lady and thus risks triviality and self-humiliation. But Sturgis's comic self-invention is more than artful camp or mere burlesque, more than simply an inversion of gender signs featuring a man imitating a woman. Such creative self-fashioning, in itself a convention of bourgeois play, would only confirm the sexual status quo.[19] Rather, his mimetic powers encompass a variety of impersonations and identities. Sturgis's "dramatic fertility" is a flowering of his "natural dignity and joy . . . in representing many things," which powerfully defy the imperative of fixed identity inculcated by Censor and custom. By demystifying the myth of the natural that is the weapon of the moralist, Sturgis's androgynous comic spirit challenges gender as absolute, self-identical, and static essence. Sturgis opens both femininity and masculinity to the play of internal incongruity and contradiction— marks of instability usually reined in by a cultural "harness" disguised as natural truth. He thereby revives the freedom of childhood, where we are "not forced to remain always consistent" and where play and masking afford "the pleasing excitement of revising our so accidental birth-certificate" (127).

As both "permanent baby" and "universal mother," Sturgis was freely expressive himself and the nurturer of expression in others. It was as a mother that his friends tended to respond to him. And the pleasure of knowing him could not help but be entwined with the pleasure of becoming a child again. Henry James, a lover of revision, mimesis, and incongruity, makes this explicit. In a letter written in 1901 he exclaimed: "My dear Howard, you are indeed as a nursing mother to me, and I, babe like, (though indeed as if you hadn't already Babe enough, to spare) gurgle back my gratitude."[20] On another occasion James called Sturgis a "richly sugared cake always on the table" (qtd. Borklund 255). Even after granting the comic hyperbole of James's luxuriant epistolary style, his passion for Sturgis's "exquisite spirit" seems vivid testimony of the exhilaration the latter could impart. By partaking of his maternal sweetness, James returned to the knitting figure of his own childhood and her steadying sympathy. Not surprisingly, when Howard the mother threatened to be eclipsed by Howard the novelist, James was distressed, gave in to selfishness, and proved a less than encouraging literary mentor. Indeed, so blunt was his criticism of *Belchamber* that Sturgis never wrote another novel and, according to Edith Wharton, "relapsed into knitting and embroidery. For the joy of his friends this was hardly to be regretted, since it left him free to give them his whole time" (235).[21] Faced with a choice between life and art, Sturgis chose life and made that his art. How relieved James must have felt to have his "nursing mother" returned to him.

Yet *Belchamber*, Sturgis's third and best novel, is not a negligible achievement, especially in its depiction of a man deeply at odds with the cultural, political, and sexual codes of the late nineteenth-century British aristocracy. Disgusted by the complacency and hypocrisy of his class, its philistine pieties and cruel indifference to the starving urban poor, Sainty Belchamber is a man trying to do good works in a society bereft of humane family traditions and social institutions. Exacerbating his sense of being a misfit is his pronounced effeminacy, which leaves him with a tormenting sense of "unlikeness to other people." Belchamber's exceptional but starved powers of empathy and love at last find an outlet in a "precious infant" who becomes "the best happiness his life had ever known." Predictably, this part of the book, where Sainty in effect serves as a male mother, elicited James's warmest praise. The child Belchamber mothers is born of the union of Sainty's wife and her lover, his cousin and boyhood friend Claude Morland. "Like some strongly scented hothouse flower . . . sweet with a strong sweetness that already suggested some subtle hint of decay," Claude has always bewitched the lame, delicate, and virginal Sainty (30). With his "ready flow of talk and perfect self-possession" and a "charming feline" seductiveness, Claude is a more sinister version of what James called the "glossy male tiger, magnificently marked" (133). Though this phrase refers to the sculptor Gloriani in *The Ambassadors* (published the same year as *Belchamber*), it applies even more to Chad Newsome (in the same novel) and to Mario in Santayana's *Last Puritan*.

In broad terms, all three works depict a worldly, glamorous man of charm and beauty who captivates a repressed "Puritan" bachelor hero. Cursed and blessed with an "unhealthy, abnormal perception of other people's feelings," the bachelor is left nearly solitary in a society populated by seductive figures of "intense egotism" (Sturgis 157, 224). Each of the novels can be said to represent, in different ways, the homoerotic energies inherent in this plot. James leaves implicit but vivid the erotic quality of the spell Chad exerts on Strether. The latter admits that he's "quite already in Chad's hands" just prior to enjoying that "rare youth's" "wonderful" ways and to discovering that "the change in him was perhaps more than anything else for the eye" (*Ambassadors* 88, 91–92). Yet for Strether Chad's allure will remain on the physical, visual plane, while the attractions of the young man's mistress, Marie de Vionnet, will be more inclusive, both sensual and emotional. In short, James does not limit Strether's awakening in Paris to homoerotic fascination but opens it to embrace heterosexual desire and, ultimately, pleasure itself as violent sensation without a fixed referent. As the next chapter will show, Strether occasionally surrenders to this primitive impulse.

Rather than diffusing his novel's eroticism across a spectrum of modes of desire and experience, Sturgis tended to suppress it. This absence of eroticism was the implicit point of James's critique of *Belchamber* that so devastated Sturgis. The failure of Sturgis's novel was its inability to dramatize, either in Sainty's consciousness or in external action, what had been made vivid from the start—that upon their first meeting Sainty had found Claude "impossible not to love." James told his friend that *Belchamber* suffers "from Sainty's having no constituted imaginative life of his own" (*Letters* 4: 294). When Sturgis justified this by explaining that "nothing happens" to Sainty after his marriage, James replied: "It is the part in which *most* happens! . . . *Claude* above all happens to him, and I regret that the relation, in which this would appear, so drops out. . . . What the subject only asks is that he [Sainty] shall *feel*" (296). Sturgis, in short, had failed to discover his deepest subject because he did not permit Sainty to bring to consciousness (in either a sublimated or direct way) his desire for Claude.

The tacit irony disclosed by James's critique is that the unabashed male mother of Queen's Acre wrote a novel marked by sexual unease and timidity. One reason *The Ambassadors* is more open to sexual desire is that James wrote it when that "glossy male tiger" Hendrik Andersen was "happening to" James. Andersen's presence doubtless helped inspire the novelist to represent Strether's sense of Chad as pervaded by a "charmed and yearning and wondering sense, a dimly envious sense" (*Letters*, Lubbock 2: 245). Thus, the play of sublimated passion nourished James's life and art. But also enriching them was his "nursing mother" Sturgis, whose personal example (if not his art) influenced James's representation of Strether's experiments with new forms of identity and sexuality. For Henry James the lesson of *Belchamber* seems to have been that its author's mimetic genius had the capacity for creating a single masterpiece, and that the masterpiece was Howard Sturgis himself.

V

Santayana might have modified that judgment, for not only was Sturgis a presiding spirit over his cousin's novel, but *Belchamber* furnished *The Last Puritan* with some characterizations and plot details.[22] Moreover, Santayana avoided the sexual timidity that hampered Sturgis's book. Santayana's fictional memoir, which he worked on intermittently for forty years, seems to have granted him the freedom to explore what his autobiography seemed to forbid: the sexual temptations, torments, and confusions of an animal psyche left unnourished by its mother. Santayana knew intimately the stunted affect and paralyzed desire that comes of this starvation, and in *The Last Puritan* he described this condition with the authority of painful experience. Yet the triumph of the novel is its depiction of, and tribute to, what he never knew save in imagination—the loving mother who nurtures and emboldens her child.

As Santayana noted more than once, *The Last Puritan* concerns "petering out," a favorite phrase that is often used in his autobiography to describe the "decline of the idle plutocracy."[23] The life and early death of Oliver Alden are meant to be understood as representative, the definitive anatomy of the social, cultural, and psychological malaise inflicted by the genteel yoke. Oliver fails to "live naturally" or to enjoy life because he lacks "the animal Epicurean faculty" of relishing it in its "arbitrariness and transiency" (*Letters* 207, 305). As is made clear throughout the novel, Oliver's emotional paralysis is rooted in "sexual suppressions" (206).

The greatest sexual pleasure of Oliver's life is swimming nude with Jim, a lover of Whitman and the sea.[24] After Jim's death, Oliver admits that his true inclination would be to sail around the world with him in a friendship "without the least reticence or hypocrisy" (*Puritan* 573). Yet even if Jim were still alive, Oliver's native priggishness would have made such a relationship impossible. Their friendship had petered out long before the sailor's death. The pagan Jim, discharged from the British navy for "immorality," had wished that Oliver had "dared call his soul his own and had the courage of his feelings." Jim understands that Oliver is "afraid of himself"—afraid of confessing (as Jim puts it) that he's "a little smitten with a friend." He reasons, "What harm can there be in showing it. . . . Poor lad! Caught before birth in a trap, born in captivity" (373–74). Oliver is blocked not only with respect to his friend. Women, too, "fail to fetch him through the senses," says Jim. "He doesn't like women as women; that sort of stickiness makes him sick; he's afraid of it; he loathes it." Oliver's inhibitions are "not very original," Jim contends, but are typical of many "respectable Americans" whose sexual nervousness often reduces them to "poor mincing ham-strung ridiculous cowards" (374–75).

Jim's enthusiasm for diving into things "blindly, before you know what will come of it" (592), embodies one alternative to genteel anhedonia. Another is offered by Oliver's cousin, Mario, in love and in pursuit of a variety of women. Mario is ultimately far more nuanced than Jim, though at first his libertine suavity seems as familiar and limited as Jim's debauched primitivism. Mario is "incalculably capricious" not in the sense of irresponsibility (he is a loyal friend to Oliver, a decorated war hero, and, finally, a husband and father) but in being inordinately empathic and curious. "Only half-human, a faun or amiable demon," his plasticity and volatility mirror the "general flux of nature." In sum, Mario embodies Santayana's comic spirit.[25] "Delicate in his strength, strangely agile and supple," though "apparently so flighty," Mario's histrionic grace has none of Oliver's stolid absolutism, his "distrust of doubleness" which cannot "admit chaos" (8–9). Refusing to fetishize sincerity and self-reliance, Mario accepts the self's contradictory impulses without seeking to cancel either. He always knows he is "producing an effect" and enjoys producing it. But his "coquetry" and "vanity" are not merely ends in themselves but express his socializing impulse to "compose" a "social figure" of grace and color that will "give people something to stare at" and enjoy (4). His is a healthy narcissism imbued with the comic power of sympathy, which modifies and complicates impulses to dominate and control.

Mario thus avoids Oliver's desolate, asocial narcissism. Oliver's confinement in his ascetic prison of the self is masked by his genuine grace and modesty. But it is his very "integrity of purpose and scorn of all compromises" that makes him incapable of the abandonment that sensuality requires. Where Mario acquired this gift of self-abandonment is a question the novel had earlier pursued, for the answer marks the crucial difference between (using Santayana's dualisms) genteel and comic, Protestant and Catholic, absolutist and naturalist. More important, the answer explains "what love really is." "I am an evil influence," Mario informs Oliver at their first meeting, when each is still an adolescent. "I explain to the boys what love really is." Mario's secret knowledge disturbs the authorities at Eton, who want him ejected (295). "And *what is love really?*" asks Oliver. He receives an answer years later, but only after Mario has asked his own question of Oliver: "Were you brought up on the bottle" or were you suckled? On the bottle, of course, Oliver replies, like everyone else in America. In this admission Mario locates the source of Oliver's unease with women: "You don't know what a woman is. You are not comfortable with women. It's all because you never loved your mother and she never loved you. That makes all the difference. My mother suckled me at her own breast" (408).

Here Mario puts in words what Oliver has already intuited—that he has been scarred by the icy tentacles of his monstrous, controlling mother, who despises all his friends and has made him feel worthless. "Because Mother never loved me she won't allow that anybody else can" (354). Oliver's realization has been virtually predestined, given his "nostalgia for femininity"(75). According to Santayana's myth of gender, this nostalgia afflicts those males born without the "generous female's" added "compensation" of emotional "buoyancy" and serene good humor, qualities necessary to offset the fact of being "unsatisfied, restless, and masculine." Bereft of the feminine, a permanent yearning will abide, a nostalgia for a "placid, motherly, comfortable fulness of life" (75).

Mario is free of this nostalgia because he has integrated femininity into his psyche; he has been suckled by a generous female. "I seem still to remember it. But suppose I couldn't remember it; the habit would be there, the impulse, the confidence, the love of softness, the sense of power" (409). The power derives from his mother, a former operatic contralto who had taught her young son how to sing and perform. But her instruction in self-representation also contains a deeper lesson concerning the power of sympathy. His mother's artistry avoids romantic self-expression in favor of a calm, impersonal style; disdaining singing that traffics in excess emotion and grand effect, she lets the music sing through her. Widowed while still young, she devotes herself to Mario and even resumes her own career so that he "should still be proud of her . . . and adore her" (411). Yet his mother's maternal "instinct" to monopolize her son's affections, not to "want anyone else to love [her] baby-boy," is not oppressive to Mario because, like her art, she is blessedly free of egotism (410). The same was true of Mario's late father, who "skipped Wagner, and worshipped his wife." Though "without mastery of any artistic medium," Harold Van Der Weyer had a virtually unrivaled capacity to be "genuinely appreciative and discriminating." Moreover, "he entirely skipped the sickly aestheticism" of the nineties (317). His refusal of mastery and deferral to his wife suggest that he is a de-Oedipalized father. The blurring of gender polarities makes it easier for Mario to internalize both parents rather than repudiate one for the other. Implicit in Mario's father and explicit in his mother is the power of sympathy, the ability of self-transport that is the basis of love, freedom, and art.

As his mother discloses, to be transported out of oneself is a paradoxical process that first requires getting "down deep, deep into oneself, down to all one might have been." To explore this realm of possibility is to enter the world of art and illusion, of playing a part. Yet this "making believe" is also sincere since it arises "out of the very depths of yourself." Freedom is the name of this state of self-transport, this shaking off of "your artificial shell" comprised of the Censor's demands to obey rules of social decorum. "Art takes you beyond all that," Mario tells Oliver, the adamant opponent of art. "And then, if you sing, everybody that hears you is transported with you" (412). Mario invites Oliver, who has a beautiful voice, to experience at first hand this life "at a different tempo." He urges him to "come to Paris and let my mother teach you to sing." She would, Mario promises, "get you out of that hole" of being a "philosophical egoist by nature." But, of course, Oliver's Puritan conscience grows uneasy at the thought of self-transport ("Wasn't it just shirking, a mere escape and delusion?") and he decides to forgo meeting the great mother, whose lessons in freedom would lift the yoke of the genteel (413). "Self-directed and inflexibly himself," Oliver's great but untrained voice remains locked within him (326).

Given the bleak facts of Santayana's own childhood, this representation of a "mother's darling" possesses a remarkable imaginative generosity by which he partly atones for his harshness to that other darling, his cousin Howard. Making possible Santayana's depiction of mother and son is the maternal spirit his novel celebrates. For what engenders Santayana's act of sympathetic imagination if not his own descent "down deep" to "all one might have been and might have felt, if all [life's] confounded accidents hadn't prevented." His mother's surgically sterilizing sword is sheathed, and Santayana can venture into the might have been of a pre-Oedipal world of maternal nurture and mutual recognition. This is the world that Mario inhabits, one founded on a "different tempo" that breeds the difference of cross-identification rather than complementarity. In content and form this realm embodies what Adorno calls a "promesse de bonheur." Such a world is untouched by the catastrophe of unitary identity and all it entails: the domination of one's inner nature, the self sacrificed to itself. Sacrifice and domination are sanctioned and disguised by the culture as mastery and invulnerability or, more familiarly, masculinity.[26] Masculinity, says Adorno, constitutes the "mutilated social character of men" that is mirrored in femininity, "the mutilated social character of women." Both are equally disfigured (*Prisms* 82). Given the disciplinary status of gender, it is no accident that Mario's access to an alternative, unmutilated, noncompulsive masculinity is tabooed as "evil" knowledge, or that Mrs. Alden, a withered and genteel matriarch, must dismiss Mario as "effeminate" (346).[27]

"Androgynous" would be a more accurate judgment, for Mario lives rooted in nature's "unspeakable variety," which Santayana addressed with subdued exaltation in his hymn to the sierras that ends his 1911 peroration on the genteel. It had concluded with the request: "Let us be content to live in the mind." In this contemplative realm of the spirit Mario will abide as an essence of complete humanity, a clue "as to what might render human existence good, excellent, beautiful, happy, and worth having as a whole" (*Character* 85). This figure of the imagination, created out of Santayana's deepest frustrations and generosity, presses back against the pressure of the coercive reality of Americanism to become "the case rich and edifying where the actuality is pretentious and vain." Henry James's insistence on "honoring the possible other case" is apposite here, for it suggests the proximity of both his and Santayana's unwavering belief that "the interest of civilization" in an important sense depends on the ability of the creative imagination to mount a campaign "on behalf of the something better" (James, *Art* 222).

In delineating "the something better," both men draw on the pre-Oedipal, which functions for Santayana's Mario and for James himself as a "long-lasting residue that accompanies other drives." In contrast, Howard Sturgis's relation to the pre-Oedipal has a regressive quality, given his abandonment of the literary vocation and surrender to the passive pleasures of embroidery.[28] Surrender to a massive, unnurturing mother defines Lambert Strether's captive state at the start of *The Ambassadors*. But he eludes this phallic mother's disciplinary yoke. With the aid of a generous female, Strether recovers his youth and, with it, the volatility and turbulence characterizing pre-Oedipal sexuality. James returns his groping, middle-aged "toddling" hero to the stage where the "living forces of nature" are beyond the Censor's reach and "something better" than obedience to genteel identity beckons.

9

Going to Smash:
Violence in *The Ambassadors*

In an 1895 notebook entry that constitutes the initial "germ" of *The Ambassadors*, James discloses that "the core of the subject" is the "revolution that takes place in the poor man" who five years later would become Lambert Strether. The word "revolution" appears twice more in the notebook entry, as well as in the 1900 "Project of Novel" and in the 1909 preface. James's repeated use of this momentous word to describe what happens to an elderly man who "has lived only for . . . effort, surrender, abstention, sacrifice" opens a gap between diction and subject. This discrepancy is always a prime source of Jamesian comedy, and nowhere more so than in a novel whose fifty-five-year-old hero happily confesses his absurdity as he finally learns to "toddle alone" (*Notebooks* 141). But granting Strether a mock-heroic stature is only one strand in a novel that is also serious about portraying him as experiencing a "revolution."[1]

On one level the term "revolution" refers to the 180-degree rotation Strether performs as he reverses his original intentions midway through the novel. But by its end Strether reverses his reversal, completing both his intended mission (he and Chad go home) and his inward revolution. As James notes in his "Project," he has proceeded "so far through his total little experience that he has come out on the other side. . . . He must go back as he came . . . " (575). Simultaneously, of course, Strether's 360-degree return, his closing of the circle, also leaves him deeply changed, "quite other. . . . He goes back other—and to other things" (575). Already implicit in James's anomalous formulation that Strether "must go back as he came—or rather, really, so quite other" is the dialectic of identity and difference that the novel will make one of its major thematic concerns. This dialectic is structurally inscribed in the internal pressures of the work James judged "quite the best" of his "productions" (*Art* 309). A source of pressure is the fact that the vagrant straying that marks Strether's inward revolution is encased in the novel's circular revolution, the basis of its much-admired formal symmetry. This tense arrangement, where one revolution jostles against another, is implied in James's claim that the novel is "very packed . . . with a good deal of one thing within another" (309). Given his belief that the novel is an art form that appears "more true to its character in proportion as it strains, or tends to burst . . . its mould," James's "packed" structure in *The Ambassadors* can be read as a strategic effort to pit one revolution against another. "Each baffles insidiously the other's ideal"; the inherent conservatism of the circular one strains to contain the implosion of Strether's change (46, 298).

James cultivates his characteristic "double pressure" (300), or friction, as a means of formally enacting a central action of the novel: a violent struggle between a disciplinary social order and one of its subjects, who is in the process of revolting against its coercive demand of identity. But James's formal pressure also mimes the friction that Strether comes to discover (and recover) as a primal source of pleasurable, exhilarating activity. My focusing upon Strether's pleasure seeks to challenge the critical tendency to immerse James's protagonist in a rhetoric of sterile negativity that portrays him as vicarious, renunciatory, prissy, fearful, and ascetic.

Igniting what James calls the process of revolution is the impact of "some great human spectacle" of "curiosity and experiment" (among other elements) that shatters the "simplicity" of Strether's original intention of bringing Chad back from Paris. In his "Project" James emphasizes that for Strether in Europe "everything is different. Nothing is manageable, nothing final—nothing, above all, for poor Strether, natural" (*Notebooks* 561). The fact of difference is the one positive term: "Difference" is what Strether finds "himself sinking [in] . . . up to his middle . . . difference from what he expected, difference in Chad, difference in everything." And "difference," says James, "is what I give" (562). To extract some causality from the above, one could say that "curiosity and experiment" unravel the simplicity of original intentions to such a degree that Strether is left nearly stranded in a quicksand of "difference." On his second morning in Paris, Strether is confronted by a "consciousness of difference. . . . What he wanted most was some idea that would simplify" (*Ambassadors* 60–61). But before too long "an uncontrollable, really, if one would, a depraved curiosity" assails Strether in Paris and never relents (72).[2]

The depravity of James's hero recalls episodes in the long trial of curiosity. In his famous remarks about Galileo, Descartes had complained that "his error is that he continually digresses and never stops to expound his material thoroughly. . . . He built without a foundation" (qtd. Blumenberg 397). Descartes's rationalism rejected the very premise of Galileo's curiosity—that "new truths are found off the side of the direct path of what method anticipates, by seizing accidental opportunities, by being ready to drop the thread of principles already established." Because the "motor quality of theoretical curiosity" easily succumbs to "objective irritations," Descartes judges it too hazardous and unreliable to achieve the rational goals of knowledge (397). Correlative with his dislike of digressive curiosity is Descartes's reliance on the notion of a centered, "true" self. As Richard Rorty notes, for Descartes "the mind and its faculties . . . were to remain as Platonism and Christianity had conceived of them" ("Freud" 13). Hence Descartes's is a morality of "self-purification," which Rorty contrasts with a morality of "self-enlargement." The desire to "purify oneself is the desire to slim down, to peel away everything that is accidental" and become simpler and more transparent. "The desire to enlarge oneself is the desire to embrace more and more possibilities, to be constantly learning, to give oneself over entirely to curiosity" (11). Rorty's contrast roughly defines the differences between William James's late quest for a transparency or "fluency" beyond language and Henry's interminable "rare curiosity." Freud is one of the great apostles of self-enlargement, "the life of unending curiosity, the life that seeks to extend its own bound rather than to find its center." Freud, says Rorty, was the "first in the twentieth century to help us rid ourselves of the notion that we have a true self" (12).[3]

Thinkers after Freud continue to interrogate this notion. Implicitly summarizing Foucault's views, William Connolly has declared: "Those who celebrate the agent as center of self-discipline, rationality, freedom, and self-consciousness are thereby unwitting vehicles of disciplinary society. To seek to dismantle the modern subject . . . is to oppose the hegemony of disciplinary society. Anything else plays into its hands" (*Terms* 237–38). Roberto Unger and Leo Bersani are among the many who have begun this dismantling process. In different contexts both distinguish between character and self in the belief that the former does not exhaust the possibilities of the latter. To "free oneself," in Unger's words, "from the tyranny of character," with its automatic, habitual responses disguised as "irrevocable fate," and "to treat character as more than a fate, to open it to revision" demands "experiments in accepted and heightened vulnerability" (*Passion* 98–99). The compulsive character of identity comprises what Unger calls character, which can be dissolved into nonidentity once one sees it "as but a partial, provisional, and pliable version of your own self" (111). Character, says Bersani, is a "partial self. Its appearance of completeness, of wholeness, may be nothing more than the illusion created by the *centralizing* of a partial self" (*Future* 313–14). Bersani pleads for an end to this centralizing illusion and an "exuberant indefiniteness about our own identity" (314).

More recently, Bersani has radicalized his position into an "ethical-erotic project" that favors an aesthetic of self-dispersing narcissism in which the "sacrosanct value of selfhood" is erased and the self reduced to a "practical convenience." Yet this reduction is "hygienic," for when the self is "promoted to the status of an ethical ideal, it is a sanction for violence." Bersani's effort to end the "tyranny of self" partly comprises his critique of what he calls the "culture of redemption," whose fundamental assumption is "about identity *as* authority." Hence redemptive discourse legitimates a view of art as a therapeutic, compensatory, "correction of life" possessed of the "authority to master" and redeem the unwieldy material of raw experience (*Culture* 1–4).

Henry James, of course, has often been enlisted to uphold a redemptive aesthetic of authority, and *The Ambassadors* has been read as an exemplary hymn to art as imaginative salvation from modernity's philistine vulgarity. But this authoritative reading so elevates the novel that we lose sight of its own kind of vulgarity, its avid mapping of Strether's depraved curiosity, which implicates him and his creator in a project of anti-Enlightenment rationalism, and an antiredemptive reduction of the self to a practical convenience. That the fictive agent of this experiment in vulnerability also hoards treasures of the imagination as solitary salvation suggests that James stages a collision between the redemptive and the vagrantly curious. In narrating this struggle, *The Ambassadors* articulates "unresolved antagonisms of reality" (Adorno, *Aesthetic* 8).

I

We can begin to pursue these matters by joining Strether on his bench in the Luxembourg Gardens. The rhythms of this scene are characteristic, for it is an episode of intensely savored deferral, a merciful "breathing-time" that repeats the unexpected and cherished "interval" Strether experiences upon arrival in Liverpool before Waymarsh appears (*Ambassadors* 60). Unlike Strether and his creator, who both relish the "waste" of time, Mrs. Newsome "had lost no time, had followed on his heels while he moved" (59), thus confirming Waymarsh's earlier taunt to Strether: "It's generally felt, you know, that she follows you up pretty close" (33). But her refusal to waste time, evidenced by her steady stream of letters, instills in Strether not commitment to his mission but its opposite—a liberating sense of escape. "Difference" is what characterizes the escape: "It was the difference, the difference of being just where he was and *as* he was. . . . This difference was so much greater than he had dreamed it would be" (60).

The "strange logic" of "difference" ruptures time, reverses intentions, and unsettles the self. Thus Strether is shocked to "find himself" free and young. So absorbing is his "consciousness of difference" that "he would have first to pull himself together . . . if he had seen Mrs. Newsome coming" (60). Strether's self has already begun a process of diffusion, an opening to otherness, that his patroness would likely condemn as sloth. In relaxing his grip on himself, he implicitly assents to Maria Gostrey's pivotal inquiry, made during their first meeting: "*Will* you give yourself up?" she had asked. "I never can," says Strether, but he quickly adds that he "unspeakably" wants to. Maria's query affirms James's remark, made in his "Project," that nothing in Paris will be "natural" for Strether, for she questions the notion of self as natural and fixed, suggesting its status as a provisional construct that can be made and unmade. It is Strether's option, Maria implies, to give up his present self and fashion a new kind of subjectivity, one not "always considering something else . . . than the thing of the moment," which is how he describes his "failure to enjoy." By the time of his momentous lunch with Marie de Vionnet, where the "thing of the moment" is nearly over-powering in its sensual palpability, Strether is able to feel that "in the matter of letting himself go, of diving deep, [he] was to feel he had touched bottom. . . . He could only give himself up" (176–77). To "let yourself go" eventually becomes Strether's advice to Waymarsh.

From the start James provides ample proof that Strether has the capacity to give up his Woollett self. "It had better be confessed at the outset," says the narrator, that Strether's "relation to his actual errand might prove none of the simplest," thanks to his "double consciousness," which mixes de-tachment and zeal, curiosity and indifference (18). Like Galileo's antira-tionalist, pragmatic improvisations, Strether's "double consciousness," his "fairly open sense of the irony of things," is "ready to drop the thread of principles already established" and seize "accidental opportunities off to the side of the direct path." With his ironic, curious sensibility, Strether leads a life of "dreadful cheerful sociable solitude" in an Enlightenment, utilitarian Woollett world (61). Thus, it is no wonder that Strether would have been startled had the first lady of Woollett suddenly appeared in the Luxembourg Gardens.

Despite his fond belief that there "was nothing in his aspect or posture to scandalise," Strether's assumption of innocence is deluded, as his defen-siveness about Mrs. Newsome suggests (60). For he is already scandalous as he relishes his "extraordinary sense of escape" (59). His "consciousness of difference," which lives on irony, complications, and contingencies, makes the simplicity of preordained, direct action an impossibility—and makes Mrs. Newsome an impossible partner. "What it comes to . . . is that you've got morally and intellectually to get rid of her," Strether concludes near the novel's end. But the seeds of this judgment are present on the garden bench, where he calls the tone of her letters "the hum of vain things" (60). What relegates Mrs. Newsome to the irrelevant or the "vain" is her implacable rationality: "She's all . . . fine cold thought," says Strether later. Her Carte-sian method "doesn't admit surprises," such as the one flooding Strether on his bench (297). In his retrospective assessment of her to Maria, Strether remarks: "She had . . . worked the whole thing out in advance, and worked it out for me as well as herself. Whenever she has done that, you see, there's no room left; no margin, as it were, for any alteration. She's filled as full, packed as tight, as she'll hold, and if you wish to get anything more or different either out or in—" (298). "You've got to make over altogether the woman herself," says Maria, completing Strether's sentence. But Mrs. New-some's is not a self to be remade. Instead, all one can do is "get rid of her." Obviously, her rigidity stands staunchly opposed to Strether's "consciousness of difference," which is rapidly dispersing his intentions and his unitary identity. As a veritable fortress against difference, surprise, or alteration, Mrs. Newsome has outlawed the "more," the margin of nonidentity.

Her rejection of margin is more than a personal quirk. Rather, it expresses her managerial prowess: she controls a prosperous "little industrial colony" in New England, a literary review, and her personal ambassador, whom she sends on a mission to tidy up domestic ambiguities. Mrs. Newsome embodies one of the "master-spirits of management" that James would encounter in 1904. In *The American Scene* James marveled at the "genius for organization," the "most ubiquitous of all" American forces, but regretted its incursions upon margin, which it would happily forsake or sacrifice in the interest of efficiency and profit (*Scene* 401, 106). But margin flourishes undisturbed in the Paris of *The Ambassadors*. In a city that seems all margin and possibility, where parts defy easy categorizing, the "imagination reacted before one could stop it" (69). And James makes margin one of the novel's pivotal motifs, embodying it architecturally in the image of the balcony, which Strether first gazes up at and eventually will gaze down from.

Clouding Strether's full recognition of Mrs. Newsome as someone to "get rid of" are his subtle rationalizations and self-deceptions which made their alliance possible in the first place. His Luxembourg Garden meditation is marked by the struggle between deception and insight, which is typical of Strether's interior monologues. Not only does he need to feel innocent of scandal but he also has "to justify" finding Mrs. Newsome's letters "vain." Groping for "some idea that would simplify," he takes refuge in a self-representation that he hopes will "become in a manner his compass and his helm." His simplifying self-image is of a Strether as "one of the weariest of men . . . done for and finished" (60–61). As if to corroborate this self-portrayal, Strether embarks on a long, melancholy excursion into his sad "grey" past of failure and passivity. But what mocks his efforts is the glaring "difference" of his present "sense of escape" into freedom and youth. This sense derives not only from the excitement of being newly arrived in Paris but also from his earlier rendezvous in England with Maria Gostrey. Alluring at dinner in her low-cut gown, Maria had occasioned a veritable orgy of "uncontrolled perceptions."

Another reason Mrs. Newsome is hard to reject is that Strether has internalized his relation to her as a dominant self-image. In describing his "acceptance of fate" as "all he had to show at fifty-five," Strether portrays himself as abjectly obedient, less a subject than an object, a mere instrument: "He would have done anything . . . been still more ridiculous" for his keeper (62). Newly revived in Paris, Strether's self-debasement is rapidly becoming irrelevant; whatever power that still lingers in it is a result of his defensive search "for some idea that would simplify." This search soon will be largely replaced by his ineluctable, if barely conscious, effort to "get rid of" Mrs. Newsome. Even at the end of the novel Strether wants to believe that his estrangement resulted solely from a "morally and intellectually" sound judgment (298). But we shall see that James portrays their rupture as disturbingly violent, saturated in imagery that plumbs the depths of Strether's repressed anger at her "close" management of him. Anger functions both as a dissolving agent of his Woollett self and as a catalyst for his renovation.

To be angry in Paris accelerates the process. "Almost any acceptance of

Paris might give one's authority away," for the city promotes disorienting flux (64). With authority and its familiar constituents—will, purpose, efficiency, and goals—beginning to give way on the Luxembourg Garden bench, before too long Strether will be sufficiently relaxed to cease being "ridiculous" for Mrs. Newsome and become "ridiculous" for himself. "I'm fantastic and ridiculous," he proudly declares to Chad near the novel's end (286). This constitutes his affirmative response to Maria's question, *"Will* you give yourself up?" But the negative sense of giving up as a form of defeat will shadow his active surrender, an ambiguity suggesting that no matter how detached Strether becomes from the compulsions of bourgeois selfhood, he remains dependent on the standards of the social order he is rejecting.

Strether's critique remains immanent even though he at times has a "breathless sense" of being beyond any standards. He feels "changed and queer" as a result of a "process somewhere deep down" so far that it cannot even be named: "It was transforming beyond recognition the simple, subtle, conveniently uniform thing that had anciently passed with him for a life of his own" (209, 334). In finding a stable identity a mere convenience rather than an essence, Strether here questions the very notion of self-ownership, the cornerstone of bourgeois individualism. William James had described the instinct of ownership as "one of the radical endowments of the race," an instinct "whose depth and primitiveness . . . would seem to cast a sort of psychological discredit in advance upon all radical forms of communistic utopia" (*Talks* 56). Ownership, noted William, is "often the antagonist of imitation." In *The Ambassadors* ownership and imitation (and its correlative terms hoarding and openness, identity and difference) clash without one giving way to the other. To give up centered identity for the fluidity of difference would be to exchange one mode of passivity for another. Rather, the reciprocal entwinement of hoarding and openness shapes Strether's behavior, anchoring his act of "giving up" to the social world that has defined him.

Paris awakens Strether's latent mimetic capacity, for "in the light of Paris one sees what things resemble." Soon he recognizes his enjoyment in "being 'like' Chad" (126). But by the novel's end Strether has become most and least like his model. Like Chad, he affirms self-ownership by rejecting his "funny alliance" with his European companion. But, unlike Chad, his impulse of ownership is compromised by a "letting go" of self that makes him less an entity to be possessed than a nexus of relations to others. In this he mimics the city of his rebirth. Like Madame de Vionnet, who has "taken all his categories by surprise," Paris eludes definition and demands relation (161). Strether imagines the city as "some huge iridescent object, a jewel brilliant and hard, in which parts were not to be discriminated nor differences comfortably marked. It twinkled and trembled and melted together, and what seemed all surface one moment seemed all depth the next" (64). In this famous passage Strether's sense of Paris as dissolving categories anticipates what has already begun to occur internally—the disintegration of his old identity based on authority and control. Trembling and melting Paris will not only come to mirror Strether but will also infiltrate his being. In short, Paris becomes an object of mimicry analogous to Henry James's imitation of American volatility and marginality.

Through his power of sympathetic identification, a capacity to impregnate himself with otherness, Strether becomes so inundated by stimuli that he not only risks incoherence but exults in it: "I seem to have a life only for other people," he tells Miss Barrace (160). Later, with Miss Gostrey, he expatiates on his diffused sense of self, which has ruptured time and monadic identity: "Of course I'm youth. . . . I began to be young, or at least get the benefit of it, the moment I met you at Chester, and that's what has been taking place ever since." The particular way Strether "cultivates" his "benefit" of youth is "out of the lives, the conditions, the feelings of other persons," particularly Chad and Marie, whose lives enter into his own. His enjoyment of his "benefit" is unabashed: "I never had the benefit at the proper time. . . . I'm having the benefit at this moment. . . . It's my surrender, it's my tribute, to youth" (197).[4]

Like the young Henry James, who "hung inveterately . . . back" and hence appeared a "dunce," Strether's surrender also appears a "poor show" to the wider world: "I don't get drunk, I don't pursue the ladies, I don't spend money" (197). Despite the absence of conventional, outward displays of unrepressed energy, Strether's middle-aged "surrender" to youth exposes the notion of "proper time" as merely another convenience that regiments and diminishes experience. Strether's "youth" returns him to the unrestrained receptivity and curiosity of childhood. He is thus immersed in the provisional pleasures of "this moment." As James observes, "He was letting himself, at present, go; there was no denying it. . . . Each day was more and more a new lesson." His letting go "might be desperation; it might be confidence," Strether muses, aware that his immersion subverts explanatory categories (203). Intellectual assessment—and the objective distancing it requires—seems to be giving way to the exhilaration of being "free to go and come" without having to explain himself to anyone, even to himself (176, 200). After he has come out "as far as it was possible to be," Strether acknowledges by the novel's end that his behavior has become "almost stupid." Yet he delights in vanquishing rational explanation:

> His heart always sank when clouds of explanation gathered. His highest ingenuity was in keeping the sky of life clear of them. . . . He held that nothing ever was in fact—for anyone else—explained. One went through the vain motions, but it was mostly a waste of life. A personal relation was a relation only so long as people either perfectly understood or, better still, didn't care if they didn't. (92)

Explanation means "keeping things straight" and "communicating quickly with Woollett" with a "quickness with which telegraphy alone would rhyme" (92). This burden of economically compressed exposition and simplification obstructs precisely what Strether most wants—"the common unattainable art of taking things as they came" (61).[5] He practices this mimetic art most intensely when he finds himself on Parisian balconies.

The balcony as the architectural embodiment of Parisian indeterminacy, of a blurred boundary, is a space that fascinates Strether at certain pivotal moments and was a spot favored by James since early childhood. "From the balcony of a hotel that hung, through the soft summer night, over the Rue de la Paix" twelve-year-old Henry intensely observed Paris. "I hung with the balcony," he noted, and helped himself to Parisian "social charm." His mimicry and observation "counted all immensely for practice in taking in" (*Autobiography* 159). Balcony hanging is a primal Jamesian activity for several reasons. Not only does it provide an ideal perch for soaking up impressions and feeding curiosity, but the balcony itself is a curious space, neither simply part of nor separate from the structure that supports it, neither wholly public nor private. In short, the balcony is redolent of "social and sensual margin, overflow and by-play," to borrow a phrase from *The American Scene*. In that book James observes the loss of margin exemplified in the ostentatious New Jersey villas: they "affirm their wealth with innocent emphasis" but fail to affirm "the highest luxury of all"—"constituted privacy." These phrases are echoed in Strether's musings as he gazes up at Chad's balcony and finds its "perched privacy" the "last of luxuries" (*Ambassadors* 70). What the balcony possesses and the villas lack is "achieved protection . . . mystery of retreat . . . saving complexity," the defining attributes of "margin and of mystery," which stimulate in the observer "ingenuities . . . of conjecture." Without this reciprocity between architecture and spectator, says James, all one is left with is "isolated opulence" and "unmitigated publicity, publicity as a condition, as a doom." Such conditions destroy not only the basis of privacy but also of manners, both of which depend on a "minimum of vagueness" (*Scene* 221, 10).

Given what James perceives as the "law" of American architecture, which holds that "every part of every house shall be . . . visible, visitable, penetrable . . . with almost no one of its indoor parts distinguishable from any other," the very idea of a balcony seems to cut against the American grain (*Scene* 167). Its rarity is perhaps one reason why Strether enjoys pausing, "without following up his advantage," "at the edge of the balcony" in order to watch the unaware Mamie Pocock "with her arms on the balustrade" (247). Lingering over this image of "perched privacy," Strether appreciates its uniqueness, recalling that typically Mamie had appeared in "the almost incessantly open doorways of home" (248). The texture of this admittedly minor moment is richly imbued with the aura of the Jamesian balcony, for it provokes "haunting curiosity" that is all the more pressing "in proportion as the social mystery, the lurking human secret, seems more shy" (*Scene* 35).

Watching little Bilham smoke on Chad's balcony is Strether's first encounter with this evocative margin. The sight prompts associations that heighten his curiosity about the "lurking human secret" it contains. "There was youth in the surrender to the balcony," Strether feels, and in his "fancy" the balcony embodies the luxury of privacy and freedom that he has missed in life (*Ambassadors* 70). Thus it is strikingly apt that, late in the novel, Strether's profoundest realization of freedom from the confines of the monadic ego occurs on a balcony, indeed, on the very balcony in which he first saw Bilham. It occurs on the evening of the day of his piercing final encounter with Woollett's second ambassador, Sarah Pocock, when her "sharp shaft of a rejoinder" severs his relation to the Newsomes and leaves him untethered.

Thus, when he hangs over Chad's balcony later that night, the "hour is full of strange suggestions, persuasions, recognitions," as if the "resolute rupture" with Woollett still reverberates, sharpening his sense of "difference." Alone on Chad's balcony, Strether notes the symmetry of the moment: "He hung over it as he had seen little Bilham hang the day of his first approach, as he had seen Mamie hang over her own" (281). Now Strether "hangs" in mimicry, commemorating these past moments and intensely responding to the present one. Below him "the great flare of the lighted city . . . brought objects into view and added to their dignity." Paris provides the aura, the "soft circle," that makes objects vibrate with a special vividness, a "mystic meaning." These vibrations form a "voice" that has never been more resonant to Strether, "proof of the change in himself" after three months in Paris. "All voices had grown thicker and meant more things; they crowded on him as he moved about—it was the way they sounded together that wouldn't let him be still" (281). This cumulative sounding—fusing emotions and objects, memories and the present moment—is the note that makes Strether's "relish quite so like a pang." And he will preserve this thickening by refusing to sort it out: "I can't separate—it's all one and that's perhaps why . . . I don't understand" (294).

Like all of James's balconies, Chad's exudes "freedom": it "was what was most in the place and the hour" (281). And freedom inevitably reminds Strether of the youth "that he had long ago missed." But the pressure of Strether's responsiveness on the balcony transmutes loss into rapt awareness of the immediate, a transformation revealed in one of James's most plangent, lyrical effusions:

> Everything represented the substance of his loss, put it within reach, within touch, made it, to a degree it had never been, an affair of the senses. That was what it became for him at this singular time, the youth he had long ago missed— a queer concrete presence, full of mystery, yet full of reality, which he could handle, taste, smell, the deep breathing of which he could positively hear. It was in the outside air as well as within; it was in the long watch, from the balcony, in the summer night, of the wide late life of Paris. (282)

Strether's own "wide late life" unsettles boundaries, enabling him to make the past live in the present, to make loss the basis of "an affair of the senses" that stirs him to a degree that won't "let him be still." In his hour on the balcony Strether discovers that what he craved as he sat in the Luxembourg Gardens—the "unattainable art of taking things as they came"—is attainable only when one recognizes this art as conditioned by the past. To take things as they come is not to possess unmediated access to them but rather to encounter objects suffused by the voices of the past ("the youth he had long ago missed") and the present: "Strether found himself in possession as he never yet had been" (281). Both voices sound together, making the act of vision sensually gratifying and the act of memory palpable to smell, taste, and touch.

To label Strether's Parisian existence as vicarious, as many critics have done, ignores the fact that his complex mingling of past and present, concrete and abstract, mystery and reality challenges the binary assumption built into the very concept of the vicarious—an opposition between mediated and unmediated experience. On the balcony, for instance, Strether's sense of lost youth is not represented as the loss of a prior plenitude that he seeks to recover. Rather, his responsiveness converts loss into plenitude.[6] To oppose the actual to the vicarious, life to art, and active to passive is antithetical to the libidinal sublimation of James's psychic economy.[7] While Strether's receptivity is itself a primary force rather than an evasion of experience, this fact does not exclude an element of the vicarious in his renewed "youth." But it is only one step in his gradual loosening of the cultural imperative of centered subjectivity. Strether's is a hazardous venture that produces pleasure not in spite of but because it courts injury at every turn. Expressing this riskiness is the hypertrophy of violent imagery pervading his always precarious ambassadorial negotiations. Indeed, violence threatens him from all sides and from various sources, including the glamour of Paris, the outrage of Woollett, the deceptions of Chad and Marie, and the anger of Strether himself.

II

If one thinks of violence at all in relation to *The Ambassadors*, it would probably be in reference to its most famous scene—Strether's shocking discovery of Chad and Marie boating on the river. The word "violence" occurs three times in two consecutive sentences. As Strether feels "relief . . . superseding mere violence," he goes "down to the water under this odd impression as of violence averted—the violence of their having 'cut' him, out there in the eye of nature" (309). The triple repetition of "violence" overrides Strether's professed sense of having "averted" it, and this is precisely James's intention. Strether's denial strains to contain what he cannot but express: his feeling of having been "cut"—in the double sense of ignored and wounded—by being excluded from the lovers' intimacy. But since Strether soon realizes that he and no one else had "dressed . . . in vagueness" the "possibility" of Chad and Marie's sexual involvement, the violent cut he receives is self-inflicted. Strether also realizes that Maria Gostrey, his deepest confidante, will have guessed his self-deception: "He was already a little afraid of her 'What on earth . . . had you then supposed?' " (313). His feeble reply, unvoiced, is that "he had really all along been trying to suppose nothing." But this response is only another effort at finding "some idea that would simplify." Like the other simplification—that being "ridiculous" for Mrs. New-some "was all he had to show"—it masks in passivity a desire to risk violence. By willfully supposing nothing but vagueness about the object of his mission, Strether has stunted his curiosity so as to preserve its purity and sharpen its intensity.

In his own life James enacted something of this titillating prohibition: "He was curious about everything . . . but his Puritan *taste* would shiver with apprehension," noted Hugh Walpole, one of the novelist's adored intimates. "There was no crudity of which he was unaware but he did not wish that crudity to be named. It must be there so that he might apprehend it, but it must not be named" (qtd. Edel, *The Master* 407).[8] Walpole here inadvertently summons up the dialectic of pure curiosity evident in both Henry James and Strether. Hans Blumenberg speaks of "a pure, as though crystallized, *curiositas*, which enjoys itself even when it stops short of its object at the last moment and leaves it alone" (363). In deferring masterful knowledge and telos, James and Strether in effect cultivate a masochistic relation to the object that is inseparable, as we shall see, from their appetite for and pleasure in shock.[9]

Strether is exposed to violence as soon as he begins "letting himself go." For instance, as Strether basks in a display of Parisian sophistication in Gloriani's garden, he realizes that he is also "on trial." The "charming smile" of his host throws a "long straight shaft . . . seasoned to steel" upon him as a "test" of his "stuff" (121). At least twice in the novel Strether conceives of his desire for violence as a "relief" and a "remedy." On the first occasion he is enjoying a lively discussion in a Parisian coffeehouse where "never in his life" had he heard "so many opinions on so many subjects." The contrast with Woollett comes readily to his mind. There, remembers Strether, "differences" are "few" and "quiet," almost "as if people had been ashamed of them," though he himself had been tempted to articulate different opinions in order "to promote intercourse." Now that he has been saturated in "the difference" of Paris and in himself, he realizes, as he sits listening to the "polyglot" talk, that he has "missed violence." When "he asked himself if none would . . . ever come at all, he might almost have passed as wondering how to provoke it . . . for relief" (109). Later, after Sarah Pocock arrives and declares her outrage, Strether seeks a "remedy for his vain tension" in "the relief of pulling down the roof on" his head and Sarah's (247). These two scenes disclose Strether's need to provoke violence as a way "to promote intercourse" founded on radical "difference" rather than identity. Instead of seizing Chad's offer to return home with him "straight off" and efficiently conclude his mission, Strether decides he is "not ready" and resolves to "stay out of curiosity" (188, 192). While Maria Gostrey applauds Strether's perversity as certain to produce "immense fun," by New England standards Strether's curiosity is so deviant that it will shatter his ties to Woollett and send forth Sarah, its latest ambassador, who Strether only half-jokingly says is "coming . . . to kill" him (270).

As Mrs. Newsome's daughter and "representative," Sarah is almost interchangeable with her; she is thus a convenient target for Strether's re-pressed hostility towards the mother of his fianceé (203). But if Sarah is the enemy, her position resembles Strether's, and he sees their kinship. Like him, she is the instrument of Mrs. Newsome, and he imagines "moments when she [Sarah] felt the fixed eyes of [her] mother fairly screw into the flat of her back." Strether finds "himself sorry for her," and there are "occasions on which she affected him as a person seated in a runaway vehicle and turning over the question of a possible jump." If she should "quit the carriage while in motion," as Strether has done by deliberately ruining his mission, their kinship would assume the violent intimacy of a collision. He fancies that if Sarah jumps "he would promptly enough become aware" because "she would alight from her headlong course more or less directly upon him; it would be appointed to him, unquestionably, to receive her entire weight" (255). To feel Sarah's weight landing on top of him is also to feel the frigid pressure of the "large iceberg" that is Mrs. Newsome, to borrow Strether's mocking image (298). In his "troubled nights" Strether is haunted by "fantastic waking dreams" of Sarah Pocock looming at him "larger than life." He imagines Sarah having "burned" him with "the blush of guilt" and sees himself "under her direction, recommitted to Woollett as juvenile offenders are committed to reformatories" (201).

Although Strether must immediately censor his own thoughts—"It wasn't of course that Woollett was really a place of discipline"—this negation is precisely how he is able to express imagery that has evidently been germinating for some time. "I'm perhaps a little afraid of her" is how Strether had first described his relation to Sarah (and implicitly to her mother), and this fear has nurtured his desire for violent revolt against that "place of discipline" (46, 201). Imagining the weighty Sarah "upon him" and being "under her" suggests the sexual subjugation involved in Strether's relationship to the Newsomes. His image of himself as a "juvenile offender" expresses his sense of being infantilized by Mrs. Newsome's virtual ownership of him. He feels himself being forced, "at the point of the bayonet" held by Mrs. Newsome, to surrender to "a whole moral or intellectual being or block," which is how Maria Gostrey and Strether describe the frozen selfhood of his patroness. What her "discipline" hopes to produce are subjects precisely like herself and her daughter—selves "packed so tight" they "can't move" (263).

"I *know* Paris," says Sarah upon her arrival, employing "a tone that breathed a certain chill upon Strether's heart" (218). Like her mother, she has "worked the whole thing out in advance," leaving no room for margin or alteration. With the help of his new friends, Strether will "get rid of her" by flaunting his support of, and intimacy with, Madame de Vionnet. This will pull the roof down upon Sarah and she will suffer the violence that Strether wishes to inflict on her mother. "She's buried alive!" exclaims an excited Miss Barrace, but Strether knows her cry of victory is premature; he "sighs" that Sarah's "not dead! It will take more than this to kill her" (263). Indeed, in their final exchange it is Sarah who nearly kills Strether: "The manner of her break, the sharp shaft of her rejoinder, had an intensity by which Strether was at first kept in arrest. She had let fly at him as from a stretched cord, and it took him a minute to recover from the sense of being pierced." This "resolute rupture" leaves him cut but also liberated from Woollett: "It probably *was* all at an end" (280). His commitment to the difference of pure curiosity has made his conduct, in Sarah's furious words, "an outrage to women" like herself and her mother (276). Wounded by Sarah's "sharp shaft," Strether nevertheless gains the "relief" of violent severance that he has long sought to provoke.

That the risk of violence is inextricable from "the matter of letting himself go, of diving deep" and "touching bottom" (176, 303), is never more vivid to Strether than during his celebrated lunch with Madame de Vionnet. Here the possibility of going "to smash" is the very source of excitement and pleasure, for "costly disorder" is the "pleasant basis" of their public lunch. Strether's undisguised rapture in her presence becomes an emotion so strong that he feels the situation "running away with him." Fused together are his heightened sensuous apprehensions and his sense of a dangerous—even calamitous—surrender to the moment. Having invited her to lunch, Strether muses:

> What did the success of his proposal in fact resemble but the smash in which a regular runaway properly ends? The smash was their walk, their déjeuner, their omelette, the Chablis, the place, the view, their present talk and his present pleasure in it. . . . It *was* clearly better to suffer as a sheep than as a lamb. One might as well perish by the sword as by famine. (177)

By the end of this quotation it is not difficult to discern a mock-heroic edge in James's diction, as he toys with Strether, whose guilty pleasures are founded upon a mere lunch. More important, however, is Strether's willingness to risk a smash for the sake of letting go. Indeed, he is more than willing: he understands that they are inextricable. Risking violence ensures his surrender to youth; what a "real smash" will do, he says later, is make him old (197).

Strether courts, inflicts, suffers, and enjoys pain as part of a process of puncturing the insulated subjectivity constructed in the reformatory of Woollett. Letting his monadic self go to smash involves the pain of violation, a pattern literalized in James's biography when he suffers the "obscure hurt" that becomes the emblem of his mimetic openness to experience.[10] In *The Ambassadors* James exposes his hero to a prolonged ordeal of vulnerability and trauma simultaneously painful and exciting. In short, Strether rehearses what James will experience in his year of repatriation.

III

The deepest affinity between James and Strether is their commitment to the "religion of doing," which in late middle age inspires a project of self-renewal through self-abandonment. What results is a shared "traumatophilia," the word Walter Benjamin used in commending Baudelaire for his genius at parrying shocks. Traumatophilia involves the subject deliberately seeking out traumatic encounters of difference rather than sameness.[11] As Eric White remarks: "Instead of a panic-stricken quest after perfect bliss, the self could make the most of desire's protean character by seeking satisfaction in the always provisional pleasures of the moment." This enjoyment of the provisional characterizes traumatophilia, "a desire to be confronted with the irreducibly other." White continues: "To refuse to be traumatized is to insist the present is nothing but a repetition of the past" (111).

The traumatophilia experienced by James and Strether is linked to their refusal to view the present as a mere repetition of the past. The pleasure of experiencing the "smash" of identity, intentions, and nearly all familiar moorings, as well as the excitement of confronting calamitous "difference" describe not only James's and Strether's "restlessness" but also recalls Leonardo's—the figure who stands as the veritable Platonic model both of curiosity (as we saw in chapter 2) and traumatophilia. The "anarchic dynamism of Leonardo's inventive will," says White, relentlessly pursues "unprecedented experience" at the price of

> acute vulnerability to the world's disruptive impact. Leonardo was in fact perpetually traumatized by his surroundings. . . . His ego was not a barricade behind which he could retreat when confronted with novel experience. Instead, it might be better thought of as a permeable membrane so open to penetration from without that Leonardo was always flooded by desires demanding satisfaction. (155)

Leonardo's masochistic economy, says White, "consents to a partial, contingent form of selfhood that never achieves a conclusive stage of realization" (107, 159). The artist embodies the powerful convergence of radical curiosity and traumatophilia with the fluid indeterminacy of pre-Oedipal sexuality. What permits him to fulfill his libidinally sublimated curiosity is the loving protection of his mother and the absence (in his first five years) of his father to inhibit and repress his energies under the Oedipal interdiction. Analogously, we have seen that maternal solicitude helps Henry James avoid the renunciations of Oedipal rivalry and the construction of a rigid selfhood. By nursing him with the "spout of her pail," Strether's maternal confidante, Maria Gostrey, emboldens him so that he can finally "toddle alone" unprotected and open to shock (196, 190).

Strether's permeability is memorialized in the novel's climactic trauma by the river. Immediately prior to his discovery of the lovers, he basks in the grass, loafing like a veritable Whitman. As he playfully alters his identity by practicing his French, Strether keeps "luxuriously quiet," with his "back on the grass . . . his tension . . . really relaxed, the peace diffused" (303). Relishing the feeling of "touching bottom," his "consciousness of difference" inevitably begins to complicate his "oblong gilt frame" of "finer harmony" as the fact of the incalculable erupts. Suddenly exposed to a "sharp,

fantastic crisis," he experiences the discovery as something "quite horrible
... some unprovoked harsh note" that breaks the "stillness" (308). Yet
Strether has known for months that the stillness of simplicity is entangled
in the shock of difference. Having repressed this dialectic, which now returns
to abash him, Strether feels foolish in his self-deception, like a "little girl"
who has "dressed her doll" (313). But if Strether's dressing up of "the truth"
of intimacy in a large "quantity of make-believe" has contributed to his
infantile state, its more important effect is to have maximized shock, thus
fulfilling his deeper need to experience the trauma of otherness.

Remaining infantile and feeding on shock is Strether's way of maintaining
the pre-Oedipal volatility of his curiosity, which breeds a masochistic relation
to the object. This relation opens him up to the vulnerability that is receptive
to masochistic pleasure. "The pleasurable unpleasurable tension of sexual
excitement" occurs, writes Leo Bersani, "when the organization of the self
is momentarily disturbed by sensations or affective processes somehow 'beyond' those connected with psychic organization" ("Sexuality" 33). "This
definition removes the sexual from the intersubjective" ("Is" 217). For Bersani human sexuality "is ontologically grounded in masochism," which makes
the latter tautologous with sexual pleasure itself. "We desire what nearly
shatters us," Bersani continues, and masochism is itself a "psychical strategy"
that "allows the infant to survive, indeed to find pleasure in, the painful
and characteristically human period during which infants are shattered with
stimuli for which they have not yet developed defensive or integrative ego
structures" ("Is" 217). Sexuality has destabilizing, subversive effects on "the
human impulse to form" ("Sexuality" 39).[12]

Strikingly, in one of his frankest (by Jamesian standards) discussions of
sexuality, James approvingly invokes the infantile, solitary, nearly masochistic appetite for physical gratification. He is evidently responding to
Hugh Walpole's confession, in an earlier letter, of having lately "wallowed"
in the pleasures of several homosexual liaisons. With the twenty-nine-year-
old Walpole the seventy-year-old James is free not to moralize: "Don't say
to me ... that I ever challenge you as to *why* you wallow, or splash, or plunge
... or whatever you may call it; as if I ever remarked on anything but the
absolute inevitability of it for you at your age and with your natural curiosities,
as it were, and passions. It's good healthy exercise, when it comes but in
bouts and brief convulsions." James goes on to stress that "the only way to
know [about passion] is to have lived and loved and cursed and floundered
and enjoyed and suffered." Regarding his own experience of the messy,
groping, promiscuous nature of passion, the usually fastidious James confesses to Walpole: "I think I don't regret a single 'excess' of my responsive
youth—I only regret, in my chilled age, certain occasions and possibilities
I *didn't* embrace" (*Letters* 4: 680). The Stretherlike tones of these last words
suggest that James's pursuit to "excess" of his "natural curiosities ... and
passions" still left unsatisfied his appetite for other possibilities, other (perhaps more directly physical) embraces and convulsions. His sexual economy,
in short, is imprinted with the "more" of the margin.

On the most primitive level, Strether's solicitation of shock and, more generally, James's emphasis on his art's obligation to represent groping bewilderment replicate the experience of convulsive loss of control that is the masochistic condition of pre-Oedipal sexual excitement. This experience simultaneously undermines the human impulse to form and organize a self and generates that objectifying, self-preserving impulse. In Freudian terms, the novel traverses both pre-Oedipal and post-Oedipal phases. James does justice to this double movement, this absence and achievement of control, by representing Strether's unraveling of his organized structure of selfhood within a densely packed symmetrical form. What this formal pressure creates is the friction that makes of art the replication of sexual pleasure as a solitary self-shattering.[13]

Friction is a crucial concept in *The American Scene*. Developed as a result of "having to reckon with a complexity of forces," friction is repressed under the weight of American culture's twin compulsions of heterosexuality and the pursuit of "active pecuniary gain only" (*Scene* 427). These demands constitute the sole "basis for any successful accommodation" to American life (236). Prohibited from contact with the repressed Puritan body is any salutary commerce with difference, the friction that loosens "prime identity." Observing the asceticism that the passion for money has inscribed on the male physiognomy, James characterizes the "unmitigated 'business man' face" as "narrowly specialized" and "commercialized," a constriction that extends to "voice, tone, utterance, and attitude" (64–65). James's suggestion that the consequences of the cultural ban on friction are manifested in the atrophy of the male's capacities for physical expressiveness underscores his understanding of the bodily reality and genesis of friction. It is this reality, as we shall see, that Jamesian mimesis (in life as well as art) hopes to recover.

When viewed in its larger context, James's project of mimetic cultural and psychic renovation emerges as both a parody of and alternative to the late nineteenth-century effort of therapeutic Protestantism to help the bourgeoisie find relief from the tensions of modernity. "Mind cure," also called the "new thought" movement, preaches the relaxing of will, an orientation that bears superficial affinities with Henry James's stance. The conjoining of these two suggests a third, mediating figure—William James. He helped give stature to the movement, beginning with his 1899 address entitled "The Gospel of Relaxation" (a phrase borrowed from Herbert Spencer). William linked his effort to ease the American malady of nervousness with the work of, among others, the Christian Science evangelist Annie Payson Call, whose *Power of Repose* was a best-seller. Three years later, in *The Varieties of Religious Experience*, William extolled this popular psychology derived from Emersonian transcendentalism as the "religion of healthy-mindedness" (78). By that time he already "counted as a chief authority," indeed, a "hero" of the movement (Meyer 315).

Whereas "official moralists advise us never to relax our strenuousness" and recommend a ceaseless vigilance of will, William notes that mind cure preaches repose, a "relaxing by letting go" (*Varieties* 109, 111). This prescription of "giving up the tension" of personal will and "giving your little private convulsive self a rest" at first seems to coincide generally with Henry James's challenge to the monadic self. Yet mind cure's next stage diverges decisively from Henry's project, for the relaxing of will and vigilance is in the service of resigning "the care of your destiny to higher powers," to a "greater Self" represented as a benevolent, omnipresent God conceived of as Universal Mind (110–11). Such loss of tension between God and man was conducive to what Ann Douglas has called the feminization of American culture. This condition satisfied the need of a post-Calvinist Protestantism to eradicate the arbitrary and contingent—indeed, otherness itself—in an orgy of identity.[14] The imperative of identity, rooted in mind cure's desire to think God's thoughts, would result in "the closure of absolute assurance" in a world fraught with indeterminacy and anxiety (Meyer 76).

The banality of mind cure's gospel of relaxation did not escape the notice of William James. He found fatuous its "moonstruck" optimism and "verbiage" (*Varieties* 96). Once again he found himself drawn into a social movement whose publicists eagerly exploited his famous name without indicating how qualified his support often was. William tacitly invited such exploitation because his characteristic ambivalence led him to support movements that he came to scorn. Describing mind cure, in 1902, as America's "only decidedly original contribution to the systematic philosophy of life," James only a few years earlier had excoriated its smug worldview (96). Spending some time, in 1896, at a Chautauqua summer adult education retreat, William was driven to jocular despair by the mediocrity that pervaded the seminar: "This order is too tame, this culture too second-rate, this goodness too uninspiring," he wrote to his wife, yearning "for something primordial and savage . . . to set the balance straight again" (qtd. Bjork 177).[15]

Like his brother, William relishes the friction of colliding impulses and imperatives that make life "really dangerous and adventurous" (*Pragmatism* 142). Pragmatism itself is a method for setting the balance straight. But William's desire for both primitive struggle and release of tension is most fully satisfied by leaving language to revel in the "fluent sense of life." In short, the "letting go" of his radical empiricism provides a kind of mind cure. In contrast, Henry avoids both Chautauqua tameness and radical empiricism's fluency by finding pleasure in "primordial" friction, which relaxes the will to control.

IV

Because "friction" necessarily involves venturing out of one's "callous shell" and possibly colliding with the unknown, it entails a temporary "state of bewilderment," a willingness to lose one's physical and mental bearings (*Art* 66). For Henry James bewilderment is the highest "degree of feeling." It initiates art, is its subject, and is imbued in the spectator. Adorno also esteems the vulnerability of bewilderment as a crucial quality of mimetic behavior. His esteem, similar to James's, is based upon a recognition that the capacity to become unsettled is precarious and precious in a world where the drive for self-preservation demands the "businessman face"—the repression of one's inner nature. The result is bourgeois coldness, that waning of affect that stunts the subject's powers of expression and encourages the manufacture of "pseudo-individuality." In a passage that reveals the proximity of traumatophilia to mimetic behavior, Adorno concludes:

> In the final analysis aesthetic behavior might be defined as the ability to be horrified, and goose pimples as a primordial aesthetic image. . . . The subject is lifeless except when it is able to shudder in response to the total spell [of reification]. . . . Shudder is a kind of premonition of subjectivity, a sense of being touched by the other. (*Aesthetic* 455)

By inducing a shudder, artworks revive the memory of our early mimetic behavior and thus have an impact on "the level of remembrance" (343). To disrupt the viewer's reified responses and tap repressed affect becomes art's aim, which Adorno describes as instilling "tremor." This is a process wherein art becomes "an historical spokesman for repressed nature" (348). Tremor manifests the return of repressed feelings of empathic openness, what Adorno calls the "concern . . . triggered by great works." Concern is experienced as tremor: the reader suffers "momentary discomfiture" and "loses his footing" as the ego, the internal agency of repression, is denied gratification and is "shaken up." Yet tremor is salutary in that the ego "becomes aware of its limits and finitude" and is permitted to "look behind the walls of the prison that it is." The disorientation of tremor pushes the reader to discover "that the truth embodied in the aesthetic image has real, tangible possibilities" in the sense of inspiring new modes of practical behavior that are not fixated on self-preservation (347–48).

In describing the experience of seeing Michelangelo's *Moses* and his other works in the Vatican, Henry James speaks of the "tremour in which they have left me," for "I stood agitated this morning by all the forces of my soul." He describes the sculptor's power as one of "melting." James feels he must "work off something of the tremour" by "writing down, in black and white and, if need be, taking my stand on it against the world, the assertion that Michelangelo is the greatest of artists" (qtd. Perry 1: 312). The "tremour" induced by Michelangelo's work in 1869 is the probable germ of a well-known prefatory passage written forty years later regarding the effect James seeks to exert upon the reader. Here he speaks not specifically of tremor but of hallucination: "One should, as an author, reduce one's reader . . . to such a state of hallucination by the images one has evoked as doesn't permit him to rest till he has noted or recorded them, set up some semblance of them in his own other medium, by his own other art" (*Art* 332). The logic of this passage recalls the "tremour" of agitation James experienced in Rome. There he felt compelled to "work off" the effect by taking a stand on the side of Michelangelo "against the world," an act that mimics Michelangelo himself, "the real man of action in art" (qtd. Perry 1: 312).

Like Adorno's instigation of "tremor" to alter consciousness, James's desire to induce hallucination also reflects his commitment to disturbing the reader's "rest" until he performs an analogous act of mimetic behavior, whereby he translates "some semblance" of the art's powerful imagery into his own "medium"—be it another act of writing or, most likely, one of thinking and feeling. In effecting this transference through the shock of "hallucination," James achieves the aim of "responsible prose": to make the reader experience a "semblance" of the "restlessness" and "bewilderment" that occurs when the barrier of the ego is loosened. This experience of tremor has a double status in *The Ambassadors*, for it describes not only the reading experience but also the novel's subject.[16]

Traumatophilia—the capacity to shudder, to suffer bewilderment or tremor—is for Adorno and James not only an artistic imperative but also a psychic state perpetually endangered by modern social and sexual arrangements. These intersecting aesthetic and historical concerns animate *The Ambassadors*. The novel locates the mimetic receptivity of James's most "exposed and assaulted" figure in a culture inimical to his mode of being. Strether will go home to a Woollett society whose sterility is based on polarized division: women are "in peerless possession" of the social field, the realm of manners and morals, while men are restricted solely to business and are therefore "out of the question" with regard to anything else (*Scene* 345).[17] The arrival of Jim and Sarah Pocock in Paris prompts Strether to connect this deadening bifurcation with "the fact of marriage." Jim, a "leading Woollett businessman," leaves "almost everything" to his wife. Thanks to Sarah's "greater acquaintance with the world," Jim "was nothing compared" to her. The "most" he can "hope to achieve socially" on his trip to Paris is a kind of infantile delight at novelty. "Small and fat and constantly facetious," Jim "gurgled his joy as they rolled through the happy streets" (*Ambassadors* 213–14).

When Strether, another infantile American male "toddling alone" for the first time, takes Jim on a tour, the former muses: "Would *his* [Strether's] relation to" marriage, "had he married ten years before, have become now the same as Jim Pocock's? Might it even become the same should he marry [Mrs. Newsome] in a few months? Should he ever know himself as much out of the question for Mrs. Newsome as Jim knew himself—in a dim way—for Mrs. Jim?" (213). What these questions bring into focus for Strether is both a disconcerting sense of his affinity with Jim and the feeling of difference his bachelorhood preserves. Not only is "he different from Pocock," but in a "society . . . essentially a society of women," Strether is socially androgynous, a male nonbusinessman preoccupied with the "feminine"—or "moral"—side of life. What "an odd situation for a man," Strether notes, but he is reluctant to forfeit its oddity through a union with Mrs. Newsome: "He should perhaps find his marriage had cost him his place" (213). To rupture his engagement, then, is one way to ensure the continued friction of his "odd situation" rather than be swallowed up in the oblivion of an American marriage. Whether the "dreadful cheerful sociable solitude" of cultural androgyny is an improvement remains an open and disconcerting question, but it is one that Strether is prepared to live. Though his embrace of androgyny, both culturally and in his masochistic pre-Oedipal orientation, is an admirably steadfast act of risk taking, he is routinely ridiculed by critics as "the most maidenly of all James's men" (Fiedler 305), a mere castrate—judgments that smack of the Woollettian standards they presume to be above.

In the context of his bleak American options, Strether's plea "Live, live all you can" (132), which James calls his novel's "essence," takes on greater urgency, for it implies that amid a desolate social order living itself becomes an achievement, as if won from hostile forces. James, then, insists on the historicity of even a concept as abstract as life. Thus Strether views his cry of "live all you can" as a "crisis." What it means to live is, of course, a theme the novel explores through Chad, the one person Strether thinks knows "how" to live (282). But Chad's knowing how to live is ultimately revealed as ominously close to the "fine cold thought" of his mother's instrumental reason. That he knows how depends on a lack of imagination and a flair for manipulation, qualities that augur well for his new management career of practicing the "art of advertisement." Chad's mastery of living comes down to his charmingly stylized passivity, a minimalism that "habitually" leaves "things to others." In one characteristic passage Strether recognizes the lazy, pampered immaturity lurking in Chad's graceful social presence. He realizes that "Chad 'put out' his excitement, or whatever emotion the matter involved, as he put out his washing." It is up to Strether to "do" Chad's emotions as a "laundress" does the wash (283).

From Chad's attenuated "art" of living to Adorno's epigraph to *Minima Moralia*—"Life does not live"—is not a great distance. James explores as a possibility what Adorno takes as a premise: the mid twentieth century is a period of the individual's "decay," since he is no longer the "dominant category." His portrait of Chad, master of the great new force of "advertising scientifically worked," prefigures the emergence of a new personality type that Adorno identifies with the rise of an "all-embracing" mass-media system. Advertising is the motor of this system, the "secret of trade," as James says, and its purveyors fashion themselves into smoothly ingratiating instruments of "serviceability, arts and dodges." Adorno describes this "belated individualism" as producing subjects who are "the good mixers liked by all. . . . They are capable of everything, even love, yet always faithlessly" (*Minima* 23–24). Given his bewildered, dazzled, mimetic response to Chad, Strether never really grasps the irony that his own act of "letting go" has been closer to one who knows how to live than has Chad's leaving "things to others." Indeed, Strether's failure to grasp this is the measure of how intensely he has lived. He finally does come to see that Chad is "only Chad," a figure constructed by the near heroic labors not only of his lover but also of others, including Strether. The latter's "high appreciation" of Madame de Vionnet's "work," he realizes, has partly "made" Chad (322).

Strether has wondered more than once "if he himself weren't perhaps changed even as Chad was changed" (281). But by the end of the novel he has become so unsettled, so transformed "beyond recognition" in his self-abandonment, that his self, unlike Chad's, resembles work that has been steadily unmade rather than made. The movement or process of change itself defines Strether. In short, he has come to embody difference. "I'm different for her," he says of his relation to Mrs. Newsome, and he will return home to a "great difference." To Maria Gostrey he pledges: "Yet I shall see what I can make of it." Rather than passively relying, as he did at first, on the uniformity and fixed identity of a "world of types," Strether is now committed to the activity of making. This is simultaneously a commitment to the incalculable and inconclusive, qualities that, for James, mark any genuine act of making. And if his making is provisional, so is his self. Rather than having healed from its many cuts and penetrations, his self has become them: "Your breach is past mending," says Maria of Strether's imperiled engagement to Mrs. Newsome (343). Strether's self now exists as an irreparable breach, just as the young Henry James's incessant gawking produced his "gaping" self. Strether's internalizing of difference and his dissolving of unitary identity estranges him (perhaps permanently) from the "iceberg" sterility of Mrs. Newsome, who remains congealed in self-identity. As Strether ruefully notes in his final talk with Maria Gostrey, "She's more than ever the same" (343).

If Mrs. Newsome remains more tightly packed than ever, Strether has become more marginal, especially after refusing Maria's "offer... of exquisite service, of lightened care." To be "right" Strether insists that he must go: "That, you see, is my only logic. Not, out of the whole affair, to have got anything for myself" (344). His justly famous self-denial can be read as expressing the melancholy of the post-Oedipal superego's moral masochism, which has renounced the excitements of pre-Oedipal turbulence.[18] Yet this interpretation still partakes of the rhetoric of negativity that informs much of the criticism of *The Ambassadors*. The basic tendency of this criticism is to understand Strether's insistence on being right in conventional terms of profit and loss. Given this premise, Strether's words do express a self-abnegating logic that renounces an active life for idealist, nostalgic contemplation.[19] This negative reading might be called the William James account of *The Ambassadors*. Although there is no record of William's response to the novel, it is not difficult to imagine that he would have found Strether a hopeless case of "ontological wonder-sickness" or diseased curiosity.

V

In 1902, a year before *The Ambassadors* was published, William inadvertently provided terms that are not only more generous when applied to Strether but, more important, can serve to dislodge the critical debate from its fixation on renunciation. In *The Varieties of Religious Experience* James remarks that "we have grown literally afraid to be poor. We despise anyone who elects to be poor in order to simplify and save his inner life. If he does not join the general scramble and pant with the money-making street, we deem him spiritless." James goes so far as to say that "the prevalent fear of poverty among the educated classes is the worst mental disease from which our civilization suffers" (*Varieties* 368–69). As a man who recovered his own sanity and strength by "accumulating grain on grain of willful choice like a very miser," William the hoarder's praise of poverty illustrates what I earlier called his dialectic of repression—advocacy of modes of being that his own psyche finds dangerous. Poverty, like saintly asceticism, permits the relaxing or "melting" of the self's "native hardness," which William can admire but not experience. Strether, also a hoarder of impressions who gains "treasures of imagination," simultaneously elects poverty and its habit of melting, of "relaxing and throwing the burden down" in an "abandonment of self-responsibility" (289).

If, for William James, hoarding and poverty conflict, Henry James reveals their compatibility with bourgeois ideology. What Strether's example suggests is that self-abandonment is enacted within, not beyond, the market-place, an understanding that he only fitfully attains. Strether's willed poverty expresses both a protest against a bourgeois calculus of profit and loss and a tribute to another moment of this ideology—a belief in the chaste immunity of aesthetic consciousness from marketplace relations, with their stress on the primacy of self-interest. More than once Strether clings "intensely to the strength of his position, which was precisely that there was nothing in it for himself. From the moment he actively pursued the charming associate of his adventure [Marie de Vionnet], from that moment his position weakened, for he was then acting in an interested way" (*Ambassadors* 201). Here Strether cannot resist his perennial temptation for "some idea that would simplify" and reduce him to morally redemptive poverty.[20]

Yet Strether's reluctance, here and elsewhere, to confront his own complicity is far outnumbered by the many times he does face up to the larger truth of his cultural embeddedness. In short, he recognizes that his subjectivity is neither natural nor autonomous but has been produced within "a place of discipline" called Woollett. We have seen that Strether's "revolution" gives subjectivity a turn toward nonidentity; this movement leaves the self situated rather than transcendent. His final decision honors this fact and thus discourages his temptation to veer toward a redemptive discourse that devalues historical experience in favor of idealizing art as "beneficently re-constructive" (Bersani, *Culture* 1). To ensure his marginality and affirm his historicity, Strether must refuse Maria's offer, which promises ideal closure. Her "haunt of ancient peace" will provide "care for the rest of his days. . . . It built him softly round, it roofed him warmly over" (*Ambassadors* 341, 344). To escape Woollett and remain in Paris would be to turn his immanent stance—his entanglement in the very structures he would revise—into a transcendent one. Evidence of such entanglement is the element of cruelty in Strether's refusal of Maria. Here he reveals that in the course of gropingly becoming receptive he has not wholly repudiated the desire to be insulated; he thus repeats the very gesture his "revolution" has been created to protest. As Adorno notes, "The very movement of withdrawal bears features of what it negates. It is forced to develop a coldness indistinguishable from that of the bourgeois" (*Minima* 26). The dialectic of ownership and mimesis is acutely revealed in this moment; Strether's act embodies both impulses, as his hoarding of himself becomes the very condition of his openness.

Yet even in the face of this immanent moment, the temptations of a transcendental reading are not easily resisted. So marginal has Strether become by the end of the novel that he has no language to describe his intentions. "What I want is a thing I've ceased to measure or even to understand" (*Ambassadors* 294). Such an elusive "thing" will avoid being reified into a possession because it can be given no name to possess; it can only be experienced. Resisting explanation and predictability, Strether's rarefied, indeterminate state of being seems to reject capitalist rationality and attain an imperial, Emersonian transparency of selfhood free of social confines, be they Paris or Woollett. But in opening himself to nearly limitless possibility, Strether actually remains within the marketplace; indeed, his freedom to dwell in indeterminacy, to hoard impressions without commitment to practical consequences, is encouraged by the particular conditions of a capitalist economy.

Georg Simmel discusses the dialectic of the self's hoarding and expansion in the *The Philosophy of Money*. Inscribed in "the inherent laws of possession," says Simmel, are "fundamental limits of ownership" that we easily overlook. Though everything we have has its own limitations, the possession with the least inherent limitations is money: "It adjusts with equal ease to every form and every purpose that the will wishes to imprint it with. Obstacles may spring only from the objects that lie behind it" (325). It follows, then, that those who only desire to own money attain the most complete freedom. "To the miser who finds his happiness in owning money without ever getting round to the acquisition and enjoyment of particular objects, his sense of power must be more profound and more valuable than any control over specific things could ever be" (327). This power comes at the price of "not attaining the objects at all and of removing all specific enjoyments that are dependent upon specific things" (328). In a striking insight Simmel defines the miser's power as essentially aesthetic. The miser's pleasure in deferral, speculation, and anticipation is a form of "aesthetic contemplation" in the sense that he shares with the aesthete the "feeling of liberation" from the limits of reality and the "dull pressure of things." Simmel illustrates his claim with an anecdote:

> I once met a man who, though no longer young, . . . spent his whole time in learning all kinds of things such as languages without ever using them—dancing without doing it, and skills of all sorts without making use of them or even-intending to do so. This is precisely the miserly type—gaining satisfaction from

having fully acquired potentialities without ever conceiving of their actualization. (328)

To this temperament of purest curiosity, the fulfillment of potential "has to be viewed as a decline" for it "must reduce the enjoyment of perfect control over things."

Simmel's logic here provides another reason why Strether, that connoisseur of deferral and hoarder of potential, must say that staying with Maria would make him "wrong," and that to be "right" he must enjoy the ineffable and endless practice of making something of "difference." By revealing that behavior seemingly furthest from capitalist rationality is also closest to it, Simmel's perspective allows us to challenge not only the negative, renunciatory reading of Strether, but also the influential transcendental one that sees him as if transported by aesthetic bliss to a realm beyond culture.[21]

Strether's decision to forego conventional forms of profit, his fidelity to being a "perfectly equipped failure" (*Ambassadors* 40), are acts that define his freedom as "the right to fling away our life at any moment irresponsibly" (*Varieties* 368). William James's description of one of the privileges of poverty anticipates Jean Baudrillard's analysis of the "chronic incapacity to wrap up victory" as an assault on the "essentially failsafe rationality" that allegedly "reigns supreme" in capitalism (204). What the dominance of purposive (instrumental) rationality outlaws, says Baudrillard, is "ambivalence," the fact that "man never really does come face to face with his own needs" (86). Suppressed by a culture of consumption incessantly producing a chaotic multiplicity of needs, values, and desires, ambivalence "is what resurges, though covertly, in failure," which "alone preserves the subject's questioning concerning his own desire" (206–7). The scandal of deliberate failure, the "refusal of fulfillment," preserves margin and nonidentity as modes of freedom. Baudrillard describes this freedom as a "mysterious economy of lost opportunity" that can "take the form of violent destruction," a "latent violence toward the principle of identity and equivalence." This violence engenders "vacillation beyond satisfaction which, in the last instance, assures the subject in his being" (207–8).

There is "latent violence," too, in Strether's "horrible sharp eye," which recognizes he is "not in real harmony with what surrounds" him, as he tells Maria. His willed dissonance destroys the certainty of fulfillment promised in her "haven of rest" (*Ambassadors* 345, 341). In sum, by electing "vacillation" and "ambivalence" Strether ensures that he "goes back other," as he affirms the elusiveness of his nonidentity. Strether's "counter-economy" of lack and difference resists purposive rationality for another form of rationality—the ends-oriented rationality of the mimetic—that he celebrates in his excited outburst: "I'm incredible. I'm fantastic and ridiculous—I don't explain myself even to myself" (286). From this perspective—of Strether's delight in his own opacity—he evades not only the repressions of post-Oedipal moral masochism but also what these repressions produce—narrative and psychological intelligibility. This evasion makes his self more than ever merely a "conveniently uniform thing" that he has dispensed with in Paris but might need if he goes back home (342). The novel's final sentence again finds him relaxing in opacity: " 'Then there we are!' said Strether." The exuberant emptiness of this remark, in response to Maria's "I can't indeed resist you," affirms the ineffable intimacy of their bond and suggests that Strether is still in touch with what Maria and Paris helped release—the child's autotelic pleasure in the indeterminacies of the pre-Oedipal. At once liberated and regressive, Strether's freedom is antinomic, situated in a field of tension.

Strether's banishing of explanation so he can take things as they come reflects his creator's commitment to representing "groping," a key word in the novel's preface. Groping cannot be known or rendered from the outside but must be experienced. Only then does it become a form of what James calls "saturation"—the capacity to be richly responsive to the point of "bewilderment." In fashioning a novelistic technique devoted to representing the meandering rhythms of groping, James does justice in fiction to the pragmatic fallibilism that suffuses the second major phase. Yet in deliberately selecting as his structural center a character who embodies the mimetic capacity in all its vagrancy, James manages both to retain and surrender control. By his "full observance of the rich rigor" of Strether's gropings (*Art* 318), James cultivates "willfulness amid spontaneity," a blending that Adorno calls the "vital element" of art (*Aesthetic* 167).

James's technical and imaginative engagement with the groping motions of curiosity is a tribute to fallibilism, to loss of control, and to the hazards of accident. Art, says Adorno, effectively represents accident not by thematically "incorporating intentional contingency"; rather, art seeks "to do justice to accident by groping in the dark." The more faithfully art gropes, "the less transparent does it become to itself" (*Aesthetic* 168). With its intense devotion to groping and opacity, *The Ambassadors* fulfills art's aim—the "creation of things of which we do not know what they are" (167). This achieved nonidentity also describes Strether's opaque selfhood by the work's end. He embodies the "blind quality" that art aims to produce as a "reenactment of objectivity" (167–68). In his loyalty to motion rather than stasis ("I must go . . . to be right"), to experience rather than explanation ("I don't explain myself even to myself"), Strether's mimetic being submits to the implacable objectivity of time and history. This realm of necessity is embodied in the objective requirements of James's symmetrical, circular form, which demand that Strether be "encaged" and returned to his point of origin—the reformatory of Woollett (*Art* 321).

Yet the novel's last scene also rejects harmonious reconciliation, as James pits the "blind quality" of mimesis (groping) against the rationality of objectification ("the compositional problem"). He maximizes pressure by having, on the expressive level, Strether violently repudiate instrumental rationality, making the logic and value of groping incommunicable save to Maria's (and the reader's) intuitive understanding: "She'd . . . understand— she always understood." Yet this repudiation of instrumentality for the mi-

metic expression of wordless, empathic understanding collides with the instrumental pressure embodied in James's self-confessed "artful expedient
for mere consistency of form" (324). This expediency centers on Maria.
Although her "ostensible connectedness" as a "ficelle" has now attained
"the dignity of a prime idea," Maria's unintended growth has made her an
impediment that must be expunged or "duly smoothed over." This will
bring to a proper end the "best 'all round' " of James's "productions" (*Art*
323). Thus formal imperatives dictate Maria's dismissal, a sacrifice carried
out by Strether's cruel rejection (324).[22]

The coercive quality of the formal symmetry here becomes charged with
social significance. James's adherence to structural "consistency" lays bare
an analogy between the coerciveness of formal discipline in his artistic practice and in American social arrangements. Thus, the cruelty of artistic shaping
in the final scene involves James in a de-idealizing of art. He reveals art's
kinship with rationalization—the "disenchantment of the world"—even as
he celebrates his hero's capacity for aesthetic impressions. In sum, implicit
in James's handling of Strether is what occurs explicitly in his relationship
to Maria: she becomes the site of art's dialectic of mimesis and rationality.
Maria exemplifies, in James's words, both the "incalculable" "fun" of art—
its propensity for "free development"—and its simultaneous insistence on
"fully economic expression" (*Art* 324). By dramatizing antinomy rather than
reconciliation between mimesis and rationality, James (to recall Adorno's
phrase) ensures "art's law of motion" (*Aesthetic* 81).

A hunger for motion, for "some such energy of direct action," helped
inspire James's repatriation the year after *The Ambassadors* was published.
Wending his way from New York to Florida, James confronted the imperative
of formal discipline in a new context: the burgeoning national trend toward
rational management and social control. The American luxury hotel became
a glamorous object of the movement's colonizing efforts. When James entered the hotel world, it was as if the tensions of the final scene of *The
Ambassadors* were being reenacted in the American scene. Fictive and social
scene were riven by the competing priorities of spontaneous, mimetic expression and technical, rational economy. James's entanglement with this dialectic in the arena of art whetted his curiosity for seeing it enacted in new
forms of American social organization.

Whereas the instrumentality of bureaucratic control (the "hotel-spirit")
aroused little but disgust in William James and most other antimodernist
intellectuals, Henry was fascinated. Surveying the triumph of the hotel
world, that monument to America's "genius for organization," James was
awed, even envious, for looming before him was an apparatus of control that
disciplined its subjects even as it granted them the "illusion of freedom."
This illusion is what Strether celebrates (equivocally) in Gloriani's garden
when he speaks of the "affair of life" as "at the best a tin mould" into which
is poured the "helpless jelly" of consciousness (*Ambassadors* 132). Strether's
speech resonates far beyond its original context, for "the illusion of freedom"
defines as well the raison d'être of a central control mechanism of modernity:

the art of advertising that Chad has taken up.[23] Strether had "marvelled" at
Chad's "skill" in pulling wires and creating scenes (*Ambassadors* 254). In
New York James salutes the craft of the Waldorf's "master spirit of management," who plays so artfully upon "boundless American material" and
transforms its "crude plasticity" (*Scene* 107). To his fellow "master" James
imputes a "wealth of. . . technical imagination [that] teaches him innumerable ways" of providing the illusion of freedom for a hotel populace. The
master "has found means to make" his guests oblivious to their status as an
"army of puppets" and to "think of themselves as delightfully free and easy"
(107). The other master, Henry James, also found the means to perfect a
similar impression in the final scene of *The Ambassadors*.

The last encounter between Strether and Maria is founded on "delightful
dissimulation," as James confesses in his preface, for it has "nothing to do
with the matter (the matter of my subject)" but "everything to do with the
manner (the manner of my presentation of the same)." In short, the scene's
function is purely technical and adds "nothing whatever" in terms of content.
Yet this empty content must be disguised; hence the need for James to treat
their last conversation "as if it were important and essential" (*Art* 324). The
logic of dissimulation that informs this last scene is virtually the same logic
by which the "hotel-spirit" rules.

This coincidence suggests an answer to the question that James poses late
in *The American Scene*. At the Breakers in Palm Beach, Florida, he muses to
himself: "Why was it ["hotel-civilization"], to the eye of the restless analyst,
. . . so to succeed in making. . . its appeal?" (*Scene* 438). The "hotel-spirit"
makes so powerful an appeal because it and James are both masters of the
simulacral "as if" effect, whereby what is "already fixed and appointed" is
treated "as if [it was] important and essential" (*Art* 324). This "as if" effect
defines the contradictory status of the bourgeois subjects James encounters
in 1904. Although treated as if they are primary and unfettered, modern
subjects are closer to "helpless jelly" waiting to be "poured" into various
"moulds" by managerial experts like Chad Newsome, Hugo Münsterberg,
or Frederick Taylor.[24]

By aligning James and the presiding masters of the hotel world in terms
of their suave instrumentality, I am not suggesting an identity without difference. James's manipulations, after all, are in the service of representing
a man of "imagination galore" whose mimetic rationality embodies the potential for making freedom more than mere illusion and experience more
than dissimulation (*Art* 310). Strether embodies the more by enacting the
less: in deflating the self he makes it less sacrosanct and more malleable to a
range of pleasures and powers. Strether's mimetic behavior consists of "the
ability to see more in things than they [sic] are. It is the gaze that transforms
empirical being into imagery. The empirical world has no trouble exposing
the inadequacy of aesthetic behavior, and yet it is aesthetic behavior alone
which is able to experience that world" (Adorno, *Aesthetic* 453). Adorno's
words aptly describe Strether's contradictory, groping, and exemplary effort
to perform a "revolution." By force of his willed opacity and submission to

the unknown, he makes potent the margin of the more to come. Strether's revolution, then, refuses to provide the consolation of redemption. Instead, all that his creator would permit himself was a belief that the reign of hotel-spirit was itself provisional rather than the telos of modernity's project (*Scene* 401).[25] The next chapter will examine James's complex response to the challenge of modernity's new "order of nature."

10
"The Amazing Hotel-World":
The American Scene of 1904

In an important essay of 1907, H. G. Dwight commends *The American Scene* as a "valuable commentary, social and aesthetic, on the democratic experiment" that supplements "the studies which have lately been making objective certain aspects of our industrial and political life." Dwight claims that "nothing of the sort has been done with the same degree of sympathetic penetration—unless by Dr. Hugo Münsterberg." Unlike most critics of James's book, Dwight perceives its multidisciplinary range and richness. Indeed, it is "fed from so many sources" that only "those of a later generation" will be able to unravel its implications (qtd. Gard 449). Thus Dwight tacitly invites us to locate James's aesthetic, social, and political commentary in its contemporary intellectual context.[1]

In taking up Dwight's challenge, this chapter to some degree mimics James's technique of cultural analysis by fashioning chains of relation connecting *The American Scene* to the leading political, social, and cultural thought of the day: Thorstein Veblen's depiction of the trophy status of women; Lincoln Steffens's muckraking exposé of psychic and urban corruption; Frederick Taylor's and Hugo Münsterberg's advocacy of efficiency and scientific management; and Theodore Roosevelt's political use of social control, as manifested in his nativism and in the larger discourse of managerial mastery central to progressivism. These contexts only partially suggest the reach of James's book. In its understanding of the impoverishing psychic effects of social control it looks back to James's most overtly political novel, *The Princess Casamassima*. His stance in 1904 embodies a mode of historicist inquiry that looks forward to the next decade, as it anticipates Randolph Bourne's powerful recasting of the role of the modern intellectual. The enveloping web of connections outlined here will, in turn, generate other strands of reference to be disclosed in the course of tracking a "train of association" (*Scene* 1).

Needless to say, none of the figures or ideas named in the preceding paragraph enter directly into *The American Scene*. Instead, James refracts his intellectual affiliations and analyses through a "complication of innuendo and associative reference on the enormous scale." William James thus accurately describes (and laments) the oblique texture of his brother's meditation on America. The book becomes, says William in wonderment, a "gigantic envelopment of suggestive atmosphere" that "grows like a germ into something vastly bigger and more substantial" (qtd. Matthiessen, *Family* 341). The presentation of a constellation of contemporaneous figures reflects an effort to make this growth visible by contextualizing its elusive references, suggestions, and innuendoes. A good place to begin is by exploring the implications of Dwight's keen, if startling, suggestion of affinity between Henry James and Hugo Münsterberg.

I

The spectre of the hotel-spirit stalks the land in 1904, a "ubiquitous American force," (*Scene* 106). One of its "thousand forms" is an unprecedented international mid September gathering in St. Louis of scholars from Europe, Asia, and America. Its announced subject is nothing less than the totality of human knowledge, and the organizational genius orchestrating each of the 320 addresses is none other than Hugo Münsterberg. Predictably, William James wishes to have nothing to do with his colleague's most ambitious venture: "I am very sorry to be so persistently disobliging, but I have nothing, absolutely nothing for which that Congress seems a proper frame. . . . As for my brother, he is less available for St. Louis than I am" (qtd. M. Münsterberg 108). Münsterberg had hoped to sign up both William and Henry for his grandest scheme—the International Congress of Arts and Sciences held in conjunction with the St. Louis Universal Exposition. William's polite refusal hides a contempt he expresses in private: "To me the whole Münsterbergian circus seems a case of the pure love of schematization running mad," he confides to a friend, denouncing it as "sheer humbug . . . for the sake of making the authority of professors inalienable . . . as if the bureaucratic mind were the full flavor of nature's revelation" (qtd. Perry 2: 151, 700).

A brief look at Münsterberg's 1903 preview of the international gathering amply conveys the reasons for William's disgust. Participants were to meet for six days in a vast conference spanning numerous divisions, departments, and sections comprising twenty-five fields of knowledge. On Monday morning, noted Münsterberg, "the subject for the whole congress is knowledge as a whole, and its marking off into theoretical and practical knowledge. Monday afternoon the seven divisions meet in seven different halls; Tuesday the seven divisional groups divide themselves into the twenty-five departments, of which the sixteen theoretical ones meet in sixteen different halls on Tuesday morning, and the nine practical on Tuesday afternoon." This description went on and on, as if the spirit of Comte, with his "ludicrous" and absurd "mania for regulation," as John Stuart Mill called it, had been reborn in the accents of German idealism (153). Unity is Münsterberg's ceaselessly reiterated theme for the congress to be convened (appropriately enough) in the city that had been home to the largest group of American Hegelians: We "must strive toward unity of thought," as befits "the American nation, with its instinctive desire for organization and unity." The mission of the congress is to bring "to the consciousness of the world the too much neglected idea of the unity of truth . . . in the specialized work of the millions spread over the globe" (qtd. Dewey, *Middle* 3: 355, 367).

"To me 'truth,' if there be any truth, would seem to exist for the express confusion of all this kind of thing . . . and to be expressly incompatible with officialism" (qtd. Perry 2: 700). Thus groused William James about Münsterberg's congress. Concurring, if less acerbically, was Dewey, who found Münsterberg's rigid plan a "reductio ad absurdum" wholly at odds with pragmatism's spirit of inquiry. Münsterberg's congress required that one passively submit to a predetermined, "ready-made" theory "representing some particular *a priori* logic" (Dewey 146–48). Declining to participate in "so presumptuous and so futile" a scheme, Dewey joined the James brothers in avoiding St. Louis. But a number of those whom Münsterberg had dubbed "star players"—"men who stand high enough to see the whole field"—did address the congress, including Max Weber, Werner Sombart, Henri Poincaré, Josiah Royce, and Woodrow Wilson. Replacing Henry James in "Department Six—History of Literature" was Chicago novelist and English professor Robert Herrick, whom Henry eventually met in Chicago after visiting St. Louis six months after the congress had ended.

It is only natural to wonder why Münsterberg invited Henry James. Perhaps it was a canny move by a consummate academic entrepreneur seeking to capitalize on the coincidence that a "star player" would be arriving in America less than three weeks before the congress convened. Or did the invitation result from Münsterberg's intuition of some affinity between himself and the novelist, an affinity that might have been sufficient reason for Henry to accept the invitation had not William foreclosed the possibility? After all, Henry, the master of formal control and impersonal craft, did not share his brother's scorn of professionalism and grand projects. Like Münsterberg, Henry was devoted to surveying the "whole field" of American habits in near microscopic detail. Both men did so as expatriates and self-conscious cosmopolitans who enjoyed the mobility of dual national identities. In 1916, the last year in each of their lives, this double-agent status became politically inflammable. An atmosphere of mounting patriotic hysteria calling for one hundred percent Americanism led to angry charges of anti-Americanism against each man. Münsterberg, long under suspicion of being a German spy, was lambasted by his Harvard colleagues for attempting to maintain a position of neutrality amid increasing German–American tensions, while James was criticized for formalizing his British citizenship.

While staying with William in Cambridge in December 1904, Henry James devoted a notebook entry to the German. William James's irritation at Münsterberg and his St. Louis "circus" apparently lingered after the summer of

1904, and he likely communicated his disgust to Henry, who, after visiting Harvard and ruminating on its future, seemed to fuse both concerns. Henry muses that "the extent of its resources" gives Harvard a "kind of incalculability" that he visualizes as a

> horizon so receding, so undetermined, that one sees not—scarce sees—the lowest or faintest blue line. THAT . . . calls up within me, however, such a desire for the glimmer of a glance at the "sinister," the ominous "Münsterberg" possibility—the sort of class of future phenomena repres[en]ted by the "foreigner" coming in and taking possession; the union of the large purchasing power with the absence of prejudice—of certain prejudices; the easy submission to foreign imposition (of attitude etc.). . . . (*Notebooks* 236)

Before concluding his entry, Henry dwells on this "Harvard professor-of-the-future light, this determined high Harvard absence-of-prejudice light" that seems to define American modernity.

This enigmatic passage touches a number of chords. It shares some of William's xenophobic dislike of Münsterberg as an intrusive, power-mad "foreigner coming in" (an anxiety already discussed in chapter 5) and, more pertinent here, it identifies the "ominous 'Münsterberg' possibility" with "absence of prejudice," a phrase invoked twice and associated with the imposition of foreign power and expertise.[2] Taken together these elements comprise the "sinister" legacy of Comtean positivism or scientism, a belief in the unreflexive neutrality and objectivity of scientific rationalism that has been called the epistemic foundation of American ideology.[3]

James puts Münsterberg's name within quotation marks perhaps to suggest that the German personifies modernity as bureaucratic rationality. For "absence of prejudice" describes the pivotal belief animating a variety of prestigious late nineteenth- and early twentieth-century political and cultural ideologies: the mugwump and subsequently the progressivist search for disinterested expertise and a neutral national state as a solution to the corruptions of special interests found in the machine politics of city bosses; the technocratic gospel of Taylorism and applied psychology (a field virtually invented by Münsterberg); the scientific socialism and bolshevism that believes it is fulfilling inevitable historical laws and aims to reeducate the working class and mold them into a technocratic intelligentsia.[4] In varying degrees, all these discourses are committed to what Max Weber, Münsterberg's onetime philosophical antagonist, regards as the engine of modernity—impersonal discipline.[5] "Of all the powers that lessen the importance of human action, the most irresistible is rational discipline." Its "offspring" is bureaucracy, an "unfailingly neutral" social structure that succeeds to the extent that it eliminates "from official business love, hatred, and all purely personal, irrational, and emotional elements which escape calculation" (*From Max Weber* 254, 216).

As James's notebook entry suggests, the future also includes elements other than the disciplinary: "Münsterberg" is a "possibility" coexisting with an incalculable, undetermined horizon. Indeed, in the rhythm of James's notebook musings the latter seems to engender the former in a dialectic of indeterminacy and control that will prove crucial to *The American Scene*. There James assumes as a virtual premise that the human subject is an effect of power but also potentially more than the passive instrument of social forces. Insisting on the individual's double status as object and subject, James finds the American "genius for organization" a "perfect riot of creation," (*Scene* 440), destructive only when its production of subjectivity obliterates margin, the capacity for curious impulse and spontaneity that unsettles or modifies discipline.

Henry made his Münsterberg notebook entry shortly after returning from New York, where he had encountered the "amazing hotel-world" of the Waldorf. There managers orchestrated the frenetic scene with a deftness as subtle "as the very air." Clearly Münsterberg, the "Harvard professor-of-the-future," with his "high Harvard absence-of-prejudice," counts as one specific referent for the Waldorf's "master-spirit of management," who plays with "boundless American material" and acts "like a master indeed" (107). This last phrase invokes the self-referentiality in James's depiction. Juxtaposing this passage from *The American Scene* with James's notebook entry suggests the possibility that the novelist tacitly recognized what Dwight made explicit—an affinity with Münsterberg. Given his inordinate curiosity, Henry might have accepted Münsterberg's invitation to St. Louis had his brother not spoken for him.

II

Watching the immigrants at Ellis Island being absorbed into their new country, Henry James was shaken as he felt the "affirmed claim of the alien" begin to "grow and grow." He declared himself a "sensitive citizen" who recognized that "one's supreme relation . . . was one's relation to one's country—a conception made up so largely of one's countrymen and one's countrywomen" (*Scene* 85). A dozen years after this declaration and only six months before his death, James was to affirm his membership in his adopted country. At that time he decided to officially change his status from American citizen to British subject. Admittedly a small, symbolic gesture, it nevertheless seems of a piece with his 1904 epiphany of citizenship. Perhaps it is surprising that one's status as a political animal would be so esteemed by the proudly expatriated novelist, who had launched his career by deliberately abandoning his national identity. But his return to America became an occasion to conduct an empirical inquiry into what it meant to be a responsible citizen, an inquiry that would culminate in his public act of affiliation a dozen years later.

In the light of Henry James's repatriation, citizenship becomes a demanding mode of behavior, for it collides with and exposes a contradiction of modern democracy: the leveling sweep of the "huge democratic broom" simultaneously discourages active, curious inquiry yet requires this restless energy if the possibility of "hotch-potch" heterogeneity is to become actual

(55, 121). James embraces citizenship as the sustaining of "mutuality within difference" (Pitkin 301). This locates citizenship's crucial element, according to the political philosopher Hanna Pitkin. She describes a "peerhood that does not presuppose total equality" but instead represents the "capacity to continue to live and act with others who are substantially, even offensively, different from oneself" (301) This is what James grasps at Ellis Island.

By 1916 the "sensitive citizen" who had watched in fascination at Ellis Island finds himself the alien (a "definite technical outsider") seeking to affirm his claim to community (*Letters* 4: 760). Apart from the obvious fact that his forty-year residence and "acquisition of some property" had made England his "supreme relation," a deeper reason for becoming a British subject was what James called his "desire to throw his moral weight and personal allegiance" into the British cause. Because the "convulsion" of war in Europe had "intensely engaged" his British "loyalty" and "affections," he now shed his "wandering loose . . . detachment." Since "one is *in* the convulsion . . . one must act accordingly" (761). Hence Henry embraced what he had spent his life deferring—unequivocal naturalized identity.

I mean to suggest that his traumatophilia, his willingness to be convulsed in 1904 America, virtually rehearses his act of 1916. Both incidents elicit his consciousness of the necessity of acting "accordingly"—as a historically alert, flexible, and responsible individual. We have seen that civic and aesthetic responsibility are deeply entwined for James. In his final preface he states that the artist "can never be responsible *enough*" and must seek "the point of view that . . . will give me most instead of least to answer for" (*Art* 328). This perspective of maximum aesthetic responsibility demands that one get "down into the arena" in order to "live and breathe and rub shoulders" with one's characters, an imperative of immersion that also guides his American travels. Such an imperative prompts the rediscovery of old connections while simultaneously making new ones, as he is reminded of his stake in community.[6] Thus James does not regard his new citizenship as a severance of his American ties. Rather, he has an enlarged sense of Anglo-American community: "Every day the difference of situation [between the two countries] diminishes and the immense fund of common sentiment increases" (*Letters* 4: 761).

James's change of citizenship was criticized in the American press as a breach of patriotism. But he would most likely have dismissed the charge of being un-American since it was founded on a theory of patriotism that he had earlier publically rejected. In reviewing Theodore Roosevelt's *American Ideals* in 1898, James had ridiculed Roosevelt's constant reiteration that "it is 'purely as an American' . . . that each of us must live and breathe" and think (*Literary* 1: 664). This logic, noted James, assumes that the "American" name is a "symbol revealed once for all." James proposed (as would Randolph Bourne) a more flexible view of patriotism as a process that "we are all making . . . as hard as we can."[7] Contingent and subject to change rather than preordained and exclusive ("Hadn't it been for the War I should certainly have gone as I was," James noted [*Letters* 4: 760]), Jamesian patriotism is not a narrowing or a wearing of "blinders," which is how he described Roosevelt's theory. Instead, patriotism is a "privilege" enriched by diverse loyalties rather than strict obedience to something called the American consciousness. What results, to cite Pitkin, is "something like a redefinition of self, an enlarged awareness of how individuality and community are connected in the self" (299–300).

In 1904 Lincoln Steffens was the American citizen most vigorously re-defining responsible citizenship in an urban world. That year he published *The Shame of the Cities*, which exposed municipal corruption and the middle-class passivity that permits party bosses to "divert our loyalty from the United States." We "are responsible, not our leaders, since we follow them" (*Shame* 11). The true shame of the cities is the hypocrisy that denies responsibility by taking refuge in willed innocence. But "the people are not innocent. That is the only 'news' in all the journalism of these articles" (14).

As an antidote to innocence, Steffens valued "educated, intelligent cu-riosity" to unsettle the "community of fixed minds" and the "satisfied, unquestioning" beliefs that comprise respectable American public opinion. The sclerotic condition of "cultured Boston"—a city "inhospitable to new ideas . . . dying of its old convictions"—was typical of the country as a whole. "We are not curious enough now as men and women," Steffens wrote in 1931, and "curiosity was the beginning and the end of education" (*Auto-biography* 644).[8] Embodying insatiable curiosity, the muckraker must "labor to change the foundation of his society, as the Russians were doing, or go along" with the society we live in, "taking care only to save our minds by seeing it all straight and thinking about it clearly" (802). Steffens chose the former option as he grew older (becoming a staunch supporter of Mussolini, Lenin, and Stalin), having attempted the latter for most of his life. To see straight, for Steffens, meant to see with the reflexive, self-correcting curiosity of pragmatic science and without the innocent egotism of the Mugwump gentry and their moralistic disgust with urban America. When E. L. Godkin, Steffens's first boss, returned to England permanently after the 1897 New York City election had put Tammany Hall back in power again, he left with a sense of futility. Thirty-three years spent in America, he said, had made him "tired of having to be continually hopeful; what I long for now is a little comfortable private gloom in despair" (qtd. Kaplan 71).

For the generation of Randolph Bourne, Walter Lippmann, and Herbert Croly—iconoclastic young intellectuals educated by Steffens in muckraking and by John Dewey and William James in pragmatism and pluralism—the rigor of the scientific method seemed the obvious path leading from genteel exhaustion to public engagement, from drift to mastery, to cite Lippmann's famous phrase. The starting point of his "applied pragmatic realism"—that "no mariner ever enters upon a more uncharted sea than does the average human being born into the twentieth century" (Lippmann, *Drift* 112)— echoes William James's insistence that the pluralist pragmatist lives in a "tramp and vagrant world" and is "willing to live on a scheme of uncertified possibilities" (*Pragmatism* 125, 142). But whereas Lippmann's response to the fact that "we are homeless in a jungle of machines" is to emphasize the "control side" of pragmatism, James's tendency is to revel in the drift of pluralistic indeterminacy.[9] Mastery, says Lippmann, substitutes "conscious intention for unconscious striving," and "science is the unfrightened, masterful and humble approach to reality" (*Drift* 150–51). Lippmann's optimism about having found a solution to immigrancy and drift helped make his book one of the bibles of self-styled "radical Progressivism."

Upon its publication in 1914, Lippmann's modernized Emersonian prometheanism swept up Randolph Bourne and many others.[10] But with the coming of war in 1917, Bourne's faith in Lippmann waned and he became disillusioned with Dewey's "keen sense of control over events" and hostility toward "any attitude that is not a cheerful and brisk setting to work" (*Will* 341). Sneering at Lippmann, an avid supporter of President Wilson's crusade, Bourne scoffs at the smug certainty of the "realists": "How soon their 'mastery' becomes 'drift' " (330). Yet confidence in the untrammeled managerial powers of the man of technical expertise remained unshaken for most pragmatists.

The war overturned—politicized—everything. It rudely brought pragmatism's sense of mastery face to face with what Bourne called the "inexorable," the "absolute, coercive situation" of imperialist power. Above all, noted Bourne, "the inexorable abolishes choices," and "nothing is so disagreeable to the pragmatic mind as any kind of an absolute" (322). Recognizing the war as inexorable, Bourne detected the blind spot of "pragmatic realists"—"that war doesn't need enthusiasm, doesn't need conviction, doesn't need hope to sustain it. Once manoeuvered it takes care of itself, provided only that" members of the industrial elite arrange for American capital to be placed "in a strategic position for world enterprise" at the war's end (321). This powerful insight exposed the political naivete at the heart of pragmatism's tough-minded rhetoric.[11] When Bourne contended that, "given efficiency at the top," our country at war "can do very well without our patriotism," he in effect delivered an ultimatum to pragmatism's followers: become an "efficient instrument of war-technique," manipulated by economic and imperialist imperatives to which you are blind, or awake and reconstruct pragmatism on a new basis—one that accepts "inexorable" capitalist efficiency rather than free will and choice as the fundamental given of modernity. Dewey was one of those who awakened.[12]

The American Scene can be said to anticipate this postwar reorientation of the intellectual's agency and civic responsibility in light of the inexorable. By 1916 history had transformed James's anticipation into participation: his declaration of British citizenship was spurred on by the inexorable forces of world convulsion.[13] Like Bourne and the postwar Dewey, James found himself in a world where the individual no longer held "all the power of origination and initiative in his hands," as William James had believed (James, *Will* 174). No longer adequate was classic liberalism's premise that individuality is "given already" (Dewey) and responsible above all to itself. In his last essay, "Old Tyrannies," Bourne had challenged the tyranny of rugged individualism and reconstructed the modern subject as a "network of representations of the various codes and institutions of society" (Bourne, *Will* 171).

The Henry James of *The American Scene* realizes that the self of possessive individualism, which he defines as "the living unit's property in himself," is "becoming more and more merely such a property as may consist with a relation to properties overwhelmingly greater" (136–37). These greater properties are the "Trusts and the weight of the new remorseless monopolies." The individual can now be conceived only in "co-existence" with corporate entities "that operate as no madnesses of ancient personal power... ever operated" (137). Modern, impersonal power, James implies, operates not by violent coercion or the mere threat of force but by fashioning subjectivity as subjection to larger economic structures. At first unnerved by industrial capitalism's shift in values and conditions, James remarks that "the freedom to grow up to be blighted... may be the only freedom in store for... future generations." Yet this is only a forecast, not a certainty; in the marginal space of the New York ghetto a "wealth of meaning" nourishes "various possibilities of the waiting spring of intelligence." The febrile intensity of the Lower East Side affirms that even "under the icy breath" of America's corporate dominion, new values, meanings, and "importances" are all being "strikingly shifted and reconstituted" in configurations and directions that defy prediction (134, 136–38).

James, like Bourne and Dewey, believes that the "reconstituted" self of modernity is capable of agency that is not limited to passive habit and obedient instrumentality. This latter image, promulgated by social control theorists and elitist progressive "realists," represents an oversocialized conception of man as a kind of puppet, of the sort that James encountered at the Waldorf. Such an objectified self is the product of order conceived as a static end in itself. Inherent in this fetishistic need to control is a flight from the possibility of a self open to the contingencies of history.[14]

In this light, James's and Dewey's belief in the potential vitality of a "reconstituted self" is not romanticism but a historicist insight that regards the eclipse of liberal individualism as evidence that subjectivity is a historical category open to revision and refashioning. In Dewey's terms, the self is "active process" and not "ready-made," a continuously precarious achievement "wrought out" from "social arrangements, laws, institutions" (*Reconstruction* 194). In 1920 Dewey had outlined the political consequences of conceiving the self dynamically: since institutions encourage certain types of individuals, "social modifications are the only means of the creation of changed personalities." Thus "inquiry into the meaning of social arrangements gets definite point and direction. We are led to ask what the specific stimulating, fostering and nurturing power of each specific social arrangement may be. The old-time separation between politics and morals is abolished at its root" (196–97).[15] Abandoning a cardinal liberal dualism that opposes self to society, Dewey affirms that the human subject has the potential to be vivified, to create meanings and values, precisely because it functions within the inexorable horizon of a preconstituted domain of practices. From within that acknowledgment of embeddedness Dewey unearths a guiding value, a reliable "point and direction": the search for and fashioning of social arrangements and practices that will create individuals possessing the maximum capacity for experimental, tolerant, communal activity. Active curiosity is the value he is particularly keen to nurture: "Is curiosity awakened or blunted? What is its quality: is it merely esthetic, dwelling on the forms and surfaces of things or is it also an intellectual searching into their meaning?" (197).

Henry James shares Dewey's valuation of curiosity in the construction of subjectivity. Something like Dewey's logic, which links politics and morals, implicitly guides James's inquiry into the forms of subjectivity that American social arrangements encourage and discourage. What alarms James is that these arrangements thwart rather than release a range of active impulses. In particular, James comes to regard the polarized relations between the sexes as an index of American society's limited capacity for mutuality within difference, the tolerating of otherness that responsible citizenship and a vital democratic public life require. The cogency and importance of James's representation of the high bourgeois American woman at the end of the century is best revealed by juxtaposing it with two other well-known examples, one contemporaneous with his own and one that he anticipated.

III

Forced into high heels, skirts, and corsets, women suffered what Thorstein Veblen in 1899 called "mutilation, undergone for the purpose of lowering the subject's vitality and rendering her permanently and obviously unfit for work" (*Leisure* 121). Five years after Veblen, James found that the American woman, "in her manner of embodying or representing her sex," had become "a new human convenience, not unlike the ingenious mechanical appliances" (*Scene* 347). Adorno and Horkheimer's *Dialectic of Enlightenment* of 1947 describes the manner in which a teenage American girl keeps "the obligatory date, the inflection on the telephone or in the most intimate situation" as bearing witness to "man's attempt to make himself a proficient apparatus. . . . Personality scarcely signifies anything more than shining white teeth and freedom from body odor and emotions" (167). One thread connecting these images is the status of middle-class women as commodities under late capitalism. All three moments can be said to register the depleted subjectivity of those who, in Adorno's words, "have escaped the sphere of production only to be absorbed all the more entirely by the sphere of consumption" (*Prisms* 82).

Adorno's 1941 essay on Veblen helps clarify James's relation not only to Veblen but also to early modern American culture.[16] While all three share an emphasis on the inherent artifice of social behavior, it is Veblen's "inability to think through the problem of mediation" (*Prisms* 91) that ultimately vitiates his critique. Informing Veblen's analysis of manners is a nostalgia for primitive nature, where efficiency and workmanship reigned, as well as a puritanical suspicion of luxury, ostentatious display, and emulation. In contrast, James refuses to liquidate mediatory functions into subjective immediacy, to make "a clean slate, to wipe away the rubble of culture and get to the bottom of things," which are Veblen's impulses as described by Adorno (84). Veblen's relish for debunking, which "defines the particular character" of his critique, expresses the attitude "of a person who does not let himself be taken in by the treachery of objects" (91). In his rage at appearances and emulation, Veblen's debunking leads him to turn "against all mediating functions." These issues can be dramatized by returning to the three images of female selfhood quoted earlier.

Veblen is writing during the New Woman movement, which he addresses toward the end of *The Theory of the Leisure Class*. He regards feminism with uncharacteristic optimism and earnestness because it promises to enact his belief that the instinct for workmanship—"the human impulse to purposeful activity"—is more powerful than, and antagonistic to, the impulse of ownership and conspicuous waste and the "motive for emulation" that drives them. "She still is the man's chattel," notes Veblen (127). In the course of economic development, women have come to exist vicariously, acquiring trophy status, evidence of their husbands' "ability to pay." Female bondage to a life of conspicuous uselessness and commodity display will be overturned by reverting to the "ancient habit" of "self-direction," a goal that the New Woman movement declares in its "double watch-word" of "Emancipation" and "Work." Veblen goes so far as to claim that "the impulse is perhaps stronger upon the woman than upon the man to live her own life in her own way and to enter the industrial process of the community at something nearer than the second remove" (*Leisure* 232).[17]

In 1907 James repeatedly discussed the polarities in American culture that exclude women from the business affairs of men. Yet his analysis of the status of women is more complex than Veblen's because James is deeply skeptical of the unconditioned sense of freedom implicit in the feminist goal of "self-direction." James begins his analysis by portraying the American woman as neither a passive consumer nor a servant to man but as an individual in "peerless possession" of the social field. Because the American businessman can never "hope to be anything but a business man," he has abdicated the social realm to his wife. Thus women provide "all the embroidery while the men supply, as it were, all the canvas" (*Scene* 66). For James, then, a creative energy of expression is nourished by a divided, unbalanced social arrangement. The American woman, whom James describes as currently "developing and extending her wonderful conquest" of the social field, possesses all of the "advantages" combined "with the absence of the drawbacks" (347). Yet this apparently unimpeded freedom is tantamount to reification. In their freedom "enjoyed very nearly for nothing," women have become one more product of modern technology—a "new human convenience, not unlike . . . stoves, refrigerators, sewing machines, typewriters, cash registers, that have done so much, in the household and the place of business, for the American name." Here James suggests that a cultural division of labor produces and packages the leisured American woman's unfettered individualism as an advertisement "for the American name," an advertisement only of a "slightly different order" than the "ingenious mechanical appliances." In short, technological development and the commodities it invents are the prior form in terms of which subjectivity in the modern age must be understood.

According to this account of the subject, James implies that (in Adorno's words) the "form of the individual itself is one proper to a society which maintains its life by means of the free market." The "peculiarity of the self," remarks Adorno, "is a monopoly commodity determined by society; it is falsely represented as natural. . . . Every advance in individuation . . . took place at the expense of the individuality in whose name it occurred" (*Dialectic* 154–55). The American woman embodies this irony: her "training for freedom," unique in its avoidance of "complications and dangers," permitted her to "develop her audacity on the basis of her security, just as she could develop her 'powers' in a medium from which criticism was consistently absent. Thus she arrived, full blown, on the general scene, the least criticized object . . . that had ever adorned it" (*Scene* 348). Absolute subjectivity engenders the mirror image of its opposite—woman as "object." "She made a convenience of me," Isabel Archer says of Madame Merle late in *The Portrait of a Lady* (475). Her remark is insightful yet incomplete. Long before meeting Madame Merle, Isabel's belief in living her own life in her own way had made her a "convenience" to herself. Her fate is caught in Adorno's remark that "the more autonomously the subject ascends above the ontic realm, the more it turns surreptitiously into an object, in ironic cancellation of its constitutive role."[18]

"Why need she originally . . . have embraced so confidently, so gleefully, yet unguardedly, the terms offered her to an end practically so perfidious? . . . Would she not have said, 'No, this is too unnatural; there must be a trap in it somewhere'?" (348). The above reads like a summary of Isabel's midnight vigil, where she finally confronts her mistaken judgment in accepting Osmond's proposal and the fact of her empty marriage. But the actual source is *The American Scene*, where James mimes the thoughts of a whole generation of Isabels. Mrs. Osmond's personal dilemma is, in a sense, American women's cultural dilemma. What they suffer is not Osmond's icy disdain but another kind of remoteness and sterility—the American husband's social "default." One solution is for the American male to "readjust" the "intersexual relation" more "proportionately." This might encourage the "repudiation of the distinctive" that James (in 1914) applauds feminists for undertaking, even though he remains skeptical that men will follow suit. A blurring of distinctive gender differences would help produce an androgynous "friction" and end the ironic reversals of subject and object, master and slave, endemic to a binary structure.[19] Meanwhile, the male's "default" continues to create a glaring absence that has made society a "lonely waste . . . [a] boundless gaping void" (345).

One reason James finds the "failure of the sexes to keep step socially" the most suggestive social fact of the country is that it is symptomatic of a larger cultural pathology that disturbs him: the attenuated public life of America (164). The social void afflicts not only intersexual relations but politics as well. James had broached the theme of political abdication in his 1898 review of E. L. Godkin's *Unforeseen Tendencies in Democracy*. What strikes James as the most surprising of unforeseen tendencies is that "so unqualified a democracy should prove . . . the society in the world least disposed to 'meddle' in politics. . . . We were counted upon rather to overdo public affairs, and it turns out that, on the whole, we do not even like them." The depoliticized politics of progressivism are a source of the sterility James finds afflicting American culture. As we shall see, *The American Scene* appeared at a historical moment when America's "genius for organization" engendered both new consolidations of power and alternative visions.

IV

A central source of depoliticization lies in the (alleged) neutral expertise of scientific management. Touted by urban progressive reform as the antidote to the reign of the machine politics of the boss, scientific management stood as an alternative to Tammany's carefully disciplined working-class, immigrant constituency which was driven by vested interests. In short, scientific management's facade of neutrality masked class politics—the legitimation of technically trained middle-class professionals. Taylorism's ability to promote this new middle class has been called "the central cause" for its success (Merkle 33). In political terms, scientific management coincided with the ambitions of late nineteenth- and early twentieth-century reform: the genteel Mugwumps of the embattled urban gentry joined with their "spiritual sons" (Hofstadter, *Reform* 167)—the middle-class progressives—to "reassert control over a society that they had been pushed out of" (Merkle 60). Godkin's favorite panacea—a merit-based civil service that would make competency and not spoils the criterion for selecting office holders—was incorporated in President Theodore Roosevelt's "gospel of efficiency" platform. Thus the patrician Roosevelt's assumption of power in 1901 pleased Mugwumps, who saw it as the promise of a genuinely new kind of leadership. "Above all he is an open instead of an underground leader," declared William James in 1905 of his former imperialist foe. William hailed him as "an enemy of red tape and quibbling and everything that in general the word 'politician' stands for" (*Letters* 2: 232). But the shift from the twilight of special interests to the daylight of "civic-minded" disinterestedness, from nineteenth-century bosses to modern experts, proved to be a less momentous change than many believed. Not only were bosses and political machines stubbornly resistant to reform, but Roosevelt himself proved a more ambiguous figure than William James and others had realized. Less staunch reformer returning government to the people than consummate careerist and image maker, Teddy

Roosevelt was ever willing to play the game with bosses and big business to gain their support (Steffens, *Autobiography* 505–6). In 1904 Henry James registered the continuity hidden beneath the public fanfare of momentous change. In the faceless, bodiless operatives of the hotel-spirit, the "underground" Boss was not buried but reborn as the master of expert organization. James imparted this fact in an incisive observation concerning an "exotic boss" he encountered on the Lower East Side: "He presented himself, to my vision, as a possibly far-reaching master-spirit" (*Scene* 207). In connecting one mode of modern power (the urban boss) to another (the "master-spirit of management"), James intuited their kinship in pursuing a common goal—securing "the blind obedience of large masses of men," to quote Godkin's scornful phrase describing one of the evils of "party spirit," the crude partisanship of machine politics that was the traditional enemy of Mugwumps (Godkin, *Unforeseen* 153–54). Mugwumps and progressives imagined themselves above such vulgarities as the imposition of "blind obedience."

Münsterberg shared this illusion and used his cachet as Harvard psychologist to promulgate the belief that his motives had nothing to do with domination. He conceived of his applied psychology, or "psychotechnics" (which aims at remedying Taylorism's neglect of psychology), as the creation of "laws" to predict and control consumer behavior. Psychotechnics spoke "the language of an exact science . . . independent of economic opinions and debatable partisan interests." Yet its ultimate goal was the "increase of industrial efficiency" on behalf of the "cultural gain which will come to the total economic life of the nation" (279, 20, 308). For Münsterberg there was no contradiction between disinterestedness and supporting increased national efficiency because he was firmly rooted in the German tradition, which idealized the state as an organic social whole to whose welfare all men were dedicated. Thus, Münsterberg spoke of America's "instinctive desire for organization and unity" (qtd. Dewey, *Middle* 3: 355). This naturalizing of organization into instinct expressed the ideal of *Gemeinschaft*, with its emphasis on the individual being subordinated to the nation's organic will or soul.

Far from being alien, Münsterberg's beliefs were in the mainstream of American progressivism, which is redolent of *Gemeinschaft* ideals. Reverence for the sovereignty of the monistic State fueled progressivism's fervent "rhetoric of the moral whole," which spoke the language of integration and unification, the "reknitting of the social body into wholeness." Unity of purpose, "a common mind" (Rodgers, *Contested* 179, 182, 184) and "single will" were the familiar clichés of the era's political leadership (Bellomy 302). Herbert Croly's influential work of 1909, *The Promise of American Life*, conceived of efficient modern democracy as a "national school" that "really teaches men how they must feel, what they must think, and what they must do in order that they may live together amicably and profitably" (284). Campaigning in 1912, Woodrow Wilson defined liberty as a "great engine" so "assembled

and united . . . that there is no friction, but a united power in all its parts."
Since the 1890s, Wilson had advocated what he called a "leaderless government" controlled by Congress and "massed opinion" (qtd. Manicas 342–
43). In 1903, while on a visit to President Roosevelt recounted in *The Future
in America*, H. G. Wells enthusiastically praised the president's reorientation
of American thought away from an "anarchistic individualism" hobbled by
"state-blindness"—the inability to perceive "the conception of a whole to
which all individual acts . . . are subordinate." Wells the scientific socialist
applauded Roosevelt's move toward a politics founded upon "synthetic effort" of "homogeneity and force" that was "closely analogous to socialism"
in its emphasis on "bringing order, control and design" to "chaotically competitive private enterprise" (153, 167). Small wonder that—at least until the
outbreak of war—Roosevelt was Münsterberg's most illustrious supporter.

As if confirming Henry James's observations regarding the barrenness of
public life, historians have described the consequences of progressivism's
zeal for social engineering and centralized management as a depoliticizing
of politics.[20] Recently Daniel Rodgers has argued that politics used in the
sense of an "open market of interests, a set of factions" was "alien to the
common talk of Progressives." His study of the rhetoric of progressivism
confirms Karl Mannheim's famous remark that "the fundamental tendency
of all bureaucratic thought is to turn all problems of politics into problems
of administration" (Mannheim 118). For progressives, the play of "interests,"
potentially a vital source of political energy, became the catchall term of
opprobrium, standing for the "predatory corporation, the unscrupulous party
boss." Interests were, "by definition, alien and predatory: sores on the body
politic" (Rodgers, *Contested* 186, 178, 182). In this context, Henry James's
insistence on the primacy of interest ("interest must be taken as a final
fact"), his suspicion of "such a term as the 'American' character," and his
acceptance of "ravage" and contempt for continuity as "criminal" monotony
strike a willfully discordant note, a pluralistic bid for "friction" in an era
devoted to imposing the homogeneity of a politics of identity (*Scene* 110,
121, 465).

To the political theorist Harold Laski, writing in 1917, the progressive
veneration of the identity principle smacked of "a certain grim Hegelianism"
that "has swept us unprotestingly on into the vortex of a great All" (*Studies*
23, 38). In search of an alternative, Laski found "vital significance for political
theory" in *A Pluralistic Universe*, especially its rejection of identity logic and
"vicious intellectualism" (*Foundations* 169). Inspired by William James's
statement that the pluralistic world is "more like a federal republic than an
empire or kingdom," Laski (along with Bourne and the Dewey of the postwar
period) may be said to represent the left's political appropriation of William
James. In contrast, Walter Lippmann's use of the latter's ideas is conservative
and control-centered. A premise of Laski's guild socialism is that the "absolute is to metaphysics" what "the State [is] to political theory" (*Studies* 6).
Both must be radically decentered, for "the very essence of liberty is the
division of authority, the multiplication of sources of experiment and re-

sponsibility." Thus Laski seeks nonbureaucratic, nonhierarchical, voluntaristic local groups free from state control. His understanding of unity as "fragmentary and incomplete" and his emphasis on the "recovery of citizenship" to combat "the dangers of obedience" (*Dangers* 68) influenced Dewey and Bourne and paralleled both William's and Henry's suspicion of monism and identity and their regard for the marginal and alien.[21] Sounding like William, Henry sees a "smaller" rather than a "greater quantity of government" as a possible solution (*Literary* 1: 692).

But Henry's gesture toward the small, like his affinity for pluralistic political theory's effort to "find a looser substitute for the sovereign State" (Rodgers, *Contested* 196), constitutes an inferential and not an explicit concern of *The American Scene*. Rather than idealizing the small, Henry is concerned with the forces of modern bureaucracy that discipline it. In dissenting from the ahistorical, organicist mystifications of mainstream progressive social theory, he analyzes the hotel-spirit as a managerial and creative force rather than an "instinct" of the national soul. The spirit animates American monopoly capitalism's project of creating an insatiable desire for consumption. In short, James locates the hotel-spirit in history, that realm of social and economic necessity that molds us and that we, in turn, shape. Implicitly situating his historicist vantage point between a positivist and individualist understanding, between a Hugo Münsterberg and a William James, Henry James concludes that the hotel world "had become the all in all and made and imposed its law." This artful triumph of "omniscient genius" intrigues James's novelistic imagination: "The effect was like nothing else of the sort one had ever known, and of surpassing interest, truly, as any supreme illustration of manners . . . is apt to be" (*Scene* 438–39).

James's insinuation that the "genius for organization" was a creative power would be repugnant to stern men of science like Münsterberg or Taylor. But we now know, at least in Taylor's case, that his fetish of neutrality and rationality merely disguised his extensive involvement in fiction making. Time-study, unit-study, labor-timing—scientific management's standard techniques of ultraprecise measurement—are "in fact shot through with guesswork" and fakery (Rodgers, *Work* 55). This fabrication of detail serves larger mystifications. Not only does Taylor claim that his conclusions merely reflect empirical "fact and law," but they also enable "you to know exactly how long the studied job *should* take" and "not only how long it *does* take in any given case" (qtd. Sohn-Rethel 154). In short, Taylor's pseudoscientific management ambiguously blurs "is" and "ought." Alfred Sohn-Rethel has identified in Taylor's thought "a tendency to progress from empirical timing to 'synthetic timing' where the time norm for a job is construed without consulting or watching the worker." Thus "pretense is inseparable from the whole intention of Taylorism," for it invents an "arbitrarily fixed" and "fictitious norm of labor timing" that is presented as "norms of independent validity . . . extracted miraculously from the bosom of nature" (154–55).[22]

Taylorism's hidden premise may be, to borrow Henry James's words, "when you haven't what you like you must . . . above all misrepresent what you have" (*Scene* 457). James thus describes another disciplinary enterprise of systematic misrepresentation—what he calls the "vast homegrown provision for entertainment," the proliferating "airy fiction" of the popular periodical press that gushes over "young gods and goddesses," with their "sword-play and gallantry and passion." However airy, this pap requires the talents of numerous professionals: the "journalist, the novelist, the dramatist, the genealogist, the historian are pressed . . . into the service" of the illustrated weeklies, which dress up American life in a haze of synthetic romance.[23] Both the popular press and Taylorism provide "the general spectacle and lesson of the scale and variety of the faking" required to organize desires and attitudes into ready-made forms (457–58). James finds that the mass production of cultural dreck (prefiguring the "culture industry," as we shall see) functions as the "pabulum provided for a great thriving democracy" (458). Ingesting insipid cultural pabulum is analogous to adherence to Taylorism's "fictitious norms": both nourish a "mental revolution" that inculcates obedience to preordained standards. "Mental revolution" is Taylor's phrase to describe what he always insisted was his primary goal. He conceived of his more famous motive—efficiency—as an epiphenomenon of inward colonization.

James's discussion of pabulum recalls his inquiry into the commercial engineering of the huge "solicitation of sugar" involved in immigrant candy consumption (see chapter 6). The organization of mass appetite posits a natural instinct only in a sense to which Münsterberg would be oblivious— as the expression of "the very order of nature" incarnated in the hotel-spirit (438). As the "very form . . . of the habitable world," the hotel-spirit becomes modernity's second nature and the source of the modern subject's manufactured instincts. "Imposing the standard, not submitting to it," the hotel-spirit not only fulfills "all American ideals" but creates "new and superior ones." It "anticipates and plucks them forth even before they dawn" (440). This emphasis on the hotel-spirit's creative power expresses James's understanding that it neither opposes nor represses individuality and freedom, two prime "American ideals." Rather, the hotel-spirit *produces* them. In an analogous way, Foucault conceives of power as not simply a force "that weighs on us and says no" but one that "produces things . . . [and] induces pleasure." The hotel-spirit is a "multiplicity of force relations" without a single, unique source, a "productive network running through the whole social body" (Foucault, *Knowledge* 119; *History* 92).

It might seem that James's characterization of the hotel-spirit as invisibly "omniscient" and "ubiquitous" smacks of Münsterbergian mystification. After all, beyond its literal reference to hotels in Florida and New York, the hotel-spirit is a symbolic construct that conspicuously fails to disclose the material identity of the much-admired masters of management. In rhapsodizing over the elegantly intricate play of the hotel-spirit, James never identifies its source and origin. At best, he fancifully visualizes this distinctly impalpable spirit as a "high-stationed orchestral" leader "waving the magical baton" (*Scene* 106). The spirit remains known only by its formal effects—

for instance, its "exquisite adjustability" to the " 'national' life"—and otherwise remains teasingly vaporous.

Yet James's seeming vagueness is far from fanciful. Rather, it vividly imparts what was soon to be uncovered by Lincoln Steffens and his onetime protégé Walter Lippmann: the disconcertingly abstract, disembodied, and elusive quality of American political power. Both spoke of political and business organizations as being "run on the same lines; both had unofficial, unresponsible, invisible actual governments back of the legal, constitutional 'fronts' " (Steffens *Autobiography* 235). The danger of this hidden structure, noted Lippmann in 1912, "is that we do not see it, cannot use it, and are compelled to submit to it" (*Preface* 21). "Invisible government" consists of an intricate facade of "dummy" directors, presidents, clerks, aldermen, mayors, and governors who serve as the puppets silently manipulated by the bosses (Steffens 233–34). The public display of "dummy" government, be it in Tammany Hall or at the highest corporate levels, has the same ontological status as the "army of puppets" James sees at the Waldorf. Its movements are endowed with verisimilitude thanks to the "master-spirit of management" who artfully pulls the puppet "strings" in "innumerable ways" (*Scene* 107).

The urge to penetrate the facade and expose the puppet masters persistently tempts Steffens, but he learns to resist. What he gradually discovers is that the "system" is designed to make the puppeteers virtually impossible to locate. Equally elusive are adequate explanations of the system. For instance, to say that " 'big business' was, and still is, the current name of the devil, the root of all evil, political and economic," matters little. Big business "is a blind phrase, useless; it leads nowhere. . . . The phrase does not cover what we mean" (Steffens 492). Yet progressivist reformers and Mugwump moralizers, like Steffens's first editor E. L. Godkin, mystify the elusive workings of American power precisely by giving it a human face— the "bad men" who run "bad government and bad journalism." His "cure," said Steffens, was "to throw the rascals out and elect good men, regardless of party" (179).[24]

Part of Steffens's famous animus against mainstream progressivism is founded on what he regards as its refusal to confront the facts of modern power. The pious humanism of reformers is useless in understanding a commercial and political power that remains ungraspable and unlocatable because it is embodied not in any single individual but in a system that, according to Lippmann, grows "independently of legal arrangements." Lippmann insists that "the whole economic life of this country . . . is controlled by groups of men whose influence extends like a web to smaller, tributary groups, cutting across all official boundaries and designations, making short work of all legal formulae, and exercising sovereignty regardless of the little fences we erect to keep it in bounds" (*Preface* 21). This system is neutral not in a positivist sense but in its inexorable operation, "without regard for persons," to cite Max Weber's phrase, the watchword of bureaucracy. It depends far more on the discipline of individual "cogs" obedient to routine than on "individual hero-ecstasy" or "spiritual enthusiasm" (Weber, *From* 228, 254). Lippmann's vision of radically decentered power is compatible with Weber's notion of bureaucracy as an "ever-moving mechanism" and anticipates Foucault's sense of a "network of power relations . . . forming a dense web that passes through apparatuses and institutions, without being exactly localized in them" (*History* 96). Foucault's definition of power as "a machinery which no one owns," to which the above analysts would assent, is confirmed in Henry James's portrayal of the hotel-spirit.

Steffens and James scrutinized the era's most compelling piece of political machinery. Steffens's portrait of Theodore Roosevelt and James's "impression" of him both revealed the gap between the ideal and the actual that is constitutive of self-representation. Roosevelt's heroic persona was just that— a public mask adroitly brandished. James relished the ultramodern efficiency of the Rooseveltian performance when he dined at the White House: "I got a rich impression of him and of his being, verily, a wonderful little machine. . . . It functions astoundingly, and is quite exciting to see. But it's really like something behind a great plate-glass window 'on' Broadway" (*Letters* 4: 341). Steffens also stressed Roosevelt's skill at representation. Concerned, above all, with publically representing "the common good," he privately had "to bribe legislators in the Senate and the House to vote for the people against the interests represented by the machines that had corrupted them." Thus, "to fight the system" Roosevelt "had to help build and maintain it" (*Autobiography* 578).

Steffens pursued the question of who was actually running the Roosevelt machine. The president himself supplied the answer: "I'm just a president," he told Steffens. The Senate boss Aldrich, claimed Roosevelt, was the "king pin in my game . . . I bow to Aldrich . . . I respect him, as he does not respect me" (506). And the man to whom Aldrich bowed was J. P. Morgan, who, according to Steffens, "sat on the American throne as the boss of bosses, as the ultimate American sovereign" (590). Yet when Steffens visited the throne, Morgan was disconcertingly elusive. Sitting alone in an unlocked room, "he was in sight all the time" yet also absent, "so alone with himself and his mind that when he did glance up he did not see me; his eyes were looking inward" (189). Thus an actual director seems indistinguishable from a dummy director. As disembodied as a "master-spirit of management," Morgan was said to have "no sense of 'absolute power' and that as a matter of fact his power . . . was very limited" (590). Steffens realized that sovereignty was not an absolute—indeed, "nothing is absolute" in America, where the throne of "actual power" is an "unidentified seat" (588). Setting aside, for the moment, the implications of Steffens's inquiry into the dislocations and vacancies of American power, that machinery which no one owns, I think that his turn toward a radical political alternative warrants scrutiny, for it suggests certain striking, if not immediately apparent, parallels to the thought of Henry James.

"There is an empty throne in every country," and "bold men can seize it—and hold it" (816). Thus Mussolini boasted to Steffens. Challenging axioms as boldly as had Einstein, Mussolini mocked the "dead logic" of Steffens's "preconceived liberal principles." In effect, Mussolini would become a boss emerging from the shadows to give the people what they were ashamed to admit: though they cried "aloud for liberty they called secretly for a boss" (590, 816). Stirred by Mussolini's unabashed will to power, his filling of the throne "to overflowing," Steffens saw in him a compelling contrast to the incorporeal spirits of an American system that refused to acknowledge man's desire to be ruled. Science would be the instrument of that rule. Lenin, the other leader whom Steffens found equally compelling, based his revolutionary government on a "scientific rearrangement of economic forces" that would evolve toward "economic democracy first and political democracy last" (796). As Steffens pointed out, a major source of his enthusiasm for Lenin and Mussolini resided not simply in their bold character and "frightening contempt" but in their "scientific confidence, in facts and in history." History, said Steffens, "told Mussolini that he was historically due—he and Lenin" (817).

Lenin was fascinated by American techniques of efficiency, particularly Taylorism. His "puritanical discipline of himself and others" predisposed him to favoring its routinizing procedures. In making Taylorism the labor policy of the Soviet state, Lenin, like Marx himself, confidently believed that efficiency was value neutral and immediately transferable to any political system (Merkle 107).[25] As Alvin Gouldner has noted, "The accent was on acquiring, not transforming, bourgeois culture; on seeing it as useful knowledge rather than as dangerous ideology" (*Against* 44). This explains the paradox of the Bolshevik leader becoming a partisan of the major technique of capitalist business organization. In short, Lenin subscribed as blindly as any Mugwump civil service reformer to the opposition between politics and administration. Conspicuously absent from Lenin's appropriation of Taylorism—and from Steffens's exuberant support of Lenin's use of American efficiency—is any critical or dialectical reflection on efficiency and bureaucratic rationality as ideologies that themselves generate social pathologies, which stunt the self's capacity for intersubjectivity, for mutuality rather than domination.

Contemporary political theorists have viewed Leninism's lack of critical reflexivity as a decisive factor in narrowing the distance between Marxism and bourgeois society. According to Russell Jacoby, "Marxists and their opponents shared the belief in science, progress and success," a convergence that has made "the history of Marxism the history of the loss of the dialectical critique of bourgeois society." The result has been an ascetic "conformist Marxism" comprised of rigid self-control and self-discipline that "serves the cold passion for science and authority" (30, 5, 27).[26] The cold passion of managerial rationality found among the revolutionary enemies of the state is a paradox explored in *The Princess Casamassima*, the first and most sustained expression of James's fascination with the ways that the "master-spirit of management" defuses democracy's defiant commitment to the incalculable.

V

The distinction between radical and bourgeois began to erode in the 1880s when European revolutionaries relied on an unreflexive faith in science and social engineering. This is the historical moment of *The Princess Casamassima*. One of the novel's shrewdest political insights concerns the effects of the social pathology of bureaucratic rationality upon a group of Bakunian anarchists. A number of years ago Lionel Trilling had identified Bakunin as the model for Hoffendahl, James's authoritarian anarchist, "the Master indeed, the very genius of a new social order," as the gushing Princess describes him (*Princess* 293).[27] Her tone is worthy of Steffens enthusing over Lenin. Hoffendahl's appellation as "Master" makes him James's first "master-spirit of management," a description that also fits Bakunin, a staunch Comtean with a "great passion for organization and revolutionary groups" of a "complexity that defies description" (Thomas 300). His love of conspiratorial fantasies and Chinese-box arrangements of political groups were strategies to protect and disguise his central authority, which "in turn would exert a sort of invisible sway over the masses" (Gouldner, *Against* 188).

This ability to dominate subtly also describes the mode of power shared by the hotel-spirit and Hoffendahl. James visualizes both modes as "orchestral" in nature, with a master-spirit "controlling and commanding" a large assembly of players (*Scene* 107). As the unmoved mover who never emerges from the shadowy underworld, Hoffendahl treats "all things, persons, institutions, ideas, as so many notes in his great symphonic massacre." James describes Hoffendahl's aesthetic of fungibility as bearing witness to a "truly German thoroughness" that "classified and subdivided" all humanity (*Princess* 295). Thus he replicates the very instrumentality that the absolute liberty of his anarchism allegedly opposes. Similarly, the case of Bakunin exposes "the ambivalent relation between anarchism and authoritarianism" (Thomas 299). Hoffendahl's "new social order" is worthy of a Münsterberg in the astonishing "manner in which it's organized"—an "immense underworld peopled with a thousand forms of revolutionary passion and devotion. . . . Invisible impalpable wires are everywhere, passing through everything" (*Princess* 290–91). Hyacinth Robinson's description strikingly prefigures the managerial finesse triumphant in the lobby of the Waldorf, where masterspirits manipulate invisible strings attached to human puppets.

Juxtaposing these passages, written over a space of twenty years, would seem to suggest that by 1904 underground "revolutionary passion" had evolved into the impersonal efficiency of the hotel-spirit. But this change never occurred, for the revolutions of scientific socialism were always far more dependent on administration than on passion. Indeed, James's point is that "revolutionary passion" is not only one of Hyacinth's romantic clichés but a virtual oxymoron when applied to the scientific socialism of a Hoffendahl, a Bakunin, or a Lenin, whose concept of a vanguard of professional revolutionaries was directly influenced by Bakunin. Asceticism, which has been called the "conceptual center of gravity of orthodox Marxism," is not only the hallmark of Bakuninism and Leninism but also the ideological crux of American social control theorists, with their dreams of a unified national state filled with silently running factories (Jacoby 35).

Modern management's ascetic imperative, be it in the service of revolution or capitalism, shapes human relations in *The Princess Casamassima*. More often than not, James represents passion as engulfed by the endless labor of preparing a "great rehearsal" for revolution, or by the endless effort merely to survive in the marketplace. A parody of passion pervades the novel. One senses it in the Princess's infatuation with the glamor and danger of radical politics, as well as in her strenuous efforts at "only trying to be natural"; in Hyacinth's florid aestheticizing, which masks his political and sexual naivete; and in Millicent Henning's "undulating" body, exhibiting "behind plate glass" the "latest new thing." The sombre chemist Paul Muniment, "moving ever in a dry, statistical and scientific air," is the perfectly passionless instrument of Hoffendahl's managerial vision. In turn, Paul regards Hyacinth as one more instrument, merely a "detail in a scheme" that he "shouldn't judge" but "simply execute" (397, 347, 294). The most that Paul does "in the way of expiation on the woes of humanity was occasionally to allude to certain statistics" (347). Yet to this man of "holy calm" both the Princess and Hyacinth become emotionally attached. The sterility of these attachments—their minimum of reciprocity and maximum of exploitation—dramatizes the loss of affect that pervades both the bourgeois world and the plottings of its allegedly revolutionary redeemers. Burdening both bourgeois and revolutionary is the discipline of "blind obedience," Hyacinth's phrase describing his vow to Hoffendahl. From the outset, the pressure of obedience is conspicuously embodied in the bulky presence of the novel's first managerial power, the female turnkey Mrs. Bowerbank, who brings Hyacinth to that "huge dark tomb" of a prison holding his mother (51).

London, of course, is the larger prison condemning most of its inhabitants to the arid reign of instrumental rationality. Its nearly unchallenged hegemony has imposed a sterility that is inevitable whenever a social order is bereft of "the due proportion of other" exemplars and possibilities (*Scene* 427). Only the creation of various other modes of reason would help to renovate instrumentality and serve as a basis for reforming moral, political, and institutional life. This alternative would comprise a social order of agonistic democracy where citizens practiced a mutuality within difference as they negotiated among contending interests. Thus James takes "comfort" that even in the progressive America of 1904 "nothing is absolute" and the "too-defiant scale of numerosity and quantity" makes efforts at definitive control of democracy an "impossibility" (121).

James intuited the importance of respecting what the contemporary political theorist Claude Lefort has called the "radical indetermination" of the democratic experience, where unity routinely dissolves into nonidentity. For both James and Lefort democracy is "the theatre of an uncontrollable adventure." It commenced, says Lefort, with the destruction of the body of the king, emblem and guarantee of integrity. With this decapitation, the "modern democratic revolution" no longer linked power to a body. "Power appears as an empty place and those who exercise it as mere mortals who occupy it only temporarily" (303). James found the empty, decentered place of power in the Waldorf, whereas Steffens found it in his botched effort to reach J. P. Morgan. Yet, as we have seen, Steffens and James responded quite differently to this discovery of the "experience of an ungraspable, uncontrollable society" where "power, law and knowledge are exposed to a radical indetermination" (Lefort 305). Ultimately Steffens (unwittingly) acceded to the bourgeois fetish of order incarnated in the alleged enemies of this order. Lefort sees the bourgeois "cult of order" as a defensive response to the democratic "disintegration of the body," a response that seeks to eliminate "a certain vertigo in face of the void created by an indeterminate society" (304). Bureaucracies function in order to maintain equilibrium by erecting regulations, establishing distances and hierarchies, and sacralizing institutions. The control mechanisms that pervaded the progressive era represent the response of the middle class to vertiginous tumult produced from below (immigrants and the disenfranchised classes) and above (unfettered monopolies and corporate power).[28]

For James bourgeois order is more complex than Lefort suggests. The hotel-spirit works by appropriating vertigo (rather than eliminating or repressing it) and converting it into a "gregarious state" of "immense promiscuity," such as the ebullient scene in the Waldorf lobby (*Scene* 103). This dialectic of control and freedom constitutes the "genius" of American social management. James stands in awe of its capacity to convert. The creation from American "social sameness" of the illusion of autonomy, of "play and range" and "practical elasticity," testifies to the hotel-spirit's "brilliancy," which absorbs all things and their contraries, including "promiscuity which manages to be at the same time . . . monotony" (*Scene* 104). In dissolving difference into "a gorgeous golden blur," the hotel-world is a paradise wherein "the general and the particular, the organized and the extemporized, the element of ingenuous joy below and of consummate management above, melted together." As a closed system, the hotel-world is "absolutely a fit to its conditions," a totality in "positively stable equilibrium" (105). However, this spirit only outwardly appears serene and in control. Its incessant need to absorb heterogeneity is precisely what makes it vulnerable, a weakness that Adorno finds in every closed system: "No matter how dynamically a system may be conceived, if it is in fact to be a closed system, to tolerate nothing outside its domain, it will become . . . finite and static." In short, closed systems are doomed to collapse (*Negative* 27).[29] "You are not final," emphasizes James. "Distinct as you are, you are not even definite." Addressing the American scene, he continues: "Thus, as you are perpetually provisional, the hotels and the Pullmans . . . represent the stages and forms of your evolution, and are not a bit, in themselves, more final than you are" (*Scene* 408).

James recognizes here that American society is a system simultaneously closed and open; its essence is only definable as a lack of essence, which he calls margin. The margin of the future dwarfs "the total of American life, huge as it already appears." America seems but a "scant central flotilla . . . on the so much vaster lake of the materially possible" (401). What James finds most characteristic is "the fact that, with so many things present, so few of them are not on the way to become quite other, and possibly different things" (402). This condition of incessant dynamism resembles Adorno's definition of the central antinomy of bourgeois society, namely, "to preserve itself, to remain the same, to 'be,' that society too must constantly expand, progress, advance its frontiers, not respect any limit, not remain the same." For Adorno, as for James and Lefort, "total socialization objectively hatches its opposite, and there is no telling yet whether it will be disaster or liberation" (*Negative* 26, 346).

Until then, James remained prophetic in his belief that "the present is more and more the day of the hotel" (*Scene* 102), a statement that predicted the hegemony of modern advertising and the whole machinery of modern media, dubbed the "culture industry" by the Frankfurt School. Coined by Adorno and Horkheimer in *Dialectic of Enlightenment* to encompass the use of mass entertainment as a means of social control, the culture industry is an "iron system" whose domain only appears to be film, radio, and the print media. The "vast home-grown provision for entertainment" that James describes as operating by large-scale "fakery" in producing the nation's cultural pabulum, is remarkably akin to the workings of the culture industry, whose "elixir of life" is advertising and administration (*Dialectic* 162). The real work of both the Jamesian and Frankfurt cultural systems is the "classifying, organizing, and labelling of consumers" (123). Forty years hence this construction of "social sameness" that James observed would produce human beings functioning like "proficient apparatuses"—in effect, like updated versions of James's "free and easy" puppets.[30] "Pseudo-individuality is rife," declares Adorno. People are now "merely centers where the general tendencies meet" (*Dialectic* 154–55).

James had encountered such deindividualized "specimens" of modern subjectivity while on a train trip to Florida. In "completely unchallenged possession" of the social landscape is the "lusty 'drummer' of the Southern trains." This type possesses a "commercial truculence" so pronounced that the drummer "promptly insist[s] on a category of his own," for James had never previously encountered such a figure (*Scene* 424). What fascinates James is the assault this type makes upon his notion of what it means to be human: "Whom were they constructed, such specimens, to talk with, to talk over, or to talk under, and what form of address or of intercourse . . . what specific human process of any sort was it possible to impute to them?" (426). The torrent of questions pours forth: "What women did they live with, what women, living with them, could yet leave them as they were?" Expressing bewilderment intermingled with disdain, James's "baffled inquiry" leads him to regard the drummers as cruelly exposed "victims and martyrs" of America's "sterility of aspect," a result of the country's singled-minded pecuniary ethos (427). Checking his temptation to blame the victim, James reflects that the drummers "hadn't *asked* . . . to be almost the only figures in the social landscape." They hadn't obliterated "other *kinds* of persons, other types, presences, classes" (427). On the same train James meets the other general social type who "share[s] the field" with the bagman—"the American girl . . . in her unrelated state . . . waving all alone in the wind" (431). Thrown into the "great glare" of publicity, drummer and girl are "monstrous" not in themselves but in their "disproportionate possession" of the social scene. James imagines the latter's "distressed consciousness" as she wonders: "Isn't it too late, and am I not . . . practically lost?" (432).

Her questions had already been answered four years earlier (1900) by Theodore Dreiser, who has a drummer and an American girl meet up on a train bound not for Florida but for Chicago. In *The American Scene* James virtually rehearses the opening tableau of *Sister Carrie*: James describes his American girl as "falsely beguiled . . . thrust forth in . . . ignorance and folly," terms that are appropriate to Carrie Meeber (431). Yet Carrie is hardly the "helpless chit" that James imagines her type to be. Curiously mute, often drifting in thought and action, addicted to cultural pabulum and thus infinitely open to suggestion, Carrie keeps afloat thanks to her fierce "self-interest." Because her anonymous self is void of any sense of interiority, her self-interest is focused upon the material world. Preternaturally receptive to objects, including her own reflection in the mirror, Carrie's mimetic genius— her effortless wealth of expressiveness—derives from her very weightlessness. In effect, she extends to an extreme the logic of the gaping, mobile Jamesian mimetic self. In merging completely with the oscillating, impersonal rhythms of the marketplace, Carrie diverges from James's self-representation, which abides in dialectical tension.[31]

The effort to sustain this tension dictates James's sense of democratic citizenship. We can find a model of James's politics of nonidentity in Lefort's conception of civic responsibility as an "adventure of interpretation," which he opposes to the closed discourse of party-line thinking. This adventure requires that you "lose the bearings which assured you of your sovereign distance from the other . . . of the distinction between subject and object, active and passive" (297). What subverts this adventure is ideology, that "principle of occultation" which habitually conceals "the enigma" of democracy's "political form" by eradicating divisiveness and restoring unity (189). By emphasizing the recovery of margin and immigrancy James seeks to preserve the nonidentical "signs of what makes a society, or humanity as such, alien to itself" (203). When the adventure of democracy flourishes, "the known remains undermined by the unknown, the present proves to be undefinable," and "the quest for identity cannot be separated from the experience of division. This society is a *historical* society, *par excellence*" (305). One remains responsible to history by sustaining "the ordeal of the division of the subject" and dislodging "the reference points of the self and the other." Lefort's statements can be read as a virtual gloss on the trajectory of James's American journey. As we shall see, the "restless analyst" repeatedly undergoes vertiginous physical and mental experiences in an effort to recover responsibility.

This effort is dramatized when James experiences an epiphany revealing America's marginality. While traveling to Charleston in a Pullman car, "the supreme seat of ease," James likens the experience to being seated in a "rushing hotel." As a self-described "spectator" enjoying this hotel on wheels, James views the shabby Carolina landscape from his seat. The "dreary land that nobody cared" for is filled with an equally bedraggled populace of poor whites and blacks, so "forlorn and depressed" that they seem indifferent to their plight. While remaining sympathetic to the scene of human insignificance and indifference passing before his eyes, James will not deny "his extraordinary, his awful modern privilege of this detached yet concentrated stare at the misery of subject populations" (*Scene* 397). Widening the gulf of class difference is the fact that his seat in the "rushing hotel" has revived in James something of the pleasure of detached spectatorship, of managerial mastery. James considers his spectatorial, class, and material privilege a "monstrous thing," but it is seemingly insurmountable: "In truth what one was perpetually doing" was to "deny to so many groups of one's fellow-creatures any claim to a 'personality.' " This is the denial that permits the social engineer—be he Muniment, Hoffendahl, or Münsterberg—to operate with scientific "absence of prejudice." Here, on his luxurious perch of spectatorship, James approaches this moral abyss of irresponsibility, recognizes his complicity in its pleasures and privileges, and turns back to a kind of solidarity with "the misery of subject populations."

Initiating this return from the void is James's literal return to earth, the "cold steel of the rails" near which James suddenly finds himself "huddled" and "stranded in the small hours of morning" (399–400). For the mighty Pullman has broken down and the passengers are roused from their sleep and forced to wait helplessly in the "February dawn." Just prior to the literal leveling that lowers him from the majestic Pullman to the earth and his fellow human stragglers, James had made an inward declaration: the "moral" of the pervasive indifference to human misery is that "it was only the restless analyst who cared" (398). The sympathetic process of caring, which James hopes will "make up for other deficiencies," is physically reinforced by his abrupt loss of privilege. This renewed sense of mutuality is further confirmed by the epiphany he experiences in the cold Carolina dawn. As if by a "click of a spring," he feels "the sense of the size of the Margin" that undermines all attempts at masterful control (400). Dislodged are the reference points of self and other, as James loses the bearings that had kept him at a safe distance from the alien. This toppling of his "mere muffled majesty of irresponsible" aloofness (to borrow a phrase from James's final preface) marks the culmination of the pattern of startling reversals that punctuate *The American Scene* (*Art* 328).

His unexpected "transfer to a dark and friendless void" prompts a "spell" of maximum suggestion, as James muses on "the sense of the size of the Margin, that was the name of it." But discovering this word—the "bare verbal statement"—is not what is most important to James. Rather, "what

had happened . . . was to make all the difference." The emotional and physical shocks of abruptly becoming marginal himself spark his recognition that
"the size of the Margin" engulfs him, undercutting his own spectatorial
immunity. The discovery of margin "couldn't have happened without one's
beginning to wander; but the lively interest was that the further one wandered the more the suggestion spoke" (*Scene* 401). In becoming a kind of
vagrant wanderer, James's adventure of being forced to "stand huddled just
where one was" operates "as by the click of a spring" to reveal his own
immigrancy to himself. In 1916 the war would serve as the catalyst in renewing this self-revelation. Now, in 1904, feeling as forlorn and ignored as
the newly arrived immigrant or the "loose human cohesion" that he had
gazed upon from his Pullman window, James remarks: "I had succeeded in
artlessly becoming a perfectly isolated traveller with nobody to warn or comfort me." He admits to finding a "charm" in this destitution, as if discovering
(to borrow Stanley Cavell's description of Emersonian abandonment) that
"shunning the cosmopolitan and embracing the immigrant" in oneself is not
"something to escape from but something to aspire to, as to the native human
condition" (158). Earlier, the powerful, if discomfiting, pull of immigrancy
had drawn James to the Jews he encountered on New York's "flaring streets"
and on Ellis Island.

VI

Not only is James himself huddled at the railroad tracks in the early morning,
but he describes America, dwarfed by margin, as also being huddled in fear.
Inscribed at the base of the Statue of Liberty are words offering a home to
the "huddled masses yearning to be free." The words are by Emma Lazarus,
the Jewish poet whom James had met and befriended in 1883. James helped
Lazarus in her efforts to gain British aid for the establishment of Palestine
as a Jewish national homeland.[32] The vibrations resulting from this "chain
of relations" are the expression of James's sympathy for the alien and the
marginal, particularly the perennially wandering Jew, for the latter is the
emblem of democracy conceived as the "uncontrollable adventure" of "radical indetermination." In short, the Jew is a repository of all that unsettles
the discipline of the hotel-spirit.

Significantly, James, Veblen, and Adorno had all nominated the Jew as
being most resistant to American homogeneity. Certainly the exiled, derac-
inated status of each man helped foster their sympathy for and identification
with the Jew. For all three the Jew expressed a compelling paradox: in his
alien status, nomadic and despised, resided his power. In his 1919 essay on
"The Intellectual Pre-Eminence of Jews in Modern Europe," Veblen stated
that the Jews are "neither a complaisant nor a contented lot, these aliens of
the uneasy feet," but their very "loss of allegiance" puts them "in the
vanguard of modern inquiry" (*Essays* 226–27).[33] For Veblen the Jew is full
of curiosity and skepticism and thus better able to escape the "inertia of
habit" that pervades gentile culture. Veblen views with alarm the Zionist

effort to establish a Jewish state, which would effectively isolate them from gentile society.

By emphasizing the vitality of the alien, James tacitly contrasts this group with the perfectly adjusted "army of puppets" at the Waldorf, that paradise of the homogenous hotel-world where Jews were unwelcome. A few miles south of the Waldorf, Jewish tenement life in the "dense Yiddish quarter" of New York's Lower East Side "hummed with the human presence beyond any" James had ever been exposed to (132). He is deeply impressed by the "intensity of the Jewish aspect," which makes "the individual Jew more of a concentrated person . . . than any other human." The Jew's intensity resides in his otherness, embodied in the "overdeveloped proboscis" noted by James. The nose is the very feature that Adorno calls the "physiognomic principle of individuality, symbol of the specific character of an individual." To Adorno the organ of smell is crucial, for smell "is more expressive than the other senses. When we see we remain what we are; but when we smell we are taken over by otherness." James subtly invokes the power of the olfactory when he describes Central Park as redolent of the "fruit of the foreign tree" that has been "shaken down with a force that has smothered everything else." To smell this fruit, James playfully remarks, is to experience the alien "as truly in possession, under the high 'aristocratic' nose" (*Scene* 117). Of course, by 1940 the otherness embodied in the Jew served to ignite a campaign of persecution and genocide. As Adorno noted, their status as "the embodiment of the negative principle"—of difference and nonidentity—branded them as the source of "absolute evil." In his discussion of the psychology of anti-Semitism, Adorno had written that "the mere existence of the Other is a provocation. Every 'Other' person who doesn't know his place must be forced back within his proper confines" (*Dialectic* 184, 168, 183).[34] Otherness, of course, is what James finds rare and most precious on the American scene, and he searches for "any faint trace" of the unassimilated immigrant.

Given the fact that James identifies with the alien, his description of this group's remarkable impact on him, culminating in his visit to Ellis Island, can be seen as a virtual rehearsal on the public stage of the intertwining of self and other that he would document in his memoirs. In James's depiction of his childhood, as we have seen, a web of associations emerges that links his earliest understanding of representation with his discovery of the mimetic nature of the self. This dialectic of identity and otherness, inseparable from his sense of sharing and participating in William's selfhood, oriented James's cultural critique of 1904, especially his response to the immigrant. In short, what happened to James on the Lower East Side and at Ellis Island has a genealogy that must be examined if one is to avoid oversimplifying his attitude toward the alien, which would inevitably lead to the familiar and inadequate verdict of snobbery at best, anti-Semitism at worst. Only when one probes James's account of the alien, the most notorious and least understood part of *The American Scene*, can one accurately gauge James's complex investment in the kind of subjectivity the Jew represents.

In James's portrayal, the Jew is "more concentrated," and "savingly possessed of everything that is in him, than any other human" (132). Here
James's irony cuts both ways: in the very act of implicitly invoking the
stereotype of the parsimonious Jew, he salutes the Jew's hoarding of subjectivity as the source of his special strength. But this hoarding, characteristic
of the bourgeois self, is modified in James's other image of the Jew as worm,
which initially must strike us as grotesque. Doubtless the brutality of the
image expresses fear and disgust, but it is also a form of self-projection, for
one need only recall James's self-characterization as "the most abject of
worms . . . suppliant flat-on-my-belly . . . crawling with my nose in the dust"
(*Letters* 4: 689).[35] The Jew recalls the worm, one of those "strange animals
. . . who, when cut into pieces, wriggle away contentedly" (*Scene* 132). Here
the hoarding self is dialectically reversed, as atomization is sublated and the
"overflow" of "swarming" ghetto life "bursts all bounds," producing in the
Jew a "diffused intensity" rather than a rigid unity. Significantly, James
associates "the unsurpassed strength of the race" not with monadic hardening
but with "the chopping into myriads of fine fragments without loss of race
quality." Like the Jew, James resembles a fragmented worm that manages
"to live in the snippet as completely as in the whole." Both use the strength
of the subject to open subjectivity to a thriving marginality. The Jew and
James both testify to Adorno's dictum that "the subject is all the more a
subject the less it is so" ("Subject" 509).

But this diffused subjectivity, at least in the case of the New York alien
of 1904, is extremely precarious, constantly on the verge of being expunged
in "the process of shedding." This "conversion of the alien" by the "great
assimilative organism" of democracy dismays James, for he recognizes the
alien not as a stranger but as the quintessential American: "Which is the
American . . . which is *not* the alien . . . and where does one put a finger on
the dividing line?" (*Scene* 124). This general recognition of commonality is
succeeded by a more particular recognition of an "equality of condition."
For James "the great fact about the alien" in America is that the members
of this group "were *at home*, really more at home . . . than they had ever in
their lives been before; and that he [James] was at home too, quite with the
same intensity" (125).

What it means to be "at home" is what James questions and redefines
here. For an alien to be at home is as oxymoronic as calling oneself—as
James does—a "restored absentee." James and the alien embody this paradox, which defies conventional understanding. "Being at home" for James
and "his companions" is not to rest securely in the stable continuity of
tradition but to embrace a "strange" contradiction—that being at home and
being an alien are identical. The "immensity of the alien presence" as the
defining fact of American life dissolves the "dividing line" between alien
and native and empties the word "home" of positive content. The sense of
unity, continuity, and closure the term usually evokes is negated, with home
becoming the locus of the alienating, the absent. The deconstruction of
home as a stable point of origin is dramatized when James confronts two

homes of his youth. Upon seeing that his "birth-house" at Washington Square is no longer extant, James feels "amputated of half" his "history." He acknowledges an even more shocking loss in Boston when he finds a "gaping void" where once had stood his "whole precious past" (229). "It was as if the bottom had fallen out of one's own biography, and one plunged backward into space without meeting anything." This plunge is emblematic, for it gives James "the whole figure of" his "connection with everything about [him]." It is a "sense of the rupture, more than of anything else," that he will carry with him (230). "Connection" in disconnection, continuity in "rupture"—as with his sense of being "at home," only paradox can express James's nonidentical relationship to America.

Significantly, his sense of vertiginous unboundedness, while acutely disconcerting, is new only in terms of degree and not in kind. Rupture and the loss of equilibrium are traumatically heightened instances of feelings full of the "precious past"—the vulnerability of a gaping, bottomless self infiltrated by vibrations. "As soon as the subject is no longer doubtlessly self-identical," writes Adorno, "no longer a closed structure of meaning, the line of demarcation with the exterior becomes blurred and the situations of inwardness become at the same time physical ones" ("Trying" 129). Loss of a sense of demarcation, conspicuous in James's account of his childhood, occurs throughout *The American Scene*. Returning in 1904 to landmarks of his birth and boyhood, James is bewildered at seeing American history being "made" and "unmade," but he is even more surprised at how physical is the impact of these relics of personal history as they abruptly loom up from the landscape. An act of recovery is required to represent this impact, which ruptures the boundary between past and present. "To recover anything," says James, is "to live over the spent experience itself." At certain moments of his repatriation James in effect relives primal experiences of nonidentity. These recovered moments can occur when he *discovers* a literal monument or ruin relating to his past, such as the "gaping void" in Boston. More frequently he relives the past by *projecting* it onto the American scene. The scene, in turn, reflects back into James's startled eyes the transmogrified, public image of his private history. Thus a double frame is tacitly imposed, analogous to James's self-described dual role as "inquiring stranger" and "initiated native." These various temporal planes and perspectives produce impressions bristling with "representative values and traceable, . . . imaginable connections" redolent of conscious and unconscious meanings (307).

Nowhere is James more entangled in a web of primal connections than in his recollections of Ellis Island. His reaction occasions one of the most remarkable passages in *The American Scene*:

The simplest account of the action of Ellis Island on the spirit of any sensitive citizen who may have happened to "look in" is that he comes back from his visit not at all the same person that he went. He has eaten of the tree of knowledge, and the taste will be forever in his mouth. He had thought he knew before, thought he had the sense of the degree in which it is his American fate to share the sanctity of his American consciousness, the intimacy of his American patriotism, with the inconceivable alien; but the truth had never come home to him with any such force. In the lurid light projected upon it . . . it shakes him . . . to the depths of his being. . . . I positively *have* to think of him as going about ever afterwards with a new look . . . in his face, the outward sign of the new chill in his heart. So is stamped, for detection, the questionably privileged person who has had an apparition, seen a ghost in his supposedly safe old house. Let not the unwary, therefore, visit Ellis Island. (85)

This passage, like others on the alien, is usually cited as proof of "what an unbearable and odious social snob James clearly revealed himself as being," in the words of his severest critic, Maxwell Geismar, whose verdict is one that many readers assent to, albeit in more temperate terms (350). While a snobbish bias is evident in his relationship to the alien, disgust does not fully measure the depth of James's response.[36] The melodramatic excess of his reaction here yields "a wild logic of its own," one beyond his full control and intentions (*Scene* 308). The "lurid light" of contorted nightmare imagery suggests an unconscious level of meaning. His unconscious "logic" discloses that the visit to Ellis Island does indeed create a trauma, but one not only of revulsion but of subterranean identification that reverberates with a sense of the past.

The extravagant rhetoric of initiation in the Ellis Island passage is modified by a sense of déjà vu: eating from the tree of knowledge is a "taste" strangely familiar. For what James confronts is not a new "truth" of experience but a new sense of the "force" of an old truth. The "degree" of that force is acutely sharpened by his visit. In the "after-sense of that acute experience," James reflects on how the shock of Ellis Island has enlarged his understanding of citizenship. Beyond what "he had thought he knew," James feels the alien's claim so sharply that under its pressure "the idea of the country itself" undergoes a "profane overhauling." Thus, "our instinct" that a country should be "simple and strong and continuous" must be readjusted to account for the "reminder not to be dodged," the one "fixed element" that haunts James: the alien's right "to share in one's supreme relation" (85–86). This statement resonates with a familiar echo—Henry's childhood memory of sharing his consciousness with his brother William. His recollection of this event is perhaps revived when he witnesses America forging its identity by accepting the alien. The "visible act of ingurgitation" on Ellis Island leaves Henry "shaken," for he is gripped with the convulsive force of empathy and kinship as he sees an uncannily literal enactment "on the part of our body politic and social" of his own primal "ingurgitation" by and of the other. Nearly dissolved is the boundary separating the political and personal body, with the physicality of James's response testifying to the blurring of distinctions.

The birth trauma of the nonidentical, open structure of American society that occurs at Ellis Island explodes the belief in the "sanctity" of consciousness, that "supposedly safe old house," as a narcissistic fiction of self-identity. "American consciousness," both national and individual, is already violated; the "ghost" of the other always haunts it. The fortunate fall into negativity—the tearing asunder of "the simple and strong and continuous"— "is a drama that goes on, without a pause, day by day and year by year" at Ellis Island. Only by visiting this primal scene of "profane overhauling" and accepting the negative can one attain any real understanding of one's American fate. However disturbing the shock of the alien's "claim" might be, one "must make the surrender and accept the orientation" of that "loud primary state of alienism which New York most offers to sight." According to James, "What we . . . seem reduced to" by this act of surrender is "*un-*settled possession" (86).

Predictably, James's uneasy "surrender" to the alien, whereby "we, not they," must go "*more* than half-way," is not readily situated in the range of early twentieth-century responses to the immigrant, whose numbers reached an all-time high of one million the year *The American Scene* was published. In the first years of the century imperialist, progressive, and Anglo-Saxon attitudes were, for all their outward differences, informed by an ideology of assimilation that James rejected. The tolerant, "assimilationist mood of the new century," prompted by a wave of prosperity and confidence, witnessed a temporary ebb of nativism and a resurgence of democratic humanism. The image of the melting pot attained renewed prominence, with one civic leader celebrating the ability of our "admirable assimilative processes" to turn out "Americans with as much facility as Dickens' sausage factory, which was capable of turning paving-stones into sausages" (qtd. Higham, *Strangers* 110, 118). As a parable of the coerciveness of the identity principle, this statement can hardly be surpassed. It vividly confirms Sartre's hypothesis that "there may not be so much difference between the anti-Semite and the democrat. The former wishes to destroy him as a man and leave nothing in him but the Jew. . . . The latter wishes to destroy him as a Jew and leave nothing in him but the man, the abstract and universal subject"—sausage, in short. The democrat, says Sartre, "recognizes neither Jew, nor Arab, nor Negro . . . but only man—man always the same in all times and all places." The blindness of the democrat to the particular is echoed in the anti-Semite's refusal of the particular, his resolve to be what Sartre calls impervious, "massive and impenetrable" as stone, the embodiment of monadic rigidity. Caught "between his enemy and his defender, the Jew is in a difficult position" because both seek to devour him (*Anti-Semite* 57, 55, 18, 58). Being neither an enemy nor a defender of the alien, James is open to experiencing their otherness as appallingly intimate. In the face of "criminal continuity" he suffers and affirms the rigors of mutuality within difference.

VII

Intellectuals belonging to a younger generation than James's would experience little of his halting struggle to affirm the alien. People half James's age, like Hutchins Hapgood and Lincoln Steffens, were unabashedly shedding their gentile identities and delighting in the urban exoticism of the Lower East Side.[37] Still younger thinkers like Randolph Bourne sought to replace the identity logic of assimilation with a "cosmopolitan ideal," which elects not a fixed national identity "but a trans-nationality, a weaving back and forth, with the other lands, of many threads of all sizes and colors. Any movement which attempts to thwart this weaving, or to dye the fabric any one color, or disentangle the threads of the strands, is false to the cosmopolitan vision" (*Will* 262). Emphasizing cosmopolitanism as a dispersed, dynamic weaving together rather than a rigid, potentially violent "welding," Bourne in effect advanced a Jamesian conception of nonidentical citizenship[38]—as well as a conception of the modern urban intellectual. As David Hollinger has argued, cosmopolitanism was a "realistic ideal" primarily for intellectuals and became the "peculiar possession" of the largely Jewish New York intellectuals, who came to prominence by the early 1940s. For them, the cosmopolitan ideal (advocated by Bourne and, more or less explicitly, by Steffens and Hapgood, among others) represented an alternative to the pessimism of alienation, the accommodationism of assimilation, and the particularism of pluralism, all of which were static doctrines (57, 73). If Bourne is considered "the founder of the modern tradition of the New York literary intellectual," then the James of *The American Scene* might be called its godfather.[39] His ambivalent, spellbound, uneasy descent into the New York "whirlpool" may reflect the unsettled pace of an older generation, but nothing could impede James's determination to bear witness for himself and affirm a shared membership.

Sharing neither Steffens's romanticism nor Bourne's universalism, James's more tentative stance partakes of both attitudes. Ultimately James's attitude eludes precise definition because it is committed above all to endless questioning and a boundless curiosity. Thus *The American Scene* cannot really come to a satisfactory conclusion; its final sentence must rank as one of the least impressive endings that James ever penned: "That was to be in fact my very next 'big' impression." James is referring to "this same criminal continuity" that "makes but a mouthful of the mighty Mississippi" (465). He breaks off here, having only completed half his intended itinerary. He never wrote his planned second volume, which would have begun with his entrance into St. Louis and the start of a western swing through the Midwest, California, and the Pacific Northwest.

But if James's abrupt last sentence defers closure, his final page leaves us with a cumulative, comprehensive image that draws together some of the deepest impulses and frustrations of his journey. Again riding in the Pullman, heading toward the Midwest, James peers at the primitive landscape, which lacks the "decency or dignity of a road." He continues: "Seated by the great square of plate-glass," the "missionary Pullman appeared to invite me to admire the achievements it proclaimed. It was in this respect the great symbolic agent; it seemed to stand for all the irresponsibility behind it." Irresponsibility resides in "the general pretension of the Pullman" (the "symbolic agent" of the country) to believe that the "general conquest of nature and space" is tantamount to achieving Enlightenment and Progress (*Scene*

463). But what the Pullman actually proclaims is merely a "pretended message of civilization," a kind of progress that has been "abandoned to monotony," to endless, mindless, growth (462). Like "some monstrous, unnatural mother" deserting her children, America increases and multiplies with impunity, bragging with "cynicism" of all that she is producing (463).

James's choice of the Pullman as the engine of the hotel-spirit—"exhaling modernity at every pore"—is particularly apt since the term "Pullman" refers to more than a mere train. By 1904 it had become a synonym for ambitious social engineering gone awry. This broader association, though unnamed by James, could not help but color his invocations of the Pullman at key moments in his text. Pullman, Illinois, George Pullman's model company town, opened to much fanfare in 1880. Advertised as a new step in corporate social responsibility and the utopian solution to the perennial conflict between labor and management, the town of Pullman was intended to house workers and, more important, to promote harmony and efficiency. Yet within twenty years the town was virtually defunct. It had achieved its greatest fame not for creating a sense of harmony but for its notorious and bitter labor strike of 1894. This dispute shattered Pullman's proclaimed aim of governance based on neutral scientific principles and revealed it as a town rife with intolerant, autocratic paternalism. As early as 1885 liberal social critics like Richard Ely had judged the model company town to be "un-American" because it deprived its inhabitants of self-government. Not even permitted to own his own home, the resident of Pullman had "everything done for him, nothing by him." According to Ely, Pullman represented "the most absolute power of capital" (qtd. Buder 103).

James's reference to Pullman, then, functions as a most evocative "symbolic agent" of the hotel-spirit. As an instrumental force of "conquest," the Pullman train and town are mechanisms of power that operate by inducing passivity, be it spectatorial—the "seat of ease" and "plate-glass" window granting that "awful modern privilege"—or civic—the attempts of a social-control ethos to reduce democratic citizenship to an act of submission to a paternalistic social order. It is not surprising that James had described the Pullman as a monument to irresponsibility. These "rushing hotels" are "the supreme social expression," for they carry "almost *all* the facts of American life" (406).

The implacable Pullman comes to possess the same emblematic status in James's representation of modernity as the "iron cage" does in Max Weber's more famous cultural discourse.[40] Both train and cage serve as master symbols of the age—in particular, its movement toward canalizing rationality into an ascetic, rigidly instrumental mode. Written upon his return from Münsterberg's St. Louis congress, Weber's famous words, occurring near the end of *The Protestant Ethic and the Spirit of Capitalism* (1905), describe the advent of the iron cage of compulsion and the hollowing out of subjectivity and moral values, which mark the Protestant ethic in its final stage of "cultural development." Now men have become "specialists without spirit, sensualists without heart; this nullity imagines that it has attained a level of civilization never before achieved" (183).[41] Weber's iron cage is a prison to all but the most heroic figures of passionate responsibility. But James's Pullman (like the model town) only outwardly appears impregnable. As he discovered in South Carolina, it is subject to breakdowns and thus must not be considered omnipotent: "You [America] are not final, complacently as you appear so much of the time to assume it"; you are merely "shaking about in the Margin" (*Scene* 407). Precisely because the hotel-spirit is "inordinately passive" in its complacency of serene mastery, it is "in *some* degree plastic."

To explore the potential plasticity of systems of power and to tap the marginality latent in their authority remains the promise of a politics of nonidentity. Rather than advocating particular parties or programs, the politics of nonidentity promotes a style of being and inquiry that conceives of subjectivity and social structures as artifacts and thus inherently amenable to revision. This attitude, of course, embodies the spirit of pragmatism and neither began nor ended with Henry James. As the "Coda" will show, his egregiously neglected pragmatic cultural inquiry reverberated beyond 1907. While James's mode of experimental flânerie in *The American Scene* cannot be said to have inaugurated an explicit tradition, his stance possesses an exceptional degree of currency and deserves to figure more prominently in our discriminations of modern modes of intellectual practice.

Coda:
The Politics of Nonidentity

Nothing is more contemporary about the thought of William and Henry James than their rejection of traditional norms of mastery and authority. In pursuing new forms of human agency and cultural inquiry that seek power and value by deliberately eluding direct identification and affiliation, each practiced a politics of nonidentity.[1] While William's mode of practice is oppositional and Henry's immanent, both Jameses questioned conventional notions of adequacy, particularly the responsibility of the intellectual in a "loose universe" where all experiences are "finite," fall back on nothing, and are "homeless." William's pragmatism—a sample of which I have just quoted—delights in mocking those refined "men of principles," the "rationalists" and "professors," who sentimentally yearn for the stability of "Reality with the big R" (*Pragmatism* 18, 125–26). We have seen that William himself—the earnest moralist of principles, proud of his oppositional authority, and preoccupied with the big R—was in many ways at odds with what his pragmatism celebrated.

An inadvertent echo of the exhilarating insouciance of William James's antifoundationalism can be heard in Foucault's jaunty dismissal of the "universal" or oppositional intellectual who speaks as a moral exemplar "in the capacity of master of truth and justice" (*Power/Knowledge* 126). For Foucault such earnestness is ill-suited to our postmodern preference for irony. He equates maturity with what he calls an ironic stance that abandons "traditional seriousness" and the "special status for truth" that supports it. To escape frivolity, the ironist must seek "those practices which offer the possibility of a new way of acting" (Dreyfus and Rabinow 117). The local, the particular, and the embedded become the focus of the "specific" intellectual's search for new modes of practice.

Whereas William James sought to outrage genteel professors of philosophy,

Foucault has his own rivals to mock, principally the French heroic intellectual tradition stretching from Zola to Sartre, which intervenes on behalf of superior moral values. Matthew Arnold was the despised moralist in the eyes of another ironist, Randolph Bourne, who sought to replace Arnold's high seriousness with a "playful attitude" that refuses "both optimism and pessimism" (*Will* 143). The ironist, says Bourne, "has lost himself completely in this world he lives in" (147). This imperative of immersion echoes Henry James's "restless analyst" and prefigures what Foucault has called his "dream of the intellectual" who is "incessantly on the move, doesn't know exactly where he is heading nor what he will think tomorrow for he is too attentive to the present" ("Power and Sex" 161).

Not only is the ironic, nontheoretical orientation of Foucault's specific intellectual familiar to pragmatism, but America's most influential neopragmatist has described irony as his favorite mode of intellectual practice. Richard Rorty's understanding of irony, like Foucault's, also indicates a willingness to forgo talk of true selves and real interests, as well as common truths and common goals.[2] In place of these is Rorty's patchwork, discontinuous stance, which separates public from private and depends on revisable, provisional beliefs as the only "final vocabulary" worth having. Rorty's brief for an ironist liberal culture captures the historicist, nominalist spirit of much contemporary American intellectual debate. As Rorty has often declared, he is inspired by Dewey's refashioning of philosophy as cultural criticism. One question the present study has weighed is which intellectual figures stand behind and parallel to Dewey. The answer—Henry James, Bourne, Adorno—though unconventional, has a certain logic. I have called that logic immanent in its assent to the "inexorable"—Bourne's term—which summarizes the new configurations of political power that have recast the responsibility of the modern intellectual.

After 1917 John Dewey modified his brand of pragmatism in a Bournian direction.[3] Although Dewey never became the "malicious" and "malcontent" ironist that Bourne saw as the intellectuals' social role (his temperament and a residual Comteanism precluded such a position), to a significant degree Dewey came to practice his own version of the politics of nonidentity. Thus he fulfilled Bourne's hope that cultural critics would keep "the intellectual waters constantly in motion" (*Will* 317). Dewey turned Bourne's "heightened energy" of tentativeness and experiment into a powerful source of vitality in mapping strategies to ventilate the inexorable (153). But Dewey's alliance is not only with Bourne but extended all the way back to Henry James. Something of the risky, restless adventurousness of *The American Scene* informs two moments in Dewey's career that stand out as exemplary instances of his nonidentical critical practice.

I

For leftist intellectuals active in the mid twenties, the most exciting social experiment was occurring in the Soviet Union. No place seemed to bristle with more possibility and potential, with what Walter Benjamin called "astonishing experimentation . . . boundless curiosity and playfulness," than Moscow (*Reflections* 106). Dewey visited the city in 1928, two years after Benjamin. In his remarkable set of "Impressions of Soviet Russia," Dewey launched an inquiry in his specific sense of an activity demanding "surrender of what is possessed, disowning of what supports one in secure ease" (*Experience* 201). In the Soviet Union Dewey became what Bourne cherished and yearned for—"the intellectual who cannot yet crystallize, who does not dread suspense" (*Will* 317). Dewey's "disowning" of ease for the precariousness of the uncrystallized began with his abandonment of all presuppositions that communism and Marxist dogma had exhausted the meaning of the Russian Revolution. He then surrendered to the exhilarated sense of curiosity and openness that suffused the streets, museums, and schools. In short, Dewey sufficiently relaxed his self to mime playfully the mood of revolution, whose essence is not "merely political and economic" but "psychic and moral" in its "release of courage, energy and confidence in life" (*Later Works* 3: 204).

The opening sentence of Dewey's first "Impression" finds him immersed in the presiding mood of tentativeness: "The alteration of Petrograd into Leningrad is without question a symbol, but the mind wavers in deciding of what" (203). Registering the fact of change and the attendant indeterminacy, Dewey manages to dwell in suspension, much as the Soviet Union dwells in a state of transition, allegedly on a path to total communism. Both remain in an "intermediate stage," resisting "premature crystallization." With his mind "dazed" and "in a whirl of new impressions" (204), Dewey's mental state approximates, to a striking degree, the open, unguarded spontaneity of mimetic behavior. Yet in modifying the urge for conceptual definition, clarity, and control (all attributes of instrumental reason), Dewey is far from oblivious to actuality, to the fragility of the Russian experiment involving the release of human powers. For this release, notes Dewey, occurs "in spite of secret police, inquisitions, arrests, and deportations . . . [including the] exiling of party opponents" (211).

At that time the Soviet Union teetered uneasily between repression and liberation, a fragile balance that was to be shattered by Stalin's consolidation of power two years later. The country itself and Dewey's response to it are riddled by paradox—what he calls "disparity." He notes that his wavering, his refusal to draw definitive conclusions about the Soviet Union's future, will offend both orthodox Marxists and anti-Communists. (Upon his return Dewey was indeed denounced by the Left and the Right.) He confesses to the "exaggerated quality" of some of his statements but lets them stand as testimony to the "depth of the impression" received, a depth founded not on the stability of fact but on the "marked disproportion" between the "breadth" of his conclusions and the "narrowness" of his experience (212–13). Analogously, there is "the sense of disparity" between the formula of Marxist doctrine that prescribes an "exact goal" and the "more basic fact of a revolution . . . of heart and mind" that liberates human possibility (246,

204–5). Dewey's wavering is founded on his suspicion that this "release of human powers on such an unprecedented scale," this psychic renovation in subjectivity prompted by economic revolution, necessarily summons new energies that exceed any preordained historical laws. To Dewey the "Marxian philosophy of history" has begun to "smell of outworn absolutist metaphysics and bygone theories of straight-line, one way 'evolution' " (207, 205).

In an important sense Dewey's thinking has here been infiltrated—not merely influenced—by the "disparity" that surrounds him. Resisting a straight line for a wavering one, Dewey enacts what Adorno has called "the volatility of thought" as he risks "exaggeration" in order to mimic the restless, "nervously active" texture of Russian life, which he finds even more mobile than that of an American frontier town (215). This indeterminacy, which threatens to make Moscow resemble an uncanny approximation of America, baffles efforts to draw definitive conclusions. All Dewey can say is that the Soviet Union's future will not only be "highly unlike" Western capitalism but "equally unlike the society which orthodox Marxist formulae call for" (223).

This land of unlikeness fosters in Dewey a sense of differential or nonidentical cognition—what Bourne calls irony, the trope of disparity. Strikingly, Dewey elects irony to embody the suspended weight of difference: "There is a peculiar tone of irony that hangs over all [one's] preconceptions," which in the Soviet Union undergo "complete reversal" (218, 244). Perhaps the most intriguing irony for Dewey is the possibility that the Russian Revolution, in terms of "creative energy," has "no intrinsic, necessary connection with communistic theory and practice," and that "the like of it might exist in any large industrial center" (214). Thus Dewey recommends close study of the Soviet experiment, which would subsequently inspire his own conversion to socialism in 1935 (249). His willingness to relax the "power of will and purpose" (Bourne), to forgo "systematic inquiries" (213), and to permit himself to be shocked and dazed, suspended in absorbed, alert contemplation, reflects a rare mode of action. His stance facilitates the experience of difference and contradiction without the imperious annexation of otherness into a system or classification or ideological commitment, the reflex of identity thinking. It also exemplifies the "flowering of human capacity" that his "renascent liberalism" will strive for, and that Adorno's emphasis on the mimetic will aim to preserve amid modernity's imperative of rationalization.

Dewey's experimental life of mimetic irony in the Soviet Union is in itself an exemplary achievement of the politics of nonidentity. The ability to perform the "toilsome labor of understanding," with its "precarious uncertainty," to steer a course between the polarized abstractions of communism and anticommunism while remaining politically astute and involved, has always been a rare feat, particularly among American intellectuals (*Experience* 46–47). Did not Dewey himself too often sound like the rationalist *malgré lui*, content with his own ceaselessly reiterated abstractions—intelligence and scientific method—which reduced the political to the technical? As Christopher Lasch has noted, the "anti-intellectualism of the intellectuals" consists in their weakness for "unequivocal answers to questions which otherwise would have prevented the kind of total political commitment that American intellectuals seem so eager to make" (305). To make vivid this flight from ambiguity we need only invoke the egregious example of Sidney Hook, whose response to the Soviet Union serves as an instructive contrast to that of his mentor, Dewey. The basis for this contrast, to borrow Michael Walzer's terms, is the difference between the oppositional (or committed) intellectual, whose arrogant belief in his "absolute clarity" of vision produces an "ideologically flattened world," and the "connected" critic, who refuses "the pleasures of absolutism" and "the exhilaration of the heights" (226, 142, 238).[4]

Looking back on his 1929 visit (a year after Dewey's), Hook has noted: "I was completely oblivious at the time to the systematic repressions that were then going on. . . . I was not even curious enough to probe and pry, possibly for fear of what I would discover." Asking himself what accounted for his timidity, Hook explained:

> I had come to the Soviet Union with the faith of someone already committed to the Socialist ideal. . . . Perhaps the most important, if not the most conscious, reason for my insensitivity during this time was the fear of losing the only animating social ideal available to someone who had rejected the system of capitalism. . . . We uncritically identified the Soviet Union with its declared socialist ideal. (Hook 123–24).

Hook here registers the idealist afflictions of identity thinking: the unification of real and ideal; the paralysis of curiosity; the refusal of immersion; and the inhibition of all affective emotion save loyalty to an ideal.

II

In the decade following his visit to the Soviet Union, Dewey's thinking again reflected a style of individual behavior and judgment that resisted the tempting certitudes of identity thinking. Dewey's old friend Sidney Hook helped persuade him to chair an inquiry into the charges Stalin had brought against Trotsky in the Moscow Trials of 1936 and 1937. In his work during the Trotsky inquiry, Dewey maintained an unaffiliated stance of nonidentity that proved especially valuable politically. Indeed, his presence as neither fellow traveler, party member, nor anti-Communist was crucial in legitimating the fairness of the proceedings. But Dewey was publically vilified for his participation, the abuse far exceeding what he endured in 1928 upon his return from the Soviet Union. This time he was attacked by many New York leftists. Most painful, perhaps, *The New Republic*, long his principal journalistic forum, opposed the inquiry. Speaking for the majority of the Left, the magazine editorialized that it saw "no reason . . . to take the Moscow Trials at other than its face value" (qtd. Hook 231). As was the case with Hook in 1929, the general refusal to question and explore for the sake of commitment was blatant.

Dewey's openness avoided this inertia and eluded as well what he saw as liberalism's endemic weakness—its "unwillingness to face the unpleasant," to "shirk when unpleasant conditions demand decisions and actions" (*Later Works* 11: 319, 335). Realizing that he risked the "bitter disillusionment" of his personal hopes for the success of the Russian experiment, Dewey nevertheless took action. Granting "that a chairman might be found... whose experience better fitted him for the difficult and delicate task to be performed," Dewey decided to accept the responsibility because, as he stated at the time, "I have given my life to the work of education... and I realized that to act otherwise would be false to my life work" (309).

Beneath his characteristic facade of blandness is the remarkable fact of the seventy-eight-year-old Dewey performing his most dramatic act of "intellectual disrobing." The work of education to which he had been committed for a lifetime assumed its own form of the inexorable—the ineradicable risk of error and failure. For Dewey inquiry demanded divestiture—the temporary shedding of the "intellectual habits we take on and wear when we assimilate" cultural norms. This "disrobing" was rooted in an openness verging on ignorance. He admitted as much to Max Eastman: "I came to the work [of the Trotsky Commission] about as ignorantly innocent of knowledge of the historic record & personalities involved as anybody could be." He would subsequently confess that "my ignorance was rather shameful" (641). At the very moment he was burdened with momentous historical responsibility, Dewey flirted with the "irresponsibility," the "blitheness springing from the volatility of thought," that Adorno saw as the necessary "license" of genuine thinking (*Minima* 127).[5]

Dwelling in ignorance, the "cultivated naivete" that can be obtained only through "the discipline of severe thought" (*Experience* 35), Dewey relaxed the coercions of unwavering rationality and approached that "calm disinterestedness of spirit" Bourne found to be the mark of the "experimental attitude toward life" (*Will* 154). His willed vulnerability and surrender had powerful consequences that went beyond the exculpation of Trotsky. This verdict reverberated, indirectly helping to consolidate the Trotskyist movement and to galvanize the rebirth of *Partisan Review*. Such were the rich fruits of Deweyan inquiry. Its fertility had its source in the sole commitment of honoring what Dewey called the universe's "character of contingency" (*Experience* 42). This adherence to the precarious, according to Adorno, produces "the concrete awareness of the conditionality of human knowledge" which alone leads us "to the threshold of truth" (*Minima* 128).

III

Whether practiced by the specific intellectual, the "connected" critic, the immanent ironist, or the "restless analyst," the politics of nonidentity challenges the idealist elevation of the intellectual into a promethean, oppositional master of truth. This figure is toppled from a position of privileged moral vision to a far less stable vantage point, one where thought and experience are "no longer 'glued' to identity." This condition, says Adorno, induces vertigo as an index of truth (*Negative* 31–33). The locus of this vertigo is on "the formidable foreground," to cite Henry James's phrase, where mastery and certainty are renounced, where "distance is not a safety-zone but a field of tension" (Adorno, *Minima* 127), and where freedom, according to Foucault, is not an essence but " 'agonism' . . . reciprocal incitation and struggle . . . permanent provocation" ("Subject" 222). In this immanent space of "immense fluidity" that James designated as "the Margin," oppositions like success and failure, passivity and resistance, impotence and power radically intermix. Here, says Dewey, "our knowledge swims in a continuum of indeterminacy" (*Later Works* 6: 275).

If, in 1917, Dewey's pragmatic faith lapsed and he supported the war, he spent the next thirty-five years revising and refining his faith, becoming splendidly adequate by surrendering the desire to achieve adequacy. He had learned Bourne's bitter lesson concerning the value of "intellectual suspense." The intellect, Bourne had noted, "craves certitude. It takes effort to keep it supple and pliable" (*Will* 315). Yet Bourne had imbibed his pragmatic suppleness from Dewey himself. In a dialectical reversal worthy of Adorno and Henry James, Dewey turned his student's taboo against "premature crystallization" into the impetus for virtually unparalleled public engagement.

Notes

Preface

1. By intellectual I mean a writer who critically examines contemporary cultural, social, and political issues. This analysis can be mediated through a work of fiction or autobiography (as in *The Ambassadors* or James's memoirs) or directly addressed to a general audience (e.g., *The American Scene*). In this latter context I describe James functioning as a public intellectual.

2. I discuss my reasons for selecting *The Ambassadors* rather than other late fiction in the first note to chapter 9.

3. This is the historian Peter Burke's phrase (qtd. Harlan, "Reply" 624).

Chapter 1

1. There is dispute among commentators regarding whether James's declaration of "ideal interests solely" conflicts with his general skepticism elsewhere of elitism and transhistorical truths. I concur with Cornel West's reading of James's conception of an intellectual class. West finds it "peculiar" in that "we find James elevating elitism" and "uncritically privileg[ing] his class," both of which are "notions he deplores elsewhere" (62). I would add that James makes his strenuous defense of individualism in the name of "the eternal forces of truth which always work in the individual" (*Letters* 2: 90). In an opposing reading, James Kloppenberg argues that James "never attempted to enshrine his values as a timeless and universal social ideal" (149).

2. Henry James's immanent relation to the instrumentality of modernity has a number of implications that are discussed in greater detail in subsequent chapters. Briefly stated, his immanence avoids the leftist romantic opposition to Enlightenment liberalism, the political philosophy of Western modernity usually regarded as en-

shrining legalistic and instrumental thinking. In the words of a recent political theorist, romantic attitudes and feelings typically "combine to make liberalism appear unbearably arid and cold, impersonal and unexpressive." A person of " 'romantic sensibility' is disposed to suffer and confess these aversions" (Rosenblum, *Another* 2). William James is one such person. Henry James's immanent stance will emerge as neither antiromantic nor anti-individualistic but as the position of a chastened romantic who, like Dewey, seeks to renovate conventional liberalism under the impetus of romantic expressivism. Although Adorno is typically associated with romantic antiliberalism, I will subsequently argue that in important ways he is actually closer in outlook to Dewey and Henry James.

3. I am referring to Story's *Roba di Roma* (1–32). I discuss Story in chapters 6 and 8.

4. For all its valuable insights, Richard Hocks's *Henry James and Pragmatistic Thought*, the only book-length study on Henry and William James, unfortunately identifies Henry's pragmatism solely with that of his brother.

5. I do not mean to imply that it is groundless to call James an anti-Semite. But critics too often make their case by quoting the incriminating evidence with no regard for context or for how James qualifies and complicates his responses. For instance, when James's descriptions of the "Hebrew conquest of New York" and of the swarming ghetto as a vast aquarium in which dwell "innumerable fish, of over-developed proboscis," are made to stand alone he appears racist (*Scene* 131–32). But this conclusion simplifies a complex attitude that expresses unease and disgust within an admiring acceptance of and identification with the alien. I argue this point repeatedly, particularly in chapter 10, where I restore original context and examine the full range of meanings in James's pronouncements.

6. Two exceptions are Thomas Bender and David Harvey. Bender finds James's reaction to the immigrants "more complex and interesting than is usually recognized" (248–49). Harvey's account of urban consciousness, the work of a Marxist geographical historian, begins with a salute to James; see my chapter 6 for quotations from Harvey's study.

7. In his superb essays on Henry James, Wright Morris declares that "he was the first American of unquestioned genius to escape from the consolations of the past, without recourse to the endless vistas of optimism" (112).

8. In a well-known essay Elizabeth Hardwick called William James an American hero, and recently Monroe Spears has reaffirmed this judgment. Frank Lentricchia has announced "the return of William James" as an exemplary intellectual model (103–33).

9. George Cotkin also describes James as an existential anarchist (174). Lentricchia exemplifies the paradox of grasping James's naivete while still extolling him. Acknowledging that capitalism "tends to be blurred and repressed by James's liberal ideology of the autonomous self," Lentricchia nevertheless somehow manages to find Jamesian pragmatism a "vision strong for criticism, self-scrutiny, and self-revision" (127, 109).

10. Despite its importance, Kloppenberg's approach to William James has some unresolved ambiguities. On the one hand, he locates the value of James's political ideas in his philosophy rather than in his political practice: "As philosophy [his] ideas were persuasive, but as politics they were problematical because they neglected the persistence of power" (194). On the other hand, Kloppenberg argues for "congruence" and a "logical relation" between James's epistemology and his politics (146). Thus James's pragmatist epistemology, which "dislodged all abstract ideas from

suprahistorical platforms and made them available for pragmatic truth testing," is at one with his political and cultural beliefs (163). The present study will argue against Kloppenberg's continuity thesis and for a view that sees conflicts and contradictions in and between James's politics and epistemology. The most obvious one is the gap between the tolerance and openness preached by his pragmatic epistemology and the content of his political pronouncements—largely repetitive, moralistic attacks on "bigness"—symptomatic of his aversion to modernity in general. Not the least reason such conflicts exist is the fact that they are rooted in the spiritual malaise that paralyzed James in his twenties and permanently shaped his temperament. And "temperaments with their cravings and refusals," as James insisted, "do determine men in their philosophies, and always will" (*Pragmatism* 24). In chapters 2 and 5 I hope to show that James's cravings and refusals are dialectically entwined and inscribe his philosophical and social thought with contradictions.

11. Virtually all of the figures mentioned (save Kallen) also had substantial reservations about James, particularly his subjectivist and moralistic fervor, which they outgrew and/or revised. In chapter 10 I discuss some of the "left" and "right" appropriations of James.

12. See Cotkin's perceptive discussion of Roosevelt's Hegelian politics (139).

13. I shall return to this image of the worm in Chapter 10, where I discuss James's comparison of New York Jews to worms wriggling "contentedly."

14. William's self-abasement is conscious of the religious tradition it resembles. He spoke of "the religious experience of the lutheran type" that "bankrupts . . . all this naturalistic self-sufficiency. . . . You are strong only by being weak, it shows" (qtd. King 196).

15. In this context, it is interesting to recall that as a young friend and intellectual admirer of the elder James, Charles Peirce's rejection of the Cartesian monadic self was likely encouraged by James's disdain for conventional modes of being. I touch on the Peirce–James senior connection in chapter 7.

16. This comment by H. G. Dwight is from his important essay, discussed in chapter 6.

17. As Fredric Jameson (most recently) and other commentators have emphasized, mimesis is a notoriously enigmatic and elusive concept in Adorno's writings (Jameson, *Late* 64, 104). Jameson's view is quoted in chapter 5. One reason for the term's slipperiness is that Adorno disregards conventional uses of mimesis as imitation or representation. For Adorno mimesis is a "process of making oneself similar to the environment" or to the other, but it is not a passive imitation of the environment or the other. I borrow this distinction from Michael Cahn's valuable essay.

Chapter 2

1. This is also true of Richard Hocks in his book on the relationship between William James's pragmatism and the literary art of Henry James. Hocks speaks of a "possible polarity expressed and embedded within the unity between" the brothers: "Henry James seems representative of the predominance of thought and reflection over that of energy and activity, and William James of energy and activity over thought and reflection" (228).

2. James's reply to Tausch was published in the same issue of *The Monist* (156).

3. In one of the most illuminating accounts of James's crisis, John Owen King

argues that, "like the ministers of early America," James "allowed his most private struggles to become public documents" and offered his life as "a moral exemplum" of a "divided self." In the tradition of Edwards and Protestant spiritual narrative, James moved from crisis to conversion (142–43, 145).

4. In various contexts, commentators have noted this propensity for doubleness in William James. John Dewey identified "two incompatible strains in the Jamesian psychology" outlined in *The Principles of Psychology*, one being "official acceptance of epistemological dualism" that sets mind and world against each other, and the other an empirical, functional account of self as interactive process. According to Dewey, this latter account, which "reduces the subject to a vanishing point," comes to the fore in James only in his 1904 essay "Does 'Consciousness' Exist?" James's answer is that consciousness does not exist as an entity, only as a function ("The Vanishing Subject in the Psychology of James," *Later Works* 14: 155–56, 166). More recently James Kloppenberg has described *The Principles of Psychology* as having a "split personality," for James "pieced together an analysis that threatened to split apart at the seams connecting its positivistic account of physical processes with its vivid descriptions of the protean character of life" (67).

5. Ironically, the Jamesian values that Veblen critiqued—prudence, equilibrium, habit—were the very functionalist, pragmatic qualities that Veblen came to celebrate fifteen years later in *The Engineers and the Price System*. The tensions discernible in Veblen between admiration for the play of "idle curiosity" and puritanical unease with it—which are evident as early as *The Theory of the Leisure Class* (1899)—reflect what David Riesman calls the ineradicable "internal contradictions of his thought" (vii).

6. Ellul would reject Veblen's use of technology as a mediating term since it disregards the fact that technology inevitably corrupts the free play of curiosity by harnessing it to the law of the one best means, technology's defining premise. In the twentieth century, notes Ellul, the speculations of scientific research became enslaved to technique, to the imperative of practical application (45).

7. Worth noting is the fact that the poem that precipitates Arnold's lament and his eventual abandonment of a poetic career concerns Empedocles, who, as one of the earliest speculative, theoretical philosophers, was an heir of the Ionians.

8. In an interesting reading of "The Sentiment of Rationality," Michael Weinstein compares James's suppression of "ontological wonder-sickness" to Heidegger's preoccupation with it. In James's escape from wonder-sickness, says Weinstein, "the possibility of an American existentialism was lost. Rather than remaining close to the lived experience of ontological insecurity . . . James uses the idea of radical contingency to show that theoretical reason does not satisfy the sentiment of rationality" (134). Significantly, Dewey critiqued what he called the "control side of pragmatism" after reading "The Sentiment of Rationality," with its flight from theoretical speculation.

9. This paradox of James's radical empiricism is explored in chapter 5.

10. To be fair to William James, he was critical of those who avoided altogether the "downward slope" of curiosity. His remarks on the temperament of one of his major philosophical antagonists, Herbert Spencer, mock the philosopher's egregious lack of "desultory curiosity, showing little interest in either books or people." Spencer once boasted to George Eliot that he had "never been puzzled." He declared that "anything like passive receptivity is foreign to my nature." With "no capacity for dreaminess or passivity," says James, Spencer was "almost incapable of believing in the reality of alien ways of feeling." His "absolute self-confidence" made him "least

divertible by casual side curiosity." James's discussion may be found in his review of Spencer's *Autobiography* (1904) (*Memories and Studies* 122).

11. The historian of American religion, William Clebsch, has described William's depression in terms of acedia. We should also note that acedia is the word Coleridge used to describe his own depression, brought on by "abstruse research," about which he felt guilty from a Christian point of view.

12. When curiosity is associated with Henry James, it tends to be satirized as an addiction to peering through the keyhole in a "rage of wonderment," to borrow the title of Max Beerbohm's famous caricature of the bloated master on his knees in front of the door of a hotel room.

13. "Perfect bliss" is White's phrase; see page 109 of his study.

14. Remarkable in James's letters to these men is not only the desire for physical contact but also its enactment (in language): "I draw you close and hold you long and am ever so tenderly yours" is a characteristic declaration. The act of reading their letters and replying obliterates "the dire gulf of space," as he informs Walpole. Speaking of himself in the third person, James tells him: "Here he is with you now, though too late at night. . . . He hardly knows how to put it strongly enough that he rejoices . . . in your company and conversation" (*Letters* 4: 678). James's love letters seem both to arouse and satisfy his fervent desire for intimacy, as if his acts of writing and reading them become in themselves pleasurable forms of sexual activity and not simply substitutes. This fusion informs the opening of a letter to Andersen: "I've had punctually all your beautiful and blessed missives, and of course I've tenderly loved you, and yearningly embraced you, and passionately thanked you for them" (4: 404). To Morton Fullerton, in 1900, James pleads: "Write me. . . . It will be, as it were, a part of yourself on which I can put my hand" (*Selected Letters* 325). Chapter 8 establishes a cultural context in which to place James's sexuality, and chapter 9 discusses the masochistic structure of his (and Lambert Strether's) sexual economy, which is grounded in the perversities of pure curiosity. These chapters, together with the present discussion, should demonstrate the inadequacy of received opinion, which still believes, in the words of a recent critic, that "James's general suppression of his homoeroticism was probably a powerful cause of his persistent unease in relation to other men. . . . The unacceptability of the homoerotic component of his desires for men means that this unease-producing gap could never safely be closed." The critic's unexamined assumption of unease derives from another false assumption— by way of Eve Sedgwick—that James and his friends participated in a "generally shared homophobic dread in masculine culture" (Derrick 51–52). I take up Sedgwick's "homosexual panic" reading of James in chapter 8.

15. Regarding the risks of radical curiosity, the following remark by William James is pertinent: "I . . . have a horror of being duped; but I can believe that worse things than being duped may happen to a man in this world." He cautions against "excessive nervousness" about "our errors" and urges a "certain lightness of heart" as the "fittest thing for the empiricist philosopher" (*Will* 25). James's will to insouciance here, as in his bid to be a "happy-go-lucky anarchistic sort of creature," represents an ideal rather than a reality that his defensive psyche achieves.

16. Another parallel is that Freud links abulia to Leonardo's inhibitions (81).

17. Leonardo's reluctance to complete his projects became part of his legendary genius. One minor instance of the nineteenth century's fascination with Leonardo, in the form of a poem by William Wetmore Story, is pertinent here, for Henry James quotes from "Leonardo" in his biography of Story. Not insignificantly, Story's poem focuses on the painter's wandering curiosity and the contempt this sparks in observers

of this "oddest man of men" (James, *Story* 2: 234). What James subtly suggests is that Story's own "extravagant waste," evident in his "caring inordinately little to present" his poems as polished and complete, makes him a Leonardo reduced to absurdity (245–46).

18. James's pungent phrase suggests the defensive, subjugating motives of canonization. He is here referring to Browning, a writer who caused him considerable psychological anxiety. See "Browning in Westminster Abbey" (*Literary* 1: 790).

Chapter 3

1. Predictably enough, Levine locates the origins of the flight from ambiguity in Puritanism. Surprisingly, he fails to mention pragmatism.

2. William Bouwsma has linked William James to Calvinism, calling him a "figure who may have a better, if a subtler, claim to be considered one of Calvin's spiritual sons than many who have thought of themselves as Calvinists" (3). Anxiety about curiosity and "horror of the unlimited" (46) are two points of connection.

3. In later chapters we shall see that for both Weber and Adorno the very success of the Enlightenment undermined its emancipatory program.

4. Henry James's participation in this effort to reunify sensibility is complicated, for although he is justly famous for seeking organic economy, he not only emphasizes the obstacles to achieving this unity but also cultivates dissonance as a source of aesthetic power. An end to social and aesthetic dissonance and fragmentation seems, at best, a perpetually deferred goal for James and not an available reality. In chapter 5 I discuss this tension.

5. For instance, Wyndham Lewis says that Henry James possessed "the overdelicate mind of the New Englander" that encouraged his predilection for a "twilit feminine universe" and his distaste for "Pagan robustness" (123, 127). In these remarks Lewis reiterates the views of Van Wyck Brooks, whom he much admires.

6. My sentence incorporates the title of Jonas Barish's useful book on the intellectual history of the antitheatrical attitude.

7. James's logic recalls Hegel's famous declaration that the "circle, which is self-enclosed and at rest, . . . is an immediate relation, the immediate continuous relation of elements with their unity." Hence it "arouses no sense of wonderment." For Hegel understanding is the "energy of thought" that shatters circular unity and attains the truth of mediation by embracing "the portentous power of the negative" (93). Breeding the monadic closure of self-identity is the Cartesian, dualistic caste of the New England mind. John Dewey of Vermont found the "sense of divisions and separations . . . borne in upon" him "as a consequence of a heritage of New England culture" (qtd. McDermott 7). "Divisions by way of isolation of self from the world, of soul from body, of nature from God, brought a painful oppression," confessed Dewey. Hegel was an antidote, for he dissolved "hard and fast dividing walls" and helped liberate Dewey from Cartesianism. In chapter 7 I return to Descartes.

8. James's challenge to masculinity, only an implicit issue in this chapter, is pursued in chapters 7 through 9. Jackson Lears (251–60) presents an interesting psychocultural reading of Brooks's fear of aestheticism and embrace of rigid masculinity. Henry James, who literally haunted Brooks's dreams, figured in Brooks's psyche as the "personification of 'feminized' European aestheticism" (256).

9. This fetishizing of the "real" is at the heart of the naive epistemology of Brooks,

Parrington, and Charles Beard. All three strikingly confirm Dewey's philosophical analysis (discussed in chapters 4 and 5) of the propensity of ideologies to appropriate the "real" as a reified entity that excludes some qualities (mutability) and sanctifies others (stability). Lionel Trilling, a former student of Dewey's at Columbia University, made a famous Deweyan critique of Parrington and the "real": "There exists, he believes, a thing called *reality*; it is one and immutable, it is wholly external, it is irreducible" (*Liberal* 2). Trilling's critique is quoted later in the present chapter.

10. Terry Eagleton's portrayal of Henry James in *Criticism and Ideology* is not only Brooksian but also seems to be inspired by his mentor Raymond Williams's view of James as ahistorical. Williams offered a retrospective clarification of his judgment (*Politics* 256–67).

11. My account draws on Richard Pells's *Radical Visions and American Dreams* and Daniel Aaron's *Writers on the Left*, two standard cultural histories of the era.

12. My emphasis on the cosmopolitan has partly been influenced by Terry Cooney's *Rise of the New York Intellectuals*. William Barrett's memoir *The Truants*, containing a valuable discussion of the early days of *Partisan Review*, stresses the marriage of Marxism and modernism.

13. For an interesting discussion (that does not include Matthiessen's ambivalent relationship to Henry James) of the discrepancies and repressions that mark the connection between Matthiessen's political commitments and aesthetic judgments, see Jonathan Arac's essay. William Cain makes a strong case for revaluating Matthiessen's achievement downward in his book on the critic.

14. Kazin's *On Native Grounds* remains one of the best accounts of Brooks's project and is eloquent on James's ability to arouse resentment in nativist mentalities.

15. This familiar charge has recently been repeated in reference to Trilling's advocacy of James. In *The Bostonians*, claims Alfred Habegger, the novelist "expressed the essential fantasy" of Trilling and *Partisan Review*: to escape from political and social reality by cultivating a "fine alienated sensibility," a stance that became "*the* central sensibility in . . . a great number of modernists" (291). Habegger's failure to distinguish between James and the uses made of him by other critics does not wholly invalidate his point. As we shall see, part of James's rise in the forties is, of course, attributable to the cultural exigencies of the day.

16. In *Theoretical Dimensions of Henry James* John Carlos Rowe offers a provocative reading of *The Princess Casamassima* that confirms Trilling's claim for the sophistication of James's political understanding. In chapter 10 I discuss the relation of James's portrayal of the anarchists in *The Princess Casamassima* to the hotel-spirit's masters of management in *The American Scene*.

17. As David Noble notes in *The End of American History*, "American historians from the Puritans in the 1630s through the writings of Charles Beard in the 1930s . . . have thought and written as if the United States was absolutely independent, standing apart in its uniqueness from the rest of human experience" (7). There is a striking analogy between progressive historiography (described later) and the genteel tradition, which also depends on an idealized space of freedom above the marketplace. In effect, American historians define the space of freedom as America itself, "an island of political and economic virtue in the surrounding sea of world corruption" (19). This vision pervades the work of the progressivist historians and accounts for their repression of capitalism. So strong is their investment in the myth of American exceptionalism that they oppose democracy to capitalism and view American history as a battle between the forces of democracy—property holders engaged in agricultural production—and the "parasitical alien capitalists" engaged in speculation with paper

money. As the historian J. G. A. Pocock has shown, this central polarity, which has many different variations, expresses a fear of capitalism that is originally not American at all but derives from an Italian tradition of republican virtue by way of seventeenth-century English republican theorists. In its American incarnation, republican theory is dualistic, positing America as a freeholding democracy whose values and laws are timeless and absolute, static and universal. In stark contrast, Europe is the center of capitalism, time, particularity, of the marketplace rather than natural law. This is the mythology that undergirded the American political imagination and historiography until the outbreak of World War II. By then an ideology of innocence and isolation could no longer be upheld in a nation thrust into international warfare. According to Noble, historians like Hofstadter began to "demythologize and to desacralize the understanding of Anglo-American history that had been dominant for almost three centuries" (10).

18. This is Russell Reising's estimate, which, for my purposes, concisely sums up the difference between Trilling's static conception of dialectic and Adorno's (and Henry James's) productive mode of dialectical thought (207).

19. William James provides a vivid example of this binary view when he declares in "Great Men and Their Environment": "Social evolution is a resultant of the interaction of *two wholly distinct forces*—the individual, deriving his peculiar gifts from the play of physiological and infra-social forces, *but bearing all the power of initiative and origination in his hands*; and second, the social environment, with its power of adopting or rejecting both him and his gifts" (*Will* 174; my emphases).

20. Taylor's emphasis on community typifies the communitarian critique of liberal individualism. Alasdair MacIntyre, Roberto Unger, and Michael Sandel are among its other leading voices. In an acute assessment of contemporary antiliberalism, Stephen Holmes notes the weighty moral burden put upon the fact that man is a social creature, a truism that some communitarians inflate into a moral panacea for liberal atomism. Holmes reminds us that "the social constitution of the individual is worthless as an argument either for or against existing institutional arrangements" (26).

21. The staying power of this genteel aesthetic idealism is impressive. Not only did it survive the nineteenth century and become reinvigorated in the mid twentieth century, but it still flourishes in our so-called age of antihumanism. For instance, in a 1988 review of a work by Saul Bellow, Leon Wieseltier quotes Bellow's urgent plea that we must keep open "access to the deepest part of ourselves . . . that part of us which is conscious of a higher consciousness. . . . The independence of this consciousness, which has the strength to be immune to the noise of history and the distractions of our immediate surroundings, is what the life struggle is all about." These "wise and beautiful sentences," says Wieseltier, discern "the far-reaching difference between intellectual life and contemplative life." The contemplative is supreme, for there what matters is soul, not mind, nature, not culture, essences, not positions. According to Wieseltier, this hierarchy suggests that "the adjective 'restless' may not be the highest compliment we can pay to the noun 'mind' " (38). Evidently the natural essence of the soul is serene contemplation. In such a hushed sanctuary, James's "restless analyst" would be an intrusive distraction.

22. Rorty quotes Lyotard in "Habermas and Lyotard on Postmodernity" (161). Ian Shapiro has argued recently that Rorty's insistence that we can get along without metanarratives constitutes his own project's metanarrative (33, 225).

23. Rorty's rejection of critique has aroused the ire of many commentators. Ian Shapiro claims that "by uncritically endorsing the values he takes to be enshrined

in our culture," Rorty "becomes inexorably wedded to a parochial conservatism, however genial" (228). Yet one might also view Rorty's "political and philosophical complacency" (226) as a willfully polemical move that disturbs the current prestige of a glibly oppositional criticism.

24. This describes Trilling's bourgeois ideal, a yearning for "freedom from pressure," which, as we shall see (chapter 8), was also a central goal of the elder James's idealism.

25. Another way Adorno resists positing an uncontaminated Other is by refusing to exempt culture from the noise of the marketplace. Art's freedom as a negation of "social purposiveness" remains "essentially bound up with the premise of a commodity economy. Pure works of art which deny the commodity society by the very fact that they obey their own laws were always wares all the same" (*Dialectic* 157). Like Rorty, Adorno repeatedly exposes bourgeois liberalism's dream of a "space of freedom" from the "coercions of the marketplace" as a nightmare of mystification. Contrary to the frequent charge of idealism, Adorno's critique of the culture industry's propaganda techniques does not assume a prior state of purity from which modern culture has fallen. Such an assumption is typical of transcendent critique, which, according to the social theorist Seyla Benhabib, promotes "the politics of collective singularity," the belief that there is a "single spot in the social structure that privileges those who occupy it with a vision of the social totality" (352). Thus atomist distortion vitiates a philosophy (Marxism) bent on eliminating such distortion.

26. Unlike transcendent critique, the function of a transcendental move within immanent critique is to "enmesh itself in its object" (to go "behind" the object rather than beyond it) in order to reveal its inner, formal logic. For a vivid illustration of this approach in the context of a discussion of Adorno's analysis of the social content of sports, see William Morgan's article "Adorno on Sport," esp. p. 836.

27. In her interesting discussion of these "conversations between one part of James's consciousness and other, discordant parts," Sharon Cameron cautions readers of *The American Scene* not to "be misled by a temptation to psychologize" and thereby conclude that in James's interior dialogues "ambivalence is externalized as ventriloquism so that James can voice both sides of the dispute" (4–5). Cameron argues instead that "disparate points of view are not significant because they exemplify conflicts in consciousness. Rather, they are significant because they exemplify the omnipresence of consciousness. . . . Conflicts become occasions for consciousness to proliferate," to freely converse with itself. The present study's emphasis on James's interrogation of normative models of social and psychic intelligibility concurs with Cameron's point that James is not restricted to a psychologically realistic context and "not delimited to a self in conventional terms" (7). But she frees *The American Scene* from psychological confines, only to restrict its referential energy to the "sheer virtuosity" of James's "performance of consciousness," which is "divorced from the strictures of situation and character." James is said to banish the given and substitute "for what is there what is *wanted* to be there" (29, 2–3). Once again a familiar, if elegant, formalism celebrates the self-reflexive purity of James's aesthetic idealism.

28. The neglect of immanent critique is beginning to be repaired. In his most recent books, including *The Company of Critics*, Michael Walzer argues for the value of criticism conducted "from within" by a "connected critic" with affective and moral ties to the societies whose practices he criticizes. Walzer's version of immanent critique (which he does not link to Frankfurt Critical Theory) contrasts the connected critic (Camus) to "the stereotype of a leftist social critic" of "absolute opposition" (Sartre), an image that Walzer finds central to the "conception of heroism that has

dominated, not the history, but the ideology of the left" (*Company* 26, 237, 225). Although Walzer discusses only one American connected critic (Randolph Bourne), Henry James can be regarded as prefiguring the critical challenge to the stereotype of leftist absolutism. The "Coda" to the present work seeks to show how two moments in Dewey's career exemplify the critical power that accrues when the Olympian posture of heroic opposition is surrendered.

29. In remarking on the passivity of certain kinds of antifoundationalism (what I've been calling neopragmatism), Roberto Unger provides an assessment helpful in describing the limitation of Rorty's and Michaels's position. Unger writes of the critic who finds in "groundlessness a new reason to reaffirm his allegiance to those historical communities as they currently exist. For what else, he tells us, is there? Thus, he turns an historicizing skepticism on its head and uses it to justify the authority of existing institutional arrangements" (*Passion* 88). Henry James's emphasis on margin and Adorno's on potential (see chapter 5) allow them to avoid what Unger calls the "ancient alliance of skepticism and surrender" (88). Whereas Adorno's understanding of immanence as a provisional stance yields insight into the potentiality inherent in what he calls the "antinomical character of systems" (*Negative* 26), New Historicism's "valorization of immanence and nominalism" can be said to produce nearly the opposite—a tendency to regard systems as closed and all-encompassing. This latter charge is made by Fredric Jameson in the course of his discussion of Michaels's work (*Postmodernism* 190). By conceiving of the market as an "all-informing totality," Michaels disregards "the way in which a radical movement toward something else is also part and parcel of the system it seeks to evade or outsmart" (211, 209). Michaels's refusal to grant systems a sense of margin results from his work's rigorous immanentism, which excludes or represses self-consciousness or reflexivity while simultaneously deploying "extreme theoretical energy" (189–90). In his powerful engagement with New Historicism, Jameson is the first to articulate and assess the importance of Michaels's "antiliberal" project. Its "interpretive brilliance and intellectual energy," he argues, make it a "signal occasion for taking the temperature" of contemporary criticism and theory (181).

30. My description of pluralism is taken from Nancy Rosenblum ("Pluralism" 221). Her book entitled *Another Liberalism* expands on her claim that in the "messy reality of pluralism" is a way to reconcile Romanticism and liberalism. By joining together liberalism and Romanticism's desire for expressive self-fashioning within a multiplicity of contexts, Rosenblum seeks to recast liberalism dramatically, making it less impersonal, legalistic, and banal. Chapter 10 will return to a discussion of James and pluralism.

31. There are, of course, exceptions to this general critical myopia toward James. An important exception is John Carlos Rowe's *The Theoretical Dimensions of Henry James*, which attempts to use the insights of contemporary theory to argue for James's historical and political depth. I share his intention to "socialize, . . . destabilize and render uncanny" James by "questioning the ways in which he has been mythologized as the master of a life-denying aestheticism" (28). Rowe's socializing places James within various modes of current literary theory (feminism, reader response, ideology critique) rather than situating his cultural critique in historical and intellectual contexts, as I attempt here. In *Henry James and the Art of Power* Mark Seltzer at first appears to challenge the image of a genteel Henry James but actually only reinscribes him more firmly as a nervous aesthete absorbed in devising ever more devious ways to "disown the shame of power." I more fully assess this effort in chapter 10. Two other exceptions that break with conventional approaches to James's aesthetics are

David Carroll's essay on the prefaces and Michael Sprinker's discussion of the political valences of James's prefatory strategies. The latter is the best Marxist reading of James I have encountered.

32. Samuel Weber offers a version of this point in noting that "Jameson's defense of Marxism is caught in a double bind: it criticizes its competitors for being ideological in the sense of practicing 'strategies of containment'. . . . But at the same time its own claim to offer an alternative to such ideological containment is itself based on a strategy of containment" (22).

33. Rorty represents the best-known example of opposing Dewey to the Frankfurt School (*Contingency* 57). Rorty's coldness to the first-generation Frankfurt School is regrettable since their project has a certain amount of affinity with Rorty's Deweyan effort to poeticize culture and reconstruct the intellectual as redescriptive ironist. Given the ferocity of Horkheimer's attack, it is surprising to find him praising Dewey in a 1941 essay entitled "Art and Mass Culture." There are also striking affinities between Horkheimer's seminal position paper of 1937, "Traditional and Critical Theory," and Dewey's 1939 *Freedom and Culture*. This suggests that Horkheimer's 1944 diatribe might have expressed an anxiety of philosophic influence, resulting in a deliberate misprision of Dewey. Horkheimer's essays are collected in his *Critical Theory*.

Chapter 4

1. Blackmur's essay is reprinted as the "Introduction" to *The Art of the Novel* (the collected prefaces).

2. This sense of aura comprises only one of its meanings for Benjamin. As is well known, he was ambivalent about the "contemporary decay of the aura." For aura is also a "unique phenomenon of distance however close it may be," a phenomenon being eclipsed by mass culture, with its bias toward homogeneity (*Illuminations* 222–23). This meaning of aura as distance, rather than as cultural fetish, would clearly be supported by Henry James, who conceives of the richest intimacy as premised on distance (see chap. 4, n. 27).

3. One of the remarkable aspects of this renewal is that it continued despite a two-year period (1909–11) when James virtually ceased writing, so afflicted was he by physical illness, depression over the financial failure of the New York Edition, and grief over William's death in 1910. That his memoirs were, to a significant degree, a therapeutic working through of his assorted troubles is a warranted and frequently mentioned inference, especially since its logic repeats an earlier dynamic established with the *Guy Domville* humiliation of 1895. Then James transformed his failure and depression into a stunning creative renewal. I concur in general, if not in particulars, with Leon Edel's estimate that despite the personal and professional tribulations of James's last two decades, during this period he becomes "looser, less formal, less distant; he writes [letters] with greater candor and with more emotional freedom. . . . [He is] less rigid and more experimental in spite of his aging" (*Letters* 4: xiii). Edel's belief that James underwent "considerable alteration in his personality" has been criticized as an exaggeration. While Edel may be typically overdramatic in his sense of discontinuity, his theory at least alerts us to the remarkable efflorescence in James's later life and work.

4. The pleasure or "*allure*," to use James's word, of surrendering "detachment

and dignity" to chaos and movement, suggests the masochistic structure of James's desire, which is also evident in his appetite for shock, discussed later in this chapter. Lambert Strether shares his creator's pleasure in self-shattering experience, a connection discussed in chapter 9.

5. This is Dewey's famous phrase to describe what he opposes.

6. Melville's novel and James's late works share a striking convergence in their effort to unsettle the repressions of monadic individualism. Their shared strategy to disorient radically the experience of reading by estranging the reader's conventional expectations is part of a larger project of seeking a more relaxed mode of being that escapes the rigid control of the bourgeois self. This effort to unsettle social and ontological vigilance is the aim of the confidence man within Melville's novel and is embodied by the "restless analyst" in *The American Scene*.

7. Despite their shared admiration of Emerson, William James stressed the latter's individualism and Dewey his status as the "Philosopher of Democracy," emphases that correlate with James's individualism and Dewey's social conception of self. In *The American Evasion of Philosophy* Cornel West makes a forceful case for the centrality of Emerson's presence in the pragmatic tradition.

8. Identity as a state of hovering in-between receives its most dramatic representation in the famous scene in *Notes of a Son and Brother* when James injures himself putting out a fire and is "jammed . . . between" two fences. I will develop this reading in chapter 7.

9. If by now *Lebensphilosophie*'s attack on deadening convention in the name of authenticity and immediacy has been largely forgotten, this is because by the 1930s it was almost completely absorbed by existentialism (Schnadelbach 139). Even so largely ascetic an antihumanism as postmodernism is not untouched by *Lebensphilosophie*, as is evident in the libidinal politics of *Anti-Oedipus* by Deleuze and Guattari and in the closing pages of the first volume of Foucault's *History of Sexuality*, where he extols "the body and its pleasures" against "sex desire" (157).

10. George Cotkin has summarized James's links to Emerson in *William James: Public Philosopher* (141). I should point out here that I use the word "Emersonian" throughout to mean radical individualism, a definition that does not reflect the actual complexities and tensions in Emerson's notion of self-reliance but rather suggests the cultural appropriation and mythologizing that simplified Emerson's thinking. This is a distinction that neither Henry (in his distrust of Emerson) nor William (in his embrace of Emerson) heeded.

11. Chapter 9 will demonstrate how James registers cultural contradictions in *The Ambassadors* by encasing the radically digressive gropings of its hero within a tightly symmetrical formal structure.

12. In the last twenty years, Quentin Anderson's book on the "imperial self" has been the most influential source of an Emersonian James, a view endorsed by such different works as Stephen Donadio's book on Henry James and Nietzsche and Carren Kaston's more recent work on James and the imagination.

13. In aligning Henry James with Mead and Dewey against William James (in chapter 5 I endorse Santayana's critique of William James), it is also important to recognize that their responses to William can hardly be called disinterested. Each was likely to harbor toward William no small amount of anxiety of influence. (In this context Henry's fraternal rivalry is analogous to the professional rivalry of the others.) After all, William was a pioneer in the field of American psychology and was the most famous American public intellectual of his time. Thus if one accepts their

reservations regarding William, it is important to realize that these qualifications are strategically defensive, judgments that help cut their towering predecessor down to size.

14. Dewey was consistently troubled by the subjectivism he found in William James's philosophy. For instance, Dewey noted that even though *The Principles of Psychology* "radically criticized" the "subjective tenor of prior psychological tradition," still "an underlying subjectivism is retained, at least in vocabulary." Dewey grants that James's "substitution of the 'stream of consciousness' for discrete elementary states" was an "enormous advance," but "nevertheless the point of view remained that of a realm of consciousness set off by itself" (qtd. McDermott 10–11).

15. This critique of subjectivism can be seen as a particular instance of the general reorientation in American thought, in the opening decades of the twentieth century, known as progressivism. As Daniel Rodgers has noted: "Part of what occurred in the Progressive era was, . . . in some measure, an assault on the idea of individualism itself. That was what the era's 'revolt against formalism' was all about," a revolt against "a particular set of formal fictions traceable to Smith, Locke and Mill—the autonomous economic man, the autonomous possessor of property rights, the autonomous man of character" ("In Search" 124). In important ways William James's individualism belonged to a preindustrial, premodern, laissez-faire era. In chapter 5 I argue that Dewey saw James in this way. In chapter 10 I discuss Henry James's dissent, in *The American Scene*, from some of the major motifs in the rhetoric and ideology of progressivism. In our own time Foucault has urged a reconsideration of the individual subject, "not to restore the theme of an originating subject, but to seize its functions" (*Language* 137). According to Richard Rorty, "Dewey and Foucault . . . agree, right down the line, about the need to abandon traditional notions of rationality, objectivity, method and truth. . . . They agree that rationality is what history and society make it—that there is no overarching ahistorical structure . . . to be discovered" (*Consequences* 204). Dissenting from Rorty's opinion, James Kloppenberg says of Dewey (and William James) that they "wanted to set epistemology on a different course rather than destroy it altogether. They denied that it could provide certainty through any 'theory of knowledge,' and to that extent Rorty is correct." Although Dewey and James sought to make philosophy more radical and experimental than idealist or empiricist models, they were not Nietzscheans (as Rorty suggests) and believed philosophy "could provide an imprecise compass for personal and political decision making" (431). Kloppenberg groups James and Dewey with the philosophers (including Wilhelm Dilthey, T. H. Green, Henry Sidgwick, and Albert Fouillée) of what he calls "the via media," a "transatlantic community of discourse in philosophy and political theory" that constructed a "radical theory of knowledge" grounded in human experience and contingency rather than transcendental truth.

16. This Comtean image of Balzac is not James's only sense of the novelist. Indeed, the Frenchman also embodies an opposite impulse of indeterminacy (see *Art* 343).

17. For this summary formulation of modernism I am indebted to Douglas Collins's important ongoing inquiry into the anthropology and psychology of the self-humiliating strategies of post-Enlightenment philosophical and aesthetic thought.

18. Indeed, Simmel is notorious for his reticence of judgment concerning his subject matter. His contemplative approach to objects explicitly derives pleasure not from touching them but from remaining reserved and remote. (See Simmel, *Philosophy* 73.) Bryan Green presents an interesting discussion of Simmel's stylistic strategies and the critical response they have drawn (92–116). David Frisby, a prominent

Simmel scholar, emphasizes the aestheticizing thrust of Simmel's works and his deep affinity with his successor, Walter Benjamin. See his *Fragments of Modernity* and *Sociological Impressionism*.

19. Though William James felt a kinship with Simmel, the latter critiqued pragmatism as a "superficial and limited" form of *Lebensphilosophie* (*Individuality* 385).

20. For some observers the career of the "two" Simmels suggests a disquieting irony. The social theorist Andrew Arato finds it a "capitulation to positivism in the very context that involved [in the pre–1914 Simmel] the beginning of a powerful critique of positivism" (152). Whereas Simmel's urban cultural criticism revealed new forms of human creativity amid alienation, this "critical edge" is lost in an irrationalist metaphysics of immediate intuition. Arato concludes that "Simmel's reconceptualization . . . left everything as it was" (158).

21. This statement is cited in David Frisby's introduction to *The Philosophy of Money* (31).

22. I am merely sketching here complex issues that remain controversial in the Benjamin–Adorno relationship. What should also be stressed is the powerful impact on Benjamin and Adorno of Lukács's *History and Class Consciousness* (1923). As a seminal work of Western Marxism, Lukács's book introduced Marxism as a method (rather than a political dogma) of cultural analysis and foregrounded the centrality of reification. Though Adorno would subsequently develop a countertheory of reification, and though both he and Benjamin would, in different ways, decisively diverge from Lukács's fierce and nostalgic dislike of avant-garde modernism, it is undeniable that in this work Lukács established the terms of critical debate for the next two generations. See the studies by Eugene Lunn and Susan Buck-Morss for a useful exposition of the above issues.

23. The organicism of the English communitarian tradition is one reason Henry James fits more comfortably in the self-consciously urban tradition of Simmel, Benjamin, and Adorno.

24. It should be noted, however, that unlike the Frankfurt School's rejection of science as merely positivism and instrumentalism, Dewey's critique of Marxism is made in the name of science pragmatically conceived.

25. Whereas, compared to William James, Dewey deepened and historicized pragmatism's critical thrust, he did not conceive of critique as the exposure of political class conflict, as did German critical theorists and American radical critics like C. Wright Mills. Chapter 5 touches on Mills's critique of Dewey.

26. The connections between Dewey and Adorno are pursued in chapter 5.

27. The fascination with the "mystic meaning of objects" shared by James, Benjamin, and Proust illustrates the positive meaning of aura.

28. Matthiessen suggests something along these lines when he describes James, before his visit to America, as needing to "break the web of his own enchantment" (*Major* 105).

29. In linking Henry James with Benjamin it is necessary to reinvoke Engels's distinction between Hegel's method and system. James's restless analysis has affinities with Benjamin's critical method, his process of producing meaning, even though the former's flâneries have nothing in common with the end point of Benjamin's system of historical materialism. This system at times professes the violent, nihilistic destruction of bourgeois culture as the prerequisite for revolutionary redemption. But it should also be remembered that more often "Benjamin's sense of revolution has more in common with an act of inspired reading than it does with seizing railroads" (Jennings 37). Like James, who consistently links artistic practice with violence and

crisis, and like many modernists since Baudelaire, Benjamin's efforts at shock are aimed at defamiliarizing readers and awakening them from their ideologically induced passivity. This idealist goal of altering consciousness seems to adhere even in the most materialist, socially engaged modernism. This is confirmed in chapter 9, where we see Adorno arguing that art is praxis because it can change readers' consciousnesses.

Chapter 5

1. James's excitement is still echoed today. A recent commentator has called Jamesian pluralism "still the liveliest American attempt to philosophize in the name of novelty and openness" (Marr 118).

2. The relation of pragmatism and radical empiricism continues to be a matter of debate, perhaps because the relation seems unclear in James's own mind. In the preface to *Pragmatism* he says there is "no logical connection" between them. Radical empiricism, he asserts, "stands on its own feet. One may entirely reject it and still be a pragmatist," a position he repeated in a letter of 1907. Yet at other times—in *The Meaning of Truth* (1909), for instance—he would nearly reverse this position. While recognizing that pragmatism and radical empiricism share a commitment to the abandonment of certainty and to the world as perpetually in the making, I side with Rorty's view that sees them as diverging in important ways. According to Ellen Suckiel, in *Essays in Radical Empiricism* James "moves beyond the principles of his pragmatism, into the very sort of metaphysics the pragmatic method is designed to circumvent" (137). The meanings of this paradox will be discussed in this chapter.

3. This is not to say that Mead and Dewey did not entwine their social thought with political ideals. By emphasizing the self as socialized, reciprocal, and cooperative they deliberately sponsor "human qualities incompatible with free-market capitalism" (Feffer 235). But, unlike Adorno, Mead and (the pre–World War I) Dewey were less radical critics of society than optimistic reformers, believing that American society would grow progressively more cooperative and rational. This helps explain their naive support of World War I as a morally righteous crusade. On this point see Feffer (254) and especially Joas, who argues that Mead's myopia confirms Bourne's critique of pragmatism (24–30; see also chap. 5, n. 19).

4. Dialectical mediation, according to Adorno, "is not a recourse to the more abstract" but a "process of resolution of the concrete in itself." He approvingly quotes Nietzsche's remark that "to perceive resemblances everywhere, making everything alike, is a sign of weak eyesight" (*Minima* 74). Adorno's eye for resemblances, like Henry James's, is dialectical in that it simultaneously heightens difference.

5. The mimetic has a peculiar status in Adorno's discourse, for it is a concept that suggests what concepts cannot encompass—wordless impulse. To define it precisely is to violate its aporetic structure. Later in this chapter I will touch on this issue.

6. Yet immediacy is not banished, for then mediation itself would become immediate and the particular would be devoured. Rather, experience is an interplay of immediate and mediated, identity and nonidentity. I owe this insight to Peter Dews's discussion of Adorno (*Logics* 42).

7. This positive concept has been far overshadowed by the book's notorious denunciation of enlightenment. My effort to portray a less pessimistic Adorno is virtually the opposite of Fredric Jameson's emphasis on an Adorno whose value for the 1990s

resides in restoring "the sense of something grim and impending within the polluted sunshine of the shopping mall," an image that epitomizes postmodern North America for Jameson (*Late* 248).

8. Thomas Haskell makes a similar point in stating that by 1900 the reality of "interdependence" made the ethic of self-reliance and the philosophy of individualism more nostalgic than meaningful for serious thinkers.

9. William James is often seen as politically naive, a view most bluntly stated in recent years by Bruce Kuklick, who believes that James is not a social and political thinker of "any stature" (306). Cornel West finds James's "obsessions with individuality" an obstacle to his reaching "intellectual maturity" (6, 54–68). James Kloppenberg—in the context of his discussion of philosophers of the "via media" exchanging "epistemology for history"—presents an eloquent reading of James's pluralism and pragmatism as historically sensitive (145–95). Yet Kloppenberg does not explore the gap between James's philosophy and his social and political views (see chap. 5, n. 13). Recently Frank Lentricchia has argued for James's political astuteness: "Though pragmatism was inchoately present in his *Principles of Psychology*, he began to know his philosophy as pragmatism only after he found the political terminus of his thought in his anti-imperialist activism at the turn of the century" (112). One reason this view is unpersuasive is that William's "political turn" is, ultimately, politically myopic. It amounts to extending his radical individualism into a sphere (international affairs) where it is irrelevant. In stressing James's alleged strength of "self-scrutiny and self-revision," Lentricchia ignores James's blindness to the insufficiency of his Emersonianism to furnish a non-naive political understanding, one responsive to the postindividual, bureaucratic character of the modern social order. His antiimperialist activity is political in the sense of representing active public engagement in a particular cause, but James had been engaged in various public crusades for years. In 1881, for instance, he spoke before the Total Abstinence League, and in 1894 he addressed the Massachusetts Legislature, arguing against the tightening of medical licensing.

10. "Prolonged" is the key word here, for temporary reflection is permissible. Thus Ross is able to explain the logic that grants him a period of aesthetic bliss: "Now that I have decided to rush into the fray . . . I can enjoy the short respite of study and contemplation without being tormented by my former doubts" (31). Precisely because it is to be succeeded by science, the aesthetic can be experienced once and for all.

11. Perhaps Ross's early literary inclinations account for his saving of the subject. He had arrived in Berlin "with the definite intention of fitting [himself] for a chair in comparative literature." But he gave it up only when he learned that no American universities provided such a chair (*Seventy* 22).

12. I stress the individualism of James's *social* thought in contrast to his philosophy of radical empiricism, which conceives of pure experience as existing prior to the split between subject and object, internal and external, and thus technically escapes the charge of subjectivism (which requires division). But, as is typical with James, his philosophical rejection of dualism conflicts with his social, personal beliefs in the primacy of the individual. This conflict represents another expression of what I have argued (in chapter 1) was the basic structure of William's psychic economy—his dialectic of repression, which philosophically advocates what temperamentally disturbs him. His temperament, his psychic balance, requires the dualisms his philosophy dissolves.

13. My view of Dewey's critique of Jamesian individualism concurs with H. S.

Thayer's discussion of the "fundamental differences of perspective" between James's subjective pragmatism and Dewey's contextual instrumentalism (422, 440–44). James Kloppenberg has challenged this familiar way of distinguishing between James and Dewey: "The difference was emphatic rather than absolute. James, like Dewey, considered experience itself to be fundamentally social. . . . James did place greater emphasis on the personal than the social dimension . . . and to that extent his pragmatism should be distinguished from Dewey's instrumentalism. I want only to insist that James recognized the necessity of social validation as well as personal validation of truth" (98). While granting the validity of this clarification, I think Kloppenberg underplays the depth of James's personal attachment to a nostalgic individualism, an attachment that Dewey implicitly and Mead explicitly (see chap. 5, n. 14) critiqued. Significantly, Kloppenberg's massive study makes no mention of Mead.

14. Mead, James's fellow pragmatist, implicitly refused to call him a pragmatist because of his assumption of a priori individualism. Instead Mead situated James's beliefs in an earlier century, describing him as representative of the American pioneer spirit of Puritan New England: "For all his analysis of the self, James's individual . . . entered in advance of the situation it helped to determine. It carried standards and criteria within itself. . . . His individual had that in him which was not fashioned in the living process" (qtd. Reck 386). Charles Horton Cooley, the other central pragmatic social thinker, observed that "although William James has insight into the social nature of the self, he did not develop this into a really organic conception of the relation of the individual to the social whole" (qtd. Coser 321). It should be noted again that despite the accuracy of Cooley's and Mead's assessments of William James, they (like Dewey) were deeply in James's intellectual debt, as they themselves acknowledged, and that their critique betrays the inevitable and anxious desire to avoid the charge of undue influence.

15. William's distress reached a climax in the summer of 1904, when Münsterberg was running an international scholarly congress at the St. Louis Exposition. Since Henry James arrived in Cambridge that same summer, he doubtless witnessed some of William's tirades against his colleague. Henry's own reaction to Münsterberg (recorded in a notebook entry and in his portrayal of the hotel world) will concern us in chapter 10.

16. In speaking of his method of industrial psychology, Münsterberg once noted that his "new science [of] psychotechnics does not stand in the service of a party, but exclusively in the service of civilization." For Münsterberg, like Frederick Taylor, science and civilization were convenient terms to disguise the interests of a managerial elite (qtd. Braverman 142).

17. Mills's important critique of Dewey is expressed in *Sociology and Pragmatism*. Cornel West shrewdly argues for Mills's anxiety of influence regarding Dewey.

18. Without trying to resolve this dispute, it seems fair to observe that Dewey's political vision is more provocative, albeit implicit, in his works of the twenties (*Experience and Nature* and *Reconstruction in Philosophy*) rather than in his social theory of the thirties. One reason is that he is less concerned with social control and clearly distinguishes between pragmatic and positivistic views of science. Pragmatism conceives of science as a self-correcting inquiry, as a "living practice" committed to the growth of intelligence rather than a "rational system" or a "fixed body of truth" (Rochberg 21, 30). In contrast, positivistic science, or Comteanism, is preoccupied with control and predictability; it assumes that society is a realm of harmony and consensus into which we are integrated. Thus man is prepared for steady obedience to the existing order (Marcuse, *Reason* 344). Dewey's philosophy adopts the pragmatic

view of science, but a residual Comteanism is evident in his social thought, especially during the crisis of the Depression era, from which emerged *Individualism Old and New*. Here Dewey remains vulnerable to charges that his work is "weakened by unacknowledged positivist elements" (Lustig 168–69). He once spoke of being "impressed deeply" in his youth by Comte's "idea of the disorganized character of Western modern culture, due to a disintegrative 'individualism' and his idea of a synthesis of science that should be a regulative method of an organized social life" (qtd. McDermott 8). Jeffrey Lustig does not differentiate between pragmatism and positivism, as I do, because he feels that pragmatism only looks emancipatory but actually has a "fundamental commitment to technical validation" that seeks to "find science-like precision and objectivity in social knowledge." According to him, "the effect of this commitment was to undermine their [pragmatists'] repeated call for the fullness of experience and to flaw their system at its heart" (165). Lustig emphasizes pragmatism's affiliation with social control and its failure to extend to political reform its radical account of action as risk and uncertainty. James Kloppenberg finds Lustig's view of the affinities between pragmatism and scientism "confused" and "polemical" (502). In chapter 10 I discuss the changes in Dewey's thought after World War I.

19. At another particularly shocking moment—America's entry into the World War I—Randolph Bourne had made a remarkably similar critique against Dewey and pragmatism (see chapter 10).

20. *Dialectic of Enlightenment* has been seen as deliberately exaggerating its argument in order to create for the reader a mimesis of the historical trauma enveloping its authors. Shock tactics were needed to penetrate the numbed psyches of an audience too eager to explain away nazism as the sheer other of Western liberal Enlightenment. It should also be pointed out that the work was self-consciously provisional, for it originally circulated in mimeograph form under the title *Philosophical Fragments*.

21. According to Adorno, Nietzsche's insistence on the primacy of the will to power made him the first to detect the predatory motive extending all the way to philosophic system building. Nietzsche also preceded Adorno (and was contemporaneous with William James) in his critique of the belief in the primacy of concepts. In Adorno's very contempt for system Fredric Jameson finds that he "retains the concept of the system and even makes it, as target and object of critique, the very center of his own anti-systematic thinking" (*Late* 27).

22. According to Peter Dews, this double refusal—of identity and the discarding of identity—defines the difference between Adorno's critique of the modern subject and that of poststructuralism. Unlike the latter, Adorno (like Henry James) refuses to abolish the identity principle but seeks to redirect its energy in order to renovate the subject.

23. Adorno's book opens with the following well-known passage:

> Philosophy, which once seemed obsolete, lives on because the moment to realize it was missed. The summary judgment that it had merely interpreted the world, that resignation in the face of reality had crippled it in itself, became a defeatism of reason after the attempt to change the world miscarried. . . . Having broken its pledge to be as one with reality or at the point of realization, philosophy is obliged ruthlessly to criticize itself. (3)

But the necessity of self-interrogation is not an end in itself but a prelude to the refashioning of the traditional tools of philosophy: systems, the abstraction of concepts, and the logic of identity.

24. Adorno wrote *Aesthetic Theory* in accord with his belief in texture rather than

thesis. His concern is in shaping a particular kind of experience for the reader; the "crux" of his book is "what happens in it." Adorno deliberately created a style for *Aesthetic Theory* that would embody nonidentity thinking and stimulate the mimetic capacity. Instead of following conventional order, Adorno "concentrically arranged" "partial complexes," giving them "the same weight and relevance." His paratactical method is to be apprehended not in "succession one by one" but as a "constellation" of fragments (*Aesthetic* 496). The texture and the experience of vertigo it induces is ignored if readers are absorbed in searching for a thesis that can be extrapolated and represent the whole. This approach treats Adorno's work as conventional aesthetics. Such reductive efforts have no patience for the "shock of inconclusiveness" that Adorno's text offers as it eludes definitive positions by maintaining a rhythm of assertion and revision. A recent example of a reductive, domesticating approach is found in John Brenkman's *Culture and Domination*. He accuses Adorno's aesthetic thought of being based on a static dualism that opposes modernism's formalism to capitalism's rationalization of reality. His misreading is worth discussing because of its typicality. According to Brenkman, Adorno asserts a "categorical and epochal opposition between art and society," as modern art becomes the "primary antagonist" of modern society. For Brenkman "such an opposition . . . marks the basic impasse of Critical Marxism's renewal of cultural theory" (118–19). There is ample evidence in Adorno's work for Brenkman's reading *if* one is willing to quote selectively and isolate one moment of the negative dialectic process. A particularly egregious instance of this approach occurs when Brenkman quotes the following passage from *Aesthetic Theory*: Art "is social primarily because it stands opposed to society. . . . By congealing into an entity unto itself—rather than . . . proving itself to be 'socially useful'—art criticizes society just by being there. . . . This social deviance of art is the determinate negation of a determinate society" (*Aesthetic* 321). Brenkman ends his quotation here and offers it as conclusive evidence in support of his argument that Adorno's dualisms idealize art as a realm uncontaminated by instrumental rationality. But this argument can stand only because Brenkman ignores the crucial sentences that follow his quotation. There Adorno explicitly qualifies his assertion regarding a "determinate society":

> It must be kept in mind that society is not co-extensive with ideology. Any society is more than sheer negativity to be indicted by the aesthetic law of form; even in its most objectionable shape, society is still capable of producing and reproducing human life. Art has had to take this aspect (no less than that of its critical task) into account. . . . And art has no way of separating affirmation and critique intentionally because it is nonjudgmental. (321)

Far from seeking to idealize art and oppose it to society, Adorno insists that inherently "every single work of art is vulnerable to the charge of false consciousness and ideology . . . because [it] *a priori* posit[s] a spiritual entity as though it were independent of any conditions of material production." In other words, all works are fetishistic, but "the fetish character of art works is a condition of their truth, including their social truth" (323). Adorno's dialectical logic neither opposes fetishism and false consciousness to art and truth nor equates society with ideology and negativity. This rejection of dualism is paramount throughout his *Aesthetic Theory*. Indeed, the work's raison d'être is its insistence that the power of modern art resides in its inherent antinomic tensions.

25. Even sympathetic critics of Adorno are troubled by his apparently self-defeating logic. Thus Susan Buck-Morss ends her valuable book by suggesting that Adorno

overreacted to the evil of instrumental reason and turned negative dialectics into a fetishistic and static dead end (189–90). One might qualify her assessment by adding that Adorno's late notions of mimetic reason and behavior act as important correctives to his negativity and preoccupation with reason as instrumental. As I have tried to show in the present chapter (and in chap. 5, n. 31), exploring mimetic behavior and reason provides an alternative to a "dead end" reading of Adorno, for they constitute a pledge redeemable in social reality. Jürgen Habermas, as we shall see, both recognized and misread this dimension of Adorno.

26. Adorno's emphasis on mimetic behavior is influenced by Walter Benjamin, who locates the mimetic mode of conduct in children's play (*Reflections* 333). But as Susan Buck-Morss notes—in a qualification applicable to Dewey and Adorno as well—Benjamin's "appreciation of childhood cognition did not imply a cult of youth. On the contrary, only people who were allowed to live out their childhood really grew up" ("Benjamin" 87).

27. Horkheimer praised *Art as Experience* in his *Critical Theory* (279, 290).

28. Laurence Holland, in *The Expense of Vision*, was the first to dissent from Blackmur's influential reading of the prefaces as magisterial and to stress their insistent eliciting of crisis, risk, and uncertainty.

29. The next chapter will reveal that prior to Lubbock's idealist reading of James's "craft of fiction," critics faulted James's fiction for its lack of organic harmony.

30. See Peter Osborne's essay on Adorno for a careful exposition of the dialectic of mimesis and rationality (28–35).

31. I mean to imply here that Habermas's reading of Adorno can be considered symptomatic of an anxiety of influence in the Bloomian sense of a deliberate misprision of the master's text that opens up a space for the ephebe. Recently critics have begun challenging Habermas's reductive interpretation of Adorno's concept of mimesis. Robert Hullot-Kentor offers a pointed critique of Habermas's misreading. Fred Alford (111–14) argues that mimesis itself is a kind of reason and behavior guided by "reconciling reason," which "respects the integrity and uniqueness of the object." In contrast, "the mimesis of instrumental reason imitates only the most rigid, routine, and routinized aspects of nature, those most subject to technical control" (113). As Adorno has stated, "If rationality is left to its own devices, or represses the aesthetic mode of behavior, . . . then rationality itself becomes feeble" (*Aesthetic* 454). The practice of art is legitimate because it prevents this enfeeblement. Fredric Jameson argues that Habermas's reading of Adorno as irrational "falls oddly flat" because the former simply regards reason as the opposite of the irrational and thus ignores Hegel's (and the Frankfurt School's) restoration of "dialectical reason" as a "superior mode of truth" (*Late* 237). One might add that Habermas's reductive sense of mimesis echoes the mimetic taboo that "places the mimetic under 'house arrest' by confining it to art." The phrase is borrowed from Michael Cahn, who is not concerned with Habermas (45).

32. According to Habermas (as reported by Seyla Benhabib), the "philosophy of consciousness" that Descartes bequeathed to Western thought posits either a lonely self cogitating upon an object or an active self shaping the world. Both models are unable to grasp "the integrity of *social* interaction: both approaches proceed from my mind to your mind, from my consciousness to your consciousness." Following an insight by George Herbert Mead, Habermas claims that ontogenetically the self becomes an "I" by interacting with other selves. "The philosophy of consciousness puts the cart before the horse: it attempts to ground sociation on individuation" (Benhabib 242–43). Discussing Habermas's reading of Adorno, Richard Wolin pre-

sents a persuasive critique: "The assimilation of [Adorno] to the . . . Cartesian frame of reference—that of a 'philosophy of consciousness'—is highly deceptive" since Adorno is a consistent critic of the "illusory purity and autonomy of 'bourgeois interiority,' " most forcefully so in his 1931 study of Kierkegaard. Thus Habermas "obscures the thematic richness, complexity and specificity" of Adorno and the first-generation Frankfurt School ("Critical" 24).

33. Mead implicitly accuses Bergson of insisting on a false opposition between science and the dynamic intuitions of life. By equating science with static laws of prediction and control, Bergson ignores pragmatism's conception of science as continual reconstruction and restatement of "hypotheses which are open to unexpected happenings." *This* conception permits one to "have the full reign of intellectual life and the control that it gives and still not stereotype your experience" (*Movements* 507).

34. I am here quoting from a study by Patricia McKee (*Commitment* 24). Her opening chapter, "An Introduction of Critical Issues," coincides with a number of emphases in the present study's stress on the antisubjectivism of Jamesian selfhood. For instance, we concur that for James "the sense of self as an independent and sufficient being is something [he] wants to get rid of rather than reach" (24).

Chapter 6

1. This last sentence borrows some phrases from Habermas's essay on Benjamin contained in *Philosophical–Political Profiles* (149).

2. For Benjamin the decline of aura involves film and photography as agents of a reorientation of "human sense perception," a shift from being trained to value "uniqueness and permanence" to being happy with "transitoriness and reproducibility" (223).

3. Bourne was also a well-known adherent of William James's pragmatism and an admirer of Bergson's vitalism. His less well-known admiration for Henry James is expressed in Bourne's various published letters (see *Letters* 199).

4. In describing his "cosmopolitan ideal" as the vital "work for a younger *intelligentsia* of America," Bourne in effect extends, with his typical polemical vigor, the logic of James's response to the alien. Bourne's extension involves identifying himself and the new class of intellectuals ("*intellegentsia*") with the alien outsider, both of whom quest for what he calls (after Josiah Royce) a "Beloved Community" (*Will* 264). Here Bourne decisively diverges from James: the former's self-styled "enterprise of integration" possesses a romantic communitarianism that points toward the movement of which he is often called a prophet—the counterculture of the 1960s.

5. My reading of Bourne contests the usual claim that he is solely a romantic individualist. Bourne's critique of Dewey's support of World War I seemed to radicalize Dewey, moving him (in the twenties) in the direction of Bourne's immanent ironist practicing a politics of nonidentity. This trajectory is sketched in the "Coda" to the present study.

6. That James consistently opposes the actual and aesthetic is Mark Seltzer's charge (104).

7. In chapter 10 I will further develop this point about James's sense of sharing his consciousness with the alien in the context of his extraordinary response to Ellis Island.

8. Bourne's plea is made in the wake of witnessing many leading thinkers capitulate to war hysteria. One Marxist historian has recently applauded James's mobility as "the only kind of intellectual stance possible in the face of a capitalism that reduces all aspects of social, cultural, and political (to say nothing of economic) life to the pure homogeneity and universality of money valuations" (Harvey xi). So begins *Consciousness and the Urban Experience*, David Harvey's attempt at "a definitive Marxian interpretation of the urban process under capitalism." While his opening invocation of James is apt, Harvey carefully sets limits to James's usefulness in analyzing urban consciousness. No sooner has Harvey praised his restless stance than he severs himself from James's "class perspective." Presumably the novelist's upper-bourgeois status prevented him from gaining further insights potentially relevant to a Marxist "historical geography of the urban process under capitalism" (xi). Though James is hardly a Marxist, it is misleading to consign him to a stable class perspective. Had Harvey fully taken James at his restless word, he might have seen that imprisonment in a monolithic class position is part of what James is eluding in his effort to make his repatriation, like his prefaces, a "*living* affair" that seeks not certainty but experience of the incalculable.

9. Chapter 9, on *The Ambassadors*, will explore James's and Strether's shared traumatophilia.

10. In the subsequent discussion of James's affinities with Benjamin, it should be stressed that the Benjamin I am presenting has been secularized and thus simplified. I neglect the fact that his cultural materialism is simultaneously an intricate theological and mystical system that invests his model of analysis (constellations) with messianic powers of redeeming the historical particulars it relies on. This secularization of Benjamin is hardly new; his first and most influential interpreter, Adorno, minimized or ignored Benjamin's theological frame in setting constellations in the direction of ideology critique. Michael Jennings makes an important point about all such appropriations of Benjamin: "When we use Benjamin to a particular end or in the service of a particular cause . . . we are always proceeding in a Benjaminian way . . . in that we 'mortify' Benjamin's own words, we rip them from their context" (213).

11. In "Dewey's Naturalist Metaphysics" Santayana complained that Dewey had gone too far and dissolved the human subject altogether. This is briefly discussed in chapter 8 of the present study.

12. My emphasis coincides with William Boelhower's important discussion of James as the virtual founder of "ethnic semiosis." Skeptical of "well-ordered taxonomies" and strategies "that favor definition and theoretical elaboration, as if a set of rigidly constructed categories could . . . control the energy of the ethnic sign," James "offers a corrective working hypothesis that dwells on the *production* of ethnic semiotic activity" (31). Boelhower's welcome, much-needed reassessment of James's relationship to the ethnic represents a major contribution to our understanding of James's seminal importance as a cultural analyst.

13. Late in *The American Scene* James reiterates the primacy of interest. This time it is not New York that casts a spell but a Florida hotel. James asks himself why "hotel-civilization" has, throughout his trip, exerted such a fascination. Why does it make so successful an appeal?: "Wasn't, for that matter, his asking of such questions as these the very state of being interested?" (438). Critics of *The American Scene* tend to neglect James's belief in the primacy of interest. James Cox, for one, concludes that James rejects America because, among other lapses, he does not visit Civil War battlefields or cornfields but prefers the Vanderbilt mansion. This accusation leaps from recognizing that James makes a *choice* of scenes, guided by an urban bias, to

the unwarranted charge that his book rejects the American Scene, as if James considers this transcendental response an actual possibility. That he doesn't consider it a possibility is the point of his elaborate declaration of interest, which renders irrelevant the very notion of rejection, if not choice and bias. In his preface he says he will "abide by the law" of his "cultivated sense," which "would react promptly in some presences only to remain imperturbably inert in others."

14. David Lloyd views the ideological function of Arnold's and Schiller's notion of culture as a harmonizing, universal totality that reconciles the individual to the bourgeois state and legitimates the ethnocentric ideology of imperialism.

15. I expand my discussion of James and the genteel tradition in chapter 8, where I also briefly discuss the connections between Henry Adams and Henry James. My subsequent discussion of the genteel tradition is indebted to Thomas Bender and John Sproat.

16. This aesthetic dilemma is also central to the prefaces, where James repeatedly stresses the "cruel crisis" of artistic creation. In his cultural analysis the aesthetic is explicitly interwoven with the political, and mutilation of the "total image" acquires critical resonance.

17. Both James and Benjamin use "roundabout"; see Benjamin, *Origin* (28).

18. Adorno's and Benjamin's examination of the atrophying of experience strikes some readers as "patrician grousing" and "*haut bourgeois* antitechnological nostalgia." This is how Terry Eagleton characterizes Adorno's passage on casement windows (*Ideology* 358).

19. Benjamin's impulse has been characterized as nihilistic: "The mood of destruction obtains its force not only from theological sources but also from a more general and vehement animus against bourgeois society.... Benjamin understood that his effort to create a new, politically useful set of images that might induce and direct political activity could succeed only if the icons of bourgeois culture were first destroyed" (Jennings 180).

20. Benjamin's method of seeking the "crystal of the total process" in the small detail was doubtless influenced by Georg Simmel's *Philosophy of Money*. In the preface to that work, Simmel declares: "The unity of these investigations ... [is] in the possibility ... of finding in each of life's details the totality of its meaning" (*Philosophy* 55).

21. My formulation here adapts Fredric Jameson's equation of the mimetic with "the tendency to narrativize the conceptual." He argues that "the mimetic possibilities of the individual [philosophical] sentence can be grasped only as the way in which they tend to form themselves into micro-narratives, and as it were to act out the content of what is in them abstractly grasped as philosophical thinking or argument" (*Late* 68, 67).

Chapter 7

1. See, for instance, Carol Holly's article, which argues that James's idealizing was quickened by the urge to recover from the nervous breakdown of 1909–11: "James did not want to represent a state of mind fathered on his own recent embarrassments and tragedies.... Instead James sought to protect himself from emotional pain and exposure by relegating his suffering to the past and by controlling the direction of his memories. For James the autobiographical act had in part to be an act of suppres-

sion" ("Drama" 23). James Cox defines James's subject and method in his memoirs as "aestheticizing experience," which seeks to acquire neither money nor things but consciousness. The motive of idealization that pervades this "rather oversweet book," says Cox, is James's strategic effort to suppress his "true image of himself as fierce aggressor and usurper," who has "crowded out"—usurped—William's place in the book (244).

2. James's untying of the knot of personality recalls similar acts by his characters—notably Lambert Strether in *The Ambassadors* but also Christopher Newman in *The American*, written nearly thirty years earlier. At the end of that novel, Newman senses that "a tight knot seemed to have loosened" as he decides to "let the Bellegardes go" (306). This moment of loosening repeats the experience he recounts at the start of the novel, when he describes the loss of sixty thousand dollars as "the sweetest thing." He takes pleasure in "letting it utterly slide" because this loss takes place "quite independently" of his "will" (34). For all their individual differences, Newman, Strether, and Henry James share a relaxation of will that permits them to open themselves up to others as well as to their own internal otherness. Newman suggests this awareness of his own nonidentity when he remarks (apropos of letting the money "slide"): "I could feel it going on inside me. You may depend upon it that there are things going on inside of us that we understand mighty little about" (34).

3. James's rejection of the literal is nicely distilled in his admission that "my face was turned." "From the first" his identity was ambiguous, a turned face eluding direct apprehension. And since to turn is to trope, a turned face suggests that one's identity is already constituted by figuration. James's impatience with the literalness of "mere actuality" appears to run counter to my emphasis on James's materialist orientation, which takes as its premise the primacy of the object. The idealist reading of James sees his "taking in" to be the hallmark of an "imperial" subjectivity, as Quentin Anderson emphasizes in his influential book *The Imperial Self*. Anderson groups James with Emerson and Whitman as three imaginations "that tend so much to incorporation" that their art in effect declares: "The world must submit to me on my terms" (223–24). This imperial annexing of reality partly describes the efforts of Emerson and Whitman, but it magnifies an impulse that Jamesian representation dialectically reverses in its effort to heighten difference and otherness. Anderson ignores the process whereby the actual is appropriated only to be crystallized. As James makes explicit, to represent something creates "the gain of charm, interest, mystery, dignity, distinction . . . over the thing . . . still unappropriated" (*Autobiography* 150). As often happens, the charge of idealism occurs when Jamesian representation, like Jamesian identity, is not grasped as a dialectical process.

4. Mead's emphasis on the mimetic capacities of the self is part of the voluminous discourse on imitation in late nineteenth-century social psychology in both Europe and America. In various ways William James, Emile Durkheim, Gabriel Tarde, Boris Sidis, Josiah Royce, and James Mark Baldwin made imitation a crucial process in the individual's social development.

5. My conclusion concerning Mrs. James is based upon James W. Anderson's persuasive analysis of her relationship to William.

6. In an important recent essay, Paul J. Eakin expressed skepticism concerning the strictly "negative" account of the relationship between William and Henry:

> The sibling rivalry has been so overplayed in recent criticism that another and equally important facet of their relationship has been obscured. William's

stardom may have generated feelings of inferiority in James, but it also supplied a kind of cover for Henry's development of his own creativity without
the family exposure that he found so inhibiting. (260)

While my own reading clearly concurs with Eakin's view, I would add that James
deliberately maximized his difference from William not only as a cover for his
own development but also to call attention to his belatedness as a mockery of authenticity.

7. Indeed, a critic writing in 1917 placed both Henry James and William Dean
Howells in the "sissy school of American literature," a judgment that, more recently,
Alfred Habegger has enthusiastically endorsed.

8. The blindness that is the condition of insulated subjectivity is incisively revealed in Henry's portrait of Henry senior, which is discussed in the next chapter.

9. It should be noted that in terms of the actual critical reception of the autobiographies, his audience deflected what I have called James's strategic estrangement.
A "general attitude of unquestioning respect" was the means of this deflection. This
uncritical veneration employed the popular Romantic category of "creative genius"
to safely defuse the audacity and peculiarities in James's self-representation. I have
gleaned the information, if not the interpretation, pertaining to Henry James's British
critical reception (which was richer and larger than the American) from Carol Holly
("British" 574–75).

10. As was established in chapter 2, libidinal sublimation is an extension of desire
rather than merely a repressive substitute. Harold Bloom is the one critic I am aware
of who has noted the following resemblance between the sexual economies of James
and Whitman: "I suspect that Henry James in his psychosexual orientation resembled
Walt Whitman more strongly than he did anyone else in literary history. Like Whitman, his desires were essentially homoerotic, and, again, like Whitman, he appears
to have evaded any merely actual fulfillment of those desires. . . . His striking originality as a novelist, nearly akin to Whitman's as a poet, has a still obscure but vital
relation to his warding-off of mere sexuality" (11–12).

11. According to Theodor Adorno, identification with the aggressor is a prehistorical
mode of mimesis derived from the "witch doctor imitating the wild animal in order
to appease it." I am quoting from Michael Cahn's account of Adorno's view. Adorno
praises "identification with" as nonrepressive behavior, in contrast to the repressiveness of "identification of" (33–34, 53).

12. From the point of view of an ideology of individualism, James's and Simmel's
rejection of binary logic commits a basic category mistake that bourgeois culture seeks
to discourage. The stranger's blurring of familiar categories of distance and proximity
produces in Simmel's reader a "degree of tension and anxiety which necessitates
some special kind of response" (Donald Levine 81). But this special response, one
equal in nuance to the position of the stranger, has not often been accorded either
Simmel or James. Both are routinely reduced to aesthetes or formalists, their valuation
of an intensely committed detachment misread as mere passivity. Indeed, the history
of Simmel's reception recalls James's. Because Simmel possesses a "persona that is
profoundly, inescapably ambiguous," his readers have "been haunted by the challenge of trying to do justice to that perplexing figure," who has been described as
both a "sociological flaneur" and a "stranger in the academy" (132). Both descriptions
suggest how deeply his theories are embedded in his own life as a Jew in the gentile
high culture of late nineteenth-century Berlin, a context that contributed to his
controversial reception.

13. The crisis of war initiating self-relinquishment occurred again during World War I. Writing to Hugh Walpole in 1915, James felt so absorbed in the war effort that he had not a scrap of identity left for a personal show: "Really one has too little of a self in these days here to be formulated in any manner at all; one's consciousness is wholly that of the Cause" (*Letters* 4: 751). This later war, like the Civil War, heightened the receptivity of James's open selfhood. He implored a correspondent to follow his [James's] lead: "Feel, feel, I say—feel for all you're worth and even if it half kills you, for that is the only way to live, especially to live at this terrible pressure, and the only way to honor and celebrate these admirable beings who are our pride and inspiration" (755). The masochistic element in this kind of self-representation is explored in chapter 9. James's formal declaration of commitment to England in 1916 is discussed in chapter 10.

14. My view differs from Eakin's reading of the "obscure hurt" episode, which he assimilates to Erik Erikson's paradigm of identity crisis. According to Eakin, Erikson depicts "an unusually gifted young man [who] undergoes a period of neurotic suffering followed by a sudden breakthrough into creativity." Eakin argues that "most of the principal features of the identity crisis are to be observed in James's behavior during the war: the need for a '*moratorium*' as a way of 'postponing the decision as to what one is and is going to be'; the temporary choice of a '*negative identity*'; . . . the experience of 'identity diffusion'; . . . a shying away from intimacy; . . . and a 'tortuous self-consciousness' " (255). Implicit in Erikson's model is the inevitable resolution of crisis through conversion, a pattern more typical of William James's life and his *Varieties of Religious Experience* (a parallel Erikson draws) than of Henry James's life. Rather than simply way stations on the road to psychic reintegration and adaptation to reality, "negative identity" and "identity diffusion" characterize James's selfhood.

15. For Adorno identity is the "universal coercive mechanism" whereby the self represses its inner nature and thereby objectifies itself. A grim paradox thus attends man's triumphant autonomy: "Man's domination over himself, which grounds his selfhood, is almost always the destruction of the subject in whose service it is undertaken; for the substance which is dominated, suppressed and dissolved by virtue of self-preservation is . . . in fact what is to be preserved" (*Dialectic* 54–55). Echoing Freud's *Civilization and Its Discontents*, Adorno equates the self's survival with repression: "The history of civilization is the history of the introversion of sacrifice. In other words: the history of renunciation" (55). Norbert Elias concurs implicitly with the equation of self and repression. He speaks of a "civilizational shift" from the Renaissance onward that involves "transition to a further stage of self-consciousness at which the inbuilt self-control of the affects grows stronger and reflective detachment greater, while the spontaneity of affective action diminishes" (258).

16. In his delineation of decentered subjectivity, Adorno resembles the Foucault of "The Subject and Power," who states that "maybe the target nowadays is not to discover what we are but to refuse what we are. . . . We have to promote new forms of subjectivity through the refusal of this kind of individuality [subjection] which has been imposed on us for several centuries" (216). Adorno puts it this way: "The question of freedom does not call for a Yes or No; it calls for theory to rise above the individuality that exists as well as above the society that exists" (*Negative* 283). The relation of Adorno and Foucault is in need of extended analysis. Such a discussion might begin with Foucault's statement that in the fifties "critical theory was hardly

known in France and the Frankfurt School was practically unheard of. . . . It is a strange case of non-penetration between two very similar types of thinking which is explained, perhaps, by that very similarity. Nothing hides the fact of a problem in common better than two similar ways of approaching it" ("Structuralism and Post-Structuralism" 200).

17. This ontology of the Jamesian theatrical self needs to be briefly situated in the much-discussed late nineteenth-century shift in American middle-class modes of self-representation. This shift is usually described as a move from an ethic of character to one of personality. While James rejects the terms of this shift (for one thing, he is skeptical of the solidity and fixity associated with "character"), he does distinguish among modes of theatricality. In *The Portrait of a Lady*, for instance, he juxtaposes three kinds: Ralph Touchett's, Madame Merle's, and Gilbert Osmond's. Madame Merle's very perfection of social art—"she's too everything. . . too complete in a word," says Ralph—forfeits the dialectic of theatricality (216), and Osmond is less a master of roles than a stable character emblematic of a social type—the Victorian dandy. Only Ralph's self-representation—which is experimental, fallible, and revisionary—approximates the dialectical tension inherent in theatricality. By the end of the nineteenth century this tension had been eroded through the assimilation of role-playing as a social norm of corporate America. The popularity of guides to success helped instrumentalize theatricality. In his article on "Role as a Cultural Concept" the sociologist George Arditi makes a useful distinction between the concepts of role-playing and social type. For a discussion of the personality/culture shift, see the studies by Sussman (271–85) and Halttunen (198–210).

18. James's unconventional sense of formalism (or aestheticism) as social practice clearly has affinities with Nietzschean aestheticism, which, as Richard Wolin notes, is "radically different than the customary senses in which the term is employed"— to posit a transcendent, separate realm. Nietzsche "transforms the *passive* aestheticism of the *l'art pour l'art* movement into an *active* one: the aesthetic attitude toward the world must transgress the boundaries of the aesthetic sphere *per se*" ("Foucault's" 73).

19. Dewey's concept of self is virtually the opposite of his understanding of experience: "Many good words get spoiled when the word self is prefixed to them. Words like pity, confidence, sacrifice, control. The reason is not far to seek. The word self infects them with a fixed introversion and isolation" (*Human* 130).

20. For a nearly opposite reading of this incident, see the article by James Cox, who finds "an alarming treachery in James's vision of himself as the forerunner" of Whitman. "James's elaborated self-interest . . . prevents him from recognizing the value of Whitman's achievement" (249).

21. The conventional "logic" of intimacy—unmediated contact—violates, in Adorno's words, "the imponderably delicate aura of the other which is his condition as a subject. . . . The flat denial of strangeness does the other supreme wrong" (*Minima* 182).

22. Stanley Cavell has described "the substantive disagreement" between Heidegger and the American antinomians Emerson and Thoreau in terms that are relevant in this context. Unlike Heidegger, Emerson and Thoreau (we could also add James) believe that "the achievement of the human requires not inhabitation and settlement but abandonment, leaving. Then everything depends upon your realization of abandonment" (138).

Chapter 8

1. Sturgis visited America in 1904, at the same time as James, and together they visited Edith Wharton at the Mount, her country home in Massachusetts. See R. W. B. Lewis (140–41). Given James's "mood of subdued ecstasy," which expressed his "immediate response" to Whitman (in Wharton's words), this scene of reading captures in miniature the change in James from "soberly fastidious" to relaxed. Wharton encountered the relaxed James, whose "quality of fun" was the "delicious surprise of his talk," as "physical ease" and "dictates of comfort" replaced formality (Wharton, 173–74, 179, 248).

2. This is not to imply that Santayana consistently did not have serious reservations about Whitman's achievement, which he dubbed "the poetry of barbarism." But for all his attention to Whitman's defects, Santayana does not hide the fact that the poet speaks to him on a powerful and intimate level unique in American literature.

3. This point is also made by Daniel Stempel in his perceptive essay "Biography as Dramatic Monologue."

4. A recent and egregious instance of indifference to the complexity of Henry James's cultural identity is provided in Lawrence Levine's yoking together of the "two Henrys" (Adams and James). Together they bemoan the immigrant, lament multiplicity, and yearn for unity (171–73). (Ignored is Adams's virulent anti-Semitism, which sharply contrasts with James's support of Dreyfus and his break with the racist Paul Bourget, to cite only two instances of his respect for Jews.) Adams's biographer, Ernest Samuels, is an honorable exception to this assimilative strategy. His reading of Adams's reaction to the Story biography, while not mentioning the sculptor's philo-Semitism, tallies with my own. "How it must have grated on Adams's nerves to read how these two congenial sensibilities [James and Story] savored their world without regrets or disenchantment" (319). Another critic who discriminates judiciously between James's social attitudes and those of Adams is Irving Howe; his observations are contained in a brief discussion in *World of Our Fathers*.

5. Despising Henry James and what he allegedly embodied, Brooks's fervent literary nationalism included a compulsive commitment to masculine autonomy and the strenuous life, preferences that did their best to conceal or deflect impulses toward aestheticism and recurrent fantasies of boundlessness. Lears links Brooks's psychic economy with Norton's; he might have added William James's.

6. Leo Bersani discusses the "de-Oedipalizing of the father" in the context of Leonardo da Vinci's childhood, where his father's absence and mother's support encouraged unlimited curiosity (*Freudian* 46–47).

7. My formulations regarding the Oedipal and pre-Oedipal here and elsewhere are indebted to the psychoanalyst Jessica Benjamin's critique of Freudian psychology's tendency to normalize the repudiation of femininity, which encourages what she calls the "Oedipal construction of difference" as polarity. Discussing the "Oedipal riddle," she claims that to "identify only with the same-sex parent" prevents the individual from "truly appreciating difference, for identification with the other parent is blocked. Identification no longer functions as a bridge to the experience of an other. . . . Real recognition of the other entails being able to perceive commonality through difference" (171). Benjamin's position is congruent with the object-relations model of a self, as described by Nancy Chodorow. According to this model, even the sense of autonomy and agency remains relational, for it "develops in the context of the early relationship with the mother and bears the meaning of her collaboration

in and response to it." Separation and autonomy are not the telos of development "because the model assumes the permeability of boundaries" (203).

8. This wondering about his mother's presence suggests the risks and precariousness of her representation of the "disinterested life." At times her self-erasure seemed to threaten her own effort to individuate and grant others recognition. Henry describes her children as accusing her of "having no other" life. "We almost contested her being separate enough to be proud of us" (*Autobiography* 342–43).

9. Henry would preserve his own flexible, nonmonadic individuality by rejecting his mother's urgings that he marry. In response to his mother's recommendation that he "harmonize the discordant elements" in his life by taking a wife, Henry opted for discordancy rather than harmony. In so doing he avoided the potential loss of selfhood latent in his mother's advice. For in the same letter his mother expressed her own ambivalence about his marrying: "I feel so often that I want to . . . fold you in my own tenderest embrace." James found a way of resisting and preserving his extreme identification with his mother. Paradoxically, he achieved this by making her his exclusive female object choice. This seems to be the wish her letter (unconsciously) implies and a wish he (unconsciously) suggests in his response to his mother's passionate plea for matrimony: "If you will provide the wife, the fortune, and the 'inclination' I will take them all" (*Letters* 1: 454). His mother, in some sense, will "provide" and be his idealized wife, leaving him free to indulge his particular form (libidinal sublimation) of homoerotic passion without disloyalty to her. Freud notes this general pattern of exceptional mother identification among some male homosexuals.

10. My claim that James was (relatively) at ease with his sexuality relates in particular to the late nineties and thereafter (at the time of his first meetings with Andersen.) Prior to this, his major heterosexual relationship was his intimate friendship with Constance Fenimore Woolson. Because of James's destruction of nearly all their correspondence, the details and meanings of this episode remain "terribly obscure," to borrow James's phrase about the "tragedy of her death" in 1894. Eve Sedgwick speculates that James used Woolson to work "out his denied homosexual panic." Because he had "something, sexually, to prove," James arrogantly subjected Woolson to a tormenting flirtation that ended in James's retreat from her in "homosexual panic," which he resolved by imposing upon himself a "specifically *hetero*sexual compulsion" in the wake of her suicide ("Beast" 163–64). The facts of James's biography suggest something far different—that Woolson's death freed him to accept fully, a few years later, his homosexual orientation. (With regard to this hypothesis, it is worth noting that he described himself as having been "extremely attached to" Miss Woolson; *Letters* 3: 465). Sedgwick not only saddles James with her interest in "*hetero*sexual compulsion" but also fails to make a sufficient distinction between James and John Marcher, a misreading that vitiates her analysis of "The Beast in the Jungle." In describing Marcher as "imprisoned by homosexual panic" and embodying the "Law of masculine self-ignorance" that enforces *hetero*sexual compulsion, she also claims that James (in Marcherlike fashion) "denies the very possibility of *difference* in desires, in objects . . . [in] erotic paths" because he is allegedly guilty of the "easy assumption . . . that sexuality and heterosexuality are always exactly translatable into one another" (178, 164). This groundless allegation not only is oblivious to the importance of nonidentity and difference to James but also ignores the fact that by the late nineties James seemed to transgress the "law" of self-ignorance and enjoyed his desires for men. In his discerning critique of Sedgwick's essay, David Van Leer notes that her preoccupation with homosexual panic makes it difficult for

her to account for "untroubled forms of male experience, both gay and straight" (a description that is apt regarding James). For individuals who are adjusted to their sexuality and who do "not accept the social definition of the normal, there is simply no closet to leave" (596–97).

11. The "dominance of the foreground" is the central claim of Santayana's famous attack on Dewey's "naturalistic metaphysics," which the former found both a contradiction in terms and "half-hearted" in its naturalism. What is perverse about Santayana's critique of Dewey is how Deweyan it is. In *Experience and Nature* Dewey's emphasis on traditional philosophy's repression of contingency and the precarious replicates Santayana's critique of the "dominance of the foreground." In his shrewd response to Santayana, Dewey noted how similar their positions were and found largely "specious and illusory" Santayana's efforts to differentiate his own system (*The Later Works* 3: 81).

12. Santayana's nonhumanistic thought is a deliberately unsettling perspective that has consistently provoked suspicion and contempt. For one thing, its corollary political beliefs tend to be antiegalitarian. In addition, he questions whether America's hegemony as a world power deserves to endure. Granting no moral privilege to the American democratic political structure and its goal of equal representation, he respects American superiority only matters of "material economy" (qtd. Lyon 220–21). Apart from Santayana's political views (which extended to affection for Mussolini), what also offends is the suave, unruffled poise of his naturalism. He professes the perspective of a disembodied spirit, transparently at one with a God's-eye view of the universe. This loftiness seemed materially embodied in Santayana's lordly bearing: "He doesn't dislike you, and doesn't like you or anyone else," an acquaintance once observed. Predictably, he was a cult figure on campus, attracting a passionate group of brilliant acolytes. Edmund Wilson quotes the above remark in an informative account of his visit with Santayana in Rome shortly after World War II ("Rome Diary" 52).

13. Robert Lowell once claimed that Santayana was the only man who could dislike William James. Dislike may be too strong a word. He respected William James's utter lack of pretension, his "undisguised limitations," which scandalized the genteel belief that a "conscientious professor ought to know everything" (*Character* 95) Yet Santayana found himself "uncomfortable in his presence. He was so extremely natural that there was no knowing what his nature was, or what to expect next; so that one was driven to behave and talk conventionally, as in the most artificial society" (*Persons* 402).

14. On rare occasions he gave vent to the wrath he suppressed. Responding in 1900 to William James's criticism of his "impertinence and superior airs" (Santayana's words), he remarked: "I wonder if you realize the years of suppressed irritation which I have passed in the midst of an unintelligible, sanctimonious and often disingenuous Protestantism, which is thoroughly alien and repulsive to me" (qtd. Perry 2: 321).

15. This description is taken from Eve Sedgwick's *Between Men* (206, 28). Her information is derived from studies by the social historian Jeffrey Weeks.

16. Sturgis's membership in the upper class facilitated his abandonment of masculinity and his adoption of a flagrant effeminacy. In the late nineteenth-century English aristocracy "the mutual exclusiveness of 'masculine' and 'feminine' traits in general was less stressed, less absolute, and less politically significant than it was to be for the nineteenth-century bourgeoisie" (Sedgwick, *Between* 207). One reason is that "the power of the individual aristocrat" was not "dependent on personal style

so much as on material and hereditary rights." Sturgis's novel *Belchamber* precisely confirms this. Lord Belchamber, as the first son of a deceased landed aristocrat, automatically accedes to his patrimony regardless of his blatant effeminacy, general incompetence, and contempt for the values of his class. Sedgwick points out that Havelock Ellis and J. A. Symonds's *Sexual Inversion* (1897) demonstrated a direct correlation between the fact that those men who openly declared their effeminacy were members of the aristocratic social class.

17. Santayana's argument that "profound philosophers" suppress the "unintelligible" and "maintain that the only reality is changeless, infinite" (*Soliloquies* 140) strikingly recalls Dewey's critique of metaphysics in *Experience and Nature*.

18. Several years prior to Santayana's remarks on the tyranny of the Censor, his critique had been echoed in the observations of Sandor Ferenczi regarding sexual repression. In 1914 Ferenczi found that much of the heterosexuality he observed in contemporary Europe seemed founded on a counterphobic "obsessive exaggeration . . . of heteroeroticism for the purpose of repressing" homosexual desire. Not only is "actual homoeroticism lacking but also the sublimation of it that appeared so obvious to the people of antiquity: enthusiastic and devoted friendship between men. It is in fact astounding to what an extent present-day men have lost the capacity for mutual affection." Instead, what prevails is "asperity, resistance, and love of disputation," which Ferenczi regards as "defense symptoms erected against affection for the same sex" (qtd. Horowitz 85). Santayana would have been sympathetic to Ferenczi's view. His memoirs record a pattern of relations cut short by the sudden chill he felt was directed at him by male friends uneasy with the intimacy required for "perfect friendship." (See, for instance, the strange coldness of his close friends Herbert Lyman and Ward Thoron.) The unexpected death of his deepest and "*last* real friend," Warwick Potter, compelled Santayana to conclude: "Modern life is not made for friendship" (*Persons* 423, 352). The taboo on homoeroticism evidently did not extend to females, at least through the nineteenth century. Far more available to middle-class women was same-sex love, which was "both emotional and sensual." The historian Carroll Smith-Rosenberg has made famous "the female world of love and ritual," where "mutual dependency and deep affection are a central existential reality coloring the world of supportive networks and rituals" (73). Only in the opening decades of the twentieth century did American male sexologists, influenced by Havelock Ellis's ascription of perversion to such female friendships, begin their successful campaign against homosocial women. On this point see Smith-Rosenberg (275–83).

19. This insight is borrowed from Martha Banta, who notes that in the 1890s and the early twentieth century playful gender experiments through masking, camouflage, inversions, and play were "not part of a subversive movement" but were entirely acceptable forms of middle-class American behavior. "Gender switches took place out in the open, sanctioned by popular romances [and] amateur theatricals." Recall the famous photograph of Santayana posing in a white dress as part of the cast of a Hasty Pudding production). This "play-dressing and poses put on for brief and special occasions" were, of course, "not in the vein of the overt political statements" made by lesbians and feminists, some of whom dressed in men's clothing. Sturgis's case is not assimilable to either the explicitly political or merely playful (280–81).

20. This passage is quoted from an unpublished letter in the Houghton Library at Harvard University, which has 142 letters from James to Sturgis written between 1899 and 1915, the period of their greatest intimacy (though they most likely met as early as 1873). Two useful accounts of the James–Sturgis friendship (apart from

Edel's) are presented by Elmer Borklund and Millicent Bell (98–118). A summary evocation (devoid of analysis and new research) of James and the Queen's Acre circle is provided by Miranda Seymour.

21. The explanation I give as to why James discouraged Sturgis's writing is an interpretation of James's not wholly conscious motivation; moreover, it overlooks the many encouragements he gave Sturgis. The degree of severity in James's reaction to *Belchamber* has been a matter of dispute. See the studies by Borklund and Edel (*The Master* 192–99).

22. Santayana's biographer characterized *Belchamber* as an "undoubted early source" (McCormick 333).

23. It seems fairly clear that Santayana's fascination with the phenomenon of petering out among his contemporaries reflected a significant degree of identification on his part with these "superfluous" men, most of whom remained lifelong bachelors. I do not mean to imply that Oliver Alden is modeled directly or exclusively on Santayana. Upon the novel's publication, readers and critics sought to align Santayana with Oliver, Mario, and other characters. He often said that although he admired and identified with Oliver, he also found him a tragic failure, as "ineffectual" as Henry Adams. Santayana once described "Oliver, Mario and the rest" as "versions of myself," perhaps the soundest judgment (*Letters* 308).

24. Santayana's care in foregrounding the homoerotic impulses suffusing Oliver's entire life made him allude to *The Last Puritan* as a "dangerous" book, "risky to publish at all" during his lifetime (*Letters* 308). He was surprised when the Book-of-the-Month Club selected it and the novel became a best-seller. Santayana wondered if readers "were not too much disturbed by my picture of... erotic friendships." And when reviewers were also undisturbed, Santayana seemed rather disappointed: "Don't people catch on or are they shy?" (qtd. Cory 158, 163).

25. Santayana makes this explicit when he writes that "Mario saw everything in comic relief... and the novelty, far from annoying him or spoiling his fun, turned everything for him into an irresponsible carnival" (*Puritan* 403). Carnival is the world viewed under the aspect of the comic vision, as Santayana notes in the chapter fittingly entitled "Carnival" in *Soliloquies in England*.

26. Influencing my formulations here and in the next paragraph is the work of Jessica Benjamin (161, 168–69, 221).

27. Adorno has described the "goal" of "hope" in ameliorating the mutilations of gender polarity: "Its goal must be a state in which the face of the grieving woman disappears simultaneously with that of the bustling, capable man, a state in which all that survives the disgrace of the difference between the sexes is the happiness that difference makes possible" (*Prisms* 82). Santayana, another philosopher who places a high valuation on happiness, has similar pronouncements that bear striking affinities with this statement.

28. "Long-lasting residue" is from Carol Armstrong's remarkable "pre-Oedipal" reading of photographer Bill Brandt's nudes. Like Brandt's uncanny photographs, Mario and Lambert Strether celebrate "another power besides that of possessing and dominating another" (69).

Chapter 9

1. I have selected *The Ambassadors* as the single work of fiction for inclusion in James's so-called second major phase because I found that the novel possesses ex-

ceptional, indeed, unique relevance to a number of the present work's particular concerns—curiosity, nonidentity, mimetic behavior, immanent critique—and mediates them through a character with deep personal resonance for James himself. While Strether is not meant to be taken as James's self-portrait, he enjoys an intimacy with his creator unique in the late fiction. My choice of this novel does not imply that it is the only relevant late fiction, that it is a representative late Jamesian novel, or that the issues I will focus on—such as the relation of violence and pleasure— represent James's only fictional rendering of such themes. Indeed, if one were to explore this thematic strand in late James, *The Golden Bowl* would be crucial to any examination. For instance, the erotic sadism in Maggie Verver's image of Charlotte as being led by a "long silken halter looped round her beautiful neck" expresses impulses in Maggie that are crucial in evaluating her moral status and underscore James's understanding that violence can be involved not only in remaking selfhood (as in *The Ambassadors*) but also in enslaving others. The darker aspects of manipulative violence are also evident in *The Sacred Fount*, which has been read as a version of *The Ambassadors* in which vampirism, paranoia, voyeurism, and monomania come to the fore. In sum, the reading of *The Ambassadors* offered here is meant to illuminate the issues central to this study rather than to assess late Jamesian thematics as a whole. Bringing together these two sets of concerns would certainly be worthwhile but is beyond the scope of this chapter.

2. My stress on Strether's practice of radical curiosity and acceptance of indeterminacy assumes his pragmatist orientation, though I suggest later in this chapter that William James would have found his exorbitant curiosity disturbing. Richard Hocks finds Strether the embodiment of his creator's "way of thinking," which he equates with William James's pluralism (152–81). While qualifying this equation, my reading, like Hocks's, stresses pragmatic openness, but beyond this initial convergence our arguments pursue different paths.

3. Whether intended or not, Rorty's celebration of a "life of unending curiosity" has overtones of acquisitive consumerism that can be correlated with the therapeutic orientation of his stance, which he describes as postmodern bourgeois liberalism. With some justification, a number of critics have disparagingly described Rorty's position as one of aestheticism. (See, for instance, the study by Nancy Fraser.) In contrast, I hope to show that in *The Ambassadors* Henry James's commitment to curiosity registers the risks of radical openness in a culture of possessive individualism and rigid gender structures.

4. James is here not simply celebrating the romantic recovery of childhood. As we will see, Strether comes to recognize that his recovery of youth is also childish and even fatuous to some degree.

5. As Patricia McKee has written in an essay on *The Ambassadors*, this art of freedom depends on "not 'making sense' or explaining experience, since both of these processes refer experience to something else, in time or space." McKee goes on to note that for Strether "lucidity is finally not at all a matter of logical clarity but a matter of seeing relations clearly without being able to explain them. . . . Even early in the novel, Strether knows that . . . explanation does not constitute a personal relation. It comes between people" ("Making" 268, 276). What explanation, in particular, obstructs is the capacity for the self to be passionately absorbed in feelings and relations. McKee concludes that "it is because passion is receptive that it is an absorbing means of responsible action" (304). One of the central claims of McKee's essay clearly coincides with the emphasis of the present work: "For James, the great mystery is not being but doing, and what it takes to *do*. . . . For James separate individuality is

not a necessary or productive condition of human being. In useful action, the self loses independence and becomes inseparable from other things as a means. To be absorbed in action is to be absorbed in others, and it is to become a relation rather than a self" (302–03). Another recent study by Michael Seidel discusses *The American Scene* and *The Ambassadors* together (131–63).

6. The most influential exception to this "negative," moralistic reading of Strether as merely vicarious is Richard Poirier's discussion of how Strether converts "life into pleasure" (*World* 136).

7. Art as action is a consistent theme in James's descriptions of great artists. Of Michelangelo, "the greatest of artists," James remarks that his "energy" and "courage" make him "the real man of action in art. . . . His greatness lay above all in the fact that he *was* this man of action" (qtd. Perry 1: 312). James describes Shakespeare's "brooding expression raised to the highest energy . . . as a primary force, a consuming, an independent passion, which was the greatest ever laid upon man" (*Literary* 1: 1211).

8. In this context, James's refusal to name the crude article responsible for the Newsome family fortune is designed to instill in the reader something of this frisson of aroused curiosity.

9. Significantly, Blumenberg's example of pure curiosity concerns Leonardo da Vinci's famous experience at the mouth of a cave, where he experienced "two contrary emotions"—fear and desire. Da Vinci's account, says Blumenberg, "remained fragmentary not only by accident—in its form—but also by virtue of its outcome" (363). Pursued later in the present chapter is an analogy between da Vinci's cultivation of shock and that sought by Strether and James.

10. John Marcher, that most insulated of Jamesian selves, experiences a similar moment of violence during his epiphany of desolation in the final moments of "The Beast in the Jungle." One "grey afternoon," while visiting the grave of May Bartram, Marcher catches a glimpse of a fellow mourner at a neighboring grave. "This face . . . looked into Marcher's own . . . with an expression like the cut of a blade. He felt it, that is, so deep down that he winced at the steady thrust." The stranger leaves, "but the raw glare of his grief" remains scarred upon Marcher's memory and ignites his recognition that "no passion had ever touched him. . . . Where had been *his* deep ravage?" The stranger's face, "an image of scarred passion," makes Marcher wonder "what wound it expressed. . . . What had the man *had* to make him, by loss of it, so bleed and yet live?" (*Complete Tales* 11: 399–400). At a certain pitch of intensity, living entails the capacity for remaining permeable, for bleeding. This is the equation the stranger reveals to Marcher. Madame de Vionnet's anguish at being "hit," at being wounded in her hopeless love for Chad, will reveal the same relationship to Strether (*Ambassadors* 330).

11. Eric White has emphasized this with reference to Jean Laplanche's theories of sublimation.

12. The context of Bersani's emphasis on the centrality of masochism is his exploration of the "speculative turbulence" produced by Freud's conflicting accounts of sexuality in *Three Essays on the Theory of Sexuality*. Freud contends, as if in spite of himself, that "infant sexuality were sexuality itself" (Bersani's phrase). Bersani shows Freud attempting (not very successfully) to domesticate his own discovery of the pre-Oedipal masochistic nature of sexual pleasure in the post-Oedipal serenity of "secure statement" ("Sexuality" 36).

13. More specifically, art or the aesthetic is the attempted elaboration and repli-

cation of the replication that is adult sexual pleasure, which repeats the infant's masochistic activity (Bersani, "Sexuality" 38).

14. Donald Meyer describes this need as the desire of mind cure that "nothing be left to sheer existence, nothing be unsusceptible to identification with mind" (76).

15. In his biographical study of William James, Daniel Bjork shrewdly probes William's contempt for Chautauqua:

> Yet was it really only Chautauqua that moved James to castigate the mediocrity of the educated American middle class? Was he not also upset with himself? After all, he had willingly prescribed self-help therapy for himself and others for years. . . . The very people who embraced the popular James were the Chautauqua crowd he loathed. He realized that . . . popular lecturing also demanded that he perpetuate Chautauquan mediocrity in himself as well as in his audience. (177)

Bjork's analysis of William James's ambivalence accords with my portrayal of his deeply conflicted psyche, structured by what I have called a dialectic of repression.

16. Bewilderment, melting, tremor, shudder, and hallucination form a nexus of affective energy transgressing and arousing formal organization on both a bodily and aesthetic level. This constellation expresses the interplay of the body and the aesthetic as sites of self-dispersing moments of intensity. "Orgasm," says Adorno, "is a bodily prototype of aesthetic experience." Sexual arousal is a process of "friction" that synthesizes incompatible moments. "During orgasm the beloved image changes, combining rigidification with extreme vividness" (*Aesthetic* 253).

17. The cultural consequences of this gender polarization are taken up in the next chapter.

18. The formulation concerning "moral masochism" is taken from Leo Bersani ("Is" 218).

19. Critics define themselves by their attitudes toward his renunciation. To see Strether's words as affirmative usually entails reading his renunciation as compensatory: his botch of the mission at least provides inward growth; the wonderful impressions that he gains will sustain him (Crews; Holland). The durability of this reading has been affirmed by more recent critics. Joyce Rowe interprets Strether's final choice as an effort to restore the "Emersonian claim that consciousness provides its own sanctification" (99). The negative view of renunciation sees Strether's words as symptomatic of James's own "negative imagination" (Sears), which prefers passive contemplation to active living, a preference reflected in the novel's ending, which depicts Strether paralyzed with "wondrous appreciation" (Matthiessen, *Major*; Philip Weinstein; Sears).

20. Laurence Holland was the first to show that Strether gradually comes to resemble Chad in his self-interested manipulation of others. In the previous quotation Strether feels compelled to impute an innocence and disinterestedness to his stance that is more self-justifying than actual. His clinging to a purity of motive and purpose blinds him to the fact that "the detached observer is as much entangled as the active participant" (Adorno, *Minima* 26).

21. Simmel's analysis converges with James's repeated insistence that art and the marketplace are inscribed in each other. As is well known, James habitually fuses artistic and economic images; the prefaces are saturated with metaphors of the writer's

activity as capitalist, and in his memoirs he visualizes the motor of imaginative activity—"taking in"—as an act of hoarding, the "seizure of property." Like Beethoven (to borrow Adorno's description), James is a "most outstanding example of the unity of those opposites, market and independence, in bourgeois art." As Adorno notes, "Those who succumb to the ideology are precisely those who cover up the contradiction instead of taking it into the consciousness of their own production as Beethoven did" (*Dialectic* 157).

22. See Laurence Holland's study (172–74, 281–82) for an important reading of Maria Gostrey's crucial sacrificial function.

23. My emphasis on the continuity of concerns between *The Ambassadors* and *The American Scene* underlines James's embeddedness in modernity, his (albeit complex) participation in its disciplinary mandate. Thus, I disagree with the implications of John Carlos Rowe's reading of the cultural resonances of *The Ambassadors*:

> Our vision of what Strether sees focuses on the hollow modernity of the twentieth century, the absence of history and the loss of discrimination and taste. Madame de Vionnet and Maria Gostrey are the last representatives of a grace and humanity being swept away by the Newsomes and the Pococks. The Chad Newsome whom Strether had fashioned in his imagination ought to have fulfilled a nineteenth-century ideal. . . . In part, Strether's inability to save his ideas of youth reflects the general failure of American idealism. (*Henry Adams* 199)

The autumnal, nostalgic texture Rowe evokes is an undeniable aspect of a novel that also suggests that modernity's very hollowness, its disenchantment of the world, engenders Strether's performance of an immanent revolution in modern subjectivity that points to new forms of grace and humanity.

24. The illusion of freedom becomes the essential product of the "omniscient genius" of the "hotel-spirit." Yet the pressure of coercion, however latent, remains perceptible to James's experienced eye. He observes "the whole housed populace move as in mild and consenting suspicion of its captured and governed state" (*Scene* 441). The hotel-spirit ensnares with such finesse that its patrons are beguiled even in their awareness of imprisonment.

25. As we shall see in the next chapter, James explicitly terms the hotel world provisional.

Chapter 10

1. Among the many critics who emphasize James's allegedly reactionary response to modernity are Peter Conn, Alan Trachtenberg, and David Furth. Valuable articles on *The American Scene* include those by Laurence Holland (411–34), Stuart Johnson, and James Kraft. Closest to my own concerns is Daniel Silver's important analysis of *The American Scene*. I discuss Maxwell Geismar's and Mark Seltzer's responses later in this chapter.

2. Contributing to this xenophobic overtone, Henry wrote to Edmund Gosse, was the presence of a "crowd of foreign experts . . . who have been at the St. Louis Congress and who appear to be turning up overwhelmingly under" William's roof (*Letters* 4: 332).

3. See the study by H. T. Wilson (15–16).

4. See Alvin Gouldner's *Against Fragmentation* (42).

5. Weber's methodological critique of Münsterberg, written in 1902, centers on the latter's positivistic penchant for static dichotomizing "between 'objectifying' and 'subjectifying' conceptions" (143). This binary thinking, according to Weber, blocks access to the central aim of sociological analysis—"interpretation," the identifying of a "complex of motives reproducible in inner experience." Without the category of interpretation, human conduct is measured by an "empirical-statistic demonstration" of calculability that effectively makes conduct "no different from the fall of the boulder from the cliff" (Weber, *Roscher and Knies* 125, 129). Weberians regard these methodological essays as signaling his breakthrough into a "multidimensional understanding of collective order" (Alexander 23). As Jeffrey Alexander notes, "Instead of action that is 'realistic' at one point in time, psychological at another, and cultural at still another, he portrays action in a generic sense as including all three modes as simultaneous reference points" (23).

6. This sentence is based upon Pitkin's *Fortune Is a Woman* (299–300). Her psychological study of gender and politics in the thought of Machiavelli is suggestive (especially its two final chapters) for conceptualizing James's stance in *The American Scene*. Especially pertinent is her linking of the capacity for "mutuality within difference" with relations with the opposite sex, particularly the pre-Oedipal bond between male child and mother (301–5).

7. Bourne mocks the "homogenous Americanism that our Rooseveltian prophets desire" (*War* 125). James shares Bourne's distaste for Rooseveltian "melting pot idealism" and its "thinly disguised panic which calls itself 'patriotism'" (*War* 125, *Will* 260).

8. Steffens's *Autobiography* delivers a powerful indictment of bourgeois genteel psychology and politics. Afflicting both realms was a significant amount of ideological mystification and self-delusion that strengthened belief in the moral purity of their antimodernism. Steffens's critique has striking affinities to that of Henry James.

9. An interesting instance of this selective use of William James is found in Lippmann's *Preface to Politics* (1913), which appropriates the "moral equivalent of war" as a "guidepost" to successful politics. Foregoing the moralistic stance of the conventional politician, Lippmann stresses that "instead of tabooing our impulses we must redirect them. . . . Every lust is capable of some civilized expression." A gang of juvenile delinquents is potentially a "force that could be made valuable to civilization through the Boy Scouts" (42–43). For Lippmann the "work of statesmanship is finding good substitutes for the bad things we want. This is the heart of a political revolution" (67). James's "moral equivalents" prefigure the "sublimations of the Freudian school." The latter, says Lippmann, represents "perhaps the greatest advance ever made towards the understanding and control of human character" (68), a statement he repeated in *Drift and Mastery*, published the following year. Contemporaneous with Lippmann's conservative appropriation of William James's belief is a more left-leaning pluralism explicitly inspired by the philosopher. This left pragmatism, to which Henry James has affinities, will be discussed later in the present chapter.

10. My characterization here is borrowed from David Hollinger (50).

11. In his critique of Dewey, Bourne enlisted William James's posthumous support ("If William James were alive would he be accepting the war-situation so easily and complacently?" (336). But Bourne's nod was not to James's anti-imperialism but rather to his indomitable spirit. Perhaps because Bourne's stress on the inexorable was profoundly at odds with a belief in the primacy of an active, individual will, the

belief that undergirded James's anti-imperialist politics, Bourne limited his salute to James's "gallant spirit," which would have called for a war "gallantly played," war as "spiritual," "creative" "adventure" (336). Bourne seems inspired here by the therapeutic James of "The Moral Equivalent of War."

12. In the coda I discuss Bourne's impact on Dewey.

13. James's change of citizenship to demonstrate his solidarity with the British cause should not be seen as contradicting Bourne's emphasis on America remaining neutral. Supporting England's war against Germany and favoring American military intervention on behalf of our European allies were quite distinct political positions.

14. Claude Lefort calls the "bureaucratic phantasy" an effort "to abolish the historical in History . . . to deny the unpredictable, the unknowable, the continual loss of the past, under the illusion of a social action, transparent to itself" (222). As will become clear later in this chapter, Lefort's understanding of democracy and ideology is strikingly congruent with that of James.

15. James Kloppenberg also draws attention to the importance of this passage (352).

16. The grounds for bringing James, Veblen, and Adorno together should be briefly mentioned. *The Theory of the Leisure Class*, which William Dean Howells dubbed an "opportunity for American fiction," and the fiction of Henry James stress the semiological character of manners, their functioning as a network of relations, a differential structure that produces public signs. For Adorno Veblen's "evil eye is fertile" (*Prisms* 80). One reason Adorno is drawn to Veblen is their shared negativity, their "constitutional inability to say yes," as Dos Passos wrote of Veblen.

17. Veblen is not alone in his belief that the work instinct will lead women out of the sphere of passive consumption. Charlotte Perkins Gilman's *Women and Economics*, published a year before Veblen's work, is based on the belief that human beings "tend to produce, as a gland to secrete. . . . The creative impulse, the desire to make . . . is the distinguishing mark of humanity." But in half of the human race, notes Gilman, this instinctual imperative is stifled, leaving an "enormous class of non-productive consumers" without "free productive expression." The American woman, in Gilman's view, remains confined as the "priestess of the temple of consumption" (116–18, 120). While Gilman's feminism is evolutionary and progressive, whereas Veblen's is anthropological or genetic, both express confidence that woman will escape from the "temple of consumption" and be free, in Veblen's words, "to live her own life in her own way" (232).

18. The ironic reversal that Adorno notes also haunts another Emersonian heroine—Edna Pontellier in Kate Chopin's *The Awakening*. Rather than enjoying a freedom nearly for nothing, Edna discovers the pain in her insistence on living her own life in her own way. But James's novel, unlike Chopin's, also dramatizes the process whereby the heroine finds a way out of this double bind. Acknowledging her status as object ultimately enables Isabel to experience a new kind of subjectivity, a dialectic suggested in Adorno's remark about Benjamin: "Everything must metamorphose into a thing in order to break the catastrophic spell of things" (*Prisms* 233). At the beginning of *The Portrait of a Lady* Isabel is the very image of self-sufficiency: She "flattered herself that . . . contradictions would never be noted in her own conduct. . . . She would be what she appeared, and she would appear what she was" (54). But this desire for perfect transparency of identity helps turn her into "an applied handled hung up tool, as senseless and convenient as mere shaped wood and iron" (459). Only when Isabel faces the fact that she has "metamorphosed into a thing" can she begin to break the "spell of things." She must shatter her narcissism, her homo-

geneity, by becoming morally stained with envy, the feeling her husband, Osmond, had blithely confessed to. But whereas his is the envy of resentment, Isabel's will be the mimetic envy of empathy. "She envied Ralph his dying," she remarks to herself during a train trip to see him for the last time, a journey during which Isabel, the applied and handled tool, dissolves into an imagined death. In an act of mimetic sympathy, she empties herself of instrumentality: "Nothing seemed of use to her today. All purpose, all intention, was suspended; all desire too. . . . She had moments indeed in her journey from Rome which were almost as good as being dead. She sat in her corner, so motionless, so passive . . . that she recalled to herself one of those Etruscan figures couched upon the receptacle of their ashes" (465). Her mimicry of death permits her to recognize otherness for the first time, as her identification with Ralph relaxes the knot of her selfhood.

19. James gains a glimpse of this "readjusted relation" on his visit to Washington, D.C. Here, in the "city of conversation" and political power, where "nobody was in 'business,' " the male has discovered that "he *can* exist in other connections than that of the Market" (*Scene* 345, 349). It is "still [too] early to say" whether Washington will remain merely the exception proving the rule.

20. Judith Merkle notes that the "goal of scientific management is the perfection of social efficiency through the elimination of politics," adding that "this apolitical stance was itself a political ideology, with the neutral, efficient 'administrative state' as its ultimate goal" (294, 68). Richard L. McCormick remarks that among the "changes of great importance" in the progressive era was the fact that "many of the government's new roles fell to independent administrative agencies which performed their tasks of investigation and adjustment well outside the public's eye" (279). Also see Russell Hanson's discussion (237–56) of the "rationalization of political discourse during the Progressive era," which tended to replace moral arguments with "argument from expediency" (237).

21. In the final chapter of *Reconstruction in Philosophy*, Dewey's critique of "the dogma of the sovereignty of the national state" and his favoring of a state of "trans-national interests" tacitly aligns him with Laski and Bourne and against Lippmann and Croly, his former colleagues at *The New Republic*. See, especially, 202–5.

22. Taylor's "synthetic timing" represented a deliberate effort to break with the English thinker Charles Babbage, his chief predecessor in the field of time-study. Babbage inquired of the worker "what quantity is considered a fair day's work . . . to enable workingmen's organizations to set fair and objective standards for measuring output" (Merkle 84). It was precisely this worker-controlled definition of a fair day's work that Taylor opposed. In noting the fakery involved in Taylorism, Judith Merkle sees its status as a pseudoscience as proof that Taylorism was above all a "powerful ideological crusade" that used "false claims of scientific objectivity for the promotion of ideologically determined goals" (29, 291).

23. This production of romance is proof, according to James, that "the aesthetic need is also intermixed with a patriotic yearning" that seeks to manufacture a past of picturesque antiquity in a country short on history. The emptiness of this trumped-up history struck James as he arrived in St. Augustine, Florida, which advertised itself as the very first American town but was actually a triumph of "fakery" *(Scene* 457).

24. Godkin's solution, in Steffens's view, is inadequate because it remains fixed purely at the level of individuals (the "who") while ignoring the impersonal, structural demands of the capitalist system (the "what") (Steffens 573). The system seems "malign" only "because we put our faith in the ideal arrangements which it disturbs,"

according to the staunch realist Lippmann. "But if we could come to face it squarely" we would see that "the nature of political power we shall not change," and "the sooner we face that fact the better." Then we could begin to "harness political power to the nation's need" (*Preface* 21–22).

25. Lenin's interest in Taylorism has been discussed by many commentators. I have benefited from studies by Judith Merkle, Russell Jacoby, and Alvin Gouldner. Gouldner locates the seeds of Lenin's attitude in the ideas of Marx: "For all of Marx's emphasis on the importance of ideology critique, he never regards science and technology as a sphere of ideology with its own impulse to social domination. Instead he sees them as a largely neutral culture capable of being transplanted into the new socialism without side effects" (*Against* 183).

26. This internal blindness within scientific Marxism also set the stage for the rigorously self-reflexive stance of critical Marxisms, such as those adopted by the Frankfurt School.

27. In addition to Trilling's seminal essay, my brief discussion of the novel enlarges upon issues raised by John Carlos Rowe—specifically his emphasis on the complicity of anarchists and aristocrats in practicing the "arts of social organization"—and Mark Seltzer—in particular his linking of Hoffendahl's kinship with the statistical mentality of sociologists. I make use of the insights of all three critics in an effort to reveal more precisely the range of affiliations at work in James's portrayal of Hoffendahl.

28. Totalitarianism represents a more radical response to democracy's "uncontrollable adventure." To "efface all signs of social division, to banish the indetermination that haunts the democratic experience" is totalitarianism's project. It seeks to revitalize the Body by adopting the idea of the People-as-One (Lefort 305).

29. My emphasis on the hotel-world as a closed system accords with Mark Seltzer's description of it as a "closed order of life" (111), "an achieved closure," an "exemplary site of power and control" (143, 112). Where we differ is that, according to my argument, James (like Adorno) finds closed systems "finite and static," whereas according to Seltzer's interpretation James (like Foucault) sees the hotel-world as embodying "the panoptic and normalizing techniques that constitute the American scene" (115). For Seltzer the hotel-world's "ultimate realization of the panoptic ideal" confirms the novelist's "own policies of aesthetic form." By "incorporating the normative and the organic, the hotel is a triumph of form, of the Jamesian imperative of organic regulation" (113). Seltzer's reading of James through Foucault reduces the novelist's work to a closed system of "circular efficiency" that is "always self-confirming[;] every deviation from the norm reaffirms the norm by providing an occasion for correction and normalization" (87). Seltzer's unfortunate insistence on the sterile circularity of James's art depends on a simplistic notion of organic form uncritically derived from Percy Lubbock. As we have seen, the organic metaphor in James's writing is always made problematical by James himself, who possesses an urge for unity—an urge inevitably compromised, and often sacrificed, to the pressures and "cruel crisis" of artistic creation. Compromised and sacrificed, too, is the disciplinary rule of the hotel-world, which is limited by its static perfection of control. For James, as for Adorno, the bourgeois norm is not discipline but antinomy. To cite a phrase from Foucault's late essay "The Subject and Power," James perceives of New York as a space of "agonism . . . a permanent provocation" (222). This Foucault might have usefully complicated Seltzer's argument and enabled him to understand New York as containing both the Waldorf puppets and the teeming intensity of the New Jerusalem. James engages both moments of modernity—the managerial and the marginal—but Seltzer's disciplinary perspective reduces the presence of the

alien Jew to a mere linguistic phenomenon, an "encroaching 'babble'" of tongues (100). Thus Seltzer's study promotes a view of James that is guilty of the very formalism it denounces, where "problems of social reference" are converted into "problems of textual self-reference" (14).

30. Jean-Christophe Agnew also singles out the "army of puppets" passage, calling it an "extraordinarily prophetic image of the managed freedom of consumer societies." Touching briefly on *The American Scene* in the course of discussing James's attitude toward consumer culture, Agnew notes that James's book "foreshadows the modern critique of the consumer culture industry as 'mass deception.' And like that critique, the book seems to look backward as well to the romantic tradition within which Marx first ventured his views on the human impoverishment of possessive individualism" (77). While Agnew's allusion to James's affinity for the Frankfurt School's views on consumerism anticipates my own argument, his description of the latter's critique as romantic is true only on the broadest level and proves inadequate when that critique is examined in detail. Although I question Agnew's emphasis on James's "elitism" and "aloofness" and his neglect of James's sympathetic identification with much of what he encountered, Agnew's essay is one of the most successful recent efforts to "break the seal of historical solipsism and idiosyncrasy surrounding James" (79).

31. American literary history tends to ignore James's and Dreiser's shared interest in this new species of subjectivity. This neglect reflects the opposed politics of their literary reputations, a subject already touched on in chapter 3. But setting James against Dreiser (a move that Lionel Trilling made canonical in his famous essay of 1950) is nearly as misleading as opposing James to Whitman. In both pairings the fastidious is opposed to the crude, the consummate genteel insider and mystified apologist for the leisure class is contrasted with the contemptuous, alien outsider bent on shattering bourgeois pieties. The James who falls outside these enduring stereotypes remains my primary subject.

32. James's correspondence with Emma Lazarus consists of eight letters—discovered by Carole Kessner—covering the years 1883–85.

33. John P. Diggins has characterized this essay as "the closest thing to a self-portrait that Veblen ever committed to print" (40).

34. The "Other," identified here with the Jew, returns us to the female "Other" discussed earlier by Veblen. Adorno and Horkheimer point to a direct relationship between hatred of women and Jews (112).

35. I am quoting one instance of a self-description that recurs in James's letters. To Edith Wharton he often referred to himself as a worm. See Bell (175–76).

36. Peter Buitenhuis wisely remarks that "Geismar vastly exaggerates" by "ingeniously quoting out of context" (a technique perfected by Lawrence Levine). But Buitenhuis still tends to regard James as far more of a conventional Brahmin than I do (188). Ambivalence toward the Jew, if not the particular mix of identification and disgust in James's response, is characteristic of American intellectual attitudes during this period. John Higham, the leading authority on American ethnicity, has written: "Most of the anti-semitism in native American circles in the late nineteenth century was entangled with a persistent sympathy" (*Send* 103).

37. Steffens worked for a time on the same newspaper with Hapgood and the Jewish fiction writer and journalist Abraham Cahan. Writing of the late 1890s, he confessed: "I at that time was almost a Jew. I had become as infatuated with the Ghetto as eastern boys were with the wild west, and nailed a mazuza on my office door" and "went to synagogue on all the great Jewish holy days" (*Autobiography* 244).

By 1916 the Jew had become less a romantic passion than the very image of contemporary existence. In "The Jew and Trans-National America," Randolph Bourne
wrote that "the Jews have lost their distinction of being a peculiar people. Dispersion
is now the lot of every race. . . . America has become a vast reservoir of dispersions."
In short, we are all Jews now (*War* 127).

38. It should be noted that toward the end of his essay on "Trans-National
America," Bourne seems to lose his dynamic emphasis on "weaving" and adopts
some of the identitarian rhetoric of the melting pot. He invokes a Roycean "Beloved
Community" as an "enterprise of integration" in which "all can unite" (*Will* 264).

39. This description of Bourne is found in Thomas Bender's study (232).

40. Although I have elected the Pullman train to serve as an analogue for Weber's
cage, more than once in *The American Scene* cage imagery—a "beguiled and caged"
populace, positively thankful" for the "definite horizon of a cage"—is used to represent the hotel-spirit's management (*Scene* 441).

41. Such a deluded belief in progress as an unmixed blessing adumbrated what
the next generation of German cultural pathologists would call the "dialectic of
enlightenment."

Coda

1. In "A Feminist Politics of Non-Identity," Leslie Rabine uses the term "nonidentity" in a manner somewhat different from the one developed in the present
work. Leaving Adorno unmentioned, she combines the beliefs of Chodorow and
Derrida, among others, to fashion an argument that rejects the "unified identity" of
both the "feminine self" and "feminist [political] positions." Although "it is necessary for feminists to take positions," Rabine urges an "oscillation between several
positions, in which the necessity of adopting a position in a given situation would
include simultaneously calling it into question" (26–27).

2. Rorty has described Foucault as "an ironist who is unwilling to be a liberal."
Unlike Rorty, Foucault does not think that "contemporary liberal society already
contains the institutions for its own improvement" (*Contingency* 61, 63).

3. In no way do I intend to imply a monocausal explanation (Bourne) for the new
direction in Dewey's thought. There is no prima facie evidence for my supposition
that Bourne influenced Dewey, though there is the fact that Dewey confessed his
error with regard to his prowar stance. Soon after the war Dewey spoke of the "pious
optimism" and "childish . . . sentimentality" of those, like himself, who supported
the war. His biographer, George Dykhuizen, implicitly links this self-critique to
Bourne's criticisms (166). I concur with Peter Manicas's claim that for Dewey "the
war was a transforming experience" that politicized his thinking (340). I have argued
that the postwar Dewey of the twenties (*Reconstruction in Philosophy* and *The Public
and Its Problems*) diverged from the pragmatic realism (and elitism) of a Lippmann
and tacitly moved toward a sympathetic engagement with Bourne. This prompted
changes in emphasis and degree, not in kind, in Dewey's philosophy.

4. Walzer's defense of the antiheroic "connected" critic has affinities with the
politics of nonidentity as practiced by Henry James and Dewey. It should be noted
that Walzer associates the "connected" critic with the "general intellectuals," which
Foucault claims have been superseded. Rejecting Foucault as a radically unsituated
"nihilist," Walzer seeks to recover the category of "general intellectual" while re-

casting it in an immanent direction. According to Walzer's revision, general intellectuals "claim no authority." They neither "inhabit a realm of pure value" nor "stand on a mountaintop, masters of all [they] survey" (202, 208, 239).

5. Adorno has written of such license that it is "resented by the positivistic spirit and [is] put down to mental disorder" (*Minima* 127). Indeed, Dewey was accused of senility by opponents of the inquiry.

Works Cited

Aaron, Daniel. *The Unwritten War*. New York: Oxford UP, 1983.
———. *Writers on the Left*. New York: Avon, 1969.
Adams, Henry. *The Letters*. Vol. 5: 1899–1905. Ed. J. C. Levenson et al. Cambridge: Harvard UP, 6 vols. 1982–88.
Adorno, Theodor W. "The Actuality of Philosophy." Trans. B. Snow. *Telos* 31 (Spring 1977): 120–33.
———. *Aesthetic Theory*. Trans. Christian Lenhardt. Boston: Routledge, 1985.
———. *The Jargon of Authenticity*. Trans. Kurt Tarnowski and Frederic Will. Evanston: Northwestern UP, 1983.
———. *Minima Moralia*. Trans. Edmund Jephcott. London: New Left, 1978.
———. *Negative Dialectics*. Trans. E. B. Ashton. New York: Continuum, 1973.
———. *Prisms*. Trans. Samuel Weber and Shierry Weber. Cambridge: MIT P, 1981.
———. "Subject and Object." Arato and Gebhart 496–511.
———. "Trying to Understand Endgame." *New German Critique* 26 (Spring–Summer 1982): 119–50.
Adorno Theodor W., and Max Horkheimer. *Dialectic of Enlightenment*. Trans. John Cummings. New York: Continuum, 1972.
Agnew, J. C. "The Consuming Vision of Henry James." *The Culture of Consumption*. Ed. Richard Fox and Jackson Lears. New York: Pantheon, 1983. 67–100.
Alexander, Jeffrey. *The Classical Attempt at Theoretical Synthesis: Max Weber*. Berkeley: U of California P. Vol. 3 of *Theoretical Logic in Sociology*. 4 vols. 1982–83.
Alford, Fred. *Narcissism: Socrates, the Frankfurt School, and Psychoanalytic Theory*. New Haven: Yale UP, 1988.
Anderson, James W. "In Search of Mary James." *Psycho-History Review* 8.1–2 (Summer–Fall 1979): 63–70.
Anderson, Quentin. "Henry James's Cultural Office." *Prospects* 8 (1983): 197–210.
———. *The Imperial Self*. New York: Knopf, 1971.
Arac, Jonathan. "F. O. Matthiessen: Authorizing an American Renaissance." *The*

American Renaissance Reconsidered. Ed. Walter Michaels and Donald Pease. Baltimore: Johns Hopkins UP, 1985. 90–112.

Arato, Andrew. "The Neo-Idealist Defense of Subjectivity." *Telos* 21 (Fall 1974): 108–61.

Arato, Andrew, and Eike Gebhardt, eds. *The Essential Frankfurt School Reader*. New York: Urizen, 1978.

Arditi, George. "Role as a Cultural Concept." *Theory and Society* 16 (1987): 565–91.

Armstrong, Carol. "The Reflexive and the Possessive View: Thoughts on Kertesz, Brandt, and the Photographic Nude." *Representations* 25 (Winter 1989): 57–69.

Arnold, Matthew. *The Portable Arnold*. Ed. Lionel Trilling. New York: Viking, 1949.

Banta, Martha. *Imaging American Women*. New York: Columbia UP, 1987.

Barish, Jonas. *The Anti-Theatrical Prejudice*. Berkeley: U of California P, 1985.

Barrett, William. *The Truants*. New York: Doubleday, 1982.

Barzun, Jacques. *A Stroll with William James*. Chicago: U of Chicago P, 1983.

Baudrillard, Jean. *For a Critique of the Political Economy of the Sign*. Trans. Charles Levin. St. Louis: Telos, 1981.

Beard, Charles. *The Rise of American Civilization*, Vol. 2. New York: Macmillan, 1927. 2 vols.

Bell, Millicent. *Edith Wharton and Henry James*. New York: Braziller, 1965.

Bellomy, Donald. "Two Generations: Modernists and Progressives, 1870–1920." *Perspectives in American History* 3 (1986): 279–306.

Bender, Thomas. *New York Intellect*. New York: Knopf, 1987.

Benhabib, Seyla. *Critique, Norm, and Utopia*. New York: Columbia UP, 1986.

Benjamin, Jessica. *The Bonds of Love*. New York: Pantheon, 1988.

Benjamin, Walter. *Illuminations*. Trans. Harry Zohn. New York: Schocken, 1969.

———. *The Origin of German Tragic Drama*. Trans. John Osborne. London: New Left, 1977.

———. *Reflections*. Trans. Edmund Jephcott. New York: Harcourt, 1978.

Bernard, Luther. *Transition to an Objective Standard of Social Control*. Chicago: U of Chicago P, 1911.

Bernstein, Richard, ed. *Habermas and Modernity*. Cambridge: MIT P, 1985.

Bersani, Leo. *The Culture of Redemption*. Cambridge: Harvard UP, 1990.

———. *The Freudian Body*. New York: Columbia UP, 1986.

———. *A Future For Astyanax*. Boston: Little, 1976.

———. "Is the Rectum a Grave?" *October* 43 (Winter 1987): 197–222.

———. "Sexuality and Aesthetics." *October* 28 (Spring 1984): 27–42.

Bjork, Daniel. *William James: The Center of His Vision*. New York: Columbia UP, 1988.

Blackmur, R. P. Introduction. *The Art of the Novel*. By Henry James. Ed. R. P. Blackmur. New York: Scribner's, 1962. xv–xlvii.

Bloom, Harold. Introduction. *Henry James: Modern Critical Views*. New York: Chelsea House, 1987.

Blumenberg, Hans. *The Legitimacy of the Modern Age*. Trans. Robert Wallace. Cambridge: MIT P, 1983.

Boelhower, William. *Through a Glass Darkly*. New York: Oxford UP, 1987.

Borklund, Elmer. "Howard Sturgis, Henry James, and *Belchamber*." *Modern Philology* 59 (May 1961): 255–69.

Bourdieu, Pierre. *Outline of a Theory of Practice*. Trans. Richard Nice. Cambridge: Cambridge UP, 1977.

Bourne, Randolph. *The Letters of Randolph Bourne*. Ed. Eric Sandeen. Troy, NY: Whitson, 1981.

———. *The Radical Will: Selected Writings, 1911–1918*. Ed. Olaf Hansen. New York: Urizen, 1977.

———. *War and the Intellectuals: Collected Essays, 1915–1919*. Ed. Carl Resek. New York: Harper, 1964.

Bouwsma, William. *John Calvin*. New York: Oxford UP, 1988.

Braverman, Harry. *Labor and Monopoly Capital*. New York: Monthly Review, 1974.

Brenkman, John. *Culture and Domination*. Ithaca: Cornell UP, 1988.

Brooks, Van Wyck. *The Pilgrimage of Henry James*. New York: Dutton, 1925.

Brown, Norman O. *Life Against Death*. Middletown: Wesleyan UP, 1959.

Buck-Morss, Susan. *The Origin of Negative Dialectics*. New York: Macmillan, 1977.

———. "Walter Benjamin: Revolutionary Writer." *New Left Review* 129 (October 1981): 77–95.

Buder, Stanley. *Pullman: An Experiment in Industrial Order and Community Planning*. New York: Oxford UP, 1967.

Buitenhuis, Peter. *The Grasping Imagination*. Toronto: U of Toronto P, 1970.

Burns, Elizabeth, and Tom Burns, eds. *Sociology of Literature and Drama*. Baltimore: Penguin, 1973.

Cahn, Michael. "Subversive Mimesis: Adorno and the Modern Impasse of Critique." *Mimesis in Contemporary Theory*. Ed. Mihai Spariosu. Philadelphia: Benjamins, 1984. 27–64.

Cain, William. *F. O. Matthiessen and the Politics of Criticism*. Madison: U of Wisconsin P, 1989.

Cameron, Sharon. *Thinking in Henry James*. Chicago: U of Chicago P, 1990.

Carroll, David. *The Subject in Question*. Chicago: U of Chicago P, 1982.

Cavell, Stanley. *The Senses of Walden*. Expanded ed. San Francisco: North Point, 1981.

Chapman, John Jay. *Selected Writings*. Ed. Jacques Barzun. New York: Farrar, 1957.

Chodorow, Nancy. "Toward a Relational Individualism." *Reconstructing Individualism*. Ed. Thomas Heller et al. Stanford: Stanford UP, 1986. 197–207.

Clark, T. J. *The Painting of Modern Life*. Princeton: Princeton UP, 1987.

Clebsch, William. *American Religious Thought*. Chicago: U of Chicago P, 1973.

Conn, Peter. *The Divided Mind*. New York: Cambridge UP, 1983.

Connolly, William. *Politics and Ambiguity*. Madison: U of Wisconsin P, 1987.

———. "Taylor, Foucault, and Otherness." *Political Theory* 13 (August 1985): 365–76.

———. *Terms of Political Discourse*. 2nd ed. Princeton: Princeton UP, 1984.

Conrad, Peter. *Imagining America*. New York: Oxford UP, 1980.

Cooney, Terry. *The Rise of the New York Intellectuals*. Madison: U of Wisconsin P, 1986.

Cory, Daniel. *George Santayana: The Later Years—A Portrait with Letters*. New York: Braziller, 1963.

Coser, Lewis. *Masters of Sociological Thought*. New York: Harcourt, 1971.

Cotkin, George. *William James: Public Philosopher*. Baltimore: Johns Hopkins UP, 1990.

Cowley, Malcolm. Rev. of *Henry James: The Major Phase*, by F. O. Matthiessen. *New Republic* 22 Jan. 1945: 122–23.

Cox, James. "The Memoirs of Henry James: Self-Interest as Autobiography." *Southern Review* 22 (1986): 231–51.

Croly, Herbert. *The Promise of American Life*. Cambridge: Harvard UP, 1965.

Crews, Frederick. *The Tragedy of Manners*. Hamden, CT: Archon, 1971.

Dallmayr, Fred. *Critical Encounters*. South Bend: Notre Dame UP, 1987.

Derrick, Scott. "A Small Boy and the Ease of Others: The Structure of Masculinity and the Autobiography of Henry James." *Arizona Quarterly* 45.4 (1989): 31–54.

Dewey, John. *Art as Experience*. New York: Putnam's, 1980.

———. *Experience and Nature*. La Salle, IL: Open Court, 1929.

———. *Human Nature and Conduct*. New York: Modern Library-Random, 1957.

———. *Individualism Old and New*. New York: Minton Balch, 1930.

———. *The Later Works, 1925–53*. Ed. JoAnn Boydston. Carbondale: Southern Illinois UP, 1986. 14 vols. 1985–.

———. *The Middle Works, 1899–1924*. Ed. JoAnn Boydston. Carbondale: Southern Illinois UP, 1977. 15 vols. 1976–83.

———. *The Quest for Certainty*. New York: Putnam's, 1960.

———. *Reconstruction in Philosophy*. Boston: Beacon, 1957.

Dews, Peter. *Logics of Disintegration*. London: Verso, 1987.

———. "Adorno, Post-Structuralism and the Critique of Identity." *New Left Review* 157 (1986): 28–44.

Diggins, John P. *The Bard of Savagery*. New York: Seabury, 1978.

Donadio, Stephen. *Nietzsche, Henry James and the Artistic Will*. New York: Oxford UP, 1978.

Dreyfus, Hubert, and Paul Rabinow. "What Is Maturity? Habermas and Foucault on 'What Is Enlightenment?' " *Foucault: A Critical Reader*. Ed. David Hoy. London: Blackwell, 1986. 109–21.

Dupee, F. W. "The Americanism of Van Wyck Brooks." *Literary Opinion in America*. Ed. Morton Zabel. Vol. 2. New York: Harper, 1962. 561–72. 2 vols.

Dykhuizen, George. *The Life and Mind of John Dewey*. Carbondale: Southern Illinois UP, 1973.

Eagleton, Terry. *Criticism and Ideology*. London: New Left, 1978.

———. *The Ideology of the Aesthetic*. London: Blackwell, 1990.

Eakin, Paul J. "Henry James and the Autobiographical Act." *Prospects* 8 (1983): 211–60. (Rpt. in *Fictions in Autobiography*. Princeton: Princeton UP, 1985.)

Edel, Leon. *The Master*. New York: Avon, 1978.

———. *The Middle Years*. New York: Avon, 1978.

———. *The Treacherous Years*. New York: Avon, 1978.

———. *The Untried Years*. New York: Avon, 1978.

Edel, Leon, and Gordon N. Ray, eds. *Henry James and H. G. Wells*. London: Hart-Davis, 1958.

Elias, Norbert. *The Civilizing Process*. Trans. Edmund Jephcott. New York: Urizen, 1978.

Ellison, Ralph. *Shadow and Act*. New York: Vintage, 1972.

Ellul, Jacques. *The Technological Society*. Trans. John Wilkinson. New York: Vintage, 1964.

Emerson, Ralph Waldo. *Essays and Lectures*. New York: Library of America, 1983.

Feffer, Andrew. "Sociability and Social Conflict in George Herbert Mead's Interactionism, 1900–1919." *Journal of the History of Ideas* 51 (April–June 1990): 233–54.

Feidelson, Charles. "Henry James and the Man of Imagination." *Language and Structure.* Ed. Frank Brady et al. New Haven: Yale UP, 1975. 331–52.

Feinstein, Howard. *Becoming William James.* Ithaca: Cornell UP, 1985.

Fiedler, Leslie. *Love and Death in the American Novel.* New York: Dell, 1969.

Foucault, Michel. *Discipline and Punish.* Trans. Alan Sheridan. New York: Vintage, 1979.

———. *History of Sexuality.* Vol. 1. Trans. Robert Hurley. New York: Vintage, 1980. 3 vols. 1978–86.

———. *Language, Counter-Memory, Practice.* Trans. Donald Bouchard. Ithaca: Cornell UP, 1977.

———. *Power/Knowledge.* Ed. Colin Gordon. New York: Pantheon, 1980.

———. "Power and Sex: An Interview with Michel Foucault." *Telos* 32 (Summer 1977): 152–61.

———. "Structuralism and Post-Structuralism: An Interview with Michel Foucault." *Telos* 55 (Spring 1983): 192–200.

———. "The Subject and Power." *Michel Foucault: Beyond Structuralism and Hermeneutics,* by Hubert Dreyfus and Paul Rabinow. 208–26.

Fox, Richard. *Reinhold Niebuhr.* New York: Pantheon, 1985.

Frankfurt Institute. *Aspects of Sociology.* Boston: Beacon, 1972.

Fraser, Nancy. "Solidarity or Singularity: Richard Rorty Between Romanticism and Technocracy." *Reading Rorty.* Ed. Alan Malachowski. Oxford: Blackwell, 1990. 303–21.

Freud, Sigmund. *Leonardo da Vinci.* Trans. Alan Tyson. New York: Norton, 1964.

Frisby, David. *Fragments of Modernity.* Cambridge: MIT P, 1986.

———. Introduction. *The Philosophy of Money.* By Georg Simmel. Trans. Tom Bottomore and David Frisby. London: Routledge, 1971. 1–49.

———. *Sociological Impressionism.* London: Heinemann, 1981.

Furth, David. *The Visionary Betrayed.* Cambridge: Harvard UP, 1978.

Gard, Roger, ed. *Henry James: The Critical Heritage.* New York: Barnes, 1968.

Geismar, Maxwell. *Henry James and the Jacobites.* Boston: Houghton, 1965.

Gilbert, James. *Work Without Salvation.* Baltimore: Johns Hopkins UP, 1977.

Gilman, Charlotte Perkins. *Women and Economics.* New York: Harper, 1966.

Godkin, Edwin L. *Problems of Modern Democracy.* Cambridge: Harvard UP, 1966.

———. *Unforeseen Tendencies of Democracy.* Boston: Houghton, 1898.

Goffman, Erving. *Frame Analysis.* New York: Harper, 1974.

Goodheart, Eugene. "A Limit to Ideology." *National Humanities Center Newsletter* 9.3–4 (Spring–Summer 1988): 1–12.

Gouldner, Alvin. *Against Fragmentation.* New York: Oxford UP, 1985.

———. *The Dialectic of Ideology and Technology.* New York: Oxford UP, 1976.

Green, Bryan. *Literary Methods and Sociological Theory.* Chicago: U of Chicago P, 1988.

Habegger, Alfred. *Gender, Fantasy and Realism in American Literature.* New York: Columbia UP, 1982.

Habermas, Jürgen. "The Entwinement of Myth and Enlightenment." *New German Critique* 26 (Spring–Summer 1982): 13–30.

———. *The Philosophical Discourse of Modernity.* Trans. Frederick Lawrence. Cambridge: MIT P, 1987.

———. *Philosophical–Political Profiles.* Trans. Frederick Lawrence. Cambridge: MIT P, 1985.

———. *The Theory of Communicative Action.* Trans. Thomas McCarthy. Vol. 1. Boston: Beacon, 1984. 2 vols. 1984–86.

Hale, Matthew. *Human Science and Social Order*. Philadelphia: Temple UP, 1980.

Halttunen, Karen. *Confidence Men and Painted Women*. New Haven: Yale UP, 1982.

Hanson, Russell. *The Democratic Imagination in America*. Princeton: Princeton UP, 1985.

Hapgood, Hutchins. *The Spirit of the Ghetto*. Cambridge: Harvard UP, 1967.

Hardwick, Elizabeth. *A View of My Own*. New York; Farrar, 1982.

Harlan, David. "Intellectual History and the Return of Literature." *American Historical Review* 94 (June 1989): 581–609.

———. "Reply to David Hollinger." *American Historical Review* 94 (June 1989): 622–26.

Harvey, David. *Consciousness and the Urban Experience*. Baltimore: Johns Hopkins UP, 1989.

Haskell, Thomas. *The Emergence of Professional Social Science*. Urbana: U of Illinois P, 1977.

Hegel, Georg Wilhelm Friedrich. *The Phenomenology of Mind*. Trans. J. Baillie. New York: Harper, 1967.

Herf, Jeffrey. *Reactionary Modernism*. Cambridge: Cambridge UP, 1984.

Higham, John. *Send These to Me*. Baltimore: Johns Hopkins UP, 1984.

———. *Strangers in the Land: Patterns of American Nativism, 1860–1925*. New York: Atheneum, 1973.

Hocks, Richard. *Henry James and Pragmatistic Thought*. Chapel Hill: U of North Carolina P, 1974.

Hofstadter, Richard. *The Age of Reform*. New York: Vintage, 1955.

———. *The Progressive Historians: Turner, Beard, Parrington*. New York: Vintage, 1970.

Holland, Laurence. *The Expense of Vision*. Baltimore: Johns Hopkins UP, 1982.

Hollinger, David. *In the American Province*. Baltimore: Johns Hopkins UP, 1989.

Holly, Carol. "The British Reception of Henry James's Autobiographies," *American Literature* 57.4 (1985): 570–87.

———. "The Drama of Intention in Henry James's *Autobiography*." *Modern Language Studies* 13.4 (Fall 1983): 22–31.

Holmes, Stephen. "The Community Trap." *New Republic* 28 Nov. 1988: 24–29.

Hook, Sidney. *Out of Step*. New York: Carroll, 1987.

Hoopes, James. *Consciousness in New England*. Baltimore: Johns Hopkins UP, 1989.

Horkheimer, Max. *Critical Theory*. Trans. Matthew O'Connell. New York: Continuum, 1982.

———. *Eclipse of Reason*. New York: Seabury, 1974.

Horowitz, Gad. *Repression*. Toronto: U of Toronto P, 1970.

Howe, Irving. Introduction. *The American Scene*. By Henry James. New York: Horizon, 1967.

———. *World of Our Fathers*. New York: Harcourt, 1977.

Hullot-Kentor, Robert. "Back to Adorno." *Telos* 81 (Fall 1989): 5–29.

Huyssen, Andreas. "Adorno in Reverse." *New German Critique* 29 (Spring 1983): 8–38.

Ingram, David. *Habermas's Recent Social Theory*. New Haven: Yale UP, 1987.

Jacoby, Russell. *Dialectic of Defeat*. New York: Cambridge UP, 1981.

James, Alice. *The Diary of Alice James*. New York: Dodd, 1964.

James, Henry. *The Ambassadors*. New York: Norton, 1964.

———. *The American*. New York: Norton, 1978.

———. *The American Essays*. Ed. Leon Edel. New York: Vintage, 1956.

———. *The American Scene*. Bloomington: Indiana UP, 1969.

———. *The Art of the Novel*, Ed. R. P. Blackmur. New York: Scribner's, 1962.

———. *Autobiography*. Ed. F. W. Dupee. New York: Criterion, 1956.

———. *The Complete Notebooks*. Ed. Leon Edel and Lyall H. Powers. New York: Oxford UP, 1987.

———. *The Complete Tales*. Ed. Leon Edel. 12 vols. Philadelphia: Lippincott, 1964.

———. *The Golden Bowl*. New York: Penguin, 1978.

———. *Letters*. Ed. Leon Edel. 4 vols. Cambridge: Harvard UP, 1974–84.

———. *Letters*. Ed. Percy Lubbock. 2 vols. New York: Scribner's, 1920.

———. *Literary Criticism: American and English Writers* [Vol. 1]. New York: Library of America, 1984.

———. *Literary Criticism: European Writers* [Vol. 2]. New York: Library of America, 1984.

———. *The Portrait of a Lady*. New York: Norton, 1975.

———. *The Princess Casamassima*. New York: Penguin, 1977.

———. *Selected Letters*. Ed. Leon Edel. Cambridge: Harvard UP, 1987.

———. *The Tragic Muse*. New York: Scribner's, 1909.

———. *William Wetmore Story and His Friends*. 2 vols. New York: Grove, 1957.

James, William. *Essays in Radical Empiricism*. Cambridge: Harvard UP, 1976.

———. *Essays, Comments and Reviews*. Cambridge: Harvard UP, 1987.

———. *The Letters*. Ed. Henry James III. 2 vols. Boston: Atlantic Monthly P, 1920.

———. *Memories and Studies*. London: Longmans, 1911.

———. *A Pluralistic Universe*. Cambridge: Harvard UP, 1977.

———. *Pragmatism*. Cambridge: Harvard UP, 1978.

———. *The Principles of Psychology*. Cambridge: Harvard UP, 1983.

———. *Talks to Teachers*. New York: Norton, 1958.

———. *The Varieties of Religious Experience*. New York: Penguin, 1982.

———. *The Will to Believe*. Cambridge: Harvard UP, 1979.

Jameson, Fredric. *Late Marxism*. London: Verso, 1990.

———. *The Political Unconscious*. Ithaca: Cornell UP, 1981.

———. *Postmodernism*. Durham: Duke UP, 1991.

Jay, Martin. *Adorno*. Cambridge: Harvard UP, 1983.

———. *The Dialectical Imagination*. Boston: Little, 1973.

Jennings, Michael. *Dialectical Images*. Ithaca: Cornell UP, 1987.

Joas, Hans. *G. H. Mead*. London: Blackwell, 1985.

Johnson, Stuart. "American Marginalia: James's *The American Scene*." *Texas Studies in Language and Literature* 24 (Spring 1982): 83–101.

Kaplan, Justin. *Lincoln Steffens*. New York: Simon, 1974.

Kaston, Carren. *Imagination and Desire in the Novels of Henry James*. New Brunswick: Rutgers UP, 1984.

Kazin, Alfred. *On Native Grounds*. New York: Doubleday, 1956.

Keller, Phyllis. *States of Belonging: German-American Intellectuals and the First World War*. Cambridge: Harvard UP, 1979.

Kessner, Carole. "The Emma Lazarus–Henry James Connection: Eight Letters." *American Literary History* 3.1 (1991). Forthcoming.

King, John Owen. *The Iron of Melancholy: Structures of Spiritual Conversion in America from the Puritan Conscience to Victorian Neurosis*. Middletown: Wesleyan UP, 1983.

Kloppenberg, James. *Uncertain Victory: Social Democracy and Progressivism in European and American Thought, 1870–1920*. New York: Oxford UP, 1986.

Kraft, James. "On Reading *The American Scene*." *Prose* 6 (1973): 115–35.

Krupnick, Mark. *Lionel Trilling and the Fate of Cultural Criticism*. Evanston: Northwestern UP, 1986.

Kuklick, Bruce. *The Rise of American Philosophy*. New Haven: Yale UP, 1977.

Lasch, Christopher. *The New Radicalism in America*. New York: Vintage, 1965.

Laski, Harold. *The Dangers of Obedience*. New York: Harper, 1930.

———. *The Foundation of Sovereignty*. New Haven: Yale UP, 1931.

———. *Studies in the Problem of Sovereignty*. New Haven: Yale UP, 1917.

Lavine, Thelma. "Pragmatism and the Constitution in the Culture of Modernism." *Transactions of the C. S. Peirce Society* 20.1 (Winter 1984): 1–17.

Lears, Jackson. *No Place of Grace*. New York: Pantheon, 1981.

Lefort, Claude. *The Political Forms of Modern Society*. Trans. John Thompson. Cambridge: MIT P, 1986.

Lentricchia, Frank. *Ariel and the Police*. Madison: U of Wisconsin P, 1987.

Levine. Donald. *The Flight from Ambiguity*. Chicago: U of Chicago P, 1986.

Levine, Lawrence. *Highbrow/Lowbrow*. Cambridge: Harvard UP, 1989.

Lewis. R. W. B. *Edith Wharton*. New York: Fromm, 1985.

Lewis, Wyndham. *Men Without Art*. Santa Rosa, CA: Black Sparrow, 1987.

Liebersohn, Harry. *Fate and Utopia in German Sociology, 1870–1923*. Cambridge: MIT P, 1988.

Lippmann, Walter. *Drift and Mastery*. Madison: U of Wisconsin P, 1985.

———. *A Preface to Politics*. Ann Arbor: U of Michigan P, 1962.

Lloyd, David. *Nationalism and Minor Literature*. Berkeley: U of California P, 1986.

Lowenthal, Leo. *An Unmastered Past*. Berkeley: U of California P, 1987.

Löwith, Karl. *Max Weber and Karl Marx*. Trans. Hans Fantel. London: Allen, 1982.

Lunn, Eugene. *Marxism and Modernism*. Berkeley: U of California P, 1984.

Lustig, Jeffrey. *Corporate Liberalism*. Berkeley: U of California P, 1986.

Lyon, Richard, ed. *Santayana on America: Essays, Notes and Letters on American Life, Literature, and Philosophy*. New York: Harcourt, 1968.

McCormick, John. *George Santayana: A Biography*. New York: Paragon, 1988.

McCormick, Richard L. *The Party Period and Public Policy*. New York: Oxford UP, 1986.

McDermott, John, ed. *The Philosophy of John Dewey*. Chicago: U of Chicago P, 1981.

Macdonald, Dwight. *Politics Past*. New York: Viking, 1970.

McKee, Patricia. *The Commitment to Excess in Richardson, Eliot and James*. Princeton: Princeton UP, 1986.

———. "Making Do: The Art of Appreciation in *The Ambassadors*." *South Atlantic Quarterly* 87.2 (Spring 1988): 253–309.

Manicas, Peter. *War and Democracy*. Oxford: Blackwell, 1989.

Mannheim, Karl. *Ideology and Utopia*. Trans. Louis Wirth and Edward Shils. New York: Harcourt, 1936.

Marcuse, Herbert. *Reason and Revolution*. Boston: Beacon, 1964.

———. "Some Social Implications of Modern Technology." Arato and Gebhardt 138–62.

Marr, David. *American Worlds Since Emerson*. Amherst: U of Massachusetts P, 1988.

Matthiessen, F. O. *Henry James: The Major Phase*. New York: Oxford UP, 1963.

———. *The James Family*. New York: Knopf, 1961.

Mead, George Herbert. *Mind, Self, and Society*. Chicago: U of Chicago P, 1934.

———. *Movements of Thought*. Chicago: U of Chicago P, 1936.

———. *Selected Writings*. Ed. Andrew Reck. Indianapolis: Bobbs, 1964.

———. "The Social Self." *Journal of Philosophy* 10 (1913): 374–80.

Merkle, Judith. *Management and Ideology.* Berkeley: U of California P, 1980.

Meyer, Donald. *The Positive Thinkers.* Middletown: Wesleyan UP, 1988.

Michaels, Walter Benn. *The Gold Standard and the Logic of Naturalism.* Berkeley: U of California P, 1987.

Mill, John Stuart. *Auguste Comte and Positivism.* London: Kegan Paul, 1907.

Mills, C. Wright. *Sociology and Pragmatism.* New York: Oxford UP, 1966.

Morgan, William. "Adorno on Sport." *Theory and Society* 17 (1988): 813–38.

Morris, Wright. *The Territory Ahead.* New York: Harcourt, 1958.

Münsterberg, Hugo. *Psychology and Industrial Efficiency.* New York: Houghton, 1913.

Münsterberg, Margaret. *Hugo Münsterberg: His Life and Work.* New York: Appleton, 1922.

Myers, Gerald. *William James: His Life and Thought.* New Haven: Yale UP, 1986.

Nietzsche, Friedrich. *On the Genealogy of Morals.* Trans. Walter Kaufmann. New York: Vintage, 1969.

Noble, David. *The End of American History.* Minneapolis: U of Minnesota P, 1985.

Novick, Peter. *That Noble Dream.* New York: Cambridge UP, 1988.

O'Neill, William. *A Better World.* New York: Simon, 1982.

Osborne, Peter. "Adorno and the Metaphysics of Modernism." *The Problem of Modernity: Adorno and Benjamin.* Ed. Andrew Benjamin. London: Routledge, 1989. 23–48.

Parrington, Vernon L. *Main Currents in American Thought.* Vol 3. New York: Harcourt, 1930. 3 vols. 1927–30.

Pater, Walter. *Selected Writings.* New York: Signet, 1974.

Peirce, Charles S. *Collected Papers.* 8 vols. Cambridge: Harvard UP, 1931–58.

Pells, Richard. *Radical Visions and American Dreams.* New York: Harper, 1973.

Perry, Ralph Barton. *The Thought and Character of William James.* 2 vols. Boston: Little, 1935.

Pitkin, Hanna F. *Fortune Is a Woman.* Berkeley: U of California P, 1984.

Poirier, Richard. "Forward." *The Expense of Vision.* By Laurence Holland. Baltimore: Johns Hopkins UP, 1982. vii–viii.

———. *The Renewal of Literature.* New York: Random, 1987.

———. *A World Elsewhere.* New York: Oxford UP, 1968.

Porte, Joel. "Santayana's Masquerade." *Raritan* 7 (Fall 1987): 129–42.

Pound, Ezra. *Literary Essays.* New York: New Directions, 1968.

Price, Martin. "The Other Self." Burns and Burns 260–79.

Przybylowicz, Donna. *Desire and Repression.* Tuscaloosa: U of Alabama P, 1986.

Rabine, Leslie. "A Feminist Politics of Non-Identity." *Feminist Studies* 14.1 (Spring 1988): 11–31.

Rahv, Philip. *Literature and the Sixth Sense.* Boston: Houghton, 1970.

Reising, Russell. *The Unusable Past.* New York: Methuen, 1987.

Ricoeur, Paul. *Freud and Interpretation.* Trans. Denis Savage. New Haven: Yale UP, 1970.

Riesman, David. *Thorstein Veblen.* New York: Seabury, 1960.

Rochberg, Eugene H. *Meaning and Modernity.* Chicago: U of Chicago P, 1986.

Rodgers, Daniel. *Contested Truths: Keywords in American Political Culture.* New York: Basic, 1986.

———. "In Search of Progressivism." *Reviews in American History* 10 (1982): 113–32.

———. *The Work Ethic in Industrial America.* Chicago: U of Chicago P, 1978.

Rorty, Richard. *The Consequences of Pragmatism.* Minneapolis: U of Minnesota P, 1982.

———. *Contingency, Irony, and Solidarity.* New York: Cambridge UP, 1989.

————. "Habermas and Lyotard on Modernity." Bernstein 161–75.

————. "Pragmatism's Freud." *Pragmatism's Freud: The Moral Disposition of Psychoanalysis.* Ed. Joseph Smith and William Kerrigan. Baltimore: Johns Hopkins UP, 1986. 1–26.

————. Rev. of *A Stroll with William James,* by Jacques Barzun. *The New Republic* 9 May 1983: 31–33.

Rosenblum, Nancy. *Another Liberalism: Romanticism and the Reconstruction of Liberal Thought.* Cambridge: Harvard UP, 1987.

————. "Pluralism and Self-Defense." *Liberalism and the Moral Life.* Ed. Nancy Rosenblum. Cambridge: Harvard UP, 1989. 207–26.

Ross, Dorothy. "On Social Science and the Idea of Progress." *The Authority of Experts.* Ed. Thomas Haskell. Bloomington: Indiana UP, 1984. 157–75.

Ross, Edward A. *Seventy Years of It: An Autobiography.* New York: Appleton, 1936.

————. *Social Control.* Cleveland: Case Western UP, 1901.

Rowe, John Carlos. *Henry Adams and Henry James.* Ithaca: Cornell UP, 1976.

————. *Theoretical Dimensions of Henry James.* Madison: U of Wisconsin P, 1984.

Rowe, Joyce. *Equivocal Endings in Classic American Novels.* New York: Cambridge UP, 1989.

Royce, Josiah. *William James and Essays on the Philosophy of Life.* New York: Macmillan, 1912.

Samuels, Ernest. *Henry Adams: The Major Phase.* Cambridge: Harvard UP, 1964.

Santayana, George. *Character and Opinion in the United States.* New York: Scribner's, 1936.

————. *The Last Puritan: A Memoir in the Form of a Novel.* New York: Scribner's, 1936.

————. *The Letters of George Santayana.* Ed. Daniel Cory. New York: Scribner's, 1955.

————. *Persons and Places.* Cambridge: MIT P, 1986.

————. *Soliloquies in England and Later Soliloquies.* New York: Scribner's, 1936.

Sartre, Jean-Paul. *Anti-Semite and Jew.* Trans. George Becker. New York: Schocken, 1965.

————. *Critique of Dialectical Reason.* Trans. Alan Sheridan-Smith. London: NLB, 1976.

Schnadelbach, Herbert. *Philosophy in Germany, 1831–1933.* Trans. Eric Matthews. Cambridge: Cambridge UP, 1984.

Sears, Sallie. *The Negative Imagination.* Ithaca: Cornell UP, 1968.

Sedgwick, Eve. *Between Men.* New York: Columbia UP, 1985.

————. "The Beast in the Closet: James and the Writing of Homosexual Panic." *Sex, Politics, and Science in the Nineteenth-Century Novel.* Ed. Ruth Yeazell. Baltimore: Johns Hopkins UP, 1986. 148–86.

Seidel, Michael. *Exile and the Narrative Imagination.* New Haven: Yale UP, 1985.

Seltzer, Mark. *Henry James and the Art of Power.* Ithaca: Cornell UP, 1984.

Seymour, Miranda. *A Ring of Conspirators.* Boston: Houghton, 1989.

Shapiro, Ian. *Political Criticism.* Berkeley: U of California P, 1990.

Silver, Daniel. "Margin and Mystery: The Fate of Intimacy in the Late Novels of Henry James." Diss. Yale U, 1981.

Simmel, Georg. *Individuality and Social Forms.* Trans. Donald Levine. Chicago: U of Chicago P, 1971.

————. "On the Theory of Theatrical Performance." Burns 304–10.

————. *The Philosophy of Money.* Trans. Tom Bottomore and David Frisby. London: Routledge, 1978.

Smith-Rosenberg, Carroll. *Disorderly Conduct.* New York: Oxford UP, 1986.

Sohn-Rethel, Alfred. *Intellectual and Manual Labor*. Trans. Martin Sohn-Rethel. Atlantic Highlands, NJ: Humanities, 1978.

Spears, Monroe. *American Ambitions*. Baltimore: Johns Hopkins UP, 1988.

Sprinker, Michael. *Imaginary Relations*. London: Verso, 1987.

Sproat, John. *"The Best Men."* Chicago: U of Chicago P, 1982.

Steffens, Lincoln. *Autobiography*. New York: Harcourt, 1931.

———. *The Shame of the Cities*. New York: Hill, 1957.

Stempel, Daniel. "Biography as Dramatic Monologue: Henry James, W. W. Story, and the Alternative Vision." *New England Quarterly* 62 (June 1989): 224–47.

Story, William Wetmore. *Roba di Roma*. Boston: Houghton, 1887.

Sturgis, Howard. *Belchamber*. New York: Oxford UP, 1986.

Suckiel, Ellen K. *The Pragmatic Philosophy of William James*. South Bend: U of Notre Dame P, 1982.

Sussman, Warren. *Culture as History*. New York: Pantheon, 1984.

Tausch, Edwin. "William James the Pragmatist: A Psychological Analysis." *The Monist* 19.1 (1909): 1–25.

Taylor, Charles. *Philosophy and the Human Sciences*. Vol. 2. Cambridge: Cambridge UP, 1985. 2 vols.

Taylor, Frederick. *The Principles of Scientific Management*. New York: Norton, 1967.

Tertulian, Nicolae. "Lukács, Adorno and Classical German Philosophy." *Telos* 63 (Spring 1985): 79–96.

Thayer, Horace L. *Meaning and Action*. Indianapolis: Bobbs, 1981.

Thomas, Paul. *Karl Marx and the Anarchists*. London: Routledge, 1980.

Tocqueville, Alexis de. *Democracy in America*. Vol. 2. New York: Vintage, 1945. 2 vols.

Trachtenberg, Alan. "The American Scene: Versions of the City." *Massachussetts Review* 8 (Summer 1967): 281–95.

Trilling, Lionel. *Beyond Culture*. New York: Viking, 1968.

———. *The Last Decade*. New York: Harcourt, 1975.

———. *The Liberal Imagination*. New York: Anchor, 1950.

———. *Sincerity and Authenticity*. Cambridge: Harvard UP, 1972.

Turner, Bryan. "The Rationalization of the Body: Reflections on Modernity and Discipline." *Max Weber, Rationality, and Modernity*. Ed. Sam Whimster and Scott Lash. London: Allen, 1987. 222–41.

Unger, Roberto. *Knowledge and Politics*. New York: Macmillan, 1975.

———. *Passion*. New York: Free, 1984.

Valéry, Paul. *Leonardo, Poe, Mallarmé*. Trans. Malcolm Cowley and James Lawler. Princeton: Princeton UP, 1972.

Van Leer, David. "The Beast of the Closet: Homosociality and the Pathology of Manhood." *Critical Inquiry* 15 (Spring 1989): 587–605.

Veblen, Thorstein. *Essays in Our Changing Order*. New York: Viking, 1934.

———. *The Place of Science in Modern Civilization*. New York: Huebsch, 1918.

———. *The Theory of the Leisure Class*. New York: Mentor, 1953.

Vidich, Arthur, and Stanford Lyman. *American Sociology*. New Haven: Yale UP, 1985.

Walzer, Michael. *The Company of Critics*. New York: Basic, 1988.

Weber, Max. *From Max Weber*. New York: Oxford UP, 1946.

———. *The Protestant Ethic and the Spirit of Capitalism*. Trans. Talcott Parsons. New York: Scribner's, 1958.

———. *Roscher and Knies: The Logical Problems of Historical Economics*. Trans. Guy Oakes. New York: Free, 1975.

Weber, Samuel. "Capitalizing History: Notes on *The Political Unconscious.*" *Diacritics* 13 (Summer 1983): 14–28.

Weinstein, Michael. *The Wilderness and the City.* Amherst: U of Massachusetts P, 1982.

Weinstein, Philip. *Henry James and the Requirements of the Imagination.* Cambridge: Harvard UP, 1971.

Wells, H. G. *The Future in America.* New York: Harper, 1906.

West, Cornel. *The American Evasion of Philosophy.* Madison: U of Wisconsin P, 1989.

Wharton, Edith. *A Backward Glance.* New York: Scribner's, 1985.

White, Eric. *Kaironomia.* Ithaca: Cornell UP, 1987.

Whitebook, Joel. "The Politics of Redemption." *Telos* 63 (Spring 1985): 156–68.

Whitman, Walt. *Leaves of Grass.* New York: Norton, 1965.

Wieseltier, Leon. Rev. of *More Die of Heartbreak*, by Saul Bellow. *The New Republic* 31 Aug. 1987: 36–38.

Williams, Raymond. *Marxism and Literature.* Oxford: Oxford UP, 1977.

———. *Politics and Letters.* London: Verso, 1981.

Wilson, Edmund. "Rome Diary: Arrival; A Visit to Santayana." *Europe Without Baedeker.* New York: Farrar, 1972. 38–55.

———. *The Shores of Light.* New York: Farrar, 1952.

Wilson, H. T. *The American Ideology.* Boston: Routledge, 1977.

Wolin, Richard. "Critical Theory and the Dialectic of Rationalism." *New German Critique* 41 (Spring–Summer 1987): 23–52.

———. "Foucault's Aesthetic Decisionism." *Telos* 67 (Spring 1986): 71–86.

———. *Walter Benjamin.* New York: Columbia UP, 1982.

Yeazell, Ruth. *The Death and Letters of Alice James.* Berkeley: U of California P, 1981.

INDEX

350 INDEX

Babbage, Charles, 331n.22
Bacon, Francis (Baconianism), 37–38, 43,
   56, 121–23
Bakunin, Mikhail, 270
Baldwin, James Mark, 316n.4
Balzac, Honoré de, 94–95, 305n.16
Banta, Martha, 323n.19
Barish, Jonas, 298n.6
Barrett, William, 64, 299n.12
Baudelaire, Charles, 5, 22, 100, 150, 179,
   194
Baudrillard, Jean, 245
Beard, Charles, 52, 60–61, 299nn.9,17
Beethoven, Ludwig van, 133, 328n.21
Bellow, Saul, 300n.21
Bender, Thomas, 7, 294n.6
Benhabib, Seyla, 301n.25
Benjamin, Jessica, 320n.7, 324n.26
Benjamin, Walter, ix, 22, 81–82, 98, 287,
   303n.2, 312n.26, 313nn.1,2,
   315nn.19,20
   and Adorno, 99–103, 306n.22, 314n.10,
      315n.18, 330n.18
   and constellations, 100, 142, 151–52
   as flaneur, 100, 141–42, 151, 179
   and Henry James, 22, 103–4, 141–42,
      145–46, 149, 151–52, 154, 156, 160–62,
      164–65, 179, 306n.29, 315n.17
   and "representation as digression," 150–
      51, 165
   and shocks, desire for (traumatophilia),
      22, 104, 150, 179, 235, 279
Bergson, Henri, 75, 81, 89, 98, 313n.3
   and Dewey, 94, 108–9, 136
   and William James, 90, 105, 125–28, 135–
      36, 207
   and Adorno, 98, 106, 125–28, 135
Bernard, Luther Lee, 120
Bersani, Leo, 46, 49, 223, 236, 320n.6,
   326n.12
Bjork, Daniel, 327nn.15,18
Blackmur, R. P., 60, 80, 312n.28
Bloch, Ernst, 98
Bloom, Harold, 317n.10
Blumenberg, Hans, 37–38, 41, 49, 232,
   326n.9
Boelhower, William, 10, 314n.1
Bourdieu, Pierre, 167, 170
Bourget, Paul, 320n.3
Bourne, Randolph, vii, 11–12, 16, 60–61,
   250, 256, 258, 264–65, 314n.8, 334n.37
   and Dewey, 146, 257, 286–88, 291,
      310n.19, 313n.5, 329n.11, 330n.12,
      331n.21, 334.3

and Henry James, 146, 149, 157, 191,
   282, 313nn.3,4, 329n.7, 330n.13
on the "inexorable," 74, 257, 286
on nonidentity of intellectuals, 149, 286,
   313n.5
on "trans-national" identity, 146, 282,
   334n.38
Bouwsma, William, 298n.2
Brecht, Bertolt, 56
Brenkman, John, 311n.24
Brooks, Van Wyck, 21, 55, 59–64, 77, 200,
   298nn.5,8, 298n.9, 299n.14, 320n.5
Brownell, W.C., 142–45, 181, 189
Browning, Robert, 298n.18
Buck-Morss, Susan, 306n.22, 311n.25,
   312n.26
Buitenhuis, Peter, 333n.36
Burke, Edmund, 99
Burke, Kenneth, ix

Cahan, Abraham, 337n.37
Cahn, Michael, 317n.11
Cain, William, 299n.13
Call, Annie Payson, 237
Calvinism, 18, 41, 54, 196, 298n.2
Cameron, Sharon, 86, 301n.27
Canonization. See James, Henry: and
   canonization
Carlyle, Thomas, 29–30
Carpenter, Edward, 209
Carroll, David, 303n.31
Cavell, Stanley, 276, 319n.22
Chapman, John Jay, 115
Chodorow, Nancy, 320n.7, 334n.1
Chopin, Kate, 330n.18
Clebsch, William, 297n.11
Coleridge, Samuel Taylor, 99, 297n.11
Collins, Douglas, 305n.17
Columbia University. See Intellectuals: New
   York
Comte, Auguste (Comteanism), 94–95, 253,
   270, 286, 305n.16, 310n.18
Connolly, William, 50, 76, 223
Conrad, Peter, 147
Contextualism, viii–ix
Cooley, Charles Horton, 16, 309n.14
Cooney, Terry, 299n.12
Cotkin, George, 16, 294n.9, 295n.11,
   304n.10
Cowley, Malcolm, 65
Cox, James, 314n.13, 316n.1, 319n.20
Croly, Herbert, 113, 256, 263, 331n.21
Curiosity, 36–54 passim, 122, 131, 134, 138,
   142–46, 154–55, 162, 166, 168, 171,

3 5282 00001 4566